Daniel in the Preterists' Den

DANIEL IN THE PRETERISTS' DEN

A Critical Look at
Preterist Interpretations of Daniel

THOMAS A. HOWE

WIPF & STOCK · Eugene, Oregon

DANIEL IN THE PRETERISTS' DEN
A Critical Look at Preterist Interpretations of Daniel

www.wipfandstock.com

ISBN 13: 978-1-55635-273-7

Manufactured in the U.S.A.

CONTENTS

FIGURES

TABLES

Hebrew Transliteration Scheme

Name	Consonant	Transliteration	Name	Vowel	Transliteration
Aleph	א	ʾ	Qames	ָ	¯a
Beth	בּ ב	_b b	Patach	ַ	a
Gimel	גּ ג	g	Qames Hatuph	ָ	o
Daleth	דּ ד	_d d	Sere	ֵ	¯e
He	ה	h	Sere Yod	ֵי	ê
Waw	ו	w	Hireq	ִ	i
Zayin	ז	z	Hireq Yod	ִי	î
Heth	ח	ḥ	Holem	ֹ	¯o
Teth	ט	ṭ	Holem Waw	וֹ	ô
Yod	י	y	Segol	ֶ	e
Kaph	ךּ כּ כ	_k k	Shureq	וּ	û
Lamed	ל	l	Qibbus	ֻ	u
Mem	ם מ	m	Shewa	ְ	ᵉ
Nun	ן נ	n	Hateph Qames	ֳ	ᵒ
Samek	ס	s	Hateph Patach	ֲ	ᵃ
Ayin	ע	ʿ	Hateph Segol	ֱ	ᵉ
Pe	פּ	p			
	ף פ	f			
Sade	ץ צ	ṣ			
Qoph	ק	q			
Resh	ר	r			
Sin	שׂ	´s			
Shin	שׁ	ˇs			
Taw	תּ ת	_t t			

Greek Transliteration Scheme

Greek Letters			Transliteration
Name	**Upper Case**	**Lower Case**	
Alpha	A	α	*a*
Beta	B	β	*b*
Gamma	Γ	γ	*g*
Delta	Δ	δ	*d*
Epsilon	E	ε	*e*
Zeta	Z	ζ	*z*
Eta	H	η	*¯e*
Theta	Θ	θ	*ht*
Iota	I	ι	*i*
Kappa	K	κ	*k*
Lambda	Λ	λ	*l*
Mu	M	μ	*m*
Nu	N	ν	*n*
Xi	Ξ	ξ	*x*
Omicron	O	ο	*o*
Pi	Π	π	*p*
Rho	P	ρ	*r*
Sigma	Σ	σ, ς	*s*
Tau	T	τ	*t*
Upsilon	Y	υ	*u*
Phi	Φ	φ	*hp*
Chi	X	χ	*hc*
Ps	Ψ	ψ	*sp*
Omega	Ω	ω	*¯o*

I

INTRODUCTION

Preliminary Matters

THERE IS, of course, a colossal debate about how one should understand the prophecies of the Old Testament in relation to the New, and there are a variety of eschatological systems designed to explain the different points of view. The debate over the end times has often taken the course of personal attack and vindictive treatment of others. Persons who present themselves as born again Christians viciously malign their brothers in Christ for not accepting a particular view. Each side accuses the other of shoddy scholarship and being too stupid to realize their own presuppositions.

As we try to make our way through this important book, we will want to consider the various views with reference to passages and interpretations. We will certainly not have the time to look at every comment or even every commentator, but we will at least want to consider the principal views, that is, those views that have had an impact upon the history of the church and are the major forces in the contemporary debate—to some degree this will be a subjective means of selection, but some selection must be made as a result of the time and space constraints. Particularly, we will be considering the two major positions that are hotly debated today, Futurism and Preterism. But throughout these considerations, I hope we can keep in mind that those who have a different view are Christian brothers and sisters, who love the Lord, and have a sincere desire to teach that which they believe is the truth. Also, we want to keep in mind our own shortcomings and be open to hear contrary views and attempt to evaluate them honestly and fairly.

Hermeneutics

In the eschatological debate, the question of hermeneutics and hermeneutical method is at the center. Kenneth Gentry, Jr. has put together a massive presentation of the Postmillennial view in his book titled *He Shall Have Dominion*. In his section on hermeneutics, Kenneth Gentry asserts, "An issue that has received much attention in the eschatological debate among evangelicals is *hermeneutics*: the principle of biblical interpretation. How are we to approach the prophecies of Scripture?"[1] Dwight Pentecost begins his *magnum opus* on eschatology, *Things to Come*, with the declaration, "No question facing the student of Eschatology is more important than the question of the method to be employed in the interpretation of the prophetic Scriptures."[2] Considering one's hermeneutic method is indeed a critical part of the process of preparing to study the Bible, but it has also been a convenient excuse for attacking one's opponents. Both sides of the issue accuse the other of bad hermeneutics, and yet both sides seem to be espousing basically the same hermeneutic methodology. It would not be possible to engage in a full length presentation of hermeneutics, but we must consider some of the factors that have been part of the debate and attempt to set forth a methodology that will form the basis of our interpretations of Daniel.

SOME IMPORTANT DISTINCTIONS

Understanding interpretation requires that some important distinctions be made. Although there are many distinctions that could be discussed, each of which would have a different level of importance for our commentary, there are at least two important distinctions that must be understood in order to be able to identify many errors that are made during the interpretive process. The first distinction is between sense and reference.

Sense and Reference

The distinction between sense and reference was first articulated by Gottlob Frege (1848–1925), a German mathematician, logician, and philosopher, a professor at the University of Jena.[3] The distinction first articulated by Frege has become a matter of technical debate in philosophy of language. This

---

1. Kenneth L. Gentry, Jr., *He Shall Have Dominion: A Postmillennial Eschatology*, 148.

2. J. Dwight Pentecost, *Things To Come: A Study in Biblical Eschatology*, 1.

3. Gottlob Ludwig Frege, "Über Sinn und Bedeutung," in *Zeitschrift für Philosophie und philosophische Kritik C* (1892): 25–50. "On Sense and Reference," in *Translations from the Philosophical Writings of Gottlob Frege*, trans. Max Black, ed. Peter Geach and Max Black (Oxford: Basil Blackwell, 1970), 56–78.

distinction is characteristically illustrated in the literature by the expressions "morning star" and "evening star." For our purposes we will use the term "sense" roughly to indicate the term's meaning, and we will use the term "referent" to indicate that to which the term refers. The expressions "morning star" and "evening star" have different senses or meanings, but they have the same referent. The sense of the expression "morning star" is a bright, shining object in the sky that can be seen from certain points on the earth in the early morning hours. The sense of the expression "evening star" is a bright, shining object in the sky that can be seen from certain points on the earth in the early evening hours. So, these two expressions have different senses or meanings, but they both refer to Venus.

The importance of this distinction can be seen in the debate concerning the use of the word "generation" in Matt 24:34: "Truly I say to you, this generation will not pass away until all these *things* take place."[4] Preterists generally criticize Futurists for understanding this statement to apply to the future. The criticism that is leveled against the Futurist interpretation is that the Futurist has changed the meaning of the term from the way it is used throughout Matthew's Gospel. For example, in his arguments against Futurists' interpretations of this verse, John Noē asserts, "a simple word study of the seventeen other New Testament uses of the identical word construction reveals that 'this generation' always means the generation then living."[5] But Noē has confused meaning with referent. Although the word "generation" in 24:34 has the same meaning as the other uses in Matthew's Gospel, it is possible that it has a different referent, that is, that it is referring to a different group.

There is precedent for understanding Jesus' use here as having the same meaning but a different referent. In Matt 23:35 Jesus says, "so that upon you may fall *the guilt of* all the righteous bloodshed on earth, from the blood of righteous Abel to the blood of Zechariah, the son of Berechiah, whom you murdered between the temple and the altar."[6] The curious part of this statement is that Jesus accuses the scribes and Pharisees to whom He is talking of murdering Zechariah between the temple and the altar. The exact accusation is found in the latter part of the verse: "whom you murdered." This is a translation of the relative clause, "ὅν ἐφονεύσατε" (*etasuenofe noh*). The verb 'murdered' is a second person plural verb, translated "you murdered."

---

4. Matt 24:34: ἀμὴν λέγω ὑμῖν ὅτι οὐ μὴ παρέλθη ἡ γενεὰ αὕτη ἕως ἂν πάντα ταῦτα γένηται.

5. John Noē, *Beyond the End Times*, 116.

6. Matt 23:35: ὅπως ἔλθη ἐφ᾽ ὑμᾶς πᾶν αἷμα δίκαιον ἐκχυννόμενον ἐπὶ τῆς γῆς ἀπὸ τοῦ αἵματος Ἅβελ τοῦ δικαίου ἕως τοῦ αἵματος Ζαχαρίου υἱοῦ Βαραχίου, ὅν ἐφονεύσατε μεταξὺ τοῦ ναοῦ καὶ τοῦ θυσιαστηρίου.

In his recent book titled *The Apocalypse Code*, Hank Hanegraaff comments on this verse: "As context makes clear, Jesus is not addressing a past generation, for he denounces as hypocrites the present generation of teachers of the law and Pharisees who say about themselves, '*If we had lived in the days of our forefathers*, we would not have taken part with them in shedding the blood of the prophets.'"[7] The obvious problem with Hanegraaff's assertion is that it was not the case that the scribes and Pharisees to whom Jesus was talking actually murdered Zechariah. This event is referred to in 2 Chron 24:20–22: "So they conspired against him [Zechariah] and at the command of the king they stoned him to death in the court of the house of the Lord."[8] The murder of Zechariah took place during the reign of Amaziah, king of Judah, between 796–767 BC. The question is, why does Jesus say these scribes and Pharisees murdered Zechariah? Jesus had already pointed out how they claimed to be different from their fathers who murdered the prophets (23:30), but by killing the one's Jesus would send to them, and ultimately killing Jesus, they demonstrated that they were of the same spirit as those who killed the prophets. In other words, they were the same kind of people as their fathers— evil and unbelieving. Although Hanegraaff acknowledges these facts, he completely misses the point that this undermines his claims about the use of the pronoun "you." Sometimes the word "you" can be directed at a person or group and yet not refer exclusively to that person or group.

Now, the relevance of this observation is that even though Jesus is using the second person form of the verb, "you murdered," He is not claiming that the scribes and Pharisees to whom He is speaking actually murdered Zechariah, but that they were just as guilty as those who did. But the "you" both does and does not refer to the scribes and Pharisees to whom Jesus is speaking. It *does* refer to them in the sense that they are the one's Jesus is directly condemning, but it *does not* refer to them in the sense that they were not the ones who actually murdered Zechariah. So, even though the meaning of the second person is the same throughout this passage, the referent is different in this verse. What this shows is that a word can have the same meaning, but a different referent. This is important when considering the similar question in 24:34. Although the word "generation" in verse 34 has the same meaning as the other uses in Matthew, it may have a different referent.

The question here is not to justify either the Futurist or the Preterist understanding of this verse, but to show that the criticism leveled against Futurists is misdirected. The question is not a question of meaning but of referent. As we have pointed out, a word can have the same meaning but a

---

7. Hank Hanegraaff, *The Apocalypse Code*, 82 (emphasis in original).

8. (2 Chron 24:21) ‏וַיִּקְשְׁרוּ עָלָיו וַיִּרְגְּמֻהוּ אֶבֶן בְּמִצְוַת הַמֶּלֶךְ בַּחֲצַר בֵּית יהוה׃‎

different referent, and the referent of the same term in other contexts is no determiner of the referent in any other context. The referent of a term must be discovered by the context in which the term occurs, not by its other uses in other contexts.

One more illustration may make this clearer. Hank Hanegraaff comments on Jesus' statement in Jn 2:19: "Destroy this temple, and in three days I will raise it up."[9] Critiquing a woodenly literal hermeneutic, Hanegraaff says, "The Jews interpreted Jesus in a wooden, literal meaning of Jesus's words to refer directly and specifically to the destruction of their temple, which had taken 'forty-six years to build' (John 2:20). Jesus, however, spiritualized his prophecy. As the apostle John explains, 'The temple he had spoken of was his body' (v. 21)."[10] However, the difference between the Jews' understanding and John's comment is not a case of literal verses spiritual meaning. Rather, it is a difference of the reference of the term "temple." The Jews understood Jesus to be literally referring to the Temple, whereas Jesus was literally referring to His body. The distinction between sense and reference is an important distinction that an interpreter needs constantly to keep before him whenever he is interpreting the text.

Meaning and Significance

Another important distinction that must be made is the distinction between Meaning and Significance. This distinction was made popular by E. D. Hirsch in his book *Validity in Interpretation*.[11] According to Hirsch, "*Meaning* is that which is represented by a text; it is what the author meant by his use of a particular sign sequence; it is what the signs represent."[12] It is always problematic to define a term by using another form of the term in the definition. To say that meaning is what the author meant hardly serves to clarify what is meant. But this is not necessarily a shortcoming in Hirsch's presentation. Meaning is a notoriously difficult concept to define, and it has been and continues to be a topic of some considerable debate. This is certainly not the place to engage or even to give a cursory survey of the issues. For our purposes we will employ a very general and popular level notion. Meaning is that which the words in their grammatical, syntactical, historical, and literary context convey to the reader.

---

9. Jn 2:19: λύσατε τὸν ναὸν τοῦτον καὶ ἐν τρισὶν ἡμέραις ἐγερῶ αὐτόν.

10. Hanegraaff, *The Apocalypse Code*, 18–19.

11. E. D. Hirsch, Jr., *Validity in Interpretation*.

12. Ibid., 8.

Hirsch defines significance as "a relationship between that meaning and a person, or a conception, or a situation, or indeed anything imaginable."[13] This definition is not altogether enlightening either. Hirsch attempts to clarify this by an explanation: "Authors, who like everyone else change their attitudes, feelings, opinions, and value criteria in the course of time, will obviously in the course of time tend to view their own work in different contexts. Clearly what changes for them is not the meaning of the work, but rather their relationship to that meaning. Significance always implies a relationship, and one constant, unchanging pole of that relationship is what the text means."[14] Essentially, what Hirsch is pointing to is that significance has to do with how an individual applies the meaning to his own life. Roughly speaking, this can be expressed in the question, "What significance does the meaning have for me?" This is certainly an inadequate account of what Hirsch is arguing, but for our purposes it will suffice.

Norman Geisler has created a chart that may be helpful in grasping the distinction we wish to make (see Table 1 below):

Table 1: Meaning and Significance

	Meaning	Significance
Nature	Interpretation	Application
Object	Text	Life
Goal	Get Knowledge (What it Means)	Get Wisdom (How it Applies)
Status	Does not Change	Does Change
Number	One	Many

Once again we must point out that this distinction does not do justice to Hirsch's arguments. Nevertheless, even at this level this is a critical distinction to make. Not only has the failure to consider this distinction been the source of confusion in theories of hermeneutics, as Hirsch points out, but it can also be a source of confusion and misunderstanding in the interpretation of actual texts. As we consider what God has said through Daniel His prophet, we must

13. Ibid.
14. Ibid.

distinguish between what the text says, what it means, from the significance it would have had for Daniel and his immediate audience, and the significance it has for the Christian today. This is not to say that a text's significance has absolutely nothing to do with the meaning of the text or that grasping the significance of the text for Daniel and his immediate audience does nothing to help us understand the text. Rather, what this means is that the significance of the text cannot be used to determine what the text means. The meaning of the text should be discovered from the words in their grammatical, historical, syntactical, and literary context. Understanding a text's significance should derive from an understanding of its meaning. However, an understanding of a text's significance will sometimes clarify a text's meaning. We hope that this will become clearer as we work through the text of Daniel.

Importance of the Original Language

Milton Terry makes an important declaration concerning the importance of the original languages: "A thorough acquaintance with the genius and grammatical structure of the original languages of the Bible is essentially the basis of all sound interpretation. A translation, however faithful, is itself an interpretation, and cannot be safely made a substitute for original and independent investigation."[15] It is important to note some aspects of Terry's assertion. First, Terry does not say that the basis of all sound interpretation is simply a knowledge of the meanings of words. In today's computer oriented culture, access to lexicons and dictionaries that provide lexical information is so user-friendly that a student need not even be able to recognize the Hebrew consonants to look up words and discover possible meanings. What Terry says, however, is that the basis of all sound interpretation is a thorough acquaintance with the "genius and grammatical structure of the original languages." It is one thing to be able to look up words in a dictionary. It is an entirely different matter to understand the grammar of the language being studied, and the grammar can make a difference between knowing which possible meaning is the actual meaning in a given text.

This point is demonstrated in Hanegraaff's assertions in the chapter titled "Grammatical Principle" in the section labeled "The Adverb *Soon*." Discussing John's introductory statement in Rev 1:1, Hanegraaff asserts, "Finally, as the whole of Revelation makes clear, Jesus used the adverb *soon* to solemnly testify to that which was near."[16] The problem with Hanegraaff's comment is that the text does not even use an adverb in this assertion. What text says is, Ἀποκά

---

15. Milton Terry, *Biblical Hermeneutics*, vol. 2, *Library of Biblical and Theological Literature*, 69.

16. Hanegraaff, *The Apocalypse Code*, 91 (emphasis in original).

λυψις Ἰησοῦ Χριστοῦ ἣν ἔδωκεν αὐτῷ ὁ θεὸς δεῖξαι τοῖς δούλοις αὐτοῦ ἃ δεῖ γενέσθαι ἐν τάχει. The statement is set out in the chart below with a word-for-word translation.

Table 2: Revelation 1:1

Ἀποκάλυψις	Ἰησοῦ	Χριστοῦ	ἣν	ἔδωκεν
Revelation	of Jesus	Christ	which	He gave
αὐτω	ὁ θεὸς	δεῖξαι	τοῖς δούλοις	αὐτοῦ
to Him	the God	to make known	to the servants	of Him
ἃ	δεῖ	γενέσθαι	ἐν	τάχει
which	is about	to be	in	a short time

The word that is usually translated "soon" is the word τάχει (*iehcat*). This is actually a noun, and in this instance it is the object of the preposition ἐν (*ne*), which usually means "in." According to the standard New Testament Greek Lexicon, this word in this prepositional construction indicates, "pert. to a relatively brief time subsequent to another point in time, ἐν τάχει as adverbial unit *soon, in a short time* . . ."[17] A lack of facility in the original language has led Hanegraaff to jump to a conclusion that is not necessarily warranted. An understanding of the original language is critical to exegesis.

SCRIPTURE INTERPRETING SCRIPTURE

In the eschatology debate, proponents of one view will often charge the proponents of the opposing view with misinterpretation and mishandling of the text, justifying their own interpretation by an appeal to the notion that Scripture interprets Scripture. In fact, Gentry identifies this principle as a basic principle of Preterist interpretation. He says, "It should always be the Christian's hermeneutic practice that: . . . (2) Scripture interprets Scripture."[18] Another interpreter asserts the following: "Many, while looking for physical and material fulfillments in the nation of Israel to these promises, have overlooked the fact that they are *spiritually* fulfilled in Christ. This is not a personal opinion or a private interpretation of Scripture—this is *Scripture interpreting*

---

17. BDAG, s.v. "τάχος."
18. Gentry, *He Shall Have Dominion*, 165.

Scripture!"[19] In his book in which he interprets the seventy sevens of Daniel's prophecy, Philip Mauro declares, "What we undertake by the grace of God to do is to make every statement and conclusion so plain, and to support it by such clear proof *from the Scriptures alone,* that the ordinary reader will be able both to see for himself the meaning of the passage, and also to comprehend perfectly the scriptural evidence by which that meaning is established. Thus he will be entirely independent of all human 'authority.'"[20] Of course this notion has had a long and illustrious career among interpreters, and it certainly sounds like the kind of thing an interpreter of the Scripture ought to do.

However, Robert Strimple correctly notes, "Perhaps there is no principle of biblical interpretation so easily abused as the familiar principle of comparing Scripture with Scripture."[21] The abuse of this practice arises from a tendency either to overlook or ignore an underlying issue—generally speaking, Scripture must be interpreted, and that includes any Scripture passage to which an interpreter appeals in his effort to support his interpretation of another Scripture passage. In other words, to claim that one is interpreting Scripture with Scripture often simply means that the interpreter has interpreted one Scripture passage in one way and is using his interpretation of that passage to support or clarify his understanding of another Scripture so as to interpret it in a comparable way. But, if an interpreter's interpretation of a given passage is questionable, his appeal to other passages does not serve to support his interpretation of the passage in question, because his interpretation of those other passages may be equally questionable. Even the choice of which Scriptures relate to which, and which do not relate at all, is an interpretive process that is influenced by the prior hermeneutical and eschatological framework of the interpreter. Stating the principle sounds very pious, but it ignores the fact that the Scripture to which appeal or reference is being made is just as subject to the interpretive approach of the interpreter as the Scripture passage to which the comparison is being made.

There is nothing that is necessarily illicit or improper in this process. The disingenuous aspect is to imply that simply because an interpreter compares one Scripture passage to another, this somehow obviates the need for interpretation and miraculously bypasses the interpreter's presuppositions and assumptions, and that by means of this process of appeal one has the herme-

---

19. Brian L. Martin, *Behind the Veil of Moses*, 19 (emphasis in original). I am using this quote only because it is convenient, not because I am trying to imply that one side is better than another.

20. Philip Mauro, *The Seventy Weeks and the Great Tribulation*, 11.

21. Robert B. Strimple, "Hyper-Preterism on the Resurrection of the Body," in *When Shall These Things Be? A Reformed Response to Hyper-Preterism,* ed. Keith A. Mathison (Phillipsburg, New Jersey: Presbyterian and Reformed Publishing Company, 2004), 303.

neutic high-ground in the debate. It is just not true that by presenting to the reader an impressive string of Scripture references thought to be relevant, that the interpreter's conclusions are thereby "entirely independent of all human 'authority,'" as Mauro claims.[22] In fact, because the situation is presented as it is, the reader of Mauro's book is dominated by Mauro's authority since to question his choice of Scriptures and the way he relates to them is tantamount to rejecting the very Word of God. There is something that smacks of spiritual arrogance for an interpreter to assume that his understanding of which Scriptures relate to which, and which do not relate at all, is the final word and is somehow above all other merely human authorities. Although we will certainly want to compare Scripture with Scripture, we cannot assume that this practice in itself somehow magically makes our interpretations necessarily objective or beyond dispute. They may be objective, and they may be true, but saying that "this is *Scripture interpreting Scripture*" does not prove or guarantee the truth of the outcome. That is just rhetoric.

Additionally, Gentry was quick to criticize others of deciding on what should be taken literally or figuratively before doing any interpretation, but Gentry's claim that one should interpret Scripture with Scripture is a presupposition that he has established before actually doing any interpretation. As true and as necessary as Scripture comparison may be, this kind of prior assumption is the very point of Gentry's criticism of Ryrie. Now Gentry is doing the very same kind of thing which he sought to disallow for the Dispensationalist. Should not Gentry "prove this, not just assume it,"[23] as he demanded of the Dispensationalist? And providing an illustration is not a proof that the approach is a valid prior assumption. Please understand. I am not saying that this approach is not a valid approach. What I am saying is that Gentry is now doing the very thing for which he vehemently criticized the Dispensationalists—assuming an approach that sets the parameters of interpretation before doing any interpreting. Who sets the standards for what counts as a comparable Scripture? Who judges whether a Scripture should or should not interpret another Scripture? And whose interpretation of the "other" Scripture should be used in making the comparison? The practice of comparing Scripture with Scripture is not some magical formula that validates one's interpretation (I do not wish to imply that this is what Gentry thinks, although some interpreters do seem to treat this approach as if it miraculously validates their interpretations). As important as the practice is, in order to be valid, the interpreter must justify and prove his interpretation of the related

---

22. Mauro, *The Seventy Weeks*, 11.

23. Gentry, *He Shall Have Dominion*, 153.

Scripture just as he must justify and prove his interpretation of the Scripture under consideration.

LITERARY GENRE

The literary nature of the text has become an important consideration in recent hermeneutic theory, particularly the notion of genre. Genre is a fancy word for "kind." In interpretation, the identification of genre has become an obligation supposedly to take place prior to interpretation. For example, in his discussion of genre considerations with regard to the book of Daniel, Ernest Lucas asserts, "Genre guides not only the expectations of readers, but also the approaches adopted by authors. An author who wants to communicate to readers in a particular culture will adopt one of the genres that belong in that culture, or else risk misunderstanding or incomprehension. Of course an author need not be a slave to a given genre, but can modify and adapt it."[24] Lucas goes on to say, "A factor I have not yet mentioned, but which some consider very important in genre classification, is the social setting, or social function, of a text. The problem with this is that the argument can get dangerously circular. The social setting has to be deduced from the text, and is then read back into it."[25] But, are not genre considerations in danger of the same kind of circularity? The genre of a given text must be discovered by reading the text, and then, when the genre is identified, these considerations are then "read back" into the text. To avoid this circularity with reference to the social setting, Lucas advises, "It seems better to let the social setting or function (as far as it can be discerned) be seen as part of the content, without giving it special emphasis."[26] But should the same not be done with reference to genre? Genre is supposed to be the grid through which proper interpretation is done. As Lucas points out, "We might expect, then, that any helpful genre classification of the stories in Dan 1–6 (i.e. one that clarifies the meaning) will rest on characteristics of both form and content."[27] Yet it was apart from any prior commitments to a specific genre classification that the interpreter understood the text in his effort to identify the patterns that might indicate genre classification. If interpretation apart from genre considerations is sufficient to identify the genre in the initial stages, why is genre then considered the grid through which interpretation must be done? Apparently, interpretation prior to genre commitment was sufficient successfully to identify the genre, why is

---

24. Ernest Lucas, *Daniel*, vol. 20, *Apollos Old Testament Commentary*, 23.

25. Ibid., 24.

26. Ibid.

27. Ibid.

it not sufficient to understand meaning apart from giving genre any "special considerations"?

How does genre classification work? In order to classify a particular piece of literature, the interpreter must read the text and attempt to discern the patterns that would indicate conformity to the characteristics of a particular genre. For example, if the text reads like a story having characters, a plot, a setting, a conflict, etc., then one might classify it as narrative. If additionally the text is presented as an account of events that actually took place, one might further classify it as historical narrative. If the text contains expressions that conform to identifiable figurative expressions, such as metaphor, simile, synecdoche, etc., being structured in short lines composed of two brief and complementary parts that seem to have some parallel relation, one might classify the material as Hebrew poetry. But, what is the interpreter doing when he reads a text in order to discover its patterns? Is he engaging in interpretation at this stage? It certainly cannot be the case that the interpreter is interpreting the text by employing a certain type of genre classification, for that is the very thing that is being sought. An interpreter cannot know the genre of a text before he identifies it in the text. The genre must be discerned and discovered in the text as one reads it. Lucas asserts, ". . . all readers have some sense of the different genres of literature that exist in their culture, and so approach a given text with expectations arising from the type of literature that they intuitively take it to be."[28] Nevertheless, even the native speaker/reader must identify, even intuitively, what kind of literature he is interpreting by reading at least some of the text, intuitively recognizing the patterns, and then reading it according to the kind of literature it is. There is some interpretation going on in the mind of the interpreter in order to understand the text sufficiently to be able to discover its patterns and identify its genre.

A particular interpreter may be alerted to a genre type before reading a given text. This alert may come because the interpreter has been taught to expect a certain kind of genre in certain places in the biblical text. For example, an interpreter may have been taught to expect historical narrative in historical books. But, poetry occurs in these books as well, so although an interpreter may expect to find historical narrative, he must still read the text in such a way as to allow the features of the text to indicate its genre. Ideally the interpreter should not impose upon the text certain genre expectations. Genre expectations should grow out of the text itself.

So, again, what is the interpreter doing as he reads a text in order to discover its genre? Is he not reading and interpreting the text prior to any genre classifications? And if so, then it must be the case that there is some mean-

---

28. Ibid., 23.

ing communicated to the interpreter apart from whether the interpreter has recognized any given genre classification. But, if genre determines meaning, then this scenario is impossible. The interpreter must know the genre before he knows the text. But this is tantamount to imposing genre expectations upon the text.

First: Read and understand at least some of the text—enough to recognize patterns

Second: Discover any patterns that may indicate genre type

Third: Relate discovered patterns to accepted genre classifications

Fourth: Test selected genre classification against text

Fifth: Use proven genre classification as aid to reading and understanding the text

The point of this brief discussion is, genre does not determine meaning. Rather, genre considerations may help us to clarify ambiguous expressions or to set the broad parameters of use, but the words and phrases of the language in their normal-historical-grammatical context determine the meaning of the text. So, we will certainly want to consider questions of genre, but we should not expect the answers to these questions to overturn the normal historical grammatical sense of the text—giving due consideration to the possibility of figure of speech, symbolic language, etc. However, we cannot, for example, use the classification "poetry" to make the Genesis creation account mean that God did not literally and actually create the heavens and the earth as the text asserts or to make the text of Genesis 1 into some kind of mythical expression of the Hebrew culture and not an actual account of God's creative activity. We cannot use the classification "Midrash" to allow for historical errors in the Gospel of Matthew. In other words, we cannot use genre to force the text to say what we want it to mean. We want to avoid this kind of procedure.

ALLEGORIZING AND SPIRITUALIZING

Allegorizing

"Allegorizing is searching for a hidden or secret meaning underlying but remote from and unrelated in reality to the more obvious meaning of a statement."[29] The allegorical method that arose among the Greek philosophers, particularly those of a Platonist persuasion, was employed by the Alexandrian Jews and was adopted by the Christian church. This is a particularly Platonist approach

---

29. Roy B. Zuck, "Highlights in the History of Hermeneutics," *Classnotes*, 1.

to hermeneutics. The meaning is the universal that exists somewhere other than the material world of the particulars of the text. The material world is only the shadow and does not impart knowledge, only opinion. Knowledge is knowledge of the forms. Consequently, since the meaning is the form that is beyond or behind the text, the meaning must be sought in the realm of the forms, not in the realm of the particulars which do not impart meaning, only opinion. A good example of allegorization is Origen's treatment of the story of the Good Samaritan. The traveler is Adam, who journeys from Jerusalem, heaven, to Jericho, the world, and is assaulted by robbers, the devil and his angels. The priest, who represents the law, and the Levite, who represents the prophets, pass by without aiding the fallen Adam. However, the good Samaritan, Christ, stops to help him, sets him on his beast, which represents Christ's body, and brings him to an inn, the church. Christ gives the innkeeper two denarii, representing the Father and the Son, and promises to come back, representing Christ's second coming. Notice how this completely ignores the historical context in which the parable is given. How would Origen's explanation fit into the context of Luke 10?

Allegory as a hermeneutical method of interpreting the Hebrew Scriptures perhaps grew out of an attempt to handle this sacred religious document so as to address contemporary issues in the way ancient myths did. The writings of ancient cultures abound in myths. H. W. F. Saggs points out that myth "was a way of making the world make sense. The primeval world was a strange, often unpredictable and frightening place: ancient peoples wanted to know where they were, how they came to be there, and why. Above all, they wanted assurance of stability. Myth gave them those answers, and that assurance."[30] Myth in ancient cultures was a way of expressing truth in terms of an experience that was not constrained by the modern "scientific" outlook.[31] The ancient myths were developed because men understood the world around them as living and themselves as vitally linked to this world, and the stories were the expressions of their lives in a living world of which they were a part. As H. Frankfort points out, "The imagery of myth is therefore by no means allegory. It is nothing less than a carefully chosen cloak for abstract thought."[32] In a manner similar to that employed by Chinese philosophers in their instruction about virtue expressed in stories of, for example, the relation between the emperor and the servant, so myths were developed to communicate truths about life, virtue, reality—addressing the same questions with which modern

---

30. H. W. F. Saggs, *Civilization Before Greece and Rome*, 290.

31. cf. H. Frankfort, et. al. *The Intellectual Adventure of Ancient Man*, 3ff.

32. Ibid., 7.

man grapples in speculative philosophy, but addressing these questions in the symbolism of myth rather than detached speculative thought.

But, the Hebrew Scriptures are an historical record of the acts of God moving His creation toward the fulfillment of His ultimate purpose. Rather than fantastical beasts or mythological personas, the Hebrew Scriptures depict the lives of real people. In an effort to use these writings in the same way myths were used by the ancients, interpreters of the Bible employed an allegorical hermeneutic to convert the real stories into symbolic communications. Whereas myth was symbolic in its nature, the Scriptures are narratives recounting the non-fantastical movement of history according to God's plan. The symbolical element needed to be added to the text in order to make it function as had the myths—hence, allegorization. As Gadamer observes, "Allegory arises from the theological need to eliminate offensive material from a religious text . . ."[33] For example, Philo takes the Genesis account of the fall and converts the various events and persons depicted in the narrative account into symbols (see quote below). A myth created to explain the same truth would have been constituted of symbolic figures as its very account. But the Hebrew Scriptures, being an historical narrative, must be converted into the necessary symbols by the hermeneutic method employed. To get around the problem of the obvious historical nature of the text, and yet the unbelievable, i.e., supernatural, character of the stories, the stories were allegorized. Interpreters looked for hidden meanings underneath the literal writings. As Justo González observes, "The Greeks also made use of allegorical interpretation in order to give new meaning to ancient myths that no longer seemed believable."[34]

Allegorization is used today to get around the fact that preachers and teachers do not know how to handle the text, particularly narrative sections, and especially the Old Testament. An example of this type of allegorizing in our culture is how some preachers approach narrative sections of the Old Testament or the Gospels. A humorous example is the command of Jesus to the disciples in Matt 21:2: "Go into the village opposite you, and immediately you will find a donkey tied, and a colt with her. Loose them and bring them to Me." The preachers application was, "Have you loosed your donkey for Jesus." The marriage feast in Cana in John 2 has been applied in the following manner. "Where we are at the end of our resources, where we have no wine, where we cannot rescue ourselves from our predicament, Jesus manifests His

---

33. Hans-Georg Gadamer, *Truth and Method*, 73. "Allegorie entsteht aus dem theologischen Bedürfnis, in religiöser Überlieferung . . ." *Wahrheit und Methode* (Tübingen: J. C. B. Mohr, 1960), 69.

34. Justo L. González, *From the Beginnings to the Council of Chalcedon*, vol. 1, *A History of Christian Thought*, 42, n.35.

glory (i.e., the saving presence and action of God)."[35] Since the features of allegory are not actually present in the text, the preacher foists upon the text an allegorical interpretation, converting the actual historical references into symbols for hidden, spiritual meaning.

Some, including Craig Blomberg, have argued that an allegorical method should be used to interpret the parables of Jesus.[36] Whether one agrees with Blomberg's proposal or not, one point is clear from his presentation; the only time an allegorical method should be used to interpret a text is when the text is an allegory. And allegories have distinctive characteristics by which they can be identified. If the text of Daniel does not exhibit the characteristics that one would expect to find in an allegory, then the allegorical method should not be employed. If an interpreter employs an allegorical method, he must demonstrate that the text being interpreted is an allegory. This cannot simply be assumed. If an interpreter is being charged with improperly employing an allegorical method, this must also be demonstrated, not simply assumed.

Spiritualizing

Spiritualizing is the disregard for the earthly, physical, and historical reality about which the text speaks and the attempt to make application by way of some spiritual analogy. Joseph being thrown into the pit in Gen 37:24 is interpreted as our being in the various pits of our lives. The stilling of the storm in Mark 4:35–41 is interpreted as Jesus stilling the storms of our lives. Jacob's struggle with the Angel of the Lord at Peniel is interpreted as our spiritual struggle with God. The problem here is the arbitrary association of only particular parts of the text with the spiritual application. If the pit of Joseph is to be taken as pits in our lives, to what will we liken Joseph's brothers? What about Joseph's coat? If the stilling the storm is to be taken as Jesus stilling the storms on the sea of life, what does the boat represent? What about the disciples—what do they represent? Does Jesus only still the storms of life that involve a group of people? The parallels are drawn on a subjective basis. No doubt Jesus is capable of stilling the storms of life, but is that what this passage means? It seems that this account is designed at least to demonstrate the glory of Christ over the physical realm. In as far as this account contributes to the knowledge of the divine nature of Christ and His authority over the realm of nature, it can be so applied to today.

There has been a tendency in the eschatology debate for the Futurists to charge the Preterists with spiritualizing the text. Of course the Futurists are

35. Sidney Greidanus, *The Modern Preacher and the Ancient Text*, 160.

36. Craig L. Blomberg, *Interpreting the Parables* (Downers Grove, Illinois: InterVarsity Press, 1990).

not immune to this practice, as the Preterists are quick to point out. But, in order to consider this question, we must understand what these terms mean. Spiritualizing, as a derogatory characterization, is the tendency to make prophetic statements that, according to their normal-grammatical-historical meaning seem to be indicating some physical phenomena, are, instead, understood to indicate *only* a spiritual reality. Philip Mauro makes a very helpful point in this regard.

> The main purpose of the present chapter is to bring clearly to view the important truth that in Scripture the contrast is not between the *spiritual* and the *literal*, but between the *spiritual* and the *natural*; for a passage of Scripture may refer, when taken "literally," either to "that which is *natural*" or to "that which is *spiritual*." In other words, the literal interpretation may call for a thing which exists in the realm of nature, or for the counterpart of that thing which exists in the realm of spiritual realities (1 Cor. 15:46). It is of the utmost importance that this be understood; for the advocates of modern Dispensationalism have wrought confusion, and have succeeded in giving plausibility to many misinterpretations of Scripture, by first taking for granted (erroneously, as will be herein shown) that a "literal" interpretation necessarily calls for something *material* or *natural*, and by then insisting strenuously that all prophecies which refer to *Israel, Jerusalem, Zion*, etc., should be interpreted "literally."[37]

Although I do not agree with Mauro's eschatological perspective, I do think this is an entirely appropriate characterization. Perhaps the word "natural" also has undesirable implications, but it seems to be the best word to use to emphasize the contrast. But we must also understand that Spiritualizing is not the same as a spiritual interpretation. Spiritualizing is the illegitimate understanding of a statement as only spiritual when it should also be understood naturally. A Spiritual interpretation is a legitimate hermeneutical methodology. It simply may be the case that some passages are to be understood spiritually. However, another dimension to this contrast is important. Simply because a passage should be understood naturally does not necessarily mean there is no spiritual dimension to it, and simply because a passage should be understood spiritually does not necessarily mean there is no natural dimension to it. People in the debate often misrepresent the other side in such matters. We must be careful to take all these factors into consideration.

Nevertheless, the appropriateness of the use of these factors in any given situation cannot simply be assumed. In other words, the interpreter must

---

37. Philip Mauro, *The Hope of Israel: What Is It?*, 14.

demonstrate that a spiritual or natural understanding of a passage is appropriate in a given instance. Nor can one necessarily be justified on the basis of one's eschatological predisposition. I say "necessarily" because there may be instances in which it is perfectly legitimate to understand a passage in terms of one's eschatological system. For example, if it were possible to demonstrate that a particular eschatological system is very likely the correct one, then it is perfectly appropriate to understand a passage in terms of the truth of the system—assuming of course the system can be demonstrated to be true and that the particular interpreter's understanding of the system is consistent and accurate. Also, to understand a passage in terms of one's eschatological system may not be inappropriate if the interpreter is attempting to show how the text would be understood from this perspective. In other words, in a given instance, an interpreter may simply be saying, "A dispensational perspective would understand this passage this way," without necessarily claiming that this is the only legitimate way to understand the passage.

WALTKE'S SELF-EVIDENT RULES OF INTERPRETATION

In his article, "Kingdom Promises as Spiritual," appearing in the book *Continuity and Discontinuity*, Bruce Waltke sets forth what he identifies as "some rules for the interpretation of Scripture that the writer holds as self-evident beyond the widely accredited grammatico-historical approach."[38] Of course, if this is self-evident, then why do we need his explanation? These "self-evident rules" are set forth with considerable comment by Waltke, and much of what he asserts cannot be dealt with here. With reference to spiritualizing, those principles that will be considered along with some of Waltke's comments are the following:

1.   The Priority of the Bible Over Other Data

2.   Priority of New Testament Interpretation Over the Interpretation of Theologians

3.   Priority of Clear Texts Over Obscure Ones

4.   Priority of Spiritual Illumination Over Scientific Exegesis

---

38. Bruce K. Waltke, "Kingdom Promises as Spiritual," in *Continuity and Discontinuity: Perspectives on the Relationship Between the Old and New Testaments*, ed. John S. Feinberg (Westchester, Illinois: Crossway Books, 1988), 263.

The Priority of the Bible Over Other Data

Waltke identifies this rule as, "The rule *sola scriptura* (the Bible alone is authoritative for faith and practice), as opposed to the authority of tradition, is too well-known to require comment here. Contemporary theologians of varying persuasions, however, are looking to the state of Israel for their interpretation of Scripture."[39] As an example of this practice, Waltke asserts, "Premillennialists plausibly appeal to the restoration of national Israel as confirmation of their cherished belief that Christ's consummate glory in history will be displayed in his reign with the church over restored national Israel."[40] Of course the problem with Waltke's charge is that on the one hand he identifies the breaking of this rule as "looking to the state of Israel for their interpretation of Scripture," and then he charges Premillennialists with "appeal to the restoration of national Israel as confirmation of the cherished belief . . ." However, confirmation of a cherished belief is not the same as looking to Israel for one's interpretation of Scripture. Although it is entirely possible that some Premillennialists do this, this is not a necessary part of a Premillennialist perspective. By way of implying guilt by association, Waltke declares, "Ancient Israel made a similar error during its last century of existence when, instead of looking solely to Scripture to understand its history, the religious establishment looked to God's remarkable deliverance of Jerusalem in 701 BC as confirmation of their tragic delusion that the temple could not fall. Superficial judgments often lead to mistaken conclusions."[41] But this does not serve as a valid criticism since the misuse of a principle does not invalidate the principle. What ancient Israel did is not analogous to what Premillennialists do since, according to Premillennialists, ancient Israel misunderstood the biblical passages in the first place. Now, if Waltke wants to make the case that Premillennialists are also misinterpreting the relevant passages, he can certainly do so. But simply making a correlation between the practices of ancient Israel and Premillennialists does not serve to call into question the practices of Premillennialists.

Premillennialists believe in *sola scriptura* as much as does Waltke. However, Waltke's criticism assumes that he has accurately interpreted the Scriptures involved. This is certainly possible, but the disingenuous aspect of Waltke's criticism is the implication that he has the hermeneutical high ground by claiming to advocate this principle while at the same time maligning Premillennialists by implying that they do not acknowledge this principle.

---

39. Ibid., 264.
40. Ibid.
41. Ibid.

The question is not who does and who does not acknowledge this principle. The question is, whose interpretation of the relevant Scripture is correct.

Also, we still have to deal with the interpretation of the Scriptures. Simply to claim *sola scriptura* does not address the question of whose understanding of the Scriptures serves as the standard on the basis of which a given interpreter can measure his own understanding. *Sola scriptura* means that the Scripture alone is authoritative, but this Scripture must still be interpreted. Simply because one interpreter differs in his conclusions from another does not mean that the one interpreter does not acknowledge the principle of *sola scriptura*. And, an appeal to *sola scriptura* does not necessarily settle a hermeneutical dispute. As we have seen, Waltke misrepresents the practice of Premillenniarians. They are not interpreting the meaning of the text by an appeal to contemporary events. Rather, they are proposing that the contemporary events may be that to which the prophecy refers or the events to which the prophecy applies. But this is not a violation of the principle of *sola scriptura*.

Priority of New Testament Interpretation over the Interpretation of Theologians

Waltke's second rule is, "the classical rule *sacra scriptura sui ipsius interpres* (the Bible interprets itself)—more specifically, the New interprets the Old—should be accepted by all Christian theologians."[42] In support of this position, Waltke presents a series of questions:

Quest. "Is it not self-evident that the author of Scripture is the final exponent of his own thoughts?"[43]

Resp. It is certainly true that the author of Scripture is the final exponent of his own thoughts. However, it is still true that the thoughts that this author expresses themselves are subject to interpretation. Simply because the author of Scripture is the final exponent of his own thoughts does not guarantee that a particular interpreter has correctly understood this exposition. Whenever an author communicates to an audience, that communication must be understood by the audience, and this goes right back to the question of interpretation. This is nothing else than the principle of Scripture interprets Scripture, which we have dealt with above.

Quest. "Should not the rule so often used by dispensationalists, who traditionally saw no connection between the OT promises and the church,

42. Ibid.
43. Ibid.

that the NT cannot contradict the OT, be reversed to say that the OT cannot contradict the NT?"[44]

Resp. This again is certainly true. However, what one theologian takes as a contradiction, another may not. What constitutes a contradiction is likewise subject to the interpretation of the one making the claim. Just because Waltke sees the interpretation of a given passage as contradictory does not necessarily mean that it is in itself. Waltke's interpretation is just as subject to his presuppositions and prior theological and eschatological commitments as are the interpretations of those with contrary views. Also, simply because Dispensationalists "traditionally saw no connection" does not mean all contemporary Dispensationalists abide by this principle.

Quest. "Should not theologians who put the enigmatic visions of prophets on a par with the most direct revelation in Christ fear?"[45]

Resp. The answer to this is, No! No one should fear putting Divine Revelation on a par with Divine Revelation! Unless Waltke is claiming that there are degrees of revelation, this principle likewise is a case of interpretation. What seems to Waltke to be an "enigmatic vision" of a prophet may not be enigmatic to another interpreter. What Waltke seems to be saying here is, "Should not theologians who put *their interpretations of* the enigmatic visions of prophets on a par with *our interpretations* of the most direct revelation in Christ fear?" The answer to this is, No! Premillennialists do not believe that Waltke's interpretations are correct. So, naturally, they will put their interpretations of visions above Waltke's interpretations of the revelation in Christ. Waltke assumes that his understanding of the "direct revelations in Christ" are necessarily the standard by which all others should be judged.

Quest. "Does not the posture that begins first with the theologian's interpretation of the OT instead of with the NT beg the issue by presuming a hermeneutic for interpreting the promises before looking to the Scriptures themselves?"[46]

Resp. This "rule" is absolutely false. The way Waltke has phrased it implies that one must interpret the OT, but one only has to read the NT. The rule should be restated so as not to be misleading: "Does not the posture that begins first with the theologian's interpretation of the OT instead of with *the theologian's interpretation of* the NT beg the issue by presuming a hermeneutic for interpreting the promises before *using a hermeneutic for*

44. Ibid.
45. Ibid.
46. Ibid.

looking to the Scriptures themselves?" Stated this way, the falsity of the claim is evident. It assumes that one can go to the NT and simply "look at the Scriptures themselves" without doing so through one's prior theological and eschatological commitments. Once again what Waltke is saying is, "You can't interpret the OT unless first you look at the Scriptures of the NT from my perspective."

Quest. "Are not dispensationalists inconsistent with their own theology, which looks to the teachings of our Lord after his moral rejection by Israel and to the apostles as normative for the faith and practice of the church, when they start not with the very literature they find normative but with their own autonomous rules for interpreting the OT?"[47]

Resp. Once again this rule is misleading and false. Why does Waltke think that the dispensationalist's rules are "autonomous rules for interpreting the OT," but he does not believe that his own rules for interpreting the NT are "autonomous rules"? The reason he thinks this is because the dispensationalists do not interpret the Scripture the way he does. I suspect that both Dispensationalists and those of opposing camps attempt to interpret the Scripture legitimately, and it is not at all clear what "autonomous rules" are.

Ultimately what Waltke seems to be saying in this rule is that there should be a priority of his understanding of what the NT says over the interpretations of theologians who interpret the OT in a contrary way. But, this is not a rule of biblical interpretation. Also, it assumes that Waltke's interpretation of the New Testament is not an interpretation of a theologian. Isn't Waltke as much a theologian as those he is critiquing? And, as such, is he not a theologian interpreting the New Testament? Ultimately then, Waltke's rule asserts the priority of his interpretation of the New Testament over any theologian who does not interpret the way he does.

Priority of Clear Texts over Obscure Ones

The third rule of Waltke's is, "Is it not self-evident that unclear texts should be interpreted in the light of clear ones and not vice versa?"[48] The answer to this is of course, Yes! Obscure texts should always be interpreted in light of clear texts. However, who determines what is and what is not a "clear text"? It is a rhetorical practice of commentators to claim that some understanding of a passage is "clear" or "obvious." But, what is obvious to one is not necessarily

47. Ibid.
48. Ibid., 265.

obvious in itself or to someone else. This is, again, a matter of interpretation. Simply because an interpreter appeals to a passage that he thinks is clear does not guarantee that he has correctly interpreted the passage or that his interpretation is not influenced by his own prior theological and eschatological commitments. What Waltke does not do is set forth any principles that clearly demonstrate what should be counted as "clear."

In support of his claim, Waltke states, "As the Law of Moses is clearer than the dreams and visions of prophets (Num 12:6–8), so also the apostolic letters and epistles are in plain speech, though admittedly containing 'some things that are hard to understand' (2 Pet 3:16), are clearer than prophetic visions and the symbolic visions of apocalyptic literature that need angels to interpret them."[49] However, Waltke's appeal to Num 12:6–8 has its own problems: "And he said, Hear now my words: If there be a prophet among you, I the LORD will make myself known unto him in a vision, and will speak unto him in a dream. My servant Moses is not so, who is faithful in all mine house. With him will I speak mouth to mouth, even apparently, and not in dark speeches; and the similitude of the LORD shall he behold: wherefore then were ye not afraid to speak against my servant Moses? And the anger of the LORD was kindled against them; and he departed." First, where in this passage does God say that what God communicates to Moses is any more clear than what He communicates to the prophets? The text simply says God will communicate to the prophets in a vision or a dream. But, visions and dreams are not necessarily less clear than are mouth to mouth communications. Simply because Waltke thinks they are does not prove that they are. This is something that must be demonstrated, not assumed, but Waltke does not present any justification for his claim.

Second, simply because God says He will not communicate to Moses in "dark speeches" does not mean that He will necessarily communicate to the prophets in dark speeches. The text simply says that God will not do this with Moses. It doesn't say he did it with the prophets. Third, if God does communicate to the prophets in dark speeches, this does not mean that the prophets could not explain in clear language what God said. Fourth, this passage has nothing to do with the "Law of Moses" as Waltke presents it. This passage has to do with the challenge of Aaron and Miriam against what appeared to be exclusivity on Moses' part of receiving communications from God. Fifth, the text says, "If there is a prophet among you . . ." which could be taken to mean that this statement applies to this particular time, not to all succeeding prophets. Now some or none of these points may be convincing, but none of them has been addressed by Waltke so as to demonstrate that his understand-

49. Ibid.

ing of this passage is the correct one. Simply to assume that he has understood
the passage correctly does not present a valid criticism of the opposing view.

Concerning Waltke's appeal to 2 Pet 3:16, there are several problems
here also. First, who decides what is "hard to understand." Second, Peter's
statement has to do with Paul's writings, not necessarily to all writings of the
NT. Third, this statement does not mean that other Scriptures are necessarily easier to understand. Fourth, what is hard for Peter to understand is not
necessarily a gauge for our level of understanding. What Peter thought was
not hard to understand may in fact be hard for people today to understand
because Peter was an apostle. Fifth, if angels have interpreted the visions and
symbolic texts, doesn't that imply they are easier to understand? Once again
the points are not convincing, but Waltke does not address any of these questions. Rather, he simply assumes that his interpretation is the correct one.
But, to take Waltke's interpretation as the standard of judgment is certainly
not a universal hermeneutical principle.

It may be true that, "Theological models should be built from the clear
teachings of our Lord and his apostles and then, and only then, adorned with
symbolic texts," as Waltke asserts.[50] But this principle does not guarantee that
the interpreter has correctly interpreted and understood the supposedly "clear
teachings" of the Lord and His apostles. It still comes down to the fact that the
interpreter must interpret the so-called clear passages as well as the so-called
obscure passages. The affirmation of this principle does not either support or
contradict any particular eschatological perspective.

Priority of Spiritual Illumination over Scientific Exegesis

This is probably the most surprising of Waltke's principles. As such, it is important to present the whole of what Waltke asserts.

> As the saint imbibes the spiritual presence of Christ while eating
> the bread and drinking the cup at the Lord's Table, so also in the
> reading of the Scriptures one participates in the life and thought
> of God through Christ Jesus in the Spirit (Eph 2:18). Moreover,
> the Holy Spirit, Scripture's divine author, both authenticates it to
> the saint by his inward witness and opens his mind to understand
> its meaning. Without God's supernatural enlightenment, which is
> granted only to the childlike, his truths about Christ and his king-
> dom are hidden from the wise and the learned (Matt 11:25–27).
> Even the apostles, whose eyes saw and whose hands touched the
> blessed Son of God (1 John 1:1), needed supernatural enlight-
> enment to know his true identity (Matt 16:17). The orthodox

50. Ibid.

Jews, who confessed the infallible authority of Scripture, did not know him (John 5:45–47), because God had drawn a veil over their unbelieving hearts (2 Corinthians 3). The rule that one must first establish what the revelation meant to the original audience is problematic, because to unbelievers it meant one thing and to believers it meant another. All too often evangelicals have interpreted the text wherein God has hidden himself according to its meaning to unenlightened minds. One must look to the Spirit's interpretation of God's thoughts (1 Cor 2:9–16). Furthermore, evangelical teachers of every persuasion, including this writer, need to repent for their brash attempts to find God, who veils himself in Scripture from the proud, through merely scientific exegesis which they control. Furthermore, he will delude any evangelical, including this writer, if he or she comes to the Scriptures with a closed mind, feigning to hear his word, even as he deluded Balaam (contrast Num 22:20 and 22) and Ahab. (cf. 1 Kgs 22:15–17)[51]

First of all, this "rule" is not only not self-evident, it is in fact unverifiable. How does someone verify that his "spiritual enlightenment" is actually from God? How can Waltke verify that his understanding of this issue is accurate? He cannot claim that he was "spiritually enlightened," because this would be circular. He cannot resort to scientific exegesis, because then he is verifying the truth about spiritual enlightenment by scientific exegesis, which is illegitimate. Second, Waltke's rule is contrary to fact. I would suspect that Waltke believes in salvation by grace through faith. Yet there are myriads of unbelievers who know that this is the message of the Gospel. Are they the recipients of "spiritual enlightenment"? If so, then Waltke's principle has lost all uniqueness and is simply another way of saying that someone understands what the Scriptures mean. Third, Waltke's characterization of establishing what the revelation meant to the original audience is in fact a mischaracterization. This "rule," if it is a rule, does not claim that the unbelievers constitute part of the original audience. Fourthly, how does Waltke know that with reference to a particular text "God has hidden himself according to its meaning to unenlightened minds"? How can this claim be verified in any given instance? Fifthly, scientific exegesis is not necessarily "controlled" by the interpreter. Sixthly, this principle and all of its support are totally subjective, being verified by subjective experience. Finally, on the basis of Waltke's principles, anyone can claim any interpretation to be "spiritual enlightenment from God," and Waltke cannot, according to his own principles, call this into question. Should he claim his own spiritual enlightenment as a counter-example, this merely becomes a he-said-she-said problem. If he claims to be able to show by

51. Ibid., 265–66.

appeal to scientific exegesis that a particular claim is false, then he has violated his own principle.

Contrary to Waltke's claim, these "rules" are not helpful in adjudicating the issue of the relationship between the testaments, nor do they supply any substantive information regarding how to evaluate conflicting hermeneutical conclusions.

DANIEL AND THE NEW TESTAMENT

A practice that is quite common when dealing with the prophecies of Daniel is to appeal to the New Testament in order to discover the meaning of the prophetic statements in Daniel. We have dealt with some of this when we interacted with Waltke's Rules under the heading "Priority of New Testament Interpretation Over the Interpretation of Theologians" (see page 20). The point here is that OT prophets like Daniel did not have the NT to which to appeal, and a basic principle of hermeneutics is to endeavor to understand the meaning of the text as the original audience would have understood it. In other words, our first effort is to try to understand the *meaning* of Daniel's text as Daniel would have understood it—without appealing to the NT first. An example of this kind of abuse of the relationship between the Testaments in the practice of interpretation is the effort by Homer Hailey to explain Dan 9:27 by a lengthy exposition of Matthew 24. Hailey declares, "Since Daniel's visions pertained to these [the end days, the latter days] and Jesus told of them, why look further and depend on speculations about antichrists and such?"[52] There are two problems with this approach. The first one is that many commentators assume that their understanding of the NT passages is necessarily correct, and they do not bother to do exegesis on those passages to demonstrate that their understanding is accurate. We have dealt with this above under the heading "Scripture Interpreting Scripture," and we do not need to add anything to that discussion.

The second problem with this approach is the fact that, as stated above, since Daniel did not have Matthew's Gospel in order to help him understand the message, and since a basic principle of interpretation is to understand the meaning of a passage in terms of how the original audience would have understood it, it is illegitimate to appeal to the NT to determine the meaning of an OT prophecy. We must be careful to make a distinction here. There is a difference between considering NT passages as examples of the fulfillment of OT prophecies, and using the NT to determine the meaning of OT text. In the case of Hailey, for example, before dealing with Daniel's statement in Dan 9:27 Hailey goes to Matthew's Gospel and expounds on various passages

52. Homer Hailey, *A Commentary on Daniel: A Prophetic Message*, 198–99.

there in order to explain what Daniel meant. Once he has appealed to the NT to determine what Daniel must have meant by the statement "abomination of desolation," he then declares that Daniel's prophecy is fulfilled in the statements of Matthew's Gospel. This is, of course, circular reasoning. He uses Matthew to determine the meaning of Daniel, then he points to Matthew as a fulfillment of Daniel in order to justify his understanding of Daniel. Regardless of the position one holds on the relationships between the Testaments, this kind of hermeneutics is clearly unacceptable.

We are not advocating the approach described by Paul Feinberg:

> A third approach to the meaning of the text associates it with the *understanding of the readers in the prophet's day.* Again, this can be the first move in the introduction of a theory of *sensus plenior.* What characterizes this view is the claim that NT writers use OT passages in ways that could not possibly have been known from their meaning derived from historical-grammatical hermeneutics. The OT text had one meaning in its historical and cultural setting that is to be derived from the understanding of the readers or hearers in the prophet's day. However, so it is argued, there are cases where the NT fulfillment would not have been understood by the OT hearers or readers.[53]

Some commentators claim that the NT authors were able to see an additional or fuller meaning in the OT prophecies than the original human authors. This view is known as *sensus plenior,* or "fuller sense." It is beyond the scope of this book to become involved in the debate about whether prophecies have a single meaning or more than one meaning. Much of this debate involves the question of whether fulfillments in the NT indicate a meaning that goes beyond the meaning that is found in the OT prophecies. Walter Kaiser makes an interesting observation on this point. After pointing out that many commentators appeal to Dan 12:6–9 in an "attempt to show that the prophets did not understand the import of what God suggested to their minds,"[54] Kaiser poses a question and a response in opposition to this view.

> So there it is, say many: "I heard, but I understood not." However, before we conclude too much, let us ask, What was it that Daniel did not understand? Was it the words he was speaking? Not at all! First, the words he did not understand were those of the angel and not his own! Second, the fact that these words of the angel were to be "closed up and sealed until the time of the end" was

---

53. Paul D. Feinberg, "Hermeneutics of Discontinuity," in *Continuity and Discontinuity*, ed. John S. Feinberg (Westchester, Illinois: Crossway Books, 1988), 113.

54. Walter C. Kaiser, Jr., *The Uses of the Old Testament in the New*, 22.

no more a sign that these events were to remain *unexplained* until the end time than was the equivalent expression used in Isaiah 8:16, "Bind up the testimony, seal the law." There, as here, the "sealing" of the testimonies was a reference primarily to the *certainty* of the predicted events.[55]

First, Kaiser's observation that the words that Daniel did not understand were the words of the angel not his own is without force. In one sense, all the words of prophecy are the words of another, not the prophet's own words. Secondly, the expression in Isaiah is not exactly like the one here in Daniel. Isaiah says, "Bind up (צוֹר, *rôs*) the testimony, seal (חֲתוֹם, *m̂ot̂ᵃh*) the law among my disciples." Although Isaiah uses the word "seal" (חָתַם, *tᵃh*), which is used by Daniel, Isaiah does not use the word "conceal" (סָתַם, *m̄ātás*), which Daniel uses in 12:9, and it is primarily this word upon which commentators base their conclusions about Daniel's lack of understanding. However, this does not necessarily support those who claim some additional or fuller meaning. Daniel was specifically told to "conceal" his prophecy, something that other prophets are not instructed to do. So, even if this word indicates that the prophecy was concealed, or that there is some fuller meaning for Daniel's prophecy, it does not indicate that all prophecies have this characteristic.

Additionally, even if the word does mean "to keep secret," it does not support the notion that there is a fuller meaning. The notion of a fuller meaning would only be indicated if Daniel did understand the initial meaning but was kept from understanding the fuller meaning. This is not the case in Daniel's prophecy. If the word means "to keep secret," then either its whole meaning is kept secret, or the word looses all of its meaning. Besides this, it is not at all clear that this is the meaning of this term. Most commentators hold that the term indicates a preservation of the prophecy for later generations, not a concealing of the meaning. In fact, when Daniel voices his lack of understanding, he does not indicate that he did not understand the meaning. In 12:8 Daniel says, "As for me, I heard but could not understand; so I said, 'My lord, what *will be* the outcome of these *events?*"[56] This does not indicate that he did not understand the meaning, but that he did not understand the outcome. If Daniel had not understood the meaning of the prophecy, then his question about the outcome makes no sense.

55. Ibid., 22–23.

56. See our comments on this verse on page 741ff.

Essentially Literal Interpretation

The approach that will be adopted here, and one that we hope to and we will endeavor to apply consistently, has been called the Essentially Literal Method (ELM). The Essentially Literal Method (ELM) attempts to understand the text according to its normal, grammatical, historical, and literary meaning. What this means is that we will endeavor correctly to grasp the grammatical and syntactical features of the original languages involved as they communicate the meaning of the text. We will attempt to understand how the language was used in its historical context. And we will endeavor to allow for the literary nature of the text including the use of figures of speech as well as straight-forward speech.

This approach has often been the target of criticism. For example, in critiquing Ryrie's "literalism," Gentry asserts, "The immediately striking point about Ryrie's first proof is that it is a preconceived hermeneutic. This is quite evident in Ryrie's statement that 'principles of interpretation are basic and ought to be established before attempting to interpret the Word . . .' Does not his approach to language function disallow the possibility of a spiritual interpretation at the very outset? Why must we begin with the assumption of literalism? May not so rich a work as the Bible, dedicated to such a lofty and spiritual theme (the infinite God's redemption of sinful man), written by many authors over 1,500 years employ a variety of literary genres?"[57] One problem with Gentry's criticism is that, regardless of which way one expresses what should constitute one's hermeneutics, the fact is, one's hermeneutic is necessarily going to set boundaries and parameters for interpretation "at the very outset." It may certainly be the case that one's stated hermeneutical methodology disallows a certain kind of interpretation, but one's methodology is necessarily prior to the actual act of interpreting. Also, Gentry's criticism of Ryrie seems to miss the point. The point is perhaps not whether the Bible does or does not contain various literary genres, and Ryrie's approach to language does not necessarily disallow any particular genre. Rather, the point is that language, in its normal function as communication, should be understood in its normal-grammatical-historical usage. This is the default approach as it were. Even spiritual interpretation must be grounded in the normal-grammatical-historical meaning in order to make sense.

Also, Gentry seems to introduce a false dichotomy in his criticism of dispensationalists. He says, "Even dispensationalists admit that biblical revelation often employs figures of speech. But this brings up the very controversy before us: *when* is prophecy to be interpreted literally, and when figuratively?"[58] The

57. Gentry, *He Shall Have Dominion*, 151.
58. Ibid.

false dichotomy is between literal and figurative, and Gentry's notion of literal interpretation may not exactly correspond to Ryrie's. The literal interpretation includes understanding some language as figurative, or even symbolic. Literal interpretation is not opposed to figures of speech. Figures of speech are a common way to communicate, both in everyday speech and in the biblical text. In fact, Ryrie quotes a statement from J. P. Lange asserting this very point: "The *literalist* (so called) is not one who denies that *figurative* language, that *symbols*, are used in prophecy, nor does he deny that great *spiritual* truths are set forth therein; his position is, simply, that the prophecies are to be *normally* interpreted (i.e., according to the received laws of language) as any other utterances are interpreted—that which is manifestly figurative being so regarded."[59] Apparently, when Gentry refers to Dispensationalists in general and Ryrie in particular as "literalists," he is not accounting for the fact that these interpreters are not accurately characterized as disavowing figurative language.

Quoting Vern Poythress, Gentry argues, "dispensationalists 'may have conveniently arranged their decision about what is figurative *after* their basic system is in place telling them what can and what cannot be fitted into the system. The decisions as to what is figurative and what is not figurative may be a product of the system as a whole rather than the inductive basis of it.'"[60] In support of this charge, Gentry quotes a statement by Ryrie: "The understanding of God's differing economies is *essential* to a proper interpretation of His revelation within those various economies."[61] However, such charges can be leveled against individual interpreters of *all* camps. Gentry objects to the notion that what counts as figurative for the Dispensationalist is established before interpretation actually begins, but Gentry is employing the same approach. The very fact that he wants to take a different approach to what counts as figurative indicates that he is making the same kind of decision prior to interpretation, just like the Dispensationalists supposedly do. It is perhaps legitimate to identify this with reference to a particular interpreter's own interpretation in given instances. But the fact that a particular interpreter makes an illicit assumption does not disqualify the entire system as illegitimate. This amounts to nothing more than an *ad hominem* attack. One may debate what constitutes figurative speech, but that such a decision is prior to the interpretive process is not a debatable point. It is prior for all interpreters regardless of what one counts as figurative.

---

59. J. P. Lange, *Commentary on the Holy Scriptures: Revelation* (New York: Charles Scribner, 1872), 98; quoted in Charles Caldwell Ryrie, *Dispensationalism Today* (Chicago: Moody Press, 1965), 87 (emphasis in original).

60. Ibid.

61. Ibid.

Gentry also criticizes the Dispensationalists for constructing a system in which "countervailing evidence" is ineffective. Of course, Gentry assumes that his objections qualify as "countervailing evidence." The fact that no dispensationalist is convinced by contrary arguments does not mean that the system is "immune to criticism" as Gentry asserts.[62] It may simply be that these arguments are not convincing. Gentry argues as if the only way he can be convinced that Dispensationalists are not stacking the deck is if they would convert to Postmillennialism. But such an argument is in fact constructed so as to be immune to criticism.

Gentry makes the bold statement, "there is no such thing as hermeneutical neutrality."[63] Of course, this is a self-defeating claim. If it is true, then there would be no way of knowing this. If there is in fact no such thing as hermeneutical neutrality, then all of Gentry's criticisms of Dispensationalism amount to nothing more than an exercise in futility. His criticisms turn out to be simply his non-neutral interpretation of dispensationalists' claims, and since his criticisms are non-neutral, then they have no objective force. If, as Gentry claims, "The interpretation of a passage is grounded in the expositor's original presupposition,"[64] then Gentry's own claim is nothing more than his interpretation grounded in his presupposition that there is no hermeneutic neutrality. If it is true of all interpreters, then it is true of Gentry and of his interpretation of interpretation.

Gentry criticizes Dwight Pentecost and John Walvoord for their assertions: "When the Old Testament is used in the New it is used only in a literal sense," and "the literal fulfillment of promises pertaining to the first coming is a foreshadowing of the literal fulfillment of promises pertaining to the second coming,"[65] respectively. Gentry declares, "Literalism *definitionally* writes off all non-literal fulfillments."[66] But, this does not follow. Granted Pentecost and Walvoord should, as Gentry says, "prove this, not just assume it,"[67] but in light of Gentry's claim that there is no hermeneutical neutrality, either his criticism makes no sense because it is merely his own non-neutral observation, or his claim about hermeneutic neutrality is wrong. If there is no hermeneutical neutrality, then how does Gentry expect the expositors to "prove" anything? And, if Gentry believes that they should prove their assertions, then hermeneutic

---

62. Ibid., 152.

63. Ibid., 153.

64. Ibid.

65. J. Dwight Pentecost, *Thy Kingdom Come* (Wheaton, Illinois: Victor, 1990), 80; quoted in Gentry, *He Shall Have Dominion*, 153.

66. Gentry, *He Shall Have Dominion*, 153.

67. Ibid.

neutrality must be possible. Just because Gentry does not accept their assertions does not mean they have not proven their point. In fact, when Gentry
charges that their definition of literalism "ignores Old Testament prophecies
of the kingdom that find fulfillment in the *ministry of Christ*, though not as a
literalistic, political conception,"[68] his criticism is merely a non-neutral interpretation grounded in his own original presupposition and consequently has
no real force except for those who already accept his system. The very fact that
Gentry thinks it is possible to critique the interpretations of others contradicts
his own claim that there is no hermeneutic neutrality.

Gentry spills much ink criticizing the claims of literalist interpretation.
However, the vast majority of his criticisms seem to be predicated on his
misunderstanding of the Essentially Literal Method. As we have said, ELM
does not reject figure of speech, typology, and other interpretive approaches.
Rather, ELM attempts, albeit perhaps sometimes unsuccessfully, to allow
the text to dictate what kind of approach must be taken with reference to
a given assertion, whether understanding it as a figure, or as a type, or what
have you.[69] That being said, it must be remembered that there is a normal-
grammatical-historical approach to the text that is the foundation of interpretation, whether it be interpreting the Bible or any other piece of literature. In
the case of literary types, or genres, the only way the interpreter can identify
the genre of a passage is to read it. But, in reading the passage, there must be
some level of understanding that takes place; else the process of recognizing
the genre would be futile. It is that level of reading and understanding that
forms the basis and the ground for all other approaches, and that is what we
call the Essentially Literal Method of interpretation.[70] The Essentially Literal
Method of interpretation seeks to understand the words and sentences of the
original text according to their normal, historical, grammatical, and literary
meanings, taking into consideration figures of speech, symbolism, idiomatic
expressions, etc., as these are indicated by the syntax, genre, and context of a
given passage.

---

68. Ibid., 153–54.

69. The notion that an interpreter can "allow the text to dictate" anything assumes the
possibility of objectivity in interpretation—a notion that has come under severe attack in
both hermeneutical and philosophical circles. The possibility of objectivity is discussed
in detail in the book, Thomas Howe, *Objectivity in Biblical Interpretation* (Longwood,
Florida: Advantage Books, 2005).

70. For further discussion of the relationship of genre to interpretation, see Thomas A.
Howe, "Does Genre Determine Meaning," *The Christian Apologetics Journal*, vol. 6, no. 1
(Spring, 2007): 1–20.

Theological Perspectives

Because of the philosophical climate, commentators and theorists alike have come to realize the importance of the perspective of the interpreter and how this perspective can influence the interpreter's understanding of a text. Virtually everyone who writes a commentary or a treatise on interpretation is faced with the necessity of addressing the presence of his own perspective and the part it plays in his work. As one author puts it, "The way in which we approach Scripture and the assumptions we bring to the text are vitally important matters, especially when we are discussing disputed doctrines like eschatology."[71] Because the issue of perspective is so important, we will set forth our theological/eschatological perspective. As Mathison points out, although we may not be able completely to set aside our own perspective, "we must at least be aware that we have these assumptions and make every attempt to recognize what they are."[72] An interpreter who has acknowledged and identified his perspective is more likely to recognize an illicit imposition of this perspective upon the text. We will endeavor to avoid this error, but it will ultimately be the reader who judges the success of our efforts.

Futurism

The theological/eschatological perspective from which this commentary will proceed is first of all Futurist. According to Norman Geisler, Futurism maintains "that the prophecies about the Tribulation, the Second Coming, and a following kingdom (relating to the Millennium) are not yet fulfilled and are all future."[73] There are many varieties of Futurism depending upon how the individual espousing the view understands the relationship between various details of the end time events. A Premillennialist, for example, is one who believes that there will be an actual, 1,000 year reign of Christ on the earth, and this reign is referred to as the Millennium. There are, of course, other views that can be identified as Futurist, but this is not the place to enter into a full exposition of each of these views. The point that is important for the purposes of this commentary is that Futurists believe that many of the prophecies of the book of Daniel are still in the future, even from our perspective. Also, the term "futurism" has been used to indicate that many of the prophecies of Daniel are future and have no historical fulfillment. That is not the way the term is being used here. The perspective of this writer is that individual prophecies of Daniel may have historical as well as future fulfillment, and many may

71. Keith A. Mathison, *Postmillennialism: An Eschatology of Hope*, 3.
72. Ibid.
73. Norman L. Geisler, *Church, Last Things*, vol. 4, *Systematic Theology*, 644.

have historical fulfillment and also function as types of future events. We will attempt to make these distinctions in the appropriate places.

Premillennialism

The second aspect of the theological perspective assumed here is Premillennialism. We have already looked briefly at this position, but a few additional comments are pertinent. Quoting Geisler again, "The essence of premillennialism is that Christ will physically return to earth and set up a worldwide thousand-year reign."[74] The designation "pre" indicates the fact that Christ will return prior to the establishing of His millennial kingdom and in fact for the purpose of establishing it on earth.

Pretribulationism

The third aspect of the theological perspective assumed in this commentary is Pretribulationism: "Pretribulationism holds that the Rapture of the church occurs *before* the Tribulation, during which the church, Christ's bride, will be in heaven, standing before His judgment seat (2 Cor 5:10) and preparing for His return to earth."[75] The Rapture is "described as Christ coming '*in the air.*' . . . Unlike Christ's return to earth, the Rapture will occur in an instant without warning, 'in a flash, in the twinkling of an eye' (v. 52; cf. 1 Thess 4:17)."[76] In this event, the saints who are raptured will be transformed from this corruptible state to the incorruptible state.

Preterism

The contrary view that we will be examining in our commentary is identified as Preterism. According to Ed Stevens, "'Preterist' means past in fulfillment, and 'Futurist' means future in fulfillment. Preterist basically means the opposite of Futurist. Futurists believe most end-time prophecies (especially the big three major ones—Parousia, Resur., and Judgment) are yet to be fulfilled. Preterists believe that most [Partial Preterism] or all [Full Preterism] of Bible Prophecy (especially the big three events) have already been fulfilled in Christ and the on-going expansion of His Kingdom."[77]

---

74. Ibid., 545.

75. Ibid., 612.

76. Ibid., 621, 633.

77. Ed Stevens, "What is the Preterist View of Bible Prophecy?" http://www.preterist .org/whatispreterism.asp.

Full Preterism

According to John Noē, "Full Preterists believe the appointed time of the end came long ago."[78] Noē goes on to give an explanation of what this means: "What the Bible says about the end of the world is *nothing*! That's right—just like the historic creeds. *Nothing*! . . . What does the Bible say about the world ending as we know it or in its present form? Again, *nothing*! . . . Not a single text, taken in context, declares the world will ever end. As unpleasant as this truth may be for some, the end of the world is simply a false, pagan doctrine that's been dragged into the Church and read into the Bible."[79] In other words, for the Full Preterist, all Bible prophecies have been fulfilled, and there is no prophecy left to be fulfilled in the future. Some refer to this view as Hyper-Preterism. Of this view Kenneth Gentry says, "The hyper-preterist believes that *all* prophecy is fulfilled in the A.D. 70 destruction of the Temple, including the Second Advent, the resurrection of the dead, the great judgment, and so forth."[80]

Partial Preterism

John Evans defines Partial Preterism as the belief that "although most of the prophecies of Daniel, the Synoptic Gospels, Revelation, and other biblical books were fulfilled by then [AD 70], some major ones remain to be fulfilled, including the coming of Christ to establish His eternal kingdom."[81] Table 3 below lists some of the key prophecies that Partial Preterists claim were fulfilled in 70 AD and those that are still in the future.

Table 3: Partial Preterism and Fulfilled Prophecies

Fulfilled in 70 A.D.	Fulfilled in the Future
A coming of Christ	The Coming of Christ
A day of the Lord	The Day of the Lord
A judgment	The Final Judgment
The End of the Jewish Age	The End of History
	The Rapture of the Living
	The Resurrection of the Dead

78. Noē, *Beyond the End Times*, 1.

79. Ibid., 42 (emphasis in original).

80. Gentry, *He Shall Have Dominion*, 555.

81. John S. Evans, *The Four Kingdoms of Daniel: A Defense of the "Roman" Sequence with AD 70 Fulfillment*, xi.

Although there are a variety of views within these overall categories, the above definitions are sufficient for our purposes. Also, in the comments and observations in the commentary, no effort will be made to distinguish between Partial Preterist views and Full Preterist views. Usually these distinctions can be inferred from what is claimed.

Family

Although the Futurist, Premillennial, Pretribulational view will be the theological/ eschatological assumption of this study of Daniel, it is hoped that we will interact with opposing views with honesty and fairness. Although it will not be possible to interact with every view on every text, we will want to spend some extra time interacting with different views when we attempt to understand Daniel's Seventy Sevens prophecy in Daniel 9 and the string of prophecies in chapter 11. During this interaction and discussion, we will endeavor to refrain from presenting contrary views in a disparaging manner, and we will endeavor to treat those who have opposing views as Christian brothers and sisters. As is customary, views that are discussed will be identified by using the names of those who hold or propose these views. This is simply a short-hand way of identifying the view in the discussion. However, no critique about contrary views should be taken as attacks against those who hold these views, and we will assume that persons who hold these views are capable and sincere scholars with whom we honestly and humbly disagree.

Introduction to the Book of Daniel

Title of Daniel

The title of the book is the name of its principle character, Daniel. In Hebrew the name is pronounced similarly, דָּנִיֵּאל (l'eŷiñaD). The name is the combination of either the verb דִּין (ñıd) which means "to judge," or the noun דִּן (nad), "judge," and the singular form of the Hebrew word "God," אֵל (le'). If the first word is a noun, then the addition of the extra *yod* (י) in the middle of the word could indicate the first person personal pronoun, in which case the name could mean, "God is my judge." If the first word is a verb, then the name could mean "God judges me." In fact, the Qal perfect form of the verb would be דָּן (nad), which is identical to the noun form, so the name 'Daniel' could be taken to have either meaning. The significance of this meaning is that it may indicate Daniel's theme. The theme of Daniel's prophecy seems to be the fact that God is the judge of all the earth, and that, in spite appearances, all things are following His schedule and are working together to fulfill His purpose. This would have been a particularly important message for the captives in Babylon and to those who were to face even greater tests in the future. God's judgment is not confined to His enemies, however. Judgment begins in the house of the Lord, and God judges Israel as well as Babylon.

Composition of Daniel

AUTHORSHIP

Daniel has probably been under as much if not more scrutiny than Isaiah. This is primarily due to the anti-supernatural bias of the critical scholars who must explain the predictive prophecies in terms of natural causes. However, there has not been an argument that has offered a reasonable alternative to the traditional view that Daniel, of the 6th century BC, is the author of this book. Because this commentary is written from an Evangelical perspective and based on the belief that the Scriptures are the inspired, inerrant Word of God, and because the primary aim is to interpret the prophecies and to address the interpretive claims of the Preterists, little time will be spent on the critical issues of authorship, date, etc.

A typical way of attempting to follow a circuitous path around the controversy is the following statement, "The question of historical basis is a complicated one. It is sufficient to say here that Daniel's main purpose is not to record detailed history but to use stories and symbols to demonstrate God's control of history."[82] This kind of assertion employs what the writers believe to be the purpose of the book to interpret the meaning of the book. The problem with this is that what one commentator believes to be the purpose of the book might not be the purpose of the book at all. In fact, there are a great many statements in the Bible about which no one knows the purpose, that is, why it was written. For example, why did God say, "Do not boil a kid in its mother's milk"? There has been an abundance of speculation, but no one has presented a definitive explanation as to why this was said. Nevertheless, it is quite clear what the statement means. And the problem of purpose is evident on the level of the whole book as well. Many commentators have assumed that the statement in Jn 20:30 is the purpose statement of the book. However, in its context, it seems better to understand this passage as a statement about post-resurrection signs that Jesus performed rather than about the purpose of the book. Using what one believes to be the purpose of the book to determine the meaning of the book is to interpret the objective text by a subjective

---

82. William Sanford LaSor, David Allan Hubbard, and Frederic Wm. Bush, *Old Testament Survey*, 2d ed. (Grand Rapids: William B. Eerdmans Publishing Company, 1996), 567.

standard. What in Daniel would lead one to think that Daniel's purpose was not to record detailed history?

Probably the most widely accepted view of the composition of the book of Daniel is that it is composed of two parts that are sharply distinguished from each other. The first six chapters have been seen to be much older in composition than chapters 7–12, and the earlier chapters have been understood as having undergone re-editing in Maccabean times to attain a redactional unity with the apocalyptic visions of chapters 7–12. Consequently, critical scholars hold that the book of Daniel is a second century BC composition deriving primarily from the Maccabean period. Typical statements like the following are made about the first six chapter: "Chs. 1–6, expressed in the third person, may well have been written by someone else about Daniel."

However, if Daniel is not the author of the book, some quite unfortunate conclusions must result. E. B. Pusey has said it well: "To write any book under the name of another, and to give it out to be his, is, in any case, a forgery, dishonest in itself, and destructive of all trustworthiness. But the case as to the book of Daniel, if it were not his, would go far beyond even this. The writer, were he not Daniel, must have lied, on a most frightful scale, ascribing to God prophecies which were never uttered, and miracles which are assumed never to have been wrought. In a word, the whole book would be one lie in the Name of God."[83]

Critical scholars who deny Daniel's authorship nevertheless attempt to extract some spiritual truth and comfort that should have been the function of the book for its intended audience. Pusey quotes one critical scholar who proposed such a view: "The truth seems that starting, like many a patriot bard of our own, from a name traditionally sacred, the writer used it with no deceptive intention, as a dramatic form which dignified his encouragement of his countrymen in their struggle against Antiochus."[84] But, as Pusey points out, "it was no encouragement at all, except on the belief of its truth."[85] If the events did not occur, if God did not intervene, if there were no visions, then there is no encouragement from God—He never did this, and there is no good reason to accept the supposed "insights" of the text. Nevertheless, assuming the Daniel of the text to be the author of the book, the most likely date of the composition of the book is about 530 BC. It is probably a collection of the memoirs of Daniel, albeit complied in a highly artistic literary structure.

83. E. B. Pusey, *Daniel The Prophet: Nine Lectures*, 75.
84. Ibid., 75–76.
85. Ibid.

STRUCTURE OF DANIEL

Literary Structure

Daniel begins with an introduction, the remainder of the book being structured into two major parts. The two parts are connected together by a hinge, chapter 7 (see Figure 1 below). From chapter 2 verse 2, the book of Daniel is written in the Chaldean language known as Aramaic. Aramaic is a cognate language of Hebrew and employs the same letters to form its alphabet. The Aramaic section of Daniel extends to the end of chapter 7. By its language, chapter 7 is connected to the first major part of the book. However, chapter 7 is connected to the second major part of the book by its content and style. Whereas in chapters 2 through 6 the visions were given to others and interpreted by Daniel, in chapter 7 and following, the visions are now given to Daniel and interpreted by an angel. Chapter 1 functions as an historical introduction. Chapters 2–6 are primarily historical accounts that contain prophecy by way of visions. Chapters 7–12 are primarily prophetic visions that concern history. There is also a contrasting parallelism between the four Hebrews who appear in the opening narrative of chapter 1, and the four beasts that appear in the prophecy given to Daniel in chapter 7.

Figure 1: Structure of Daniel

STRUCTURE OF DANIEL				
INTRO 1:1-2:1	GENTILE DOMINION 2:2-6:28		HINGE 7:1-28	ISRAELITE EXALTATION 7:1-12:13
H E F B O R U E R W S	NEBUCHADNEZZAR 2:2-4:37		B F E O A U S R T S	RAM AND GOAT 8:1-27
	BELSHAZZAR 5:1-30			SEVENTY SEVENS 9:1-27
	DARIUS 5:31-6:28			LATTER DAYS 10:1-12:13

Another way to look at the structure of the book of Daniel is presented in the graphic in Figure 2 on page 41. This graphic demonstrates some of the interrelationships between the various parts of the book. The first part is identified as a nadir, which is the opposite of a climax. A nadir starts at a high point and descends to a low point. The record of the empire of Babylon is at its highest point under Nebuchadnezzar and is so illustrated in his vision being represented by the head of gold in chapter 2. It descends to its lowest point under Belshazzar when it is ultimately overthrown by the Medes and the Persians, and Darius takes the throne. The empire of the Medes and Persians is represented by the breast and arms of silver, a less precious metal, indicating an inferior quality of this new empire. Also, a chiasm exists between chapters 2 through 7. This is another indicator that chapter seven is the pivotal chapter of this book.

A closer look at chapters 2–7 will present further confirmation of the pivotal role of chapter 7. The graphic in Figure 2 depicts the chiastic arrangement of these chapters. Chapter 2 identifies the four kingdoms that will come upon the earth, starting with the head of gold representing Babylon under Nebuchadnezzar. The decrease in the value of the metals may indicate a corresponding deterioration in the political cohesiveness, while the increasing ferocity of the beasts in chapter 7 indicates a corresponding increase in the ruthlessness of the representative kingdoms. So, chapter 7 is part of the chiastic structure that unites chapters 2 through 7. Yet chapter 7 is also part of the structure of the final chapters by the fact that it introduces the visions of Daniel that are interpreted by the angel. Chapter 7 is the hinge on which the book pivots.

Logical Structure

A primary focus of this commentary is to examine the Preterist interpretations of the prophecies of Daniel and to evaluate their success in explaining these prophecies in light of the text and history. Unfortunately, few Preterists have undertaken the task of providing a commentary on the whole book of Daniel. Most of the writing from the Preterist camp deals with specific prophetic passages such as the Seventy Sevens prophecy of chapter 9.

This may be due to the fact that the first six chapters of Daniel do not seem to present any prophetic material that is directly related to the issues that divide Preterists and Futurists. It is a contention of this commentary that these first six chapters do more than simply provide a historical background to the prophetic section or provide important lessons on how the people of God should live and act in hostile environments. The dream of Nebuchadnezzar recounted in chapter 2 is a major prophecy in of the book of Daniel and provides the framework into which the later prophecies fit. The fact that this material comes so early in the book rather than being contained with those chapters that have traditionally been taken to be the prophetic material seems to suggest that these first six chapters are more crucial to understanding the prophecies of chapter 7–12 than simply providing the historical or moral background.

Figure 2: Graphic Structure of Daniel

Figure 2: Graphic Structure of Daniel

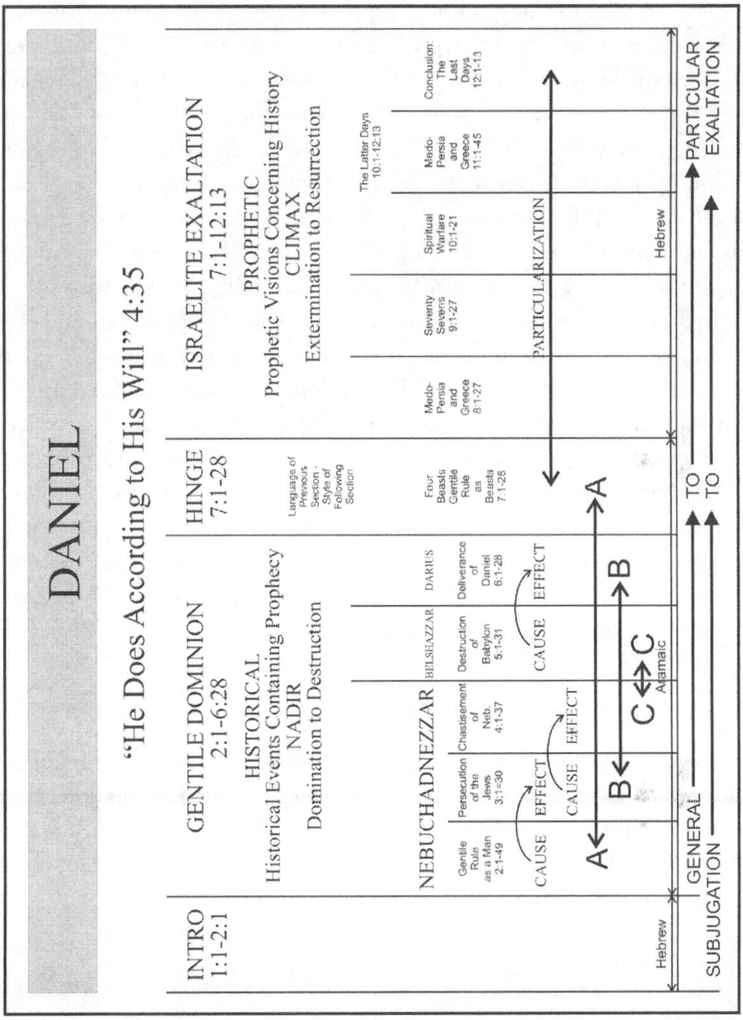

The relationship of chapters 1–6 to the second major section of the book, chapters 7–12, we will refer to as the Logical or Thematic Structure of Daniel's book. This material is integral to the prophecies of the later chapters and, as such, will be as subject to the eschatological view point of the interpreter as are the later chapters. Consequently, the "Introduction" is not the place to set forth this what we perceive to be the logical or thematic structure. One aim of this commentary is to consider the prophecies of Daniel in terms of the original languages and the historical contexts so as to evaluate whether the Preterist interpretations can successfully explain these relationships and account for all that the text asserts. In other words, we want to see how the Preterists interpret the language of the prophecies and, for example, how they associate the prophecies with facts of history in order to see if their interpretations can explain this relationship. Once we have examined in detail whether or not the Preterist interpretations can explain the prophecies of Daniel in light of the text and of the facts of history, we believe that this examination will demonstrate the failure of the Preterist view. At the same time, we want to set forth in detail the Futurist interpretation in terms of these same relationships and demonstrate how the Futurist can successfully relate the language of the prophecies to the facts of history. This being our aim, we want the logical and thematic structure to grow out of the details of the text rather than impose this structure upon the text. Although it may not be possible for any interpreter completely to avoid an imposition upon the text of his prior eschatological commitment, we endeavor to prevent this as much as is possible. Consequently, our presentation of the logical and thematic structure of the book of Daniel in which we argue for the relationship of the first six chapters to the later prophetic section will come at the end of our commentary. For the reader who wants to see this material before entering into the presentation of the commentary itself, you may refer to the section titled "Structure of Daniel's Prophecies" beginning on page 695.

Historical Background

It is important to have a basic grasp of the historical background situation against which the book of Daniel is set. Much of this information will be dealt with in the course of the commentary itself. However, there are some few general background considerations that form the basic historical setting and can be dealt with here.

THE KINGDOM OF JUDAH

By the time of Daniel's captivity to Nebuchadnezzar and Babylon, the northern kingdom of Israel had already been destroyed, and the people of Israel have been scattered by the Assyrians throughout the Assyrian empire. Daniel would probably have been born during the reign of Josiah, king of Judah who reigned from 640 to 609 BC. Josiah died at Megiddo in 609 BC, and his son Jehoahaz took over the kingdom. Jehoahaz reigned for only about three months and was deposed by Pharaoh Neco. Neco placed Jehoiakim on the throne of Judah, and he reigned from 609–597 BC. It was during the reign of Jehoiakim that Nebuchadnezzar II defeated Pharaoh Neco and the Egyptian army at Carchemish in 605 BC, after which he invaded Judah and Jerusalem and took many of the best people and the vessels of the temple back to his own temple. Stephen Miller offers a helpful summary of the period.

> Jehoiakim promised loyalty to Nebuchadnezzar but soon rebelled, bringing Babylon's wrath upon the nation. The Judean king died rather mysteriously during Nebuchadnezzar's siege of Jerusalem, and his son, Jehoiachin (2 Kgs 24:6–16), reigned for three months in 598/597 B.C. After surrendering the city of Jerusalem to Nebuchadnezzar on March 15/16, 597 B.C., Jehoiachin was taken captive to Babylon along with ten thousand Judean citizens (2 Kgs 24:12–16), including the prophet Ezekiel (cf. Ezek 1:1–2). Zedekiah (2 Kgs 24:17–25:21), another son of Josiah, then became the last king of Judah (597–586 B.C.). Eventually the new king also defied Babylonian authority, and Nebuchadnezzar determined to put an end to the rebellious nation. He laid siege to Jerusalem on January 15, 588 B.C. (cf. 2 Kgs 25:1; Jer 39:1; 52:4; Ezek 24:1–2) and succeeded in capturing it on July 18, 586 B.C. (cf. 2 Kgs 25:2–3; Jer 39:2; 52:5–7). The final destruction of Jerusalem (which included the demolition of Solomon's temple) began on August 14, 586 B.C. (cf. 2 Kgs 25:8–10). Daniel, therefore, lived through the reigns of five Judean monarchs and saw the fall of the nation and the destruction of Jerusalem.[86]

Daniel was probably about 15 years old when he and his companions were taken to Babylon. Daniel lived in Babylon throughout the existence of the Neo-Babylonian Empire and into the time of Cyrus the Persian (580–529 BC).

MESOPOTAMIAN RELIGION

As far back as the time of the Sumerians, perhaps as far back as 3000 BC, there are indications of the deification of nature, or at least the postulating of a deity responsible for a particular natural phenomenon or celestial object, such as the sun. As Jean Bottéro describes it, "the ancient Mesopotamians doubled their universe with a parallel universe of supernatural personalities whose names reflected their roles: An was Heaven, and the god who presided over Heaven; Utu/Šamaš was the sun and the sun god; Namtar was not only 'decisions' (this is the meaning of that Sumerian term), presiding over the turning point in our 'destiny' (*item*), but also the god who governed them;"[87] Bottéro goes on to point out that recent calculations have discovered as many

86. Stephen R. Miller, *Daniel: An Exegetical and Theological Exposition of Holy Scripture*, vol. 18, *The American Commentary*, 43–44.

87. Jean Bottéro, *Religion in Ancient Mesopotamia*, 44.

as 3,000 gods in the Sumerian pantheon, "but the list was not, and still is not, complete: new documents, as they are discovered, continue to present us with names of deities that were hitherto unknown."[88]

The Akkadians, following the Sumerians, syncretized the Sumerian pantheon with their own and managed to reduce the overall number of deities. Bottéro explains, "The gods were countless and teeming in the time of their Sumerian creators; but the Akkadians, less at ease before so many supernatural beings, apparently gradually introduced many fewer of them from their own pantheon (in the oldest catalogs, from around 2600, we still count only three Akkadian gods out of more than five hundred; and the overall total, a few centuries later, was never more than thirty!). It was as if, faced with that Sumerian legacy, the Akkadians preferred to elevate the dignity and power of their gods as they were simultaneously reducing the number of them."[89]

Through the centuries the Akkadians organized and reorganized the massive pantheon of gods until, at the rise of the Neo-Babylonian Empire, Marduk, "the lord," also referred to as *bêlu*, and *bêl*, began to emerge as the principal deity. Although Marduk was believed to be the destroyer of the mountains, indicating his omnipotence, he was nevertheless conceived after the pattern of humans. As Bottéro explains, "Thus 'the god' was first imagined via his *superiority*—his superiority over everything else, but especially over humans, since in this anthropomorphic regime of the local religion, the divine was represented in an exalted and superior form based on the human model. Every god was thus perceived as having been formed in our image but was believed to be superior to us in everything, both positive and negative."[90] That to Marduk was given worship and trust even by Nebuchadnezzar II is demonstrated in a prayer to Marduk:

> Without Thee, Lord, what has existence?
> For the king Thou lovest, whose name Thou didst call,
> who pleaseth Thee, Thou advancest his fame,
> Thou assignest him a straightforward path.
> I am a prince Thou favorest, a creature of thine hands,
> Thou madest me, entrusted to me the kingship over all people.
> Of Thy grace, O Lord, who providest for all of them,
> cause me to love Thy exalted rule.
> Let fear of Thy godhead be in my heart,
> grant me what seemeth good to Thee;
> Thou wilt do, verily, what profiteth me.[91]

88. Ibid., 45.
89. Ibid., 48.
90. Ibid., 58–59.
91. Thorkild Jacobsen, *The Treasures of Darkness: A History of Mesopotamian Religion*

Marduk was the patron god of Babylon. Through the centuries, Marduk rose to prominence ultimately "simply known as Bēl (Lord)."[92] The Snake-Dragon is a companion of Maruk: "By comparing the figure depicted on the gates and processionals way at Babylon with the description of the building operations given by King Nebuchadnezzar II (reigned 504–562 BC), it has been possible to identify with certainty the creature's Akkadian name as mušhuššu, 'furious snake.'"[93]

THE BABYLONIAN EMPIRE

It was Nebuchadnezzar I (1124–1103 BC) who ushered in the new rise to prominence of Babylonia. After him the next significant ruler was Nabu-nasir (747–734 BC), which led to the first of the new dynasty of Babylonian rulers, Nebopolassar (625–605 BC), the father of Nebuchadnezzar II. As Oppenheim explains,

> Under Nabopolassar's son, Nebuchadnezzar II, Babylonia invaded and took over the provinces of the Assyrian Empire from the Mediterranean Sea to the Persian Gulf. Nebuchadnezzar was married to Amyitis, the daughter of the king of the Medes, and thus Babylonia was protected by an alliance with that kingdom. Quite in Assyrian style, the Babylonian king began then to appear annually with his army to collect tribute and to conquer and punish recalcitrant cities such as Jerusalem in 597 and 586 B.C. He repeatedly fought with the Egyptian army. The last ruler of Babylonia, Nabonidus (555–539 B.C.), provided a somewhat queer "fins" to the independence of Babylonia (see above, p. 152). Cyrus moved into the capital without encountering resistance and treated Nabonidus with his characteristic leniency toward defeated kings. This was the end of Babylonian sovereignty, but that the spirit of the country was not yet dead is brought home by the fact that two later pretenders to the Babylonian throne took the magic name of Nebuchadnezzar.[94]

The Chaldeans, to whom reference is made in various parts of the book of Daniel, first appear in historical records of Babylonia in about the ninth century BC. According to Oppenheim, "They seem to have lived in a region of swamps, lakes, and canebrakes along the lower course of the two

(New Haven, Connecticut: Yale University Press, 1976), 238–39.

92. Jeremy Black and Anthony Green, *Gods, Demons and Symbols of Ancient Mesopotamia: An Illustrated Dictionary*, 128.

93. Ibid., 166.

94. A. Leo Oppenheim, *Ancient Mesopotamia: Portrait of a Dead Civilization*, 163.

rivers between the shores of the Persian Gulf and the southernmost cities of Babylonia."[95] At this time the Chaldeans were mostly composed of individual politically independent groups called "houses." These groups were composed of backward peoples, at least by the measure of the large cities of people such as Babylon. Evidence seems to indicate that even at this time these Chaldeans spoke a dialect of Aramaic.

In the forty-third year of his reign, about 562 BC, Nebuchadnezzar II died. The succession to the throne was a confused set of circumstances complicated by intrigue and murder. Nebuchadnezzar's son Amel-Marduk, who is referred to in 2 Kgs 25:27 as Evil-Merodach אֱוִיל־מְרֹדַךְ _(kador^eM lɩw^e^>)_, ruled over Babylon from 561 to 560 BC. His successor was his brother-in-law, Nergal-shar-usur (Neriglissar) who came to power in 559 BC. He ruled from 559 to 556 BC. and was succeeded by his young son, Labashi-Marduk. Labashi was murdered in 556, having been on the throne for only two months. Nabonidus was thereupon named the King of Babylon. Historical records indicate that Nabonidus may have been mentally unstable. When he went into a self imposed exile in the Oasis of Temâ in the Arabian desert, he was absent from Babylon for almost ten years. His oldest son Belshazzar became the co-regent of Babylon. Daniel 5:1–4 records the great feast that Belshazzar held in Babylon on the occasion of which God announced the ultimate defeat and overthrow of Babylon. The feast is in fact confirmed by the Greek historian, Herodotus. It was shortly after this event, in 539, that Cyrus invaded Babylon. Gobyras, Cyrus' commander, entered Babylon and took it without any resistance. Shortly thereafter Cyrus allowed as many as 40,000 Jews to return to Jerusalem. However, it was not until the Artaxerxes I allowed Nehemiah to return to Jerusalem in 445 B.C. that there is a specific mention of the opportunity to rebuild Jerusalem. Futurists believe that the Seventy Sevens of Daniel's prophecy, which is declared to begin with the "decree to restore and build Jerusalem," is calculated from this 445 BC date. Below is a brief overview of the history of Mesopotamia indicating the dates of the reigns of various kings, and also indicating the dates of significant events.

95. Ibid., 160.

Table 4: Brief Overview of the History of Mesopotamia

	Prehistoric Era
Sixth millennium	The region emerges little by little from north to south as a great lowland between the Tigris and the Euphrates. It was populated by unknown ethnic groups who had come from the piedmonts of the north and the east. There is no doubt that those groups included Semites from the northern edges of the Syro-Arabian desert.
Fourth millennium (at the latest)	After the arrival of the Sumerians (most probably from the southeast), a process of interaction and exchange began to form the first major civilization in the area. An urban society soon arose through the unification of more or less autonomous primitive villages.
	Historical Era
Ca. 3200	Early Dynastic Period: invention of writing.
2900–2330	First Dynasty of Ur (Ur I), the dynasty of Lagasˆ: time of independent city-states.
2330–2100	Old Akkadian Period: the first Semitic empire founded by Sargon the Great (Akkadian dynasty); invasion of the Guti and the time of "Anarchy."
2100–2000	The kingdom of Ur (Third Dynasty of Ur, Ur III): first arrivals of new Semitic tribes, the Amorites.
2000–1750	Rival kingdoms: the dynasties of Isin, Larsa, Ešnun, Mari, etc.
	Old Assyrian Period: first rulers of Assyria. Old Babylonian Period (begins in 1894): First Dynasty of Babylon (Babylon I).
1750–1600	Hegemony of Babylon. Hammurabi (1792–1750) reunites the country in a kingdom centered on Babylon, which his five successors would maintain.
1600–1100	Middle Babylonian Period: invasion and control by the Kassites, who draw the country into a political torpor, which favors a vigorous cultural development.
	Middle Assyrian Period: ca. 1300, Assyria (capitals: first Aššur, later Kalhu, and then Nineveh) gains its independence.

1100–1000	First infiltrations of new Semitic tribes: the Arameans. Second Dynasty of Isin: ca. 1100, Babylonian revival. Battle for hegemony between Assyria and Babylonia. Even when the latter was politically dominated, it maintained its cultural supremacy.
1000–609	Neo-Assyrian Period: Assyrian dominance, time of the Sargonids (Esarhaddon, Assurbanipal).
609–539	Neo-Babylonian Period and Chaldean dynasty: Babylon takes control of Assyria in 609; Aramaization continues.
539–330	Persian Period: in 539 Babylon falls to the Achaemenid Cyrus, and Mesopotamia is incorporated into the Persian Empire; Aramaization intensifies.
330–130	Seleucid Period: in 330 Alexander conquers and takes over from the Persians and brings the entire Near East into the Hellenistic cultural orbit; his successors, the Seleucid rulers, maintained their hold over Mesopotamia.
130–	Arsacid Period: in 127 Mesopotamia passes into the hands of the Parthians, under the Arsacid dynasty. The land lost not only all autonomy but all contemporary political and cultural significance. Another era begins.

Flow of Daniel's Narrative

The flow of Daniel's narrative begins with the account of the captivity of the tribes of Judah and Benjamin, the Southern Kingdom, by Nebuchadnezzar. Chapter one recounts how Daniel, Hananiah, Mishael, and Azariah come to their place of leadership and position in the kingdom of Babylon. Against the background of the rebellion and apostasy that led to the captivity—see for example Jer 1:16: "I will pronounce My judgments on them concerning all their wickedness, whereby they have forsaken Me and have offered sacrifices to other gods, and worshiped the works of their own hands"—Daniel demonstrates a commitment to the God of Israel, not wanting to "defile himself" (יִתְגָּאָל, laʾagtiy) by partaking "in the portion of the king and in the wine of his feasts" (בְּפַתְבַּג הַמֶּלֶךְ וּבְיֵין מִשְׁתָּיו, kelemmah gaḇtafʿb wyaʾtsim ñeybu). This same word, "defile" (גָּאַל, laʾag) is used in Isaiah and Lamentations to refer to the fact that Israel's hands are defiled by blood from murder (Isa. 59:3; Lam. 4:14), and in Zechariah in parallel with rebellion: "Woe to her who is rebellious [מֹרְאָה, haʾrom] and defiled [וְנִגְאָלָה, hālaʾginʿw]" (Zech 3:1). Part of God's complaint against Israel was that they had defiled themselves. Daniel is determined not to follow the practices that have led to the captivity of his people.

There is a very curious passage in Jeremiah 29. The text points out that Jeremiah had sent a letter to the exiles who had been taken into captivity by Nebuchadnezzar. In the letter Jeremiah encourages the people to live and prosper in the land: "Work to see that the city where I sent you as exiles enjoys peace and prosperity. Pray to the Lord for it. For as it prospers, you will prosper" (29:7). Then the text says something very curious in light of Daniel's prophecy: "For the Lord God of Israel Who rules overall says, 'Do not let the prophets or those among you who claim to be able to predict the future by divination deceive you. And do not pay any attention to the dreams that you are encouraging them to dream. They are prophesying lies to you and claiming my authority to do so. But I did not send them. I, the Lord, affirm it!'" (Jer 29:8–9). As was the case in Jerusalem before the exile, the false prophets would be plying their trade in Babylon also. As Charles Feinberg describes, "In Babylon, as in Judah, false prophecy was flourishing (cf. vv. 15, 21). The theme was always the same: a speedy return to the homeland. Rosy predictions were the stock in trade of the falsifiers. . . . The deceivers must not be trusted because they had never been commissioned by the Lord (v. 9)."[96] God would ultimately use Daniel as the channel through whom to inform His people of the future of Israel, but God would also use the heathen kings as His instruments to bring the prophetic word to the people. Interestingly, God would use the dreams of the heathen and the visions of Daniel to instruct His people. Whereas God had warned Israel not to listen to the false prophets who claim that they had received dreams from God, God would use the dream of Nebuchadnezzar to lay out the history of His people and show them that He is still in control.

Chapters 2 through 6 record God's communications through the foreigners He had chosen. But the chapters of Daniel's prophecies and visions are not in chronological order. The chart in Figure 3 illustrates the chronology of Daniel's visions and prophecies.

---

96. Charles L. Feinberg, *Jeremiah: A Commentary*, 198.

Figure 3: Chronology of Daniel's Visions

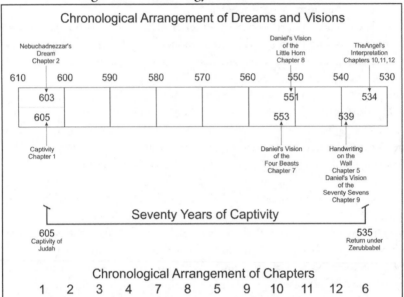

Daniel's narrative is organized according to Daniel's themes. Chapters 2 through 6 present the view of the gentile world powers and their relation to God's people primarily as this is seen from the perspective of man. In chapter 2 the world powers are depicted as a magnificent king in his earthly glory. The world powers appear in orderly fashion succeeding one another in descending order of the purity of the kingdoms represented. This contrasts strongly with the picture of these same kingdoms in Daniel 7, which is the view from God's perspective. These kingdoms are presented there as ravenous and self-destructive beasts whose succession is based on the destruction of the previous regime. Chapter 2 includes the dream of Nebuchadnezzar depicting the succession of kingdoms ultimately culminating in the establishing of the Messianic kingdom symbolized by the stone that grows into a mountain to cover the entire earth. This chapter also includes Daniel's interpretation.

Chapter 3 depicts Nebuchadnezzar in his pride and reveals him in his effort to cause the world to worship his image. The three Hebrew young men who refuse to bow are cast into the furnace, but are delivered by the intervention of the God of Israel. Chapter 4 recounts Nebuchadnezzar's humiliation at the hands of the God of Israel. Chapter 5 depicts the story of the blasphemy of Belshazzar and the message that God sends to him by means of the handwriting on the wall. It is this event that immediately precedes the overthrow of Babylon by the forces of Cyrus. Chapter 6 is the famous account of Daniel's deliverance from the mouths of the lions.

Chapter 7 at once concludes the previous section by its parallelism with the vision in chapter 2 and the fact that it was written in Aramaic and begins the following section by introducing the visions of Daniel. Chapters 8 through 12 are presented as following immediately one upon another, although chapter 8 is separated from chapter 9 by almost 12 years, and chapter 9 is separated from chapters 10–12 by almost 5 years. Nevertheless, these chapters basically form a prophetic unit presenting in amazing detail the future of the people of Israel. Chapter 12 functions as the conclusion to the book. The graphic in Figure 2 on page 41 depicts the overall structure of the book, while the chart in Table 5 below presents some of the parallelisms between the chapters in the first major section of the book.

Table 5: Overview of Daniel 2–7

OVERVIEW OF DANIEL 2–7						
CONTENTS						
Chapter	2	3	4	5	6	7
Chiasm	A	B	C	C'	B'	A'
Subject	Four Metals	Nebuchadnezzar's Proclamation	Nebuchadnezzar's Writing	Belshazzar's Writing	Darius' Proclamation	Four Beasts
Theme	Future	Faith	Character	Character	Faith	Future
Narrative	1–Test Daniel vs Wise men	2–Trial Fiery Furnace	3–Prophecy Dream (Past)	1–Test Daniel vs Wise men	2–Trial Lion's Den	3–Prophecy Dream (Future)

STRUCTURE						
Chapter	2	3	4	5	6	7
Setting	Nebuchadnezzar's Dream	Image and Proclamation	Pride and Arrogance	Feast and Arrogance	Promotion and Proclamation	Daniel's Vision
Crisis	Daniel vs. Wise men	Accusation	Details	Wise men vs. Daniel	Accusation	Details
Resolution	Interpretation	Deliverance	Realization	Interpretation	Deliverance	Realization
Conclusion	Reward	Reward	Praise	Reward	Reward	Perplexity

Theological Context of Daniel

Daniel's prophecy is directed ultimately at the restoration of the people of God and the city of God from their rebellion and from the curse upon them. Jeremiah warned the people of the coming judgment.

> Therefore thus says the Lord of hosts, "Because you have not obeyed My words, behold, I will send and take all the families of the north," declares the Lord, "and I will send to Nebuchadnezzar king of Babylon, My servant, and will bring them against this land and against its inhabitants and against all these nations round about; and I will utterly destroy them and make them a horror and a hissing, and an everlasting desolation. Moreover, I will take from them the voice of joy and the voice of gladness, the voice of the bridegroom and the voice of the bride, the sound of the millstones and the light of the lamp. This whole land will be a desolation and a horror, and these nations will serve the king of Babylon seventy years." (Jer 25:8–11)

As the writer of Chronicles describes, the destruction of the land and the captivity to Babylon for seventy years was because, among other things, the people did not observe the Sabbath years as God had instructed.

> The Lord, the God of their fathers, sent word to them again and again by His messengers, because He had compassion on His people and on His dwelling place; but they continually mocked the messengers of God, despised His words and scoffed at His prophets, until the wrath of the Lord arose against His people, until there was no remedy. Therefore He brought up against them the king of the Chaldeans who slew their young men with the sword in the house of their sanctuary, and had no compassion on young man or virgin, old man or infirm; He gave *them* all into his hand. All the articles of the house of God, great and small, and the treasures of the house of the Lord, and the treasures of the king and of his officers, he brought them all to Babylon. Then they burned the house of God and broke down the wall of Jerusalem, and burned all its fortified buildings with fire and destroyed all its valuable articles. Those who had escaped from the sword he carried away to Babylon; and they were servants to him and to his sons until the rule of the kingdom of Persia, to fulfill the word of the Lord by the mouth of Jeremiah, until the land had enjoyed its Sabbaths. All the days of its desolation it kept Sabbath until seventy years were complete. (2 Chr 36:15–21)

The judgment that came upon Judah and Jerusalem returned it to the empty wilderness from which it came: "'For My people are foolish, they know Me not; They are stupid children and have no understanding. They are shrewd to do evil, but to do good they do not know.' I looked on the earth, and behold, empty and uninhabitable [וְהִנֵּה־תֹהוּ וָבֹהוּ, *uhobaw^ uhot hennih*e*w*]; And to the heavens, and they had no light" (Jer 4:22–23). Because of the rebellion of God's people, the land would return to an uninhabitable wilderness as it was at the very beginning of God's creative activity. But the hope of God's people was the restoration of the city and the sanctuary and the reestablishing of the people in the land of promise. In fact, Daniel's prayer, although including God's people, was primarily for the restoration of God's city:

> And now, O Lord our God, Who has brought Your people out of the land of Egypt with a mighty hand and has made a name for Yourself, as it is this day—we have sinned, we have been wicked. O Lord, in accordance with all Your righteous acts, let now Your anger and Your wrath turn away from Your city Jerusalem, Your holy mountain; for because of our sins and the iniquities of our fathers, Jerusalem and Your people have become a reproach to all those around us. So now, our God, listen to the prayer of Your servant and to his supplications, and for Your sake, O Lord, let Your face shine on Your desolate sanctuary. O my God, incline Your ear and hear! Open Your eyes and see our desolations and the city which is called by Your name; for we are not presenting our supplications before You on account of any merits of our own, but on account of Your great compassion. O Lord, hear! O Lord, forgive! O Lord, listen and take action! For Your own sake, O my God, do not delay, because Your city and Your people are called by Your name." (Dan 9:15–19)

The primary concern of Daniel was that God would honor His name in restoring His city and His people. Indeed, as Warren Gage states, "The foundational hope of all prophecy is 'the restoration of all things' (Acts 3:21), and the consummating expectation of faith is the return of Edenic bliss in the dwelling together of God and man in the holy city, the New Jerusalem (cf. Rev. 21:2–4; 22:1–4)."[97] The movement of the Pentateuch, and indeed the history of Israel, has been toward the re-establishing of the Garden paradise, ultimately established by the descending from Heaven of the New Jerusalem—Zion. The importance of the city motif is seen in the fact that, as Oppenheim points out, the earliest records of Mesopotamia indicate "spontaneous urbanization." He goes on to observe, "It is true that cities rose here and there around royal

97. Warren Austin Gage, *The Gospel of Genesis: Studies in Protology and Eschatology* (Winona Lake, Indiana: Carpenter Books, 1984), 49.

residences, trading settlements (ports of trade), wells, and certain sanctuaries, but nowhere do we find such an agglomeration of urban settlements as in southern Babylonia—and so early in history at that. In this dark and remote period originated the basic attitude of Mesopotamian civilization toward the city as a social phenomenon. This attitude is one of unconditional acceptance of the city as the one and only communal organization."[98] This seems also to be the motivation behind Cain's decision to build a city, i.e., not to wander, and to build a community. Consequently, the New Jerusalem will be the epitome of community and fellowship of God and mankind.

Zion, of course, is the "mountain of God" as depicted in Ezek 28:13–14: "You were in Eden, the garden of God; . . . You were the anointed cherub who covers, and I placed you there. You were on the holy mountain of God; you walked in the midst of the stones of fire." The association of Zion with Eden is not unique to Ezekiel. Once again Gage puts it succinctly: "The restoration of the Edenic mountain in scripture is to be identified with the eschatological exaltation of Zion as the cosmic mountain of the north."[99] This association is set forth in Isa 14:13: "But you said in your heart, 'I will ascend to heaven; I will raise my throne above the stars of God, and I will sit on the mount of assembly in the sides of the north [בְּיַרְכְּתֵי צָפוֹן, *ñoʃas̱ˆ eṯᵉkrayᵉb*].'" Many have attempted to make this a reference to Satan, but Ps 48:2 specifically identifies the "recesses of the North" as Zion: "Beautiful in elevation, the joy of the whole earth, is Mount Zion in the recesses of the north [יַרְכְּתֵי צָפוֹן, *ñoʃas̱ˆ eṯᵉkray*], the city of the great King." The expression "beautiful in elevation" identifies Zion as transcendent above all the mountains, which is the final state of Zion as depicted by Isaiah: "Now it will come about that in the last days the mountain of the house of the Lord will be established as the chief of the mountains, and will be raised above the hills; and all the nations will stream to it" (Isa 2:2). Even Daniel identifies Jerusalem as God's holy mountain: "O Lord, according to all your justice, please turn your raging anger away from your city Jerusalem, your holy mountain [יְרוּשָׁלַ ם הַר־קָדְשֶׁ ךָ, *ˉakĕs̱daq rah miālās̱urᵉy*]" (Dan 9:16).

In view of this, Daniel's prophecy begins with allusions to the first family driven out of the garden to the east and the rise of the opposition forces in the construction of Babel in the land of Shinar. In Genesis, the bringing of the curse is coordinated by the serpent/dragon (נָחָשׁ, *s̱aḥan*) who deceives the couple so that they "eat" from the forbidden tree. Correspondingly, the bringing of the people of God to the opposition city is coordinated by Nebuchadnezzar who, in the development of the book of Daniel, comes to

98. Oppenheim, *Ancient Mesopotamia*, 111.

99. Ibid., 51.

symbolize the Anti-Christ who is empowered by the Dragon: ". . . one of his heads as if it had been slain, and his fatal wound was healed. And the whole earth was amazed *and followed* after the beast; they worshiped the dragon [δράκων] because he gave his authority to the beast; and they worshiped the beast, saying, 'Who is like the beast, and who is able to wage war with him?'" (Rev 13:3–4). Daniel's book opens with the captivity of the people of God and the domination of the City of God by the Dragon and his city. One reason the far ranging prophecies are given through Daniel at this time is because this is the beginning of the subjugation of Jerusalem, the City of God/ Zion, the Mountain of God. The prophecies of Daniel present to the people of God the plan of God to overcome the Dragon and his minions, ultimately establishing Zion over all mountains.

Interestingly, the exaltation of Zion over all the mountains includes the exaltation over the mount of Olives. This mountain is referred to in 2 Kgs 23:13 as "the Mountain of Destruction." This is the mountain upon which Solomon built altars to Milcom, the god/king of the Ammonites, and Chemosh, the destroyer/war god of the Moabites. It is, of course, on the Mount of Olives where the Olivet Discourse occurs in which, among other things, Jesus predicts the destruction of the Temple in Jerusalem.

A correlation exists between the pre-flood city of Enoch built by Cain and the post-flood Babel/Babylon (בָּבֶל, *lebab*) built by Nimrod. Babel/ Babylon in the plains of Shinar becomes the site for the Tower "whose top *will be* in the heavens" (Gen 11:4). This is not only an attempt to build a mountain in which their god can dwell. It is also an effort to reestablish the Edenic mountain. The correlation between Eden and Jerusalem, the Holy Mountain of God, implies that Eden was also a mountain. This notion is strengthened by the New Zion or New Jerusalem that comes down from heaven. It is a holy mountain, its height measuring 1,500 miles: "The city is laid out as a square, and its length is as great as the width; and he measured the city with the rod, fifteen hundred miles; its length and width and height are equal" (Rev 21:16).

Nebuchadnezzar, the new king of Babel/Babylon, is compared to the serpent (תַּנִּין, *ñnnat*) in Jer 51:34: "Nebuchadnezzar king of Babylon has devoured me and crushed me, he has set me down like an empty vessel; he has swallowed me like the serpent [כַּתַּנִּין, *ñnnatak*], he has filled his stomach with my delicacies; he has washed me away." The Hebrew term "serpent" (תַּנִּין, *ñnnat*) is translated in the LXX by the Greek word (δράκων, *ñokard*). Nebuchadnezzar is not necessarily identified as the serpent, but is compared

Table 6: Cities of Enoch and Babel

City of Enoch	Babel/Babylon
God cursed Cain to "be a vagrant and a wanderer on the earth." (Gen 4:12)	The people were commanded to be scattered across the world: "And God blessed Noah and his sons and said to them, 'Be fruitful and multiply, and fill the earth.'" (Gen 9:1)
"Then Cain went out from the presence of the Lord, and settled in the land of Nod, east of Eden." (Gen 4:16)	Babel/Babylon was built in the east: "It came about as they journeyed east, that they found a plain in the land of Shinar and settled there." (Gen 11:2)
Cain builds a city to prevent having to wander according to God's judgment: "and he built a city, and called the name of the city Enoch, after the name of his son." (Gen 4:17)	Babel/Babylon was built in order to prevent the people from being scattered, contrary to God's command: "They said, 'Come, let us build for ourselves a city, and a tower whose top will reach into heaven, and let us make for ourselves a name, otherwise we will be scattered abroad over the face of the whole earth.'" (Gen 11:4)
Cain, the founder and builder of the city of Enoch, murdered his brother: "And it came about when they were in the field, that Cain rose up against Abel his brother and killed him." (Gen 4:8)	Nimrod, the founder and builder of Babylon, was a mighty hunter before the Lord. (Gen 10:9)

to the serpent—the Dragon. The Dragon is Pharaoh who, as the pattern followed by Nebuchadnezzar and Babylon, held the people of God captive: "Speak and say, 'Thus says the Lord God, "Behold, I am against you, Pharaoh king of Egypt, the great monster [הַתַּנִּים, δράκων] that lies in the midst of his rivers, that has said, 'My Nile is mine, and I myself have made [it]'"'" (Ezek 29:3); and again, "Son of man, take up a lamentation over Pharaoh king of Egypt and say to him, 'You compared yourself to a young lion of the nations, yet you are like the monster [הַתַּנִּים, δράκων] in the seas; and you burst forth in your rivers and muddied the waters with your feet and fouled their rivers'" (Ezek 32:2). The Dragon/Serpent is none other than Satan, the accuser of the brethren: "And he laid hold of the dragon (δράκων), the serpent (ὄφις, sifo)of old, who is the devil and Satan, and bound him for a thousand years;" (Rev 20:2).

Daniel's book is set within this theological development. The city of the Great God and King is laid to ruin, and the people of God are in captivity to the opposition forces. Many commentators have proposed that one function of Daniel's prophecy is to encourage the people of God in Babylonian captivity of the ultimate triumph of the God of Israel over the opposition forces. This may certainly have been one function. However, there is a problem with this notion. If the prophecy of Daniel was put into its final form before it was made known to the people, then the message of the prophecy of Daniel would have been given to Israel at the end, not at the beginning, or even in the midst of their captivity. Even supposing that Daniel distributed his prophecies to captive Israel soon after they were given, this would still put their distribution close to the end of the captivity. The prophetic messages of chapters 7 through 12, and even the handwriting on the wall of chapter 5, did not occur until 553 BC. If the seventy years of captivity were ended in 536 or 535 BC, then these messages could hardly have been given for the purposes of encouraging Israel to endure their captivity. Their captivity was almost over, and by this time they must have learned to endure. As Robert Culver notes, "It is not only possible, but entirely probable, that Daniel's book was not issued to the reading public in the Babylonian era at all, but during the Persian era."[100]

This implies that perhaps the prophecies were given for another purpose. What that purpose is will perhaps become clear as we study the details of the book itself. Although it is certainly true that purpose does not determine meaning, it is often true that purpose can shed light on the meaning. However, we do not wish to allow it to do what it is not designed to do. So, at this stage we will refrain from proposing a purpose for Daniel's book in hopes that our presupposition will not distort our understanding of the text.

Outline of the Book of Daniel

I. Historical Introduction		1:1–6:28
A. The Preparation of Daniel		1:1–21
1. The Captivity of Daniel and His Friends		1:1–7
a. Nebuchadnezzar Spoils Jerusalem		1:1–3
b. Nebuchadnezzar Selects Jews		1:4–7
2. The Faithfulness of Daniel and His Friends		1:8–16
a. Faithfulness to the Lord		1:8–11
b. Faith in the Lord		1:12–16
3. The Advancement of Daniel and His Friends		1:17–21
a. Examined Before Nebuchadnezzar		1:17–19
b. Exalted By Nebuchadnezzar		1:20–21

100. Robert Duncan Culver, *Daniel and the Latter Days*, 108.

2

THE PREPARATION OF DANIEL: 1:1–21

Introduction

THE BOOK of Daniel begins with the invasion of Jerusalem by Nebuchadnezzar, king of Babylon, and the captivity of Jehoiakim. This event was the culmination of hundreds of years of steady decline of Israel's relationship with God. Back in Deuteronomy, God through Moses had warned Israel over and over not to go after other gods to worship and serve them. In fact, in Deuteronomy 12 Moses had given Israel specific instructions about heathen worship: "You shall utterly destroy all the places where the nations whom you shall dispossess serve their gods, on the high mountains and on the hills and under every green tree. And you shall tear down their altars and smash their sacred pillars and burn their Asherim with fire, and you shall cut down the engraved images of their gods and you shall obliterate their name from that place" (vv. 2–3).

God had also specifically warned Israel, "be careful that you do not offer your burnt offering in every place you see, but in the place which the Lord chooses in one of your tribes, there you shall offer your burnt offerings, and there you shall do all that I command you" (Deut 12:13–14). However, when Israel had settled the land, they brought the tabernacle to Shiloh but allowed it to deteriorate. During this time even Samuel worshiped God in the high places. Apparently God tolerated this, but this became a major stumbling block to Israel. After the temple was built, the people continued to worship at the high places, but this time under the influence of pagan religions. Eventually they had compromised the worship of YHWH to such a degree that they had incorporated much of pagan worship into Judaism. They had begun to go after other gods to worship them. Although God sent His servants the prophets to warn them of impending judgment, they refused to hear until God brought in His rod of correction, the invading armies of the Assyrians and ultimately those of Nebuchadnezzar.

In chapter one, the reader is introduced to this judgment event in the history of Israel, and the consequences of Israel's spiritual adultery. Many people from Jerusalem are taken into captivity to Babylon along with the treasures of the temple. At this point the reader is also introduced to Daniel and his three companions. The character of these four young Hebrew men serves as a stark contrast to the character of the people as a whole. Whereas Israel, as a nation, had become unfaithful to the covenant relation even though they lived and prospered in the promised land, Daniel and his three friends demonstrate a strong and unwavering commitment to the God of Israel, and they do this in the most difficult circumstances imaginable—as slaves to a foreign nation and a pagan king.

J. E. Goldingay has set forth the structure of chapter one as a chiasm, and a modified version of his diagram is illustrated below.[1]

A	Historical Introduction		1–2
	B	The young men taken for training	3–7
		C The story of the test	8–16
	B′	The young men taken for training	17–20
A′	Historical Conclusion		21

A chiastic structure is one that is patterned on the shape of the Greek letter *chi* (X), following one side of its angular shape. The purpose of the chiastic structure seems to be to focus the attention of the reader on the center point of the story, in this case, the testing of Daniel and his friends.

The Captivity of Daniel and His Friends: 1:1–7

NEBUCHADNEZZAR SPOILS JERUSALEM: 1:1–2

1— In the third year of the reign of Jehoiakim king of Judah, Nebuchadnezzar king of Babylon came to Jerusalem and besieged it.

2— The Lord gave Jehoiakim king of Judah into his hand, along with some of the vessels of the house of God; and he brought them to the land of Shinar, to the house of his god, and he brought the vessels into the treasury of his god.

1. John E. Goldingay, *Daniel*, 8.

Verse one states that Nebuchadnezzar invaded Jerusalem in the third year of the reign of Jehoiakim. However, Jer 46:2 states that this event took place in the fourth year of the reign of Jehoiakim. A typical criticism leveled against the book of Daniel by critical scholars is that this conflict is a clear contradiction and undermines the historical integrity of the book. The difficulty is resolved, however, when it is understood that the difference is the result of two systems of dating. Daniel employed the Tishri calendar system in which the first month of the year was Tishri, around October in our modern calendar. Jeremiah employed an Assyrian calendar system that marked Nisan (around April) as the first month of the year. Jehoiakim became king in the month of Tishri in 609 BC. Nebuchadnezzar's invasion took place in the summer of 605 BC, between the months of Nisan and Tishri. The official reckoning of a king's first year starts on the first day of the new year. Since Jehoiakim became king of Judah several days after the first day of the new year, his first official year as king did not begin until the first day of the following year. For Daniel, this meant that Jehoiakim's first official year began almost a whole year after he took the throne. For Jeremiah, this meant that Jehoiakim's first official year began about six months later on the first day of Nisan. So, when Nebuchadnezzar invaded, it was only the third official year according to Daniel's reckoning, but the fourth year according to Jeremiah's reckoning (see Figure 4 below).

Figure 4: Invasion Calendars

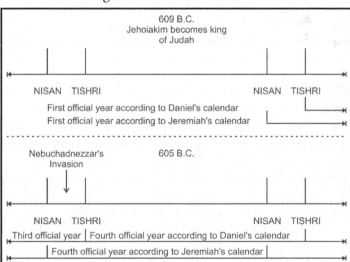

It is important to note that Nebuchadnezzar's success against Judah and Jerusalem was not attributed to his forces, but to the fact that, "The Lord gave Jehoiakim king of Judah into his hand." This is a specific reference to the fulfillment of God's promise to destroy Jerusalem if the people of Israel did not repent. Their sin was to worship and serve other gods, and God was driving them out of the promised land as a result of worshiping other gods. He had done the same with Adam and Eve, who were driven out of the garden for going after worshiping other gods, namely, themselves. They took the prerogative of God upon themselves to decide for themselves what is and is not good. The first deportation of the people of Jerusalem was in 605, the second was in 597, and the third was in 586 with the destruction of Jerusalem.

Notice that the text does not use the covenant name of God, Yahweh (יהוה, YHWH). Rather, Daniel uses the term 'Adonai' (אֲדֹנָי, yaḏoḏaʾ). It is not as the covenant God of Israel that God gives them into Nebuchadnezzar's hand, but as the Lord and Master Who is in control and Who is rendering judgment upon the people and the land. Nebuchadnezzar does not take the land or the vessels of the temple. Rather, they are "given" (וַיִּתֵּן, ñetiyyaw) by the Lord into his hand. As Leon Wood puts it, "*Adonai* speaks of God as supreme master. The significance of using this name here is to say that, though outward signs did not seem to show it, God was the master of this situation . . ."[2]

Verse 2 states that Nebuchadnezzar brought some of the vessels that he had taken from the house of God to the land of Shinar: וַיְבִיאֵם אֶרֶץ־שִׁנְעָר (ra'nîs sereʾ ñeʾıbyaw). This does not seem to be a mere geographical notation. The author could certainly have used the name "Babylon" (בָּבֶל, leḇaḇ) since in verse 1 Nebuchadnezzar is identified as the King of Babylon. The first occurrence of this name Shinar is in Gen 10:10: "The beginning of his [Nimrod's] kingdom was Babel and Erech and Accad and Calneh, in the land of Shinar." The beginning of the Tower of Babel narrative is the next place we encounter Shinar: "It came about as they journeyed east, that they found a plain in the land of Shinar and settled there" (Gen 11:2). Shinar is the reference to the area, whereas Babel/Babylon is the name of the city located in the land of Shinar. There is a parallelism between Babylon in the post-flood account and the city of Enoch built by Cain in the pre-flood narrative. Whereas Cain was cursed by God to wander, yet he built a city and called it Enoch, so the people after the flood, who were commanded by God to fill the earth and subdue it, rebelled against God by building a city and a tower by which they could prevent themselves from being "scattered abroad over the face of the whole earth" (Gen 11:4). Babylon takes on the character of Cain as

---

2. Leon Wood, *A Commentary on Daniel*, 30 (emphasis in original).

symbolic of the organized opposition to the plan and the commands of God, the slayer of his brother.

Nebuchadnezzar also took some of the vessels of the temple. This is a fulfillment of the prophecy declared in Jer 20:5: "I will also give over all the wealth of this city, all its produce and all its costly things; even all the treasures of the kings of Judah I will give over to the hand of their enemies, and they will plunder them, take them away and bring them to Babylon." Of course this will also be important in chapter 5 when Belshazzar will bring these vessels out of the treasury. Nebuchadnezzar takes some of the vessels from the house of God and puts them in the treasury (אוֹצַר, *raṣoʾ*) of his god. This act was meant as a demonstration of the superiority of the god of Nebuchadnezzar, perhaps Marduk, over the God of Israel, and his bringing them to the temple of his god was meant as an act of worship of his god. The word "treasury" is used in Isa 39:2 to refer to the treasury that Hezekiah showed to the representatives of Merodach-baladan. Hezekiah was judged by God for this act so that he was condemned to die. Hezekiah pleaded with God for deliverance from death, and God gave him fifteen more years of life. Nevertheless, God through Isaiah pronounced judgment upon Judah. "Then Isaiah said to Hezekiah, 'Hear the word of the Lord of hosts, "Behold, the days are coming when all that is in your house and all that your fathers have laid up in store to this day will be carried to Babylon; nothing will be left," says the Lord. "And some of your sons who will issue from you, whom you will beget, will be taken away, and they will become officials in the palace of the king of Babylon"'" (Isa 39:5–7).

There may be the additional notion that Nebuchadnezzar believed that by taking the accouterments of the temple that the God of Israel Himself was also being taken away. Oppenheim observes, "The role of the image was central in the cult as well as in private worship, as the wide distribution of cheap replicas of such images shows. Fundamentally, the deity was considered present in its image if it showed certain specific features and paraphernalia and was cared for in the appropriate manner, both established and sanctified by the tradition of the sanctuary. The god moved with the image when the latter was carried off—expressing thus his anger against his city or the entire country."[3]

Nebuchadnezzar Selects Jews: 1:3–7

3— Then the king ordered Ashpenaz, the chief of his officials, to bring in some of the sons of Israel, including some of the royal family and of the nobles,

---

3. Oppenheim, *Ancient Mesopotamia*, 184.

4—   youths in whom was no defect, who were good-looking, showing
          intelligence in every branch of wisdom, endowed with understand-
          ing and discerning knowledge, and who had ability for serving in
          the king's court; and he ordered him to teach them the literature and
          language of the Chaldeans.

5—   The king appointed for them a daily ration from the king's choice
          food and from the wine which he drank, and appointed that they
          should be educated three years, at the end of which they were to
          enter the king's personal service.

6—   Now among them from the sons of Judah were Daniel, Hananiah,
          Mishael, and Azariah.

7—   Then the commander of the officials assigned new names to them;
          and to Daniel he assigned the name Belteshazzar, to Hananiah
          Shadrach, to Mishael Meshach and to Azariah Abed-nego.

Nebuchadnezzar had taken captive some of the young people who were of
royal blood, descendants of Hezekiah. Once these individuals had been carried to Babylon, it was the king's plan to assimilate them into the Babylonian
culture. "Those carried away captive could well serve as hostages to help keep
the royal family of the kingdom of Judah in line. Their presence in the king's
court also would be a pleasant reminder to the Babylonian king of his conquest and success in battle. Further, their careful training and preparation to
be his servants might serve Nebuchadnezzar well in later administration of
Jewish affairs."[4] The text asserts that Nebuchadnezzar wanted men "who have
the strength to stand in the temple of the king" (Dan 1:4). It fell to Ashpenaz,
the chief of the eunuchs, to bring such men before the king.

    The fact that Ashpenaz is referred to as the "chief of his eunuchs"
(רַב סָרִיסָיו‎, ras̱ bariwas̄) does not necessarily mean that Ashpenaz was a
true eunuch. Potiphar is referred to as a eunuch in Gen 37:36, yet he was a
married man: "Meanwhile, the Midianites sold him in Egypt to Potiphar,
Pharaoh's officer [סָרִיס פַּרְעֹה‎, hoʿrap sirʿs], the captain of the bodyguard."
Here the word is translated "officer." Also, Isaiah prophesied that some of
Hezekiah's descendants would be made eunuchs in Babylon: "And some of
your sons who will issue from you, whom you will beget, will be taken away,
and they will become officials [סָרִיסִים‎, misiras] in the palace of the king
of Babylon" (Isa 39:7). Although the text of Daniel does not specifically state
that these three young men were made eunuchs, if the term is taken to refer to
an official in the court of Babylon, it is implied in the process of their training
and appointments.

---

    4. John F. Walvoord, *Daniel: The Key to Prophetic Revelation*, 34.

According to Lucas, "The giving of a new name is a sign of new ownership and so, by implication, new allegiance, was common court practice (Gen. 41:45; 2 Kgs. 23:34; 25:17 . . .)"[5] The recording of the changing of the names of the Hebrew youths emphasizes the significance of these names.

Daniel	=	God is Judge, or my Judge is God
Hananiah	=	YHWH is gracious
Mishael	=	Who is what God is, or Who is like God
Azariah	=	YHWH is my help

The Babylonians changed the names of these young men in order to emphasize Nebuchadnezzar's victory over them and their God, to attempt to obliterate any remembrance of the God of Israel, and to signify their subjugation to the gods of Babylon.

Belteshazzar	=	Lady, protect the king
Shadrach	=	I am fearful (of god)
Meshach	=	I am despised, contemptible, humbled (before god)
Abednego	=	Servant of Nebo (son of Bel/Marduk, Babylonian god)

Interestingly, the name "Daniel" occurs 65 times throughout the book, while the name "Belteshazzar" occurs only 8 times. The names of Daniel's three companions occur in precisely the same pattern each time—Shadrach, Meshach, and Abednego. Their Hebrew names occur 5 times, 4 in chapter 1 and 1 in chapter 2. Their Babylonian names occur 14 times, once in chapter 2 and 13 times in chapter 3. Their names do not occur after chapter 3.

THE FAITHFULNESS OF DANIEL AND HIS FRIENDS: 1:8–16

Faithfulness to the Lord: 1:8–11

8—   But Daniel made up his mind that he would not defile himself with the king's choice food or with the wine which he drank; so he sought permission from the commander of the officials that he might not defile himself.

---

5. Lucas, *Daniel*, 53.

9—   Now God granted Daniel favor and compassion in the sight of the commander of the officials,

10—   and the commander of the officials said to Daniel, "I am afraid of my lord the king, who has appointed your food and your drink; for why should he see your faces looking more haggard than the youths who are your own age? Then you would make me forfeit my head to the king."

11—   But Daniel said to the overseer whom the commander of the officials had appointed over Daniel, Hananiah, Mishael and Azariah.

Having been entrusted into the care of the chief of the eunuchs, Daniel and his companions were to be given food and wine from the King's portion. However, Daniel decided not to defile himself with the king's choice food. In the previous verses the text records that Nebuchadnezzar had called for young men who were intelligent, quick of mind, and able to learn well. They were to have the wisdom to make distinctions and proper decisions. The fact that Daniel sets upon his heart not to defile himself establishes these very characteristics of Daniel. Daniel possessed knowledge of the history of Israel and the cause of the captivity. He demonstrated understanding of the nature of God and His law, and he demonstrated the courage to do the right thing in the midst of unfavorable circumstances. Daniel did not confront his captors with a harsh demand. Rather, Daniel exhibits the maturity to persuade others toward his point of view without offending and the capacity to be a leader among men. In this situation Daniel exhibits all the characteristics for which Nebuchadnezzar was looking in the young men of Israel.

There have been a number of speculations about why Daniel refused to eat the king's food. Since Daniel said he did not wish to defile himself (אֶל אֶגְאָ֫לְ, laʾagtiy), some have proposed that Daniel is observing the Mosaic law. However, it is curious that the text does not state this, and one commentator asserts, "the fact that the Mosaic food laws do not include reference to wine (except in the case of the Nazarite vow, Num. 6:2–4) suggests that this cannot be more than a partial reason for Daniel's decision."[6] Also, when Daniel presents his proposal to the chief of the eunuchs (שַׂר הַסָּרִיסִים, mûsîrassah rás, that this is a different expression than the one in verse 3 may imply that this was a different person), the chief responded, "I am afraid of my lord the king, who has appointed your food and your drink; for why should he see your faces looking more haggard than the youths who are your own age? Then you would make me forfeit my head to the king." (1:9). There was no reason for the chief to think that eating vegetables and drinking water would make Daniel and his

6. Ernest Lucas, *Daniel*, 54.

friends appear gaunt or deprived, but the chief probably would have believed that eating the king's food would make them much stronger, more intelligent, and with a much better appearance than one eating the food of mere mortals. The chief's objection is not that they would appear as starving and deprived, but that they would appear more haggard by comparison to the other youths. In other words, it was not that they would look emaciated, but they would not look as good as the other youths. One commentator describes the situation as "a poorer condition of health . . . which would show in a saddened facial appearance."[7] However, this is not a necessary conclusion. They would not necessarily have been of poor health and saddened countenance. Rather, it was believed that the food dedicated to the gods of Babylon would engender a much greater vitality than the normal condition of Daniel and his friends, and they would look haggard by comparison.

By this stage in the process, Daniel and his friends would have known that the king had selected them for preparation to function in the royal court and in the temple. Oppenheim gives an account of the daily care and feeding of the gods that may shed light on why Daniel refused the king's food: "Having been presented to the image, the dishes from the god's meal were sent to the king for his consumption. Clearly the food offered to the deity was considered blessed by contact with the divine and capable of transferring that blessing to the person who was to eat it."[8] The food offered to the idol was usually given only to the king since the divine blessing would be conferred upon the king by eating the food. In this case, the king's food was given to these young men apparently in the expectation that they would receive the blessing and become the kinds of servants that Nebuchadnezzar desired—men of character, strength, knowledge, and understanding. This may indicate that one reason Daniel refused the king's food is that he did not want his condition to be attributed to the gods of Nebuchadnezzar. By refusing the king's food, Daniel's condition would be attributed to his God, the God of Israel. We see Daniel expressing this very notion in chapter 2 where he insists that the king understand that the wisdom and insight that Daniel exhibited came from the God of Israel: "there is a God in heaven who reveals secrets, and makes known to the king Nebuchadnezzar what shall be in the latter days" (2:28). By eating the king's portion, Daniel would defile himself before God in the same way that Israel did, by abandoning the true and living God and by compromising with foreigners. By eating the king's food, any superior intelligence, skill, or health in Daniel would have been attributed to the gods of Babylon, not to the God of Daniel. In this way, Daniel would actually misrepresent his God to

7. Wood, *Daniel*, 39.

8. Oppenheim, *Ancient Mesopotamia*, 189.

his pagan captors. Daniel was unwilling to do the very thing that precipitated the captivity in the first place—unflinching compromise with foreigners in their dedication and service to their gods. Daniel would have them know that his condition was the result of the power of His God, not the gods of Nebuchadnezzar.

Also, the word that is used to refer to the king's food, פַּת־בַּג (gab tap), is used in Dan 11:26: "Yea, they that feed of the portion of his meat shall destroy him, and his army shall overflow: and many shall fall down slain." The point here is that those who ate the king's food were supposed to be loyal servants and devotees of the king and of his god. Turning against the king after having eaten the king's food was an act of great disloyalty. Daniel refused to eat the king's food because he did not want to be perceived as a loyal servant or devotee of the king of Babylon or of his god. Daniel's loyalty was toward the God of Israel. This dedication is also demonstrated by Daniel's three friends when they refuse to pay homage to the image that Nebuchadnezzar has set up: "But if not, be it known unto you, O king, that we will not serve your gods, nor worship the golden image which you have set up" (3:18). In Ps 141:4, David prays, "Do not incline my heart to any evil thing, to practice deeds of wickedness with men who do iniquity; and do not let me eat of their delicacies." Eating their delicacies would be a sign of being joined with them and abandoning his God. Speaking about evil men, Prov 4:17 says, "For they eat the bread of wickedness, and drink the wine of violence." Daniel did not want willfully to participate in the wickedness of Babylon. Eating the king's food and drinking his wine was, at least as far as Daniel was concerned, an act of complicity.

The danger that Daniel saw in acquiescing to the plan of the king was not necessarily in the actual eating of the king's portion, but in the appearance that would compromise his profession to be dedicated to the God of Israel. Eating the king's portion would tell his captors that his God is not worthy of complete devotion. For us, and even perhaps for Daniel's captors, refusing to eat the king's portion to avoid being defiled might seem like a small thing: "It is only food, after all, and there's no clear, undisputed statement in Torah that demands that you not eat the king's portion." But what seems like a small thing to us was an important thing to Daniel. Daniel was faithful in the small things, and God gave him responsibility over big things. As Lucas points out, "The chapter centres on the internal, personal struggle to remain true to one's convictions and commitments when it would be much easier to go with the crowd."[9]

9. Lucas, *Daniel*, 94.

But there is yet another curious aspect to this. Verse 4 points out that Daniel and his friends were to be educated in the "learning [literally "literature" סֵפֶר, *refes*] and the tongue of the Chaldeans." Although Daniel set upon his heart not to defile himself with the food of the king, he does not refuse to take in the learning of the Chaldeans. This is particularly interesting since Jesus said, "*It is* not what enters into the mouth *that* defiles the man, but what proceeds out of the mouth, this defiles the man" (Matt 15:11). It seems that the defilement of which Daniel refused to partake is not so much from the food itself, but from the appearance of participation and complicity in the rituals and blessing bestowed by foreign gods. By taking the food, there would be no way for them to demonstrate to these pagans the true nature of their God. Daniel demonstrated the very essence of the principle that Jesus had set forth in Matt 10:16: "so be shrewd as serpents and innocent as doves."

Lucas makes a very important observation about the test: "it sets out the basic issue that underlies all the stories: can a Jew function successfully as a courtier to a pagan king and still remain loyal to the God of Israel?"[10] This would be an important lesson for Israel not only because they were captive in Babylon, but because, as Daniel's prophecy will declare later, the people of Israel would be scattered among the nations until the re-gathering, and they needed to see that even among the nations they could remain faithful to their God. But functioning in a foreign environment meant not only having inward purity, but having outward faithfulness that would be a testimony to those outside of the covenant.

It is interesting to note that although it was God who allowed Daniel and his friends to be captured and taken to Babylon, Daniel did not become bitter against God. Rather, he continued in obedience to God's law. He trusted in God in the most adverse circumstances. As Daniel's prayer would later reveal (chapter 9), Daniel realized that God's actions were just and righteous because of the unfaithfulness of the people. Daniel proposed in his heart that he would be faithful, both inwardly and outwardly.

Faith in the Lord: 1:12–16

12— "Please test your servants for ten days, and let us be given some vegetables to eat and water to drink."

13— "Then let our appearance be observed in your presence and the appearance of the youths who are eating the king's choice food; and deal with your servants according to what you see."

14— So he listened to them in this matter and tested them for ten days.

10. Ibid., 50.

15—   At the end of ten days their appearance seemed better and they were fatter than all the youths who had been eating the king's choice food.

16—   So the overseer continued to withhold their choice food and the wine they were to drink, and kept giving them vegetables.

Concerning the ten-day trial that Daniel proposed, Leon Wood asserts, "It shows remarkable faith on Daniel's part to believe that in ten days God would so improve their appearance that this man would be convinced of the propriety of the menu."[11] Interestingly, there is no statement by Daniel, or by the narrator, that Daniel's action is performed in the belief that God would "improve their appearance." Daniel certainly believed that in 10 days the physical condition of himself and his companions would be better than that of the youths eating the king's portion, yet there is no direct statement in the text that the favorable result was the work of God. The text merely states, "At the end of ten days their appearance seemed better and they were fatter than all the youths who had been eating the king's choice food. So the overseer continued to withhold their choice food and the wine they were to drink and kept giving them vegetables" (Dan 1:15–16). Yet because Daniel set the test in terms of defilement, there does seem to be the dimension of trust. And the image of eating, which, in the OT is indicative of man's mortality and his need to trust in God's provision, implies the fact that Daniel was willing to trust in God's provision. Vegetables and water were the alternatives to eating the king's food, and since the king's food was rejected on spiritual grounds, the only alternative was the only provision available—God's provision. Unlike the people of Israel who were dissatisfied with God's provision, Daniel relied on God's provision not only to sustain his life, but to prosper him and his friends.

The Advancement of Daniel and His Friends: 1:17–21

Examined Before Nebuchadnezzar: 1:17–19

17—   As for these four youths, God gave them knowledge and intelligence in every branch of literature and wisdom; Daniel even understood all kinds of visions and dreams.

18—   Then at the end of the days which the king had specified for presenting them, the commander of the officials presented them before Nebuchadnezzar.

---

11. Wood, *Daniel*, 40.

19— The king talked with them, and out of them all not one was found like Daniel, Hananiah, Mishael and Azariah; so they entered the king's personal service.

The text seems to imply that it was Daniel's faithfulness to God and his steadfast adherence to God's law that resulted in God's favor. God blessed these young Hebrew men and gave them prominence among the captives. The text states that God gave these faithful young men "knowledge and intelligence in all literature and wisdom; Daniel even understood all visions and dreams" (Dan 1:17). Several commentators in fact assert that these gifts *were* given to them "for their faithfulness,"[12] and one commentator asserts that the text "does seem to be making the point that faithfulness to the God of Israel is the way to success, even in the Gentile world."[13] But neither of these is a necessary conclusion. If God is rewarding these faithful Jews, then the acceptance of their efforts is predicated on the fact that they were already part of the covenant people.

There is yet another dimension to the refusal of Daniel to eat the king's portion. As we set forth in the introduction, the theological context of Daniel is the flow of God's purpose. We argued that there are some parallels between the Babylon of Daniel's day and the Babel of Genesis, which was set as the antithesis of the Holy Mountain. Perhaps the refusal of Daniel to eat continues this association. Unlike the couple in the garden who ate the fruit of the tree, Daniel refuses to eat the king's portions. It is also interesting that Daniel refuses to eat the king's portion, but rather opts for the הַזֵּרֹעִים (*miʿōrezzah*). This word is literally translated, "the things sown." In other words, Daniel opted to eat the fruit of the ground rather than the meat from that which had been sacrificed to the god of Babylon.

It is also interesting that they are given "knowledge and intelligence" for eating the sown things. The term 'knowledge' (מַדָּע, *ʿadam*) here is from the same root as the word 'knowledge' (דַּעַת, *taʿad*) in Gen. 2:17 that is used with reference to the tree of knowledge. The woman saw that the tree was able to make one wise (לְהַשְׂכִּיל, *liksahel*). Daniel and his companions were given not only knowledge, but "intelligence" or "wisdom" (וְהַשְׂכֵּל, *leksahew*). Whereas the couple sought knowledge and wisdom and violated the command of God and ate, Daniel sought to follow the command of God, refused to eat, and thereby gained knowledge and wisdom.

But in addition to the knowledge and wisdom that was given to each of the young Hebrews, Daniel was also given the capacity to understand dreams and visions. As Oppenheim points out,

12. Miller, *Daniel*, 70.
13. Lucas, *Daniel*, 55.

The importance of divination in Mesopotamian civilization is emphasized by the large number of omen collections and related cuneiform texts that have been preserved. . . . Basically, divination represents a technique of communication with the supernatural forces that are supposed to shape the history of the individual as well as that of the group. It presupposes the belief that these powers are able and, at times, willing to communicate their intentions and that they are interested in the well-being of the individual or the group—in other words, that if evil is predicted or threatened, it can be averted through appropriate means. . . . Normally the dream offers nothing more than an 'omen,' which means that the dream is meaningful only when correctly interpreted by an expert.[14]

The importance of the interpretation of dreams, and the capacity of Daniel to do this accurately, would insure his rise in importance and influence, not only in the Neo-Babylonian kingdom, but in the Medo-Persian kingdom that would take over under Cyrus. It was important for Daniel to distinguish his source of understanding from that which was claimed by Nebuchadnezzar's wise men.

Exalted By Nebuchadnezzar: 1:20–21

20—   As for every matter of wisdom and understanding about which the king consulted them, he found them ten times better than all the magicians and conjurers who were in all his realm.

21—   And Daniel continued until the first year of Cyrus the king.

The closing verses of this chapter provide a summary of the three years of training of Daniel and his three friends. This chapter provides the historical and spiritual background upon which the remainder of the book is built. We have been introduced to Daniel and provided with all the information we need to recognize him as a man of God and a prophet. Also, the reader is prepared to understand Daniel's rise to prominence as the work of Daniel's God, even as Daniel persistently points out to his earthly masters.

The statement in verse 21, "וַיְהִי דָּנִיֵּאל עַד־שְׁנַת אַחַת לְכוֹרֶשׁ הַמֶּלֶךְ" _(kelemmah ˘seʾokᵉl _ṭahaʾ _tanᵉṣ daʿ lᵉeŷiñaD ˆiʰᵉyaw)—"And Daniel continued until the first year of Cyrus the king," does not indicate that Daniel died in the first year of Cyrus, but that Daniel was still alive in the first year of Cyrus. This testifies to the faithfulness of God. Daniel was taken captive by the Babylonians, and yet Daniel would outlive the Babylonian empire to which he had been subjugated.

14. Oppenheim, *Ancient Mesopotamia*, 206–7, 222.

3

NEBUCHADNEZZAR'S DREAM OF WORLD HISTORY: 2:1–49

Introduction

OF THIS chapter, John Walvoord states, "Few chapters of the Bible are more determinative in establishing both principle and content of prophecy than this chapter; and its study, accordingly, is crucial to any system of prophetic interpretation."[1] The bulk of this chapter is the reporting of and the interpretation of the dream of Nebuchadnezzar. There seems to be a balanced literary structure in the vision:

A   Nebuchadnezzar—King of Kings
    B   The Second Kingdom—Represented by two arms
        C   The Third Kingdom—Represented by a single torso
    B´   The Fourth Kingdom—Represented by two legs
A´   Messiah—King of Kings

Usually a chiastic structure focuses upon the center of the shape, but this is not necessarily its only or primary function. In this case, the emphasis may be on the beginning and ending structures, and the purpose of the chiasm may be to establish a parallel relationship between the kingdom of Nebuchadnezzar and the kingdom of the Messiah. This relationship may emphasize the symbolic role played by Nebuchadnezzar as the anti-Messiah of Babylon, functioning as a literary foil to the Messiah.

---

1. Walvoord, *Daniel*, 45.

Nebuchadnezzar's Dream: 2:1–18

A Dream Troubles the King: 2:1

1—   Now in the second year of the reign of Nebuchadnezzar, Nebuchadnezzar had dreams; and his spirit was troubled and his sleep left him.

Chapter 2 begins, "And in the second year of the reign of Nebuchadnezzar, Nebuchadnezzar dreamed dreams, and his spirit was troubled, and his sleep left him." There have been some accusations lodged against the historical accuracy of the text with reference to this statement. In chapter 1, the four Hebrew youths are entered into a program of training that is, according to the text, to last for three years (Dan 1:5). Since chapter 2 begins with the reference to the second year of the reign of Nebuchadnezzar, many critical scholars have argued that these passages are in conflict. However, there are several ways to explain these passages. Donald Campbell's explanation about why Daniel and his friends were not called to the king with the other wise men is applied to this situation as well: "The fact that Daniel and his friends were not included in this group is probable evidence that this whole incident took place while Daniel was still in training (see 'in the second year,' 2:1)."[2] The parenthetical reference indicates that Campbell intended this explanation to be applied here as well. This explanation seems to account not only for the fact that chapter 2 opens on the second year of Nebuchadnezzar's reign, and the fact that Daniel and his friends were not called by the king, but also it seems to explain why Nebuchadnezzar seems not to recognize Daniel and his friends. This solution does not contradict the closing statements in chapter 1: "Then at the end of the days which the king had specified for presenting them, the commander of the officials presented them before Nebuchadnezzar" (Dan 1:18). The very last statement skips over all the intervening events when it refers to the fact that Daniel continued to the first year of Cyrus. So there is no contradiction for the text to observe that Daniel and his friends were presented before the king. This statement simply skips over the intervening events to present the outcome of Daniel's training.

However, there is a serious problem with Campbell's solution. Dan 2:48 states that Daniel is promoted by Nebuchadnezzar as a reward for his actions: "Then the king promoted Daniel and gave him many great gifts, and he made him ruler over the whole province of Babylon and chief prefect over all the wise men of Babylon." This seems to obviate Campbell's explanation. How could the statement in 1:19—"The king talked with them, and out of them all not one was found like Daniel, Hananiah, Mishael, and Azariah; so they

2. Donald K. Campbell, *Daniel: Decoder of Dreams*, 17.

entered the king's personal service"—be accurate if Daniel and his friends, or at least Daniel, had already been promoted?

Another explanation offered by several scholars has to do with the calculating of the reigns of kings. According to this argument, the last year of a dying king's reign is not counted as the first year of his successor's reign. So, when Nebuchadnezzar took the throne, Daniel and his friends entered into service for the three year period. When the third year was nearing a close, it would have been Nebuchadnezzar's second official year as king. Walvoord offers the following chronology of events to explain the calculations.

> May–June, 605 BC: Babylonian victory over the Egyptians at Carcherish
>
> June–August, 605 BC: Fall of Jerusalem to Nebuchadnezzar, and Daniel and companions taken captive
>
> September 7, 605 BC: Nebuchadnezzar, the general of the army, made king over Babylon after the death of his father, Nabopolassar
>
> September 7, 605 BC to Nisan (Mardi–April) 604 BC: Year of accession of Nebuchadnezzar as king, and first year of Daniel's training
>
> Nisan (March–April) 604 BC to Nisan (March–April) 603 BC: First year of the reign of Nebuchadnezzar, second year of training of Daniel
>
> Nisan (March–April) 603 BC to Nisan (March–April) 602 BC: Second year of the reign of Nebuchadnezzar, third year of training of Daniel, also the year of Nebuchadnezzar's dream[3]

Also, Edward Young offers the following schema to illustrate the relationship between the training years and the years of Nebuchadnezzar's reign.[4]

3. Walvoord, *Daniel*, 46.

4. Edward J. Young, *The Prophecy of Daniel: A Commentary* (Grand Rapids: William B. Eerdmans Publishing Company, 1978), 56.

Table 7: Training Years

Years of Training		Nebuchadnezzar
First Year	=	Year of Accession.
Second Year	=	First Year.
Third Year	=	Second Year (in which dream occurred).

What these charts show is that when the Hebrew youths entered the service of the king, it was Nebuchadnezzar's accession year, which is not counted in the calculation of the years of the king's reign. When the Hebrew youths had completed their third year of training, it would have been Nebuchadnezzar's second official year as king. This last explanation, along with the chronology proposed by Walvoord, serves to alleviate the conflict between the statements in question without introducing additional problems as Campbell's explanation does.

THE WISE MEN FAIL THE KING: 2:2–11

2— Then the king gave orders to call in the magicians, the conjurers, the sorcerers and the Chaldeans to tell the king his dreams. So they came in and stood before the king.

3— The king said to them, "I had a dream and my spirit is anxious to understand the dream."

4— Then the Chaldeans spoke to the king in Aramaic: "O king, live forever! Tell the dream to your servants, and we will declare the interpretation."

5— The king replied to the Chaldeans, "The command from me is firm: if you do not make known to me the dream and its interpretation, you will be torn limb from limb and your houses will be made a rubbish heap.

6— "But if you declare the dream and its interpretation, you will receive from me gifts and a reward and great honor; therefore declare to me the dream and its interpretation."

7— They answered a second time and said, "Let the king tell the dream to his servants, and we will declare the interpretation."

8— The king replied, "I know for certain that you are bargaining for time, inasmuch as you have seen that the command from me is firm,

9—   that if you do not make the dream known to me, there is only one decree for you. For you have agreed together to speak lying and corrupt words before me until the situation is changed; therefore tell me the dream, that I may know that you can declare to me its interpretation."

10—   The Chaldeans answered the king and said, "There is not a man on earth who could declare the matter for the king, inasmuch as no great king or ruler has [ever] asked anything like this of any magician, conjurer or Chaldean.

11—   "Moreover, the thing which the king demands is difficult, and there is no one else who could declare it to the king except gods, whose dwelling place is not with [mortal] flesh."

As a result of his dream and the worry this caused him, the king called for his counselors to come before him to "tell to the king his dreams." The verb "to tell" (לְהַגִּיד, *dıggahᵉl*) seems to indicate that the king did not simply want them to relate an interpretation, but to declare to him the actual content of the dreams themselves. There is a debate over whether the king actually forgot the dream or simply put the wise men to the test by demanding that they recite the dream before proposing an interpretation. It is certainly the case that he was testing these would-be wise men. The KJV of verse 5 reads, "The thing is gone from me," but many commentators propose that this is not the best translation of this phrase. The phrase is מִלְּתָא מִנִּי אַזְדָּא (*atᵉllim ᵓadza ᵓınnim*), which is translated by many to read, "The command from me is firm." If Nebuchadnezzar had completely forgotten the dream, how would he have been able to tell whether his wise men were accurately reporting the dream? Also, apparently the wise men themselves did not understand him to be saying he forgot the dream. As Miller observes, the wise men "continued to plead with him to reveal it."[5] Either he completely remembered the dream, or he remembered enough of it to be able to test his wise men. Nebuchadnezzar believed that if they were able to tell him his dream, then he could trust their interpretation.

Of course they were unable to comply with the king's demand, and Nebuchadnezzar decreed that they all be put to death. The situation is not dissimilar to the attempts of Pharaoh's magicians to duplicate the judgments of God upon Egypt. Although the magicians could counterfeit some of these judgments, they could not produce lice, and the magicians declared, "This is the finger of God:" (Ex 8:19). Nebuchadnezzar's wise men could not tell him his dream because this was the finger of God. Even the wise men themselves

5. Miller, *Daniel*, 81.

testified to this fact: "There is not a man on earth who can do what the king asks! No king, however great and mighty, has ever asked such a thing of any magician, or enchanter, or astrologer. What the king asks is too difficult. No one can reveal it to the king except the gods, and they do not live among us" (Dan 2:10–11). Of course these wise men were supposed to be in contact with the gods, and here they practically admit that they cannot do what they claimed to be able to do.

Many people mistakenly attribute the modern practice of astrology to the astrologers of Nebuchadnezzar's court. However, according to A. Pannekoek, astrology in ancient Assyria was principally the discovery and interpretation of omens: "The court astrologers had to find omens for every large enterprise; and from all important sites the king received regular reports of what was happening in the sky and its interpretation."[6] Marie-Louise Thomsen confirms this assertion: "The main reason for astronomical observations in ancient Babylonia was the belief that celestial phenomena could foretell what would happen in the future."[7] Thomsen observes that "a large compendium of omens called from the initial line *Enuma Anu Enlil*, 'When Anu and Enlil,' and containing about 7,000 omens written on a total of 70 tablets," contained omens concerning the "country and king, never the fate of an individual."[8] This absence of reference to the individual indicates a fundamental difference between astrology as it would later be practiced by the Greeks and ultimately in modern times. That Assyrian astrology was not the developed system commonly practiced in Greece some centuries later is also attested by the fact that "not all omens were derived from the stars. Omens were to be found everywhere; in the livers of the sacrificial victims, a variable and thus prolific object; in the flight of birds; in miscarriages, earthquakes, clouds, rainbows, and haloes."[9] The efforts to predict future conditions of plenty or famine, or the rise or fall of lords, by observing the planets and the moon, called for more precise measurement of the motions of the planets. As Pannekoek goes on to point out, "Detailed knowledge of the heavenly phenomena thus obtained could not have been the result of observations for mere time-reckoning and orientation, but there was still no trace of scientific purpose. . . . The connection between the phenomena was seen not as cause and effect but as sign and meaning."[10] Astrology in the time of Nebuchadnezzar was not like the

6. A. Pannekoek, *A History of Astronomy*, 38.

7. Marie-Louise Thomsen, "Witchcraft and Magic in Ancient Mesopotamia," 88.

8. Ibid.

9. Pannekoek, *A History of Astronomy*, 38.

10. Ibid., 48.

popular practice today. It was principally a source of information to advise the king.

THE KING ORDERS AN EXECUTION: 2:12–13

12— Because of this the king became indignant and very furious and gave orders to destroy all the wise men of Babylon.

13— So the decree went forth that the wise men should be slain; and they looked for Daniel and his friends to kill *them.*

The king assumed that the wise men were stalling, so he issued a decree that all the wise men be put to death. This decree included Daniel and his three companions, so the king sent men to find them in order to put them to death. It is very likely that the wise men would have been assembled for a mass execution. The fact that Daniel and the three Hebrew youths were not present is no criticism against the integrity of the text. It is possible that they did not assemble with the other wise men when the king called because they were considered junior members of the guild, or perhaps they were left out because of the fact that they were Hebrews and not native Babylonians. Whatever the reason, to claim that this introduces a contradiction into the text is reading too much into their absence.

DANIEL CALLS ON GOD: 2:14–16

14— Then Daniel replied with discretion and discernment to Arioch, the captain of the king's bodyguard, who had gone forth to slay the wise men of Babylon;

15— he said to Arioch, the king's commander, "For what reason is the decree from the king [so] urgent?" Then Arioch informed Daniel about the matter.

16— So Daniel went in and requested of the king that he would give him time, in order that he might declare the interpretation to the king.

When Daniel heard of the king's decree, he asked Arioch, the captain of the guard, to explain the nature of this decree. As soon as Daniel understood the circumstances, he sought the king to give him some time, and he assured the king that he would be able to comply with the king's demands. It is interesting that when the king thought that the wise men were "bargaining for time," he was unwilling to accede to their request. However, when Daniel comes before the king and "requested of the king that he would give him time," apparently the king agreed. There is no indication that the king's actions were because of any intervention of God. This may simply have been because of the relationship that Daniel had with the king or, perhaps, Daniel's reputation, or even the simple fact that he assured the king that he would be able to do what the king demanded. We are not denying supernatural intervention. It is simply an observation that the text makes no comment one way or the other.

Daniel Prays to God: 2:17–18

17— Then Daniel went to his house and informed his friends, Hananiah, Mishael and Azariah, about the matter,

18— so that they might request compassion from the God of heaven concerning this mystery, so that Daniel and his friends would not be destroyed with the rest of the wise men of Babylon.

Daniel and his three friends gather together to seek God and ask for wisdom. Notice that the text states, "so that they might request compassion from the God of heaven concerning this mystery" (Dan 2:18). The Hebrew equivalent to the Aramaic term "compassion" (וְרַחֲמִין, ûumᵃhrᵉw) is used in Gen 43:14 when Jacob agrees to send Benjamin with his other sons back to Egypt: "And God Almighty give you mercy [רַחֲמִים, ûumᵃhar] before the man, that he may send away your other brother, and Benjamin." Here these four Hebrew youths are asking God to have mercy upon them before the vicious and angered king.

Daniel's Interpretation: 2:19–49

Daniel Relates the Dream: 2:19–35

19— Then the mystery was revealed to Daniel in a night vision. Then Daniel blessed the God of heaven;

20— Daniel said, "Let the name of God be blessed forever and ever, for wisdom and power belong to Him."

21— "It is He who changes the times and the epochs; He removes kings and establishes kings; He gives wisdom to wise men and knowledge to men of understanding."

22— "It is He who reveals the profound and hidden things; He knows what is in the darkness, and the light dwells with Him."

23— "To You, O God of my fathers, I give thanks and praise, For You have given me wisdom and power; Even now You have made known to me what we requested of You, For You have made known to us the king's matter."

24— Therefore, Daniel went in to Arioch, whom the king had appointed to destroy the wise men of Babylon; he went and spoke to him as follows: "Do not destroy the wise men of Babylon! Take me into the king's presence, and I will declare the interpretation to the king."

25— Then Arioch hurriedly brought Daniel into the king's presence and spoke to him as follows: "I have found a man among the exiles from Judah who can make the interpretation known to the king!"

26— The king said to Daniel, whose name was Belteshazzar, "Are you able to make known to me the dream which I have seen and its interpretation?"

27— Daniel answered before the king and said, "As for the mystery about which the king has inquired, neither wise men, conjurers, magicians nor diviners are able to declare it to the king."

28— "However, there is a God in heaven who reveals mysteries, and He has made known to King Nebuchadnezzar what will take place in the latter days. This was your dream and the visions in your mind while on your bed."

29— "As for you, O king, while on your bed your thoughts turned to what would take place in the future; and He who reveals mysteries has made known to you what will take place."

30— "But as for me, this mystery has not been revealed to me for any wisdom residing in me more than in any other living man, but for the purpose of making the interpretation known to the king, and that you may understand the thoughts of your mind."

31— "You, O king, were looking and behold, there was a single great statue; that statue, which was large and of extraordinary splendor, was standing in front of you, and its appearance was awesome."

32— "The head of that statue was made of fine gold, its breast and its arms of silver, its belly and its thighs of bronze,

33— its legs of iron, its feet partly of iron and partly of clay."

34— "You continued looking until a stone was cut out without hands, and it struck the statue on its feet of iron and clay and crushed them."

35— "Then the iron, the clay, the bronze, the silver and the gold were crushed all at the same time and became like chaff from the summer threshing floors; and the wind carried them away so that not a trace

of them was found. But the stone that struck the statue became a
great mountain and filled the whole earth."

In response to the prayers of Daniel and his friends, God granted Daniel a
night vision by which the mystery of the dream and its interpretation were
given to Daniel. Immediately he offered praise and thanksgiving to God. The
prayer is an acknowledgment of God's sovereignty over their situation and
over the world which He has created.

Daniel reported to Arioch and told him not to destroy the wise men
because he would make known to the king the interpretation of the dream.
Arioch took Daniel to the king, and notice what Arioch says: "I have found
a man among the exiles from Judah who can tell the king what his dream
means" (Dan 2:25). Of course Arioch did not "find" Daniel. Daniel found
him.

Daniel is careful to make known to the king that the reason he is able to
fulfill the king's request is because the God of Heaven has revealed this mystery. After this statement, Daniel begins to relate to the king the dream he had.
Daniel makes sure that the king realizes that no human being could have met
the king's demand. Daniel exalts God and points out that it was not Daniel's
own wisdom or power that could answer the king. This is of particular interest
since Nebuchadnezzar had just spent three years of the kingdom's time and
money training Daniel. Yet, neither this training nor the wisdom of the wise
men of Babylon, but only the God of the heavens, could accomplish this task.
In this initial statement, Daniel makes it clear that, through the dream, God
had made known to the king what would take place in the future.

Daniel declares to the king that God "has made known to King
Nebuchadnezzar what will take place in the latter days [בְּאַחֲרִית, $\it{tir^{a}ha^{\,e}b}$]"
(Dan 2:28). This phrase is extremely significant in that it becomes the first
point of division between the various schools of eschatological thought. For
example, Young states, "It thus has primary reference to that period which
would begin to run its course with the appearance of God upon earth, i.e., the
days of the Messiah. While it is true that the entire contents of the dream do
not fall within the Messianic age, nevertheless the principal point, the establishment of the Messiah's Kingdom, does fall therein."[11] James Montgomery
makes an observation about the phrase that is contrary to Young's: "An expression which occurs fourteen times in the O.T., and which always denotes the
closing period of the future so far as it falls within the range of the view of the
writer using it. The sense expressed by it is thus relative, not absolute, varying
with the context. . . . Here, as the sequel shows, it is similarly the period of the

---

11. Young, *Prophecy of Daniel*, 70.

establishment of the Divine Kingdom, which is principally denoted by it."[12] The various eschatological perspectives begin to show themselves even with this one small phrase.

Robert Culver notes several important aspects of this phrase:

> *First*, this phrase is an exact Aramaic translation of the Hebrew *b᾿ᵃchᵃrîth hôyyāmîn* and is an idea lifted *en toto* out of the general prophetical literature of Israel. It is spoken by a Jew who was versed in that literature. Hence, its meaning is to be determined by its usage in that literature, not in any other. *Second*, "the latter days" cannot be restricted in meaning to the understanding which the heathen King Nebuchadnezzar may have had of it. . . . *Third*, "the latter days" in the prophetical literature of the Old Testament refers to the future of God's dealings with mankind as to be consummated and concluded historically in the times of the Messiah. . . . *Fourth*, this term in the Greek translation is used by the New Testament writers with the same meaning. . . . *Fifth*, interpretation of "the latter days" must allow it to include not only the first advent and the second advent with the coming of Messiah's future Kingdom, but also the age intervening between the advents in which we now live. . . . *Sixth*, and finally, the term "the latter days" is to be distinguished from "the time of the end," which is mentioned in Daniel. The ideas are related but not identical, as is seen later.[13]

It is clear that much of what Culver asserts is derived from his Premillennial perspective. However, it also seems clear that what is in view in the dream is the span of Gentile kingdoms that are brought to an end by the stone that strikes the foot of the statue, and that the expression "the latter days" must include all of this period. We will consider these expressions in more detail when we come to Daniel's interpretation.

DANIEL INTERPRETS THE DREAM: 2:36–43

36—   "This *was* the dream; now we will tell its interpretation before the king.

37—   "You, O king, are the king of kings, to whom the God of heaven has given the kingdom, the power, the strength and the glory;

---

12. James A. Montgomery, *A Critical and Exegetical Commentary on the Book of Daniel*, 162.

13. Robert Duncan Culver, *Daniel and the Latter Days*, 116–18.

38—   and wherever the sons of men dwell, *or* the beasts of the field, or the birds of the sky, He has given *them* into your hand and has caused you to rule over them all. You are the head of gold.

39—   "After you there will arise another kingdom inferior to you, then another third kingdom of bronze, which will rule over all the earth.

40—   "Then there will be a fourth kingdom as strong as iron; inasmuch as iron crushes and shatters all things, so, like iron that breaks in pieces, it will crush and break all these in pieces.

41—   "In that you saw the feet and toes, partly of potter's clay and partly of iron, it will be a divided kingdom; but it will have in it the toughness of iron, inasmuch as you saw the iron mixed with common clay.

42—   "*As* the toes of the feet *were* partly of iron and partly of pottery, *so* some of the kingdom will be strong and part of it will be brittle.

43—   "And in that you saw the iron mixed with common clay, they will combine with one another in the seed of men; but they will not adhere to one another, even as iron does not combine with pottery.

It is a common sound to be heard from critical camps that Daniel's prophecy is not to be understood as depicting actual kingdoms. As one critical scholar put it, "All too often, readers of Dan. 2 get so caught up in trying to interpret the details of the dream that they more or less ignore the point of it. The 'mystery' it reveals is not the details of the course of events in history, but the fact that history is under the control of God and that it has a purpose, which will be achieved. In the interpretation of the dream (25–45) there is no detailed exposition of the meaning of the four metals."[14] Of course critical scholars never explain why a make-believe interpretation that really tells no one anything true about the actual history of events will nevertheless communicate the fact that God controls history. If the story is not true, then how does this tell us anything true about God's control? Unless the prophecy of Daniel actually tells us about the unfolding events of human history, it tells us nothing about God's control of that history.

First, Daniel recites the dream as the king had commanded. As the king was looking, he saw a single great statue. The head of the statue was made of fine gold; its breast and arms were made of silver; its belly and its thighs were made of bronze; its legs were made of iron, and its feet were made of iron mixed with clay.

As the king continued to look at the statue, without hands a stone was cut out of a mountain, and it struck the statue in the feet of iron and clay, and

14. Lucas, *Daniel,* 79.

it crushed them. Then, the entire statue and all of its magnificent metals were crushed "at the same time," and they became as chaff so that the wind blew them away without leaving a trace. Then the stone grew into a great mountain that filled the whole earth.

Take note of the different elements of this dream.

1. A statue—large, extraordinary splendor, awesome in appearance stood before the king.

2. Gold—pure gold—head

3. Silver—breast and arms

4. Bronze—belly and thighs

5. Iron—legs and feet

6. Iron mixed with Clay—not a metal, soft pliable material—feet

7. Stone—cut without hands

8. Mountain—great mountain filling the whole earth

Note some observations about the dream:

1) The dream is of a single statue, not several statues, indicating that it is a unity. As Young observes, "Darby is correct when he says, 'We may first observe that the Gentile kingdoms are seen as a whole. It is neither historical succession nor moral features with respect to God and man, but the kingdoms all together forming, as it were, a personage before God, the man of the earth . . .'"[15]

2) The metals descend in value from gold to iron mixed with clay.

3) Daniel's interpretation of the symbolism indicates that the statue represents a movement through time from the time of Nebuchadnezzar to the time of the final kingdom, moving through time as one descends down from the head to the toes, so that the kingdom symbolized by the feet and toes is chronologically later than the kingdom symbolized by the head of gold.

4) Verse 41 makes reference to the toes. In objecting to a dispensationalist interpretation, Young asserts, "We are not expressly told that there are ten toes."[16] However, it is not an unreasonable assumption that there were ten toes, since there is no indication that the statue represents a deformed man. Whatever the toes may or may not represent, it is unreasonable to assume that there were not ten of them. Young vacates his own principle when later he declares, "The stone is represented as not being cut out of the mountain

15. Young, *Prophecy of Daniel*, 76.

16. Ibid., 78.

by hands in order to show that it is prepared, not by men, but by God."[17] Of course "We are not expressly told that" the stone was prepared by God. This certainly seems to be a reasonable inference, but according to Young's principle, it cannot be legitimate if we are not "expressly told" this.

5) When the stone strikes the statute on the feet, the text states that the feet are crushed. Young also argues, "the image was not smitten upon the toes but upon the feet (2:34)."[18] But the text also says that the stone struck the statue "on its feet of iron and clay and crushed them." Are we to assume that just because the text does not mention the toes that they were not crushed? That would be absurd. The fact that the stone struck the feet requires that the toes also were struck.

6) But, the text goes on to say that the entire statue is crushed "as one" (הַדָּ֫קָה, *hadᵃhak*). At first glance it appears as if the feet were crushed and then the rest of the statue together. However, the text actually enumerates the parts that are crushed as one: "As a result, was the iron, the clay, the brass, the silver, and the gold, broken to pieces as one . . ." So, the text indicates that when the stone struck the feet, the entire statue was broken to pieces as one whole thing. This necessarily means that the toes were crushed along with the feet.

7) Once the statue was crushed, there was nothing of it to be found. All of it was blown away. There was no residue remaining. In fact, the text states that "no place was found for them."

8) The stone struck the statue so that it was crushed and disappeared before the stone grew into a mountain to cover the entire earth. Mathison asserts that this kingdom "is destined to overcome all opposing kingdoms and grow into a kingdom that will fill all the earth. It is characterized by the gradual subjection of all the enemies of God . . . the growth of the kingdom is gradual. The kingdom of God begins as a stone, but does not remain a stone, and it certainly does not shrink into a pebble. Instead, it grows into a mountain that fills the whole earth."[19] However, contrary to Mathison's claim, the text does not present the growth of the kingdom of God as a gradual subjection of all the enemies of God. The text asserts, "Then the iron, the clay, the bronze, the silver and the gold were crushed all at the same time and became like chaff from the summer threshing floors; and the wind carried them away so that not a trace of them was found. And the stone that struck the statue became a great mountain and filled the whole earth" (Dan 2:35). Although the text does present the kingdom of God as becoming a great mountain, the text

17. Ibid., 79.

18. Ibid., 78.

19. Mathison, *Postmillennialism*, 94.

presents this as an action that takes place after the destruction and sweeping away of the other kingdoms. The destruction of the statue is presented as a single, sudden catastrophic event. There is no sense of a gradual overcoming of the statute, or a gradual replacing of the statue by the growing stone. The statue is destroyed, and then the stone grows into a mountain.

9) The stone struck the statute and then became a great mountain. It was not another or a different stone that became a mountain. It was that very stone. The mountain filled "the whole earth." Not part of it, but all of it. The stone grew to fill the whole earth only after the statue was completely gone. Also, strictly speaking, the text does not say that the stone gradually grew into a great mountain. The text simply says, "And the stone that struck the statue became a great mountain and filled the whole earth" (Dan 2:35).[20] The text does not use the word "gradually" in its description. Although it may seem reasonable to think that the kingdom grew gradually because this is the way kingdoms grow, this is nevertheless an assumption that is not derived from the text. Since the stone was cut out without hands, indicating that the kingdom was not made by man, there is no reason to think that the growth would necessarily be like the growth of manmade kingdoms. It is just as reasonable to conclude that the kingdom of God immediately engulfed the whole earth, or did so rapidly, not gradually. The point is, to conclude, as Mathison does, that the "growth of the kingdom is gradual,"[21] simply does not derive from the statements of the text. This is an assumption on Mathison's part—an assumption for which he presents no arguments. We are not saying this is a false assumption or that it is not legitimate to make this assumption. We are simply pointing out that the text does not state this, and therefore this is an assumption, and Mathison presents no argument why anyone should believe that this assumption is legitimate.

DANIEL EXPLAINS THE DREAM: 2:44–45

44— "In the days of those kings the God of heaven will set up a kingdom which will never be destroyed, and *that* kingdom will not be left for another people; it will crush and put an end to all these kingdoms, but it will itself endure forever.

45— "Inasmuch as you saw that a stone was cut out of the mountain without hands and that it crushed the iron, the bronze, the clay, the silver and the gold, the great God has made known to the king what

---

20. (Dan 2:35) וְאַבְנָא דִּי־מְחָת לְצַלְמָא הֲוָת לְטוּר רַב וּמְלָת כָּל־אַרְעָא׃

21. Ibid.

will take place in the future; so the dream is true and its interpretation is trustworthy."

Daniel moves immediately into the interpretation of the dream. Notice first that Daniel does not explain the statue as a whole. Rather he begins immediately to explain the significance of the various parts of the statue.

Interpretation of the Parts

Head of Gold—Nebuchadnezzar is the head of gold. Daniel refers to him as "the king of kings" (מֶלֶךְ מַלְכַיָּא, *'ayyaklam kelem*). Daniel says, "the God of heaven has given you dominion and power and might and glory." This is the same God of whom Daniel said He "reveals secrets, and makes known to the king Nebuchadnezzar what shall be in the latter days" (Dan 2:26). The purity of the gold is representative of the pure power and sovereignty of Nebuchadnezzar's rule, as verse 38 points out.

Breast and arms of Silver—A subsequent kingdom that will be composed of two parts, corresponding to the two arms. This kingdom will be inferior to Babylon, although not necessarily smaller. This statement has been the cause of much debate. Critical scholars have been quick to attack Daniel's comment because, historically, each succeeding kingdom actually gets progressively larger in its territory. However, there is no reason to think that this is necessarily what Daniel meant by the term "inferior." There is no question that the metals are progressively less valuable, and this may imply that the form of government is less desirable in each case. Although our modern view holds that a republic is the best form of government, this is predicated on the assumption that men are inherently evil, and therefore there must be checks and balances in order to protect the helpless. However, the best form of government would be an all-powerful, all-loving, all-knowing King. Nebuchadnezzar's kingdom was an absolute monarchy. Each successive kingdom is a messier more complex and more difficult form of government. As Lucas points out, "Although, in one way, that dream was flattering to Nebuchadnezzar, because he was the head of gold, it also reminded him that human kingdoms come and go, and that disunity makes them fragile and prone to collapse."[22] There may be a sense in which the statue symbolizes a progressive disunity. This is certainly true for the feet of clay and iron. It may be this notion of disunity and instability that is indicated by Daniel's comment concerning the inferiority of the second kingdom.

22. Lucas, *Daniel*, 93.

Figure 5: Neb's Statue

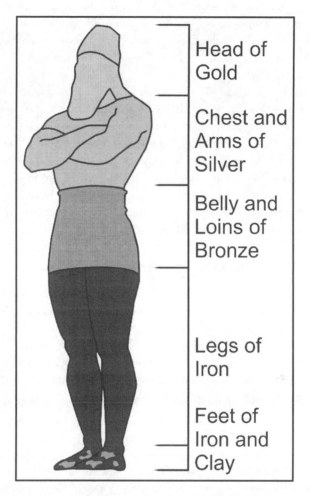

Head of
Gold

Chest and
Arms of
Silver

Belly and
Loins of
Bronze

Legs of
Iron

Feet of
Iron and
Clay

Belly and thighs of Bronze—At first the third kingdom seems also to be composed of two parts corresponding to the thighs. The Aramaic term translated "thighs" is יַרְכָה (ḥakray). Its Hebrew equivalent, (יָרֵךְ, keray), has, according to *The Hebrew & Aramaic Lexicon of the Old Testament*, "the same meaning."[23] The Hebrew term is often used to refer to the "loins," in the sense of the seat of procreative power. This is, of course, not referring to the thighs in the sense of the upper part of the legs. In several places the word is used to refer to the flank in a military sense. In Ex 26:22 it is translated "rear"

---

23. *The Hebrew & Aramaic Lexicon of the Old Testament* (2001), s.v. "יַרְכָה." Hereinafter referred to as KBH.

in the NASBU—"For the rear of the tabernacle, to the west, you shall make six boards"—and "sides" in the KJV—"And for the sides of the tabernacle westward thou shalt make six boards." It is possible that the description of this part of the statue includes the torso and the area of the hips. Otherwise, it seems difficult to understand the term "legs" if it does not refer to the whole leg from the hip down.

Legs of iron and feet of iron and clay—The fourth kingdom will be as strong as iron. Although the metals decline in value, they increase in strength, gold being the most pliable and iron being the hardest and strongest. This last kingdom will crush and demolish "all these." However, the final state of this kingdom will be extremely unstable inasmuch as iron and clay do not mix. Daniel spends more time on this kingdom than on the previous kingdoms. One reason this may be the case is because, whether Preterist or Futurist, and assuming that this is a reference to the Roman Empire, it is during the time(s) of the Roman Empire that Messiah comes.

Identity of the Fourth Kingdom

Milton Terry argues against the notion that the fourth kingdom depicts Rome. Before we consider Terry's arguments, it is necessary to point out that there is no inconsistency in accepting Terry's hermeneutic principles and rejecting his hermeneutic conclusions. There are many factors in addition to one's hermeneutic principles that forge one's conclusions. Terry's conclusions may not be a result of a simple application of his own principles, and this will become evident in his first argument against the Roman view.

> Great stress has been laid by the advocates of the Roman theory upon three considerations: (1) First they urge that Rome was too important to be left out of sight in such a vision of world-empire. "The Roman kingdom," says Keil, "was the first universal monarchy in the full sense. Along with the three earlier world-kingdoms, the nations of the world-historical future remained still unsubdued." But such presumption cannot properly be allowed to weigh at all. It matters not in the least how great Rome was, or how important a place it occupies in universal history. The sole question with the interpreter of Daniel must be, What world-powers, great or small, fell within his circle of prophetic vision? This presumption in favour of Rome is more than off set by the consideration that geographically and politically that later empire had its seat and centre of influence far aside from the territory of the Asiatic kingdoms. But the Graeco-Macedonian Empire, in all its relations to Israel, and, indeed, in its principal component elements, was an Asiatic, not a European, world-power. The prophet, moreover,

makes repeated allusion to kings of Greece (יָוָן, Javan), but never mentions Rome.[24]

Terry's restatement of the question is out of the question. There is nothing in the vision or the interpretation that requires one to confine the "circle of prophetic vision" within the territory of the Asiatic kingdoms. Simply because the first two kingdoms are so confined does not require the remaining two to be thus also confined. Terry's attempt to confine the empire of Greece to this territory is at best a stretch. The fact that the prophet never mentions Rome is no mark against this view, since the prophet likewise never mentions Medo-Persia. Here Terry's conclusion is not based on the application of his hermeneutic principles, but on the prior assumption that Rome is not part of the prophecy.

Terry's second argument concerns the image of the iron as depicting the strength of the Roman Empire.

> (2) It is further argued that the strong and terrible character of the fourth kingdom is best fulfilled in Rome. No previous dominion, it is said, was of such an iron nature, breaking all things in pieces. Here again we must insist that the question is not so much whether the imagery fits Rome, but whether it may not also appropriately depict some other kingdom. The description of iron strength and violence is, no doubt, appropriate to Rome, but for anyone to aver that the conquests and rule of Alex and his successors did not "break in pieces and bruise" (Dan. ii, 40), and trample with terrible violence the kingdoms of many nations, is to exhibit a marvelous obtuseness in reading the facts of history. The Graeco-Macedonian power broke up the older civilizations, and trampled in pieces the various elements of the Asiatic monarchies more completely than had ever been done before. Rome never had any such triumph in the Orient, and, indeed, no great Asiatic world-power, comparable for magnitude and power with that of Alexander, ever succeeded his. If now we keep in mind this utter overthrow and destruction of the older dynasties by Alexander, and then observe what seems especially to have affected Daniel, namely, the wrath and violence of the "little horn," and note how, in different forms, this bitter and relentless persecutor is made prominent in this book (chapters viii and xi), we may safely say that the conquests of Alexander, and the blasphemous fury of Antiochus Epiphanes, in his violence against the chosen people, amply fulfilled the prophecies of the fourth kingdom.[25]

24. Terry, *Biblical Hermeneutics*, 420 (emphasis in original).
25. Ibid., 420–21.

Once again Terry's argument is not a result of the simple application of his principles. To argue that the iron also depicts Greece ignores the very statement of Daniel in verse 40: "Then there will be a fourth kingdom as strong as iron." According to Terry's view, Greece would have to be both the third and the fourth kingdoms, which seems contrary to the scheme of Daniel's interpretation thus far. Daniel presents each succeeding kingdom as a new and different kingdom, not a continuation of a previous kingdom. Also, Evans demonstrates the inaccuracy of ascribing to Antiochus Epiphanes the strength of iron: "Inasmuch as Antiochus IV was intimidated out of invading Egypt in 168 BC by the Roman envoy to that land, his kingdom simply does not match that description."[26] In fact, even Alexander's kingdom does not match this description. There is no doubt that Alexander did crush many enemies, but he did not crush the Jews once they told him that God had spoken of him in the Scriptures, as Josephus reports.[27] Alexander often demonstrated a compassion that was absent from the ruthless Roman military machine.

Terry goes on to argue, "The advocates of the Roman theory are continually laying stress upon the supposed import of the *two* arms, and *two* legs, and *ten* toes of the image; whereas these are merely the natural parts of a human image, and necessary to complete a coherent outline. The prophet lays no stress upon them in his exposition, and it is nowhere said that the image had *ten* toes."[28] Of course nowhere does the exposition explicitly say there are two arms. Rather, Daniel reports only that the statue had arms. Likewise, there is no explicit statement that there were two legs, only that the statue had legs. Yet Terry accepts the notion of the two arms and two legs as necessary to "complete a coherent outline." Likewise, the conclusion that there are ten toes is equally necessary to complete a coherent outline. The fact that nowhere is it said that the image had ten toes is no argument against the Roman view.

The Kingdom of God

The final kingdom is established by the God of heaven. This kingdom will be set up by way of crushing the previous kingdoms. The fact that the residue of the previous kingdoms is completely swept away, coupled with the fact that the stone is cut out of the mountain without hands, indicates that this kingdom is not in the succession of earthly kingdoms and is not established by mankind. The text asserts, תְּקוּם לְעָלְמַיָּא, (ʾayyamla ʿel muqʿt) which is usually translated "it will stand forever." For the word used here, עָלַם

---

26. Evans, *Four Kingdoms*, 119–20.

27. Josephus, *Antiquities of the Jews*, XI.8.4–6.

28. Terry, *Hermeneutics*, 421.

(*mala'*), KBH lists the following definitions: "remote time, eternity."[29] The fact that this word does not necessarily mean "eternity" can be illustrated from its use in Ezra 4:15: "so that a search may be made in the record books of your fathers. And you will discover in the record books and learn that that city is a rebellious city and damaging to kings and provinces, and that they have incited revolt within it in past days [מִן־יוֹמָת עָלְמָא, *'amla' 'amoy_ nim*, lit. 'from days of remote time']; therefore that city was laid waste." Obviously the word cannot be understood as referring to eternity in this context since this city and its records did not exist from eternity. So, in the Daniel passage, the phrase can certainly be referring to an eternal kingdom, but the word itself does not require this meaning. It could be referring to a kingdom that lasts for a long time, but not necessarily eternally, or it could indicate the quality of the kingdom rather than its duration—it is the kind of kingdom that lasts for eternity even though it may not actually last for eternity.

Taking the cue from Daniel's own identification of the first kingdom as that of Nebuchadnezzar, it is a matter of investigating history to see how Daniel's prophecies fit. The second kingdom was Medo-Persia, indicated by the two arms. The Medo-Persian Empire was not a pure monarchy, nor would many say it was as glorious a kingdom as that of Nebuchadnezzar's. The third kingdom is the kingdom of Greece. Although most translations read "belly and thighs," this could be translated "belly and loins" or "belly and sides." The fourth kingdom is the kingdom of Rome. The representation of the kingdom of Rome as two legs has spawned a great deal of debate. It may be that the two legs correspond to the two geographical areas, Europe and Asia, which the Roman Empire dominated. It may be because the Roman Empire divided into the eastern and western empires. It may be representative of two aspects of the empire, namely the political and spiritual. Each one of these views has been taken by commentators, and we will address this in more detail when we consider Daniel's interpretation.

Some have argued that Daniel's interpretation does not reflect the truth of Nebuchadnezzar's kingdom. Daniel's interpretation indicates that Nebuchadnezzar's dominion extended over the entire earth: "wherever the sons of men dwell, or the beasts of the field, or the birds of the sky, He has given them into your hand and has caused you to rule over them all" (Dan 2:38). In fact, Nebuchadnezzar did not exercise dominion over the entire earth as Daniel's prophecy indicates. However, there is no discrepancy between Daniel's interpretation and the reality of Nebuchadnezzar's rule. Daniel declared that God had given this dominion to Nebuchadnezzar. He did not say that Nebuchadnezzar actually exercised the dominion that God had given

29. KBH, s.v. "עָלַם."

to him. This is not a unique circumstance. God told Joshua, "Every place on which the sole of your foot treads, I have given it to you, just as I spoke to Moses. From the wilderness and this Lebanon, even as far as the great river, the river Euphrates, all the land of the Hittites, and as far as the Great Sea toward the setting of the sun will be your territory. No man will be able to stand before you all the days of your life" (Josh. 1:3–5). However, the account of the books of Joshua and Judges testifies to the fact that Israel did not take possession of the land that God had already given to them. Their unfaithfulness to the covenant relation led to their increasing failure to drive out the inhabitants. Likewise, dominion over the world had been given to Nebuchadnezzar, but for whatever reason, Nebuchadnezzar did not actually exercise this dominion. There is no discrepancy between Daniel's interpretation and the facts of Nebuchadnezzar's reign.

Walvoord reports, "The description of the stone as being cut out 'of the mountain without hands' has sometimes been referred to Mount Zion specifically, but it is better to consider this as a symbolic picture of political sovereignty."[30] However, as we pointed out in the introduction, in Scripture, Jerusalem is often referred to as the Mountain of God. This is true even in the book of Daniel: "O Lord, according to all your justice, please turn your raging anger away from your city Jerusalem, your holy mountain [יְרוּשָׁלַ͏ִם, הַר־קָדְשֶׁךָ *akĕṣdaq rah miālāsurᵉy*]" (Dan 9:16). The mountain here may in fact be symbolic of the Holy Mountain of God out of which comes Messiah, Who becomes a man not by the agency of men, but by the Holy Spirit. This also fits well with the depiction of the kingdom as a stone. Psalm 118:22 declares, "The stone which the builders rejected has become the chief corner *stone*." Almost all commentators understand this to be a reference to Christ.

Generally speaking, two of the major eschatological camps, Preterism and Futurism, agree as to the identification of the first three kingdoms, Babylon, Medo-Persia, Greece. The differences begin to emerge with reference to the fourth kingdom and the identity and timing of the kingdom represented by the stone becoming a mountain covering the entire earth. Although both Preterists and Futurists agree that the fourth kingdom is Rome, they disagree as to the extent of the Roman Empire and how it relates to the stone that was cut out without hands. These differences are discussed below, and the relevant verses are dealt with in that discussion.

---

30. Walvoord, *Daniel*, 76.

DANIEL RECEIVES HONORS: 2:46–49

46— Then King Nebuchadnezzar fell on his face and did homage to Daniel, and gave orders to present to him an offering and fragrant incense.

47— The king answered Daniel and said, "Surely your God is a God of gods and a Lord of kings and a revealer of mysteries, since you have been able to reveal this mystery."

48— Then the king promoted Daniel and gave him many great gifts, and he made him ruler over the whole province of Babylon and chief prefect over all the wise men of Babylon.

49— And Daniel made request of the king, and he appointed Shadrach, Meshach and Abed-nego over the administration of the province of Babylon, while Daniel [was] at the king's court.

As a result of Daniel's successful interpretation of the king's dream, Daniel is promoted to a prominent position in the kingdom. Although Nebuchadnezzar confesses, "Surely your God is a God of gods and a Lord of kings and a revealer of mysteries, since you have been able to reveal this mystery" (2:47), this does not indicate that Nebuchadnezzar had experienced a conversion in the strict sense. It is probably the case that Nebuchadnezzar simply recognized the superiority of Daniel's God without confessing Him as the only true and living God. This chapter provides the basic framework upon which the whole of prophetic history will be built. Through this vision, God set before Nebuchadnezzar His plan for history from the time of Nebuchadnezzar to the "latter days." The reference to Daniel's three companions sets the reader up for the events of chapter 3.

The Kingdom of God

Having given a brief overview of the chapter, we now want to focus on the various eschatological views with respect to the prophecy of chapter 2. There are several Preterist views that have been proposed in recent years. This does not necessarily indicate that the Preterist view is faulty. There are, no doubt, as many different views among the Futurists as among the Preterists. It would not be possible to consider all the claims of all the Preterist authors and their views on the nature of the kingdom of God. Additionally, this is not a theological textbook on eschatology, but a commentary on the book of Daniel. Consequently, we will consider only a few representatives from this perspective. We will confine our comments to those authors who actually comment on the prophetic passages of Daniel chapter 2. Since it is the understanding of the nature of the kingdom of God as this is described in this prophecy that distinguishes the Preterist from the Futurist interpretations, we will primarily focus on these passages and this issue.

Preterist Views

PRETERIST VIEW OF JESSIE MILLS

One Preterist view of the kingdom of God as it is depicted in Daniel's prophecy is explained by Jessie Mills. He declares, "The establishment of the kingdom of God was to appear during the fourth kingdom, or the fourth phase of the image. To this Paul the Apostle testifies, Col. 1:13; see also Mark 1:14–15 and Rev. 1:9. Since the New Testament testifies of the establishment of the kingdom during the Roman period, I conclude that the Roman kingdom was the fourth kingdom."[31] Mills goes on to present an interpretation of the various kingdoms. The second kingdom, according to Mills, is Medo-Persia, the third Greece, and the fourth Rome. Having dealt with the four metals and the four kingdoms, Mills turns his attention to verses 44–49. Mills quotes the first part of verse 44, then he asserts, "Notice here that the inference is to a spiritual kingdom, not an earthly one."[32] In support of this "inference" he quotes Jesus' statement in Jn 18:36. Apparently Mills does not consider it necessary to defend his understanding of this NT passage, nor his understanding of Daniel's interpretation of the kingdom. As a result, there are several questions that go unanswered. First of all, although Mills has no reluctance to identify the head of Gold with Nebuchadnezzar and the earthly kingdom of Babylon, and the kingdoms of Medo-Persia, Greece, and Rome as earthly kingdoms, Mills declares that the reference to the kingdom of God is an inference "to a spiritual kingdom, not an earthly one."[33]

However, to take this as a reference to a spiritual kingdom instead of a kingdom on the earth seems to cause the imagery in Daniel to become inexplicably inconsistent. If the stone cut out without hands that grows into a mountain covering the entire earth, does not indicate a kingdom on this earth, then it is inconsistent not only with the previous references, which were all to be kingdoms on this earth, but with Daniel's own interpretation. The text says, "But the stone that struck the statue became a great mountain and filled the whole earth" (Dan 2:35). The Aramaic text employs the word "earth" or "land" in the expression "all the earth": כָּל־אַרְעָא (ʾaʿraʾ□□lak). This same expression is found in Daniel's interpretation of the vision: "After

31. Jessie E. Mills, Jr., *Daniel: Fulfilled Prophecy*, 17.
32. Ibid., 18–19.
33. Ibid.

you [Nebuchadnezzar] there will arise another kingdom inferior to you, then another third kingdom of bronze, which will rule over all the earth" (Dan 2:39). The specific phrase occurs at the end of the sentence: "בְּכָל־אַרְעָא" (*ᵓaʿraᵓ lakᵉb*), "over all the earth." Here Mills seems to have no problem with understanding this as a reference to a physical kingdom actually existing on the earth. Why does he suddenly take the reference to God's kingdom as a spiritual rather than a physical kingdom when the same wording is used to refer to Greece in verse 39, a kingdom on the earth, and to God's kingdom in verse 35?

To support of his assertion he appeals to a statement by Jesus: "Jesus said, 'My kingdom is not of this earth.'"[34] Of course this very statement is not as clear-cut as Mills would have us think. The statement comes from John's Gospel: "My kingdom is not of this world [κόσμου, *uomsok*]. If My kingdom were of this world [κόσμου, *uomsok*], then My servants would be fighting so that I would not be handed over to the Jews; but as it is, My kingdom is not of this realm [ἐντεῦθεν, *nehtuetne*]" (Jn 18:36). What is problematic for Mills' assertion is that it is not necessary to take Jesus' statement as saying that His kingdom is not a kingdom on this earth. Jesus could be saying, though His kingdom is *on* the earth, it is not an *earthly* kingdom. There are two phrases that call Mills' understanding into question. The first is the prepositional phrase, "out of this world," (ἐκ τοῦ κόσμου τούτου, *uotuot uomsok uot ke*). This prepositional phrase does not necessarily mean that the kingdom is not *on* the world. To express this spatial relation, the preposition ἐπί (*ipe*, "on" or "upon") would probably have been used. In fact, according to Daniel Wallace,[35] Herbert Weir Smyth,[36] James Hope Moulton,[37] and Maximilian Zerwick,[38] to name a few, the preposition ἐκ is never used to indicate "on" in a spatial sense. Additionally, Jesus' own statement adds a qualification to the phrase when He says, "but My kingdom is not of this realm [δὲ ἡ βασιλεία ἡ ἐμὴ οὐκ ἔστιν ἐντεῦθεν, *etneⁿnitse kuō emē eh aielisab̄ eh eduneht*]." Here the word translated "realm," (ἐντεῦθεν) is given the following definitions in BDAG: "pert. to extension from a source near the speaker, *from here*. . . . ἡ βασιλεία ἡ ἐμὴ οὐκ ἔστιν ἐ. *my kingdom is not from here*= ἐκ τοῦ κόσμου τούτου J 18:36."[39] According to the standard NT Greek lexicon, the

---

34. Ibid., 19.

35. Daniel Wallace, *Greek Grammar Beyond the Basics*, 371.

36. Herbert Weir Smyth, *Greek Grammar*, §1688.

37. James Hope Moulton, *Prolegomena*, 72, 102, 246, et. al.

38. Maximilian Zerwick, *Biblical Greek* (Rome: Scripta Pontificii Instituti Biblici, 1963), §62.

39. *A Greek-English Lexicon of the New Testament* (2005), s.v. "ἐντεῦθεν." Hereinafter referred to as BDAG.

phrase "not of this world" is indicating that Christ's kingdom does not have its source in this world. The statement is not claiming that His kingdom is not located on this earth. Additionally, both William Hendricksen and R. C. H. Lenski, neither of whom are dispensational or premillennial, take Jesus' comment to indicate the source and character of His kingdom, not whether it will or will not be "on the earth." Hendricksen says, "the kingship of Jesus is not like an earthly kingship. It does not spring from the earth: it was not given to him by earthly power, and it is totally different in character."[40] And Lenski states, "The origin of Jesus' kingship explains its unique character: it is 'not of this world.' Take the whole wide world as it is. It has produced many earthly kings and rulers. They all sprang out of (ἐκ) this world and were kings that corresponded to such an origin."[41] In fact, Hendricksen does propose that this statement, "does not have reference to God's dominion (hence, also the dominion of the second person of the Trinity) over all his creatures, but distinctly to *Christ's spiritual kingship* in the hearts and lives of his followers,"[42] but this does not disturb our point. The point we are making is that the statement "My kingdom is not of this world" is a statement about the character and the source of His kingdom, not whether it is on the earth—the sense that Hendrickson acknowledges. Consequently, this statement cannot provide evidence for Mills' point unless and until he demonstrates that his meaning is *the correct* meaning of this text. Simply quoting Scripture is not sufficient to provide evidence for his claim.[43]

Mills goes on to assert, "The spiritual kingdom would destroy Judaism and the Hebrew kingdom."[44] It is not at all clear how this statement relates to the Daniel passage. There is no clear indication that any one of the kingdoms symbolized in Nebuchadnezzar's dream is "Judaism or the Hebrew kingdom." Mills cites several verses that one assumes he believes are somehow related to this claim: "This is the rock cut out by unseen hands, the rock of offense, Isa. 8:14, a tried stone, Isa. 28:16, a stone engraved, Zech. 3:9."[45] First of all, Daniel's text does not say "cut out by unseen hands." The text says, "You continued looking until a stone was cut out *without hands* [דִּי בְיָדַיִן] א

---

40. William Hendricksen, *Exposition of the Gospel According to John*, 408–9.

41. R. C. H. Lenski, *The Interpretation of St. John's Gospel*, 1229.

42. Hendricksen, *Exposition of John*, 408.

43. This is an example of the "Scripture interprets Scripture" approach that is taken by many in the debate. Simply to refer to another passage or to quote it is not sufficient to show that one Scripture supports one's view of another. The interpreter must show that his interpretation of the related Scripture is correct before he can use it to support his claim about the original passage.

44. Mills, *Daniel*, 19.

45. Ibid.

לֹ, *niyaḏib ʾal*]," literally, "not by hands." It is not clear why Mills misquotes the passage, and this misquote does not seem to be crucial to his argument. However, it does alert the reader to the possibility that the passages to which Mills appeals may be similarly misunderstood by Mills. Also, Mills may be implying that the references to the stone in the passages he quotes are subtly implying the crucifixion of Christ—with unseen hands may be an allusion for Mills to the human hands that crucified Christ. However, this is not stated by Mills and cannot be used against his argument.

Mills refers to Isa 8:14 as if this verse lends support to his claim that the rock will "destroy Judaism and the Hebrew kingdom." Isa 8:14–15 states, "Then He shall become a sanctuary; but to both the houses of Israel, a stone to strike and a rock to stumble over, and a snare and a trap for the inhabitants of Jerusalem. Many will stumble over them, then they will fall and be broken; they will even be snared and caught." This is a prophecy about the inhabitants of Jerusalem going into Babylonian captivity as a result of abandoning God. Paul refers to this verse in Rom 9:33, but Paul's use is to emphasize faith in Christ, in contrast to the Jews who were not willing to trust God to deliver them from impending destruction. There does not seem to be anything in either of these passages that deals with "destroying Judaism and the Hebrew kingdom." Unfortunately, since Mills did not see fit to explain the connection he apparently saw, we have no way of dealing with his claims. Since the connection is unclear, the appeal to these passages does not help Mills' assertions.

The second passage to which Mills refers is Isa 28:16: "Therefore thus says the Lord God, 'Behold, I am laying in Zion a stone, a tested stone, a costly cornerstone for the foundation, firmly placed. He who believes in it will not be disturbed.'" This is in fact the other part of the reference to which Paul appeals in the Romans passage above. Once again there is nothing in these passages about destroying Judaism or the Hebrew kingdom.

The last passage is Zech 3:9: "'For behold, the stone that I have set before Joshua; on one stone are seven eyes. Behold, I will engrave an inscription on it,' declares the Lord of hosts, 'and I will remove the iniquity of that land in one day. In that day,' declares the Lord of hosts, 'every one of you will invite his neighbor to sit under his vine and under his fig tree'" (Zech 3:9–10). Again there is no reference in the verse or in the context to the destruction of Judaism or the Hebrew kingdom. One is at a complete loss to understand how Mills related these verses to his claim. Mills also declares, "We are to know this kingdom will destroy all other kingdoms, Gal 4:22–31; Mt. 15:13–14."[46] Once again these verses say nothing about destroying

46. Ibid.

Judaism and the Hebrew kingdom, and Mills' claim that this kingdom "will destroy all other kingdoms" is not supported by Daniel's vision. The stone that strikes the statue destroys all of the kingdoms represented by the statue, but it would be illegitimate, without some justification, to conclude that this means *all* kingdoms will be destroyed. This may be a valid inference, but it must be supported by argument, not simply stated.

Additionally, this seems to be a problem for Mills' thesis. If the kingdom represented by the stone is to destroy all kingdoms, and yet there are kingdoms today that have not been so destroyed, this seems to imply that either Daniel's prophecy was faulty, or the kingdom to which his prophecy points has yet to be established. One reason the stone may not be said to destroy "all kingdoms" is because when the stone strikes the feet of the statue, many kingdoms no longer exist, for example, the Hebrew kingdom. But this also implies that there is some sense in which the kingdoms of the statue still exist at the time the stone strikes the feet. This question will be addressed later.

PRETERIST VIEW OF JAMES S. EVANS

James Evans presents another Preterist view. He appeals to the fact that the stone striking the feet of the statue destroyed the entire statue as one whole as evidence that "suggests that the first three kingdoms survive in some sense (or senses) until the demise of the fourth . . ."[47] Without directly delineating in what sense or senses these three kingdoms continue, Evans uses this assumption to reject Walvoord's claims about the toes of the statue. Evans asserts,

> You sometimes read that the passage "In the time of those kings" in 2:44 does not refer to the predecessors of the fourth kingdom, but to kingdoms that arise late in the history of the fourth kingdom that are perhaps symbolized by the toes of the statue. The prominent dispensationalist John F. Walvoord (1910–2002) followed this interpretation, though he did not quite promote the toes into kingdoms. Since Daniel 2 says *nothing* about the toes symbolizing kingdoms while it explicitly states that other parts of the statue *do* symbolize kingdoms, and since 7:12 explicitly states that the first three kingdoms survive into the time of the fourth, this idea is suspect.[48]

There are a couple of serious problems with Evans' claim, however. First, although the text says nothing *specific* about the toes being kingdoms, this is implied by the fact that the material of each portion of the statue is the

47. Evans, *The Four Kingdoms*, 114.
48. Ibid., 116 (emphasis in original).

material that constituted the kingdom symbolized. Suddenly to suppose that the clay, just because it is clay, represents something other than the symbol of the character of the kingdom represented is to change hermeneutical horses in the middle of the stream without the least hermeneutical indicator that this should be done. If the gold, silver, bronze, and iron indicate separate kingdoms, why does not the clay also indicate separate kingdoms? The fact that the clay is mixed with the iron is no basis for rejecting the clay as representative of a kingdom of separate kingdoms.

Second, chapter 2 of Daniel does not explain the sense in which the previous kingdoms extend into the time of the fourth kingdom. This "extension," in whatever sense it is true, could not be in the sense that one kingdom continues to exist as a kingdom until the last kingdom. It could be in the sense of the previous kingdom(s) influencing the following kingdoms, or could be by lineage in that the kingdoms of this world all come from the same source—sinful man. But, the fact that the end of one metal and the beginning of another is explained by Daniel as the cessation of one kingdom and the beginning of another eliminates the notion that one kingdom survived its destruction as a kingdom.

Third, it is not at all clear that 7:12 "explicitly states that the first three kingdoms survive into the time of the fourth." This verse states, "As concerning the rest of the beasts, they had their dominion taken away: yet their lives were prolonged for a season and time." Evans states, "If exegesis is to be sound, mere supposition must be kept to a minimum,"[49] but to get out of this statement that it "explicitly states that the first three kingdoms survive into the time of the fourth" seems to be the very kind of supposition that Evans warns against. In fact, the verse seems to say precisely the opposite. The text explicitly states that "their dominion [שָׁלְטָן, *ñaﬂâs*] was taken away [הֶעְדִּיו, *wıd ʿeh*]" even though the lives of the beasts were prolonged for a set period of time. Besides the fact that the "set period of time" (עַד־זְמַן וְעִדָּן, *namʿz̲ daʿ ñadiʿʿw*) is not explicitly defined as "extending into the time of the fourth" kingdom, as Evans claims, although this is perhaps as valid inference, the dominions of these beasts are explicitly declared to have been "taken away" (הֶעְדִּיו, *wıd ʿeh*). We will say more about this in the commentary on that section of chapter 7, but this is sufficient to demonstrate that Evans' idea is suspect.

Evans attempts to argue that the iron and clay of the feet and toes "symbolizes the incorporation into the fourth kingdom of a distinctive people relatively late in the kingdom's existence."[50] He even declares, ". . . Pompey

---

49. Ibid.

50. Ibid., 120.

effectively incorporated Judea into the Roman Empire seven decades later
. . ."[51] But this is in fact not true since in the time of Pompey there was no
such thing as the Roman Empire. At the time of Pompey, Rome was still a
Republic. As Chester Starr points out, the Roman Empire dates "from 27 B.C.
onward."[52] Pompey died almost 20 years earlier, in 48 B.C. In other words, as
far as Nebuchadnezzar's statue is concerned, Pompey existed during that time
that the kingdom symbolized by the bronze is still alive. Evans admits that
"the Hasmoneans continued to wield some political and religious power in
Judea until 37 BC,"[53] some 10 years before the Empire was established under
Octavian-Augustus. Since the Jews did not fulfill the symbolism of the clay,
because they were brought under the heal of the "autocratic Herod as Judea's
sole ruler,"[54] as Evans himself points out, his interpretation of the symbolism
is faulty and is in fact a misrepresentation of the history.

Evans makes his claim about the "distinctive people" on the strength of
his argument that, "The listing of the clay with the statue's other component
materials suggests that it shares something in common with them. If the common element is not that these substances all symbolize ruling dynasties, what
is it? I suggest that the common element is that the five substances symbolize
distinctive *peoples*: the Babylonians, the Medes and Persians, the Greeks, and
the Romans, and the people represented by the clay."[55] In fact, later Evans
proposes, "*The clay in the feet of the great statue of Daniel 2 can be interpreted
as symbolizing the Jews living* (sic) *the Roman Empire. This is the interpretation
of the clay that makes by far the most sense, and it must have made sense to many
residents of Judea in the second half of the second century BC.*"[56] But Evans chides
others for introducing "speculative detail" and charges that, "Such efforts are
dangerous . . ."[57] In another place he declares, "*The emergence of an independent Judea can thus be viewed as being equivalent to moving all the way down
the statue to the lower ankles of the feet composed of a mixture of iron and clay.*"[58]
But, as any standard history book shows, the supposed "independent Judea"
was born and died before the Roman Empire even started. The faulty aspect
of Evans' claims is that he is identifying the clay that is mixed with the iron
as the influence of the Jews, particularly the independent Judean state under

---

51. Ibid., 234.

52. Chester Starr, *A History of the Ancient World*, 547.

53. Evans, *Four Kingdoms*, 235.

54. Ibid.

55. Ibid., 120 (emphasis in original).

56. Ibid., 235 (emphasis in original).

57. Ibid., 121 (emphasis in original).

58. Ibid., 237 (emphasis in original).

the Hasmoneans which, according to Evans' own statement ended in 63 BC.[59] However, Daniel's own interpretation of the statue places the feet at the bottom of the statute, which indicates that the iron mixed with clay occurs at the end of the Roman Empire, not before it even began. Evans must turn the lower part of the statue upside down in order to make it fit his eschatological scheme.

Additionally, the claim that these materials represent "peoples" or that the residents of Judea in the second half of the second century BC must have understood this to be the case, when there is absolutely no historical evidence to support this claim, and when the text states that they represent kingdoms, is, again, the very kind of speculation that Evans rejects in the interpretations of others. There is nothing in the text of Daniel that would even imply that these metals represent "peoples." Daniel specifically refers to them as kingdoms (מַלְכְוָתָא, *ātaw*ᵉ*klam* Dan 2:44).

However, there is an indication that the clay mixed with iron is not symbolic of either peoples or kingdoms, but of the instability of the final form of the Roman Empire. Daniel has already told Nebuchadnezzar that the subsequent kingdoms are "inferior," and the inferiority seems primarily to be the instability of the respective empires from pure absolute monarchy to virtual anarchy. Evans takes his supposition that these are "peoples" and then treats it as a fact: "After all, does not the refusal of the followers of the Maccabees to be assimilated into the dominant Greco-Syrian culture of the Seleucid Empire demonstrate the kind of cultural incompatibility envisioned in Daniel 2?"[60] Evans' speculation about the clay representing "people" has developed into a "cultural incompatibility," and yet there are no indications of this in the text.

Evans also asserts, "the quantity of time that elapses increases as one moves down the statue . . ."[61] But this assumption has not been proven. Is there some proportional relationship between the length of the head and the length of the reign of Nebuchadnezzar? No such case has been convincingly made, and yet Evans employs this assumption to ridicule the Futurists interpretation: "But when was the last stage of the fourth kingdom's existence? For futurists, it would somehow seem to lie ahead of us, but if this is the case, then we must ask if we are to assume that the statue should be envisioned as having enormously distended lower legs and feet."[62] But according to Evans' view, the Roman kingdom was crushed by the kingdom of God at the com-

---

59. See Ibid., 246.
60. Ibid., 121–22.
61. Ibid., 122.
62. Ibid.

ing of Christ. Since Palestine was conquered in 64 BC, and the beginning of the Roman Empire traditionally dates from about 31 BC with the victory of Octavian over Mark Antony, this means that its destruction took place at most some 70 years after its inception. In fact, the mainland of Greece was not taken over until 146 BC. Does Evans' statue have curtly contracted lower legs and feet? Additionally, Evans completely ignores his own principle of prophetic abridgement, taken up later, which he employs to try to explain the final kingdom as a possible explanation of the Futurist view of the legs. If Evans can use it for the final kingdom, why cannot the Futurist use it for the legs?

Evans states a characteristic Preterist position on the identity of the feet and toes: "The conclusion that logically follows is that the clay in the feet and toes of the great statue symbolizes the large pre-Christian Jewish minority that lived in much of the Roman Empire and resisted full cultural assimilation into the empire."[63] But this "conclusion" faces a major difficulty. Evans, who has been diligent to make sure that things are "explicitly stated," seems completely to ignore the fact that his conclusion does not explain why there are ten toes, or any toes at all. Although there is no direct statement of there being *ten* toes, Daniel's text does specifically refer to the toes of the statue in 2:41 and 42: "In that you saw the feet and toes, partly of potter's clay and partly of iron" (2:41) and "*As* the toes of the feet *were* partly of iron and partly of pottery" (2:43). Since there is no direct statement in the text that there were *two* arms or *two* legs, and yet all commentators infer that there were, there is no reason not to infer that there were ten toes. Daniel specifically refers to the toes, and we must conclude that there were ten of them, unless the statue is deformed. Evans' claims simply do not account for this.

In an effort to support his view, Evans refers to the fact that in Isa. 64:8(H7) the people of Israel are referred to as "clay." However, besides the fact that the word in Daniel is Aramaic (חֲסַף, *fasᵃh*), and the word in Isaiah is Hebrew (חֹמֶר, *remoh*), the Aramaic and Hebrew terms are not even cognates, as TWOT points out, "חֲסַף, (*fasᵃh*) *clay, potsherd*. The word is not used in Hebrew."[64] So, an appeal to any other passage in which Israel is figuratively referred to as clay does not support Evans' claim. Contrary to Evans' claim that "surely it is reasonable to conclude that the references to the clay in the feet of the great statue in Daniel 2 would have been understood by some Jews in the centuries before the birth of Christ to be a reference to the Jewish people,"[65] assuming that a given Jew could read both Hebrew and

---

63. Ibid., 123.

64. Theological Wordbook of the Old Testament (1980), s.v. "חֲסַף." Hereinafter referred to as TWOT.

65. Evans, *Four Kingdoms*, 123.

Aramaic, which, after the captivity became an ever decreasing possibility, such a Jew would most certainly not have understood this to be the case. Such a Jew would have known the respective languages, and he would have seen that these words are not cognates and not talking about the same thing. But whether some Jews would think this or not does not support Evans' theory. It is not a question of what the Jews may have understood, since, as the NT demonstrates, the Jews have a long history of misunderstanding their own Scriptures. Rather, it is a question of what the text says, and the text does not support Evans' claims.

In an effort to coordinate a Preterist view with the question of the relation between the prophetic depiction of the stone striking the feet as a sudden, catastrophic event, Evans introduces the notion of a "prophetic gap." He explains: "Sequential passages of the Bible sometimes display such gaps. For example, when Daniel informs Nebuchadnezzar that 'You are the head of gold' (v. 2:38) and them [*sic*] immediately tells him that 'After you, another kingdom will rise' (v. 2:39), the prophet ignores a time interval of about twenty-three years between the king's death and the fall of Babylon to the Medes and Persians."[66] Evans then attempts to apply this notion to his problem.

> By considering the action of striking the statue to be a prophetic abridgement inserted for the purpose of telescoping a lengthy but continuous process into a dramatically short one, however, you can reconcile the striking action of the rock with the First Advent approach. Furthermore, the rock as the First Advent approach does not require the striking action to be a drawn-out process. Perhaps it signals the relatively short period of the First Advent and the time of the Apostles that culminated in the events of AD 70. Then, relying on the concept of Prophetic abridgement you can argue that following that period, the process of collecting and removing the debris prophesied in verse 35 set in, and that although this process has been working itself out over a long period of time, the foreshortening was essential to achieve brevity, dramatic effect, and the encouragement of the faithful. *Imagine, for example, what the impact upon its intended audience would have been had Daniel 2 stated that the process of removing the debris and turning the rock into a mountain would extend for over 2,000 years!*[67]

Even if we grant Evans' placement of the prophetic gap is reasonable, his thesis goes against historical fact. In fact it was not the Christian church

---

66. Ibid., 127 (emphasis in original).

67. Ibid. (emphasis in original). Later in his book (page 362ff) Evans' criticizes the Futurists for inferring a two thousand year gap, and yet Evans is not reluctant to use this kind of inference when it supports his view.

that undermined the Roman Empire, a fact that Augustine takes great pains to prove in *The City of God*. As Augustine argued, it was the corruption of the empire from within that caused it to collapse, and most historians concur with his estimation. Additionally, in what would "removing the debris" consist? How can the church be said to be "removing the debris"? Further, the claim that the final kingdom would involve a process of progressive building contradicts the continuity of the prophetic vision. Each kingdom is succeeded by another kingdom, but each kingdom is replaced by the following kingdom so that the prior kingdom is ended and the new kingdom starts. The notion of the continuation of one kingdom into the next does not have to do with the kingdoms *qua* kingdoms, but with the influence of one upon the next. Daniel states that one kingdom ends and the next begins. To have an overlap of the continuation of the final human kingdom and the kingdom of God disrupts this continuity and goes against the symbolism. Daniel states that the stone will "put an end to these kingdoms" (וְתָסֵיף כָּל־אִלֵּין מַלְכְוָתָא, *ātawᵉklam ūñelli' ūlak ĵeṣatᵉw*), and this is done before the stone begins to grow into a mountain. There is no basis in Daniel's interpretation of the image or the image itself for understanding this kind of overlap.

Evans anticipates contrary arguments and prepares himself against those who point out that the history seems to show that the church is in fact not growing into a mountain to cover the entire earth. Evans asserts, "In the preterist view, by contrast, building the mountain that will eventually take over the whole earth is a work in process, and one should not necessarily assume that the decline in spirituality that many claim to see is irreversible. *The theology of preterism is one of religious optimism in which the world's understanding of God's true nature and presence has grown in the past 2,000 years and continues to do so.*"[68] However, Evans' scenario does not either fit history or Daniel's prophecy. First, the stone that strikes the statue does not begin to grow into a mountain until the statue is completely destroyed and the debris is "swept away." So, to claim that there is a prophetic gap does not help Evans' claim. The prophecy clearly depicts these two as successive, not simultaneous, events. To understand the growth of the kingdom as simultaneous with the "sweeping away" of the kingdoms departs from the hermeneutic that Evans himself has applied up to this point. There is no sense of simultaneity when one kingdom replaces another, and this is also true of the Kingdom of God. Daniel clearly states that one kingdom ends and another begins. Second, it is not simply the case that the church is in the midst of a spiritual decline. In fact, Christianity is losing ground throughout the world, and Islam is becoming a world dominating religious movement. Christianity seems to be experi-

---

68. Ibid., 128–29 (emphasis in original).

encing a progressive decline, not simply a bump in the road. Although this is certainly reversible, it takes more than optimism to demonstrate a consistency between the actual state of affairs and the prophecies of Daniel. The fact is, the history does not coincide with Evans' characterization of the prophecy, and his position requires more evidence and argument than Evans has provided.

ARGUMENTS BY E. J. YOUNG

Although E. J. Young would perhaps reject the label "Preterist," some of his arguments concerning the kingdom of God coincide with the Preterist view, so we will treat his comments here. Young argues, "The kingdom of God is of divine *origin* and eternal *duration*. For this reason, it cannot be the millennium, which is but 1,000 years in length. Since the kingdom is divine, it is therefore eternal."[69] First of all we have seen that the word translated "eternal" does not necessarily mean eternal in temporal duration. It can be used to refer to a long though limited period of time. In these instances, the word would be qualitative, not quantitative. Secondly, simply because the kingdom is divine in its origin does not mean that it is therefore eternal. The world itself is of divine origin, but it will be destroyed with intense heat. Man is divine in origin, but he must die. That the kingdom will not be conquered does not indicate an eternal kingdom either, since Jesus was not conquered by any foe, yet He died on the cross. The notion that the kingdom will not be conquered simply indicates that it is unconquerable. If the kingdom comes to an end, it is not as a result of being conquered.

Also, Young is adamant about the fact that there is no explicit statement that there are ten toes. However, he argues that the stone strikes the statue on the feet "because such a blow will cause it to totter and fall. Where else would one strike a blow that would cause the entire image to fall?"[70] However, there is no explicit statement that the statue tottered and fell, nor is there an implication that this occurred. The statement of the text indicates that the feet and the statue together were "crushed in pieces [דָּקַת, *qiddat*]." According to KBH, the Aramaic term indicates "to crush,"[71] and the Hebrew cognate indicates "to pulverize."[72] In fact the text indicates that the statue is crushed and pulverized into dust, not that it tottered and fell. So, Young's claim that the striking on the feet is "symbolical and does not necessarily have any particular reference to the fourth kingdom" itself totters and falls. Besides the fact that the feet and toes are declared to be part of the fourth kingdom, the striking

69. Young, *Prophecy of Daniel*, 78.

70. Ibid.

71. KBH, s.v. "דָּקַק."

72. KBH, s.v. "דָּקַק."

on the feet indicates that the stone struck the fourth kingdom at this point in time.

POSTMILLENNIAL VIEW OF KENNETH GENTRY

Kenneth Gentry presents the following understanding of Daniel's prophecy: "In Daniel 2:31–45 the kingdom of Christ comes down to the earth as a stone smiting the world kingdom, which exists under a fourth imperial rule. As we read through the passage we learn that the kingdom grows to become a great mountain in the earth:"[73] After quoting the passage, including verse 44, Gentry asserts, "In this imagery we have both linear continuity over time and remarkable upwardly progressive development: the stone *grows* to become a 'great mountain.' We also witness struggle and resistance: the stone eventually smashes the image."[74] Unfortunately for his reader, Gentry offers no support from the text to justify his claim that there is "struggle and resistance." In fact, the text seems to indicate that there is no struggle and resistance, but that the stone pulverizes the statue without any resistance at all. There is simply nothing in the text that indicates struggle and resistance. Gentry also asserts, "the stone eventually smashes the image." But there is no sense of "eventuality" in the description. The stone is cut out of the mountain and then strikes the statue, which is crushed and blown away.

Gentry goes on to say, "Finally, we rejoice in its fortunes: the God-defying image is thoroughly crushed. This gradual progress to victory against opposition is portrayed also in Daniel 7:26, where we witness victory as 'the result of *many* blows rather than one.'"[75] There are several problems with Gentry's claims, however. First, there is no sense in the description of the stone striking the feet of the statue that there is any "gradual" progress toward victory. The destruction is immediate and catastrophic. Second, the appeal to Dan 7:26 does not support Gentry's claim. This verse states, "But the court will sit *for judgment,* and his dominion will be taken away, annihilated, and destroyed forever." The verse is set out below with a word-for-word translation.

Table 8: Daniel 7:26

יְהַעְדּוֹן	וְשָׁלְטָנֵהּ	יִתִּב	וְדִינָא
will be taken away	and his dominion	will sit	And the council

---

73. Gentry, *He Shall Have Dominion,* 259.
74. Ibid. (emphasis in original).
75. Ibid. (emphasis in original).

לְהַשְׁמָדָה	וּלְהוֹבָדָה	עַד־	סוֹפָא׃
to annihilate	and to destroy	until	the end.

Interestingly, KBH offers the following translation: "and in the end to destroy it and to annihilate it."[76] There is simply no reference here to "many blows" as Gentry claims. The term "until" is not necessarily indicating some process that takes place over time. Rather, it is simply making the statement, "In the end, the dominion of this king will be destroyed and annihilated." But regardless of how one translates this verse, the text of Daniel 2 clearly portrays the growth of the kingdom of God as taking place after the destruction of the world kingdoms. It is after the statue is crushed and blown away that the stone grows into a mountain.

PRETERIST VIEWS OF THE KINGDOM OF GOD

Preterists do not believe that this prophecy of Daniel speaks of a physical, material kingdom of God to be established on the earth as the Futurists' depict. In so far as those who are believers embody the kingdom of Christ on earth, it is certainly on earth. According Ed Stevens,

> Christ's kingdom is here now. Paradise has been restored in Christ (spiritually-speaking). Christ has conquered all His enemies and has given us the Kingdom. . . . Bible prophecy absolutely makes sense when approached from this past-fulfillment (preterist) perspective! It puts emphasis on the spiritual nature of God's Kingdom, not on the physical, materialistic, sensual, and sensational. It teaches a realized spiritual salvation in Christ and the Church now, instead of a frustrated hope for a postponed sensually-gratifying paradise way off in the future. It has an optimistic worldview that gets involved, makes a positive difference, and lights a candle, rather than cursing the darkness, longing for a rapture-escape, or retreating from society. It doesn't engage in wild-eyed speculation like futurist views. It's just simple, straight-forward Bible interpretation.[77]

76. KBH, s.v. "סוֹף."

77. Stevens, "What is the Preterist View of Bible Prophecy?" This kind of rhetoric is, unfortunately, quite common in the debate. Stevens characterizes the Preterist view as one that "gets involved, makes a positive difference, lights a candle, rather than cursing the darkness, longing for a rapture, or retreating from society." This rhetoric is meant to imply that those who oppose his view are not doing the things that are spiritually desirable. Perhaps Stevens has forgotten that it is because of those who went before him in spreading the Gospel throughout Europe and America that he is able to promote his view now. Many of these very people who brought the Gospel to America had diametrically opposed

According to Preterists, the kingdom of God is spiritual, not physical, and was established by the establishing of the Church. Of course this raises the question, briefly dealt with above, about how the Preterists explain the fact that earthly kingdoms were not "crushed" so that there is no place found for them. Preterists will argue that these statements should be taken in a spiritual sense, not an earthly, physical sense, but this is a hermeneutic shift that requires explanation and justification. Preterists take the descriptions of the text as indicating earthly and physical kingdoms up to the point that the text begins to talk about God's kingdom. Since the description of God's kingdom uses many of the same expressions used to describe the other kingdoms, why should an interpreter not take them in the same sense? Preterists offer no hermeneutical justification other than the fact that the text is referring to God's kingdom. But this is begging the question. However, since Preterists seem to deal with the kingdom of God more thoroughly when commenting on Daniel chapters 7 and 9, further analysis and comment on this will be taken up there.

Futurist View

The Fourth Kingdom

The Futurist View holds that the kingdom of God as it is depicted in the prophecy of Daniel as the stone cut out without hands striking the statue on the feet and becoming a mountain filling the whole earth are yet future from our perspective. The feet and ten toes of the statue represent a final state of the Roman Empire. Futurists hold that the fourth kingdom of Daniel's prophecy is the Roman Empire and that the feet and toes represent a stage in this empire that has not yet appeared on the historical scene. It must be understood that because Futurists hold that the kingdom as it is described in this prophecy refers to the future this does not mean that Futurists do not believe that the kingdom is now in some sense. Most Futurists hold that the kingdom of Christ is indeed established now in a spiritual sense, but it also awaits a physical stage that corresponds to Daniel's descriptions.

Daniel characterizes the fourth kingdom as iron that "crushes [דְּקַק, *qqd*] and shatters [חֲשַׁל, *lăsᵃh*] all things, so, like iron that breaks in pieces [רְעַע, *ʾaᶜr*], it will crush [דְּקַק, *qqd*] and all these it will shatter [חֲשַׁל, *lăsᵃh*]" (Dan 2:40). Interestingly, the word translated "crush" (דְּקַק, *qqd*) is used to describe the actions of the stone that is cut out of the mountain. In verse 34 the stone will "break them in pieces" using the word דְּקַק (*qqd*), and in verse 44 it will "break in pieces and consume all these kingdoms," using

---

eschatological views to Stevens'.

the words דקק (*qqd*) for "break in pieces" and סוף (*fus*), for "consume," which literally means "to bring to an end." Again in verse 45 the text says that the stone will "brake in pieces the iron, the brass, the clay, the silver, and the gold," using the word דקק (*qqd*).

One often finds among Futurist interpreters an effort to verify the claim that the fourth kingdom represents Rome by statements such as the following: "The first aspect of interpretation of the fourth kingdom stresses the strength of the iron legs and their power to break in pieces and subdue all that opposes. This, of course, was precisely what characterized ancient Rome. As Leupold states it, 'The Roman legions were noted for their ability to crush all resistance with an iron heel. There is apparently little that is constructive in the program of this empire in spite of Roman law and Roman roads and civilization be-cause the destructive work outweighed all else, for we have the double verb "crush and demolish ['break in pieces and bruise,' AV].'""[78] However, if this characterization is supposed to illustrate the description that Daniel gives, must we not also draw the same conclusions about the Kingdom of God since it also "breaks in pieces"? Perhaps the breaking and crushing does not have specifically to do with the Roman soldiers, but with the policies of the empire itself. As Norman Davies puts it,

> There is a quality of cohesiveness about the Roman world which applied neither to Greece nor perhaps to any other civilization, an-cient or modern. Like the stones of a Roman wall, which were held together both by the regularity of the design and by that peculiarly powerful Roman cement, so the various parts of the Roman realm were bonded into a massive, monolithic entity by physical, organi-zational, and psychological controls. The physical bonds included the network of military garrisons which were stationed in every province, and the network of stone-built roads which linked the provinces with Rome. The organizational bonds were based on the common principles of law and administration, and on the univer-sal army of officials who enforced common standards of conduct. The psychological controls were built on fear and punishment—on the absolute certainty that anyone or anything that threatened the authority of Rome would be utterly destroyed.[79]

Rome's policy of utterly overpowering nations and peoples and subju-gating them under the Roman rule fits Daniel's description and can be equally applied to the Kingdom of God. Messiah will rule with a rod of iron (Rev 2:27) subduing any who oppose His kingdom. But Messiah will not employ

78. Walvoord, *Daniel*, 68–69.

79. Norman Davies, *Europe: A History*, 149.

the practices that are usually viewed as characteristic of the Roman legions. The correlation between the rule of Rome and the rule of Messiah characterized by the use of the word "crush" (דקק, *qqd*) is perhaps best not associated with the reputation of the Roman legions, but with the policy of Rome to rule with an iron fist as Messiah rules with an iron rod. The fact that there is apparently a correlation between the iron rule of Rome and the iron rod of Messiah does not require that they each used the same methods or tools, nor that they exhibited the same demeanor toward their subjects.

According to a Futurist interpretation, the clay is not symbolic of a people group or of a kingdom, but is used to indicate the instability of the kingdom in its final stages. As Walvoord says, "What Daniel implies is simply that the material which forms the feet portion of the image is not all one kind but is composed of iron and pottery, which do not adhere well one to the other. This is what Daniel himself brings out in subsequent explanation."[80] Walvoord is referring to Daniel's statement in verse 43, "but they shall not cleave one to another, even as iron is not mixed with clay."

The statement in verse 43, "they will combine with one another in the seed of men," is, as Walvoord observes, "not entirely clear," and, as he goes on to say, "it has given commentators a good deal of latitude in using their imagination."[81] There are some peculiarities that merit comment. First, the word translated "combine" is the Aramaic עֲרַב (*bar*ᵃ) and is equivalent to the Hebrew term עֵרֶב (*bere*ᶜ), meaning "mixture" or "mixed company." The peculiar thing is that the Hebrew term occurs in only two places in the entire OT: Ex 12:38 and Neh 13:3. In the Exodus passage the NASBU translates the term "mixed multitude," while the same term in Nehemiah is translated "foreigners." In both instances this term indicates a group of people who were foreigners in some sense. John Sailhamer describes the people in the Exodus account "as those who had been impressed by the miracles that Moses had performed. Later, in Numbers 11:4, this group is called 'the rabble' and is seen as the cause of Israel's incessant complaining against God's good provisions."[82] Likewise, in Nehemiah the group is identified as foreigners who would not be allowed to associate with the Israelites. This may indicate that what Daniel is alluding to is the mixing of contrary peoples, perhaps non-citizens, or those who are not dedicated to the Empire or its ideals, or even rulers, like kings or governments, that generate instability in the government.

The second peculiarity is that Daniel's phrase actually says, "they will combine with one another in the seed of *the man* [אֲנָשָׁא, *ʾāsan*ᵃ];" In

---

80. Walvoord, *Daniel*, 69.

81. Ibid., 70.

82. John Sailhamer, *The Pentateuch as Narrative: A Biblical-Theological Commentary*, 264.

Aramaic, the final *aleph* (**א**) is the suffix indicating definiteness. The text does not comment on who precisely is "the man." It may, however, indicate the notion of mixing the divine with the merely human. The mythological beginnings of the Roman state involve the legend of Romulus and Remus who were reputedly descendants of Aeneas, the son of prince Anchises, a descendant of Zeus, and the goddess Aphrodite (Venus in Roman mythology). This belief in a semi-divine founding of Rome may be implied in Daniel's statement. In fact, the Emperors of Rome often claimed the worship of the people and presented themselves as divine rulers. Attempting to mix the divine rulers with mere humans, indicating the attempt to establish some democratic participation by the masses, may have been the mixture to which Daniel refers. In light of the definiteness of the word "the man," it may be possible that Daniel is referring to an unholy alliance with anti-Christ. This is, of course, speculation, and there does not seem to be any way definitively to substantiate these notions. Whatever else the mixture indicates, it clearly indicates an instability that leads to failure.

THE TWO LEGS

Walvoord draws attention to the significance of the two legs of the statue. Quoting Geoffrey King, Walvoord identifies some of the points at issue here: "This is where I find I have to join issue with the commonly accepted interpretation. I have heard it said more than once or twice that the two legs of the image represent the Roman Empire, because in AD 364 the Roman Empire split into two. There was the Eastern Empire, with its capital at Constantinople and the Western Empire, with its capital at Rome. Two legs, you see. All right. But wait a minute! To begin with, the division occurs before you get to the iron! The two legs begin under the copper, unless this image was a freak."[83]

However, it is not necessary to conclude, as King does, that the division of the legs began "under the *copper*." As we pointed out above, the word translated "thighs" can also be translated "loins" and can refer to the lower part of the torso including the hips and buttocks. The way the statue is usually depicted is with the bronze extending to the top portion of the thighs. However, it is possible to understand the text to be depicting the bronze extending only to the top of legs at the hip, thus depicting no division in the kingdom represented by the bronze (see Figure 6 below). Consequently, it is possible to understand the statue as depicting the division beginning with the establishment of the Roman Empire. Of course that still does not address the question about this division with respect to the Roman Empire itself. Some

83. Geoffrey R. King, *Daniel* (Grand Rapis: William B. Eerdmans Publishing Company, 1966), 72–73; quoted in Walvoord, *Daniel*, 71.

have argued that the division of the Empire into East and West did not occur immediately upon the establishment of the Empire, and in fact did not occur until at least 330 AD However, Norman Davies characterizes the division differently.

Figure 6: Division in the Fourth Kingdom

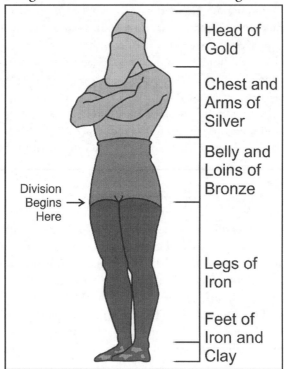

Head of Gold

Chest and Arms of Silver

Belly and Loins of Bronze

Division Begins Here →

Legs of Iron

Feet of Iron and Clay

The growing divergence of East and West was so slow that it was virtually imperceptible to contemporaries. For them, it was far less impressive than the sturdy strands of continuity. What is more, there is no general consensus about the point where "Rome" was truly supplanted by "Byzantium." In its origins, the split can be traced back to Octavius and Mark Antony, whose rivalry had briefly divided the Roman world for the first time. In which case the gradual emergence of Byzantium, and the supremacy of the East, might be seen as belated compensation for the tragedy of Antony and Cleopatra.[84]

84. Davies, *Europe*, 239.

So, there is a sense in which the Roman Empire was divided from its very inception, an inheritance, so to speak, from the final stages of the Roman Republic. Some have argued that the depiction of Greece as the torso of the statue, with or without the inclusion of the thighs, does not depict this empire in its entirety since it was divided into four parts after Alexander's death. However, just as the head of gold depicts Nebuchadnezzar, as Daniel himself asserted, yet passes over the reign of Belshazzar and depicts the next kingdom as Medo-Persia, so in this instance Greece under Alexander is pictured, and the division is passed over and moves on to the depiction of Rome. Also, even though Alexander's empire was divided, the four kings who took over the realm still reigned over the one Grecian Empire much as Alexander had built it.

Much has been made of the unity of the image as that of a single man. The Preterists, as represented by Evans, argue that this unity must mean that in some sense the previous kingdoms are present at the time the stone strikes the statue on the feet. However, this unity need not indicate the political presence of the previous kingdoms. As Leon Wood puts it, "The Roman kingdom would break the three earlier ones. The thought is not that Babylonia and Medo-Persia would still exist at the time Greece was overrun by Rome. History indicates that each was destroyed by its predecessor in turn, which is implied also in this passage (vs. 39) by the use of 'after' (*batrak*, literally, 'in your place') and in 8:3–8, where Medo-Persia and Greece are each represented as destroying its predecessors."[85] In the theological context that was discussed in the introduction, the basic principle of Babylon is the idea of man's rebellion against God, and man's effort to establish a city and a home on this earth. Consequently, the unifying theme of the statue is not the political oneness, but the oneness of purpose, that is, to establish a permanent residence, a kingdom of men, upon this earth in which mankind can "make a name for themselves" and be their own masters. The establishing of the Kingdom of God destroys man's effort to build his own city and kingdom and establishes the Kingdom of God with its capitol city the New Jerusalem.

The Days of Those Kingdoms

Verse 44 is another controversial verse: "In the days of those kingdoms the God of heaven will set up a kingdom which will never be destroyed, and that kingdom will not be left for another people; it will crush and put an end to all these kingdoms, but it will itself endure forever." The debated point is to which kingdoms is Daniel referring. Preterists take this to refer to the kings of the four kingdoms, Babylon, Medo-Persia, Greece, and Rome. However,

85. Wood, *Daniel*, 69.

in many instances, Daniel does make a distinction between the word "king" (מֶלֶךְ, *kelem*) and the word "kingdom" (מַלְכוּ, *uklam*). Since Daniel uses the word "kingdom" in this verse, it is unlikely that he is referring to the kings themselves. This coupled with the fact that the word "day" (יוֹם, *moy*) can be used in a figurative sense to refer to a period or even an age, this could simply be referring to the period or age of the rule of the Gentiles. Consequently, it is not necessary to conclude that this implies that the previous kingdoms were somehow present at this time.

Additionally, the word translated "never" is simply the adverbial negative "not" (לָא, *'al*). This could be a temporal reference, but it could also be a qualitative reference, not attempting to indicate the duration of the kingdom but the stability of the kingdom. This would be a fitting contrast to the progressive instability of the kingdoms of men. In other words, the statement could be saying, "this is the kind of kingdom that cannot be destroyed." It is not necessarily indicating that the kingdom would last forever. Of course, if, as the Futurists assert, the kingdom of God has both a Spiritual dimension, which was established when Christ sent the Holy Spirit, and a physical dimension, which will be established at Christ's second coming, there is a sense in which His kingdom will last forever even if the physical dimension is ended.

FUTURIST VIEW OF THE KINGDOM OF GOD

According to the Futurist view, the final kingdom, the Kingdom which, according to Daniel's interpretation, would be set up by the God of heaven, has yet to be established. As Donald Campbell explains,

> But what about the statue's feet and toes? According to the context, they, too, represented a form of the fourth kingdom, the Roman Empire, a form that has not yet appeared on the scene of history. And what about the stone that pulverizes the image and then fills the earth? How and when is that to be fulfilled? It seems best to recognize that Daniel's prophecy passes over the present age and that this rather extended period of time belongs between verses 40 and 41. From our vantage point, verses 37–40 are history; verse 41–45 are prophecy. The prophetic dream reveals that the fourth empire, Rome, would appear and have a dramatic history only to go into an eclipse till the end times, when it will reappear.[86]

Evans argues that the Futurist has a problem with explaining the intervening kingdoms in a scenario such as the one presented above by Campbell:

---

86. Campbell, *Daniel*, 25.

"Since the futurist approach to the prophecy of the rock views its striking of the statue as an event that has yet to occur, an obvious question for its advocates is how do you deal with the fact that more than fifteen centuries have elapsed since the Roman Empire, the presumed fourth kingdom, ceased to be a political and military entity?"[87] Dwight Pentecost, although not addressing this question specifically, has indicated a solution to this problem.

> The "times of the Gentiles" has been defined by the Lord as that period of time in which Jerusalem was under the dominion of Gentile authority (Luke 21:24). This period began with the Babylonian captivity when Jerusalem fell into the hands of Gentiles. It has continued unto the present time and will continue through the tribulation period, in which era the Gentile powers will be judged. The dominion of the Gentiles ends at the second advent of Messiah to the earth. . . . The first prophetic outline of the course of this period is given in Daniel 2, where, through the medium of the great image, the successive empires that would exercise dominion over Jerusalem are outlined.[88]

What Pentecost has pointed to is the fact that the kingdoms that are the focus of Daniel's prophecy are those kingdoms that have exercised dominion over Jerusalem. Since the Roman Empire, there have been no kingdoms to exercise such dominion. Although there have certainly been groups who have controlled Jerusalem, there have been no kingdoms on the scale of these four to exercise dominion. So, it is not necessary to "deal with" the intervening centuries. They are not within the scope of Daniel's prophecy.

Campbell points out several important characteristics related to the kingdom of God as this is understood by Futurists:

> Note several things that will be true of the future revived Roman Empire: (1) it will be a federation of 10 kings (see Dan. 7:24) that will no doubt be formed after believers have been taken to be with Christ (1 Thes. 4:13–17); (2) the revived Roman Empire will combine strong and weak kingdoms (Dan.2:42); (3) it will have internal problems especially before the rise of Antichrist (2:43; 7:24–25); (4) it will be in existence just prior to the return of Jesus Christ to establish His millennial kingdom, and (5) it will be destroyed by Jesus Christ at His second advent (2:45). He is the "stone cut out of the mountain" who will deliver a devastating and final blow against the nations before commencing His reign on earth. This passage is expanded in the Book of Revelation

87. Evans, *Four Kingdoms*, 129.

88. J. Dwight Pentecost, *Things To Come: A Study in Biblical Eschatology*, 315–16.

(19:11–21). There John declares, "And out of His mouth goeth a sharp sword, that with it He should smite the nations, and He shall rule them with a rod of iron." (Rev 19:15)[89]

The prophetic gap to which the above quotes refer is not an explanation peculiar to Futurists. As Evans himself pointed out, "Sequential passages of the Bible sometimes display such gaps."[90] Evans' gap was an effort to explain why the text does not indicate a gradual overcoming of the kingdoms of men, a gap which, according to Evans has lasted some 2,000 years. The Futurist gap is an effort to explain the distance between the first and the second comings of Christ. The graphic in Figure 7 below illustrates the principle. A prophet looking forward in time sees the high points of events in the future, not being able to see the valleys separating them. So, Nebuchadnezzar's statue depicts the Roman Empire in its beginning stages and in its final stage at the return of Christ, passing over the intervening period.

Figure 7: Prophetic Gap

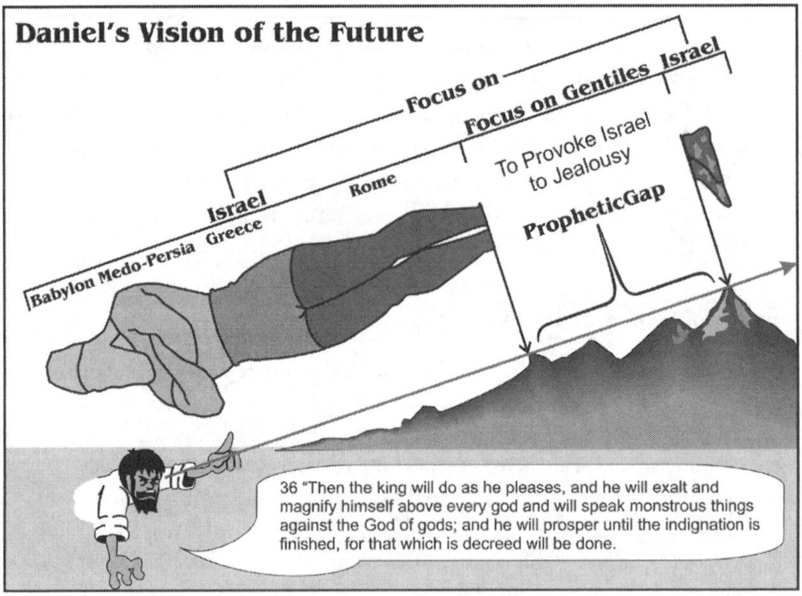

89. Campbell, *Daniel*, 25–26.
90. Evans, *Four Kingdoms*, 127.

4

Nebuchadnezzar's Dream of Greatness: 3:1–30

Introduction

Lucas presents the organization of this chapter in a chiastic structure. The following layout has been adapted from the one presented by Lucas:[1]

A Nebuchadnezzar's Decree to Worship the Golden Image (1–7)
  B The Three Hebrews Accused (8–12)
    C The Three Hebrews Threatened (13–15)
      D The Three Hebrews Confess Their Faith (16–18)
    C′ The Three Hebrews Punished (19–23)
  B′ The Three Hebrews Vindicated (24–27)
A′ Nebuchadnezzar's Decree to Honor the Hebrews and Their God (28–30)

Lucas goes on to point out, "This shows a chiastic structure that highlights the words spoken by Shadrach, Meshach, and Abednego in vv. 16–18, which are the only words they speak in the whole story. This is clearly a key point in the story."[2] Lucas also points out how the literary technique of Daniel serves to present a picture of the Babylonians as automatons, blindly and mechanically following the commands of their king. Various repetitions serve to give this feeling of mechanism. In the five verses from 2 to 7, the verb "set up" occurs four times:

---

1. Lucas, *Daniel*, 86.
2. Ibid.

v. 2   the image that Nebuchadnezzar the king had set up

v. 3   the image that Nebuchadnezzar the king had set up

v. 5   the golden image that Nebuchadnezzar the king has set up.

v. 7   the golden image that Nebuchadnezzar the king had set up.

Twice the author presents the long list of officials:

v. 2   the satraps, the prefects and the governors, the counselors, the treasurers, the judges, the magistrates, and all the rulers of the provinces

v. 3   the satraps, the prefects and the governors, the counselors, the treasurers, the judges, the magistrates, and all the rulers of the provinces

Four times the author presents the long list of musical instruments:

v. 5   the horn, flute, lyre, trigon, psaltery, bagpipe, and all kinds of music

v. 7   the horn, flute, lyre, trigon, psaltery, bagpipe, and all kinds of music

v. 10   the horn, flute, lyre, trigon, psaltery, and bagpipe, and all kinds of music

v. 15   the horn, flute, lyre, trigon, psaltery and bagpipe, and all kinds of music

Eight times the author refers to the furnace with the same description:

v. 6   a furnace of blazing fire

v. 11   a furnace of blazing fire

v. 15   a furnace of blazing fire

v. 17   the furnace of blazing fire

v. 20   the furnace of blazing fire

v. 21   the furnace of blazing fire

v. 23   the furnace of blazing fire

v. 26   the furnace of blazing fire

Beginning with verse 12, the three Hebrews are repeatedly referred to by all three names. Not once after this point does the author use a pronoun or any other shortened form to refer to them:

v. 12   Shadrach, Meshach, and Abed-nego

v. 13   Shadrach, Meshach, and Abed-nego

v. 14 Shadrach, Meshach, and Abed-nego

v. 16 Shadrach, Meshach, and Abed-nego

v. 19 Shadrach, Meshach, and Abed-nego

v. 20 Shadrach, Meshach, and Abed-nego

v. 22 Shadrach, Meshach, and Abed-nego

v. 23 Shadrach, Meshach, and Abed-nego

v. 26 Shadrach, Meshach, and Abed-nego (twice in this verse)

v. 26 Shadrach, Meshach, and Abed-nego

v. 28 Shadrach, Meshach, and Abed-nego

v. 29 Shadrach, Meshach, and Abed-nego

v. 30 Shadrach, Meshach, and Abed-nego

The worship of the image commanded by Nebuchadnezzar is presented as a mechanical response, as Lucas describes: "Avalos argues that the repetition of the lists of officials and instruments is used to 'portray those pagans as a version of Pavlov's dogs.' The officials act like automatons, responding mechanically to the king's command (2–3) and to the musical cue (4–7)."[3] The mechanical response of the worshipers serves as a foil against the intentional and willful response of the three Hebrews. The Pagan worshipers simply do what they are told when they are told. As Lucas puts it, "They lose something of their humanness."[4] By contrast, the three Hebrews are committed to their God not out of a mechanical or non-human response, but by choice and against the flow of the circumstances and even the culture in which they live. This contrast is heightened by the fact that the three Hebrews will not worship the image even if their God does not deliver them from the immediate effects of the fiery furnace.

As Lucas points out, the lack of humanness of the pagans is depicted in the seeming necessary flow of cause and effect which follows in a automaton-like description of the worship of the image. The signal goes out, and everyone falls down—the signal goes out, and everyone falls down—the signal goes out, and everyone falls down. The pattern is presented in an unwavering process of cause and effect—automatic and predictable. However, the three Hebrews believe that God is able to deliver them from the threat of death. But the God of the Hebrews is not some cosmic mechanism that responds with a predictable effect from the prescribed cause. The God of the Hebrews is the living God Who is able to deliver the Hebrews, but Who is also able to decide

3. Ibid., 87.

4. Ibid., 93.

to take action as He sees fit. He is not manipulated by the actions of men. The God of the Hebrews is trustworthy, but He is also the Living God.

The Danger 3:1–15

Nebuchadnezzar's Decree to Worship the Golden Image: 3:1–7

1—   Nebuchadnezzar the king made an image of gold, the height of which *was* sixty cubits *and* its width six cubits; he set it up on the plain of Dura in the province of Babylon.

2—   Then Nebuchadnezzar the king sent to assemble the satraps, the prefects and the governors, the counselors, the treasurers, the judges, the magistrates and all the rulers of the provinces to come to the dedication of the image that Nebuchadnezzar the king had set up.

3—   Then the satraps, the prefects and the governors, the counselors, the treasurers, the judges, the magistrates and all the rulers of the provinces were assembled for the dedication of the image that Nebuchadnezzar the king had set up; and they stood before the image that Nebuchadnezzar had set up.

4—   Then the herald loudly proclaimed: "To you the command is given, O peoples, nations and language,

5—   that at the moment you hear the sound of the horn, flute, lyre, trigon, psaltery, bagpipe and all kinds of music, you are to fall down and worship the golden image that Nebuchadnezzar the king has set up.

6—   But whoever does not fall down and worship shall immediately be cast into the midst of a furnace of blazing fire."

7—   Therefore at that time, when all the peoples heard the sound of the horn, flute, lyre, trigon, psaltery, bagpipe and all kinds of music, all the peoples, nations and *men of every* language fell down *and* worshiped the golden image that Nebuchadnezzar the king had set up.

Apparently, the impact of the dream upon the king in which the king is presented as the head of gold leads Nebuchadnezzar to an act of extravagant pride. Although there is a debate about whether this statue was patterned after Nebuchadnezzar's dream, there seems to be a deliberate attempt on the part of the author to connect the opening of this chapter with the previous chapter. In chapter 2 Nebuchadnezzar saw in his dream a stature of extraordinary splendor in which he is represented by the head of gold, and in chapter 3,

"Nebuchadnezzar the king made an image of gold" (Dan 3:1). Also, the final verse of chapter 2 makes reference to the three Hebrew youths, Shadrach, Meshach and Abed-nego, who become the focus of chapter 3. Finally, verse 1 of chapter three has no conjunction or connector as a signal to the reader that a new section is beginning. Rather, the verse simply starts off, "Nebuchadnezzar the king made an image of gold . . ." The lack of any conjunction or connector seems to bring these two chapters into very close relationship, the one flowing into the other without a break or transition.

Nebuchadnezzar constructs a statue and sends forth a decree that all people should bow down to worship this image. The compulsion to worship the image was probably more of a political than a religious necessity. To bow down and worship the image would have been an outward expression of loyalty to the king and would avoid the unpleasant consequences. The command does not allow for freedom of expression on the part of Nebuchadnezzar's subjects. Consequently, their response is more mechanical and not indicative of any real devotion either to the king or to the pantheon of gods.

Lucas speculates that perhaps Nebuchadnezzar is attempting to demonstrate his belief in the sempiternal character of his own kingdom. Quoting Fewell, Lucas observes, "'His created image remedies the weaknesses inherent in his dream image: his is made of a unified substance; his has no feet of clay.' He is concerned about the strength and unity of his kingdom, because the two things are interrelated. So he seeks a demonstration of unity, one that is marked by great pomp and circumstance."[5] In fact this characterization not only fits well into the sense of this chapter, but it also captures the perspective of Nebuchadnezzar's attitude demonstrated in chapter 4.

Nebuchadnezzar declares that "whoever does not fall down and worship shall immediately be cast into the midst of a furnace of blazing fire" (Dan 3:6). There is no question that this is a case of commanding an action that is contrary to the Law of the God of Israel. It is interesting that the captivity in Egypt was characterized by Moses as an "iron furnace": "But the Lord has taken you and brought you out of the iron furnace [מִכּוּר הַבַּרְזֶל, *lezrabah rukim*], from Egypt, to be a people for His own possession, as today" (Deut 4:20). Jeremiah had likened the captivity in Babylon that Judah and Jerusalem faced because of breaking the covenant to the bondage in the iron furnace of Egypt:

> The word which came to Jeremiah from the Lord, saying, "Hear the words of this covenant, and speak to the men of Judah and to the inhabitants of Jerusalem; and say to them, 'Thus says the Lord, the God of Israel, "Cursed is the man who does not heed the words of this covenant which I commanded your forefathers in the

5. Lucas, *Daniel*, 93.

day that I brought them out of the land of Egypt, from the iron furnace (מִכּוּר הַבַּרְזֶל, *lezrabah rukim*), saying, 'Listen to My voice, and do according to all which I command you; so you shall be My people, and I will be your God,' in order to confirm the oath which I swore to your forefathers, to give them a land flowing with milk and honey, as it is this day.'"' Then I said, "Amen, O Lord." And the Lord said to me, "Proclaim all these words in the cities of Judah and in the streets of Jerusalem, saying, 'Hear the words of this covenant and do them. For I solemnly warned your fathers in the day that I brought them up from the land of Egypt, even to this day, warning persistently, saying, "Listen to My voice." Yet they did not obey or incline their ear, but walked, each one, in the stubbornness of his evil heart; therefore I brought on them all the words of this covenant, which I commanded them to do, but they did not.'" (Jer 11:1–8)

The Babylonian captivity is a re-enactment of Egyptian bondage, with the exception that Judah and Jerusalem have gone into Babylonian captivity because they have broken the covenant. To break the covenant is to go after worshiping other gods. In light of this background, the stubbornness of these three Hebrews in their refusal to bow down takes on a new perspective. Unlike their ancestors who would rather go back to Egypt than die in the heat of the desert, the three Hebrew youths refuse to bow to the pagan gods. They choose rather to die in the heat of the fiery furnace.

It is also interesting that the dimensions of the image are sixty cubits, about ninety feet, by six cubits, about nine feet. In other words, the image was very tall and very thin—its height ten times its width. It is very unlikely that the image was only the image of a man, since these proportions would have made for a much distorted figure. It is likely that the human part of the image was set upon a tall pedestal (see Figure 8 below). Placing this statue on an extremely tall pedestal may have been the symbolism of a mountain at the top of which stood the great god and king. The fact that Nebuchadnezzar's command was given to "peoples, nations, and *men of every* language" is reminiscent of the tower of Babel/Babylon in which "the whole earth used the same language and the same words" and were gathered on the plain of Shinar to build a tower to reach up to heaven. If this association is correct, there once again seems to be connections with the Babel/Babylon of Genesis. The multitude constructed a tower in the plain of Shinar in order to make a name for themselves. In chapter 4 Nebuchadnezzar as much as exalts himself to the position of a god, having made a name for himself. This image may have been his effort to express his aspirations to deity. In fact, Young states, "Thus, the image represented the deified Neb."[6]

6. Young, *Prophecy of Daniel*, 84.

Figure 8: Nebuchadnezzar's Statue

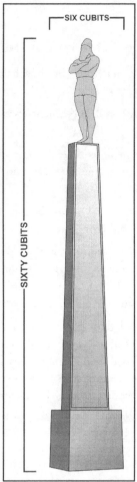

Also, the use of the number six seems to function symbolically as well. Numerology was a common practice in the Ancient Near East, and Bottéro points out that "the number 60 is associated with Anu," who is "the sovereign god, the father and founder of the divine dynasty."[7] Nebuchadnezzar may have used the dimensions intentionally to associate himself with the principal god of the pantheon. But there may be a symbolism that was not Nebuchadnezzar's intent to convey. Rev 13:18 states, "Here is wisdom. Let him who has understanding calculate the number of the beast, for the number is that of a man; and his number is six hundred and sixty-six." As symbolic of

7. Bottéro, *Religion in Ancient Mesopotamia*, 70, 30.

Antichrist, Nebuchadnezzar's use of these dimensions reinforces his role to be a type of Antichrist.

The Three Hebrews Accused: 3:8–12

8—   For this reason at that time certain Chaldeans came forward and brought charges against the Jews.

9—   They responded and said to Nebuchadnezzar the king: "O king, live forever!

10—   You, O king, have made a decree that every man who hears the sound of the horn, flute, lyre, trigon, psaltery, and bagpipe and all kinds of music, is to fall down and worship the golden image.

11—   But whoever does not fall down and worship shall be cast into the midst of a furnace of blazing fire.

12—   There are certain Jews whom you have appointed over the administration of the province of Babylon, Shadrach, Meshach and Abed-nego. These men, O king, have disregarded you; they do not serve your gods or worship the golden image which you have set up."

The commandment decreed that any who would not worship the image would be cast into a furnace of fire and burned alive. The constant repetition of the expression "the king had set up" emphasizes the character of the image as man-made, not divine in any sense, in contrast to the stone of chapter 2.

The text states that "certain Chaldeans came forward and brought charges against the Jews" (v. 8). They were probably already upset that these youths had been given high offices, and they were probably quite happy to report their treason. These officials point out that these young men do not worship the gods that Nebuchadnezzar serves. This accusation probably could not be gleaned from their refusal to obey this single command. This accusation seems to come from a prior disdain of these Jews on the part of the officials and is added here for the purpose of casting their one act in a much graver context in Nebuchadnezzar's mind. In other words, they want to make them look as bad as possible.

The Three Hebrews Threatened: 3:13–15

13—   Then Nebuchadnezzar in rage and anger gave orders to bring Shadrach, Meshach and Abed-nego; then these men were brought before the king.

14—   Nebuchadnezzar responded and said to them, "Is it true, Shadrach, Meshach and Abed-nego, that you do not serve my gods or worship the golden image that I have set up?

15—   "Now if you are ready, at the moment you hear the sound of the horn, flute, lyre, trigon, psaltery and bagpipe and all kinds of music, to fall down and worship the image that I have made. But if you do not worship, you will immediately be cast into the midst of a furnace of blazing fire; and what god is there who can deliver you out of my hands?"

Whether bowing down to the image was viewed by the Babylonians as a political expression or not, it was certainly understood by the three Hebrew youths to be a religious act and an act of idolatrous worship. The herald had in fact declared that all were commanded to "fall down and worship" the image. Consequently, in order to remain faithful to the Lord their God, Shadrach, Meshach, and Abednego refused to bow down to the image. This refusal led to the accusation by the officials. Their refusal to submit to this religious act is presented as an act of political rebellion. Because they do not worship the gods of Nebuchadnezzar, they cannot be trusted with the positions of responsibility to which Nebuchadnezzar has appointed them. It is also significant that in twelve instances in which their names are used, not once are their Hebrew names used. The three Hebrews are clearly presented as subjects of the kingdom, not as aliens or outsiders and therefore perhaps exempt from the requirement. However, when the officials report to the king, they emphasize that these youths are Jews and were put in a place of authority by the king.

For Nebuchadnezzar there would have been no contradiction in worshiping one's own god and worshiping this image. It is understandable, then, why Nebuchadnezzar seems to express surprise when he interrogates the three: "Is it true, Shadrach, Meshach, and Abed-nego, that you do not serve my gods or worship the golden image that I have set up?" (Dan 3:14). Nebuchadnezzar offers them the opportunity to comply. This may indicate the reason why the Chaldeans brought the accusation in the first place. It seems very strange that the king would give someone who had purposely disobeyed the king's decree a second chance. In fact, it seems almost as if Nebuchadnezzar is attempting to reason with them to get them to comply. The decree clearly stated that anyone who would not comply would "immediately [שָׁעֲתָא, ʾatⁱ ʿ ās] be cast into the midst of a furnace of blazing fire." Yet the king does not follow the dictates of his own decree, but attempts to persuade the three Hebrews. This may indicate that these three Hebrews were held in very high esteem by the king, and perhaps he was reluctant to put them to death. Perhaps Nebuchadnezzar was aware of the jealousy of the Chaldeans and was making his own inquiry of the three Hebrews if perchance the Chaldeans had brought a trumped up charge for the purpose of destroying their rivals. Whatever the situation, it seems that the Chaldeans were bent on ridding themselves of these intruders who had captured the king's ear, so to speak.

There is no contradiction here between Nebuchadnezzar's question— "and what god is there who can deliver you out of my hands?"—and the fact that at the end of chapter 2 Nebuchadnezzar had acknowledged, "Surely your God is a God of gods and a Lord of kings and a revealer of mysteries, since you have been able to reveal this mystery" (Dan 2:47). In the earlier instance, Nebuchadnezzar had acknowledged the greatness of Daniel's God to be able to reveal mysteries, but there is no indication in this obeisance that Nebuchadnezzar recognized any power or strength in the God of Daniel. Here, Nebuchadnezzar is implying, "I know about your God. He is able to reveal secrets, but He is not strong enough to resist my will or to deliver you out of my hand." Nebuchadnezzar had learned one lesson about the God of heaven, namely, His omniscience. He is about to learn the second lesson— God's omnipotence.

The Declaration 3:16–18

16— Shadrach, Meshach and Abed-nego replied to the king, "O Nebuchadnezzar, we do not need to give you an answer concerning this matter.

17— If it be, our God whom we serve is able to deliver us from the furnace of blazing fire; and He will deliver us out of your hand, O king.

18— But if not, let it be known to you, O king, that we are not going to serve your gods or worship the golden image that you have set up."

Nebuchadnezzar's pride is no more visible than when he interrogates the youths: "Who is that God that shall deliver you out of my hand?" These young Hebrews have no need to answer the charges that have been laid against them. They readily admit their having disobeyed the king's command. But the translation of their response has caused much misunderstanding. Some have translated the phrase as, "If God exists . . ." But this translation is very unlikely. Nebuchadnezzar did not question the existence of the God of these Hebrews. Rather, he questioned their God's ability to deliver them. However, the KJV and the NASBU translations do not adequately communicate the idea either. These translations state something like this: "If God is able to deliver us . . ." But young Hebrew men are not questioning God's ability. In fact they emphatically declare, "our God whom we serve is able to deliver us."

It was not a question of whether God was able, at least not in the minds of the three Hebrews. Rather, they are responding in kind to Nebuchadnezzar's challenge. It is as if they are saying, "OK, God is able to deliver, of that we have no doubt. And if He chooses to do so, He will deliver us. But, if He chooses to deliver us, then you have to acknowledge that He is more powerful than you and your god." It is not as if they do not believe God is able to do this. Rather, they are not willing to presume upon God's goodness to declare that He will certainly do something He has not committed Himself to do. God is able to deliver them, and they know it. But, they also know that God is worthy of their dedication whether He delivers them or not. Their commitment to God is not predicated on any earthly benefits God may bestow, but on who He is. This is very similar to the charge against Job: "Does Job fear God for nothing?" (Job 1:9). After the Satan had done his worst, the text declares, "Through all this Job did not sin nor did he blame God" (Job 1:22). These young Jews had the faith of Job: "Though He slay me, yet will I trust in Him" (Job 13:15).

There is a stark contrast here between the gods of Babylon and the God of Israel. Nebuchadnezzar declared that the people of his kingdom either bow down and pay homage to the image he had set up or die. The three Hebrews declared that they would worship their God by being faithful to Him even if they die. The dedication to the pagan gods was imposed from the outside and could be practiced regardless of one's internal conviction. Nebuchadnezzar did not ask the three Jews whether they had come to trust in the gods of Babylon or whether they were convinced of the greatness of Nebuchadnezzar's gods. He did not inquire about some spiritual experience that would mark a conversion to the gods of Babylon. In fact, Nebuchadnezzar did not ask them to abandon their God. He did not demand that they stop being Jews. He merely required them to bow down and pay homage to the image. However, for these Hebrew youths, worship meant an undivided commitment to God based in a personal trust in His goodness and His power. The commitment of these pagans to Nebuchadnezzar and the gods of Babylon was outward and ritualistic. The commitment of Shadrach, Meshach, and Abednego was inward and unwavering that showed itself in an outward willingness to remain faithful in the face of death.

Throughout the story there has been no mention of Daniel. No doubt, if he had been present, he would not have bowed to the image. At least one aspect of Daniel's absence is that it clearly demonstrates the independent integrity and courage of the three Hebrew youths. They do not need the presence of Daniel to led them or encourage them to act, and they do not need Daniel in order to know what it is they should do. At the end of chapter 1 the text points out that "God had given to them knowledge and intelligence in all literature and wisdom" (Dan 1:17). This incident demonstrates the reality of God's gracious gifts to these three youths.

The Deliverance: 3:19–30

The Three Hebrews Punished: 3:19–23

19— Then Nebuchadnezzar was filled with wrath, and his facial expression was altered toward Shadrach, Meshach and Abed-nego. He answered by giving orders to heat the furnace seven times more than it was usually heated.

20— He commanded certain valiant warriors who *were* in his army to tie up Shadrach, Meshach and Abed-nego in order to cast *them* into the furnace of blazing fire.

21— Then these men were tied up in their trousers, their coats, their caps and their clothes, and were cast into the midst of the furnace of blazing fire.

22— For this reason, because the king's command *was* urgent and the furnace had been made extremely hot, the flame of the fire slew those men who carried up Shadrach, Meshach and Abed-nego.

23— But these three men, Shadrach, Meshach and Abed-nego, fell into the midst of the furnace of blazing fire tied up.

Verse 19 states, "Then Nebuchadnezzar was filled with anger, and the image of his face changed toward Shadrach, Meshach, and Abed-nego." The word translated "facial expression" in the NASBU and "form of his visage" in the KJV is the same word that has been used throughout this chapter to refer to the image (צְלֵם, *ṣelēs*) that Nebuchadnezzar had set up (קוּם, *ḿuq*). In chapter 2, it is the Kingdom of the God of Heaven set up (קוּם, *ḿuq*) by God that would destroy the image (צְלֵם, *ṣelēs*). Here it is the commitment of God's servants that changes the image of Nebuchadnezzar.

In his rage, Nebuchadnezzar heats up the oven. The text states that Nebuchadnezzar commanded that the oven be heated "one seven over what was customary to heat it." Nebuchadnezzar was not able to control the fate of the image in chapter 2. The image was destroyed by the stone from the mountain. Here Nebuchadnezzar is not able to control himself or the fate of the Hebrews. The command to heat the oven was an act of uncontrolled rage. That it was folly to command that the furnace be heated so hot is seen in the fact that it killed the valiant warriors who carried up the three Hebrews. Not only does Nebuchadnezzar not destroy the Jews, but he loses valuable men in the process.

The Three Hebrews Vindicated: 3:24–27

24— Then Nebuchadnezzar the king was astounded and stood up in haste; he said to his high officials, "Was it not three men we cast bound into the midst of the fire?" They replied to the king, "Certainly, O king."

25— He said, "Look! I see four men loosed *and* walking *about* in the midst of the fire without harm, and the appearance of the fourth is like a son of *the* gods!"

26— Then Nebuchadnezzar came near to the door of the furnace of blazing fire; he responded and said, "Shadrach, Meshach and Abed-nego, come out, you servants of the Most High God, and come here!" Then Shadrach, Meshach and Abed-nego came out of the midst of the fire.

27— The satraps, the prefects, the governors and the king's high officials gathered around *and* saw in regard to these men that the fire had no effect on the bodies of these men nor was the hair of their head singed, nor were their trousers damaged, nor had the smell of fire *even* come upon them.

Verse 24 states, "Then Nebuchadnezzar the king was astounded and stood up in haste." It is interesting that the word "stood up" is the same word used throughout this chapter for "set up." The king set up the image, but the fourth man in the fire made the king sit up. As Walvoord puts it, "Instead of three men, there were four; instead of being bound, they were free; instead of writhing in anguish in the flames, they were walking about in the fire and making no attempt to come out; further, it was quite apparent that they were not hurt; most astounding of all, he had the impression that 'the form of the fourth is like the Son of God.'"[8] The text can be translated in at least two ways: אֱלָהִין דָּמֵה לְבַר־, *ûihaleʾ rabᵉl hemad*—"like the Son of God," or "like a son of gods." In favor of the later translation, Walvoord argues, "While it is entirely possible that the fourth person in the fiery furnace was indeed the Son of God, it would be doubtful whether Nebuchadnezzar would comprehend this, unless he had prophetic insight."[9]

Many have taken this to be a pre-incarnate appearance of Christ. In Isa 43:1–2, the prophet announces the miraculous protection that God would

8. Walvoord, *Daniel*, 91.
9. Ibid., 91.

give to His people and that He would be with them in times of trial: "But now, thus says the Lord, your Creator, O Jacob, And He who formed you, O Israel, 'Do not fear, for I have redeemed you; I have called you by name; you are Mine! When you pass through the waters, I will be with you; And through the rivers, they will not overflow you. When you walk through the fire, you will not be scorched, nor will the flame burn you.'" However, in light of the later revelation of the spiritual warfare going on behind the scenes, it is also very likely that this was an angel, perhaps Michael, who, according to 12:1, is "the great prince who stands guard over the sons of your people."

It has often been pointed out that the three Hebrews were not delivered from the fire, but were delivered through the fire. But this is not accurate, at least not in the sense that this distinction is usually made. Generally speaking, when this distinction is made there is no assumption that the individuals who have been brought through some tragedy have come through completely unscathed. Usually this characterization indicates that although someone has suffered, they have not been overcome. However, in this case, these three Hebrews are completely untouched by the fire, and are in fact walking around in it. This is a miraculous deliverance from the fire and from the fiery trial. This is, perhaps, a picture of Israel who would be miraculously protected from harm throughout their captivity in Babylon. In fact, one aspect of this is seen in the book of Esther in which the people of God are miraculously protected even though God is not mentioned in the book.

Nebuchadnezzar's Decree to Honor the Hebrews and Their God: 3:28–30

28—   Nebuchadnezzar responded and said, "Blessed be the God of Shadrach, Meshach and Abed-nego, who has sent His angel and delivered His servants who put their trust in Him, violating the king's command, and yielded up their bodies so as not to serve or worship any god except their own God.

29—   "Therefore I make a decree that any people, nation or tongue that speaks anything offensive against the God of Shadrach, Meshach and Abed-nego shall be torn limb from limb and their houses reduced to a rubbish heap, inasmuch as there is no other god who is able to deliver in this way."

30—   Then the king caused Shadrach, Meshach and Abed-nego to prosper in the province of Babylon.

This is the second time that God had demonstrated His sovereignty and majesty to Nebuchadnezzar. First, through Daniel God demonstrated His superiority over the gods of Babylon by giving Nebuchadnezzar a revelation of the future and providing one of His servants to interpret the revelation. At that time Daniel told the king that he had his position only because of the grace of the God of heaven. Now, God reveals to Nebuchadnezzar His power. Nebuchadnezzar had asked, "Who is that God that shall deliver you out of my hand?" God has provided the answer. Will the king get the point?

Daniel's Absence

Verse 2 states that Nebuchadnezzar "sent word to assemble . . . all the rulers of the provinces to come to the dedication." As Leon Wood points out, "Since the official people named came from all the provinces of the empire, the king had to send for them, no doubt, by established lines of communication. Some time would have been required for the communication to go and the invited persons to come to Babylon."[10] Mills supposes that, "with his added authority, Daniel could have been out of town at the time."[11] However, since all the rulers from all over the empire were commanded to come to the dedication, it seems extremely unlikely that Daniel was not present simply because he was away on business. Although it is true that we may not be able to propose a definitive explanation as to why Daniel is not mentioned, some have proposed a symbolic significance to his absence.

From a Futurist point of view, the tribulation is predicted to be a fiery trial upon Israel who will be miraculously preserved through the ordeal. Futurists in general, and Premillennialists in particular, identify this as the "Tribulation," or "time of Jacob's trouble" as referred to in Jer 30:7. According to the Premillennialists, the church will have been translated at the Rapture prior to the beginning of this time of Jacob's trouble. Some have proposed that Daniel's absence is symbolic of the church while the three Hebrews are symbolic of Israel. The church, like Daniel, will be inexplicably gone from the scene while Israel, like the three Hebrews, will be tried by fire. There certainly is nothing in the text that would require this explanation, nor are there any direct statements or actions on the part of any of the characters that would call for this conclusion. It is the prior assumption of a Premillennial-Pretribulational perspective that sees this symbolism here. If one accepts this eschatological perspective, then a case might be made that this is perhaps the symbolism. However, one cannot use this as a means of arguing that the

10. Wood, *Daniel*, 91.
11. Mills, *Daniel*, 21.

Premill-Pretrib perspective is true since this perspective must be assumed in order to see this symbolism here. Although it cannot be used to prove the Futurist position, it can be called upon as supporting evidence if a Futurist position can be established by other means.

5

Nebuchadnezzar's Dream of Humiliation: 4:1–37

Introduction

CHAPTER FOUR is an account given by Nebuchadnezzar of how God humbled him and brought about his conversion. He begins this account by praising God for His goodness in showing him great signs and wonders, and it ends with praising and exalting God. This chapter seems to be built on a chiastic structure:

A Salutation (4:1–3)
   B The Dream Given (4:4–9)
      C The Dream Related (4:10–18)
      C′ The Dream Interpreted (4:19–27)
   B′ The Dream Fulfilled (4:28–36)
A′ Benediction (4:37)

Salutation: 4:1–3

1— Nebuchadnezzar the king to all the peoples, nations, and men of every language that live in all the earth: "May your peace abound!

2— It has seemed good to me to declare the signs and wonders which the Most High God has done for me.

3—   How great are His signs, and how mighty are His wonders! His king-
       dom is an everlasting kingdom, and His dominion is from genera-
       tion to generation."

The opening verses of this chapter indicate that this material perhaps took
the form of an encyclical letter personally written or dictated by the king to
be distributed and read throughout his empire: "Nebuchadnezzar the king to
all the peoples, nations, and men of every language that live in all the earth:
May your peace abound! It has seemed good to me to declare the signs and
wonders which the Most High God has done for me. How great are His signs,
and how mighty are His wonders! His kingdom is an everlasting kingdom,
and His dominion is from generation to generation" (4:1–3(A3:31–33)). This
salutation indicates quite a change in the king's attitude about himself and
about his subjects. Whereas in the past, Nebuchadnezzar presented himself
as the absolute ruler whom his subjects were required to worship and serve,
now the king is wishing peace to all people—peace on earth. Also, the praises
of God that are voiced by the king present a decided advance in his understanding and attitude toward the God of Israel. There is a controversy over
whether the king was converted as a result of his experience presented in this
chapter. Notice, for example, that he does not identify God as "the God of
Israel," but as "the Most High God." This may indicate that Nebuchadnezzar
still believed in the other gods but held the God of Israel to be the highest
of them all. However, the other things said about God seem to suggest that
Nebuchadnezzar has undergone an actual conversion experience. But whether
we accept that it was or not, these words certainly indicate a progression in his
understanding and appreciation for who the God of the Hebrews is.

The Dream Given: 4:4–9

Nebuchadnezzar's Fear: 4:4–5

4—   "I, Nebuchadnezzar, was at ease in my house and flourishing in my
       palace."

5—   "I saw a dream and it made me fearful; and these fantasies as I lay on
       my bed and the visions in my mind kept alarming me."

Nebuchadnezzar's testimony begins with a description of his prosperity and
ease. Apparently this was at a time in which all Nebuchadnezzar's enemies
had been subdued and at the end of his many building projects. According to
verse 30, he was at ease and secure in his domain having built the strongest
kingdom and the most glorious city in the ancient world in his day. This is
quite similar to another person who voiced a similar self-satisfaction: "And

I will say to my soul, 'Soul, you have many goods laid up for many years to come; take your ease, eat, drink and be merry.'" But God said to him, 'You fool! This very night your soul is required of you; and now who will own what you have prepared?'" (Lk 12:19–20).

At this point, Nebuchadnezzar states that he "saw a dream." There is no indication in the text that at this point Nebuchadnezzar suspects that the dream had been given to him by Daniel's God. The text states that Nebuchadnezzar was very much afraid because of the dream. In fact, the word used indicates sheer terror. Nebuchadnezzar describes himself lying in his bed, "and the visions in my mind kept alarming me" (v. 5). Apparently he could not sleep as the visions continued to race through his mind and robbed him of any peace. Since Nebuchadnezzar's opening words indicated that he was at ease and secure in his prosperity in the safety of his palace, what could possibly have terrified the king? Perhaps he understood enough to know that all that he had built was threatened. The very things that made him feel at ease and secure may be taken away from him, and this terrified him. This time the vision was particularly concerning Nebuchadnezzar's own future, rather than the future of the Gentile world as in chapter 2.

Nebuchadnezzar's Appeal: 4:6–9

NEBUCHADNEZZAR'S CALL: 4:6–7

6—   "So I gave orders to bring into my presence all the wise men of Babylon, that they might make known to me the interpretation of the dream."

7—   "Then the magicians, the conjurers, the Chaldeans and the diviners came in and I related the dream to them, but they could not make its interpretation known to me."

Nebuchadnezzar ordered that all of the wise men of Babylon be called in to tell him his dream. As before, the wise men of Babylon were unable to interpret the dream. Unlike before, however, the king relates to the wise men the dream he had, and unlike before, it does not seem to be the case that the king was suspicious that the wise men would try to make up some story. Either they had learned their lesson, or this was a completely new group who had heard of the fate threatened of the previous group. The text simply states that they were unable to tell him the interpretation.

DANIEL'S APPEARANCE: 4:8

8—   "But finally Daniel came in before me, whose name is Belteshazzar according to the name of my god, and in whom is a spirit of the holy gods; and I related the dream to him, saying,"

For whatever reason, Daniel was not among the group of wise men who initially came to the king. Daniel finally appears, and the king turns immediately to him for help. The king points out to his readers that Daniel's name is Belteshazzar. Much has been made of this, and critical scholars attempt to impugn the book's integrity on the basis of this assertion. Critical scholars point out there would be no reason to identify Daniel in this way if this were an actual historical account. However, Walvoord's explanation accounts for this use: "This decree was going throughout the kingdom where most people would know Daniel by his Babylonian name, Belteshazzar."[1] The king explains that this name was given according to the name of his god. This was probably Bel who is also known as Marduk. There is no contradiction here with the fact that it appears that Nebuchadnezzar has had a conversion as a result of this dream. He could simply be saying that this name was given to Daniel when Nebuchadnezzar's god was Marduk.

NEBUCHADNEZZAR'S PLEA: 4:9

9—   'O Belteshazzar, chief of the magicians, since I know that a spirit of the holy gods is in you and no mystery baffles you, tell me the visions of my dream which I have seen, along with its interpretation.'

The king calls upon Daniel to explain to him the meaning of the visions. He declares, "I know that a spirit of the holy gods is in you and no mystery baffles you." Of course the word "gods" could be singular or plural. Since Nebuchadnezzar uses the adjective "holy," it is very likely that Nebuchadnezzar is referring to Daniel's God: "the Spirit of the Holy God is in you."

1. Walvoord, *Daniel*, 100.

Figure 9: Structure of Tree Prophecy

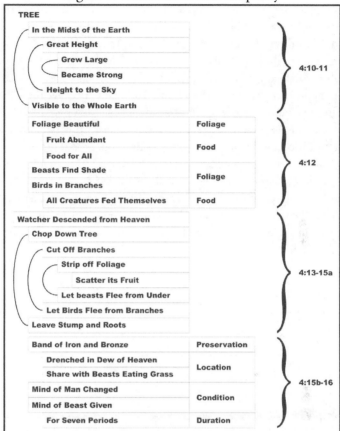

The Dream Related: 4:10–18

Description of the Tree: 4:10–12

10— 'Now these were the visions in my mind as I lay on my bed: I was looking, and behold, there was a tree in the midst of the earth and its height was great.'

11— 'The tree grew large and became strong And its height reached to the sky, And it was visible to the end of the whole earth.'

12— 'Its foliage was beautiful and its fruit abundant, And in it was food for all. The beasts of the field found shade under it, And the birds of the sky dwelt in its branches, And all living creatures fed themselves from it.'

Having enlisted Daniel as his interpreter, Nebuchadnezzar relates to Daniel the dream that has frightened him (see Figure 9 above for structure of the tree prophecy). As he was looking, Nebuchadnezzar saw a tree "in the midst of the earth." The word translated "earth" could also be translated "land" (verse 7 in the Aramaic text): (בְּגוֹא אַרְעָא, ᵓaʿraᵓ ᵓogᵉb). Whether this be taken to refer to the whole earth, or the land of Babylonia, it is certain that the tree is situated in a place of prominence. Jeremy Black and Anthony Green give the following explanation of the use of tree symbolism in ancient Mesopotamia: "Stylised trees of one type or another are commonly portrayed in Mesopotamian art from prehistoric times through to the Neo-Babylonian Period. At one time the tree will be very formalised, often elaborate, at another tending towards naturalism, but in either case it will usually be set upon an elevation of some kind or placed in a position of prominence with respect to the other elements of a design. The tree is often flanked by animals, or by supernatural figures."[2] The graphic in Figure 10, provided by Black and Green, give an example of this kind of stylized tree.[3]

Figure 10: Stylized Mesopotamian Tree

Nebuchadnezzar describes the tree as it appeared to him in his vision. Its height was great, and yet it grew even larger. It became strong, and its height reached to the sky. The word translated "sky" could also be translated "heavens" (שְׁמַיָּא, ᵓayyamᵉs). Because of its height, it was visible to the end

2. Black and Anthony, *Gods, Demons, and Symbols*, 170–71.

3. The image in Figure 10 comes from Black, *Gods, Demons and Symbols*, 170.

of the whole earth. The foliage of the tree was beautiful with abundant fruit that provided fruit for all. The beasts found shade under the foliage and the birds of the heavens nested in the branches of this great tree. It was so large, powerful, and fruitful that it provided food for all the creatures of the world.

Of course the symbolism fits the character of Babylon, which, according to history, has always been a great city and a city of great mystery. Babylon was like a great tree. However, under Nebuchadnezzar, it became a world power, and his kingdom was very strong. Because of the power and prosperity of the kingdom, the whole world was aware of Nebuchadnezzar and the prominence of Babylon. Of course Nebuchadnezzar would think of the impact of his kingdom in the most positive terms, providing food and shelter for the whole world. The construction of the golden statue as depicted in chapter 3 is evidence of Nebuchadnezzar's aspirations to be a god and that Babylon might be seen as the holy mountain in which the seat of his kingdom rests. The obvious symbolism of the kingdom of Nebuchadnezzar may explain why he was terrified. Apparently he understood enough to know that whatever might be the details of the meaning, it had something to do with him and his kingdom, and it wasn't pretty.

Words of the Watcher: 4:13–17

FELLING THE TREE: 4:12–15A

13— 'I was looking in the visions in my mind as I lay on my bed, and behold, an angelic watcher, a holy one, descended from heaven.'

14— 'He shouted out and spoke as follows: "Chop down the tree and cut off its branches, Strip off its foliage and scatter its fruit; Let the beasts flee from under it And the birds from its branches."'

15a—"Yet leave the stump with its roots in the ground, but with a band of iron and bronze around it in the new grass of the field;

As Nebuchadnezzar was watching, he saw a "watcher" (עִיר, *îr*ʿ) coming down from heaven. The word "angelic" that is found in many translations is not a separate word in the text, but is usually added in an effort to try to explain what is meant by the term "watcher." The use of the term "holy one" (קַדִּישׁ, *šiddaq*) perhaps indicates that this should be understood as an angel sent from God. Nebuchadnezzar is probably using the term that is most familiar to him. As Walvoord points out, "That angels are watchers, or better translated 'vigilant, making a sleepless watch,' is not foreign to the concept of angels in Scripture."[4] The Aramaic term for "angel" (מַלְאָךְ, *ka'lam*), like

4. Walvoord, *Daniel*, 102.

its Hebrew cognate (מַלְאָךְ, *ka'lam*), means "messenger" primarily because angels are the one who often carry messages from God to men.

The watcher sends out a decree that the tree should be cut down, its branches cut off and stripped of foliage, and its fruit should be scattered. The beasts and birds will flee, but the stump should be bound with a band of iron and bronze. The symbolism is fairly clear up to the reference to the band of iron and bronze. There has been much discussion and controversy over what exactly the band of iron and bronze symbolizes. Oddly enough, in his interpretation of the dream, Daniel does not make reference to the iron and bronze. Some have proposed that this is some kind of arboricultural practice to preserve the life of the tree. However, there is no historical information that such a practice was ever performed in ancient cultures. Others have suggested that the band is symbolic of Nebuchadnezzar's madness that holds him bound during his ordeal. However, there is no clear reason why iron and bronze are used instead of a single metal or perhaps just a reference to a chain. It is interesting that iron and bronze, the two metals symbolic of the third and fourth kingdoms, are used. Although Babylon falls to the Medes and the Persians, Babylon as an entity continues to exist, and Darius the Mede is appointed as the ruler of Babylon under this second kingdom. However, under the rule of the Greeks and the Romans, Babylon does not continue as a separate entity, and the seat of government shifts toward the west. This band may be symbolic of the fact that the stump will be held together until the rise of the bronze and iron kingdoms. This is speculation, and no commentators have proposed an explanation that is completely satisfactory.

HUMBLING THE MAN: 4:15B–16

15b— And let him be drenched with the dew of heaven, and let him share with the beasts in the grass of the earth."

16— "Let his mind be changed from that of a man and let a beast's mind be given to him, and let seven periods of time pass over him."

At this point the references suddenly change from references to the tree to references to a man: "Let his heart be changed from that of a man" [v. 16 (A13)]. Some translations have the word 'mind' instead of 'heart.' The Aramaic word is לְבַב (*bab[e]l*), which is a cognate of the Hebrew term and can be translated "heart" or "mind." Lucas points out however, "in Semitic languages the metaphorical use of the word 'heart' corresponds more closely to the English word 'mind,'" and Lucas makes reference to verse 34 (A31) as an example.[5] In this

---

5. Lucas, *Daniel*, 100.

verse Nebuchadnezzar states that he lifted his eyes to heaven and his "reason [וּמַנְדְּעִי, *i ʿednamu*] returned." The word "reason" (מַנְדַּע, *ʿadnam*) refers to the power of reason or knowledge. So, the watcher's words probably indicate the mind rather than the heart.

This man is given a mind of beasts, indicating that he will lose his capacity to reason.[6] Being drenched with the dew from heaven indicates that he will make his home out in the open. His food will be the grass of the field. He will not only have the mind of a beast, but he will live like a beast. This condition will last for seven periods. This probably refers to seven years. A similar experience is reported to have happened to Nabonidus. The description is almost identical to this, and the period of his condition was specifically stated to have been seven years. This is important for understanding the symbolism of the seventy sevens later. Here we have an instance in which the word "seven" is used of a determined length of time, most probably seven years.

EXALTING THE LORD: 4:17

17— "This sentence is by the decree of the angelic watchers and the decision is a command of the holy ones, in order that the living may know that the Most High is ruler over the realm of mankind, and bestows it on whom He wishes and sets over it the lowliest of men."

The watcher declares that this is a decree that will be carried out, and its purpose is to make the king realize that the Most High is the ruler over the realm of men, He gives it to whom He pleases, and He sets up over it the lowliest of men. It is interesting that the text uses the word "sets up" (יְקִים, *mûqʿy*(A14)). This is the same word that was used so frequently in chapter 3 to refer to the image that Nebuchadnezzar set up. Nebuchadnezzar set up the image which was supposed to be a symbol of his divine power, but it is God who sets up kingdoms and the men who rule them, and those whom God sets over kingdoms are "the lowliest of men." Why does God give the kingdoms of men to the lowliest? Perhaps because of a principle which Paul explains in 1 Cor 1:28: "the base things of the world and the despised God has chosen, the things that are not, so that He may nullify the things that are." God is the one who controls the kingdoms of men, and when these kingdoms accomplish that for which God has established them, it is ultimately God's doing. Also, for Nebuchadnezzar to admit that he is one of the lowliest of men whom God has set over the kingdom of Babylon would be a diametrically opposite

---

6. There are unmistakable implications here for the biblical view of the difference between man and animals. The text implies that there is a difference in kind, not simply a difference in degree, and that difference is at least in part due to man's reason.

attitude from the kind of attitude he demonstrated in chapter 3 and even in the beginning of chapter 4.

How would "the living" know that the Most High rules in the kingdom of men? Because of the wide influence of Babylon and Nebuchadnezzar throughout the ancient world. In fact, this very chapter is presented as a letter from Nebuchadnezzar to the world of people under his influence and the influence of his empire. Therefore, there is a sense in which this letter is a fulfillment of this prediction. The world of the living heard from the greatest king in the world at the time that the God of Israel is the Most High Who rules in the kingdom of men.

Enlisting the Interpreter: 4:18

18—   'This is the dream *which* I, King Nebuchadnezzar, have seen. Now you, Belteshazzar, tell *me* its interpretation, inasmuch as none of the wise men of my kingdom is able to make known to me the interpretation; but you are able, for a spirit of the holy gods is in you.'

This section concludes with Nebuchadnezzar pleading with Daniel to make the interpretation of the dream known to him. Once again Nebuchadnezzar acknowledges that Daniel has the Spirit of God and is able to understand these kinds of matters. It seems that Nebuchadnezzar is already beginning to experience a change of attitude as he pleads with this Hebrew to help him in his time of need. An interesting question is, why did God give this kind of dream to Nebuchadnezzar at all? Why not give it at a different time to a different ruler? Why Nebuchadnezzar? We will consider these questions later. Now we want to look at Daniel's interpretation.

The Dream Interpreted: 4:19–27

Daniel's Desire Expressed: 4:19

19—   "Then Daniel, whose name is Belteshazzar, was appalled for a while as his thoughts alarmed him. The king responded and said, 'Belteshazzar, do not let the dream or its interpretation alarm you.' Belteshazzar replied, 'My lord, if only the dream applied to those who hate you and its interpretation to your adversaries!'"

As soon as Daniel heard the details of the dream, he became troubled at what he realized was the significance of the dream. The text says he became troubled "for a while." The KJV has "one hour," but the NASBU is probably the better translation. Daniel was appalled at the thought of what would happen to the king. He expressed his consternation: "My lord, if only the dream applied to those who hate you and its interpretation to your adversaries!" (v. 19). Apparently over the years Daniel had developed a good relationship with the king and did not want to see him experience such suffering.

Daniel's Interpretation Explained: 4:20–26

The Tree is the King: 4:20–22

20— 'The tree that you saw, which became large and grew strong, whose height reached to the sky and was visible to all the earth'

21— 'and whose foliage was beautiful and its fruit abundant, and in which [was] food for all, under which the beasts of the field dwelt and in whose branches the birds of the sky lodged–'

22— 'it is you, O king; for you have become great and grown strong, and your majesty has become great and reached to the sky and your dominion to the end of the earth.'

Daniel describes the character of the dream, that it is a prophetic warning of an unpleasant future for Nebuchadnezzar. There is one significant difference between Daniel's interpretation of this dream and the interpretation of the previous dream of the king. Here Daniel says nothing about how the interpretation of dreams and the understanding of secret things comes from the Most High God. In verse 24 Daniel does say, "this is the decree of the Most High," but there is no longer the elaborate explanation as is found in the previous instance. Perhaps this indicates that Nebuchadnezzar no longer needs convincing.

Daniel rehearses the dream for the king with the added information that this definitely applies to him: "The tree that you saw, which became large and grew strong, whose height reached to the sky and was visible to all the earth and whose foliage was beautiful and its fruit abundant, and in which was food for all, under which the beasts of the field dwelt and in whose branches the birds of the sky lodged–it is you, O king; for you have become great and grown strong, and your majesty has become great and reached to the sky and your dominion to the end of the earth" (vv. 20–22).

Daniel recalls that the vision depicted the tree whose height "reached to the heavens and was visible to all the earth . . ." This is Daniel's rendition of what the dream depicted as being "in the midst of the earth." This is reminiscent of another tree. Gen. 2:9 states that the tree of life was "in the midst of the garden": (וְעֵץ הַחַיִּים בְּתוֹךְ הַגָּן, *naggah̲ kot̲b m̂iyyah̲ah̲ se ᶜ ew*). Historians have often associated the tree depictions in Mesopotamian art and religion with the tree of life. As Jeremy Black notes, "Interest in the stylised tree [of Mesopotamia] has been provoked, and interpretation of it often influenced, by the 'tree of life' (and the 'tree of the knowledge of good and evil') in the Garden of Eden, in Genesis 2–3. There is no reason, however, to connect the two traditions."[7] There is a sense in which Black's statement is true. There is no extant evidence that the tree myths of Mesopotamia can be traced to the Garden trees. However, there seems to be a conceptual connection here. Babylon is not only the false city, in opposition to the city whose builder and maker is God, but in it is also the false tree of life. The similarity with the tree in the city of God in Revelation is significant: "On either side of the river was the tree of life, bearing twelve kinds of fruit, yielding its fruit every month; and the leaves of the tree were for the healing of the nations" (Rev 22:2). According to Lucas, there was "widespread 'cosmic tree' imagery" in the ancient near east.[8] As the depiction in Figure 10 on page 144 shows, the tree is usually accompanied by symbols depicting a cleansing or purification ritual. The tree of Mesopotamia serves a similar purpose of symbolism as the tree of Revelation.

Of course Babylon itself is symbolic of the organized opposition to God by presenting a false hope. This symbolism is indicated by the features that characterized Babylon. It is outside the promise land, yet it has the outward appearance of the garden paradise. Under Nebuchadnezzar, Babylon was adorned with the famous Hanging Gardens. Also, the river Euphrates ran through the midst of the city. Gen 2:9 states, "Out of the ground the Lord God caused to grow every tree that is pleasing to the sight and good for food;" This is quite similar to the description of the tree in Dan 4:11–12: "The tree grew large and became strong and its height reached to the sky, and it was visible to the end of the whole earth. Its foliage was beautiful and its fruit abundant, and in it was food for all. The beasts of the field found shade under it, and the birds of the sky dwelt in its branches, and all living creatures fed themselves from it." Babylon is depicted as the "cosmic tree" of life and prosperity, yet it is the false tree of life that resides in the false garden in the city on earth whose builder and maker is Nebuchadnezzar, the false messiah. Babylon offers food and protection, but it cannot offer life everlasting.

THE KING IS HUMBLED: 4:23–25

23—   'In that the king saw a watcher, a holy one, descending from heaven and saying, "Chop down the tree and destroy it; yet leave the stump with its roots in the ground, but with a band of iron and bronze in

7. Black, *Gods, Demons and Symbols*, 171.

8. Lucas, *Daniel*, 110.

the new grass of the field, and let him be drenched with the dew of heaven, and let him share with the beasts of the field until seven periods of time pass over him'"

24—   'this is the interpretation, O king, and this is the decree of the Most High, which has come upon my lord the king:'

25—   'that you be driven away from mankind and your dwelling place be with the beasts of the field, and you be given grass to eat like cattle and be drenched with the dew of heaven; and seven periods of time will pass over you, until you recognize that the Most High is ruler over the realm of mankind and bestows it on whomever He wishes.'

The tree was beautiful to look upon and good for food. However, God would bring down this haughty tree that offers false hope. In Ezek 17:22–24 God declares, "I will also take a sprig from the lofty top of the cedar and set it out; I will pluck from the topmost of its young twigs a tender one and I will plant it on a high and lofty mountain. On the high mountain of Israel I will plant it, that it may bring forth boughs and bear fruit and become a stately cedar. And birds of every kind will nest under it; they will nest in the shade of its branches. All the trees of the field will know that I am the Lord; I bring down the high tree, exalt the low tree, dry up the green tree and make the dry tree flourish. I am the Lord; I have spoken, and I will perform it." Daniel's interpretation reveals that the king will be judged by God for his pride and arrogance, and that he will be cut off from mankind until he recognizes that "the Most High is ruler over the realm of mankind, and bestows it on whomever He wishes" (v. 25).

This imagery also brings up associations with the fall of Adam as a result of eating the fruit of the tree of knowledge. In his kingdom, Nebuchadnezzar had access to the abundance of fruit that was secured by his rule. However, in judgment he will not be able to eat the fruit, but will eat the grass that grows up out of the ground. Whereas Nebuchadnezzar's kingdom offered shelter to all the beasts, he will no longer be sheltered by his kingdom, but will live among the beasts in the open, drenched with the dew from heaven.

THE KINGDOM IS PRESERVED: 4:26

26—   'And in that it was commanded to leave the stump with the roots of the tree, your kingdom will be assured to you after you recognize that *it is* Heaven *that* rules.'

Daniel then predicts the king's preservation throughout the ordeal: "And in that it was commanded to leave the stump with the roots of the tree, your kingdom will be assured to you after you recognize that Heaven rules" (v. 26). Notice that there is no reference here to the iron and bronze band that surrounded the stump. If this band is designed in some way to preserve the stump, perhaps indicating that even with the absence of the king, the kingdom would not be split up and given to a variety of leaders, this is perhaps the reason Daniel interprets this part of the dream as the preservation of the kingdom for Nebuchadnezzar's return.

Daniel's Advice Given: 4:27

27— 'Therefore, O king, may my advice be pleasing to you: break away now from your sins by *doing* righteousness and from your iniquities by showing mercy to *the* poor, in case there may be a prolonging of your prosperity.'

At this point Daniel seeks to encourage the king to change his ways in order to avoid this time of suffering. Some have argued that this is tantamount to promoting a works salvation—if you change your ways, you will be saved from judgment. But this is not a necessary conclusion. In other instances in the OT the threat of judgment was followed by encouragement to alter one's life in order to avoid the coming temporal judgment. There may be no eternal results in view here, only the escape from this terrible ordeal. This is comparable to Jonah's preaching to Nineveh to repent in order to avoid the coming judgment. The fact that Daniel encourages the king to "break away now from your sins by doing righteousness and from your iniquities by showing mercy to the poor," may indicate the outward acts that signal an inward attitude of repentance.

The Dream Fulfilled: 4:28–36

Nebuchadnezzar's Pride: 4:28–30

28— "All *this* happened to Nebuchadnezzar the king."

29— "Twelve months later he was walking on the *roof of* the royal palace of Babylon."

30— "The king reflected and said, 'Is this not Babylon the great, which I myself have built as a royal residence by the might of my power and for the glory of my majesty?'"

Even though Daniel had warned the king to turn from his wickedness and pride, twelve months later, while surveying his realm, the king swells up with pride over his accomplishments. No doubt the twelve month period was to give Nebuchadnezzar ample time to repent and to change his ways—but this was not to happen. The king was surveying all that he had created and made, as he says, "by the might of my power and for the glory of my majesty" (v. 30). Of course there were many great kings in history who boasted of their achievements and were proud and arrogant. Why was Nebuchadnezzar singled out as the one to receive this kind of opportunity to repent and this kind of chastisement from God leading to his realization of the truth? As Lucas points out, "Pride, especially the hubris of rulers who think they can 'play god,' is a theme that runs through the book of Daniel."[9] In fact, Nebuchadnezzar's declaration sounds similar to the kinds of praises of God that are found in the Bible. It would seem that Nebuchadnezzar is not merely taking pride in his accomplishments, but is, once again, aspiring to be like God. Although there were no doubt many kings who aspired to be like God throughout history, none occupied the special place that was occupied by Nebuchadnezzar, as the head of the city that became symbolic of all such leaders and aspirations. If Babylon and Nebuchadnezzar are symbolic of all such leaders and their aspirations, then the humbling of Nebuchadnezzar may also be symbolic of the fact that God will ultimately make all nations and their leaders bow before Him and acknowledge that He is the Most High God who rules the kingdoms of men.

Nebuchadnezzar's Conversion: 4:31–36

Nebuchadnezzar's Trial: 4:31–33

31— "While the word was in the king's mouth, a voice came from heaven, saying, 'King Nebuchadnezzar, to you it is declared: sovereignty has been removed from you,'"

32— 'and you will be driven away from mankind, and your dwelling place *will be* with the beasts of the field. You will be given grass to eat like cattle, and seven periods of time will pass over you until you recognize that the Most High is ruler over the realm of mankind and bestows it on whomever He wishes.'

33— "Immediately the word concerning Nebuchadnezzar was fulfilled; and he was driven away from mankind and began eating grass like cattle, and his body was drenched with the dew of heaven until his hair had grown like eagles' *feathers* and his nails like birds' *claws*."

9. Ibid., 116.

According to the dream and its interpretation, the judgment of God falls upon Nebuchadnezzar, and a voice announces that seven times would pass over him until he recognized that God is sovereign in the affairs of men. The phrase "seven times" is probably symbolic of seven years. The use of the term "time" to stand for a year will come up again in the later part of Daniel's prophecy. The text states once again what will fall upon Nebuchadnezzar. The repetition of this scenario is reminiscent of the repetitions in the previous chapter. Here, however, the repetition is not to an absurd degree and serves to emphasize the severity of the decree.

NEBUCHADNEZZAR'S CONFESSION: 4:34–35

34— "But at the end of that period, I, Nebuchadnezzar, raised my eyes toward heaven and my reason returned to me, and I blessed the Most High and praised and honored Him who lives forever; For His dominion is an everlasting dominion, and His kingdom *endures* from generation to generation."

35— "All the inhabitants of the earth are accounted as nothing, But He does according to His will in the host of heaven and *among* the inhabitants of earth; And no one can ward off His hand Or say to Him, 'What have You done?'"

At the end of the appointed time, Nebuchadnezzar lifted up his eyes toward heaven, indicative of his looking up to God in humble submission. Realizing his state, he acknowledges that the dominion of the Most High God is an everlasting dominion and that His kingdom endures from generation to generation. This is very similar to the prodigal son who realized his condition and humbled himself before his father. It is important that Nebuchadnezzar's reason returns to him, and then he acknowledges God. As a free moral agent, Nebuchadnezzar could have cursed God for his experience, but he realizes who God is and humbles himself.

Although there is much disagreement over whether the king was actually converted, it seems that the language provides enough evidence to conclude that he was. However, this question seems to be a side issue. The point is that this prideful world leader was brought to his knees to acknowledge that the Lord is God, and He rules in the kingdom of men. In Nebuchadnezzar is pictured all the world powers that exalt themselves against God. They will all be brought low, whether they are thereby converted or not. This chapter is typical of the outcome of every proud and arrogant nation. God is the one who sets up nations and brings them down. God is in control of who is in control. Throughout the history of Gentile dominance, God will judge the proud and control the wicked to accomplish His own ends. This chapter surely provided a great deal of encouragement to Israel. They were not lost. God had not forsaken them. Ultimately, in the latter days when persecution of Israel will be at its worst, this will be true then also. God will not forsake His people, and the ruthless, proud, arrogant, and merciless rulers of the world are only there because God has a purpose. It is God who rules in the kingdom of men, and He gives this kingdom to whomsoever He wills.

NEBUCHADNEZZAR'S RESTORATION: 4:36

36—   "At that time my reason returned to me. And my majesty and splendor were restored to me for the glory of my kingdom, and my counselors and my nobles began seeking me out; so I was reestablished in my sovereignty, and surpassing greatness was added to me."

Like the loving father of the parable, God restored Nebuchadnezzar to his throne. In this place of power and influence, he was well placed to announce to the world the truth about the Most High God. Notice also that not only did God restore Nebuchadnezzar, but also, "surpassing greatness was added to me." God restored more to him than he lost. This is similar to the case of Job who is restored with twice what he lost.

Benediction: 4:37

37—   "Now I, Nebuchadnezzar, praise, exalt and honor the King of heaven, for all His works are true and His ways just, and He is able to humble those who walk in pride."

The benediction is a praise and honor of the Most High God: "Now I, Nebuchadnezzar, praise, exalt and honor the King of heaven, for all His works are true and His ways just, and He is able to humble those who walk in pride" (v. 37). This final praise offers a closing *enclusio* connecting the beginning and the ending.

6

Belshazzar's Humiliation: 5:1–30

Introduction

THIS CHAPTER seems to be constructed as a chiasm introduced by a small section that sets the scene for the action. The chiasm itself focuses in on the king's praise of Daniel, the request for Daniel's help, and Daniel's recounting of the king's past and present. This recounting consists of reminding the king about his father's experiences and rebuking the king for his sin.

Introduction: 5:1–4
    A   Omen Appears (5:5–6)
        B   Wise Men Fail the King (5:7–9)
            C   The King Requests Daniel's Help (5:10–16)
            C´   Daniel Rebukes the King's Sin (5:17–24)
        B´   Daniel Interprets the Writing (5:25–29)
    A´   Omen Fulfilled (5:30–31)

Belshazzar's Arrogance: 5:1–4

1—   Belshazzar the king held a great feast for a thousand of his nobles, and he was drinking wine in the presence of the thousand.

2—   When Belshazzar tasted the wine, he gave orders to bring the gold and silver vessels which Nebuchadnezzar his father had taken out of the temple which *was* in Jerusalem, so that the king and his nobles, his wives and his concubines might drink from them.

3—   Then they brought the gold vessels that had been taken out of the temple, the house of God which [was] in Jerusalem; and the king and his nobles, his wives and his concubines drank from them.

4—   They drank the wine and praised the gods of gold and silver, of bronze, iron, wood and stone.

It is odd that there is no introduction to Belshazzar. There is no reference to the year of his reign, and there is no explanation of what happened to Nebuchadnezzar. Only in verse two of the story does the reader learn that Nebuchadnezzar was the ancestor of Belshazzar.[1] The explanation for the absence of this material may be the connection that it has with the previous chapter. Chapter 4 ends with Nebuchadnezzar making the following declarations: "Now I, Nebuchadnezzar, praise, exalt, and honor the King of heaven, for all His works are true and His ways just, and He is able to humble those who walk in pride" (Dan 4:37). There is not even the usual conjunction introducing a new section; "Now Belshazzar . . ." There is only the name that appears first in the sentence, "Belshazzar the king . . ." which itself is contrary to normal Semitic word order that usually placed the verb before the subject. The way this chapter starts off is as if to say, "God is able to humble those who walk in pride, like Belshazzar."

There is also a similarity between the beginning of this chapter and the beginning of chapter 3. Chapter 5 begins, "Belshazzar the king made a feast . . ." (בֵּלְשַׁאצַּר מַלְכָּא עֲבַד לְחֶם, *meḥᵉl dabᵃʿ ʾaklam rᵃṣṣ ʾăŝleb*). Similarly, chapter 3 begins, "Nebuchadnezzar the king made an image . . . (נְבוּכַדְנֶצַּר מַלְכָּא עֲבַד צְלֵם, *mel°s dabᵃʿ ʾaklam rᵃssendakubᵉN*). In fact, there is even a similarity in the sound between these two phrases. The contrast that is thereby set up is between the humble realization of Nebuchadnezzar, and the prideful defiance of Belshazzar. Also, there is the contrast between the Babylon of Nebuchadnezzar that reaches its greatest height, and the Babylon of Belshazzar that meets its end. Another interesting note to consider is that the name "Belshazzar" probably means "O Bel [Marduk], protect the king." Not only does Belshazzar fail as a leader, but Bel fails as a protector.

The experience of Belshazzar is similar to that of Nebuchadnezzar in that he experiences the judgment of God upon him and his nation. However, it is different and thereby adds another ingredient to the prophetic revelation of the character of the age. Belshazzar's party is typical of the attitude of the Gentile world toward sacred things as the time of the fall of Babylon draws near. Jesus made the observation in Matthew 24, "For the coming of the Son of Man will be just like the days of Noah, for as in those days which

---

1. Neither Hebrew nor Aramaic have a separate word for "ancestor" other than the word "father," אָב, *'ab*.

were before the flood they were eating and drinking, they were marrying and giving in marriage, until the day that Noah entered the ark, and they did not understand until the flood came and took them all away, so shall the coming of the Son of Man be" (Matt 24:37–39). Although Nebuchadnezzar exhibited an attitude of self-reliance, pride, and arrogance, he did not exhibit a lack of reverence for holy things. On three occasions he acknowledged the holiness and power of the God of Daniel. Whereas Nebuchadnezzar places the vessels of the Temple in the temple of his god, Belshazzar exhibits no such reverence, but profanes the holy vessels that were taken from the temple of God.

Belshazzar holds a feast during which he commands that the vessels of gold and silver that Nebuchadnezzar brought from the temple in Jerusalem be brought to the banquet so that they could drink wine from them. No doubt Nebuchadnezzar's treasury was filled with vessels of gold and silver that had been seized by him during his many campaigns. Yet Belshazzar specifically requests that the ones from the temple of Jerusalem be brought out. This seems to be an act intentionally aimed either at the Jews themselves or at the God of Israel, perhaps instigated by a force behind the scenes. Later Daniel reminds the king that he knows the truths that Daniel had told him about Nebuchadnezzar: "Yet you, his son, Belshazzar, have not humbled your heart, even though you knew all this" (5:22). Perhaps this was a calculated act of defiance on the part of Belshazzar. Belshazzar is exhibiting a lack of reverence for the vessels that even Nebuchadnezzar did not show. Although Nebuchadnezzar looted the temple and brought the vessels back from the temple in Jerusalem, he at least had enough respect to put them in the treasury of the temple of his god (1:2). As Lucas observes, "Belshazzar is prepared to put them to profane use."[2]

Omen Appears: 5:5–6

The Fingers Appear: 5:5a

5a— Suddenly the fingers of a man's hand emerged and began writing opposite the lampstand on the plaster of the wall of the king's palace,

The text states, "Suddenly the fingers of a man's hand emerged and began writing . . ." The appearance of the hand occurred as the group "drank the wine and praised the gods of gold and silver, of bronze, iron, wood, and stone" (v. 4). As Lucas observes, "When Daniel later condemns Belshazzar's use of the temple vessels to praise other gods, he says of these gods that they 'do not see or hear or know' (23). This impotence of the gods of 'silver and gold, of

---

2. Lucas, *Daniel*, 138.

bronze, iron, wood, and stone' is a constant theme in the attacks on idolatry by the Hebrew prophets . . . Yahweh is contrasted with them as the god who is living and active."[3] The appearance of a human hand and fingers depicts the God of Israel, the God whose vessels these are, as a living being able to communicate and condemn the actions of Belshazzar. In other words, this is not a communication that is seen or heard only by some specifically designated person that must then be related to others. This is an appearance for all to see of the living and active God. Although the meaning would need to be interpreted and explained, all could see the presence of the God of Daniel even if they did not recognize Him as such.

The Hand Writes: 5:5b

5b— and the king saw the back of the hand that did the writing.

Figure 11: Handwriting

As the king is watching, the hand writes on the wall. The writing was very possibly an ancient Aramaic script, much like what is depicted in Figure 11. Apparently the writing was unintelligible to the king and ultimately to his wise men. There has been some speculation about how this writing could have been unintelligible to the very people whose native language is Aramaic. But this is not difficult to conceive. Even in English, the separate words "numbered, numbered, weighed, lacking," do not make sense apart from a larger context in which the meaning can be understood. Also, since Aramaic was written without vowel points, an unpointed group of words outside of a context would be ambiguous at best. For example, the Hebrew word דבר could be a noun meaning "word," or it could be a verb meaning "he spoke." Without a context, even a Hebrew would not know which word is intended even though within a sufficiently rich context, a Hebrew would have no problem at all identifying which unpointed word would fit. This is not differ-

3. Ibid., 129.

ent from English or any other language. Without a sufficiently rich context, understanding what a group of individual words is meant to communicate is sometimes impossible.

The King Panics: 5:6

6—   Then the king's face grew pale and his thoughts alarmed him, and his hip joints went slack and his knees began knocking together.

The text gives a graphic description of the king's panic: "Then the king's face grew pale and his thoughts alarmed him, and his hip joints went slack, and his knees began knocking together." One commentator has argued that the phrase "his hip joints went slack" should actually be translated, "the knots of his loins were loosed," referring to the fact that he soiled his pants.[4] Whether this is correct or not, the picture is of one in shear panic. Since we know from Daniel's testimony that Belshazzar was familiar with the experiences of Nebuchadnezzar, perhaps the king immediately recognized the similarity of this event and realized that it must mean something bad is in store. Even though the king could not understand the meaning of the words, the sight of a hand and fingers writing on the wall would perhaps be enough to frighten anyone into a panic.

Wise Men Fail the King: 5:7–9

Call for the Wise Men: 5:7

7—   The king called aloud to bring in the conjurers, the Chaldeans and the diviners. The king spoke and said to the wise men of Babylon, "Any man who can read this inscription and explain its interpretation to me shall be clothed with purple and a necklace of gold around his neck, and have authority as third in the kingdom."

Belshazzar calls for the wise men to read the words and explain their meaning. He promises great rewards to anyone able to do this, even to the point of giving that person "authority as third in the kingdom." The traditional conservative view of this statement is that, since Belshazzar was second in the kingdom behind his father Nabonidus, Belshazzar is offering this person the third place in the kingdom. However, Montgomery offers a convincing explanation that this is actually an official title.

> The reff. have been conveniently collated by Klauber . . . We are dealing here, then, with a customary official title, the numerical

---

4. Ibid., 121.

denotation of which has been lost. [The Hebrew-Aramaic text] has preserved the two Akk. case-forms of the word, *taltâ* and *taltqî*, by true reminiscence . . . *N.b.* that תלתי is not emph. but abs., hence not 'the third ruler,' so AV RVV, but rather 'one of three,' with JV, and we might translate 'Thirdling'; and תלתא שליט, v. 29, is the same although on its surface it might mean 'ruler of the third.' In a word Dan. was appointed a high dignitary in the kingdom, with a title which had lost its original significance, like 'tetrarch,' or 'chamberlain' and 'knight' in English. The recognition of this Akk. origin accordingly antiquates Kau.'s notion of 'an abnormal stat. emph. to תַּלְתִי . . .⁵

Whichever way the expression is taken, there can be no doubt about the antiquity and historical accuracy of Daniel's statement.

The Wise Men Fail: 5:8

8— Then all the king's wise men came in, but they could not read the inscription or make known its interpretation to the king.

As was the case in the past, the wise men are unable either to read the inscription or tell its meaning. This had already occurred in the previous chapters, so it almost seems redundant to mention it here. However, it is a particularly important point in light of Belshazzar's actions. It is very likely that Belshazzar's actions were a deliberate attempt to demonstrate the superiority of the gods of Babylon, gold, silver, etc., over the God of Israel. Consequently, when the wise men who are servants of the very gods that Belshazzar sought to elevate are unable to read the message or communicate its meaning, and this has the unmistakable ring of Nebuchadnezzar's confrontations with the God of Israel.

The King is Terrified: 5:9

9— Then King Belshazzar was greatly alarmed, his face grew paler, and his nobles were perplexed.

It is no wonder that when they are unable to perform, the king and his nobles are in great fear. The text says the king's face grew even paler. The failure of the wise men has once again proven the superiority of the Hebrew God to the gods of Babylon, and now even the nobles are dumbfounded and alarmed at the situation.

---

5. Montgomery, *Daniel*, 256.

The King Requests Daniel's Help: 5:10–16

The King Hears of Daniel: 5:10–12

10— The queen entered the banquet hall because of the words of the king and his nobles; the queen spoke and said, "O king, live forever! Do not let your thoughts alarm you or your face be pale."

11— "There is a man in your kingdom in whom is a spirit of the holy gods; and in the days of your father, illumination, insight and wisdom like the wisdom of the gods were found in him. And King Nebuchadnezzar, your father, your father the king, appointed him chief of the magicians, conjurers, Chaldeans *and* diviners."

12— "Because an extraordinary spirit, knowledge and insight, interpretation of dreams, explanation of enigmas and solving of difficult problems were found in this Daniel, whom the king named Belteshazzar. Let Daniel now be summoned and he will declare the interpretation."

The scene is reminiscent of the previous instance in which Daniel comes in later than the other wise men. In each instance the wise men are given ample opportunity to demonstrate their inadequacies before Daniel comes on the scene. Perhaps in this case, Belshazzar had actually forgotten about Daniel and his reputation and ability. It was probably not the queen, but the queen mother who came in to remind Belshazzar about Daniel. Wood offers two convincing reasons: "One is that verse three states that the king's wives were already present, and this person arrived only after the writing appeared. The other is that this person showed firsthand acquaintance with the affairs of Nebuchadnezzar, as if she had lived during his time, telling of times when Daniel had helped this great predecessor of Belshazzar."[6] Belshazzar was made co-regent in 553 BC, and he was killed in 539. Nebuchadnezzar died in 562 BC, so there was only about nine or ten years between the time of Nebuchadnezzar's death and the time Belshazzar is made co-regent with his father Nabonidus.

Table 9: The Kings of Babylon

Nabu-apla-usur (Nabopolassar) 626—605 BC
Nabu-kudurri-usur (Nebuchadrezzar) II 605—562 BC
Amel-Marduk 562—560 BC

6. Wood, *Daniel*, 140.

Nergal-šar-usur (Nergal-sharezer) 560—556 BC
Labaši-Marduk 556 BC
Nabu-na'id (Nabonidus) 556—539 BC Belshazzar (co-regent) 553—539 BC

The description of Daniel given by the queen mother is reminiscent of the previous descriptions. Daniel is portrayed as one having supernatural gifts in whom the "spirit of the gods" or "Spirit of God" dwells. The queen-mother points out to Belshazzar that Nebuchadnezzar appointed Daniel as chief of the "magicians, conjurers, Chaldeans, and diviners," implying that Belshazzar is somewhat less a king than Nebuchadnezzar who had enough sense to appoint Daniel to this position. By contrast, Belshazzar has either forgotten, does not know of the existence of this great man, or perhaps willfully ignored Daniel. The queen-mother instructs the king on what he should do. One commentator believes that this is designed to present Belshazzar as a buffoon who needs his mommy to tell him how to run his kingdom.

The King Enlists Daniel: 5:13–16

13— Then Daniel was brought in before the king. The king spoke and said to Daniel, "Are you that Daniel who is one of the exiles from Judah, whom my father the king brought from Judah?"

14— "Now I have heard about you that a spirit of the gods is in you, and that illumination, insight and extraordinary wisdom have been found in you."

15— "Just now the wise men *and* the conjurers were brought in before me that they might read this inscription and make its interpretation known to me, but they could not declare the interpretation of the message."

16— "But I personally have heard about you, that you are able to give interpretations and solve difficult problems. Now if you are able to read the inscription and make its interpretation known to me, you will be clothed with purple and a necklace of gold around your neck, and you will have authority as the third in the kingdom."

When Daniel comes before the king, the king presents the case as if he had heard about Daniel for some time: "Now I have heard about you that a spirit of the gods is in you, and that illumination, insight, and extraordinary wisdom have been found in you" (v. 13). Of course Belshazzar neglected to point out that he heard only a few minutes before Daniel came in. Belshazzar states that he has heard about Daniel almost in a sense of challenge: "I have heard this about you, and I want you to prove that it is true." The king challenges Daniel, "if you are able," and then offers him the same rewards that were offered to the wise men. Clearly, Belshazzar does not understand either Daniel or his God.

Daniel Rebukes the King's Sin: 5:17–24

Daniel Tells of Nebuchadnezzar: 5:17–21

17—   Then Daniel answered and said before the king, "Keep your gifts for yourself or give your rewards to someone else; however, I will read the inscription to the king and make the interpretation known to him."

18—   "O king, the Most High God granted sovereignty, grandeur, glory and majesty to Nebuchadnezzar your father."

19—   "Because of the grandeur which He bestowed on him, all the peoples, nations and language feared and trembled before him; whomever he wished he killed and whomever he wished he spared alive; and whomever he wished he elevated and whomever he wished he humbled."

20—   "But when his heart was lifted up and his spirit became so proud that he behaved arrogantly, he was deposed from his royal throne and glory was taken away from him."

21—   "He was also driven away from mankind, and his heart was made like beasts, and his dwelling place with the wild donkeys. He was given grass to eat like cattle, and his body was drenched with the dew of heaven until he recognized that the Most High God is ruler over the realm of mankind and He sets over it whomever He wishes."

Of course Daniel is not motivated by the same desires that characterize the pagan wise men, and he refuses the gifts of the king. Nevertheless, he will comply with the king's request—since he asked so nicely. Throughout the narrative Belshazzar has been depicted as a man desperately trying to pass himself off as someone of importance and achievement. Belshazzar is not responsible for building the great city, although he will be responsible for its destruction. Daniel's statement in verse 18 is virtually a taunt, as Lucas points out: "It starts like a description of how God has blessed him [Belshazzar], but then is seen to refer to Nebuchadnezzar (lit): 'You, O king, the Most High God kingship, greatness, honour and glory has been given . . . to Nebuchadnezzar your father.'"[7]

Both the queen-mother's references to Nebuchadnezzar and now Daniel's reference to him stress the fact that the author wants the reader to make a comparison between the two kings. Whereas Nebuchadnezzar exhibited the same kind of pride and arrogance that is now seen in Belshazzar, Nebuchadnezzar was wise enough to learn from his mistakes and to humble himself before the Most High God. Belshazzar seems to be a complete opposite of his ancestor, and accordingly he will not be given the opportunity to repent.

Daniel enumerates the various successes and achievements of Nebuchadnezzar: "Because of the grandeur which He [God] bestowed on him [Nebuchadnezzar], all the peoples, nations, and men of every language feared and trembled before him [Nebuchadnezzar]; whomever he wished he killed, and whomever he wished he spared alive; and whomever he wished he elevated, and whomever he wished he humbled" (v. 19). Nebuchadnezzar had, by the grace of God, built a magnificent empire and won the respect and fear of the whole world. By contrast, the best that Belshazzar can muster is a large feast. One commentator observes, "Belshazzar's pride arises from his insecurity due to a lack of achievement. . . . Belshazzar's feast was an attempt to win the political allegiance of his subjects and to consolidate his political power."[8] By arrogantly using the vessels of the temple of Jerusalem in his pagan feast, Belshazzar hopes to show his guests that he is a man of courage and self-determination. His arrogance is exhibited in the fact that he makes this move while the Persian army is besieging the city. It is very unlikely that the people of the city were unaware of the move against Babylon taking place at this very time.

Daniel goes on to describe how Nebuchadnezzar's heart was also lifted up in pride and how God humbled him by driving him from mankind. Eventually, Nebuchadnezzar's reason returned to him, and he acknowledged that the Most High is the ruler in the kingdom of men. Belshazzar tries to portray himself as a ruler, but the text portrays him as an arrogant, ignorant child who has no understanding.

Daniel Tells of Belshazzar: 5:22–24

22— "Yet you, his son, Belshazzar, have not humbled your heart, even though you knew all this,"

---

7. Lucas, *Daniel*, 139.

8. Ibid., 138.

23—   "but you have exalted yourself against the Lord of heaven; and they
       have brought the vessels of His house before you, and you and your
       nobles, your wives and your concubines have been drinking wine
       from them; and you have praised the gods of silver and gold, of
       bronze, iron, wood and stone, which do not see, hear or understand.
       But the God in whose hand are your life-breath and your ways, you
       have not glorified."

24—   "Then the hand was sent from Him and this inscription was written
       out."

Daniel enumerates the sins that have led to Belshazzar's demise: "Yet you,
his son, Belshazzar, have not humbled your heart, even though you knew all
this, but you have exalted yourself against the Lord of heaven; and they have
brought the vessels of His house before you, and you and your nobles, your
wives, and your concubines have been drinking wine from them; and you have
praised the gods of silver and gold, of bronze, iron, wood, and stone, which do
not see, hear, or understand. But the God in whose hand are your life-breath
and your ways, you have not glorified" (vv. 22–23). Now Daniel alludes to the
significance of the hand writing the message on the wall. The hand indicates
the hand of God who holds the very "life-breath" of Belshazzar.

       Daniel states, "Then the hand was sent from Him and this inscription
was written out." The word "then" implies a causal connection. The reason
the hand was sent was because of the arrogance and pride of Belshazzar and
the fact that he defiled the vessels of the Lord's temple. What Daniel's analysis
indicates is that it was not the case that Belshazzar had forgotten Daniel or
Nebuchadnezzar. Rather, Belshazzar willfully ignored the truth of what he
knew and arrogantly defied the God of Daniel. Belshazzar was attempting to
show his guests that he was not intimidated by this heritage, but that he is his
own man. But God has weighed him and found him falling short of the standard. The hand that holds the life of Belshazzar has written out his demise.

Daniel Interprets the Writing: 5:25–29

Daniel Identifies the Words: 5:25

25—   "Now this is the inscription that was written out: 'MENE, MENE,
       TEKEL, UPHARSIN.'"

Daniel now reads the inscription: 'Mene, Mene, Tekel, Upharsin' (מְנֵא מְנֵא
תְּקֵל וּפַרְסִין, *m̄isrāfu leqᵉt ᵓenᵉm ᵓenᵉm*). According to KBH, there is some
controversy about the meaning of the term "Mene" (מְנֵא, *ᵓenᵉm*). It could be

from the verb מְנָה which means "to count."[9] Of course the fact that modern lexicographers have difficulty identifying the meaning and how the lexical structure of Aramaic words relates says nothing about Daniel's understanding of the meanings of the words.

"Tekel" (תְּקֵל, *teqᵉt*) means "shekel, unit of measure, and of weight."[10] The word "Upharsin" is actually the combination of the *waw* conjunction taking the form וּ (*û*), and the noun *šerᵉp* (פְּרֵס): וּפַרְסִין, *nisrāfu*. Concerning this word, KBH says, "traditionally *one-half of a mina*, rather *one-half of a shekel* . . . according to Eissfeldt פַּרְסִין is not to be taken here as pl., but as dual, 'two half-shekels.' But the traditional treatment as a plural still remains possible, and it is perhaps to be preferred."[11] The resulting meaning is quite similar to the standard translations: "numbered, numbered, weighed, divided."

Daniel Explains the Meaning: 5:26–28

26— "This is the interpretation of the message: 'MENE'–God has numbered your kingdom and put an end to it."

27— "'TEKEL'–you have been weighed on the scales and found deficient."

28— "'PERES'–your kingdom has been divided and given over to the Medes and Persians."

Daniel now gives the interpretation of the message: "'MENE'–God has numbered your kingdom and put an end to it." The reason this word is written twice is for emphasis. God is the one who has numbered the length of Belshazzar's kingdom. The very one whom Belshazzar defied by defiling the vessels of His temple is now the one who has numbered Belshazzar's days. "'TEKEL'–you have been weighed on the scales and found deficient." The idea of weighing in order to find whether something is good or bad is not unknown to ancient Mesopotamian culture and religion. Figure 12 depicts Šamaš, the sun god, dispensing divine justice by the use of balances.[12] This is the concept here. Belshazzar has been placed in the balances and found to be deficient. Finally, Daniel explains the last word: "'PERES'–your kingdom has been divided and given over to the Medes and Persians."

---

9. KBH, s.v. "מְנָא."

10. KBH, s.v. "תְּקֵל."

11. KBH, s.v. "פְּרֵס."

12. The graphic is from Black, *Gods, Demons and Symbols*, 183.

Figure 12: Šamaš Dispensing Divine Justice

Daniel interprets this word as meaning "divided" or "broken." There seems to be a play on sounds in this instance. The word written "PERES' פְּרֵס (serep) comes from the Aramaic word "Peres," indicating that Belshazzar's kingdom would be divided and given to the Persians, פָּרַס, saraf. In the Aramaic text the words sound very much alike: *Upharsin*, divided and given to the *Upharas*. It is interesting that Daniel interprets the word as "divided" since the statue in Nebuchadnezzar's dream depicted the Medo-Persian Empire as being composed of two arms, though united by one chest.

In what was Belshazzar's kingdom lacking? Taking the word 'kingdom' as a metonymy for the king himself, and since the rebuke of the king concerned his arrogance and pride and his unwillingness to humble himself before the Most High God, the reference seems to be to Belshazzar's lack of any spiritual weight or value.

Daniel Receives the Reward: 5:29

29—   Then Belshazzar gave orders, and they clothed Daniel with purple and a necklace of gold around his neck, and issued a proclamation concerning him that he had authority as the third in the kingdom.

Even though Daniel had refused the gifts offered by the king, the king bestowed them upon Daniel. Interestingly, the command of the king that these rewards be given to Daniel is the only recorded response of the king to the message of the writing. There is no indication that he became angry. Indeed the implication is the reverse. This could indicate that the king was not convinced of the truth of Daniel's words, or that the king had resigned himself to the predicted end and put on a façade pretending to be unmoved by Daniel's warning. Miller points out, "He [Daniel] did not refuse the gifts since to receive them now could not influence his message, and at any rate the gifts were meaningless. What good was it to be 'proclaimed' (to the people in the room, not throughout the empire) the third ruler in an empire that would collapse in only a few hours?"[13] Apparently, Belshazzar was defiant to the end, being true to his character and demonstrating the very character that brought about his demise.

Omen Fulfilled: 5:30–31

Belshazzar is Killed: 5:30

30— That same night Belshazzar the Chaldean king was slain.

The omen had been given, and the warning had been sounded, and that very night the king was slain. Historical accounts all agree that there was very little bloodshed in the conquering of Babylon. Certainly Daniel was not killed. This seems to emphasize the point that it was the king's arrogance and pride that led to the downfall of Babylon and his own death.

Babylon is Taken: 5:31

31— So Darius the Mede received the kingdom at about the age of sixty-two.

There are many speculations about how the Persians and the Medes conquered Babylon. Probably one of the most popular notions is that the army rerouted the Euphrates river and came in under the wall on the river bed. This account is reported by both Herodotus (ca. fifth century BC) and Xenophon (ca. 434–355 BC). Whether this is historically accurate, the text indicates that the very night of the feast, the city was in such a state that it was even possible to kill the king. It must certainly have been a swift take-over.

It is ironic that the very empire that destroyed Jerusalem and carried the Hebrews into captivity would have as its last official act the exaltation of the very people that it once dominated. The downfall of Belshazzar's Babylon is a type of the ultimate downfall of Babylon that would take place in Daniel's future. Unlike the chastisement that fell upon Nebuchadnezzar, this is a judgment of destruction.

13. Miller, *Daniel*, 166.

7

Darius the Mede's Realization: 6:1–28

Introduction

This chapter seems to be organized as two complementary chiastic structures.

Figure 13: Structure of Chapter 6

	Introduction: Plan of the King	6:1-2
Man Seeks to Destroy	A Darius Wants to Promote Daniel	6:3
	B Daniel is Not Corrupt	6:4
	C Law of God	6:5
	D Agreement of the Officials	6:6
	E No One Can Pray	6:7
	F Establish a Decree	6:8-9
	E Daniel Prays	6:10
	D Agreement of the Officials	6:11
	C Law of the Medes	6:12
	B Daniel is a Criminal	6:13
	A Darius Wants to Rescue Daniel	6:14
God is Able to Deliver	A Agreement of the Officials Together	6:15
	B Orders to Throw Into the Pit	6:16
	C Mouth of the Den Shut	6:17
	D A Troubled King	6:18-19
	E Is God Able to Deliver?	6:20
	D Don't Be Troubled	6:21
	C Lions' Mouths Shut	6:22
	B Orders to Take Up Out of the Pit	6:23
	A Execution of the Officials Together	6:24
	Conclusions: Decree of the King	6:25-28

The complementary structures have contrary themes. The first chiasm focuses on Darius' decree to punish anyone who attempts to pray or call upon any god without Darius' control. However, the contrary theme is that God is able to deliver His people from the destructive control of evil men and evil powers. Israel would face the forces of evil that would attempt to use Israel's commitment to God as a means of destroying them and the works of God through them, but God would deliver them from these destructive forces.

In the Hebrew Bible, the text of chapter 6 begins with what is versified as 5:31 in the English Bible: "So Darius the Mede received the kingdom at about the age of sixty-two." Because this chapter opens with a reference to Darius receiving the kingdom, it has been dated to about 538 BC. Chapter 6 recounts Daniel's miraculous preservation among the lions and his release from the lions' den. This may have served as a metaphor for the preservation the people of Israel in Babylonian captivity and their subsequent release from the lion's den.

According to Jeremy Black, in Mesopotamian literature, "the lion is a favourite metaphor for warlike kings and fierce deities, especially *Ninurta* or *Inana*."[1] Ninurta was the Sumerian and Akkadian lord of the earth, and Inana was the foremost female deity in ancient Mesopotamia, the patron goddess of the Sumerian city of Uruk, and the hero-king of the Gilgamesh Epic. The frieze that surrounds the Palace of Darius I, dating from about 510 BC, is composed of images of lions.[2] The lion represented the warlike power of the king and of the gods thus represented. Daniel's protection from the lions depicts his victory over both the kings and the gods of this world.

There has been much controversy over the identity of the Darius named in this chapter. In fact, according to H. H. Rowley, "The references to Darius the Mede in the book of Daniel have long been recognized as providing the most serious historical problem in the book."[3] Miller summarizes the most commonly proposed identities: 1) Darius is one Gubaru (Gobryas) who was governor of Babylon and mentioned in the Nabonidus Chronicle; 2) Darius is a literary fiction; 3) "Darius is a title for Cyrus, the first ruler of the Medo-Persian Empire."[4] Miller concludes that there is "convincing evidence" that Darius the Mede is a title for Cyrus.[5] Some have in fact proposed that the

---

1. Black, *Gods, Demons and Symbols*, 118.

2. A frieze was a decorative band that was built into a wall or structure. Often, the band was extended around the entire structure.

3. H. H. Rowley, *Darius the Mede and the Four World Empires in the Book of Daniel*, 9 (page citations are to the reprint edition).

4. Miller, *Daniel*, 172–75.

5. Ibid., 175.

name 'Darius' is not a proper name, but is a title along the lines of the title Pharaoh for the Egyptian kings.

Parallelisms Between Chapters 6 and 3

There are a number of interesting parallels between chapters 6 and 3 that invite the comparison and contrast of these two chapters (Table 10) below.

Table 10: Parallel Structures in Daniel 3 and 6

Parallel Structures in Daniel	
DANIEL 3	DANIEL 6
SIMILARITIES	
The height of the image was 60 (שִׁתִּין) cubits high and 6 cubits wide.	Darius received the kingdom at age 60 (שִׁתִּין) and two years.
Nebuchadnezzar set up (אֲקִימֵהּ) an image in the plain of Dura.	Darius set up (וַהֲקִים) officials over the kingdom.
The image was 60 cubits high and 6 cubits wide. 60 x 2 = 120 6 ÷ 2 = 3	The officials were 120 satraps and 3 overseers. 120 ÷ 2 = 60 3 x 2 = 6
THE GATHERING Nebuchadnezzar sent to gather together his official to bow down to the image he set up.	THE GATHERING The officials considered together to set up a statute of Darius to which all must bow down.
THE COMMAND (טְעֵם) OF NEB In the time you hear the music, you will fall down and do homage to the image of gold, and whosoever does not, will be thrown (יִתְרְמֵא) into the midst (לְגוֹא) of the furnace of burning fire.	THE COMMAND (טְעֵם) OF DARIUS Anyone seeking a petition from any god or man until thirty days except from Darius the king will be thrown (יִתְרְמֵא) into the den (לְגֹב) of lions.
v. 8 Certain men "devoured the pieces" of the Jews. (וַאֲכַלוּ קַרְצֵיהוֹן דִּי יְהוּדָיֵא)	v. 25 Certain men "devoured the pieces" of Daniel. (אֲכַלוּ קַרְצוֹהִי דִּי דָנִיֵּאל)

Parallel Structures in Daniel	
DANIEL 3	**DANIEL 6**
REMIND THE KING OF HIS COMMAND V. 10 You, O King, made a command that every man who hears the sound . . . should fall down and do homage to the image of gold and whosoever does not . . .	REMIND THE KING OF HIS COMMAND V. 13 Did not an interdict you inscribe that any man who seeks from any god or man until thirty days except from you, O King, will be . . .
IDENTIFYING THE OFFENDERS v. 12 There are men of the Jews whom you appointed over the service of the provinces of Babylon, Shadrak, Meshak, and Abed-nego.	IDENTIFYING THE OFFENDER v. 13 Daniel who is from the sons of the exiles who is a Jew.
IDENTIFYING THE OFFENCE v. 12 They have not placed due regard to you, O King, or the command (לָא־שָׂמוּ עֲלָיךְ מַלְכָּא טְעֵם)	IDENTIFYING THE OFFENCE v. 14 He has not placed due regard to you, O King, or the command (לָא־שָׂם עֲלָיךְ מַלְכָּא טְעֵם)
ATTEMPT TO PREVENT PUNISHMENT v. 15 Nebuchadnezzar offers the Hebrew youths the opportunity to fulfill the command and avoid punishment.	ATTEMPT TO PREVENT PUNISHMENT v. 15 Darius attempts to reverse the command in an effort to rescue Daniel from punishment.
REFUSAL TO SUBMIT vv. 16-18 The three Hebrews refuse to submit to the command from the king to pay reverence to the gods of the king or to pay homage to the image of the king.	REFUSAL TO SUBMIT v. 11 When Daniel knew that the writing had been inscribed, he went up to his roof chamber where the windows were already opened to face Jerusalem, and he prayed and praised God three times a day just as he had been doing before the command was issued.
ENACTMENT OF PUNISHMENT The three youths were bound and thrown into the furnace.	ENACTMENT OF PUNISHMENT Daniel was brought and thrown into the den of lions.

Parallel Structures in Daniel	
DANIEL 3	**DANIEL 6**
KING'S RESPONSE v. 24 Thereupon Nebuchadnezzar was startled and rose up in haste (תְּוַהּ וְקָם בְּהִתְבְּהָלָה)	KING'S RESPONSE v. 20 (19) Thereupon the king in the dawn rose up in the daylight and in haste (יְקוּם בְּנָגְהָא וּבְהִתְבְּהָלָה)
DIVINE DELIVERANCE vv. 25-28 The Hebrew youths were delivered so that they were not harmed (וַחֲבָל לָא־אִיתַי בְּהוֹן) because their God sent His angel to deliver them. (אֱלָהֲהוֹן ... שְׁלַח מַלְאֲכֵהּ וְשֵׁיזִב) v. 17 The youths had said that their God would deliver them from the hand of the king. (וּמִן־יְדָךְ מַלְכָּא יְשֵׁיזִב)	DIVINE DELIVERANCE v. 23 Daniel was alive the next morning because his God sent His angel and closed the mouth of the lions. (אֱלָהִי שְׁלַח מַלְאֲכֵהּ וּסֲגַר) v. 28 Darius said that Daniel had been delivered from the hand of the lions. (דִּי שֵׁיזִיב לְדָנִיֵּאל מִן־יַד אַרְיָוָתָא)
THE COMMAND FROM THE KING v. 29 And from me was made a command that (וּמִנִּי שִׂים טְעֵם דִּי) all people, nations and tongues who say anything remiss against the God of Shadrak, Meshak, and Abed-nego will be dismembered and his house will be made a refuse heap.	THE COMMAND FROM THE KING v. 27 From before me was made a command that (מִן־קֳדָמַי שִׂים טְעֵם דִּי) in all the dominion of my kingdom there will be trembling and fear from before the God of Daniel.
PROSPERING THE HEBREWS v. 30 The king caused Shadrak, Meshak and Abed-nego to prosper (הַצְלַח) in the provinces of Babylon.	PROSPERING DANIEL v. 29 And this Daniel was caused to prosper (הַצְלַח) in the kingdom of Darius and the kingdom of Cyrus the Persian.
EXALTATION OF GOD This section ends in a poem that praises the God of Israel.	EXALTATION OF GOD This section ends in a poem that praises the God of Israel.

Parallel Structures in Daniel	
DANIEL 3	DANIEL 6
DIFFERENCES	
Nebuchadnezzar was building an image of gold.	Darius was building a kingdom with officials.
vv. 13, 19 Nebuchadnezzar was enraged because the Hebrews disobeyed his command.	v. 14 Darius was distressed because his officials had brought this evil upon him and Daniel.
v. 15 The three Hebrews were not paying reverence to Neb's god or paying homage to the image, so Neb said, "Who is the god who can deliver you from my hand?"	v. 17 Daniel did not follow the interdict of the king, but Darius said, "Your God to whom you are continually paying reverence, He will deliver you."
v. 23 The youths were taken up (סְלִק) to the furnace and thrown in.	v. 24 Daniel was taken up (סְלִק) from the den and brought out.
v. 28 The youths were delivered from the fire and thereby changed (שְׁנָא) the king's word.	v. 16 The king could not change (שְׁנָא) his word and thereby deliver Daniel from the lions.

The similarities and differences invite the reader to investigate other possible parallelisms and ultimately validate the structural depiction of chapters 2 through 7 displayed in Figure 2 on page 41. Similar charts can be constructed in the comparisons of these other chapters. Indeed, there seems to be a chiastic structure of these chapters:

Figure 14: Chapter Comparisons

Chapter 2   Gentile world powers exist according to God's plans
Chapter 3   Gentile world powers will attempt to corrupt God's people
Chapter 4   Gentile world powers are still under the control of God
Chapter 5   Gentile world powers are still under the control of God
Chapter 6   Gentile world powers will attempt to destroy God's people
Chapter 7   Gentile world powers will be judged by Messiah

There are, no doubt, other themes and points of comparison that could be identified. These comparisons give the basic concept that is perhaps invited by the similarities like those presented in Table 10. These comparisons also imply some of the reasons why these chapters and these accounts are included in Daniel's prophecy. God's people have certainly faced these fortunes in their history, but God is in control, things are progressing according to His plan, and Messiah will ultimately be triumphant. This point of encouragement would be particularly relevant to the people of Israel as they are being released from Babylonian captivity. They should not suppose that this freedom to return to their land marks the end of their struggles. They will again face persecution and hardship, but they must be continually reminded that God is in control, and His plan and His Man will accomplish the end that He has destined.

Introduction: Plan of the King: 6:1–2

5:31—So Darius the Mede received the kingdom at about the age of sixty-two.

6:1—It seemed good to Darius to appoint 120 satraps over the kingdom, that they would be in charge of the whole kingdom,

2—and over them three commissioners (of whom Daniel was one), that these satraps might be accountable to them, and that the king might not suffer loss.

This chapter begins with the notice that Darius the Mede has become king in Babylon (5:31). Although 5:31 fits into the structure of the previous chapter, it also fits well into the structure of chapter 6. Verse 31 seems to be a hinge between these two chapters tying them together in some way. Perhaps this connection invites a comparison and contrast between Belshazzar and Darius.

The Medes and Persians were known for their organizational structures, and Darius immediately begins exercising his power by establishing order in his kingdom. Daniel is placed in a high position in the order under Darius as one of the three commissioners who would oversee the activity of the 120 satrapes (אֲחַשְׁדַּרְפְּנַיָּא, radsaha'i'ayyan'). The three commissioners were placed in these positions so that the king and the kingdom might not "suffer loss."

Man Seeks to Destroy: 6:3–14

Darius Wants to Promote Daniel: 6:3

3—   Then this Daniel began distinguishing himself among the commissioners and satraps because he possessed an extraordinary spirit, and the king planned to appoint him over the entire kingdom.

Verse 3 states that Darius wanted to promote Daniel over the whole empire. Because of Daniel's excellent character and skill, which facilitated his promotion and rise to prominence in Nebuchadnezzar's kingdom, Darius offered to promote him "over the entire kingdom" (v. 3) (see Figure 15 below). At first it appears that the other officials in the realm became jealous of Daniel. However, there is evidence that perhaps they wanted to remove Daniel because he made it impossible for them to rob the government.

The text states that Darius appointed 120 satraps over the kingdom and that they would be in charge of the whole kingdom. Over these satraps, he appointed three commissioners, and Daniel was one of these. Verse 2 states that these satraps were accountable to commissioners so that "the king might not suffer loss." As Miller points out, "Evidently this means that the administrators [commissioners] watched over the satraps so that all tax moneys were properly collected and so that none of these lesser officials could steal from the king."[6] When Darius planned to place Daniel over the whole kingdom, the other commissioners and officials realized that they would not be able to continue their practices of stealing from the government. Daniel's honesty and integrity would certainly cut into their profits.

Daniel is Not Corrupt: 6:4

4—   Then the commissioners and satraps began trying to find a ground of accusation against Daniel in regard to government affairs; but they could find no ground of accusation or corruption, inasmuch as he was faithful, and no negligence or corruption was found in him.

---

6. Ibid., 178.

Figure 15: Darius' Organizational Plan

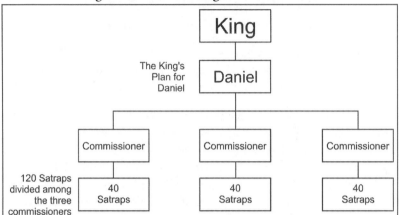

Whether it was jealousy or greed that motivated them, they hatched a plot to destroy Daniel. However, they could not find any basis of accusation against Daniel in any of his responsibilities or loyalties to his duties and to the king. This observation seems to support the notion that these officials were motivated by greed. Usually people will look for flaws in others in precisely the areas of their own weaknesses. Perhaps these officials simply assumed that Daniel must certainly be like everyone else. Particularly, the text points out that they could find in him no "corruption, because he was trustworthy and neither corrupt nor negligent." As Lucas points out, "the main point of these verses, in the context of the story, is the reference to Daniel's exemplary fulfillment of his duties due to his 'extraordinary spirit.' The implication seems to be that this 'spirit' is, in some sense, of divine origin (cf. Dan. 4:8[5]; 5:11)."[7] This point is particularly important in that Daniel's rescue thereby symbolizes the superiority of the God of Israel over the gods of Babylon or the Medes and Persians.

Law of God: 6:5

5—   Then these men said, "We will not find any ground of accusation against this Daniel unless we find against him with regard to the law of his God."

Because the officials could find no grounds for any accusation against Daniel with regard to the execution of his duties, they decided they must find a way to use his devotion to his God as a means of accusing him. The text reports

7. Lucas, *Daniel*, 148.

their plan: "We will not find any ground of accusation against this Daniel unless we find against him with regard to the law of his God." This implies that they would either have to learn about the law of his God, or that they knew about it. The fact that they must find something with regard to the law of Daniel's God establishes an interesting contrast with the "law of the Medes and Persians, which may not be revoked" (v. 8). Because Daniel prays at an open window, his enemies would have no problem in verifying his guilt in breaking the law of the decree. However, they had totally misunderstood both Daniel's devotion and God's law. Nowhere in the OT is anyone commanded to pray three times a day facing Jerusalem. This practice was Daniel's custom, not an aspect of "the law of his God" (בְּדָת אֱלָהֵהּ, *heha1e˒ 1ade b*). Daniel was indeed thrown into the lions' den, but Daniel's rescue, according to Daniel's testimony, is because he did not break the law, either of God or man: "I was found innocent before Him; and also toward you, O king, I have committed no crime" (v. 22). The law of the Medes and Persians that could not be broken was in fact "broken" by God, but Daniel's custom, which was in fact not a law of God, could not be broken by the plotting of these conniving officials.

Agreement of the Officials: 6:6

6—   Then these commissioners and satraps came by agreement to the king and spoke to him as follows: "King Darius, live forever!"

The text indicates that they "came by agreement" (v. 6). This expression appears three times in this chapter. In fact, this English phrase translates the one Aramaic word רְגַשׁ (*sage r*), which indicates "to enter in a crowd."[8] The idea is more of an uncontrolled tumult than an organized movement. Commentators usually argue that the idea of an uncontrolled mob does not fit the context, and many argue that the word is used in order to give a sense of conspiracy. However, one commentator suggests that there is "a strong element of ridicule in the portrayal of them all rushing around in a throng."[9] This group of officials, who are supposed to be responsible to their higher-ups in the organization of and administration of the kingdom, are running about like unorganized, frantic madmen in order to attempt to accuse and trap Daniel. This is in contrast to Daniel's ordered routine of praying three times a day and still being without fault in the carrying out of the duties for the kingdom.

8. KBH, s.v. "רְגַשׁ."

9. Lucas, *Daniel*, 149.

No One Can Pray: 6:7

7—   "All the commissioners of the kingdom, the prefects and the satraps, the high officials and the governors have consulted together that the king should establish a statute and enforce an injunction that anyone who makes a petition to any god or man besides you, O king, for thirty days, shall be cast into the lions' den."

This plot involved convincing Darius to make a decree prohibiting anyone from consulting any god or man besides the king for a period of thirty days. Of course they lied when they said, "All the commissioners of the kingdom . . . have consulted together," since they obviously did not consult Daniel. The statement, "anyone who makes a petition to any god or man besides you, O king," implies that the decree was meant to prevent anyone from praying to any god or man other than the king himself. Some have understood this simply to be a regulatory statement, that is, no one can pray to any god or man unless it is first cleared through Darius. It is not too difficult to understand what the regulation means with reference to the gods. No man should "request a request" to any god. However, to say the same thing with reference to a man is more difficult to grasp. Miller argues that "it seems to allude to the priests through whom petitions were mediated to the gods. Thus Darius was to be the only priestly mediator during this period."[10] This explains a great deal. What these officials have proposed is that for this period of time, Darius would become the only mediator between man and the gods.

Establish a Decree: 6:8–9

8—   "Now, O king, establish the injunction and sign the document so that it may not be changed, according to the law of the Medes and Persians, which may not be revoked."

9—   Therefore King Darius signed the document, that is, the injunction.

Most commentators assert that it was because of his pride that Darius agreed to the decree and the punishment of offenders by casting them into a den of hungry lions. However, it may have been another organizational procedure in these early days of the new empire. By agreeing to issue the decree, Darius may have thought that he could demonstrate that he is the new king and that the populace of Babylon would have to resign themselves to the presence of a new authority. Also, Darius may have looked upon this as an opportunity to get a handle on the religious activities in this new kingdom. As Miller points out, "In his role as mediator, prayers to the gods were to be offered through

10. Miller, *Daniel*, 180.

him rather than the priests. Such a law might have been allowed for political reasons, and Darius may also have permitted a decree of this kind as a test of loyalty to his new government."[11] The decree may not have prohibited offering prayers or petitions through the priests, but may have simply required that anyone get permission through Darius first. Also, by going through Darius, he would get a sense of who is worshiping whom. But, whether it was pride or a sense of expedient organizational planning, the text demonstrates a serious weakness in Darius. As Lucas observes, "There is also an element of ridicule in the picture of the king that is presented here. The one who is put on a (semi-) divine pedestal is at the same time shown to be naive and conceited, and therefore open to manipulation by his courtiers."[12]

Daniel Prays: 6:10

10—   Now when Daniel knew that the document was signed, he entered his house (now in his roof chamber he had windows open toward Jerusalem); and he continued kneeling on his knees three times a day, praying and giving thanks before his God, as he had been doing previously.

The text states that when Daniel heard that the decree had been passed, "he entered his house (now in his roof chamber he had windows open toward Jerusalem); and he continued kneeling on his knees three times a day, praying and giving thanks before his God, as he had been doing previously" (v. 10). The wording seems to imply a causal relation, not merely a temporal sequence. It was upon the occasion of hearing this decree that Daniel went to his house to pray. There is no sense of defiance in this description. This was a practice that was Daniel's custom. Also, he did not go home and fling open his windows to flaunt his faithfulness to his God. Rather, the windows were already open toward Jerusalem. Although Daniel did not pray in defiance of the king's order, neither did he attempt to conceal his actions. There is a sense in which this event makes a nice *inclusio* with Daniel's stand in chapter 1. There was no sense of defiance in that act either. With reference to that action, we proposed that one of Daniel's principal concerns was that eating the king's portion would tell his captors that his God is not worthy of complete devotion. In this case, perhaps the same motivation is in view. As Lucas asserts, Daniel "could have withdrawn to a more private place of prayer, and still gone on praying. However, given that his piety was apparently well-

11. Ibid., 180.
12. Lucas, *Daniel*, 149.

known, to do so would have been to compromise."[13] Daniel does not attempt to hide his practice, even knowing that these officials were well aware of his custom. Daniel does not alter his custom because he does not want to give the appearance that his God is not worthy of this kind of dedication, or that his devotion to the king takes precedence over the devotion to his God.

Agreement of the Officials: 6:11

11—   Then these men came by agreement and found Daniel making petition and supplication before his God.

This is the second instance of the word "agreement." Verse 11 states that these officials "found Daniel making petition and supplication before his God." The word translated "making petition" (בָּעֵא, 'b) is the verb form of which the noun appears in verse 7 in the decree: "anyone who makes a petition [בָּעוּ, u'b] to any god or man besides you, O king, for thirty days, shall be cast into the lions' den." The officials had found Daniel doing precisely what the king's decree had forbidden. It is also important that the text states that they "found" Daniel praying and making supplication before his God. The word "found" or "find" occurs five times in this chapter. In verses 4 and 5 the officials are trying to *find* some fault in Daniel, but they could *find* no corruption in him. In verse 11, they *find* Daniel praying. In verse 22 Daniel declares that he was *found* innocent of any crime, and in verse 23 Darius could *find* no harm in him.

Law of Medes: 6:12

12—   Then they approached and spoke before the king about the king's injunction, "Did you not sign an injunction that any man who makes a petition to any god or man besides you, O king, for thirty days, is to be cast into the lions' den?" The king replied, "The statement is true, according to the law of the Medes and Persians, which may not be revoked."

Having found Daniel in violation of the decree, they approach the king to make accusation against Daniel. However, before they break the news to him that it is Daniel who has violated the decree, they remind him that he himself made the decree, and the king declares, "The statement is true, according to the law of the Medes and Persians, which may not be revoked." This situation is similar to the one faced by David when Nathan the prophet proposed the scenario to him about a man taking another's lamb. Upon hearing of the

13. Ibid., 154.

situation, the text states, "Then David's anger burned greatly against the man, and he said to Nathan, 'As the Lord lives, surely the man who has done this deserves to die'" (2 Sam. 12:5). When Nathan declared "You are the man!" David confessed his sin, but was unable to avoid the consequences. In our passage, the text later indicates that Darius regrets the consequences of his impulsive decree, but, although he apparently tries to free Daniel, he can find no way to get around the law of the Medes and Persians.

Daniel is a Criminal: 6:13

13— Then they answered and spoke before the king, "Daniel, who is one of the exiles from Judah, pays no attention to you, O king, or to the injunction which you signed, but keeps making his petition three times a day."

Once the officials had Darius in their trap, they gave him the punch line: "Daniel, who is one of the exiles from Judah, pays no attention to you, O king, or to the injunction which you signed, but keeps making his petition three times a day." Miller provides a very helpful characterization of this event:

> Thereupon they promptly reported that Daniel had violated the king's command and attempted to put as bad a light on the situation as possible. First, they emphasized that Daniel was not truly one of them; he was an exile captured from Judah. There was no reason for mentioning that Daniel had been a captive other than to humiliate him and make him seem more likely to be disloyal. Second, Daniel's actions were said to have been due to disrespect, not merely of the king's law ("the decree") but of the king himself. They declared that Daniel "pays no attention" to the king, which means that Daniel did not consider the king significant. It also was emphasized that the decree was signed personally by the king, further proof that Daniel did not honor the king. Not only had Daniel disobeyed the king and broken the law, but he did it three times every day ("prays three times a day"). It was not a mere lapse on Daniel's part.[14]

Of course these accusations are more revealing of the perspective and motivation of these officials than they were convincing to Darius. They could not find anything by which they could accuse Daniel of criminal activity, so they made him into a criminal.

14. Miller, *Daniel*, 184.

Darius Wants to Rescue Daniel: 6:14

14— Then, as soon as the king heard this statement, he was deeply distressed and set [his] mind on delivering Daniel; and even until sunset he kept exerting himself to rescue him.

It is important that even Daniel's enemies counted upon Daniel's faithfulness to God. They knew that he would not obey the edict, and it was Daniel's faithfulness that insured the success of their plot. When Daniel prayed as he always did, the officials sprang their trap. Because the laws of the Medes and Persians could not be revoked, even by the king, Daniel's execution was certain. This aspect of the Medo-Persian law illustrates a marked difference with the Babylonian law under Nebuchadnezzar and justifies the representation of Nebuchadnezzar as a head of gold and the Medo-Persian empire as the less precious silver. Nebuchadnezzar was absolute ruler and could make and change laws according to his sovereign rule. In fact, in the accusation of the three Hebrews, Nebuchadnezzar simply ignored his own decree that dictated that an offender must be *immediately* thrown into the furnace. Not so in the new order. A decree of a king in the Medo-Persian Empire could not be revoked even by the very king who issued it.

As Lucas points out, "There is dramatic irony in the conspirators' first audience with the king. While the king is readily accepting semi-divine status, the readers see him only as a gullible mortal who is being manipulated by his officials. In the second audience, the irony of the king's situation is made plain. The very law that elevated him to semi-divine status is now the trap in which he is caught."[15] This is now twice that this king, who saw himself as the absolute ruler, was unable to fulfill his own desires. In verse 3 the text states that the king planned to put Daniel over the whole kingdom. Now, he wants to rescue Daniel. Men try to control their circumstances and are often controlled by them.

God is Able to Deliver: 6:15–24

Agreement of the Officials: 6:15

15— Then these men came by agreement to the king and said to the king, "Recognize, O king, that it is a law of the Medes and Persians that no injunction or statute which the king establishes may be changed."

This is the third time the expression "they came in agreement" has been used. This time they come together to pressure the king to carry out his mandate.

15. Lucas, *Daniel*, 154.

Although Darius tried every means to free Daniel from what appeared to be certain doom, Darius was ultimately unsuccessful, and Daniel had to face the lions. Once again they point out that it is the law of the Medes and Persians that no injunction can be changed. This is the third time in this chapter that reference has been made to the law of the Medes and the Persians.

Orders to Throw Into the Pit: 6:16

16—   Then the king gave orders, and Daniel was brought in and cast into the lions' den. The king spoke and said to Daniel, "Your God whom you constantly serve will Himself deliver you."

Finally the king had to relent. Daniel was brought in and cast into the lions' den. When the punishment was finally carried out, the king said to Daniel, "Your God whom you constantly serve will Himself deliver you." It is not clear whether this is a statement of confidence on the part of Darius or an expression of his hope. However, there was no question that Darius believed that Daniel's fate rested ultimately with his God—not with the gods of Babylon or the gods of the Medes and the Persians. In the king's statement we see the influence that Daniel has had. Daniel's life and testimony must have been sufficient to account for the fact that the king knew that Daniel constantly served his God and that his God might have the power to rescue Daniel.

Mouth of the Den Shut: 6:17

17—   A stone was brought and laid over the mouth of the den; and the king sealed it with his own signet ring and with the signet rings of his nobles, so that nothing would be changed in regard to Daniel.

After Daniel is thrown into the pit, a stone is placed over the mouth of the pit to prevent anyone from changing Daniel's situation or rescuing him. To add insult to injury, the stone was then sealed with the king's own signet ring and with the signet rings of his nobles. This would be similar to the Romans placing the seal over the stone that had been rolled over the mouth of the tomb of Jesus. The signet ring was a sign of the authority of the kingdom of Darius. Anyone breaking the seal and moving the stone in order to rescue Daniel would bring down upon him the might of the kingdom. Lucas points out, "There is irony in the fact that the king who sought to portray himself as the one through whom everyone's petitions could be answered finds that he cannot bring about the one thing he wants to happen."[16] Darius' decree placed him as the only mediator between the gods and men. Now Darius

16. Ibid., 151.

himself faces the fact that Daniel's fate does not rest in Darius' gods. In fact, Daniel's fate rests in the power of Daniel's God to Whom Daniel has direct access, apart even from Darius' understanding, much less mediatorship.

A Troubled King: 6:18–19

18—   Then the king went off to his palace and spent the night fasting, and no entertainment was brought before him; and his sleep fled from him.

19—   Then the king arose at dawn, at the break of day, and went in haste to the lions' den.

The text states that the king did not eat and he did not bring in any entertainment. This indicates that the king did not want any distractions from thinking about the day's events and the fate of Daniel. Or perhaps he hoped that he could sleep early and hasten the night. But sleep fled from him, probably because of his worry over Daniel. Early in the morning the king made his way to the pit to discover the outcome of Daniel's night with the lions. Interestingly, there was nothing in the decree that stated that there would be only one night in the lions' den. In fact, no time limit was set on how long an individual must remain in the lions' den. No doubt that is because no one ever expected that someone could last more than a few minutes with a group of hungry lions. Miller refers to the fact that Daniel's release fits with "the perspective of the ancient Babylonian custom that the victim would be pardoned if he were tortured and had not died by the following day."[17]

Is God Able to Deliver? 6:20

20—   When he had come near the den to Daniel, he cried out with a troubled voice. The king spoke and said to Daniel, "Daniel, servant of the living God, has your God, whom you constantly serve, been able to deliver you from the lions?"

When Darius calls out to Daniel he refers to Daniel as the servant of "the living God [חַיָּא אֱלָהָא, kaḥal[e] ᵓayyąh]." Lucas explains that, "To speak of God as 'the living God' is to imply that he is powerful and active. . . . The commonest use of the epithet in the HB outside Daniel is to contrast the God of Israel with the idols worshipped by the other nations."[18] It seems very likely that the only source available to Darius to learn about the true nature of

---

17. Miller, *Daniel*, 186. Miller is actually quoting A. Lacocque, *The Book of Daniel*, trans. D. Pellauer (Atlanta: John Knox Press, 1979), 118.

18. Lucas, *Daniel*, 157.

the God of Israel was from Daniel himself. Perhaps it was Daniel's influence on Darius in this spiritual capacity that engendered the care and concern that Darius exhibits for Daniel. In fact, if Darius was in fact a title for Cyrus, as Miller argues, then Daniel's influence may have been the foundation for Cyrus' decree to free the Jews. What appeared at the beginning to be a terrible tragedy, the captivity of the people of Israel, proves again to be God's planning—to have His man at the right place at the right time.

Don't Be Troubled: 6:21

21— Then Daniel spoke to the king, "O king, live forever!"

The God of Daniel is the living God, but from the bottom of the pit Daniel wished for the king, "O king, live forever!" This juxtaposition of the reference to the living God and to Darius "honors Darius' kingship, implying that it has a share in God's life and power, and yet relativizes it, implying that it is God-given."[19] Notice also that Daniel does not speak disrespectfully to the king. Daniel's attitude toward the king is a marked contrast to the attitude of the other officials. They are not reluctant to manipulate the king for their own ends. Daniel, on the other hand, is not bitter as a result of his experience.

Lion's Mouths Shut: 6:22

22— "My God sent His angel and shut the lions' mouths and they have not harmed me, inasmuch as I was found innocent before Him; and also toward you, O king, I have committed no crime."

To seal Daniel in the pit of death so that none could change the decree and rescue Daniel, the mouth of the pit was shut and sealed with a stone and a signet ring. Now Daniel testifies that God sent an angel to shut the mouths of the lions. The wicked officials had found Daniel praying and accused him of a crime, but God had found Daniel innocent of any crime either towards the king or towards God. This implies that if Daniel had been guilty of some crime against the king, that God would not have delivered him from the punishment that would rightly be applied.

Orders to Take Up out of the Pit: 6:23

23— Then the king was very pleased and gave orders for Daniel to be taken up out of the den. So Daniel was taken up out of the den and

19. Ibid.

> no injury whatever was found on him, because he had trusted in his
> God.

Daniel was cast into the pit. Now he is taken up out of the pit of death to
a new life. Not only did God find Daniel innocent, but Darius did not find
any harm had come to Daniel. He was protected from harm "because he had
trusted in his God." Interestingly, there is no indication in the account that
Daniel uttered a single word in his defense.

Execution of the Officials Together: 6:24

24—   The king then gave orders, and they brought those men who had
        maliciously accused Daniel, and they cast them, their children and
        their wives into the lions' den; and they had not reached the bottom
        of the den before the lions overpowered them and crushed all their
        bones.

Through this ordeal, however, God preserved Daniel by shutting the mouths
of the lions. The next morning, when Darius found Daniel perfectly safe, he
arrested those who had accused Daniel. Three times in this chapter the officials
act "in agreement." Here they are all together cast into the lions' den, with
their children and their wives. Not having eaten all night, and perhaps not the
day before in anticipation of the arrival of Daniel, "they had not reached the
bottom of the den before the lions overpowered them and crushed all their
bones." The fate that they had planned for Daniel became theirs.

Conclusion: Decree of the King: 6:25–28

25—   Then Darius the king wrote to all the peoples, nations and language
        who were living in all the land: "May your peace abound!"

26—   "I make a decree that in all the dominion of my kingdom men are
        to fear and tremble before the God of Daniel; For He is the living
        God and enduring forever, And His kingdom is one which will not
        be destroyed, And His dominion forever."

27—   "He delivers and rescues and performs signs and wonders in heaven
        and on earth, Who has delivered Daniel from the power of the
        lions."

28—   So this Daniel enjoyed success in the reign of Darius and in the reign
        of Cyrus the Persian.

This time the king wrote a decree that "in all the dominion of my kingdom men
are to fear and tremble before the God of Daniel; For He is the living God and

enduring forever, and His kingdom is one which will not be destroyed, and His dominion forever." Darius goes even beyond Nebuchadnezzar in his praise of God and declaration to all in his empire. As Lucas observes, "Nebuchadnezzar forbade blasphemy against the God of the Jews; Darius enjoins respect for this God. Nebuchadnezzar confessed God's power to deliver; Darius makes a far fuller confession, which has many echoes of those in ch. 4."[20]

Verse 28 states that Daniel had success "in the reign of Darius and in the reign of Cyrus the Persian." It is possible to translate this verse as saying, "in the reign of Darius, even in the reign of Cyrus the Persian," indicating that Darius is in fact Cyrus. This last statement makes an *inclusio* with the final observation of chapter 1, "And Daniel continued until the first year of Cyrus the king" (1:21).

The final note on this section concerns the exaltation of Daniel's God and the preservation of Daniel. Again this chapter is typical of the ultimate deliverance of Israel from all their enemies. It is also reminiscent of the judgment of the nations which Jesus describes in Matthew 25. In that chapter there are three groups, the sheep, the goats, and "My brethren." The sheep are accepted into the joy of the Lord because they have "done it unto the least of these My brethren," and the goats are condemned to outer darkness because they "have not done it unto the least of these My brethren." This is a fulfillment of the Abrahamic covenant—those that bless you, I will bless. Those that curse you, I will curse. In chapter 6, Darius is not condemned, but those who attempted to destroy Daniel were condemned. So it will be in the judgment of the nations. Those who attempt to destroy Israel will be judged. Those who help Israel will be saved.

The idea of the ultimate judgment of the nations and the preservation of God's people to enter the kingdom is demonstrated by the repeated occurrence of poetic sections that offer praise to the God of Daniel. W. S. Towner identifies a pattern that is developed throughout the first six chapters of Daniel's prophecy as set forth in these poetic sections:

> A succinct description of the pattern is as follows; (1) In a narrative, an impossibly dangerous situation is forced upon a righteous fearer of God by the most powerful and alien force imaginable; however it is alleviated by a miraculous intervention which is identified as an act of God; (2) the narrative sequence is then bracketed by a prayer in which the afflicted person (or his wondering alien afflictor) is moved to utter phrases adapted by the learned writer of the material from the hymnic and thanksgiving traditions of prayer—phrases which praise the powerful and eternal God who alone can do such wonders as those reported in the narrative. The

20. Ibid., 153.

effect of the universalist-theodicy logic when fully employed is to denigrate the power of evil to prevail and to testify in a dramatic and convincing way of the superiority of Israel's Creator-Redeemer over any king or people on earth.[21]

In a sense, chapter 6 is the culmination of this pattern. Not only does this chapter conclude the section that deals primarily with the kings of the nations, but this chapter also sets forth the basis for the ultimate victory for God's people. It does this in what seems to be a series of parallelisms between Daniel and Jesus as depicted in Table 11.

Table 11: Parallelisms Between Daniel and Jesus

Daniel	Jesus
Can find no fault in Daniel	Can find no fault in Him
Must accuse by the Law of his God	Must accuse by the Law of God
Darius manipulated by his officials	Pilate manipulated by the Jews
Darius Powerless to Save Daniel	Pilate Powerless to Save Jesus
Was Faithful in his Practice	Was Faithful in the Father's Plan
Cast into the Lions' Den	Nailed to the Cross
The den is sealed by a stone	The grave is sealed by a stone
Victory over death by Rescue	Victory over death by Resurrection
Found Innocent Before God and man	Found Innocent Before God and man
Committed no Crime	Committed no Sin
Daniel Taken up Out of the Pit	Jesus Taken up Out of the Grave
King Acknowledges God	Kings Acknowledge God
Daniel, Servant of the Living God	Jesus, Son of the Living God

Conclusion

With chapter 6, the first major portion of the book is concluded. Chapter 7 functions as the hinge that will connect the two major portions together. In their studies of this book, commentators and theologians focus primarily on

21. W. Sibley Towner, "Poetic Passages of Daniel 1–6," *Catholic Biblical Quarterly* 31 (1969), 325.

the prophetic portions of Daniel and spend little time on the other chapters. However, these chapters have presented the historical background against which the prophetic sections are set. As we have seen in the introduction to the book (Figure 3 page 50), the chronology of the chapters follows a specific pattern. However, that diagram shows only the relation of the prophetic dreams and visions. The following diagram illustrates the chronological relation of the narrative chapters to the prophetic dreams and visions.

Figure 16: Chronological Relation of Chapters

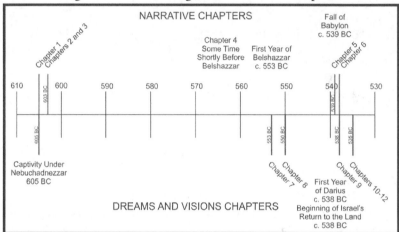

Although some of the dates are debated, the above graphic does show the relationships between the various chapters. The diagram also shows that the visions of Daniel, which begin in chapter 7, all took place from the time of Belshazzar's reign to a time about three years after Cyrus began to release the captives to return to the land of Israel. What this seems to indicate is that the visions of Daniel were not given to encourage Israel during the time of their captivity, since these visions took place at the end of the captivity. Rather, these visions look forward in time, warning the people of God that the worst times are yet to come, and they will need to trust God to deliver them through these times. Ultimately God will triumph, and all the history that is about to be poured out upon God's people is still under His sovereign control.

8

Daniel's Vision of the Kingdoms of the Gentiles: 7:1–28

Introduction

AccordinG to W. S. Towner, "Modern commentators are generally agreed that chapter 7 is the single most important chapter of the Book of Daniel. Its position is pivotal, both in terms of the architecture of the book as a whole and in terms of the brilliance of the vision which it contains."[1] And Walvoord declares, "As interpreted by conservative expositors, the vision of Daniel [in chapter 7] provides the most comprehensive and detailed prophecy of future events to be found anywhere in the Old Testament."[2] With chapter 7 we have reached the second major part of the structure of the book of Daniel. Chapter 7 is the last chapter to be written in Aramaic, but it is also the beginning of the visions of Daniel. Consequently, it forms a hinge between the first and second major parts of the book. This chapter seems to be composed of two major parts, an introduction, and a conclusion:

Introduction: 7:1
Giving of the Vision (7:2–14)
Interpretation of the Vision (7:15–27)
Conclusion: (7:28)

The structure of chapter 7 is similar to the structure of the entire book, being composed of two major parts with an introduction and a conclusion.

1. Towner, *Daniel*, 91.
2. Walvoord, *Daniel*, 145.

Similarly, verses 15 and 16, in which Daniel expresses his distress and requests an interpretation, serve as a hinge between the two major parts.

As a transition chapter between the two major parts of the book, it is important to consider the relations of these two parts. The material from chapter 2 to chapter 7 has given a view of the Gentile world powers from the time of Daniel into the future. The use of the Aramaic language signals the Gentile perspective. Also, the fact that the statue of Nebuchadnezzar's dream presented these world powers in the dignity and strength of a man indicates that this is also the perspective as seen through the eyes of man. As Mills puts it, "When a Gentile had a vision of the course of world-empires, he saw the image of a man—a stately and noble figure, one that filled him with such admiration that he set up a similar statue to be worshiped as a god."[3] By contrast, the view of the same kingdoms as they are presented to Daniel in chapter 7 is the view from God's perspective. God presents the true nature of the Gentile world powers as mutually destructive beasts.

But we must not write off chapters 2–6 as merely preparatory material leading up to the prophecies of chapters 7–12. These early chapters have a distinct message that is critical in assisting us to understand the later chapters. Perhaps the most important message that comes from these chapters is expressed by two of the Gentile kings who were eye witnesses of the power of the God of Israel:

> "Surely your God is a God of gods and a Lord of kings and a revealer of mysteries, since you have been able to reveal this mystery." 2:47 Nebuchadnezzar

> ". . . there is no other god who is able to deliver in this way." 3:29 Nebuchadnezzar

> "Now I, Nebuchadnezzar, praise, exalt and honor the King of heaven, for all His works are true and His ways just, and He is able to humble those who walk in pride." 4:37 Nebuchadnezzar

> "For He is the living God and enduring forever, and His kingdom is one which will not be destroyed, and His dominion forever. He delivers and rescues and performs signs and wonders in heaven and on earth, who has delivered Daniel from the power of the lions." 6:26–27 Darius

As was pointed out in the introduction to Daniel (Table 5 on page 51, and Figure 17 below), this message is presented by means of the parallelism that constitutes the structure of this material. Chapter 2 presents the grand scope of the history of Gentile world powers in Nebuchadnezzar's dream, and

3. Mills, *Daniel*, 63.

God shows Himself to be the one who reveals mysteries. In chapter 3, the three Hebrews are rescued from destruction in the fiery furnace, and God shows Himself to be the one who is able to deliver. In chapter 4, Nebuchadnezzar is brought to his knees until he confesses that God is the Ruler in the kingdoms of men. In the conclusion to chapter 4, Nebuchadnezzar declares that God is able to humble those who walk in pride. This captures the basic thrust of chapter 5 and Belteshazzar's arrogant defiance of the God of Israel. Besides chapter 1, which functions as an introduction to the book, chapter 5 is the only chapter that does not end with the Gentile ruler praising the God of Israel. In the conclusion to chapter 6, Darius sums up what has been revealed about the God of Israel throughout these early chapters: "He is the living God and enduring forever, and His kingdom is one which will not be destroyed, and His dominion is forever. He delivers and rescues and performs signs and wonders in heaven and on earth" (Dan 6:26–27).

Figure 17: Themes of Chapters 2–6

Subject	4 Metals	Nebuchadnezzar's Proclamation	Nebuchadnezzar's Writing	Belshazzar's Writing	Darius' Proclamation	4 Beasts
Theme	Future	Faith	Character	Character	Faith	Future
Perspective	Test Daniel v. Wise Men	Trial Fiery Furnace	Testimony Dream (Past)	Test Daniel v. Wise Men	Trial Lions' Den	Testimony Dream (Future)

There are additional parallelisms and themes among these chapters that form a complex interrelation of meaning and significance.

God is the revealer of mysteries   — statue

God is able to deliver   —fiery furnace

God is the ruler over the realm of mankind   —controls the kingdom

God is able to humble   —man to beast

God is the living God   —lions' den

The short chiastic structure of ideas is supported by the chiastic structure of the chapters themselves:

A   Dream of Four Earthly Kingdoms and God's Heavenly Kingdom (ch 2)

  B   Faithful Jews in the Face of Death (ch 3)

    C   Proud King Humbled by God (ch 4)

    C′   Proud King Humbled by God (ch 5)

  B′   Faithful Jew in the Face of Death (ch 6)

A′   Dream of Four Earthly Kingdoms and God's Heavenly Kingdom (ch 7)

The focus of the chiastic structure is that God is the ruler in the kingdoms of men, and He gives it to whom He wills. All these characteristics are important for understanding the prophecies in chapters 7–12. As chapters 2–6 have demonstrated the superiority of the God of Israel over all pagan gods and have focused on revealing the ultimate demise of Gentile world rule, so chapters 7–12 demonstrate the power of the God of Israel to fulfill His promises to His people even through the confusing maze of world events and rebellious kingdoms. So, chapters 2–6 primarily focus on the future of the Gentile world powers, and chapters 7–12 primarily focus on the future of the nation of Israel in this unfolding history.

There can be no doubt that chapter 7 is replete with imagery and symbolism. According to Miller, "Symbolism is a key element in apocalyptic, and these symbols sometimes have baffled readers of books like Daniel and Revelation."[4] Jessie Mills asserts, "The majority of Bible scholars agree that when the prophets described what was to occur to tyrants in the future, they conveyed their oracles in a comparatively dark and obscure manner, yet so as to be clear when the events should occur."[5] Although there is a wide divergence of interpretation with regard to many aspects of this chapter, as Walvoord observes, "conservative scholars generally are agreed, with few exceptions, that Daniel traces the course of four great world empires, namely, Babylon, Medo-Persia, Greece, and Rome . . ."[6] And, whether one is a Preterist, like Mills, or a Futurist, like Miller, proponents from either camp would agree that there are certainly some aspects of the prophecy of chapter 7 that have been fulfilled. However, if it were true, as Mills asserts, that the prophecies were to be "clear when the events should occur," then we are at a loss to explain why there are so many differences among interpreters concerning some portions of the

4. Miller, *Daniel*, 193.

5. Mills, *Daniel*, 64.

6. Walvoord, *Daniel*, 145.

prophecy. If the prophecy is to be clear when the events prophesied have occurred, and since the controversy between the Preterist and Futurist camps primarily concerns the Fourth Beast, could it be that a lack of clarity indicates that the event has not yet occurred? Mills would most certainly not agree with this conclusion, but if we accept his principle, then this is certainly a logical possibility and seems to follow from it.

Such a prophetic panorama would have been a great encouragement to those who were in captivity to the Gentiles in Babylon, even though for only a few more years, or to those who would experience the wrath of pagan powers in future circumstances. Daniel's prophecy would have been a significant source of strength by the realization that God would not abandon His people. As Miller points out, "Eschatological promises of a better world have always encouraged believers in the here and now."[7]

Introduction: 7:1

1—   In the first year of Belshazzar king of Babylon Daniel saw a dream and visions in his mind as he lay on his bed; then he wrote the dream down and related the following summary of it.

Verse 1 functions as an introduction to this chapter and sets the stage for the events that will be described by Daniel. That this chapter opens with a reference to the first year of the reign of Belshazzar is another indicator of the structure of this material. Chapters 1 through 6 were presented in chronological order beginning with the capture of Jerusalem by Nebuchadnezzar in 604 or 605 BC and ending with the events of chapter 6 which took place in the early years of the reign of Darius, perhaps about 539 BC. Chapters 7 through 12 are also presented in chronological order, but chapter 7 goes back to a period prior to the events recorded in chapter 5. Miller gives the following as the chronology of chapters 7–12: "(1) chap. 7—first year of Belshazzar, (2) chap. 8—third year of Belshazzar, (3) chap. 9—first year of Darius the Mede, (4) chaps. 10–12—third year of Cyrus."[8] Miller speculates on the reason for choosing this as the time and Belshazzar as the ruler to give this vision to Daniel. He says, "Possibly the Jews were concerned about their future under the rule of the wicked Belshazzar, and the vision was imparted to assure the Jewish people that they were secure."[9] However, it is likely that the Jews in captivity were always concerned about their future, and it is also very likely that this material was not even made available until the end of Daniel's life. A

---

7. Miller, *Daniel*, 193.

8. Ibid.

9. Ibid., 194.

more likely reason is that chapters 2 and 7 form an *inclusio* with the beginning and ending of the Babylonian Empire. The parallelism of these two chapters supports this notion. Indeed, as in the case of the captivity of the people of Jerusalem, many were absorbed into the political and religious structure of Babylon under Nebuchadnezzar. So also many of the people of Babylon were absorbed into the political structure of Babylon under Darius—whereas Daniel was absorbed into the political structure and promoted to a high position under Nebuchadnezzar, so he is absorbed into the political structure and promoted to a high position under Darius.

Daniel says he is going to report a "summary" of his dream and vision. The Aramaic expression is רֵאשׁ מִלִּין (*rêllim s'er*), which literally means, "the head of the matter." As Miller puts it, "Here the phrase denotes the foremost details of what Daniel had seen."[10] What this indicates is that Daniel will not either state or explain all of the details of what he saw in his dream/vision, but he will present what he takes to be the most important matters.

Giving of the Vision: 7:2–14

According to Lucas, this section is constructed as a chiasm.[11] On the basis of this evaluation, Lucas proposes, "The structure of this chapter makes clear what it is that the author wants to emphasize. Both the central place it holds in the palinstrophic structure of the main vision report, and its poetic form, highlight the importance of the throne scene. Human kings may seem to be free to rampage at will, but there is a throne in heaven and One on it to whom they are ultimately subject."[12] This evaluation fits very well with what seems to have been the major emphasis of the first 6 chapters, namely, the Most High is the Ruler in the kingdoms of men, and He gives it to whom He will.

A   Four Beasts Appear (2b–3)
  B   The First Three Beasts (4–6)
    C   The Fourth Beast Appears (7)
      D   A Small Horn Makes Great Claims (8)
        E   A Throne Scene (9)
      D´   The Small Horn Makes Great Claims (11a)
    C´   The Fourth Beast Destroyed (11b)
  B´   The Fate of the First Three Beasts (12)
A´   A Human-Like Figure Appears (13–14)[13]

10. Ibid.

11. Lucas, *Daniel*, 164.

12. Ibid., 165.

13. This structural arrangement is adapted from the one developed by Lucas, *Daniel*, 164.

Vision of Four Beasts: 7:2–12

FOUR WINDS: 7:2

2—   Daniel said, "I was looking in my vision by night, and behold, the four winds of heaven were stirring up the great sea."

Daniel's vision begins with the observation that "the four winds of heaven were stirring up the great sea." In many places in the OT the reference to "the great sea" is a reference to the Mediterranean Sea. There is a sense in which this is the sea around which all these empires stand. Some commentators hold that the sea is symbolic of the mass of humanity out of which these empires come. In creation God overcame the chaotic sea by His Word. The raging, restless sea symbolizes the chaos of the world system. This chaos re-emerges here to produce these destructive beasts who, unchecked, will return the world to an uninhabitable wasteland (see Mk 13:20). "The cosmic sea, however, also symbolizes the continued threat that forces of chaos pose against God and creation. . . . As the home of the chaos monster who can be roused, the sea symbolizes the threat of the reemergence of chaos (Job 3:8). In fact, the evil world powers and the antichrist of the last days which oppose God and his people are symbolized as beasts arising from the sea (Dan. 7:3; Rev. 13:1)."[14] Concerning the symbolism of the sea, J. J. Collins asserts, "Out of this sea, four great beasts arise, but the sea is the source, and the beasts are its offshoots. There is no further reference to the sea in Daniel 7, and its presence in the visions must be explained from its traditional associations."[15] However, this statement seems to be inaccurate. In the interpretation of the vision/dream, verse 17 states that these beasts come up "from the land/earth" (מִן־אַרְעָא, ʾaʿraʾ nim), where the term "אֲרַע" (ʿaraʾ) can be understood as the "land" or the "earth." In other words, whereas in Daniel's vision the beasts come up out of the sea, the interpretation explains that they are coming up out of the earth. As Goldingay puts it, "The Great Sea in the symbolic vision stands for the world."[16] In verse 17 the earth is best understood in the sense of the earthly powers or the world of people. Also, Isa 57:20 declares, "But the wicked are like the tossing sea, for it cannot be quiet, whose waves cast up mire and mud." In fact, the sea is mentioned again, this time in terms of the reality for which the sea is a symbol.

---

14. *Dictionary of Biblical Imagery* (1998), s.v. "SEA."

15. J. J. Collins, "Stirring Up the Great Sea: The Religio-Historical Background of Daniel 7," in *The Book of Daniel in the Light of New Findings*, ed., A. S. Van Der Woude (Leuven: Leuven University Press, 1993), 126.

16. Goldingay, *Daniel*, 173.

Walvoord argues that the wind is perhaps symbolic of the sovereignty and power of God: "Although the Scriptures do not tell us, inasmuch as the wind striving with the world is a symbol of the sovereign power of God striving with men (Gen 6:3; Jn 3:8), the prophetic meaning may be the sovereign power of God in conflict with sinful man. . . . In Daniel, wind is uniformly used to represent the sovereign power of God, which is the viewpoint of the book. The history of the Gentiles is the record of God striving with the nations and ultimately bringing them into subjection when Christ returns to reign (Ps. 2)."[17] However, Wood argues that, "The winds stand for various forces which play upon the nations, serving to bring strife and trouble. That they come contrary to nature, from the four directions at the same time, indicates the severity and confusion of this strife and world-turmoil."[18] It is perhaps instructive that in the corresponding section in which these images are interpreted, there is nothing said about the four winds. Lucas claims, "it is probable, as we shall see, that each of the compass-points produces a beast."[19] This proposal does not stand up to scrutiny once one looks at a map. The four winds may simply indicate that these kingdoms encompass the known world.

FOUR BEASTS: 7:3–11

Beasts from the Sea: 7:3

3— "And four great beasts were coming up from the sea, different from one another."

Daniel reports, "four great beasts were coming up from the sea" (v. 3). The picture of the four winds of the heavens stirring up the sea seems to be a causal factor in the emergence of the beasts. The views of Walvoord and Wood expressed above do not necessarily indicate contrary positions. It is certainly the sovereignty of God that orchestrates the affairs of the world, and as the previous chapters have demonstrated, God is the Ruler in the kingdoms of men. In the Exodus, the wind of God caused the walls of water to cover the armies of Pharaoh for the purpose of destruction so that "the Lord overthrew the Egyptians in the midst of the sea" (Ex 14:27). Now the winds blow upon the sea to bring forth the armies of the nations to do battle with each other and with the people of God. God is no doubt in control, even if the wind symbolizes the forces of this world system.

17. Walvoord, *Daniel*, 152.
18. Wood, *Daniel*, 180.
19. Lucas, *Daniel*, 178.

First Beast: 7:4

4—   "The first was like a lion and had the wings of an eagle. I kept looking
until its wings were plucked, and it was lifted up from the ground
and made to stand on two feet like a man; a human mind also was
given to it."

Figure 18: Lion Griffin

Daniel describes the first beast coming out of the sea as "a lion and had the
wings of an eagle." Of course the lion was often used as a symbol of royalty,
and in Babylon, the winged lion was a common symbol of the king. However,
this symbol usually consisted of a lion's body, the wings of a bird, and the
head of a man. Even the so-called lion-dragon or lion-griffin was a combination of a "lion's foreparts and bird's hind-legs, tail and wings . . ." (see Figure
18).[20] Daniel's description, however, seems to depict a normal looking lion yet
having eagles' wings. These simple differences between the actual images and
the description given by Daniel have caused many commentators to look elsewhere for the meaning of the symbolism. Yet commentators are almost unani-
mously agreed that this beast is symbolic, whatever else the lion and wings
may signify, either of Nebuchadnezzar himself, or the Babylonian Empire
that he represents, or both. Daniel continues, "I kept looking until its wings
were plucked, and it was lifted up from the ground and made to stand on two

20. Black, *Gods, Demons and Symbols*, 121.

feet like a man; a human mind also was given to it." There is also an almost unanimous agreement that this refers to the experience of Nebuchadnezzar in the narrative of chapter 4. The plucking of the two wings is understood to be symbolic of Nebuchadnezzar's loss of his ruthlessness as conqueror.

Second Beast: 7:5

5—   "And behold, another beast, a second one, resembling a bear. And it was raised up on one side, and three ribs were in its mouth between its teeth; and thus they said to it, 'Arise, devour much meat!'"

The second beast is described as "resembling a bear." As Daniel looked, he saw that "it was raised up on one side, and three ribs were in its mouth between its teeth; and thus they said to it, 'Arise, devour much meat!'" Although there is less unanimity among commentators regarding the symbolism of this beast, most conservative scholars associate the bear with the kingdom of Medo-Persia. Historians have attempted to discover any relationship between a bear and either the Median or Persian empires, but nothing definitive has been proposed. Similarly, nothing satisfactory has been said about the significance of the three ribs in the teeth of the bear. The most likely meaning relates to the usual characteristics of the animal in the wild.

MEDO-PERSIA OR THE MEDIAN EMPIRE?

Critical scholars have generally held that the second beast is Media, and the third is Persia. One of the principal reasons argued by conservative scholars for rejecting this association is that the Median Empire was absorbed by the Persian Empire some 11 years prior to the fall of Babylon. According to C. C. Caragounis, one of the reasons conservatives reject identifying the second beast with the Median Empire is, "they assume that each succeeding empire must come into being first after the dissolution of each preceding empire."[21] However, this is in fact not an assumption of conservative commentators. In the statue of Nebuchadnezzar, each succeeding metal follows where the preceding metal ends. Of course one might argue that this is merely the necessities of illustration. However, in Daniel's interpretation he declares, "After you there will arise another kingdom inferior to you . . ." The word translated "after" is וּבָתְרָךְ (karṭabu) from אֲתַר (raṭaʾ). According to KBH, אֲתַר can be used to mean "place, location."[22] Since this noun is prefixed with the inseparable preposition בְּ, and suffixed with the second person singular

21. C. C. Caragounis, "History and Supra-History: Daniel and the Four Empires," in *The Book of Daniel*, 388.

22. KBH, s.v. "אֲתַר."

pronominal suffix ך ָ, the resulting meaning seems to be "in your place." Taking the reference to Nebuchadnezzar as a metonymy for Babylon, this seems to indicate that the kingdom of Babylon will be replaced by the second kingdom. But, this could not have been Media since Media did not replace Babylon. Of course it will be argued that even Medo-Persia was in existence before Babylon fell, so it does not seem to fit the criterion of historical succession. However, this objection is tied to the next assumption that Caragounis attributes to the conservative view.

He claims that conservatives "make ruling the Babylonian territory the implicit criterion for being one of the four empires."[23] Caragounis argues against this assumption by claiming, "The center of interest for our Author is not Babylon or the Babylonians, but Judaea and the Jews."[24] Having rejected what he believes to be the conservatives' assumption and refocused attention to the Jews and Judaea, he asserts, "Once this is realized it becomes apparent that a great power could be regarded as one of the empires by the Jews even though it did not actually rule over Babylon."[25] However, after providing an impressive account of the history of the Median Empire, Caragounis offers no reasons why the Jews should consider them one of the four empires. If the focus is on the Jews and Judaea, then what has Media to do with the Jews? In Caragounis' account, there is nothing in the history of the Median Empire that relates to the Jews or Judaea except how Media relates to Babylon. In fact, having refocused attention to the Jews, Caragounis completely loses sight of the Jews and Judaea in his recounting of the history of Media.

Since the center of Daniel's focus is the Jews, it requires that the four empires be understood in relation to the nation of Israel, and Media had no dealings with Israel. It was only because the Medo-Persian Empire replaced the Babylonian Empire and thus became the "caretakers" of the captive Jews that this empire becomes significant in Daniel's vision. Since the Median Empire did not capture Babylon, and did not either oppress or hold captive the people of Israel, according to Caragounis' own principle, Daniel has no interest in the separate kingdom of Media. This also explains why there is this historical succession. Even though the Persian Empire was in existence some 75 years before the fall of Babylon, this kingdom did not enter into the purview of Daniel because they had no dealings directly with the Jews. Once they captured Babylon and took over the Babylonian Empire, they became the masters of captive Israel. Caragounis' argument falls on its own principle of refocus. Historically, and in terms of the testimony of the text, there is no

23. Caragounis, "History and Supra-History," 388.

24. Ibid., 390.

25. Ibid., 390–91.

good reason to believe that the second beast refers to any other kingdom than that historically identified as the Medo-Persian Empire.

RAISING AND BEING RAISED

Concerning the raising up on one side of the bear-like beast, Mills asserts, "The bear being raised up on one side would denote a kingdom that had been quiet and at rest, but that was now rousing up deliberately for the conquest of war."[26] Montgomery says, "The animal then is pausing to devour a mouthful before springing again on its prey, to which feat an oracular voice encourages it."[27] However, there is nothing in the text to indicate that this is the significance of this observation. Also, the notion that being raised up on one side indicates a moving bear seems contrary to the way bears move. The brown bear seems to move with an opposing gate. When one front paw is going forward, the back paw on the same side is back. Although bears are generally classified as pacers, indicating that they move one side of the body at a time, they will also change their gate with a change of speed. Even pacers do not "raise up" on one side to walk. Even a charging or running bear does not raise up on one side. Attacking bears will often raise up on their hind legs, but not on one side. Another view is that the raising up on one side indicates the superiority of the Persians in the Medo-Persian alliance. Wood explains this view:

> The words of this much-disputed phrase are best translated as given here, indicating that the bear was seen to have its two feet on the same side raised at one time, making that side to be higher than the other. Two points of symbolism should be noted. First, that the animal had one side rise higher than the other points to the greater importance assumed by the Persian division over the Median, in the Medo-Persian empire—a symbolism formed also by the two horns of the ram in Daniel's second vision (8:3), the second being made to grow higher than the first. Second that the legs were lifted, as if the animal was about to move forward, points to the great Medo-Persian desire for conquest, carried out so dramatically by Cyrus.[28]

Walvoord agrees the significance indicates "the one-sided union of the Persian and Median Empires," although his understanding of the picture is a bit different: "The bear pictured apparently lying down is described as raising itself up on one side. Such an action, of course, is typical of an awkward ani-

26. Mills, *Daniel*, 67.

27. Montgomery, *Daniel*, 288.

28. Wood, *Daniel*, 183.

mal like the bear."[29] There are some problems with this view, however. First, to assume that the beast was "lying down," as Walvoord surmises, is contrary to the picture of the beast "coming up from the sea." Although this is not individually stated with reference to each individual beast, it is certainly implied from the statement in verse 3 that Daniel saw the four beasts coming up from the sea. Coming up is not consistent with lying down. Second, as we have seen, the notion of rising up on one side is not characteristic of the movement of a bear, or even of preparation for movement, and it is certainly not "typical" of a bear. I doubt that anyone who has been threatened by a bear would call it "awkward." Third, neither the translations nor the interpretations seem to take into consideration the stem of the verb. That the verb is Hoph'al would seem to imply a causal passive nuance.

Another explanation may be found in the use of the term to describe the bear that takes into account the fact that the verb is Hoph'al. The text states, "it was raised up on one side." The phrase "it was raised up" translates a single Aramaic word, הֳקִמַת _(tamiqªh)_. Since this is a Hoph'al form, it seems to indicate a causal idea as well as a passive idea. The bear was caused to rise up on the one side. The word used here is the same word in the same form used in verse 4 to indicate that the lion was caused to rise up on two feet like a man. In other words, this was done to the lion, not something that it did to itself.

There is another Aramaic word that could have been used in either case, namely, סלק, _(qls)_. In fact, it is used in Dan 6:23 (A24) to refer to taking up, lifting up, or causing Daniel to be raised out of the pit. Most translations and interpretations treat the word in Dan 7:4 as a causal passive idea indicating that the lion "was made to stand." Perhaps the bear is made to rise up on one side in the same way that the lion was made to raise up on its hind legs. The incident with the lion is generally understood to symbolize Nebuchadnezzar's experience in chapter 4 where he was given the heart of a beast until seven periods passed over him, and at the end his "reason" returned to him and he stood up like a man. Perhaps the fact that the bear is caused to raise up on one side indicates a partial "conversion" after the manner of Nebuchadnezzar's experience. If this is the case it would certainly coincide with the experience of Darius the Mede in his recognition that the God of Daniel is "the living God." At this point, however, there is no way of verifying this understanding, and it may be that the corresponding passage in chapter 8 will shed additional light on this passage.

---

29. Walvoord, _Daniel_, 156.

THREE RIBS

Although there have been no proposals that have convinced all commentators of the significance of the three ribs, Miller's observations seem fairly satisfactory: "The bear 'had three ribs in its mouth,' which may safely be understood to represent the conquests of the empire. . . . Although Young considers the three ribs to represent 'the insatiable nature of the beast . . . since, not being content with one body, it devoured many,' others (probably correctly) have taken the ribs to represent Medo-Persia's three major conquests—Babylon (539 B.C.), Lydia (546 B.C.), and Egypt (525 B.C.)."[30] The bear-like creature is told, "Arise, devour much meat!" Walvoord proposes that this indicates the continued conquests of the Medo-Persian Empire after it captures Babylon. If the three ribs are symbolic of the three major conquests, then understanding the command to devour much meat fits with this.

Third Beast: 7:6

6—   "After this I kept looking, and behold, another one, like a leopard, which had on its back four wings of a bird; the beast also had four heads, and dominion was given to it."

Daniel continues to look, and a third beast comes out of the sea, and Daniel describes it as, "another one, like a leopard, which had on its back four wings of a bird; the beast also had four heads, and dominion was given to it." The conservative camp almost universally identifies this beast as representing Greece. The four wings are usually associated with the increased speed of an already swift animal. If the male goat in Dan 8:5 is also a reference to Greece in general and Alexander in particular, his speed was so great that he appeared to come across the earth "without touching the ground." Lucas proposes that the four wings and four heads are more likely "the echo of 'the four corners of the earth' mentioned above (see vv. 2b–3), implying the wide extent of this power's empire."[31] However, if these were to symbolize the four corners of the globe, one wonders why there are both four wings and four heads. Would not one set be sufficient for such an indication? Miller proposed that the four wings not only symbolize the swiftness of Alexander's campaigns, but also "the four quarters of the earth, thus signifying world dominion."[32]

Again most conservative authors tend to hold that the four heads symbolize the four generals among whom Alexander's empire was divided: "(1) Antipater, and later Cassander, gained control of Greece and Macedonia;

30. Miller, *Daniel*, 198–99.
31. Lucas, *Daniel*, 180.
32. Miller, *Daniel*, 199–200.

(2) Lysimachus ruled Thrace and a large part of Asia Minor; (3) Seleucus I Nicator governed Syria, Babylon, and much of the Middle East (all of Asia except Asia Minor and Palestine); and (4) Ptolemy I Soter controlled Egypt and Palestine."[33] The use of both the four wings and the four heads may be the way the symbolism captures the two stages of this empire. The four wings are symbolic of the empire under Alexander's rule, which was primarily the stage of the warring history of the empire. The four heads symbolize the second stage of the empire in its state under the four separate kingdoms. Heads are usually symbolic of kings or kingdoms, and wings are symbolic of warfare or military power. These two groups of four symbolize the whole of the Macedonian empire.

Fourth Beast: 7:7–8

Without doubt, many aspects of the symbolism of the fourth beast have generated more controversy than all of the others together. Not only is their divergence of opinion between conservative and critical scholars, but even among conservative interpreters there are conflicting points of view. And yet as Walvoord points out, "The crucial issue in the interpretation of the entire book of Daniel, and especially of chapter 7, is the identification of the fourth beast."[34] Although most conservatives identify the fourth beast as Rome, the interpretation of the details reveals divergent views on eschatology.

DESCRIPTION OF THE FOURTH BEAST: 7:7

7— "After this I kept looking in the night visions, and behold, a fourth beast, dreadful and terrifying and extremely strong; and it had large iron teeth. It devoured and crushed and trampled down the remainder with its feet; and it was different from all the beasts that were before it, and it had ten horns."

It is significant that Daniel does not offer any zoological category for this beast. Montgomery points out that the fourth beast "is so horrible that it defies any zoological category."[35] Most conservative scholars identify the fourth beast as the Roman Empire. Caragounis attempts to demonstrate that the fourth beast is Greece. Examining the number of words dedicated to the descriptions of the four metals in chapter 2 and the four beasts in chapter 7, Caragounis shows that by far the concentration of discourse focuses on the fourth beast. He says, "In the Vision of ch. 7 the fourth empire not only receives about four

33. Ibid., 200.
34. Walvoord, *Daniel*, 159.
35. Montgomery, *Daniel*, 282.

times as much space, but it is also the only one that is deemed worthy of interpretation . . ."[36] Caragounis then considers the amount of space dedicated to the description and interpretation of Greece in chapter 8, showing that in the "Vision of chapter 8, where only two of the four empires—Persia and Greece—figure, Greece receives an enormous amount of attention as compared with Persia."[37] He then jumps to the conclusion, "Though the matter cannot be settled conclusively on this point alone, this evidence suggests that the fourth empire is considered as the most important one and as identical with Greece."[38] However, although Caragounis' study of the relative space dedicated to the various beasts is informative, his conclusion is a *non sequitur*. This is like saying, since in the first discussion of A, B, C, and D, D is given the most space, and since in the second discussion of B and C, C is given more space than B, C and D must be identical. This simply does not follow.

His next argument relating to what he identifies as a "progression of treatment in the various empires" that in chapter 8 serves to narrow "the span of time by concentrating on only two of the empires," he once again concludes, "Since the emphasis given to the second of these is comparable to that given of the fourth empire in chs. 2 and 7 the fourth empire should be none other than Greece."[39] However, the logic in this argument is identical to the logic in the previous argument. Just because the emphasis is identical does not mean that the fourth beast in chapter 7 is the same as the second entity in chapter 8. This simply does not follow. The fourth beast is described as being "dreadful and terrifying and extremely strong" and "different from all the beasts that were before it." This hardly seems an apt description of a goat, which is the imagery of Greece in chapter 8. There is simply no way to reconcile the description of the fourth beast in chapter 7 with the imagery of Greece in chapter 8.

According to Miller, "Just as this monster was 'different' from all the others, so the Roman Empire differed from those that had preceded it. Rome possessed a power and longevity unlike anything the world had ever known. Nations were crushed under the iron boot of the Roman legions, its power was virtually irresistible, and the extent of its influence surpassed the other three kingdoms."[40] And as Walvoord observes, "This hardly is descriptive of either Alexander or the four divisions of his empire which followed."[41]

---

36. Caragounis, "History and Supra-History," 389.

37. Ibid.

38. Ibid.

39. Ibid., 389–90.

40. Miller, *Daniel*, 201.

41. Walvoord, *Daniel*, 161.

Almost all commentators associate the fourth beast with the iron and iron and clay of the statue in chapter 2. In fact, Young asserts, "There can be no question that it is intended to be identical with the iron of the image of ch. 2."[42] Its teeth of iron are usually the characteristic to which most commentators point to support this view. If this association is correct, then it is important to note that the beast has ten horns, which is comparable to the ten toes of the statue's feet. As Miller points out, "'Horns,' like heads, commonly symbolize kings or kingdoms in Scripture (cp. Rev 13:1 and 17:12; also Ps 132:17; Zech 1:18), and the 'horns' in this verse are specifically identified as 'kings' (or 'kingdoms') in v. 24."[43] Consequently, if the ten horns are symbolic of ten kings or kingdoms, then the ten toes ought to be understood similarly as symbolizing ten kings or kingdoms. In fact, Young states, "it is only by inference that we can say the image of ch. 2 has ten toes."[44] But this is not accurate. In 2:47 Daniel makes specific reference to the toes of the statue, and unless we surmise that the statue was in some way deformed, it follows that the statue had ten toes. The inference from the ten horns is supporting evidence, not constitutive evidence.

Aramaic has distinct words for "king" (מֶלֶךְ) and "kingdom" (מַלְכוּ). "King" is used in only 3 verses in chapter 7—Dan. 7:1, 17, 24—while the word "kingdom" is used in six verses—Dan. 7:14, 18, 22, 23, 24, 27. Although sometimes the word "king" is used to represent a kingdom, these terms seem to be used distinctly in chapter seven. This seems to be illustrated especially in verse 24 where both terms are used: "As for the ten horns, out of this kingdom (מַלְכוּתָה, ḥaṭuklam) ten kings (מַלְכִין, n̄iklam) will arise; and another *king* will arise after them, and he will be different from the previous ones and will subdue three kings (מַלְכִין, n̄iklam)."

Lucas points out, "In the ANE, horns represented power and strength. By metonymy they came to symbolize the holders of power. In Mesopotamian art, gods and deified kings have horned headgear."[45] Black reports that, "From the early third millennium BC onwards a cap with up to seven superimposed pairs of horns is the distinctive head-dress of divinity."[46] However, the fact that Daniel observes ten horns is a problem for the view that this beast is symbolic of the Roman Empire. Of course it is no less problematic for those who claim that the beast represents the Greek empire. As Walvoord notes, "This and the succeeding matter has no correspondence either to the history of

---

42. Young, *Prophecy of Daniel*, 146.

43. Miller, *Daniel*, 201.

44. Young, *Prophecy of Daniel*, 147.

45. Lucas, *Daniel*, 180.

46. Black, *Gods, Demons and Symbols*, 102.

Greece or to the history of Rome."[47] Young attempts to circumvent the problem by asserting, "Since the number *ten* indicates completeness, we need not regard the horns as representing then specific *contemporary* kings."[48] However, Young's take here seems contrary to other instances in which he takes the numbers as actually representing that number of realities. For example, with reference to the four metals, Young holds the view that these are four actual kingdoms referring to "the four empires of this prophecy . . ."[49] Some may argue that Young takes this as four empires because Daniel interprets it this way. However, the same is true of the ten horns. In verse 24 the interpreter identifies the ten horns as ten kings that will come up out of the fourth kingdom: "As for the ten horns, out of this kingdom ten kings will arise." For Young to take the four metals as symbolizing four actual kingdoms, and then to take the ten horns as a symbolic number that does not represent ten actual kings, either in succession or simultaneously, betrays an arbitrary and inconsistent application of his hermeneutic principles.

Walvoord gives a helpful summary of the primary divergent views on the significance of the ten horns.

> Interpreters of this chapter who agree that it is Roman divide three ways in their explanation of how this relates to the Roman Empire. Amillennial scholars like Young and Leupold tend to spiritualize both the number ten and the number three, and thus escape the necessity of finding any literal fulfillment. Both of them find literal fulfillment impossible because there are no ten kings reigning simultaneously in the Roman period. Young, however, considers fulfillment in the Roman Empire in the past, and no further fulfillment is necessary. Leupold finds ultimate fulfillment at the second coming of Christ, rather than in past history. Premillennialists offer a third view, providing literal fulfillment: ten actual kingdoms will exist simultaneously in the future consummation.[50]

Walvoord's characterization of Young's view is similar to the Preterist view in that the Preterists consider some or all of the prophecies fulfilled in the past, particularly in the events of 70 AD. Many Preterists hold that the kingdom of God, symbolized by the stone in Daniel 2, to have been established in the death, burial, and resurrection of Christ, but that the kingdom is now growing into a mountain. Stanley Paher is representative of this view: "Therefore, the kingdom of God was meant to endure throughout the ages,

---

47. Walvoord, *Daniel*, 162.

48. Young, *Prophecy of Daniel*, 147.

49. Ibid., 74.

50. Walvoord, *Daniel*, 162.

increasing in its influence like Daniel's description of the stone cut from the mountain (2:34–36, 45), which itself 'became a great mountain and filled the whole earth' (v. 35). The kingdom would grow, and operate like the mustard seed and the leaven, until it accomplished its heavenly purpose among men."[51]

Although the Amillennial view does not seem to be correct, it does not seem to be correct to characterize this view as spiritualizing the numbers ten and three as Walvoord claims. That Young, for example, takes the number ten as symbolic of completeness is not strictly spiritualizing, and Walvoord does the same thing with the four wings of the leopard. He does not hold that there are four literal *somethings* of the Greek empire that literally correspond to the four wings. So, the fact that Young and others take the number ten as symbolic rather than actual does not of itself disqualify this view. If it did, then it would be necessary for Walvoord and other conservatives to disqualify their own view about the four wings of the leopard. One way to avoid this criticism is to propose that the four wings of the leopard are symbolic of the four *somethings*, e.g., the four winds or the four directions, either one of which is applicable to Alexander's empire.

COMING OF THE LITTLE HORN: 7:8

8—   "While I was contemplating the horns, behold, another horn, a little one, came up among them, and three of the first horns were pulled out by the roots before it; and behold, this horn possessed eyes like the eyes of a man and a mouth uttering great boasts."

The fourth beast and the ten horns intrigued Daniel such that he stopped to contemplate them: "While I was contemplating the horns, behold, another horn, a little one, came up among them, and three of the first horns were pulled out by the roots before it; and behold, this horn possessed eyes like the eyes of a man and a mouth uttering great boasts." Young argues that this horn is not like the horn in chapter 8 because "this horn is not described as growing in stature."[52] At least one more time Young refers to the fact that this horn is not described as growing. However, the word used, though in the Pa'el stem, indicates ascending or coming up. Although the stem does not allow the idea of a continued growing, the meaning certainly has the idea of the process of coming up. The little horn did grow. It simply did not continue to grow. In fact, unless the horn suddenly appeared full grown, it would certainly have to grow to get to the height it was when Daniel began to describe it. Also,

51. Stanley W. Paher, *Matthew 24: First Century Fulfillment or End-Time Expectation?*, 45.
52. Young, *Prophecy of Daniel*, 147.

the growing of the little horn is implied when, in verse 20, the description of this horn states that it was "larger in appearance than its associates." Since when Daniel first saw it he described it as a "little horn," it would certainly have to grow to become larger than the other horns. The difference between this description and the one in chapter 8 is that here Daniel is simply not commenting on its growing, but on its actions. Wood states, "'Little' indicates only that this horn started small, as it gradually emerged among the grown horns, not that it remained small; for the context, especially verse twenty, shows that it finally became the greatest of all."[53]

Mills argues that the little horn is Vespasian who comes up after the three previous kings, each of which, according to Mills, "will be disposed of in his own order."[54] This requires a succession of kings, and such a succession is evident in Mills' presentation. Against this view is the fact that the little horn is said to come up "between" the ten horns. The preposition בֵּין (*ñeb*), which is used only one other time in the Aramaic texts of the Bible, Dan 7:5. There it is used to describe the position of the three ribs "in its mouth between בֵּין its teeth."[55] This certainly cannot indicate a succession in the sense of "after its teeth," but must be understood spatially. Some may argue that the conquest of the three great world powers by the Medo-Persian Empire necessarily involved a succession. The problem with this argument, however, is that the word "between" is not used with reference to the relation of the ribs to each other, but of the three ribs to the teeth. That the conquests of the three world empires were successive is certainly true, but it is also certainly true that all of these conquests took place while the teeth existed. The conquests did not take place after the teeth existed, but during the existence of the teeth.

If the same preposition in the same chapter is used in the same way here, it indicates that the little horn comes up at a time when all the other ten horns are in existence, that is, not successively but simultaneously. Perhaps the ten horns arose in succession, but they are all in existence when the little horn comes up. In fact, Evans asserts, "it is hard to avoid recognizing that the three uprooted horns must be contemporaneous,"[56] and he acknowledges that the language indicates "the ten horns appear to be present on the fourth beast when it arrives on the scene (v. 7) . . ."[57] Later, however, he says, "Remember, however, that the text of Daniel 7 states that the ten horns and the little horn are kings, not kingdoms (v. 24). That fact would seem to conclusively

53. Wood, *Daniel*, 187.

54. Mills, *Daniel*, 75.

55. See KBH, s.v. "בֵּין."

56. Evans, *Four Kingdoms*, 396.

57. Ibid., 177.

favor having the horns be sequential unless they can be taken to represent ten contemporary Hellenistic rulers. To argue that as many as ten Hellenistic kings existed who ruled contemporaneously with Antiochus IV seems a highly dubious endeavor."[58] What Evans is saying here is that those who hold that Antiochus IV is the little horn must propose the actual simultaneous reign of ten kings in the Hellenistic Empire, which, as he says, is a doubtful possibility. But the same problem holds for those who hold that this refers to the Roman Empire in the time of Christ or shortly thereafter. To argue that as many as ten Roman kings existed who ruled contemporaneously also seems to be a highly dubious endeavor, to use Evans' expressions.

Wood argues, "The word 'uprooted' (*raqª*) connotes a gradual process, where new growth pushes out old. The new king will not take control of all three areas at once, then, but over a period of time."[59] However, there is no lexicographical evidence that this is the connotation of this word. TWOT points out, "Its usage is paralleled closely by Hebrew."[60] The Hebrew cognate is used in Ecc 3:2: "A time to plant and a time to uproot [לַעֲקוֹר, *rôqaʿ al*] what is planted." In fact, KBH gives the meaning, "to be plucked out Da 7$_8$."[61] There is no sense here of a "gradual process" in which "new growth pushes out old." Rather as Miller notes, "The uprooting of three horns symbolizes that three kings or kingdoms (nations) will be conquered by the new ruler. Being 'uprooted' denotes a violent overthrow and does not imply that an individual will merely succeed a previous king (or kings) to the throne. Nor does it mean that the king will simply displace other rivals for his position of leadership."[62] Also, the word "uproot" in verse 8 indicates that the word "subdue" in verse 24 should not be taken merely to mean "to humble," as it is used elsewhere in Daniel. The term "uproot" implies a violent subjugation, not merely a humbling of the previous kings.

Concerning the problem of the "uprooting" of the three horns, Evans proposes an explanation. He recognizes the fact that, "With regard to the three emperors, one can argue that Vespasian did not actually uproot (v. 8) or subdue (v. 24) them."[63] After making this concession, however, he goes on to argue, "it does not seem at all farfetched to view Vespasian's becoming emperor as equivalent to the 'uprooting' of the three 'kings.' The uprooting in the vision could simply be a symbol of the operation of impersonal historical

---

58. Ibid.
59. Wood, *Daniel*, 188.
60. TWOT, s.v. "עָקַר."
61. KBH, s.v. "עקר."
62. Miller, *Daniel*, 203.
63. Evans, *Four Kingdoms*, 405.

forces—the pushing aside of three inconsequential rulers to make room for a more imposing one."[64] The problem with this proposed solution is that it contradicts what the text actually says. Verse 24 states that "he will subdue three kings." Since verse 24 is the interpretation of Daniel's vision in verse 8, this means that the "uprooting" is done by the little horn, not by "impersonal historical forces." Evans makes additional proposals, floats other hypothetical scenarios, and offers more speculation, but these are sufficient to demonstrate that, the notion that Vespasian is the little horn of Daniel 7 is both historically inaccurate and forced.

Little Horn as Antiochus IV Epiphanes

Towner proposes that the little horn is Antiochus IV Epiphanes but admits that this conclusion "is open to considerable question."[65] However, Young mounts a devastating criticism of this view, some of which is presented below, and he demonstrates that the little horn cannot be Antiochus IV.[66]

> Nearly all expositors are in agreement that this horn [in chapter 8] has reference to Antiochus Epiphanes. Now, the basic question is, Are we to identify this horn with the "little horn" of ch. 7? If such identification can be made, then we must conclude that the fourth empire is Greece. If, however, such identification cannot be made, we are forced to the conclusion that the fourth empire is not Grecian. Such a comparison must, of course, be a just one. We must not overrate the importance of minor divergences in the descriptions, but must seek to discover whether or not there are major divergences. What, then do we discover? This question may be answered by presenting in tabular form the representations of the two horns.

---

64. Ibid., 404–5.
65. Towner, *Daniel*, 95.
66. Young, *Prophecy of Daniel*, 275–79.

Table 12: Young's Comparison of the Horns in Chapters 7 and 8

Ch. 7	Ch. 8
1. The horn is called a little horn.	1. The horn is said to come forth from littleness.
2. Diverse from the horns which preceded it.	2. No similar statement made concerning this horn.
3. The horn "comes up."	3. The horn "goes out."
4. In coming up, the little horn uproots three of the ten previous horns.	4. The horn goes out from one of the four horns which had come up in place of the great horn upon the head of the he-goat. It does not uproot any horns before it.
5. Personalized traits—eyes as the eyes of a man and a mouth speaking great things—are given to this horn.	5. No personalized traits, unless possibly the words "and trampled them" of 8:10 might be so considered.
6. Nothing is said about a growth in size of this horn. On the other hand, the little horn acts as though it were great. Its mouth speaks great things; it has a look more stout than its fellows, it makes war with the saints and prevails against them, it wears out the saints, and thinks to change times and laws, and the saints are given into its hand until a time, times and the dividing of a time, but nowhere is this "little" horn described as becoming great.	6. Stress is immediately placed upon the great growth in size of this horn.

7. The little horn carries on his warfare until the final judgment. He, together with the fourth beast from which he rose, is destroyed by Divine judgment. In order to introduce the statement of his destruction the reader is given a majestic judgment scene, and from this supreme judgment council the books are opened, and the beast was slain and given to the burning fire.

7. Wholly different is the end of this horn. Of him it is merely said that "he shall be broken without hand." Hardly any stress is placed upon his death.

8. The saints who are persecuted by the "little" horn receive the kingdom.

8. Nothing is said of any reward being given to those who were persecuted by this horn.

Of the various differences above listed, some are obviously more important than others. The purpose of ch. 7 seems to be to stress the unique character of the "little" horn. This appears first of all in the explicit statement of the diversity of this horn from those which had preceded it. Wholly in keeping with this description is the fact that the beast itself from which the horn grows, is diverse from the three beasts which had preceded it. In ch. 7 the reader's attention is thus drawn to the unique character of the beast and also of the "little" horn.[67]

Perhaps the best brief refutation of the view that the little horn of chapter 7 is Antiochus IV Epiphanes is made by Gleason Archer.

> There can be no question that the little horn in chapter 8 points to a ruler of the Greek empire, that is, Antiochus Epiphanes (cf. 8:9). The critics therefore assume that since the same term is used, the little horn in chapter 7 must refer to the same individual. This, however, can hardly be the case, since the four-winged leopard of chapter 7 (i.e., 7:24) clearly corresponds to the four-horned goat of chapter 8; that is, both represent the Greek empire which divided into four after Alexander's death. The only reasonable deduction to draw is that there are two little horns involved in the symbolic visions of Daniel. One of them emerges from the third empire, and the other is to emerge from the fourth.[68]

---

67. Ibid., 276–77.

68. Gleason L. Archer, Jr., *A Survey of Old Testament Introduction*, 398.

One of the most difficult problems in identifying the little horn of chapter 7 as Antiochus Epiphanes is that, with reference to the Roman Republic in the time of Antiochus, there are no historical kings to correspond to the ten horns. Of course the same problem faces those who conclude that the fourth beast is Roman Empire—neither are there ten kings of the Roman Empire.

Little Horn is a Man

As Daniel was looking, he saw that the little horn had "eyes like the eyes of a man and a mouth uttering great boasts" (v. 8). C. F. Keil points out the peculiarity of this observation: "But why the eyes of a *man*? Certainly this is not merely to indicate to the reader that the horn signified a man. This is already distinctly enough shown by the fact that eyes, a mouth, and speech were attributed to it."[69] Keil proposes that the eyes are said to be of a man not in contrast to the beast, but in contrast to "a higher celestial being, for whom the ruler denoted by the horn might be mistaken on account of the terribleness of his rule and government."[70] It seems highly unlikely, however, that this designation would be given simply to avoid a possible misunderstanding. If that were the case, then it would seem necessary to add a multitude of additional descriptions in order to avoid the many misunderstandings that no doubt have come from the other parts of the vision. Keil's notion does not seem too far off, however. It may be that the eyes are said to be "of a man" in order to emphasize the fact that this is just a man in contrast to some heavenly being, not to avoid a misunderstanding, but to stress the fact already indicated otherwise that this is only a man, not a demon, or an angel, or Satan. Montgomery points out, "It is universally accepted that these two human traits, the most expressive of the individual person, interpret the little horn as an individual."[71]

Daniel states that the mouth uttered "great boasts." Miller proposes that these great boasts are "the king's arrogant assertions, particularly his blasphemies against the true God (cf. 7:25)."[72] This seems certainly to be the case in light of the fact that the interpreter of the dream states, "he will speak out against the Most High" (7:25) as Miller suggests. However, at this point in the vision, it is not made clear that the "great things" that the mouth of the horn boasts are blasphemous. As Lucas puts it, "At this point no particular attitude

---

69. C. F. Keil, *Biblical Commentary on the Book of Daniel*, in *Ezekiel, Daniel*, vol. 9, *Commentary on the Old Testament in Ten Volumes*, C. F. Keil and F. Delitzsch (Grand Rapids: William B. Eerdmans Publishing Company, 1978), 229.

70. Ibid.

71. Montgomery, *Daniel*, 291.

72. Miller, *Daniel*, 202.

is explicitly attributed to the small horn. It is simply said to have human eyes and to speak impressively."[73] However, in the flow of Daniel's book, "speaking great things" is reminiscent of Nebuchadnezzar's pride and arrogance for which he was "humbled." Although at this point the expression "speaking great things" may not necessarily imply blasphemies, it certainly seems to suggest pride and arrogance to an extreme.

Concerning the Preterist view of the identity of the little horn, Evans remarks, "It must be conceded, however, that they [Preterists] lack a single consensus interpretation of the little horn that can be said to be *the* preterist interpretation."[74] Futurists claim that there are no historical events nor historical personages that can be said to coincide with the prophecies of the rise of the little horn and the demise of the fourth beast, therefore these events must yet be future. Consequently, they generally associate the little horn with the Antichrist of Revelation. But we will deal with this in more detail as the prophecy progresses.

Appearance of the Ancient of Days: 7:9

9—   "I kept looking until thrones were set up, And the Ancient of Days took His seat; His vesture was like white snow and the hair of His head like pure wool. His throne was ablaze with flames, its wheels were a burning fire."

As we have seen, Lucas holds that this is the focal point of the chiastic structure that began in verse 2b. As Daniel continued to look he saw that "thrones were set up, and the Ancient of Days took His seat; His vesture was like white snow and the hair of His head like pure wool. His throne was ablaze with flames, its wheels were a burning fire." Jeffrey Niehaus remarks that Daniel's vision "is perhaps the most 'human' glory theophany yet portrayed in the Old Testament."[75] Walvoord claims that what Daniel saw was "thrones in heaven."[76] This seems to be the generally accepted view. However, Daniel does not say that the thrones are set up "in heaven," or any other particular place. Verse 22 states that "the Ancient of Days came and judgment was passed in favor of the saints of the Highest One." This implies that the Ancient of Days came to where the saints were and then passed judgment, and verse 13 states, "I kept looking in the night visions, and behold, with the clouds of heaven

73. Lucas, *Daniel*, 180–81.

74. Evans, *Four Kingdoms*, 162.

75. Jeffrey J. Niehaus, *God At Sinai: Covenant and Theophany in the Bible and Ancient Near East*, 323.

76. Walvoord, *Daniel*, 163.

one like a Son of Man was coming, and He came up to the Ancient of Days and was presented before Him." If the one like a Son of Man was coming with the clouds of heaven, to where was He "coming" if not to where the throne of the Ancient of Days was set? Goldingay argues, "the opening phrase of v. 9 implies a continuity of perspective: Daniel continues to look in the direction he had been looking. That the scene takes place on earth is presupposed by v. 22," since the Ancient One is said to come.[77] Lucas points out that elsewhere Goldingay argues, "in the HB, where specifically God is judging, the scene is normally on earth (Jer. 49:38; Joel 3[4]:1–2, 12; Zech. 14:1–5; Pss. 50; 96:10–13)."[78] Lucas rejects this notion and asserts, "it is questionable whether any part of the vision in Dan 7 is to be thought of as located anywhere other than in 'mythic space,' as Collins puts it."[79] However, if this appearance is a theophany, as Niehaus supposes, this indicates that the thrones were probably set up in heaven, but the throne of the Ancient of Days moves down to earth, where most theophanies take place.

The symbolism depicting the appearance of the Ancient of Days is variously interpreted. Most commentators hold that the snow white clothing depicts God's purity. Although the Ancient of Days is engaged in judging the kingdoms of the world, He is not soiled by their presence, nor is His judgment in any way swayed by their influence. God's justice is pure and righteous without favoritism or unjust prejudice. Many commentators hold that the hair that is white like wool also depicts purity. But, in this judgment scene, it is more likely that the white hair is designed to signify the wisdom of the Ancient of Days. As Towner puts it, "God has white hair, appropriate for one called the Ancient of Days. The early rabbis thought that God appeared at the Exodus as a young, black-haired holy warrior—but here as at Sinai, God appears as a wise and honorable judge."[80] These are the two qualities most desperately needed in a judge—absolute moral purity that is not persuaded by outside influence and wisdom that comes from mature experience. In other words, God is not judging the fourth beast simply because this beast makes war with His people. God judges righteously, and the judgment of the fourth beast is because of the sin of the beast itself.

The throne of the Ancient of Days is "ablaze with flames." Miller well captures the significance of this imagery: "'Fire' is commonly a symbol of judgment, and God's throne being engulfed in flames signifies the wrath of

---

77. Goldingay, *Daniel*, 164.

78. Lucas, *Daniel*, 181.

79. Ibid.

80. Towner, *Daniel*, 98.

God that is here being poured out upon the wicked."[81] The intensity of God's judgment is signified by the fact that the throne itself is "ablaze." This is comparable to Nebuchadnezzar heating up the furnace seven times more than usual. God's anger against the fourth beast and the little horn is great and furious. It is also interesting that the throne of the Ancient of Days has wheels (גַלְגַּל, *laglag*), depicting this as a chariot-throne, an image that would have had particular significance in this culture. The chariot-throne would have depicted the Ancient of Days as the Warrior God coming to defeat the fourth beast. The wheels are "a burning fire." This, of course, brings up associations with the vision of Ezekiel. The wheels indicate the universality of God's justice in that it reaches to every place, and none can escape. That God's throne has wheels further supports the notion that the Ancient of Days comes from heaven to the earth to execute justice upon the beast. A curious point is that whereas even the chariots of the gods of Mesopotamia were pulled by some animal, frequently a lion-griffin or lion-dragon (see Figure 19 below[82]), there is no indication that the chariot of the Ancient of Days is pulled by anything or anyone.

Figure 19: Ishkur's Chariot Pulled by a Lion-Dragon

Judgment of Fourth Beast: 7:10

10—   "A river of fire was flowing and coming out from before Him; Thousands upon thousands were attending Him, and myriads upon myriads were standing before Him; The court sat, and the books were opened."

---

81. Miller, *Daniel*, 205.

82. This graphic comes from Black, *Gods, Demons and Symbols*, 52.

In this scene Daniel also sees a "river of fire was flowing and coming out from before Him; Thousands upon thousands were attending Him, and myriads upon myriads were standing before Him; the court sat, and the books were opened." The river of fire seems to depict God's purifying judgment as being poured out at this moment. God is the righteous Judge, but the dispensing of justice takes place at a time of God's choosing. The flowing river of fire indicates that this is one of those times. God's judgment is being poured out on the wicked as Daniel is watching. The great multitude standing before the throne indicates the vastness of God's kingdom and the fact that God's judgment takes place in the open, not in secret. The judgment upon the beast and the little horn will be for all to see and to realize the rightness of God's judgment. Many have identified this as a great multitude of angels, and this may certainly be correct. However, the text does not say they are angels, nor does the text assert that those who constitute the multitude are there for service. They seem to be there as witnesses to God's judgment.

As Daniel is looking he sees this whole scene as a cosmic court in which the books were opened. These books, no doubt, are the records from which the evidence is presented concerning the guilt of the beast. Miller asserts, "In Scripture 'the books' are symbolic of God's memory of the deeds, words, and thoughts of every person who has ever lived (cf. Exod 32:32; Dan 12:1; Luke 10:20; Rev 20:12)."[83] The fact that Daniel characterizes the scene as a court and the fact that he witnesses the books being opened supports the idea that the river of fire depicts the judgment that is now flowing out upon the beast. As such, it may be that the great multitude depicts God's army prepared to go to war against the beast in order to carry out the judgment of God.

Destruction of the Fourth Beast: 7:11

11—   "Then I kept looking because of the sound of the boastful words which the horn was speaking; I kept looking until the beast was slain, and its body was destroyed and given to the burning fire."

Many commentators argue that the scene of the great multitude depicts God's angelic army prepared to execute God's judgment upon the beast. They point out that this is supported by the fact that Daniel next sees that "the beast was slain, and its body was destroyed and given to the burning fire." The "sound of the boastful words which the horn was speaking" grabbed Daniel's attention and caused him to continue looking. No doubt the reference to the boastful words spoken by the horn is mentioned so as to provide the explanation for the present judgment. Since we have concluded that the fourth beast

83. Miller, *Daniel*, 205.

signifies the Roman Empire, this verse clearly states that the empire will be destroyed. As Evans points out, "The destruction of the beast poses a problem for Preterist exegesis because the Roman Empire lasted well beyond the first century AD."[84]

Evans also asserts, "although 7:11 informs us that the fourth beast is slain and his body is thrown into a blazing fire, Daniel 7 does not tell us how the little horn meets his end. It is commonly assumed that the beast and the little horn are destroyed at the same time, and it must be conceded that the fact that verse 11 precedes the passage about the slaying of the beast with one about the little horn speaking boastfully inclines the reader toward that view. I suggest, however, that *the vision allows room for the possibility that the beast survives the little horn.*"[85] Evans is arguing that the little horn is destroyed, but the fourth kingdom/beast lives on after the destruction of the little horn. It will be necessary to quote his entire argument in order to address it in its context.

> Of considerable relevance here is the next verse, which informs us that although they were stripped of their authority, the other beasts "were allowed to live for a period of time." Commentators commonly state that verse 12 indicates that the first three beasts are allowed to live after the fourth beast has been killed, but this interpretation is unsound. For my authority on this I rely on Allan MacRae, who stated that the context of Daniel 7 "makes it very clear that when the fourth beast was destroyed it meant the final end of all four, though each of the first three had been permitted to continue to live for a time." Although MacRae also assumed, as futurists generally do, that "the fate of the little horn . . . is to be understood as included in the destruction of the beast," that assumption rests upon a futurist analytical framework. From the preterist perspective, it is easily undermined. I therefore conclude that the text of Daniel 7 allows the inference that all four beasts survive the little horn. I conclude further that the text does not pursue the matter of the successor kings to the little horn because it was irrelevant to Jewish history—and it should be kept in mind that the history of the Jewish people is central to Daniel 7, as well as to the other three visions of Daniel.[86]

Evans claims that to conclude that the fate of the little horn is included in the destruction of the beast is based upon a Futurist analytical framework. However, Evans fails to prove this or even supply any evidence that would

84. Evans, *Four Kingdoms*, 395.
85. Ibid., 399 (emphasis in original).
86. Ibid.

make one think this is possibly correct. By the same token we can charge Evans with basing his conclusions on a Preterist analytical framework. The fact that the fate of the little horn and the beast go together is not the result of a Futurist analytical framework, but is rather indicated by what the text states. Ultimately Evans argues that Vespasian is the little horn, a view that is inspired by Mills' presentation.

In support of the notion that Vespasian is the little horn, Evans presents Jessie Mills argument that the calculation of the ten kings leading up to Vespasian should begin with Pompey: "As Jessie Mills has sagely observed, *it makes sense from the Jewish perspective to begin the enumeration of Roman rulers with Pompey, the man who brought Judea into the Roman Empire in 63 BC.*"[87] An argumet that has been leveled against this reasoning is that Pompey was never King. Concerning the objection that Pompey was never emperor or king, Evans responds, "Does it necessarily follow, however, that a vision pertaining to Roman rulers in the distant future received by a prophet living in Babylon in the sixth century BC would embody a concept of 'king' that would be identical to the concept of an 'emperor' fixed in the mind of a Roman subject living in the first or second century AD?"[88] Evans goes on to claim, "That such a vision might treat Pompey as a 'king' seems perfectly credible . . ."[89] But the more Evans argues, the more his argument rests suppositions on speculations on unproven hypotheses. Although it is not logically impossible that Pompey might be treated as a "king" by someone in the past, there simply is no evidence that Daniel in fact did this. And if conclusions are to be based on speculations and unproven hypotheses, then anything can be proposed as a solution to the question of who is the little horn. If the interpreter has the option of instilling a meaning into the text according to his own understanding, then terms loose all determinate meaning, and the text can mean whatever an interpreter wants it to mean. It is not legitimate to superimpose a meaning from a possible future use upon a term in its own context. Such a practice makes the text completely unintelligible to Daniel in his own time, and such an approach seems contrary to the fact that Daniel said the angel "made known to me the interpretation" (Dan 7:16). If the angel is using terms in the way Evans proposes, then Daniel would not be able to "know" the interpretation. The fact of the matter is, the term "king" as it is used by Daniel has a determinate range of meaning, none of which could reasonably be applied to Pompey, either in Daniel's time or in the time of the Roman Republic. He simply was not a king. And although Daniel, as a mere

87. Ibid., 404 (emphasis in original).
88. Ibid.
89. Ibid.

human, might make that mistake, using the term 'king' with reference to someone who was not a king, God certainly would not.

Three Beasts: 7:12

12—   "As for the rest of the beasts, their dominion was taken away, but an extension of life was granted to them for an appointed period of time."

Verse 12 states, "As for the rest of the beasts, their dominion was taken away, but an extension of life was granted to them for an appointed period of time." This statement has generated some misunderstandings. Some have proposed that, even though their dominion is taken away, the other three kingdoms continue to exist after the destruction of the fourth beast. For example, Goldingay argues, "The vision in chap. 2 pictures the whole statue being destroyed at once. Here, similarly, all four creatures lose authority together, though v 12b adds a nuance to the picture. . . . More likely, the vision is making a theological point, taken up in vv 14 and 27: the kingdoms submit to God and his people either in receiving judgment or in doing honor."[90] In other words, these three kingdoms either submit and continue on after the destruction of the fourth beast, or they are destroyed along with the fourth beast. However, taking this view sets up a contradiction with the parallel passages in chapter 2. In chapter 2, when the fourth kingdom is destroyed, the entire statue, and consequently the other three kingdoms, is also destroyed. They do not simply "lose their authority." Since these kings lose their dominion, in what sense could they be said to continue?

What is being explained here is the fate of the other three beasts. Now that Daniel sees the fate of the fourth beast, he then sees the fate of the other three beasts. Each beast in turn lost his dominion, but was given an extended time of life (וְאַרְכָה בְחַיִּין, *ʾewaﬁtyyaḥ*ᵉ*b ḥakr*). In fact, the expression "of life" could be translated "in life." Waltke and O'Connor refer to the circumstantial use of the בְ (ᵉ*b*) preposition in which it "serves to qualify the realm with regard to which the verbal action obtains . . ."[91] The text could be saying that these three beasts are given an extension of influence in the realm of the living, not that they themselves continue to exist.

Wood explains, "Whereas the fourth empire and its closing ruler were fully destroyed at the time of this divine judgment, the other three had been given an extension of time. That is, when each of the previous three had

---

90. Goldingay, *Daniel*, 167.

91. Bruce K. Waltke and M. O'Connor, *An Introduction to Biblical Hebrew Syntax*, 11.2.5e.

been brought to an end by the beginning of its respective successor, it had continued on in some sense that was not true of the fourth."[92] In other words, this description is looking back over the span of time from the demise of the fourth beast back to the first. For each of the three previous beasts, his dominion was taken away, but he continued to live on in the following beasts. This is a well known feature of the history of kingdoms, as Mieroop points out: "History rarely knows clear-cut endings. Even when states are definitively destroyed, they leave an impact, the duration of which depends on whether one looks at political, economic, cultural, or other aspects of history."[93]

This notion of influence can perhaps best be illustrated in the relationship between the Greek Empire and the Roman Empire. There was, of course, a long history of development that issued in the Roman Empire as it stood in the time of Christ's earthly ministry and the beginnings of Christianity. However, the spread and gradual dominance of Greek culture resulting from the campaigns of Alexander ultimately issued in a more "unified cultural" environment around the Mediterranean lands, which "underlies the rise and endurance of the Roman empire."[94] Although at the birth of Christianity Rome ruled the world, nevertheless, "The most advanced civilization in the world of Jesus and of Caesar alike was Hellenistic."[95] This civilization influenced the world in virtually all areas, but particularly in science, arts, and language. As Ronald Nash put it, "While Rome achieved military and political supremacy throughout the Mediterranean world, it adopted the culture of the Hellenistic world that preceded its rise to power. Thus, while political control of the Mediterranean belonged to Rome, the culture continued to be Hellenistic."[96] Although the Greek Empire came to an end, because of its influence upon the Roman Empire, it was given an extention of life.

The three previous kingdoms did not continue as kingdoms once they were destroyed, yet they were given an extension of life in that the impact and influence of each previous kingdom on its successors lived on in these kingdoms until they were all ultimately destroyed along with the fourth kingdom. When the fourth beast is destroyed, he and all the other kings are completely destroyed so that they do not continue to live on in any succeeding kingdom (see Figure 20). The "appointed time" is the time of the judgment of the fourth beast and the establishing of the kingdom of God.

92. Wood, *Daniel*, 191.

93. Marc Van De Mieroop, *A History of the Ancient Near East: ca. 3000–323 BC*, 2.

94. Chester G. Starr, *A History of the Ancient World*, 414.

95. Ibid., 431.

96. Ronald Nash, *Christianity and the Hellenistic World*, 19.

Figure 20: Extension In Life

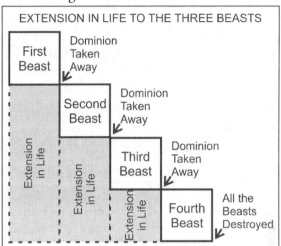

This is precisely what the statue in Daniel 2 indicates. When the stone struck the statue on the feet, the entire statue was destroyed. This implies that there was something of the previous kingdoms in each succeeding kingdom, but all were destroyed when the stone struck the statue, and the text specifically states that "the wind carried them away so that not a trace of them was found" (Dan 2:35). The point here is that once the fourth beast is destroyed, nothing of it or the previous three kingdoms remains. There is nothing in the final kingdom, the kingdom of God, that is infected with the influence of the previous kingdoms.

JESSIE MILLS' ARGUMENTS CONCERNING THE FOURTH BEAST AND THE TEN HORNS

Mills declares that the horns represent "the first eleven rulers" of Rome. Mills provides some historical information and, on the basis of this, concludes, "With all this evidence, I cannot but see that Pompey was the first of the Roman rulers, or the first horn, in Daniel's vision."[97] The first eleven rulers of the Roman Empire, according to Mills, are presented in Figure 21.[98] Mills claims that Vespasian is represented by the little horn that grows up among the ten.

97. Mills, *Daniel*, 74.
98. Ibid., 72.

Figure 21: Mills' Eleven Kings

The *Fourth Beast* in Daniel 7

The "Beast" represents the Roman Empire
Its "Horns" represent the first eleven rulers:

1. *Pompey* (52-49 BC) sole ruler of Rome
2. *Julius* (47-44 BC)
3. *Augustus* (*Octavian*) (31 BC–14 AD)
4. *Tiberius* (AD 14-37)
5. *Caligula* (*Gaius*) (AD 37-41)
6. *Claudius* (AD 41-54)
7. *Nero* (AD 54-68)

8. **Galba (AD 68-69)** ⎫   *These three had very short*
9. **Otho (AD 69)**   ⎬   *reigns, less than a year –*
10. **Vitellius (AD 69)** ⎭   **Vespasian** *"pulled these out"*

11. *Vespasian* (AD 69-79)
    He ruled over theocratic Israel
    only until August 10th, AD 70–
    a very short reign (AD 69-70).

There are several problems with Mills' presentation however. First of all, Pompey was never a king and certainly not a ruler in the Roman Empire. Pompey received the sole consulship as the leader of the senatorial party in 52 BC. In fact, at this time there was not even a Roman Empire. At this time it was the Roman Republic, and Pompey was in fact not even the first consul. As Davies points out, "The Roman Republic presided over the city's growth from provincial obscurity to mastery of the whole Mediterranean. The process began in 509 BC with the first election of the ruling consuls . . ."[99] and later Davies states, "Actium [the battle] was decisive; it ended the civil wars, finished off the Republic, and gave Octavian the supreme title of Augustus."[100]

The battle of Actium was between Antony and Cleopatra on the one side and Octavian on the other and took place in 31 BC, approximately 18 years after the death of Pompey. Historians almost universally identify this event as precipitating the formation of the Empire. So, there was no Roman Empire in the time of either Pompey or Julius. Also, Pompey was not the first ruler in the Roman Republic. The office of temporary dictator was part of the political structure of the Republic, as Klaus Bringmann describes:

> If necessary any of the three senior magistrates could be entrusted
> with military or civil duties. The reorganization of the government

99. Davies, *Euorpe*, 153.
100. Ibid., 158.

did not end with this. Precautions were taken to ensure that differences of opinion among the office holders did not lead to a blockage in the ability of the leaders of the government to act. To avert this danger one of the consuls was permitted, if necessary under pressure from the senate, to appoint a dictator for six months (this term corresponded to the usual length of a military campaign), to whom a deputy, the so-called master of the horse (*magister equitum*), and the regular office holders were answerable.[101]

Lucius Quinctius Cincinnatus (c. 519 BC), was twice appointed to the office of dictator.[102] His first appointment was made so that he might defend Rome against the attacks of the combined forces of the Volscians, Aequians, and the Sabines. After defeating the enemy, Cincinnatus laid down his office as dictator. In 439 Capitolinus again urged the elders to appoint Cincinnatus as dictator to defend Rome against another invader.

According to Davies, Sulla Felix was another dictator: "In 82–79 L. Sulla Felix declared himself Dictator after defeating the partisans of G. Marius (157–86), the greatest soldier of his age."[103] Mills himself quotes a source that states this very fact, but Mills seems to ignore this: "The half century after Sulla's death was one of the greatest confusion and witnessed the final collapse of the Roman republic; sometimes the senate was in full control, sometimes the assembly, and sometimes, a strong man, or dictator; the strong man usually had the support of either the senate or the assembly, but always the army. One of these strong men . . . was Pompey until 48."[104] Since Mills' own research shows that there were other dictators, Mills' conclusion that Pompey was the first is simply not true, and to begin his calculation of the 11 kings with Pompey is arbitrary and motivated by his already present eschatological commitment. Also, Mills asserts, "Most scholars do not accept Pompey as a ruler of Rome. Perhaps the question can be solved if we understand that Pompey did rise in power and become the sole ruler in his period, although Julius did not at the time approve of Pompey as sole ruler of Rome. Nevertheless the Senate approved of Pompey in the absence of Julius . . ."[105] However, from the historical record and Mills' own report we know that other strong men or dictators also were supported by the senate. Even if we grant Mills' claim that Pompey was a ruler of Rome, he was not the first.

101. Klaus Bringmann, *A History of the Roman Republic*, 42.

102. See Philip Matyszak, *Chronicle of the Roman Republic*, 52.

103. Ibid., 156.

104. Ross John Swartz Hoffman, *Man and His History: World History and Western Civilization* (Garden City, New York: Doubleday & Company, 1964), 142; quoted in Mills, *Daniel*, 73.

105. Mills, *Daniel*, 74.

In fact, according to Bringmann, Pompey was never elected dictator and was never, as Mills claims, sole ruler of Rome: "And so the Optimates gradually came round to the plan of using Pompey for their own purposes, initially to restore order in the city and later to topple Caesar. Although Pompey was not to become dictator, it was agreed that for at least two months he would be appointed consul without a colleague."[106] Throughout his career in Rome, Pompey was always under the authority of the senate, and in 50 BC, Gaius Scribonius Curio, a supporter of Caesar, "put forward the proposal in the senate that both proconsuls, Pompey and Caesar, should step down simultaneously from their commands. Although Pompey and his allies were adamantly opposed to this, the proposal was adopted by an overwhelming majority of 370 to 22 votes."[107] This proposal, and other events, ultimately lead to civil war: "But when the rumour spread that Caesar was already marching on Rome, the consul Claudius Marcellus went with a group of allies to Pompey's house and, without authorization by the senate, granted him powers for the military protection of the state and the command over the two legions which had been destined for Syria and empowered him to levy new troops."[108]

Additionally, Mills actually seems to misrepresent the support he claims to have. For his second point about Pompey, Mills provides the following quote: "Pompey [was] commissioned by [the Roman senate] to restore order in the empire in 52 B.C. and elected sole consul, [he] was virtually dictator of the empire until 49 B.C."[109] Mills claims that this quote comes from the "*Illustrated World History*, pp. 238–247."[110] In his "Bibliography of Works Consulted," Mills lists this work as, "Barnes, Harry Elmer. *Illustrated World History*, New York, N.Y. Wm. H. Wise & Co. 1939."[111] However, the quote appears nowhere in this book. Parts of the quote do appear, however. For example, on page 246 the quote actually reads, ". . . senatorial tribune Milo Cicero, who on his return found himself surprisingly popular, had nothing better to propose than that Pompey should be invested with dictatorial powers for the restoration of order."[112] There is no reference to "the empire" as Mills purports. Another partial quote is found on page 249: "Pompey, com-

---

106. Bringmann, *A History of the Roman Republic*, 251.

107. Ibid., 254.

108. Ibid.

109. Mills, *Daniel*, 73.

110. Ibid.

111. Ibid., 201.

112. Harry Elmer Barnes, *Illustrated World History* (New York: Wm. H. Wise & Co. 1939), 246.

missioned by the Senate, left Rome to raise more troops in Italy."[113] Nowhere in this entire chapter does this book refer to the political entity as the "Roman Empire." Mills' evidence seems to turn out to be no evidence after all.

Although Pompey was appointed consul in 52, as Mills notes, Pompey's authority was still subject to the dictates of the Roman senate. In the first of the great civil wars, Pompey had cornered Caesar and planned simply to starve him into submission. However, the senate wanted Pompey to crush Caesar: "They saw an enemy on the ropes, and were impatient for the final blow. . . . Finally, the senate forced Pompey to stake everything that he had fought and campaigned for in his life on a single battle. It was fought at Pharsalus in 48, and Pompey lost."[114] Far from being king of Rome, Pompey was in fact a commander of the army at the ultimate behest of the Roman senate. Pompey was defeated by Caesar at the battle of Pharsalus. Thereupon, Pompey "fled to Egypt, where Aulus Gabinius had left three legions to protect the king he had reinstalled on the throne, but on the orders of the Ptolemaic government Pompey was murdered on his arrival in Alexandria on 28 September 48."[115] Contrary to Mills' claims, Pompey was never elected as dictator and was never the sole ruler of Rome. In fact, it was not until Octavian that "something new, namely the consolidation of the rule of an individual" came about, "which resulted from the process of the collapse of the Republic . . ."[116]

Second, Julius was not king or emperor either. Julius was, "C. Iulius Caesar" who "shared the first triumvirate from 60 BC with Pompey and Crassus," and from 56 BC he served as "Proconsul of the two Gauls."[117] Matyszak describes how, "In 44 he [Caesar] declared himself 'perpetual dictator for the restoration of the commonwealth'—dictator for life, if he so chose," although, "He made no fundamental social, economic or political changes" in the organization of Rome.[118] Caesar did not have the opportunity to declare himself dictator for life, however, for he was assassinated on the fifteenth of March, 44 BC. Julius Caesar was not an emperor of Rome. In fact, all historians of the history of the Roman Empire identify Augustus as the first emperor. Even the Preterist John Evans recognizes that, "Although Julius acquired dictatorial powers before his assassination in March 44 BC, he was never crowned emperor."[119] The most difficult problem for Mills is

113. Ibid., 249.

114. Matyszak, *Chronicle of the Roman Republic*, 189–90.

115. Bringmann, *A History of the Roman Republic*, 259.

116. Ibid., 305.

117. Davies, *Europe*, 158.

118. Matyszak, *Chronicle of the Roman Republic*, 208.

119. Evans, *Four Kingdoms*, 401.

that, if he is going to count from Pompey and Julius who were consuls and proconsuls of the Roman Republic, why not count all of the previous consuls and proconsuls back to 509 BC? To begin the count at this point is arbitrary and seems to be motivated by an attempt to make the history fit the prior eschatological commitment.

Third, contrary to Mills' assertions, Vespasian did not "pull out" the three previous emperors. Mills declares, "There can be no doubt that Vespasian did subdue three kings . . ."[120] But the history does not support this assertion. According to Davies, "The Emperor Galba (r. 68–9), a military man, was killed by the mutinous military in 'the year of the four emperors,' as were his successors Otho and Vitellius."[121] Galba was murdered as the result of a plan conceived and orchestrated by Marcus Salvius Otho, governor of Lusitania (Portugal).[122] Otho had spent much time, money, and effort to ingratiate himself to the emperor Galba to no avail. Galba, who had no natural heir, had chosen to adopt one Lucius Calpurnius Pisco Licinianus as his son and heir. Otho was in enormous debt, but he had "laid hands on a million sesterces a day or so before, and with this war chest he launched a plan to assassinate Galba and Pisco," a plan that was successfully carried out on the fifteenth of January, 69 AD.[123] When Galba was assassinated, Vespasian was in Syria awaiting instruction from Galba, the new emperor, as to how he should continue the execution of the subjugation of the revolt in Judea. Vespasian had sent Titus his son to attempt to ingratiate himself to the new emperor, but as Morgan points out, "Titus had reached only Corinth in Greece when he received the news that Galba had been assassinated, and that Otho and Vitellius were fighting for the throne."[124] Vespasian was no part of the plot, the execution of the plan, or the execution of Galba.

Upon the assassination of Galba, Otho became emperor, but Aulus Vitellius, who had been appointed by Galba to command the legions in Upper Germany, had already begun to move his troops back to Rome to seize power. When Vitellius had arrived at his new post in November of 68, there was great dissatisfaction among the troops, and Vitellius had taken action to secure their favor. When tensions reached their peak, "On 2 January Fabius Valens rode into Colonia Agrippinensis from Bonna with an escort of legionary and auxiliary cavalry (to show that Roman and non-Roman forces were

120. Mills, *Daniel*, 75.
121. Davies, *Europe*, 189.
122. Gwyn Morgan, *69 A.D.: The Year of the Four Emperors*, 63ff.
123. Ibid., 63.
124. Ibid., 179.

equally enthusiastic), and hailed Vitellius emperor."[125] The march of Vitellius' forces to Rome, which had probably begun on the fifth or ninth of January, 69 AD, was designed to depose Galba. It was not until late January that the troops learned that Galba had been assassinated by Otho.

Otho was designated emperor, but reigned only a few months. Vitellius' army was already in route, and Otho gathered his troops to meet this "usurper" in northern Italy. After a few skirmishes, the major battle took place on the road to Cremona. Vitellius' army won the battle and the war, and Otho's forces surrendered the next day. However, Otho's forces who were with him in Brixellum "were not ready to surrender. There would have been more slaughter and suffering, had Otho not committed suicide at dawn that same morning, so ending the campaign and with it, the war."[126] During the struggle between Vitellius and Otho, Vespasian was "playing a waiting game, planning—according to Tacitus—to sit on the sidelines while Otho and Vitellius slugged it out."[127] Once again Vespasian had nothing whatever to do with the circumstances of Otho's suicide.

The fact that Vespasian could not have "uprooted" three kings before him is emphasized by his own reluctance even to conduct a rebellion against Vitellius. Josephus describes how the soldiers and commanders of Vespasian's troops began to speak openly about ousting Vitellius and making Vespasian emperor. Both Licinius Mucianus, governor of Syria, and Tiberius Julius Alexander, prefect of Egypt, encouraged him to make a bid for the throne. Yet in the face of this, Josephus points out, "when he [Vespasian] had shown his reluctance a great while, and had endeavored to thrust away this dominion from him, he at length, being not able to persuade them, yielded to their solicitations that would salute him emperor."[128] Morgan corroborates Josephus testimony: "In the face of this hesitation Vespasian's friends and commanders did all they could to reassure him."[129]

The war that ultimately issued in the death of Vitellius on the twentieth of December, 69 AD was one that Vespasian had hoped would produce a minimal amount of bloodshed. Vespasian had hoped that his advancing troops and the defection of many who had been mistreated by Vitellians would force Vitellius to surrender and abdicate the throne. Instead, Vitellius was unwilling to end the war peacefully, and, consequently, the war extended into Rome

125. Ibid., 55.

126. Ibid., 138.

127. Ibid., 180.

128. Josephus, *The Wars of the Jews*, 10.4.604. πολλὰ δὲ πρὸς αὐτοὺς διατει—νάμενος ἐξ ὧν διωθεῖτο τὴν ἀρχὴν τελευταῖον, ὡς οὐκ ἔπειθεν, εἴκει τοῖς ὀνομάσασι.

129. Morgan, *69 A.D.*, 183.

and finally to the very palace of the emperor where he hid himself from the advancing troops: "Finally, worn out by his wretchedness and his aimless wanderings, he concealed himself in 'a shameful hiding place,' and from this he was dragged by the tribune Julius Placidus (the man is otherwise unknown)."[130] Vitellius was finally slain and beheaded. It is perhaps only Vitellius of whom it can be said that Vespasian "uprooted him." But, the facts of history show that it is simply false for Mills to claim, "There can be no doubt that Vespasian did subdue three kings . . ."[131]

In order to avoid a contradiction between the historical record and his interpretation, Mills seems to want to change the statements in Daniel by re-interpreting them. He says, "Notice v. 20, 'and the meaning of the ten horns that were in its head, and the other horn which came up, and before which three fell.' What the interpretation is speaking of is this: before Vespasian comes to power, three small kings will reign each for a short period, and each will be disposed of in his own order."[132] But, if each of these kings is disposed of "in his own order," then there does not seem to be any basis upon which Mills can claim that Vespasian "subdued" these three kings. In fact, Vespasian had nothing to do with the demise of Galba or Otho, and Vespasian had to be forced into accepting the place as Emperor against his wishes and at the point of a sword. As Josephus points out, "But on his declining, the officers pressed him more insistently and the soldiers, flocking round with drawn swords, threatened him with death, if he refused to live with dignity."[133] In Daniel's vision, the little horn had "a mouth uttering great *boasts*." Considering the fact that Vespasian emphatically resisted the encouragement of his troops to overthrow Vitellius, and the extent to which Vespasian had to be threatened by his men into accepting their wish to see him become emperor, Vespasian is hardly presented as a man who would utter great boasts.

With reference to this king, verse 20 states, "before which three of them fell [וּנְפַל, *ulafnu*]." This can be taken in a chronological sense to indicate that the three previous kings fell before the fourth king came to power. However, this interpretation is eliminated by the interpretation in verse 24 which states that this king "will subdue [יְהַשְׁפִּל, *lipsah^e^y*] three kings." The word translated "subdue" is a Haphel verb which means "to cause to be made low," or "to put down" or "subdue by power." This verb in this form occurs 3 other times in Daniel (see Table 13).

130. Ibid., 253.

131. Mills, *Daniel*, 75.

132. Ibid.

133. Josephus, *The Wars of the Jews*, 10.4. ἀρνουμένῳ δὲ μᾶλλον οἱ ἡγεμόνες ἐπέκειντο καὶ περιχυθέντες οἱ στρατιῶται ξιφήρεις ἀναιπεῖν αὐτὸν ἠπείλουν, εἰ μὴ βούλοιτο ζῆν ἀξίως.

Table 13: שְׁפַל in Daniel

Dan 4:37 (A 34)	"Now I, Nebuchadnezzar, praise, exalt and honor the King of heaven, for all His works are true and His ways just, and He is able to humble [לְהַשְׁפָּלָה, lᵉhašpᵉsah] those who walk in pride." כְּעַן אֲנָה נְבוּכַדְנֶצַּר מְשַׁבַּח וּמְרוֹמֵם וּמְהַדַּר לְמֶלֶךְ שְׁמַיָּא דִּי כָל־מַעֲבָדוֹהִי קְשֹׁט וְאֹרְחָתֵהּ דִּין וְדִי מַהְלְכִין בְּגֵוָה יָכִל לְהַשְׁפָּלָה:
Dan 5:19	"Because of the grandeur which He bestowed on him, all the peoples, nations and language feared and trembled before him; whomever he wished he killed and whomever he wished he spared alive; and whomever he wished he elevated and whomever he wished he humbled [מַשְׁפִּיל, lišsam]." וּמִן־רְבוּתָא דִּי יְהַב־לֵהּ כֹּל עַמְמַיָּא אֻמַיָּא וְלִשָּׁנַיָּא הֲווֹ זָאֲעִין וְדָחֲלִין דִּי־הֲוָה מִן־קֳדָמוֹהִי צָבֵא הֲוָא קָטֵל וְדִי־הֲוָה צָבֵא הֲוָה מַחֵא וְדִי־הֲוָה צָבֵא הֲוָה מָרִים וְדִי־הֲוָה צָבֵא הֲוָה מַשְׁפִּיל:
Dan 5:22	"Yet you, his son, Belshazzar, have not humbled [הַשְׁפֵּלְתְּ, lᵗlepšahᵉ] your heart, even though you knew all this," וְאַנְתְּה בְּרֵהּ בֵּלְשַׁאצַּר לָא הַשְׁפֵּלְתְּ לִבְבָךְ כָּל־קֳבֵל דִּי כָל־דְּנָה יְדַעְתָּ:

In each of the other three cases the word is a Haphel indicating a causal action. In each of the three previous instances it is used to mean "to humble" or "to bring low." God did this to Nebuchadnezzar by giving him the mind of a beast and forcing him to eat grass, crawl, and live outside to be drenched by the dew. God did this to Belshazzar by destroying his kingdom at the hands of the Persians. The idea here in chapter 7 is that this king will humble or bring low three previous kings by destroying them. What Mills is doing here, however, is taking the preposition קֳדָם (m̄adᵃq) in the expressions "pulled out by the roots before it," in verse 8 and "before which three of them fell" in verse 20 as indicating a temporal relation. However, this preposition can also be used to indicate a spatial relation in the sense of being in front of someone. For Mills to take it as temporal without any argument does not prove his point. Since the preposition can be taken spatially, Mills must prove his understanding of its use, not merely assert it. Also, Mills himself declared that Vespasian "did subdue three kings . . ."[134]

The text seems to indicate that the three kings will be subdued at the same time. The fact that the ten horns already exist on the head of the beast when the little horn comes up suggests that these kings are not to be thought of as existing in succession, but simultaneously. That the little horn "comes up" after the ten horns, as described by Daniel, implies that the ten horns are in existence at the time the little horn arises. This may not be a necessary conclusion at this point, but it seems to be supported by the description. But, to think of them as in a succession rather than simultaneously existing is also not a necessary conclusion at this point, and Mills has not attempted to support or prove his position. Whether taken as successive kings or simultaneously existing kings, the fact is, there is no historical evidence to support Mills' claims about the eleven rulers of Rome or about Vespasian subduing three kings.

The fourth problem with Mills' presentation, and perhaps the most devastating critique of the notion that Vespasian is the little horn, is the fact that in verse 24 it is said that the little horn "will be different from the previous ones." Mills does not address this issue, and there is nothing in the historical record and all the descriptions and arguments presented by Mills that indicates that Vespasian is in any way "different" from the other "rulers" in Rome. Missing this critical point seems seriously to weaken Mills' arguments. With all this evidence, one cannot but see that Pompey cannot be the first of the Roman rulers, or the first horn, in Daniel's vision, nor can Vespasian be the little horn.

THE TEN HORNS, SIMULTANEOUS OR SUCCESSIVE?

Miller makes a very important observation about the ten horns: "Since the 'horns' protrude from the fourth beast, these 'kings' (or 'kingdoms') must have a connection with the empire. Therefore one's interpretation of the ten horns will be determined by the identification of the fourth empire."[135] And Wood points out that, "Since the beast had ten horns, which Daniel saw at the same time, the symbolism is that Rome, at the time depicted, would have ten contemporaneous kings, presumably ruling over the same number of subdivisions of the empire."[136] In other words, according to Wood, Daniel's vision did not depict a series of successively appearing horns, but all ten at once. Although this argument seems impressive at first, it is not as significant as it seems. The image of Nebuchadnezzar's dream was the image of a man

134. Ibid.

135. Miller, *Daniel*, 201.

136. Wood, *Daniel*, 186.

that Nebuchadnezzar saw "at the same time," and yet all interpreters agree that it depicts a chronological progression of successive kingdoms. The fact that the horns appear together and that Daniel saw them together is not a decisive point after all. However, neither does it require a series of successive rulers. The two arms of the statue depicted the simultaneous existence of the two parts of the empire, Media and Persia, and the two legs of the statue indicated the simultaneous existence of those two parts. So, seeing the horns together does not necessitate either a succession or simultaneous existence of these kings or kingdoms. But, that they come from the head of the beast certainly indicates that they are associated with the empire symbolized.

However, there is one factor that supports the notion that the ten horns exist simultaneously. The fact that the little horn comes up among the ten horns indicates that the little horn comes up while the other horns are present, and he comes up in the midst of them. So, the act of "coming up" (סִלְקָת, *īaqlis*) indicates the chronological succession. However, none of the other horns are said to "come up," but they are present on the head of the fourth beast when it comes up out of the sea. The text asserts that this horn came up *among* them (בֵּינֵיהוֹן, *ñoheñeb*), not "after them" which would have been expressed אַחֲרֵיהוֹן (*ñoherᵃha'*).

In fact, in verse 24 this horn is said to "arise after them," referring to the previous ten horns: "As for the ten horns, out of this kingdom ten kings will arise; and another will arise after them [אַחֲרֵיהוֹן, *ñoherᵃha'*], and he will be different from the previous ones and will subdue three kings." Earlier we used an interpretive passage to help understand the meaning of a word in the vision passage. We objected to Mills' understanding of the word 'fell' in verse 20 and used verse 24 to clarify its meaning. Verse 24 said that the three horns were "subdued" by the little horn, not that they merely "fell" prior to the little horn "coming up." If we can do this with reference to these two words, why cannot the Preterist do so with reference to the words "among" and "after." The problem is, the word "fell" in verse 20 can be used to mean "fall before as slain" or "humiliated," and that possible meaning is supported by verse 24. However, "to come after" is not one of the possible meanings of "to come up between" or "among." However, to come up "after" can be used to mean "come up after they came up." The later interpretation cannot be used to contradict the earlier vision; else we have a problem with the inerrancy of the text. They must in some way complement each other. So, to "come up after" must mean something that complements the observation that this horn "came up among" or "between" the other horns. In other words, "come up among" cannot mean "to come up after." However, "to come up after" can be used to indicate that the other horns had already come up, were there in existence, so that the little horn comes up after they had come up and while there were still in existence. Verse 24 is saying that the ten horns came up, the ten horns are in existence, and the little horn comes up after them and among them. So, whereas Mills' use introduces an inconsistency between the vision and the interpretation, this use does not introduce such an inconsistency.

It seems we have reached several conclusions thus far in this survey: 1) It is inconsistent to take the ten as a symbolic number, so it must then refer, as the interpreter states, to ten actual kings. 2) The ten horns come up out of the head of the fourth beast, so the ten kings must in some way be associated with the fourth empire. 3) The empire symbolized by this fourth beast is Rome. 4) The proposal of Mills is historically inaccurate and forced in order to make it fit his eschatological scheme, and it would seem that, historically, any other attempt to identify ten kings of the Roman Empire in the same manner would be equally arbitrary. However, that determination must wait for the consideration of the remainder of the vision/dream.

Vision of the Kingdom: 7:13–14

COMING OF THE SON OF MAN: 7:13

13—   "I kept looking in the night visions, And behold, with the clouds of heaven One like a Son of Man was coming, And He came up to the Ancient of Days And was presented before Him."

Lucas remarks, "The introductory formula echoes that used to introduce the vision as a whole (2b) and the vision of the fourth beast (7). This indicates the importance of this final scene."[137] However, this is the eighth time that Daniel has used exactly the same expression, "I kept looking . . ." (הָוֵית חָזֵה, _ŧewᵃh ḥeẓah), so it is doubtful that this expression indicates any particular importance above the surrounding material. Daniel reports, "I kept looking in the night visions, and behold, with the clouds of heaven One like a Son of Man was coming, and He came up to the Ancient of Days and was presented before Him." If there is any greater importance to this final scene, it is because of the presence of the one "like a Son of Man." Walvoord declares that this is the "climax of the vision,"[138] and Miller concurs: "With these two verses [vv. 13–14] the grand climax of the vision is reached."[139]

Daniel sees one "like a Son of Man [כְּבַר אֱנָשׁ, ʾšanᵉʾ rabᵉk]" coming "with clouds of heaven." Niehaus points out that "clouds are theophanic attri-

---

137. Lucas, *Daniel*, 183.

138. Walvoord, *Daniel*, 167.

139. Miller, *Daniel*, 207.

butes—as so often in Old Testament and ancient Near Eastern theophanies."[140] He also points out, "The phrase 'son of man' can indicate simply a human being or humanity (Ps 8:5[4]). Both Ezekiel (Eze 2:1; et al.) and Daniel (Da 8:17; et al.) are addressed as 'son of man'—to emphasize their humanity when angels speak to them."[141] However, in this instance, as theophanic attributes, the clouds indicate that the personage in the appearance is deity. The use of the expression אֱנָשׁ כְּבַר (*san^(e᾿) rab^ek*) for this person, then, implies that this divine being is in some sense human. In fact, in Matt 26:64 Jesus uses the phrase "Son of man" in a way that is strikingly similar to this instance: "nevertheless I tell you, hereafter you will see the Son of Man (τὸν υἱὸν τοῦ ἀνθρώπου, *uoporhtna uot noiuh not*) sitting at the right hand of Power, and coming upon the clouds of heaven." This statement of Jesus is rather peculiar. If He is "sitting," how can He at the same time be "coming"? This statement implies that, having been "presented before" the Ancient of Days, He sits at His right hand on the chariot-throne of the Ancient of Days (remember, Daniel's description of the throne having wheels). It may be that the Son of Man is coming on the clouds of heaven sitting on the chariot-throne at the right hand of the Ancient of Days. This description by Jesus would most likely have generated the image of Daniel's description in the minds of these Jews.

The Son of Man does not simply approach the throne of the Ancient of Days, but is presented to Him. This implies the submission to the king on the part of the one being presented. Of course this perfectly fits Jesus who humbled Himself and became obedient. This and other associations have supported the long held belief that the Son of Man here is none other than the Messiah, Jesus Christ. However, this view is not universally held by commentators. In critiquing this view, Lucas asserts, "Its weakness is that the book of Daniel seems devoid of any messianic hope as usually understood. The 'anointed ones' of 9:25–26 are enigmatic figures, with nothing to suggest that either of them is the Davidic Messiah of later Judaism."[142] However, to claim that the book of Daniel "seems devoid of any messianic hope" seems to require that one completely ignore the imagery of the stone cut out without hands that destroys the statue and grows into a great mountain that covers the entire earth. In his interpretation, Daniel declares, "In the days of those kings the God of heaven will set up a kingdom which will never be destroyed, and that kingdom will not be left for another people; it will crush and put an end to all these kingdoms, but it will itself endure forever." And the use of the stone imagery cannot be merely accidental. The stone associated with

140. Niehaus, *God At Sinai*, 325.

141. Ibid., 324.

142. Lucas, *Daniel*, 185.

the kingdom brings to mind the references to the stone that is rejected by
the builders having become the chief cornerstone (e.g. Ps 118:22). There can
hardly be a more descriptive messianic hope than this. Lucas rejects the identification of the "Son of Man" with Jesus Christ:

> However, it seems both unwise and unnecessary to press the im-
> agery much beyond the observation made by Goldingay (1989:
> 169) that the point of it is establishment of God's rule in a new
> and direct way. Since this rule is later also invested in "the holy
> ones of the Most High," the "one like a human being" is in some
> way symbolic of them, but that does not require a simple one-to-
> one correspondence. Perhaps the significance of the theophanic
> element in the symbolism is to make the point that it is God's rule
> that is being established, even though it is exercised through crea-
> tures. The "human" element in the imagery, as contrasted with the
> beasts, is probably rooted in the Hebrew understanding of humans
> as created in "the image and likeness" of God to have dominion
> over the animals.[143]

In other words, this could be anything except a pre-incarnate Christ.
Lucas' view is not the only alternative to understanding the "Son of Man"
as Jesus. Miller summarizes two other popular views: One view is that "the
'one like a son of man' represents the archangel Michael, and the 'holy ones'
('saints'; cf. vv. 18, 27) of Dan 7 are his angelic followers on whose behalf
he receives the kingdom."[144] The principal problem with this view is the indications in the text of Daniel and also in related texts in the NT that this
individual is divine in nature, not merely angelic. In support of the deity of
the Son of Man, Miller points out:

> However, the most compelling evidence for the messianic iden-
> tification of the son of man is furnished by Christ himself. In
> Mark 14:61–62 he identified himself as that "Son of Man sitting
> at the right hand of the Mighty One and coming on the clouds of
> heaven." There is no other passage in the Old Testament to which
> Christ could have been referring. Furthermore, when Christ made
> the claim, the high priest said, "You have heard the blasphemy"
> (Mark 14:64), demonstrating that Jesus was understood to ascribe
> deity to himself. Young asserts, "The employment of this title by
> Jesus Christ is one of the strongest evidences that He attributed
> Deity to Himself."[145]

143. Ibid., 187.
144. Miller, *Daniel*, 207.
145. Ibid., 209.

The second alternative view that Miller summarizes argues that the "son of man" is "the personification of the people of god, the Jewish nation. They contend that since believers receive the kingdom (vv. 18, 22, 27), the son of man who also receives the kingdom must be symbolic of God's people."[146] Besides the evidence that the Son of Man is deity, a problem with this view is that an expression like "sons of Israel" or "sons of Jacob" is not used here. There is no precedent for using the expression "son of man" to refer to the sons of Israel.

Along a similar line, Towner argues that the phrase "a son of man" is interpreted in later verses as "the saints of the Most High."[147] Towner argues that the reader must understand the "son of man" as interpreted in the same way the beasts were interpreted. In other words, the reference to the saints receiving the kingdom in verse 22 should be taken as the interpretation of the identity of the "son of man." According to Towner, since the beasts apparently refer to collective entities, the expression "son of man" should be taken to refer to a collective entity. Towner argues, "No matter who the son of man may have been in the tradition lying behind Daniel 7, these three texts make clear that he has now been radically interpreted as an identifiable and specific collective entity."[148] This collective entity is, according to Towner, "those *hasidim* [holy ones] by and for whom the Book of Daniel itself was written and for whom the apocalyptic expectation of vindication was a source of particularly crucial comfort. These are the saints who even as the book was being written were experiencing the pangs of persecution at the hands of the Syrian king."[149] In Towner's argument the word "*hasidim*" refers to what Towner describes as "the observant party known in I Maccabees 2:42 and 7:13–17 as the 'Hasideans.'"[150]

So, the saints who receive the kingdom, referred to as the "son of man," is confined to this small sect of persecuted Jews who lived in the second century BC. Besides being a very narrow view, against this view Keil argues, "But the delivering of the kingdom to the people of God does not, according to the prophetic mode of contemplation, exclude the Messiah as its king, but much rather includes Him, inasmuch as Daniel, like the other prophets, knows nothing of a kingdom without a head, a Messianic kingdom without the King Messiah."[151] Additionally, it seems unwarranted to think that the

---

146. Ibid., 208.

147. Towner, *Daniel*, 105.

148. Ibid.

149. Ibid., 106.

150. Ibid., 7.

151. Keil, *Book of Daniel*, 235.

everlasting kingdom, "one which will not be destroyed" (v. 14), would be given to this small band of Jews, or that such language would be used with reference only to them. Notwithstanding the exclusivity of such an event, Towner holds that, "It is they [the *hasidim*] who expect the reward of their devotion in the form of an everlasting dominion."[152] Of course by this Towner means that they will participate in this kingdom along with others, not be the exclusive participants. However, to conclude this goes beyond the statements of the text in the way Towner has interpreted it. The text says, "the saints took possession of the kingdom" (v. 22). If the saints are the *hasidim*, as Towner argues, then they are the ones who take possession of the kingdom, and no others are mentioned or included. Additionally, they are not said simply to participate in the everlasting kingdom, but to "take possession of it." Towner's identification of the "son of man" with this exclusive group simply does not fit the text. Also, Walvoord effectively argues,

> Obviously, the expression the Son of man should be interpreted by the context. In verse 13, He is presented as being near the Ancient of days, and in verse 14 given dominion over all peoples and nations. This could not be an angel, nor could it be the body of saints, as it corresponds clearly to other Scriptures which predict that Christ will rule over all nations (Ps 72:11; Rev 19:15–16). Only Christ will come with clouds of heaven, and be the King of kings and Lord of lords over all nations throughout eternity. Inasmuch as all the nations which survive His purging judgment and come under His dominion are saints, it would be tautology to make the Son of man the personification of the saints.[153]

Walvoord makes what seems to be an observation that is devastating to Towner's thesis. This "son of man" is said in Daniel's vision to come "on the clouds of heaven." If the expression "son of man" refers to the *Hasidim*, how can it be said of them that they come on the clouds of heaven? There does not seem to be a convincing reason to take this reference as anything other than an appearance of the pre-incarnate Christ. It is also important to notice that the kings—in 7:17 Daniel says, "These great beasts, which are four in number, are four kings," using the word מַלְכִין (*ñiklam*), "kings," not מַלְכוּת (*ṯuklam*) "kingdoms" as in 7:27—are portrayed as vicious and destructive animals, while this one is presented as being like a human being. The world-wide kingdom that the beasts endeavored to gain by their ferocity and destructive tactics they ultimately lose and the "Son of Man" gains and holds forever.

152. Towner, *Daniel*, 106.
153. Walvoord, *Daniel*, 168.

The contrast between the kings portrayed as beasts in comparison to the one who receives the eternal kingdom, who is portrayed as a man, may help to clarify why the little horn has eyes like a man. The first beast, portrayed as a lion with the wings of an eagle, is made to stand on his hind feet like a man once the wings are plucked. Most commentators associate this with Nebuchadnezzar's experience in chapter 4. It is when Nebuchadnezzar raised his eyes toward heaven and his reason returned to him that he "blessed the Most High and praised and honored Him who lives forever." As was related in the dream, his mind was changed from that of a man, and he was given a beast's mind. Once he acknowledged that the Most High rules in the kingdoms of men, he was given back the mind of a man, indicated by the fact that his reason "returned" to him. In a sense, the beast became a man when he humbled himself before God. By contrast, out of the head of the fourth beast comes up a little horn with eyes like a man, and a mouth speaking great things—reminiscent of the "great things" spoken by Nebuchadnezzar that brought about his demise. Perhaps the imagery here is that this little horn aspires to be a man, but is unable to become a man because he blasphemes the Most High rather than humbly submitting to God's authority. Perhaps what is being portrayed here is that the little horn aspires to present himself as "the son of man." Perhaps the little horn is presenting himself as the Messiah, boasting that he is the one who has destroyed or subdued all the other kingdoms and is the rightful ruler of the world. If this is accurate, it also forms an *inclusio* by contrast with the first beast. Whereas the first beast becomes a man through humility, the last beast aspires to be the son of man but is destroyed because of his arrogance—beastliness.

GIVING OF THE EVERLASTING KINGDOM: 7:14

14—   "And to Him was given dominion, glory and a kingdom, that all the peoples, nations and men of every language might serve Him. His dominion is an everlasting dominion which will not pass away; and His kingdom is one which will not be destroyed."

It is not clear how Daniel obtained this information. The fact that the dominion is everlasting and the kingdom is one that cannot be destroyed are not things that can be seen with the eyes. In other words, they are not specifically represented by any particular symbol in the vision. Rather, they are concepts. Perhaps some voice announced this to him, or he was given this impression as he was witnessing the presenting of the Son of Man to the Ancient of Days. Perhaps this is one of the things that was announced by the angel to Daniel which he does not report. This notion might be an inference from the theology of the Messianic kingdom of which Daniel was most certainly aware. As

Isaiah declared, "There will be no end to the increase of *His* government or of peace, on the throne of David and over his kingdom, to establish it and to uphold it with justice and righteousness from then on and forevermore. The zeal of the LORD of hosts will accomplish this" (Isa 9:7).

The language used here occurs earlier in Daniel, as Lucas points out: "The phrase 'people of every race, nation, and language' has been used before of the rule claimed by Nebuchadnezzar (3:4, 7, 29; 4:1[3:31]; 5:19) and Darius (6:25), but only God's rule is said to be everlasting (2:44; 4:3[3:33]; 4:34[31]; 6:26)."[154] Also, in Daniel's interpretation of the meaning of Nebuchadnezzar's dream he points out to the king, "wherever the sons of men dwell, or the beasts of the field, or the birds of the sky, He has given them into your hand and has caused you to rule over them all" (2:38). The parallelism between chapters 2 and 7 have already been noted and is acknowledged by all interpreters. Correspondingly, Nebuchadnezzar's reign is comparable in description to the kingdom of the "one like a son of man." Assuming that the "Son of Man" is Christ, this seems to set up a relationship between Nebuchadnezzar and Christ, that the first is perhaps a type of the second. In fact, the contrasts between Nebuchadnezzar and Christ, as well as the correspondences, may indicate that Nebuchadnezzar functions as a type of Anti-Christ (see Table 14 below).

Table 14: Parallelisms Between Nebuchadnezzar and Jesus

Nebuchadnezzar	Jesus
Dominion and a Kingdom Are Given to Him by God	Dominion and a Kingdom Are Given to Him by God
Nebuchadnezzar's Kingdom is World-wide	Christ's Kingdom is World-wide
Nebuchadnezzar is Absolute Ruler	Christ is the Absolute Theocratic King
Nebuchadnezzar Forces All to Worship His Image	Everyone Will Worship Him the Image of the Invisible God
Nebuchadnezzar's Kingdom is Destroyed	Christ's Kingdom is Never Destroyed
Nebuchadnezzar Attempts to Kill the Jews	Christ is Killed by the Jews
Nebuchadnezzar is Humbled by God	Christ Humbles Himself
Is Given the Heart of a Man	Became a Man

154. Lucas, *Daniel*, 185.

Additional comparisons and contrasts may suggest themselves, but these are sufficient to illustrate the possible parallelism that exists. Nevertheless, the text describes the kingdom of the "Son of Man" in terms not applied together to any other kingdom, and some terms are not applied at all to any other kingdom. In contrast to the kingdoms of the beasts, His kingdom will never be destroyed. Interestingly, the word translated here "destroyed" (חבל, *lbḥ*) is not the one used to refer to the destruction of the fourth beast in 7:11. That word is אבד (*db'*). In fact, of the five times that חבל (*lbḥ*) is used in Daniel, only once is it used of actually destroying something. In the other four instances, it is used of not being destroyed—three of those are with reference to the kingdom, and one is when, in 6:22[23], Daniel declares to the king, "My God sent His angel and shut the lions' mouths and they have not destroyed me." The one instance in which חבל (*lbḥ*) is used of actual destruction is in 4:23[20] when, in interpreting the king's dream of the tree, Daniel relates the watcher's words as, "Chop down the tree and destroy it." KBH indicates that while the word אבד (*db'*) is used to mean "perish" or "destroy,"[155] the word חבל (*lbḥ*) is given the meaning "hurt" or "damage."[156] It may be that חבל (*lbḥ*) is used for emphasis. That is, unlike the kingdoms of men that will be utterly destroyed, the kingdom of the "Son of Man" will not even suffer harm.

Interpretation of the Vision: 7:15–27

Interpretation of the Vision Requested: 7:15–16

DANIEL DISTRESSED: 7:15

15—   "As for me, Daniel, my spirit was distressed within me, and the visions in my mind kept alarming me."

Having seen the vision of the beasts and the Son of Man, Daniel is distressed, particularly to understand the meaning of the fourth beast. We must not forget that this vision occurs in the first year of Belshazzar, about 553 BC. Even if Nebuchadnezzar's dream of chapter 4 occurred in the final years of his reign, it would still have been as much as 15 years since that experience. There is no indication that Daniel experienced any other such events in this period. After 10 to 15 years of silence, all of a sudden to be confronted with this dream must certainly have been disturbing. The text says, "As for me, Daniel, my spirit was distressed within me, and the visions in my mind kept alarming me."

155. KBH, s.v. "אבד."
156. KBH, s.v. "חבל."

The parallelisms between this chapter and chapter 2 are strengthened here. Daniel's response to the vision is similar to Nebuchadnezzar's response to his dream. Nebuchadnezzar's spirit is troubled, and he anxiously desired to know the meaning of it. The images are ominous and frightful in themselves, and, unlike Nebuchadnezzar's distress in chapter 4, perhaps brought on by a sense that it applied to him, there is no indication that Daniel's distress was due even to a partial grasp of the meaning of the vision.

INTERPRETATION REQUESTED: 7:16

16—   "I approached one of those who were standing by and began asking him the exact meaning of all this. So he told me and made known to me the interpretation of these things:"

It is particularly interesting that Daniel, of whom it is said in 1:17, "Daniel even understood all kinds of visions and dreams," apparently is unable to understand this vision. There is an interesting shift that begins here in chapter 7. Whereas in the previous chapters, others received visions or had dreams that Daniel interpreted, now Daniel is having a vision for which he needs an interpreter. With the greatness of Daniel's gift, he is still a limited human being, and the things of God ultimately go beyond the grasp of even the wisest and most gifted. The text states that Daniel "approached one of those who were standing by and began asking him the exact meaning of all this." The following material is Daniel's account of the meaning as this is communicated to him. The one whom Daniel approached is generally understood to be an angel. Although the text does not state this, it certainly seems to make sense. There is no reason to think that anyone else was in the room with Daniel when he was experiencing the vision, and there is no reason to think that Daniel would think that any other man would be able to interpret the vision.

The word that is used here and translated "meaning" is פְּשַׁר, (răsᵉp). As TWOT points out, "The word became a standard introduction to the exegetical sentences in the commentaries written in Qumran. A sentence of scripture is followed by ͑orhsip 'its interpretation is:'"[157] The text is saying that this angelic being told Daniel that he would give him an exegesis or explanation of the vision—"its interpretation is . . ."

157. TWOT, s.v. "פְּשַׁר."

Summary of the Vision Given: 7:17–18

FOUR KINGS: 7:17

17— 'These great beasts, which are four in number, are four kings who will arise from the earth.'

The interpreter initially gives a very brief summary of the meaning of the entire vision. The word "kings" is used here, rather than "kingdoms," and this may be a metonymy for the kingdoms, as Goldingay suggests. Goldingay also refers to the "forces of disorder symbolized by the crashing waters" of the sea.[158] This disorder, or chaos, is reminiscent of the waters of the great deep over which the Spirit of God hovered in the creation account. The great deep was indicative of the chaos and disorder out of which God brings order by the force of His Word. That the sea is symbolic of the world of mankind is made plane here. As Walvoord explains, "the sea represents symbolically the nations covering the earth, and what is symbolic in Daniel 7:3 is literal in Daniel 7:17."[159]

EVERLASTING KINGDOM: 7:18

18— 'But the saints of the Highest One will receive the kingdom and possess the kingdom forever, for all ages to come.'

Although the beasts will arise out of the earth, they will not possess the earth. As the text states, "But the saints of the Highest One will receive the kingdom and possess the kingdom forever, for all ages to come." Lucas points out that, "The phrase 'the holy ones of the Most High' has produced almost as much debate as the phrase 'one like a human being.'"[160] Many have proposed that these are angelic beings. One argument put forward for this view, using Goldingay as an example, points out that, "In the OT, קְדוֹשִׁים [holy ones] most commonly denotes heavenly beings."[161] Lucas explains this position more thoroughly: "The strength of this position is that there is general agreement that, when the adjective *mîšodᵉq* is used as a noun in the HB, it usually refers to heavenly beings. The only undisputed use of it to refer to humans is Ps. 34:10, with Deut. 33:2 and Ps. 16:3 as debatable cases."[162] Several arguments have been made opposing this interpretation, but the most devastating is that verse 21 declares that the "other horn" will overpower or prevail against

158. Goldingay, *Daniel*, 173.
159. Walvoord, *Daniel*, 172.
160. Lucas, *Daniel*, 191.
161. Goldingay, *Daniel*, 176.
162. Lucas, *Daniel*, 191.

the saints/holy ones. Also, verse 25 states that the horn that arises after the ten will "wear down the saints of the Highest One." The term "wear down" is בְּלָא (ʾlb), which has the idea of being worn out from constant harassment. The cognate Hebrew term, בלה (hlb), is used in Ps 32:3 to refer to one's body wasting away: "When I kept silent, my body wasted away through my groaning all day long." It is also used in various places in the Pentateuch to refer to clothes or shoes that are worn out. It is difficult to think that this merely human king would be able to overpower and prevail or do anything that would "wear out" an angelic being, much less many of them.

In response some have argued that Dan 8:10 indicates that the small horn of verse 9, presumably a man, "grew up to the host of heaven and caused some of the host and some of the stars to fall to the earth, and it trampled them down." This statement seems to indicate that this man had the power to cause some of these "stars" to fall to the earth and to trample them. However, this objection assumes that the stars are angelic beings. Too much is assumed in this objection to attempt to deal with it here. The details of this passage and its relation to the issues of the identity of the saints in Dan 8:10 will be dealt with at the appropriate point. Also, Walvoord short-circuits this objection by including in the reference to holy ones "the saved of all ages as well as the holy angels which may be described as 'the holy ones.'"[163] Whether the word 'saints' includes the angels or not may not admit of a definitive answer at this point, a position that Goldingay takes: "Dan 7 is too allusive to enable us to decide with certainty whether the holy ones are celestial beings, earthly beings, or both."[164]

However, it seems fairly clear that this group at least includes the human beings who are, by faith, the children of God. It is perhaps instructive that Daniel does not ask about the identity of the saints of the Most High. This may indicate that he naturally understood them to be the people of Israel, and this seems to be the way any reader contemporary with Daniel would have understood the reference. At present this seems to be the most likely group to constitute at least part of those indicated by the word "saints," that is, the people of Israel who are, as Paul says, "a Jew inwardly" (Rom 2:29).

These saints or "holy ones" will "receive the kingdom and possess the kingdom forever." There is very little room for difference of opinion about the fact that these "saints" will receive the kingdom and possess it forever. As Young points out, "They are not to establish or found the kingdom by their own power."[165] However, what exactly is mean by "the kingdom" is a

163. Walvoord, Daniel, 172.

164. Waltke, "Kingdom Promises as Spiritual," 263.

165. Young, Prophecy of Daniel, 158.

point of bitter controversy between the Preterists and the Futurists. Preterists generally hold that the kingdom of God, symbolized by the rock striking the feet of the statue in Daniel 2 and growing to become a mountain covering the entire world, "can be viewed as the advent of the Christian religion in the first century AD and that the process of the rock growing into a mountain that fills the earth has continued unto our day."[166] Jessie Mills argues, "Dan. 7:20–25 indicates when the saints will receive the kingdom of God and reign therein without religious competition. It was established during the days of 'those kings' in AD 33 Roman calendar, and was relieved of any divine religious competition when the temple in Jerusalem was destroyed in AD 70." Bruce Waltke describes this view as follows: "By 'kingdom promises as spiritual' is meant God's OT promises in covenants, types, and prophecy to come into the world in the person of his king and establish his righteous, universal, everlasting, beneficent reign as fulfilled, according to the NT witness, in the advent of the Lord Jesus Christ. His advent occurred in two phases: First in flesh, and then, after his ascension to his heavenly throne, in the Holy Spirit, by whom he forms his body, the church, in the world."[167]

Futurists generally identify the kingdom of God in Daniel 2 and 7 as ultimately fulfilled in the Millennial kingdom on earth to be established at the second coming of Jesus Christ.

> Premillennarians of course recognize the validity of more than one aspect of the kingdom. They insist, however, that the millennial form of the kingdom of God is not fulfilled by the eternal state, nor a present rule of God in the hearts of men. . . . It should be obvious, however, that the millennial kingdom, though in some respects the consummation of much kingdom truth in Scripture, is not the sum total of God's kingdom purpose. There is, of course, a validity to the concept of an eternal kingdom to be identified with God's government of the universe. In contrast, however, to this universal aspect, the millennial kingdom is the culmination of the prophetic program of God relative to the theocratic kingdom or rule of the earth. This in one sense began in the creation of Adam in the Garden of Eden, continued through human government, was manifested in the kingly line which ruled Israel, and has its consummation in the millennial kingdom which in turn is superseded by the timeless eternity which follows. Though there is a rule of God in the present age which can properly be described

---

166. Evans, *Four Kingdoms*, 413.

167. Bruce K. Waltke, "Kingdom Promises as Spiritual," in *Continuity and Discontinuity: Perspectives on the Relationship Between the Old and New Testaments*, ed. John S. Feinberg (Westchester, Illinois: Crossway Books, 1988), 263.

by the word kingdom, it is not the fulfillment of those prophecies
that pertain to the millennial reign of Christ upon the earth.[168]

It will not be possible to enter into the debate on the nature of the
kingdom of God. However, as we progress through various passages of the
rest of Daniel's prophecy, we will consider those statements that relate to the
kingdom of God and attempt to discover what view these passages seem to
support or promote.[169] So far in Daniel's prophecy we have seen the kingdom
of God as the final world kingdom. In chapter 2, as the kingdoms represented
by the metals were kingdoms on this earth, so the stone that grew into a
mountain indicates a kingdom on this earth. Various texts have declared that
the kingdom is an everlasting kingdom that cannot and will not be destroyed
or harmed in any way. In chapter 7 we have seen that the kingdom will be
received by the Son of Man and by the saints of the Most High. The saints will
receive the kingdom and possess it forever. There is nothing in any of these
texts so far encountered that would indicate that the various passages are not
referring to the same kingdom. In other words, there is no reason at present
to think that the kingdom in chapter 2 is a different kingdom than the one
referred to in chapter 7. Nor is there any reason given in the various texts that
the references to the kingdom as an everlasting kingdom, an everlasting dominion, etc., are not talking about the same kingdom referred to in chapters
2 and 7. Although more may be added as we continue through the book, and
some things may change, this seems to be what has been presented thus far
about the kingdom of God.

Vision of the Fourth Beast Extended: 7:19–22

Meaning of the Fourth Beast: 7:19

19—   "Then I desired to know the exact meaning of the fourth beast, which
was different from all the others, exceedingly dreadful, with its teeth
of iron and its claws of bronze, and which devoured, crushed and
trampled down the remainder with its feet,"

Apparently Daniel is not satisfied with simply a general overview of the meaning. He is principally interested in the meaning of the fourth beast and the
other horn that came up among the ten horns. There are some interesting

---

168. John F. Walvoord, *The Millennial Kingdom*, 297.

169. Although it is certainly true that this author approaches these texts from a Futurist, particularly Premillennial perspective, an honest attempt will be made to understand
these texts as objectively as is possible.

differences between the description of this beast in verses 7–8 and the one in verses 19–20 (see Table 15).

Table 15: Comparison of Descriptions

7–8	19–20
dreadful	exceedingly dreadful
terrifying	
extremely strong	
large iron teeth	teeth of iron
	claws of bronze
devoured	devoured
crushed and trampled down the remainder with its feet	crushed and trampled down the remainder with its feet
it was different from all the beasts that were before it	which was different from all the others
ten horns	ten horns on its head
another horn	other horn
came up among them	came up
three of the first horns were pulled out by the roots before it	before which three of them fell
eyes like the eyes of a man	eyes
a mouth uttering great boasts.	mouth uttering great boasts
a little horn	larger in appearance than its associates

In the first description, Daniel sees that the beast is "terrifying and extremely strong," two points that are not repeated in the second description. Also, though he mentions the teeth of iron in both instances, in the first he states that they are large, and in the second he adds that the beast had "claws of bronze."[170] There is no comment on the part either of Daniel or of the interpreter why there is the added reference to the "bronze claws." It is of note, however, that the reference to iron teeth and bronze claws recalls the

170. FYI it is interesting that the Aramaic word for 'bronze' is נְחָשׁ (ṣaḥen), pronounced *nechash*, where the 'ch' is a guttural sound. The Hebrew word 'serpent' is similar in sound and spelling, נָחָשׁ (ṣaḥan). It is pronounced with a long a sound in the first syllable, *nachash*, rather than a short e sound, *nechash*, of Aramaic. The point of interest here is the association of the serpent, the נָחָשׁ (ṣaḥan), referred to as a "fiery serpent," הַשְּׂרָפִים הַנְּחָשִׁים (mîṣarᵉssah mîṣaḥᵉnnah), in Num. 21:6, with the "fiery *serpent*," identified only as the שָׂרָף (fārás), or *seraph*, in verse 8, and the "bronze serpent," נְחַשׁ נְחֹשֶׁת (ṣaḥⁿ tēsoḥᵉn), of verse 9. The serpent in the garden is a נָחָשׁ (ṣaḥan) as well.

reference in chapter 4 to the iron and bronze bands around the stump that was cut down. Finally, whereas the horn is referred to as a "little horn" in the first description, it is said to be "larger in appearance than its associates" in the second. This certainly seems to imply growth.

Meaning of the Little Horn: 7:20

20—   "and the meaning of the ten horns that were on its head and the other horn which came up, and before which three of them fell, namely, that horn which had eyes and a mouth uttering great boasts and which was larger in appearance than its associates."

Daniel wanted to know the meaning of the vision. As we observed in the chart above, in the first description Daniel describes the other horn as "a little one" (זְעֵירָה, haŕeʿez), in verse 20 he describes this horn as "larger in appearance than its associates" (רַב מִן־חַבְרָתַהּ, hāṯarḇah nim bar). TWOT points out that the usage of זְעֵיר (r̄eʿez) is "similar to Hebrew."[171] Consequently, it can be used to mean small in stature or less important or less significant in appearance. It seems out of place, however, to think that the word "small" as it is used in verse 8 would mean anything other than small in stature, since it is only after Daniel sees that little horn come up that it begins to "speak." It seems more likely that Daniel sees the horn as smaller in size rather than being less important or significant in appearance. Correspondingly, the observation in verse 20 that this horn is "larger" would also indicate size rather than importance or impressiveness of outward appearance of demeanor. The words translated "larger" are actually the combination of the word "great" (רַב, bar) and the comparative use of the preposition "from" (מִן, nim) to form the construction meaning "greater than" or "larger than." This seems to indicate that although the horn was small when it appeared, it grew to become larger than all the other horns. Miller also points out that this horn was now "more imposing" not only because it was "probably larger in size," but also "because of the eyes and mouth."[172]

Horn Waging War Against Saints: 7:21

21—   "I kept looking, and that horn was waging war with the saints and overpowering them"

Before the interpreter responds to Daniel, Daniel sees the other horn "waging war with the saints and overpowering them." The word translated "over-

---

171. TWOT, s.v. "זְעֵיר."
172. Miller, *Daniel*, 212.

powering," יְכִל (*likᵉy*), indicates "to prevail against, defeat."[173] This is not a case of the horn merely threatening the saints by demonstrating his superior power, but actually defeating the saints of the Most High. This is in fact a new aspect of the vision, something that Daniel did not report seeing in the previous account. Many commentators take this vision to depict the persecution of the saints. Evans specifically identifies this as such: "The climactic events in Daniel 7 are . . . the little horn's persecution of the 'saints' (v. 21, 25) . . ."[174] Miller also takes this to indicate persecution: "The fact that the little horn would successfully persecute believers had not been expressed previously . . . the little horn will continue his persecution . . ."[175] However, the idea of persecution usually involves the inability of those persecuted to respond in any way to resist the harm or to inflict harm on the persecutors. However, the term "war" indicates a battle between combatants, each attempting to inflict damage on the other. Persecution seems to be primarily one directional, whereas war indicates movement in both directions. Persecution implies only a receiving, while war indicates a giving and receiving. It is not at all clear that Evans and others are using the term in any technical sense. Some may look upon a one-sided conflict as "persecution" because the losing side does not have sufficient forces or power to resist the oppressor. However, it seems more accurate to refer to this action as war rather than persecution. This implies that the saints are at least attempting to fight back even if they are ultimately unsuccessful. Hebrew has a term that is regularly translated "persecute" (רָדַף, *fᴀdar*), and KBH indicates that this is an Aramaic loan-word.[176] So Aramaic had a word for "persecution" which is not used here. These factors indicate that what is being described is more of a conflict than a persecution.

It may ultimately turn out that what is being described is a persecution in a non-technical sense—e.g., if the war is so one-sided that the losing side has no possible chance, and yet the winning side is not predisposed to exercise mercy. But that information is not present in this chapter, and it is perhaps expedient not to read back into this statement information that may be imposed on the basis of a preferred eschatological perspective. Wood captures the idea: "The thought is that saints will be opposed by this person so symbolized, and will be made to suffer."[177]

---

173. KBH, s.v. "יְכִל."
174. Evans, *Four Kingdoms*, 409.
175. Miller, *Daniel*, 212–13.
176. KBH, s.v. "רָדַף."
177. Wood, *Daniel*, 198.

Saints Take Possession of the Kingdom: 7:22

22—   "until the Ancient of Days came and judgment was passed in favor of the saints of the Highest One, and the time arrived when the saints took possession of the kingdom."

The victory of the horn over the saints continues "until the Ancient of Days came and judgment was passed in favor of the saints of the Highest One, and the time arrived when the saints took possession of the kingdom." This statement implies that the war was over who would have possession of the kingdom, and the Ancient of Days rendered His verdict in favor of the saints, which is the basis upon which they take possession of the kingdom. This phrase "judgment was passed" gives the distinct impression of a court scene. This certainly coincides with the observation in verse 10. The word "judgment" here is the same word used in verse 10 and translated "court"— דִּין, *n̄ıd*. This word can also be translated "justice." In fact, the word is used in Dan 4:34 and is translated "just": "Now I, Nebuchadnezzar, praise, exalt, and honor the King of heaven, for all His works are true and His ways just [דִּין, *n̄ıd*] . . ." What is being expressed here is that justice is being rendered, not simply the exercising of superior power to turn the tide in favor of one side over the other.

In the earlier part of the vision, the judgment that was pronounced upon the little horn was death. The word used there, קְטַל (*laṭᵉq*), simply means "to kill." Hebrew has a word that indicates the action of executing someone in the carrying out of a sentence—יָקַע (*ʾaqay*).[178] It is used in Num 25:4 and 2 Sam 21:6, 9. It is strange that Daniel uses the word "kill" rather than an Aramaic equivalent to the Hebrew word "execute," since this seems to be the carrying out of the sentence. Perhaps the added perspective of a "war" indicates the reason. It may be that the little horn is not simply executed as the function of a court, but is sentenced to death by being killed in the war.

Verse 18 states that the saints would "receive the kingdom and possess the kingdom," whereas here it is said they "took possession of the kingdom." The same word is used in both verses—the word is חְסַן (*nasᵃh*)—and in both verses it is in the same stem. The Aramaic Haphel stem is related to the Hebrew Hiphil,[179] which indicates that they in fact "took" the kingdom. KBH also gives the meaning "occupy."[180] This sense seems to coincide with the idea that this is warfare. The idea in both verses is that the saints take possession of the kingdom. The saints cannot take possession of the kingdom

---

178. KBH, s.v. "יקע."

179. See Waltke and M. O'Connor, *Biblical Hebrew Syntax*, §26n1.

180. KBH, s.v. "חסן."

until the appointed time (וְזִמְנָא, *'anmiz^ew*), and that appointed time has been reached with the arrival of the Ancient of Days.

Judgment of the Fourth Beast Explained: 7:23–26

INTERPRETATION OF THE FOURTH BEAST: 7:23

23—   "Thus he said: 'The fourth beast will be a fourth kingdom on the earth, which will be different from all the other kingdoms and will devour the whole earth and tread it down and crush it.'

At this point, the interpreter begins to explain to Daniel the meaning of the fourth beast, the little horn, and those parts that troubled Daniel. The fourth beast will be a fourth kingdom. Whereas in verse 7 the interpreter used the word "kings" to refer to the four beasts, here he uses the word "kingdom" (מַלְכוּ, *uklam*) to refer to the fourth beast. This indicates that the kings are used as standing for the kingdoms they rule, and the kingdoms for the kings that rule them. Daniel had observed on two occasions, verse 7 and verse 19, that this beast was different from the others. Now the interpreter makes the same statement: "which will be different from all the other kingdoms." The word used here, שְׁנָה (*hañăs*), in the Pe'al stem, can be used to mean "be different," indicating a state of being, or "be changed," indicating an action. This word is used 19 times in Daniel and usually has the sense of being changed as an action. The word occurs 6 times in chapter 7 (Dan 7:3, 7, 19, 23, 24, 25, 28). In verse 25 it is used to refer to the fact that the other horn will attempt to "change" the times and the law, and in verse 28 it is used to refer to Daniel's face that "changed" because of the alarm that plagued him. Interestingly, in verse 3 the word is used to indicate that the beasts were "different from one another," indicating a state of being. But there seems to be something more intended in stating three times that the fourth beast is different from all the others. Unfortunately, what constitutes that difference is not specifically stated. It cannot simply be the ruthlessness or ferocity of the beast, since this is simply a matter of degree, not difference in the sense of being changed from one thing or state to another (this is the significance of the word in its other uses).

Some have proposed that the difference is in the fact that the fourth beast will "devour the whole earth and tread it down and crush it." But this doesn't seem to be the case for several reasons: 1) Several times in Daniel, Nebuchadnezzar's kingdom is said to cover the whole earth. For example, in 4:22 Daniel interprets Nebuchadnezzar's dream of the tree and says, "your dominion [is] to the end of the earth." Also, in Jer 27:7 God says, he will give Nebuchadnezzar, "all the nations" so that they will "serve him and his son and his grandson until the time of his own land comes." 2) The fourth kingdom is not the only one that devours. The second beast, the bear, has three ribs in its mouth, and it is told, "Arise, devour much meat!" 3) Treading down and crushing the whole earth seems to be a matter of the degree to which destruction is carried out. It is not different in kind from the kind of actions of the previous beasts. In fact, in verse 7, the first time the phrase occurs, this characteristic is not associated with its destructive power or the extent of destruction. In fact, this observation is made after all the other observations are made, except the fact that the beast had ten horns: "and it was different from all the beasts that were before it, and it had ten horns." The fact that the phrase moves around in the description in relation to the other parts over the three instances indicates that this characteristic is not associated with any particular characteristic listed. 4) Of course the difference could be the cumulative impact of all the attributes attributed to the fourth beast. But this does not seem to work either, since in different instances not all of the attributes are named. 5) Although the conjunction *waw* (ו) can be used to indicate a causal relation, one thing happening because of another, there are other constructions that make this more explicit. Most frequently the *waw* expresses a simple conjunctive idea expressed by the word "and." It does not seem to be the case that the trampling and crushing of the whole earth is that factor that makes it different from all the other beasts.

Interestingly, although all commentators make reference to the fact that the fourth beast is different from the others, no one seems to spend much time attempting to understand why this is the case, and yet this seems to be an important ingredient having been mentioned twice by the interpreter. It seems that most commentators assume that the difference is obvious. Miller states, "This empire will be 'different' in power and duration of its rule from the other kingdoms."[181] But of course that can be said of each kingdom. Each kingdom's power and duration is different from every other kingdom. When comparing the three instances in this chapter in which the fourth beast is described (see Table 16), the only significant difference is the added information about the "other horn" and what it does.

---

181. Miller, *Daniel*, 213.

Table 16: Descriptions of the Fourth Beast

7–8	19–20	23–24
dreadful	exceedingly dreadful	
terrifying		
extremely strong		
large iron teeth	teeth of iron	
	claws of bronze	
devoured	devoured	will devour the whole earth
crushed and trampled down the remainder with its feet	crushed and trampled down the remainder with its feet	tread it down and crush
it was different from all the beasts that were before it	which was different from all the others	which will be different from all the other kingdoms
ten horns	ten horns on its head	ten horns
another horn a little one	other horn	another
came up among them	came up	will arise
three of the first horns were pulled out by the roots before it	before which three of them fell	will subdue three kings
eyes like the eyes of a man	eyes	
a mouth uttering great boasts	mouth uttering great boasts	He will speak out against the Most High
it was different from all the beasts that were before it	larger in appearance than its associates	he will be different from the previous ones

The first instance in which the difference is noted is in verse 7. The text says, "and it was different from all the beasts that were before it, and it had ten horns." This is referring to the beast, not to the little horn. Table 17 sets out this verse with a word-for-word translation.

Table 17: Daniel 7:7

חֵיוְתָא	כָּל־	מִן־	מְשַׁנְּיָה	וְהִיא
beast	every	from	different	And he
לַהּ׃	עֲשַׂר	וְקַרְנַיִן	קָדָמַיהּ	דִּי
to it.	ten	and horns	before it	which

The final clause is simply, "and horns ten to it." In this instance, the conjunction "and" (וְ, *w*) can be translated "even" or "that is": "even ten horns to it," or "that is, ten horns." Waltke-O'Connor refer to this as the epexegetical *waw*: "on the clausal level may serve the goal of introducing a clause restating or paraphrasing the previous clause."[182] In other words, the conjunction may be indicating that this is the characteristic that distinguishes this beast from every other beast. Other beasts had kings in successive rules. The Seleucid kingdom had 31 kings stretching from Seleucus I Nicator in 305 BC to Philip II Philoromaeus (65–63 BC). The Ptolemaic kingdom had as many as 18 kings from Ptolemy I Soter in 282 BC to the co-regency of Cleopatra VII Philopator and Ptolemy XV Caesarian in 31 BC. However, no other kingdom had ten kings ruling together at the same time. In fact, there is no kingdom in history that has had ten kings all ruling in the same kingdom at the same time. The text may be using this very characteristic to distinguish this kingdom from all the others, and expressing it by this single clause: "And *it* was different from every beast which was before it, that is, it had ten horns." This seems to be an argument in favor of the fact that the kingdoms are simultaneous, not consecutive.

INTERPRETATION OF THE LITTLE HORN: 7:24

24—   'As for the ten horns, out of this kingdom ten kings will arise; and another will arise after them, and he will be different from the previous ones and will subdue three kings.'

A limited amount of new information is given in this description. The interpreter states that the ten horns are kingdoms that arise out of the fourth kingdom. What is new in this description is the explicit assertion that the ten horns are ten kings arising out of the fourth kingdom. This was implied in the earlier symbolism, but here it is specifically asserted by the interpreter. This also supports the view that the distinguishing characteristic of this kingdom is that it is constituted of ten simultaneously existing kingdoms. The interpreter

---

182. Waltke and O'Connor, *Biblical Hebrew Syntax*, 39.2.4c.

goes on to describe the "arising" of "another" that will come after them. As was indicated in the earlier symbolism, this king will subdue three kings.

The interpreter does add some interesting new information about this king that arises. The interpreter states, "he will be different from the previous ones." It is perhaps worth noting that just as the fourth beast is said to be "different" from all the other beasts, so the "other horn" is "different from the previous *horns*." The following things are all said of this "other horn":

1.   he will subdue three kings

2.   he will speak out against the Most High

3.   he will wear down the saints of the Highest One

4.   he will intend to make alterations in times and in law

5.   they will be given into his hand for a time, times, and half a time

6.   he will be different from the previous horns

7.   his dominion will be taken away

8.   his dominion will be annihilated and destroyed forever

Except for 1 and 7, and perhaps 8, which can be said of the other beast/kingdoms, this horn/king does do things that are not said of the other beasts or of the ten horns, 1–5. Unfortunately, no very detailed description is given of the other horns other than the fact that they are kings, so to discover how that difference might be identified may be withheld from the reader at this point. But, since the little horn is distinguished from the other horns in that it had the eyes of a man and a mouth speaking great things, this may be the very characteristic that distinguishes it from the other horns.

There is another important point here with regard to the proposal that Vespasian is the little horn. This verse states, "out of this kingdom ten kings will arise; and another will arise after them." According to the historical information on the rulers that preceded Vespasian, each was killed in his turn, and according to Mills own statement, they all "came up and went down in a year and a half . . ."[183] They did not all lose their lives at the same time, but in succession over a period of 1½ years. Mills goes on to point out that these three "were followed by Vespasian"[184] clearly indicating that Vespasian did not become ruler until after them. Since the text states that this horn came up after the ten, and then subdued three kings, this cannot possibly have been Vespasian since, according to the historical information, at least the first two of the three kings were already dead and gone before Vespasian became ruler/

183. Mills, *Daniel*, 75.
184. Ibid.

horn. Indeed, Mills himself acknowledges, "before Vespasian comes to power, three small kings will reign each for a short period, and each will be disposed of in his own order."[185] Also, if, according to the text, this one became king *after* the ten, and then subdued three, these three would of necessity have to be kings at the time this one was raised up as king. This clearly did not happen at the time of Vespasian. Although his three predecessors "went down" in a very short time, it is still an historical fact that at least two of them were gone before Vespasian came to power, and since the text states that this king did not subdue the other three until after he came to power, this clearly disqualifies Vespasian as a candidate for this king. Vespasian clearly could not have "subdued" kings that were already dead and gone by the time he became a ruler/horn.

Jay Adams and Milton Fisher agree that the fourth beast is the Roman Empire, but they propose that the ten horns are ten provinces: "But the text makes clear that it [Rome] would be *different* (cf. v. 7). Look at those ten horns! The other empires were under an emperor. In its early days Rome was a republic, ruled by the senate. And perhaps even more to the point in relation to the ten horns, the Roman Empire consisted of ten provinces, each governed by rulers (proconsuls and praetors) who acted like kings."[186] There are two serious problems with Adams' proposal. First, the text does not say that the ten horns are ten provinces. Rather, the text refers to the ten horns as ten kings. The way the text interchanges the words "king" and "kingdom," these ten horns represent ten kings or ten kingdoms, not ten provinces in a single kingdom. Second, the text does not say the ten horns are ten proconsuls or praetors *acting like kings*. Rather, it refers to them as kings. Additionally, the office of proconsul and praetor existed during the time of the Roman Republic, not in the Roman Empire. Since the prophecy concerns Rome as the Empire, and not as the Republic, these proposals do not even fall within the historical period indicated by the prophecy.

Additionally, Rome was not the only world power that was organized into provinces. The Persian Empire was also organized into provinces. According to Mieroop, "In response [to political problems], the Persians developed a more systematized form of governance: from a union of states held together by the person of the king, it evolved into an empire with provinces. Darius is usually credited with instituting drastic reforms, but he probably regularized a system that had gradually grown under his predecessors."[187] In fact, the Romans actually adopted an organizational structure that was similar to that

185. Ibid.

186. Jay E. Adams and Milton C. Fisher, *The Time of the End: Daniel's Prophecy Reclaimed*, 19.

187. Mieroop, *History of the Ancient Near East*, 296–97.

of the Persians: "The organization of the Persian Empire was more successful than that of earlier empires, and its value is shown by the fact that the
Romans, quite independently, found the same solution to governing a mixture of many peoples."[188] Although there may have been a difference in the
number of provinces, the division of the Roman government into provinces
was not different in kind from that of the Persians, and does not seem to fit
the characterization of being "different from the others."

Adams goes on to propose that Nero is the little horn: "Daniel's little
horn seems to be the same as one of the 'heads' of Revelation. . . . We can more
readily place him in line with the rest of the heads—all Roman Emperors."[189]
This is a very curious observation on the part of Adams since earlier on this
very page he declared that the horns were proconsuls and praetors who "acted
like kings" ruling simultaneously over ten provinces. Now, seemingly without
foundation, at least one of these proconsuls has become an emperor and that
consecutively. He continues, "In Revelation, he is further identified as the
man whose name numbers 666 (13:18). This seems to point rather definitively to Nero Caesar."[190] However, Nero simply does not fit the profile. He
did not subdue three kings. He did not rule at a time when there were ten
kings also ruling in the same kingdom. And he was not essentially different
from the other horns/emperors, and many names of many people throughout
history have been associated with the numbers 666.

Horn Victorious in War Against Saints: 7:25

25—   'He will speak out against the Most High and wear down the saints
        of the Highest One, and he will intend to make alterations in times
        and in law; and they will be given into his hand for a time, times,
        and half a time.'

The interpreter gives a further description of the horn/king/kingdom: "He
will speak out against the Most High and wear down the saints of the Highest
One, and he will intend to make alterations in times and in law; and they
will be given into his hand for a time, times, and half a time." As was described earlier, the horn/king/kingdom had a mouth that was "uttering great
boasts." The expression "great boasts" is a translation of the single Aramaic
word רַבְרְבָן (n̲ab̲ᵉrbar). This is simply the feminine plural form of the word
רַב (bar) used in verse 20 that simply means "great." The horn was "uttering
great *things*." It is not until this verse that we learn that the great things he

188. Joseph R. Strayer and Hans W. Gatzke, *The Mainstream of Civilization*, 23.
189. Adams and Fisher, *The Time of the End*, 19.
190. Ibid.

is uttering are "against the Most High." This indicates that these great things were boastful blasphemes, perhaps claims to deity, equality with or perhaps even superiority to the God of Israel. Such claims were not unusual in the ancient near east. Sennacherib uttered similar boasts as recorded in Isa 14:14: "I will ascend above the heights of the clouds; I will make myself like the Most High."

This is also another nail in the coffin of the notion that the little horn is Vespasian. According to A. B. du Toit, "When Vespasian died on 23 June 79, his last words were reputedly, '*Vae! Puto deus fio*', which may be translated, 'Alas! I think I am becoming a god'—from which we may infer that he was none too happy with the Roman custom of making their emperors divine. For all that, he was immediately declared a god. His humble attitude went a long way towards winning the favour of the aristocrats. Tacitus asserted that he was the first emperor to change for the better (*Hist.* 1:50). He was a hard worker, and the simplicity of his life was an example to the senators of his day."[191] A hard working man with a humble attitude hardly qualifies as a man "speaking great blasphemies."

This king will "intend to make alterations in times and in law." The term "times" is the plural of זְמָן (*nam^ez*), which indicates "appointed times." Neither the Hebrew nor Aramaic word is used in a dual form. This word occurs in verse twelve to refer to the other beasts given an extension of life for "an appointed time." It also occurs in verse 22 to refer to the "appointed time" for the saints to take possession of the kingdom. In Esther the cognate Hebrew term is used to refer to the appointed time set for the celebration of Purim (Est 9:27, 31), and it occurs in Ecclesiastes in the statement, "There is an appointed time for everything" (Ecc 3:1). Montgomery declares that the word "appointed time," which he translates as "seasons," refers to "the calendar feasts."[192] Young states, "not necessarily fixed times for religious observances, but times or seasons ordained by God (cf. Gen. 1:14; 17:21; 18:14)."[193] Wood asserts, "With no indication to the contrary, it is logical to take the words for 'times' (*ñummiz*) and 'law' (*tad*) in a general sense, referring to God's laws of the universe, both moral and spiritual (Gen. 1:14; 17:21; 18:14)."[194] Walvoord says something quite similar: "He will also attempt to 'change times and laws,' that is, to change times of religious observances and religious traditions such as characterize those who worship God."[195] It would

---

191. A. B. du Toit, ed., *The New Testament Milieu*, 4.4.10.

192. Montgomery, *Daniel*, 311.

193. Young, *Prophecy of Daniel*, 161.

194. Wood, *Daniel*, 201.

195. Walvoord, *Daniel*, 175.

seem that most commentators take this expression as being connected with religious observance.

It is perhaps significant that the term translated "law" (דָּת, *dad*) is singular, not plural. Whether this is a reference to the Law of God is not necessarily indicated simply by the fact that this is singular. If the structure of Daniel as was proposed in the introduction to this study is accurate, this would indicate that chapter 7, although functioning as a hinge, is connected by content and perspective with the last major section of the book. This perspective is with reference to Israel. As such, this would suggest that the "appointed times and law" would imply the prescribed observances and the Law of God. The singular form of the word may support this notion as well. The fact that the text states that he "will intend" (סְבַר, *rabᵉs*) to change these may indicate that either he simply does not do it, or perhaps that his efforts are resisted. This may be indicated also by the reference to "wearing down" the saints (see comments above about this term).

The saints will be given over to the horn/king/kingdom for a period of time specified as "time, times, and half a time." There is some debate about the length of time, if it is in fact an actual length of time, that this expression might indicate. Wood presents some convincing reasons why this should be taken as a period of 3½ years.

> First, the placing of a singular (time), a plural (times), and a half (half a time) together makes sense only if these refer to a total of three and one-half of some unit of time (day, week, month, year), a conclusion to which most expositors agree. Second, that this unit of time must be a year follows from a comparison with parallel passages, of which there are several. (1) It has been seen that seven "times" in 4:16 (cf. 4:23, 25) means seven years, and the word for "year" there is the same as here. (2) The Hebrew equivalent of the same phrase, "time, times, and half a time," is used in 12:7 and is best taken to be approximately equal to the 1,290 days of 12:11 and the 1,335 days of 12:12, both of which are just over three and one-half years . . .[196]

Some commentators understand this to be symbolic of an indefinite period, but Montgomery points out that "the 'half' still militates against the theory of a round number."[197] In other words, symbolic numbers do not customarily come in halves. If the number was symbolic, the preciseness of indicating a half would be superfluous. That this expression indicates a period of 3½ years is important as this passage relates to others in Daniel and in the NT.

---

196. Wood, *Daniel*, 201–2.
197. Montgomery, *Daniel*, 314.

Many Futurist commentators associate this period with the mid-week action in Dan 9:27. This certainly seems to coordinate with this period of time when the "saints" of the Most High will suffer under the power of the horn/king/kingdom. If the changing of appointed times and law is related specifically to Israel, then the relation to 9:27 seems to fit, particularly since the verse also points out that he will "put a stop to sacrifice and grain offering." Putting a stop to the sacrifice and grain offering would certainly qualify as changing the appointed times and law.

Also, many commentators see this little horn as pointing to the actions of Antiochus Epiphanes depicted in chapter 11. Antiochus did send out decrees commanding that all religious observances be suspended and replaced with the standard observances as prescribed by the worship of the Caesar. Antiochus encouraged all Jews to renounce their allegiance to the God of Israel and to adopt the observances indicative of allegiance to Rome and Caesar. Whether the statements here are a reference to Antiochus perhaps cannot be settled at this point, but it will be taken up again in chapters 9 and 11.

HORN DESTROYED BY JUDGMENT OF COURT: 7:26

26—   'But the court will sit for judgment, and his dominion will be taken away, annihilated and destroyed forever.'

Although this king will prevail over the saints for an appointed time, the time will come when his dominion will be taken away: "But the court will sit for judgment, and his dominion will be taken away, annihilated and destroyed forever." Here the word "court" is the same one occurring earlier and translated as "judgment," in verse 22, and "court" in verse 10. This is, of course, a description of the same vision Daniel reported in verse 10. The judgment against the king will be that his dominion will be taken away, annihilated, and destroyed forever. It is curious, however, that the text says his dominion will be annihilated and destroyed "forever." Of course the actual annihilation and destruction of the dominion will not continue forever. Rather, the annihilation and destruction will render his dominion incapable of ever being able to be revived. It will be gone forever. The curious point, however, is that the idea of annihilation and destruction would seem to indicate this without the added expression "forever." The addition of the term "forever" seems to emphasize that the kingdom can never be re-established or reinstituted. The term translated "annihilated" is שְׁמַד (dam⁴s) and is used only here in the HB. The Hebrew cognate is used in Dan 11:44 to describe the rampage of the king who will "go forth with great wrath to annihilate [שְׁמַד,dam⁴s] and destroy many."

The term translated "forever" is עַד־סוֹפָא (ʾáfos daʿ), which is the combination of the preposition עַד (daʿ), which means "until," and the noun סוֹף (fos), which means "the end." This is an idiom literally translated, "until the end." As Keil points out, its significance is "to the end of the days, *i.e.* forever."[198] To say that the kingdom will be "annihilated and destroyed" to the end of the days does not mean that the destruction would continue on, but that the results of the destruction would be an everlasting kind of result. In other words, the expression is more a qualifier than a quantifier. Once again this does not fit with Vespasian. Vespasian actually died of an illness, as Suetonius describes:

> In his ninth consulship he had a slight illness in Campania, and returning at once to the city, he left for Cutiliae and the country about Reate, where he spent the summer every year. There, in addition to an increase in his illness, having contracted a bowel complaint by too free use of the cold waters, he nevertheless continued to perform his duties as emperor, even receiving embassies as he lay in bed. Taken on a sudden with such an attack of diarrhoea that he all but swooned, he said: "An emperor ought to die standing," and while he was struggling to get on his feet, he died in the arms of those who tried to help him, on the ninth day before the Kalends of July, at the age of sixty-nine years, seven months and seven days.[199]

As A. B. du Toit puts it, "Vespasian died in 79 A.D. at the age of sixty-nine, the first emperor since Augustus over whom there was no doubt that he died a natural death."[200] This is hardly a description of one who is judged by God and killed. Vespasian's son Titus took over the kingdom, and the Roman Empire continued for hundreds of years. Again this does not fit the characterization of a dominion that is annihilated and destroyed forever. In fact, Vespasian's dominion was not annihilated and destroyed forever. His empire continued on in the reign of his son.

---

198. Keil, *Book of Daniel*, 244.

199. C. Suetonius Tranquillus, *The Lives of the Twelve Caesars*, in *Loeb Classical Series*, trans. J. C. Rolfe (Cambridge, Massachusetts: Harvard University Press, 1914), 24. 320–21. "MCMXIII Consulatu suo nono temptatus in Campania motiunculis levibus protinusque urbe repetita, Cutilias ac Reatina rura, ubi aestivare quotannis solebat, petit. Hic cum super urgentem valitudinem creberrimo frigidae aquae usu etiam intestina vitiasset nec eo minus muneribus imperatoriis ex consuetudine fungeretur, ut etiam legationes audiret cubans, alvo repente usque ad defectionem soluta, imperatorem ait stantem mori oportere; dumque consurgit acnititur, inter manus sublevantium extinctus est VIIII. Kal. Iul. annum agens aetatis sexagensimum ac nonum superque mensem ac diem septimum."

200. Toit, *The New Testament Milieu*, 4.4.11.

Having gone through the verses relating the meaning of the ten horns and the "other horn," some further comments on the statement in verse 24 may be in order. In verse 24 the interpreter described the "little horn" as "another" king or kingdom that will "arise after them [the ten horns], and he will be different from the previous ones." As we observed with reference to verse 24, there were not very many new things said about the "little horn" or "other king/kingdom" from what was described earlier in the chapter. However, that the "other king/kingdom" would be different from all the previous ones was a completely new piece of information given in this verse. It may be that the way in which this horn/king/kingdom is different from the other horns is comparable to the way in which the fourth beast is different from the other beasts, and likewise in the reverse. Although there is very little information given about the other horns, there is one characteristic in the horn/king/kingdom that stands out as quite different from the others. This horn is the only one that was said to have eyes like a man and a mouth speaking great things. Earlier we speculated that perhaps the appearance of the eyes like the eyes of a man may indicate that this horn aspired to be "the man," that is, "the Son of Man," the Messiah. Commenting on the statement in verse 25 that this horn will "speak out against the Most High," Young asserts, "He will employ language in which he will endeavor to set God aside and will arrogate unto himself prerogatives which belong alone to God, cf. 2 Thess. 2:4."[201] If the difference between this horn and the other horns is analogous to the difference between the fourth beast and the other beasts, perhaps that difference is in an aspiration to be like God, that is, to take the place of God. In other words, perhaps there is a relationship between the beast and the other horn that is analogous to be relationship between the Ancient of Days and the Son of Man.

That this difference relates to an effort to be "like God" fits with the other descriptions given by the interpreter. Speaking against the Most High could certainly indicate blasphemy in such a way as to denigrate the God of Israel and promote himself, as Young described. Prevailing against the saints of the Most High could also be a part of this aspiration. This king would endeavor to annihilate the followers of the God of Israel in order to establish a kingdom populated only with his own followers. The fact that the war with the saints seems to be over the kingdom also fits this scenario. Consequently, that which makes the fourth beast different from the other beasts is the very thing that makes the "other" horn different from the previous horns—the aspiration to establish a kingdom in the stead of the kingdom of God, with

---

201. Young, *Prophecy of Daniel*, 160–61.

the beast in the place of the Most High, and the little horn in the place of the "Son of Man." Of course, at present this is just speculation.

Establishing of the Everlasting Kingdom: 7:27

27—   'Then the sovereignty, the dominion and the greatness of all the kingdoms under the whole heaven will be given to the people of the saints of the Highest One; His kingdom will be an everlasting kingdom, and all the dominions will serve and obey Him.'

The final description of the interpreter concerns the establishing of the kingdom. This is another ingredient that seems to support the notion that the characteristic that makes the fourth beast different from the others is the fact that it aspires to be a replacement for the kingdom of God. Here the text states, "all the dominions will serve and obey Him." Just like the kingdom of God in which all dominions serve God, so in the false kingdom, in which this kingdom is constituted by ten other kingdoms, the little horn seeks to exercise dominion over all other dominions.

This is yet another characteristic that bodes ill for the claim that Vespasian is the little horn. It can hardly be claimed that at the end of Vespasian's reign, or even the reign of Titus, that "all the kingdoms under the whole of heaven" were given to the "people of the saints of the Highest One," or that "all dominions" served and obeyed Him.

As we have proposed, the word "saints" seems to refer at least in part to the people of Israel. However, it may not be that the reference should be confined only to this group. Nevertheless, at this point, after the kingdoms of this world have been destroyed, they will receive the kingdom "forever." That the text states that the kingdom will be "an everlasting kingdom" has led many to reject the Futurists' proposal that this could be a reference to the millennial kingdom. However, to say that the kingdom is an everlasting kingdom does not require that it remain in one state or condition forever. The term "everlasting" can be a qualitative reference rather than a quantitative reference. It other words, it is the kind of kingdom that lasts forever. The same kind of expression is used to describe of the fourth beast. As we pointed out with reference to verse 26, the expression "to the end of days" is a qualifier, not a quantifier. So here the term everlasting could be taken as a qualifier indicating the kind of kingdom, not necessarily that the kingdom would continue on as simply an earthly kingdom.

We have already seen that the Son of Man receives the kingdom from the Ancient of Days. It follows that here the kingdom is given to the saints by the Son of Man. But this does not mean that there is no king. As Walvoord puts it, "At the destruction of the fourth empire, the kingdom then becomes the possession of 'the people of the saints of the most High.' This does not mean that God will not rule, as verse 14 plainly states that dominion is given to the Son of man, but it does indicate that the kingdom will be for the benefit and the welfare of the saints in contrast to their previous experience of persecution."[202] The King and His saints possess the kingdom together. It is important that the expression, "His kingdom" (מַלְכוּתֵהּ, ḥêṭuklam), uses a singular personal pronoun, rather than a plural personal pronoun which one would expect if the antecedent were "saints." This indicates that the "He" to which the pronoun refers is the Son of Man.

Wood presents an interesting observation about the next phrase, "all the dominions will serve and obey Him": "A further reason for rejecting the idea of this kingdom being Christ's spiritual rule may be noted at this point. Certainly in the age now existent one does not see the dominions of the world serving and obeying 'saints.' Furthermore, if one holds that this becomes true only after Christ comes again, at which time the eternal state begins (held by those who hold to the idea of a spiritual kingdom), there is little meaning for saying that dominions serve and obey saints then. During the eternal state, all wicked will be suffering the torment of hell."[203] That this kingdom is a physical kingdom on the earth seems to be required by the parallelism with chapter 2. In chapter 2 the stone that destroyed the statue became a mountain the covered the entire earth. As the metals of the statue signified physical kingdoms, there is no reason to think that suddenly the imagery switches to representing a spiritual rather than a physical kingdom. The only reason for concluding this would be a prior theological or eschatological commitment. If the parallelism holds, the kingdom described here is the final kingdom of chapter 2, and the implication is that it will also be an earthly, physical kingdom.

Conclusion: 7:28

28—   "At this point the revelation ended. As for me, Daniel, my thoughts were greatly alarming me and my face grew pale, but I kept the mat-ter to myself."

The translations of this final statement are misleading. The word translated "revelation," מִלְּתָא (ʾaṭ ellim), simply means "matter" or "word" or "affair."[204] It is comparable to the Hebrew word דָּבָר (rabad), which has a comparable range of meaning. The Hebrew word is certainly used to refer to the "word of

---

202. Walvoord, Daniel, 176.

203. Wood, Daniel, 205.

204. KBH, s.v. "מִלָּה."

God," and in that sense it is speaking of a revelation. It is perhaps the same here. The vision given to Daniel no doubt is given to him by God and as such constitutes revelation. Nevertheless, this is not the "revelation." Perhaps a better translation would be, "At this point the word ended," or "the matter ended," or "the communication ended." The revelation may have continued, but not in the form of a vision.

Even though the vision had come to an end, Daniel's thoughts continued to generate great alarm for Daniel. The word "alarm" may indicate dismay rather than simply fear. No doubt Daniel was fearful, but the word may contain the notion that this "alarm" was generated, at least in part, from the fact that many things remained unclear to Daniel. The fact that there was indeed fear along with the dismay is indicated by the fact that Daniel's "face grew pale," literally, "my brightness changed" (וְזִיוַי יִשְׁתַּנּוֹן, *yañiz* *w ñonnaïtsiy*). Daniel did not immediately begin declaring what had been given to him. Rather, the text points out that he kept the matter in his heart (וּמִלְּתָא בְּלִבִּי נִטְרֵת, *ïertin ïbbil* *b* *at* *llimu*).

As we have pointed out several times, virtually all commentators see a parallelism between chapter 2 and chapter 7. Because of this, some have raised the question about the reason for giving Daniel a vision that basically covers the same information that was presented in Nebuchadnezzar's dream. Miller has some helpful observations on this point.

> What was the purpose of repeating the prophecy of the four kingdoms? First, the two accounts complement each other in that they each provide details not found in the other. Second, there may be truth to the idea that the image with its glittering metals portrays the world's kingdoms from humanity's viewpoint—impressive and great, whereas the beasts depict these earthly kingdoms from God's perspective—vicious and destructive. Third, the message probably was repeated to emphasize its certainty. In Gen 41 Pharaoh had two dreams that taught the same truth—a famine was coming upon the land. Joseph told Pharaoh, "The reason the dream was given to Pharaoh in two forms is that the matter has been firmly decided by God, and God will do it soon" (Gen 41:32). Thus the revelation of the four kingdoms in Daniel may have been presented in two forms in order to underscore the certainty of this amazing prophecy.[205]

There is another reason why this vision is given to Daniel and why he placed it in the place he did in his book. The first six chapters have demonstrated that the people of God can expect to live under the yoke of the

205. Miller, *Daniel*, 218.

Gentiles until the establishing of the kingdom of God. However, the children of God can also expect to be able to live and even prosper under these circumstances in many cases. They are to be faithful to God, and He will be faithful to His covenant relation with them. They are to understand the times and the seasons.

In chapter 2, the Gentile world powers that will dominate the world scene until the coming of the Messiah have been presented in a way that does not reveal their true character. That information is given in the vision in chapter 7. The viciousness and the terror of these world powers, especially as they relate to the people of God, is portrayed in these four beasts. But the revelation of the true nature of these kingdoms is placed after the people have been shown that they can not only survive during this time, but even prosper, and that through it all, God will be faithful. As Miller noted, chapter 7 reveals many details that are not included in chapter 2. Although chapters 1–6 are certainly more than simply a preparation for the information in chapter 7, they are certainly not less than that. The revelation of chapters 1–6 has prepared the reader for the harsh realities that are presented in chapter 7. But chapter 7 concludes with the hope of God's people, the establishment of His kingdom.

9

Daniel's Vision of the Ram and Goat: 8:1–27

Introduction

With the beginning of chapter 8, the language of the text reverts to Hebrew. As Lucas observes, "Scholars have long been puzzled by the change back to Hebrew at this point, rather than, say, at 7:2, where there is a shift from referring to Daniel in the third person to first-person speech by Daniel."[1] However, as we proposed in the introduction, it seems clear that with the change of focus from the Gentile world powers specifically to Israel comes the change from the language of the Gentiles, Aramaic, to the language of Israel, Hebrew. Chapter 7 does not have this change because, even though it is part of the change of focus, it serves as a hinge (see Figure 22) to connect the two parts of the prophecy together so that they are not seen as unrelated.

Figure 22: Hinge Structure of Chapter 7

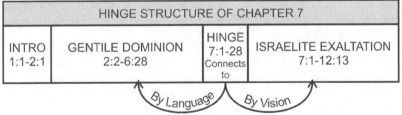

HINGE STRUCTURE OF CHAPTER 7			
INTRO 1:1-2:1	GENTILE DOMINION 2:2-6:28	HINGE 7:1-28 Connects to	ISRAELITE EXALTATION 7:1-12:13

Almost all commentators hold that the visions related in chapter 8 primarily concern the Medo-Persian Empire and the empire of Greece, although

---

1. Lucas, *Daniel*, 212.

there is some divergence of agreement later in the chapter. This vision, then, covers a portion of the same period of history treated in the previous chapter. It seems that beginning with chapter 8, the period of time becomes more focused and narrower in its scope. However, this is not a grid through which later chapters must be interpreted. Rather, it is simply an observation about chapter 8. Young postulates that one reason for this focus is "that the author now intends to deal more in detail with the development of the kingdom of God."[2]

Another reason for dealing with these two kingdoms in more detail is perhaps to focus in on the Greek Empire and to make clear the distinction between the horn in chapter 8 and the Little Horn in chapter 7. Perhaps the goal is to insure that there is no confusion between these two so that the horn is chapter 8 is not mistaken for the final stage of Gentile world powers. Most commentators identify the horn of chapter 8 with Antiochus IV Epiphanes. If it is correct to understand the Little Horn of chapter 7 as the Anti-Christ who will be in power when the Stone strikes the kingdoms of men and destroys them, then it is important for those who will be alive at the time of rise to power of the horn in chapter 8 that they not mistake these events for the time of the establishing of the Kingdom. The history leading up to this person, and the events surrounding his career and demise clearly distinguish this horn from the Little Horn of chapter 7. Additionally, focusing on the horn of chapter 8 may serve to introduce this figure who seems to become a type of the final ruler, the Little Horn of chapter 7, who persecutes the Jews. This symbolism will also be discussed in the commentary on chapter 11.

Several commentators point out that the opening phrase of this chapter tends to link it with the events of chapter 5 such that Belshazzar is a type of the blasphemous horn whose actions directed against God and the people of God are described in such detail here. As such, Towner's comment may capture a major theme of this chapter. He states, "If God's own ground can be invaded, and the very ordinances which he himself established as an abiding assurance of a vital relationship between his people and himself can be rudely set aside by a pagan idolater, can the very security of the universe itself be relied upon? Will not profound questions be raised about God's ability to protect his interests and his people and to complete his saving plan?"[3] In this comment there is the reminiscence of God's declarations at the Exodus: "The Egyptians shall know that I am the Lord, when I stretch out My hand on Egypt and bring out the sons of Israel from their midst" (Ex. 7:5). God proves His superiority again through these blasphemous leaders.

2. Young, *Prophecy of Daniel*, 165.

3. Towner, *Daniel*, 123.

Introduction to the Vision: 8:1

1— In the third year of the reign of Belshazzar the king a vision appeared to me, Daniel, subsequent to the one which appeared to me previously.

The vision that Daniel is about to relate was given to him in the third year of Belshazzar the king. This was probably about 551 BC, probably 12 years before the fall of Babylon. Consequently, this vision occurred before the handwriting experience related in chapter 5.

The Vision Presented: 8:2–14

The Vision of the Ram: 8:2–4

2— I looked in the vision, and while I was looking I was in the citadel of Susa, which is in the province of Elam; and I looked in the vision and I myself was beside the Ulai Canal.

3— Then I lifted my eyes and looked, and behold, a ram which had two horns was standing in front of the canal. Now the two horns were long, but one was longer than the other, with the longer one coming up last.

4— I saw the ram butting westward, northward, and southward, and no other beasts could stand before him nor was there anyone to rescue from his power, but he did as he pleased and magnified himself.

Daniel in Susa

In the third year of Belshazzar, Daniel had another vision. In the vision that came to Daniel, he saw himself in the citadel of Susa beside the Ulai canal. Goldingay points out that although many of the ancient place names remain the same even today, many of the names of the waterways have long since been changed: "The ruins of Susa lie near the River Karun, but the names and the locations of the watercourses in the area seem to have changed over the centuries. Ulay is an ancient name for a waterway near Susa. The vision is located at a gate opening toward a waterway, in the tradition of Ezekiel's vision by the Kebar canal . . ."[4] Susa is approximately 200 miles East of Babylon. In the KJV of Nehemiah it is referred to as Shushan. Nehemiah was the cupbearer in the palace of Susa during the reign of Artaxerxes I from 465 BC to 424 BC.

---

4. Goldingay, *Daniel*, 208.

Capital of the non-Semitic people and district of Elam. Susa (modern Shūh, KJV Shushan) is located in southwest Iran, about 150 miles north of the Persian Gulf and due east of the well-known city of Babylon. French archaeologists have been excavating the site since 1884, discovering that it was occupied as long ago as about 4000 B.C. Its importance in the OT derives mainly from the fact that it was incorporated into the Persian Empire founded by Cyrus in 550 B.C. It became a royal city along with Ecbatana (the other main city in Elam), Babylon, and Persepolis. This was the great period of importance for Susa, although it had known an earlier golden age in the 12th century B.C. (The first copy found of the law code of Hammurabi was discovered at Susa, dated in the 12th century B.C.). The center of Persian Susa was an acropolis or citadel which rose above the city as a rectangular platform surrounded by a massive wall. This was the royal quarter within which the palace stood. The palace was the winter residence of the Persian kings.[5]

DANIEL SEES A RAM

As Daniel looked up he saw a ram that had two horns. One of the horns was longer than the other even though it had come up later. As Daniel watched, the ram charged to the west, to the north, and to the south. It was so powerful that no other animal could stand against it, and none of the animals it confronted could be rescued from its power. Most commentators recognize this ram as symbolic of the Medo-Persian Empire. The fact that one horn is longer than the other may help to clarify the significance of the bear in chapter 7 having one side raised up. As Miller Explains, "Before Cyrus came to power, Media already was a major force, while Persia was a small country holding less than fifty thousand square miles of territory. But Cyrus succeeded in gaining control of powerful Media to the north (ca. 550 B.C.) and then made Persia the more important of the two states. With these nations united, he established the vast Medo-Persian Empire."[6] This description is comparable to the symbolism in chapter 7 and seems to indicate that the raising up of the beast on one side ought to be understood in the same way the longer horn of the ram should be understood. If this is correct, both images indicate the uneven distribution of power and authority in the Medo-Persian alliance, Persia being the dominate force. Although several commentators refer to the testimony of Ammianus Marcellinus, that Persian rulers carried the gold head of a ram

5. Walter A. Elwell and Barry J. Beitzel, *Baker Encyclopedia of the Bible*, 2005.
6. Miller, *Daniel*, 222.

when marching in procession, Lucas points out, "this relates to Shaqur II at the battle of Amida in the early fourth century AD. There is no evidence of crowns or helmets with ram's horns being worn by Persian kings earlier than the third century AD."[7] Perhaps the use of the ram imagery depicts the power without the ferocity of the bear, lion, or leopard.

As Daniel watched the ram, he reports, "He did as he pleased and became great." Goldingay proposes, "There is nothing inherently wrong about 'doing great things' (הִגְדִּיל); but the expression is only used in an unequivocally good sense of God (1 Sam 12:24; Ps 126:2, 3); of human beings it tends to suggest arrogance (Jer 48:26; Joel 2:20; Zeph 2:10; Ps 35:26; Ps 55:13 [12])."[8] The text is translated differently by different translations and commentators. The word translated "magnified" is גָּדַל (*ladag*) and simply means, "made great" or "magnified," but without a stated object it is assumed that he made himself great. Whichever way it is translated, it certainly is reminiscent of other instances in Daniel where a ruler becomes arrogant because of his accomplishments.

The Vision of the Goat: 8:5–8

DANIEL SEES THE GOAT—8:5A

5a— While I was observing, behold, a male goat was coming from the west over the surface of the whole earth without touching the ground;

Next, Daniel saw a male goat coming from the west. He was moving so fast that he did not even touch the ground. This goat had a conspicuous horn between its eyes. It attacked the ram which was still present in Daniel's vision. It destroyed the horns of the ram, threw him to the ground, and trampled on him. There was no one to rescue the ram from the anger of the goat. As soon as the goat began to magnify himself, the large horn was broken and four horns came up in its place.

The references to the ram and the he goat are translations of two different Hebrew words. The word "ram" is אַיִל (*liya*˒), whereas the word translated "he goat" is צָפִיר (*rifas*). Although a sheep and a goat are certainly different, the term "ram" is often used for the adult male of either. Traditionally, however, it has been assumed that the ram, the אַיִל (*liya*˒), refers to a sheep, while the צָפִיר (*rifas*) is a reference to the goat. The goat is usually of "lighter build than the sheep."[9] The difference may have been chosen in order to depict the difference in the kind of military campaigns each ruler conducted.

7. Lucas, *Daniel*, 213.

8. Goldingay, *Daniel*, 209.

9. Elwell and Beitzel, *Baker Encyclopedia*, 103.

Alexander's campaign was swift, indicated by the fact that the feet of the goat did not touch the ground. This swiftness fits with the lighter build of a goat. Lucas makes a similar proposal: "The choice of the goat is best explained by the fact that it is a fiercer and stronger animal than a ram (cf. Jer. 50:8)";[10] as does Wood: "Compared with a ram, a he-goat has greater strength and agility, features significant in the symbolism."[11] Perhaps a ram and a goat are used because of their well-known similarities and differences implying both similarities and differences between the two successive empires.

THE GOAT'S HORN—8:5B

5b—and the goat had a conspicuous horn between his eyes.

Daniel states, "the goat had a conspicuous horn between his eyes." Goats generally have two horns that are straighter than the horns of a sheep, and usually they slant backwards. Apparently this horn pointed forward similar to what one thinks of when picturing a unicorn. This single horn represents Alexander himself. As Miller points out, "The rest of the symbolism is not explained in the text but is clear from history. Coming 'from the west' points to the position of Greece, which was to the west of Medo-Persia (and Palestine). 'Crossing the whole earth' means that Alexander conquered the world of his day, and the goat speeding across the globe 'without touching the ground' portrays the swiftness of Alexander's conquests."[12] Alexander had conquered the entire Near East in only three years.

THE GOAT'S POWER—8:6–7

6—   He came up to the ram that had the two horns, which I had seen standing in front of the canal, and rushed at him in his mighty wrath.

7—   I saw him come beside the ram, and he was enraged at him; and he struck the ram and shattered his two horns, and the ram had no strength to withstand him. So he hurled him to the ground and trampled on him, and there was none to rescue the ram from his power.

Daniel describes the power of the goat: "He came up to the ram that had the two horns, which I had seen standing in front of the canal, and rushed at him in his mighty wrath. I saw him come beside the ram, and he was enraged at

10. Lucas, *Daniel*, 214.

11. Wood, *Daniel*, 209.

12. Miller, *Daniel*, 223.

him; and he struck the ram and shattered his two horns, and the ram had no strength to withstand him. So he hurled him to the ground and trampled on him, and there was none to rescue the ram from his power" (vv. 6–7). The hatred of the Greeks, especially that of Alexander, for the Persians had apparently been growing for years, and, as Wood points out, "Normal strength becomes heightened when backed by emotional heat."[13] The two horns of the ram were broken, symbolizing the utter destruction of the Medo-Persian Empire, and the strength that once characterized the power of the Persians evaporated in the face of the onslaught of Alexander and his army.

THE FOUR HORNS ARISE—8:8

8—   Then the male goat magnified himself exceedingly. But as soon as he was mighty, the large horn was broken; and in its place there came up four conspicuous horns toward the four winds of heaven.

As Daniel continued to watch, "the male goat magnified himself exceedingly." Whereas the ram magnified himself, the goat magnified himself *exceedingly* (מְאֹד, *mᵉʾdoʾ*). This speaks of arrogance that exceeds that demonstrated by the Persian kings. However, "as soon as he was mighty, the large horn was broken . . ." At the height of his power, after having subjugated the entire Medo-Persian Empire, Alexander died in Babylon at age 33 having contracted a fever. Subsequently, his empire was divided between four of Alexander's generals: "and in its place there came up four conspicuous horns toward the four winds of heaven." These military leaders are commonly referred to as the Diadochi (διαδοχαί, *iahcodaid*) meaning "successors."[14] According to Montgomery, understanding the four "conspicuous horns" as symbolic of the Diadochi "has been the almost constant interpretation of the four, with variations as to the names of the Diadochi, since the beginning."[15] This also corresponds to the four heads of the leopard in chapter 7. Also, the fact that the four horns that are said to be "toward the four winds of heaven" perhaps also clarifies the question about the four wings of the leopard in chapter 7. The four heads symbolize the Diadochi who take over the kingdom, and the four wings symbolize the four directions of the compass or the "four winds of heaven."

13. Wood, *Daniel*, 210.
14. *A Greek-English Lexicon* (1996), s.v. "διαδοχή, ἡ."
15. Montgomery, *Book of Daniel*, 332.

The Vision of the Little Horn: 8:9–14

THE SMALL HORN—8:9

9— Out of one of them came forth a rather small horn which grew exceedingly great toward the south, toward the east, and toward the
Beautiful Land.

Daniel reports that, "Out of one of the four horns grew a small horn . . ."
The expression is literally, "and from the one from them . . ." (מֵהֶם אַחַת
וּמִן־הָ, *mehem̱ tạha'ah nim̂u*). This certainly seems to indicate that this new
horn actually grows out of one of the four already present on the head of the
goat. Wood asserts, "The symbolism of this single horn is clear. From one of
the divisions would emerge a king of unusual significance, of which Daniel
was now to take note."[16] Almost all commentators take this horn to represent
Antiochus IV Epiphanes (175–163 BC). Antiochus IV became the eighth
ruler of the Seleucid Empire. This horn "became great against the south, the
east, and the Beautiful Land." The term "land" in the expression "Beautiful
land" is not actually a separate word in the text. However, since the symbolism seems to be that this king, represented by the horn, becomes great against
the south and east, most commentators hold that it is consistent to think
that this is referring to the beautiful "land." Also, there seems to be a connection with this statement and the one that occurs in 11:16 in which the
expression "the beautiful land" is used with the presence of the word "land":
(בְּאֶרֶץ־הַצְּבִי, *ib̂e ssah sere'eb*). The term "the beautiful" is הַצְּבִי (*ib̂essah*)
and also occurs in various places in the Old Testament often referring to Israel:
e.g., "Your beauty, O Israel [הַצְּבִי יִשְׂרָאֵל, *le'arsiy̱ ib̂e ssah*), is slain on your
high places!" (2 Sam 1:19).

Miller gives a helpful explanation of this part of the vision.

> Starting "small" (Heb, *ri't̂as*, "little with the idea of insignificant")
> indicates that Antiochus would have an insignificant beginning.
> Although his nephew, son of his older brother Seleucus IV, was the
> rightful heir to the throne, Antiochus gained this position through
> bribery and flattery. He made notable conquests in "the south"
> (Egypt), "the east" (Persia, Parthia, Armenia), and "the Beautiful
> Land" (Palestine). Palestine is called "Beautiful" (*sēbî*, "place of
> beauty or honor"; cf. 11:16,41; Jer 3:19) not because of its scenery
> but because of its spiritual significance. It was a place of beauty
> and honor because Yahweh God had chosen it as the center of his
> operations on the earth and because his people lived there. Though
> Palestine was in the southern regions, it is singled out because the

16. Wood, *Daniel*, 212.

little horn's rule over the holy land would have enormous consequences for the Jewish people.[17]

TRAMPLING THE STARS OF HEAVEN—8:10

10—　　It grew up to the host of heaven and caused some of the host and
some of the stars to fall to the earth, and it trampled them down.

This horn "grew up to the host of heaven [צְבָא הַשָּׁמַיִם, *miyamaśsah ˀabˁs*]
and caused some of the host and some of the stars to fall to the earth,
and it trampled them down." The phrase "host of heaven" has caused no
little comment and divergence of opinion. The fact that the word "stars"
(הַכּוֹכָבִים, *mibakokah*) also occurs in this description has led some to conclude that this must be a reference to heavenly beings. However, Dan 12:3
associates the imagery of stars with the people of God: "those who lead the
many to righteousness, like the stars forever and ever." Interestingly, those
who identify the "host of heaven" as heavenly beings such as angels usually
confess that, as a result, the meaning is obscure. However, since the parallel
passages in chapter 7 seem to refer to the people of God, there is no reason
not to understand the "host of heaven" also to refer to the people of God.
Goldingay provides a helpful discussion of this issue.

> In the interpretation of the small horn's attack on the heavenly
> army (צבא השמים) similar issues arise to those raised by chap.
> 7. References to the earthly sanctuary in vv 11–12 could suggest
> that the heavenly army is the Jewish people, or the priesthood in
> particular, viewed as of heavenly significance because of their rela-
> tionship with the God of heaven. They are the Lord's armies (Exod
> 7:4; cf. 6:26; 12:17, 51; Num 33:1); they are his heavenly children
> (2 Macc 7:34). It is they who are attacked by Antiochus (1 Macc
> 1:29–38). Yet the people attacked include "some of the stars,"
> which rather points to the heavenly army being a supernatural
> body. Elsewhere "the heavenly army" denotes the actual stars in the
> heavens (Isa 34:4; cf. Gen 2: 1 ; Ps 33:6), and more commonly the
> stars as personalized objects of worship (Deut 4:19; Jer 8:2; Zeph
> 1:5). The stars in the heavens are Yahweh's servants (Judg 5:20).
> Dan 12:3, however, promises that the faithful are destined to shine
> like the stars. The notion of attacking the stars, which goes back to
> Isa 14:13, is applied retrospectively to Antiochus in 2 Macc 9:10;
> and from 169 B.C. Antiochus's coins picture his head surmounted
> with a star, and he entitles himself King Antiochus God Manifest
> (Βασιλευς Αντιοχος Θεος Επιφανης). Perhaps it is the case,

17. Miller, *Daniel*, 225.

then, that an attack on the Jerusalem temple, the people of Israel, and the priesthood is presupposed to be implicitly an attack on the God worshiped there and on his supernatural associates who identify with Israel.[18]

Goldingay commented that the attack was upon "the heavenly army," is a possible translation of the word "host" (צָבָא, *ab^es*). This indicates that perhaps the ones who are attacked are actually an army of the people of Israel, rather than simply the priesthood. "When Antiochus Epiphanes ruled (176–164 B.C.), he attempted to abolish Jewish worship and institute purely Greek rites; the Hasidim and the majority of the people rose up to preserve the old faith."[19] In 1 Macc. 2:42 the Hasideans, who resisted the efforts of Antiochus Epiphanes, are referred to as a "mighty army of Israel": "Then came there united with them a company of Hasidans, mighty warriors of Israel (ἰσχυρὶ δυνάμει ἀπὸ Ισραηλ), all who offered themselves willingly for the law" (1 Macc. 2:42).[20] The support for understanding this reference as applying to the people of God seems sufficient to hold this view to be correct. This seems to go against the arguments discussed in chapter 7 (see page 245f) that the "saints" are angelic beings. If the "host of heaven" are the people of God, particularly Israel and perhaps an army of Israel, then the "saints" must also be a reference to the people of God, at least including the people of Israel if not confined to this group.

The reference to throwing down and trampling upon these "stars" implies severe persecution of the Jews. As Miller explains,

> Antiochus's persecution of the Jews may be considered to have begun in 170 B.C. with the assassination of the high priest Onias III and terminated in 163 B.C. at his death (or even a few months earlier when the temple was rededicated in December 164 B.C.). During this period he executed thousands of Jews who resisted his unfair regulations. In 169 B.C., after a humiliating experience in Egypt when Antiochus was turned back by the Roman commander Popilius Laenas . . . the Syrian king plundered the temple in Jerusalem (taking its treasures, including the furniture that was adorned with precious metals) and committed 'deeds of murder' (cf. 1 Macc 1:20–24; 2 Macc 5:1ff). In 2 Macc 5:11–14 these 'deeds of murder' are said to have included the slaughter of eighty thousand men, women, boys, and girls, even infants by Antiochus's soldiers during this attack upon Jerusalem. Many

18. Goldingay, *Daniel*, 209–10.

19. Elwell and Beitzel, *Baker Encyclopedia*, 931.

20. Bruce M. Metzger and Roland E. Murphy, ed., *1 Maccabees*, in *The New Oxford Annotated Apocrypha*, 191.

other ways in which Antiochus 'trampled' upon the Jewish saints are recorded in 1 Maccabees (e.g., 1 Macc 1:29–32, 41–64). In December 167 B.C., Antiochus committed his crowning act of sacrilege against the Jewish religion by erecting an altar to Zeus in the temple precincts and offering swine on it (cf. 1 Macc 1:37, 39, 44–47, 54, 50; 2 Macc 6:2–5).[21]

MAGNIFYING ITSELF—8:11A

11a— It even magnified itself to be equal with the Commander of the host;

The translation "Commander of the host" is שַׂר־הַצָּבָא הִגְדִּיל (ʾabassah rás lɩdgih), "the great prince of the host." Goldingay points out that "שַׂר־הצבא is a standard term for an army leader (e.g., Gen 21:22; 1 Sam 12:9), and the compound expression needs to be understood in the light of the reference to 'the army' in v 10."[22] Coupled with the fact that this one is referred to as "the Prince of princes" in verse 25, it is interesting that in Josh. 5:14, in what seems to be an appearance of the pre-incarnate Christ, the One who confronts Joshua identifies Himself as "captain of the host of the Lord" (צְבָא־יְהוָה־שַׂר, ḥawhᵉy ʾabᵉs ras). In this declaration, the word 'captain' is a translation of the same Hebrew word used here in Daniel—שַׂר (rás). Many commentators take this to be a reference to God, and understanding this as a reference to God the Son certainly seems to fit the "Captain/Prince/Commander of the host of the Lord." It would not be necessary for Antiochus to know against whom he was magnifying himself. Perhaps Antiochus believed he was magnifying himself against the God of the Hebrews. What someone thinks he is doing, and what he is actually doing, are often incommensurate. Nevertheless, the expression "Commander of the host" could be a reference to the person who orchestrated the rebellion against Antiochus, and the reference to "his sanctuary" may indicate that this person was a priest or high priest.

Although some commentators attempt to identify the "prince" with Onias III, the high priest at this period of time, the events described in verse 10 actually antedate the murder of Onias. To get around this problem, Goldingay proposes, "Perhaps, then, the reference is more generally to Antiochus's usurping the authority of the priesthood over the religious life of the Jerusalem temple."[23] But this involves Goldingay in an inconsistent treatment of the text. If this reference is general, why is not the supposed reference

---

21. Miller, *Daniel*, 226.

22. Goldingay, *Daniel*, 210.

23. Ibid.

to Antiochus likewise general and referring to the general tendency of some
Hellenistic influence? Goldingay, along with most other commentators, has
understood the references up to this point to be rather specific. Suddenly to
shift to a general sense is to engage in hermeneutic inconsistency to avoid an
unpleasant conclusion. If the Prince is a reference to Christ as the Captain
of the army, this implies that the army may be more than simply the Jews.
This seems to have been the case in the conquest. Perhaps "host" includes the
angels of God as well. However, even if this is a reference to Christ as the captain of the army whose sanctuary is thrown down, this would not necessarily
make the reference include angels. In this instance, for Antiochus to oppose
the mighty army of Israel would be to oppose God whose people they are, and
the captain whose army they are.

Sacrifice and Sanctuary—8:11b

11b— and it removed the regular sacrifice from Him, and the place of His
sanctuary was thrown down.

Young believes that the next part of the verse—"he removed the regular sacrifice from Him, and the place of His sanctuary was thrown down"—"relates
wherein this 'acting greatly' consisted. It was the removal of the Temple
sacrifices."[24] In other words, magnifying himself against the Prince was the
act of removing the sacrifices and throwing down the sanctuary. The word
"sacrifice" does not actually occur in the verse. The word so translated is
הַתָּמִיד (dimattah) and, as an adverb, simply means "lasting, continually."[25]
Here the presence of the definite article converts the adverb to a substantive,
literally indicating "the continual." Miller points out that "the term is merely
an abbreviated form of 'ōlat tāmîd, 'a continual burnt offering' (Exod 29:42),
which specifically designates the daily sacrifices."[26]

Montgomery declares that verses 11 and 12 "constitute the most difficult short passage in the bk."[27] There are many different views, but these are
summarized by Walvoord into three general classes:

> First, the critical view that Daniel was a second-century forgery
> written by a pseudo-Daniel regards this prophecy as simply his-
> tory written after the fact and completely fulfilled in Antiochus
> Epiphanes. This, of course, has been rejected by the great major-
> ity of conservative scholars. Second, the view that this is genuine

24. Young, *Prophecy of Daniel*, 172.
25. KBH, s.v. "תָּמִיד."
26. Miller, *Daniel*, 227.
27. Montgomery, *Daniel*, 335.

sixth-century B.C. prophecy, but completely fulfilled historically in Antiochus Epiphanes. Edward J. Young is strongly in favor of this interpretation and speaks in general for many amillenarians who are conservative interpreters. Third, the view that the prophecy is genuine prediction fulfilled historically in the second century B.C., but typical and anticipatory of the final conflict between God and Gentile rulers at the time of the persecution of Israel prior to the second advent of Christ.[28]

One criticism of the third view, the Futurist view, is that there is nothing in the text itself that would indicate a fulfillment beyond Antiochus. However, with types, there is never anything overt in the text containing the type that directly asserts its fulfillment in an antitype. The writer to the Hebrews understands various aspects of the tabernacle and the priesthood as typical of Christ even though the relevant passages in the Old Testament are not prophetic and do not specifically refer to the future. Even though this objection does not have any force in the sense of making the typical interpretation impossible, it is true that there is nothing directly stated in the text that requires a fulfillment beyond the historical fulfillment in Antiochus' actions. Judgment of this view must wait at least until more of the interpretation of Daniel is complete.

The text states, "the place of His sanctuary was thrown down." The verb "was thrown down" (הֻשְׁלַ֖ךְ, *kalsuhᵉw*) does not necessarily indicate a physical destruction. Antiochus did not actually destroy the temple of Jerusalem. To "cast down" can be used in a figurative sense and is so here.[29] Miller explains that this term "does not mean that the temple was destroyed but that it would be desecrated,"[30] and Young points out that, "Antiochus did not actually tear down the temple, although evidently he desecrated it to such a point that it was hardly fit for use."[31] In other words, the temple was desecrated so that it was unusable for sacred things, as if it has been thrown down and destroyed.

TRANSGRESSION AND TRUTH—8:12

12—   And on account of transgression the host will be given over to the horn along with the regular sacrifice; and it will fling truth to the ground and perform its will and prosper.

---

28. Walvoord, *Daniel*, 186.

29. Ezek 18: 31 is an example of a figurative use of this word: "Cast away (הַשְׁלִ֣יכוּ, *ukilsah*) from you all your transgressions which you have committed and make yourselves a new heart and a new spirit!"

30. Miller, *Daniel*, 227.

31. Young, *Prophecy of Daniel*, 172.

The term "transgression" (פֶּשַׁע, ʿăsep) is also translated "rebellion." Some commentators have proposed that this could be a reference to the rebellion of the people of Israel issuing in their being given over to the power of the horn. Others propose that this is a reference to the sin of Antiochus. Miller claims that it most likely is referring to Israel, "because the books of 1 Maccabees and 2 Maccabees report that many in Israel were not faithful to their God and even adopted the idolatrous Greek religion (cf. 1 Macc 1:11–15, 43). These sins would have brought about God's chastening in order to purify the nation."[32] It seems unlikely, however, that because "many in Israel" were not faithful and adopted idolatry that God would chasten the whole nation with such persecution. Israel was rebellious for hundreds of years prior to the captivity, and God's patience forestalled His chastening until virtually the entire nation was rebellious.

Walvoord holds that the transgression is the transgression of Antiochus. He argues, "The statement that *an host was given him* apparently refers to the fact that the people of Israel were under his power with divine permission. The phrase *against the daily sacrifice* can be translated 'with the daily sacrifice,' that is, the daily sacrifices were also in his power and he was able to substitute heathen worship. The phrase *by reason of transgression* should be understood as an extension of this, that is, the daily sacrifices are given in his power in order to permit him to transgress against God."[33] Lucas proposes that the word "host" refers to "the army of Antiochus," indicating that the reference is to "the garrison that Antiochus Epiphanes established in Jerusalem to suppress the Jewish cult."[34] In other words, the meaning would be, "By reason of Antiochus' army that was set over the daily sacrifices . . ." The meaning is obscure, and no simple solution has been proposed that satisfies everyone.

Regardless of whose transgression it is, it seems clear that the host refers to the people of Israel, particularly since this word is used earlier and is a reference to them. Also, the daily sacrifices come under the power of Antiochus. It would be incongruent to say that the host refers to Antiochus' army and the daily sacrifice refers to the Jewish sacrifice. Regardless of who committed the transgression, it is because of the transgression that the host and the daily sacrifice are given over to the horn. This seems to indicate that being given over to the horn is an adverse result of the transgression, but why would it be an adverse result for Antiochus' army to be given over to him? It seems to make more sense to take this as referring to the people of Israel and the daily sacrifice at the temple. The text would then be saying, "And on account of

32. Miller, *Daniel*, 227.

33. Walvoord, *Daniel*, 188.

34. Lucas, *Daniel*, 217.

transgression the host [Israel] will be given over to the horn [Antiochus] along with the regular [Jewish] sacrifice."

"As a result, he will fling truth to the ground." The word translated "fling" is the same word used in verse 11 to refer to the throwing down of the sanctuary. In the same manner as Antiochus would make the sanctuary unfit for use, so he would make it too costly to hold on to the truth. A passage from 1 Maccabees demonstrates this:

> Then the king wrote to his whole kingdom that all should be one people, and that all should give up their particular customs. All the Gentiles accepted the command of the king. Many even from Israel gladly adopted his religion; they sacrificed to idols and profaned the sabbath. And the king sent letters by messengers to Jerusalem and the towns of Judah; he directed them to follow customs strange to the land, to forbid burnt offerings and sacrifices and drink offerings in the sanctuary, to profane sabbaths and festivals, to defile the sanctuary and the priests, to build altars and sacred precincts and shrines for idols, to sacrifice swine and other unclean animals, and to leave their sons uncircumcised. They were to make themselves abominable by everything unclean and profane, so that they would forget the law and change all the ordinances. He added, "And whoever does not obey the command of the king shall die." (1 Macc. 1:41–50)[35]

Lucas points out that, "The 'truth' that is 'thrown down to the ground' is no doubt the Jewish Torah. Antiochus' agents burnt any copies they could find, and executed those in whose possession they were found (1 Macc. 1:56–57)."[36]

---

35. Metzger and Murphy, *I Maccabees*, 189. "Καὶ ἔγραψεν ὁ βασιλεὺς πάσῃ τῇ βασιλείᾳ αὐτοῦ εἶναι πάντας εἰς λαὸν ἕνα καὶ ἐγκαταλιπεῖν ἕκαστον τὰ νόμιμα αὐτοῦ. καὶ ἐπεδέξαντο πάντα τὰ ἔθνη κατὰ τὸν λόγον τοῦ βασιλέως. καὶ πολλοὶ ἀπὸ Ισραηλ εὐδόκησαν τῇ λατρείᾳ αὐτοῦ καὶ ἔθυσαν τοῖς εἰδώλοις καὶ ἐβεβήλωσαν τὸ σάββατον. καὶ ἀπέστειλεν ὁ βασιλεὺς βιβλία ἐν χειρὶ ἀγγέλων εἰς Ιερουσαλημ καὶ τὰς πόλεις Ιουδα πορευθῆναι ὀπίσω νομίμων ἀλλοτρίων τῆς γῆς καὶ κωλῦσαι ὁλοκαυτώματα καὶ θυσίαν καὶ σπονδὴν ἐκ τοῦ ἁγιάσματος καὶ βεβηλῶσαι σάββατα καὶ ἑορτὰς καὶ μιᾶναι ἁγίασμα καὶ ἁγίους, οἰκοδομῆσαι βωμοὺς καὶ τεμένη καὶ εἰδώλια καὶ θύειν ὕεια καὶ κτήνη κοινὰ καὶ ἀφιέναι τοὺς υἱοὺς αὐτῶν ἀπεριτμήτους βδελύξαι τὰς ψυχὰς αὐτῶν ἐν παντὶ ἀκαθάρτῳ καὶ βεβηλώσει ὥστε ἐπιλαθέσθαι τοῦ νόμου καὶ ἀλλάξαι πάντα τὰ δικαιώματα, καὶ ὃς ἂν μὴ ποιήσῃ κατὰ τὸν λόγον τοῦ βασιλέως, ἀποθανεῖται."

36. Lucas, *Daniel*, 217. "The books of the law that they found they tore to pieces and burned with fire. Anyone found possessing the book of the covenant, or anyone who adhered to the law, was condemned to death by decree of the king" (1 Macc 1:56–57). "καὶ τὰ βιβλία τοῦ νόμου, ἃ εὗρον, ἐνεπύρισαν ἐν πυρὶ κατασχίσαντες. καὶ ὅπου

Horror for 2300 Days—8:13–14

13— Then I heard a holy one speaking, and another holy one said to that particular one who was speaking, "How long will the vision about the regular sacrifice apply, while the transgression causes horror, so as to allow both the holy place and the host to be trampled?"

14— He said to me, "For 2,300 evenings and mornings; then the holy place will be properly restored."

Daniel now reports the words of two "holy ones" speaking. As Walvoord observes, "The answer given in verse 14 has touched off almost endless exegetical controversy."[37] One of the holy ones, apparently an angel, is speaking, but Daniel does not report what that one is saying. He rather reports a question posed by a second one to the one that was speaking: "How long..." The question concerns the events recorded in verse 12. The expression "transgression causes horror" (הַפֶּשַׁע שֹׁמֵם תֵּת, *tet* *mĕmōs* *ʾǎseppah*) is translated in the KJV as "transgression of desolation." Wood understands the meaning of the question to be, "how long the transgression that brought desolation on the regular ceremonial observances would last."[38] Goldingay translates it as "Desolating rebellion," concerning which he says, "According to 1 Macc 1:54, the abomination was erected on the altar of sacrifice, and this has usually suggested it was an image of Zeus (and of Antiochus, according to Porphyry). 1 Macc 1:59, however, speaks of there being a (pagan) altar erected on the altar of sacrifice. . . . This implies rather that the setting up of the abomination consists in the rebuilding of the altar for it to serve a different cult (as in Judg 6:25–26): Antiochus had it turned into an old-fashioned high place . . ."[39]

    Some have argued that the expression, 2,300 evenings and mornings (עֶרֶב בֹּקֶר אַלְפַּיִם וּשְׁלֹשׁ מֵאוֹת, *to'em* *soĩsu miyapla'* *reqob̲ bere'*) refers to 1,150 evenings and 1,150 mornings, equaling 1,150 whole days. For example, Evans argues, "If we interpret the peculiar wording 'evenings and mornings' so as to make one evening and one morning equivalent to one day, we arrive at 1,150 days, which equals three 365-day years plus 55 days; i.e., we come considerably close to the actual period of three years plus a few days for the profanation of the Temple than we do with the three and one-half years of 7:25, 9:27, and 12:7."[40] Of course what is "peculiar wording" to Evans might

---

εὑρίσκετο παρά τινι βιβλίον. διαθήκης, καὶ εἴς τις συνευδόκει τῷ νόμῳ, τὸ σύ γκριμα τοῦ βασιλέως ἐθανάτου αὐτόν."

37. Walvoord, *Daniel*, 188.

38. Wood, *Daniel*, 217.

39. Goldingay, *Daniel*, 212.

40. Evans, *Four Kingdoms*, 185.

not have been peculiar wording to the Hebrew ear. Also, the text does not actually say, "evenings and mornings." Literally, the sentence reads:

Table 18: Daniel 8:14

עַד	אֵלַי	וַיֹּאמֶר
until	to me	And he said
אַלְפַּיִם	בֹּקֶר	עֶרֶב
thousands	morning	evening
וְנִצְדַּק	מֵאוֹת	וּשְׁלֹשׁ
and will be put right	hundreds	and three
		קֹדֶשׁ׃
		holy *place*.

The text says, "until evening morning (two) thousands and three hundreds." This is not the same as saying, "2,300 evenings *and* mornings." Since there is no conjunction "and" between the words "evening" and "morning," the two are treated as one thing. It is not saying, 1,150 evenings and 1,150 mornings, but 2,300 evening-mornings. This can only refer to a single day involving both an evening and a morning sacrifice. Keil presents a lengthy argument to support the 2,300 days interpretation, and Miller gives a helpful summary of it: "First, Keil points out that in the Hebrew text the phrase is literally 'until evening morning, 2,300.' He then demonstrates that in Old Testament usage an evening and morning specified a day (e.g., Gen 1). Second, he shows that when the Hebrews wished to make a distinction between the two parts of a day, the number of both was given, for example, 'forty days and forty nights' (Gen 7:4,12). Third, Keil correctly observes that appeal to Dan 7:25 and 9:27 to support a period of three and one-half years here is not valid since these passages do not describe the activities of Antiochus IV. Neither does Dan 12:11–12 speak of Antiochus."[41] Also, as was pointed out earlier, the word translated "daily sacrifice" or "regular sacrifice" is the single word "continually" with the definite article (הַתָּמִיד, *dumattah*), "the continual." The word is singular and refers to both the evening and morning sacrifices as one thing, not two distinct things. The period in question, then, covers six years and 140 days, calculating on the basis of 360 day years, or six years and 110 days, calculating on the basis of 365 day years.

41. Miller, *Daniel*, 229.

Miller argues,

> December 164 (the reconsecration of the sanctuary) is the termi-
> nation date given in the text, thus the 2,300 days began in the fall
> of 170 B.C. Something significant must have occurred at that time
> that marked the beginning of the persecution, and such an event
> did take place. In 170 B.C. Onias III (a former high priest) was
> murdered at the urging of the wicked high priest Menelaus, whom
> Antiochus had appointed to that position for a bribe. From this
> point trouble between Antiochus's administration and the Jews
> began to brew (cf. 2 Macc 4:7–50). In 169 B.C. Antiochus looted
> the temple and murdered some of the Jewish people (cf. 1 Macc
> 1:20–28). The altar to Zeus was not set up until 167 B.C., but the
> persecution had been going on long before that event.[42]

Evans objects to Miller's argument: "A more serious flaw in Miller's argument, however, is his assumption that Antiochus initiated his persecution
of the Jews in 169. While the verses he cites in 1 Maccabees 1 may seem to
warrant that finding, the account in 1 Maccabees is highly suspect, as I noted
earlier in this chapter. Antiochus did raid the Temple in 169, but he did not
thoroughly loot it as described in 1 Maccabees 1:21–23; and while it stands
to reason that there was violence associated with his raid, nothing indicates
that the systematic and thorough suppression of the Jewish faith began that
year."[43] Of course Miller did not claim that a "systematic and thorough suppression of the Jewish faith began that year," as Evans implies that he does.
Also, Evans' earlier arguments about the highly suspect nature of 1 Maccabees
are grounded in speculation and actually only question the exaggerated claim,
not the historical facts.

There are many proposals that attempt to explain the historical fulfillment of the 2,300 days. Walvoord summarizes what seems to be the best explanation: "Taking all the evidence into consideration, the best conclusion is
that the twenty-three hundred days of Daniel are fulfilled in the period from
171 B.C. and culminated in the death of Antiochus Epiphanes in 164 B.C.
The period when the sacrifices ceased was the latter part of this longer period.
Although the evidence available today does not offer fulfillment to the precise
day, the twenty-three hundred days, obviously a round number, is relatively
accurate in defining the period when the Jewish religion began to erode under
the persecution of Antiochus, and the period as a whole concluded with his
death."[44]

42. Ibid., 229–30.

43. Evans, *Four Kingdoms*, 187.

44. Walvoord, *Daniel*, 190.

The Vision Interpreted: 8:15–27

With verse 15 we have moved into the second part of this chapter. The vision is complete, and Daniel seeks to understand. Although the text does not state that Daniel asked for an interpretation, it does say that he "sought to understand" (וָאֲבַקְשָׁה בִינָה, *ḥanib ḥăsqbᵃʾaw*).

The Interpretation of the Vision of the Ram: 8:15–20

A Human-like Figure—8:15–16

15— When I, Daniel, had seen the vision, I sought to understand it; and behold, standing before me was one who looked like a man.

16— And I heard the voice of a man between the banks of Ulai, and he called out and said, "Gabriel, give this man an understanding of the vision."

While Daniel was contemplating the vision, suddenly an individual like a man stood before him. In expressing this event, Daniel uses the word "behold" (וְהִנֵּה, *ḥenniḥᵉw*) as if saying, "I wanted to understand, and, behold, suddenly there stood someone before me who could explain it all!" This is reminiscent of chapter 7. The first part of the chapter is the vision, the second part is the interpretation, and the interpreter is like a man. At this point Daniel hears a voice: "And I heard the voice of a man between the banks of Ulai, and he called out and said, 'Gabriel, give this man an understanding of the vision'" (v. 16). Miller argues that the "one like a man" whom Daniel saw first is in fact God: "Though the angel Gabriel has been suggested, this being is best understood to be God himself. In the following verse it seems to be the 'voice' of this same person heard ordering Gabriel to explain the vision, demonstrating his superiority over that important angel."[45] However, it is interesting that when Daniel says he saw one that looked like a man, he uses the word גֶּבֶר (*reḇag*), which comes from the verb גָּבַר (*raḇag*) which usually is used to mean "be strong" or "prevail."[46] The word גִּבּוֹר (*ḡobbig*), which usually refers to a warrior, also comes from this root—e.g., "Mighty God" or "Warrior God" (אֵל גִּבּוֹר, *ḡobbig ʾleʾ*). This also forms part of the name of the angel addressed by the voice—Gabriel, גַּבְרִיאֵל (*leʾ ɪrbag*), which means "man of God" or "warrior of God." Perhaps the man, *reḇag*, whom Daniel sees, is Gabriel even though the voice is God's. This seems to be supported by the fact that the expression "voice of a man" does not use *reḇag*, but *mᵃ̄da*ʾ

45. Miller, *Daniel*, 231.
46. KBH, s.v. "גבר."

(קוֹל־אָדָם, *m̤ada' loq*). Most commentators understand the voice to be the voice of God, and the one who looks like a man to be the angel Gabriel.

There may be another explanation of who this person is. There are some interesting parallels that may suggest an identity. In the chart below (Figure 23), the parallel relation between Daniel and Matthew suggests that perhaps the man in Daniel is a theophanic appearance of the Pre-Incarnate Christ. There are several factors that may support this suggestion. A. D. A. Moses has argued that the literary structure of material surrounding the Transfiguration in Matthew chapter 17 suggests that there is an apocalyptic background to the transfiguration reminiscent of Daniel 7. He points to a "Son of Man *inclusio* in Mt. 16.27; 16.28–17.1–8–17.9; 17.12 . . ."[47] According to Moses, this *inclusio* yields the following chiastic structure:

> 16.27   The Son of Man coming for deliverance and judgment
> 16.28   The Son of Man coming in His kingdom
> 17.1–8 The transfiguration (The glory of the Son of Man)
> 17.9   The Son of Man and the resurrection
> 17.12   The suffering of Son of Man[48]

The Son of Man *inclusio* and the parallel structure of Dan 7:13–18 with Matt 17:1–13 along with the parallelisms between Dan 8:15–26 and Matt 17:5–10 suggest that perhaps either Gabriel is a type of Christ, the Warrior of God, or that this is an appearance of the Pre-Incarnate Christ.

The point is that the parallelisms and the apocalyptic features of the transfiguration in Matthew suggest that the transfiguration is an apocalyptic and eschatological revelation. Notice that in Matt 17:10 the disciples seek to understand by asking about Elijah: "Why then do the scribes say that Elijah must come first?" Why would they ask this question about Elijah? They asked because they understood the transfiguration as "the coming of the Son of Man in His kingdom" just as Jesus had said in Matt 16:28. If the transfiguration is the coming of the Son of Man in His kingdom, then why do some say that Elijah must come first? In other words, the disciples understood the transfiguration to be the coming that Jesus referred to in 16:28, but it had not been preceded by Elijah as some said would happen. But, Jesus clarifies the situation for them: "And He answered and said, 'Elijah is coming and will restore all things; but I say to you that Elijah already came, and they did not recognize him, but did to him whatever they wished. So also the Son of Man is going to suffer at their hands'" (Matt 17:11–12). These factors are taken by

---

47. A. D. A. Moses, *Matthew's Transfiguration Story and Jewish-Christian Controversy* (Sheffield, England: Sheffield Academic Press, 1996), 99.

48. Ibid.

some to indicate that the man presented here in Daniel is Christ. However, these images connect more favorably with chapter 7 than with chapter 8, and are ultimately inconclusive.

Figure 23: Comparison of Daniel and Matthew

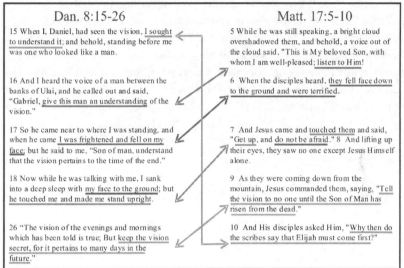

Dan. 8:15-26	Matt. 17:5-10
15 When I, Daniel, had seen the vision, I sought to understand it; and behold, standing before me was one who looked like a man.	5 While he was still speaking, a bright cloud overshadowed them, and behold, a voice out of the cloud said, "This is My beloved Son, with whom I am well-pleased; listen to Him!
16 And I heard the voice of a man between the banks of Ulai, and he called out and said, "Gabriel, give this man an understanding of the vision."	6 When the disciples heard, they fell face down to the ground and were terrified.
17 So he came near to where I was standing, and when he came I was frightened and fell on my face; but he said to me, "Son of man, understand that the vision pertains to the time of the end."	7 And Jesus came and touched them and said, "Get up, and do not be afraid." 8 And lifting up their eyes, they saw no one except Jesus Himself alone.
18 Now while he was talking with me, I sank into a deep sleep with my face to the ground; but he touched me and made me stand upright.	9 As they were coming down from the mountain, Jesus commanded them, saying, "Tell the vision to no one until the Son of Man has risen from the dead."
26 "The vision of the evenings and mornings which has been told is true; But keep the vision secret, for it pertains to many days in the future."	10 And His disciples asked Him, "Why then do the scribes say that Elijah must come first?"

THE TIME OF THE END—8:17

17—   So he came near to where I was standing, and when he came I was frightened and fell on my face; but he said to me, "Son of man, understand that the vision pertains to the time of the end."

Since Gabriel had been commanded to give Daniel understanding about the vision, the angel came up to where Daniel was, and Daniel became frightened and fell on his face. As Walvoord puts it, "Because of the whole context of the vision, the powerful presence of Gabriel, and the mysterious voice which may be the voice of Deity, Daniel is afraid, actually panic-stricken, and falls on his face."[49] This may be here in order to identify Gabriel as a formidable angelic being, a warrior, striking terror in Daniel. Gabriel spoke to Daniel, "Son of man, understand that the vision pertains to the time of the end." Interestingly, there is no statement that Gabriel touched Daniel or instructed him to stand at this point. Gabriel addresses Daniel as "son of man": בֶּן־אָדָם (*mada' neb*). Perhaps this was sufficient reassurance to calm Daniel's fears.

49. Walvoord, *Daniel*, 191.

The address "son of man" is used 93 times in Ezekiel and only 14 times outside of the book of Ezekiel. Outside of the book of Daniel, the expression, "I fell on my face," specifically using the first person reference is found only in Ezekiel (Ezek 1:28; 3:23; 11:13). In two of the three instances in which the expression "I fell on my face" occurs in Ezekiel, the "glory" of the Lord is present. In Ezek 1:28, the Lord speaks to Ezekiel using the "son of man" appellation: "Son of man, stand on your feet that I may speak with you!" These may be present here in order to present a picture similar to the one found in Ezekiel, indicating that this is a communication from God himself.

Gabriel then begins to explain the vision to him. He says, "understand that the vision pertains to the time of the end" (v. 17). One problem here is that the word "pertains" is used to translate the inseparable preposition ל (*l*) on the word "time" (עֵת, *ie*ʿ, see Table 19 below). This preposition has a wide range of meaning, but most frequently simply means "to." The entire phrase is set out below.

Table 19: Daniel 8:17

הָבֵן	בֶּן־	אָדָם	כִּי
Understand	son of	man	that
לְעֶת־	קֵץ	הֶחָזוֹן:	
to time of	end	the vision.	

Preterists argue that this is referring to the time when Christ came, died, was buried, and raised again bringing an end to Judaism and establishing the kingdom of God. For example, Mills asserts, "In the future time when the divine indignation shall be manifested toward the Hebrew people, the beginning of these calamities would therefore bring forth the end, seen in chapter 8 as beginning with Antiochus. It therefore pertains to a series of events which are to introduce the latter days, when the kingdom of God (Christ) will be established, and Judaism abolished."[50] Of course Mills does not mean the future from the perspective of the year 2007, but the future from the perspective of Daniel. In support of his statement he refers to 1 Cor 10:11: "Now all these things happened unto them for ensamples: and they are written for our admonition, upon whom the ends of the ages have come."[51] Of course the Corinthian passage does not say the end of Judaism, and the plural form

50. Mills, *Daniel*, 116.

51. ταῦτα δὲ τυπικῶς συνέβαινεν ἐκείνοις, ἐγράφη δὲ πρὸς νουθεσίαν ἡμῶν εἰς οὓς τὰ τέλη τῶν αἰώνων κατήντηκεν. (1 Cor 10:11).

"ends" and "ages" calls into question the very notion that this relates to the passage in Daniel, which uses singular forms. Neither in the Corinthian passage nor in any passages in Daniel is there a statement that uses the phrase "the end of Judaism."

In fact, Evans summarizes an argument that calls Mills' association into question: "Joyce Baldwin . . . stated that the passages in verses 17 and 19 pertaining to the 'time of the end' do not necessarily refer to the end of all things, 'but may refer to the question asked in verse 13' pertaining to the desolation of the sanctuary, and she gave examples of cases in other books of the Old Testament in which 'the end' refers to the conclusion of an historical period in which there had been a rebellion by Jews against God."[52] Of course Evans is using this argument to support his Preterist view, but it also works against his view. If this verse is referring to the question in verse 13 and is not referring to the "end of the ages," then not only is Mills' association incorrect, but the notion that this is the end of Judaism can also be called into question. This may not refer to any such event, but simply to the end of the persecution under Antiochus. However, most commentators take this verse along with verse 19, so the discussion of the meaning will be taken up at that point.

A serious problem in the Preterist interpretation of this point is that although Jerusalem was physically destroyed, Judaism itself survived the war of 70 AD, and Jerusalem itself was repopulated over the seventy years until the Bar Kokhba revolt in AD 132. There was in fact another Jewish revolt in 116–117 AD, also indicating that 70 AD did not mark the end of Judaism. Peter Schäfer describes how Judaism, rather than being destroyed, recast itself in the form of what is now referred to as Rabbinic Judaism:

> The reconstitution of Judaism as rabbinic Judaism is closely linked to the figure of Johanan b. Zakkai and the city of Jabneh/Jamnia. . . . Jabneh's importance after 70 CE as the geographical and spiritual centre of rabbinic Judaism was so great that one may justifiably refer to the period from the destruction of the Temple to the Bar Kochba uprising as the "Jabneh period." It was here that, under Johanan b. Zakkai and Gamaliel II, the son of Simon/Shimon h. Gamaliel I (the leader of the Pharisees before 70 and during the war), the foundation of rabbinic Judaism was laid, and the material which was later to make up the Mishnah was first formulated and sifted through. This is why the period of Jabneh is often referred to as the formative period of rabbinic Judaism.[53]

52. Evans, *Four Kingdoms*, 174.
53. Peter Schäfer, *The History of the Jews in the Greco-Roman World*, 137, 139.

The Bar Kochba revolt fueled the flame of revolt by minting coins with inscriptions such as, "Year One of the Redemption of Israel," and "For the Freedom/Liberation of Jerusalem."[54] Schäfer also points out that research on the Bar Kochba revolt focuses on several points, one of which is the following: "Did the rebels conquer Jerusalem and perhaps even attempt to rebuild the Temple (now the third Temple) and resume sacrificial worship in this 'new' capital of Bar Kochba's Messianic Kingdom?"[55] In fact, Schäfer, commenting on the coin inscriptions states, "These coins have been used to infer, in the first years of the revolt, Jerusalem was in the hands of the rebels: the legends on the coins dating from the first and second years proclaim the successful liberation or redemption of Israel."[56] However, Schäfer points out that there are several problems with the notion that Jerusalem was taken over for purposes of the revolt, and that "Jerusalem was still in ruins and would hardly have been particularly well fortified by the Romans."[57] However, the very question implies that indeed Jerusalem was repopulated to some degree and apparently held by the Romans. Schäfer notes that after the 70 AD war, the Roman legion *legio X Fretensis* was actually headquartered in Jerusalem.[58]

David Dungan gives a brief description of the consequences following the Bar Kochba revolt.

> Fifteen years later in 132, about seventy years after the first re-volt in 66, a second, massive rebellion broke out in Judea once again, led by a coalition of Pharisaic leaders and a Jewish 'king' or messiah named Bar Kokhba. Recent archaeological discoveries indicate that there was substantial advance preparation for this revolt, including the digging of underground staging centers, food and weapons storage depots, and the like. The Bar Kokhba rebellion took the Romans three years to suppress, at great expense and bloodshed. This time, the Roman Senate was not inclined to be lenient. Circumcision was made a crime, Jews were forbidden to serve in any civic positions anywhere in the empire, Jerusalem was turned into a colony of Rome with a new legal foundation and a new temple and a new name—Aelia Capitolina (thus destroying the old shekel-based Jewish economy), and Jews were forbidden on pain of death to come even within eyesight of their former capital city.[59]

54. Ibid., 155.

55. Ibid., 154.

56. Ibid., 155.

57. Ibid., 154–55.

58. Ibid., 131.

59. David Laird Dungan, *A History of the Synoptic Problem: The Canon, the Text, the*

The map in Figure 24 below shows the region of Palestine, Judean Shephelah, in which the underground staging centers referred to by Dungan were found.[60] The Bar Kochba war ranged from the Judean Shephelah possibly as far north as Galilee and certainly included Jerusalem. Schäfer points out, "The consequences of the [Bar Kochba] revolt were perhaps even more catastrophic and far-reaching than those of the first war [of 70 AD]. . . . The economic structure of the country was largely destroyed. The entire spiritual and economic life of the Palestinian Jews moved to Galilee."[61]

Contrary to the claims of the Preterists, history shows that in fact the 70 AD war was not the end either of Judaism or Jerusalem. After the Bar Kochba war Jerusalem became a Roman colony, and, as Schäfer notes, "The Jews were forbidden on pain of death to set foot in the new Roman city. Aelia [Jerusalem] thus became a completely pagan city, no doubt with the corresponding public buildings and temples."[62] In other words, even after the more devastating war of Bar Kochba Jerusalem was not annihilated, but was repopulated as a Roman city.

Of course the response of the Preterist is that by saying that this was the destruction of Judaism, they are not referring to the physical dissolution of the practice of Judaism or of the complete physical destruction of Jerusalem in 70 AD. What they seem to be claiming is that this was the end of Judaism as a spiritual basis for a relationship with God. The sacrificial system was dissolved and discontinued with the sacrifice of Christ as the Lamb of God.

Composition, and the Interpretation of the Gospels, 46–47.

60. This map was taken from Amos Kloner, "Underground Hiding Complexes from the Bar Kochba War in the Judean Shephelah," *Biblical Archaeologist*, 215.

61. Schäfer, *The History of the Jews*, 159.

62. Ibid.

Figure 24: Bar Kochba Regional Map

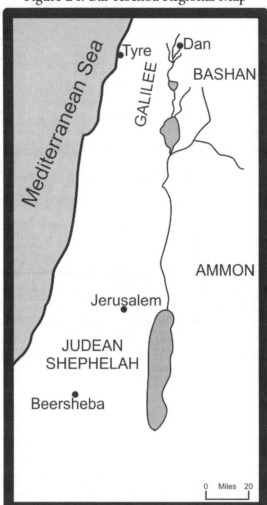

There are several problems with this claim, however. First of all, the text seems to be referring not to a spiritual conflict, but to a physical one. The interpretation of the angel in verse 25 describes a physical conflict by such statements as "He will destroy many while *they are* at ease," and "he will even oppose the Prince of princes." Preterists cannot take this last phrase as indicative of any spiritual conflict. If it is taken as a spiritual conflict, then it is not a conflict with Judaism, but with Christ and therefore cannot indicate an end to the validity of the sacrificial system. Second, by the time of the persecutions of Antiochus, the Pharisees had already corrupted Judaism from its Old

Testament beginnings. The Pharisees had made the principle of keeping the law as the means of entering the Kingdom of God. So, what is ended in 70 AD was not the legitimate sacrificial system, but the corrupt system of the ruling Jewish parties. Third, if the descriptions of the physical end are taken as the basis upon which one understands the end of the sacrificial system, then there is a serious problem with the fact that the history shows that the physical practice did not end with the death, burial, and resurrection of Christ, but continued on until the destruction of the temple in 70 AD. If the physical is the basis of the spiritual significance, then the history shows that the spiritual significance of the sacrificial system was not ended at the time of Christ because the physical end on which the spiritual interpretation is based did not occur. In fact, S. Safrai points out that the destruction of the temple in 70 AD was not even the end of the nation:

> The Great Revolt, which lasted for more than four years and involved all parts of the country, together with the various sieges, the conquest of Jerusalem and the destruction of the Temple, was a heavy blow to the Jewish people as well as the towns and villages of the Land of Israel. . . . However, the demographic and economic impoverishment of the population did not last; the Jewish people in the Land of Israel was [*sic*] not reduced to total devastation. Not only was it able to wage a great war only one generation after the destruction, but the population had to a remarkable degree recovered its numeric and economic strength by the end of the first century.[63]

It is certainly true that Christ's sacrifice replaced the sacrificial system in the sense of fulfilling it. However, the point here is, this fact is not the subject of these prophecies. This is not the "end" to which these prophecies are making reference. At least these verses are not sufficient to make the Preterist interpretation beyond question. The historical factors as well as the statements of the text seem to indicate that this is referring to a physical destruction culminating in the breaking of this evil person, the little horn, as stated in verse 26. If the Preterists are going to claim that this is referring to the "end of Judaism," more argument and support will need to be mustered. Simply asserting this view is insufficient to establish its validity. Not only is it necessary for the Preterists to explain the text in relation to this view; they must also explain the history that seems to go against their understanding. If 70 AD was not the "end" of Judaism physically, how can it signify the end of

63. S. Safrai, "The Jews in the Land of Israel (70–335 CE)," in *A History of the Jewish People*, ed. H. H. Ben-Sasson (Cambridge, Massachusetts: Harvard University Press, 2002), 314.

Judaism spiritually? And if this passage is not talking about the physical end of Judaism, then it is not making reference to the spiritual end of Judaism as the Preterists claim. The reference to the end in these verses is simply not talking about the end of Judaism as the Preterists claim, either physically or spiritually.

It is certainly true that the destruction of the Temple in Jerusalem marked the end of the sacrificial system. However, Israel had faced such an "end" before when, in 586 BC the Babylonians destroyed Jerusalem and sacked the Temple treasury. To many the destruction of Jerusalem and the Temple may have seemed permanent. However, with the return of the people to the land, the Temple and the city were rebuilt. Since the events of 70 AD nor the outcome of the Bar Kochba revolt marked the end of the Jews or Judaism, and though it may seem a permanent state of affairs, it is still possible that the Jews could return to the land and rebuild the Temple and begin the sacrificial system once again. For the Preterists to claim that 70 AD marked the end of the sacrificial system assumes that they are capable of predicting the future. Both history and prophecy testify to the fact that Israel will indeed return to the land to rebuild their Temple and reinstitute the sacrificial system. As to the notion of the end of the validity of the sacrificial system, Preterists cannot claim with certainty that the sacrificial system will not be reinstituted, and its validity was compromised by the corruption of the ruling priests long before Christ appeared in the flesh. Preterists may respond that they are talking about its spiritual validity regardless of the actual practice, but this goes beyond the statements of the text. Nowhere in the text is such a distinction made. It must be imposed upon the text by the prior eschatological commitment of the Preterist view.

THE FINAL PERIOD—8:18–19

18—   Now while he was talking with me, I sank into a deep sleep with my face to the ground; but he touched me and made me stand upright.

19—   He said, "Behold, I am going to let you know what will occur at the final period of the indignation, for it pertains to the appointed time of the end.

While Gabriel was talking to Daniel, he sank into a deep sleep with his face to the ground. This is also quite similar to the statements in Ezekiel. Goldingay comments that the "deep sleep" is not an everyday term and "denotes a coma-like state of deep sleep brought about by supernatural agency, especially in connection with visionary experiences."[64] Without citing any textual support,

---

64. Goldingay, *Daniel*, 214–15.

Wood declares, "It is better taken to mean 'I fainted' here, however, for Daniel experienced an abnormal loss of consciousness because of extreme emotional excitement, and the period of time implied for the unconscious state is not long. This 'fainting' occurred no doubt for the same reason that he had already fallen on his face. His sense of unworthiness continued, Gabriel's words not having been understood sufficiently to give the reassurance intended."[65] However, as we pointed out, Wood offers no support for his understanding of the expression "deep sleep" as fainting. He merely asserts this.

Since so much of Daniel's vision involves symbolism, perhaps Daniel's deep sleep or "fainting" has a symbolic purpose as well. Walvoord comments that Daniel's deep sleep "is not a natural sleep but the result of his fear described in verse 17."[66] It may be symbolic of the kind of reaction that will be typical of those who experience the persecution that has been described thus far, that is, they respond in great fear to the point of falling into a stupor. But, just as Gabriel touched Daniel and made him stand upright, so after the period of suffering, the people will be made to stand up. In other words, not only is Daniel so frightened that he falls into a deep sleep, but those who experience this time will also succumb to the great fear that overtakes them, perhaps both physically and spiritually. Alternately, the concept of a "deep sleep" is sometimes used symbolically of death. If Daniel somehow represents his people, this may picture a "death" of Israel. Since Gabriel's name means "My warrior is God," the touching of Daniel to cause him to stand may depict the resurrection of the nation of Israel after the manner of the prophecy of Ezekiel 36ff. And if this is accurate, this cannot be referring to the events of 70 AD since there was no "death" of Israel, nor was there any resurrection of the nation.

Goldingay also points out, "The terms 'time' (עֵת), 'end' (קֵץ), 'closing part [of the wrath]' (הַזַּעַם [אַחֲרִית]), and 'set moment' (מוֹעֵד) appear in vv 17, 19. . . . Like their English equivalents, all are everyday words. None inherently refers to the absolute End, and only their contexts tell us whether the expressions in the various combinations refer to the end of a particular period of time or to the End of Time."[67] Keil makes a similar observation: "'Time of the end' is the general prophetic expression for the time which, as the period of fulfillment, lies at the end of the existing prophetic horizon—in the present case the time of Antiochus."[68] Walvoord observes that there are basically four major positions on the interpretation of this phrase: "(1) the historical view

65. Wood, *Daniel*, 221.

66. Walvoord, *Daniel*, 191.

67. Goldingay, *Daniel*, 215.

68. Keil, *Book of Daniel*, 310.

that all of Daniel 8 has been fulfilled; (2) the futuristic view, the idea that it is entirely future [from our perspective]; (3) the view based upon the principle of dual fulfillment of prophecy, that Daniel 8 is intentionally a prophetic reference both to Antiochus Epiphanes, now fulfilled, and to the end of the age and the final world ruler who persecutes Israel before the second advent; (4) the view that the passage is prophecy, historically fulfilled but intentionally typical of similar events and personages at the end of the age."[69] These issues are much too involved to attempt to discuss them at this point, and the fact that one's view must take into consideration passages from chapters 9–12, any additional comments on these issues will be taken up as the relevant passages are encountered in the remaining chapters.

Many commentators take the reference to "indignation" to refer to the wrath of God. For example, Young argues, "The *indignation* amounts to being a technical term for designating the wrath of God and His displeasure; cf. Isa. 10:5, 25; 26:20. 'It plainly means here the *season of indignation* on the part of God, who gives up his people to punishment, because they have sinned against him' (Stuart)."[70] Contrary to this view, Goldingay argues,

> The notion of a period characterized by wrath is one of the aspects of Dan 8 that reflects Zech 1, where the exile is a period of wrath (1:12). The context there indicates that reference to wrath does not denote that God is punishing Israel for their sin: although their sin was the original cause of the exile, the ongoing period of wrath is one in which they are continuing to be treated harshly rather than compassionately because of the hostility of their enemies rather than because of their own sin. In a parallel way 1 Macc 1:64 speaks of Antiochus's persecution as the coming of very great wrath on Israel (cf. 2 Kgs 3:27). There, too, Israel's transgressions contributed to what happened (1:11–15, 43, 52–53), but 1 Maccabees hardly implies that Antiochus's persecution is simply God's punishment of Israel's sin. Neither in Dan 8 is it likely that the seer views Israel's experience as God's punishment for their sin . . .[71]

Lucas supports Goldingay's view with some additional points:

> In the HB *ma'az* nearly always refers to the wrath of God. It can refer to a brief period of divine judgment (Is. 26:20). However, in Zech. 1:12 (a passage which, as we have seen, has various similarities with this chapter), God is said to have been "wrathful" or "indignant" with Israel for the seventy years of the exile. There is a

---

69. Walvoord, *Daniel*, 192.

70. Young, *Prophecy of Daniel*, 177.

71. Goldingay, *Daniel*, 215.

parallel to this in the concept of "the age of wrath" in the Qumran literature. In CD [Qumran *Damascus Document*] 1:5 the "age of wrath" seems to be the 390 years of Israel's punishment prophesied in Ezek. 4:5 (see Collins 1993: 338). However, it is important to note that, in Zechariah, although the exile was caused by Israel's sin, the "ongoing" wrath is not seen as a continuing, deserved punishment for Israel's sins, but rather as the harsh treatment of Israel by the nations into whose power God has delivered her. The implication of the first three visions is that this has gone well beyond anything Israel deserved, and that is why the call for divine mercy in Zech. 1:12 is appropriate. The meaning of "the time of wrath" in Dan. 8:19 seems to be the same, because in this chapter all the rebellion and transgression mentioned seems to be that of the earthly kings, and especially of the small horn. So "the time of wrath" is to be understood as the whole period from the beginning of the exile onwards, the period covered by the four kingdoms of Dan. 2 and 7. The "last days of the time of wrath" refers to the Antiochene persecution, as v. 24 indicates.[72]

However, Lucas' characterization seems contrary to the notion of mercy. If, as Lucas claims, the treatment of Israel has gone "well beyond anything Israel deserved," then it is not mercy that Israel needs, but rather justice. The reason Zech. 1:12 calls for mercy is because mercy involves God's grace to help those who have no claim to favorable treatment. Also, according to Miller, "Lacocque remarks that except for Hos 7:16, this word [indignation] 'always designates the wrath of God.' The Idea is that God's 'wrath' is the demonstration of his righteous 'indignation' against sin. In this context the recipients of this wrath are Antiochus and the unfaithful Israelites of the Maccabean period."[73] The term "wrath" or "indignation" (זַעַם, *ma'az*) occurs in Daniel only here and in 11:36. In Daniel, the actions of Antiochus are not characterized as "indignation." However, there remains the problem of the prophecy of Amos 8:11–13: "'Behold, days are coming,' declares the Lord God, 'When I will send a famine on the land, not a famine for bread or a thirst for water, but rather for hearing the words of the Lord. People will stagger from sea to sea and from the north even to the east; they will go to and fro to seek the word of the Lord, but they will not find. In that day the beautiful virgins and the young men will faint from thirst.'" Although it certainly does not seem to be a case of "hearing the words of the Lord" (דִּבְרֵי יְהוָה, *hawh'y erbid*), Amos' prophecy seems to be more than simply not physically hearing God's word. Certainly the Word of God was studied, read, and taught during this

72. Lucas, *Daniel*, 219–20.
73. Miller, *Daniel*, 233.

whole time. Rather, it seems to be a prophecy indicating that God has, at least for a time, abandoned Israel. In a sense, God had become like one of Israel's idols—not seeing, hearing, speaking, or acting for Israel. If this is the case, then it is difficult to see how the indignation would be God's indignation for Israel's sins. The judgment of God was often seen as God's communicating to Israel, and the wrath of God during this time was God's silence, not His activity. Indeed, a lack of communicative activity is what constituted the famine. The indignation that concerns the appointed time of the end seems to refer rather to the wrath of Antiochus than to the wrath of God. Nevertheless, a good case can be made for the opposing view, and more light might be shed on this issue as the other relevant verses are considered.

THE IDENTITY OF THE RAM—8:20

20—   "The ram which you saw with the two horns represents the kings of Media and Persia.

The references to the "appointed time of the end" forms the context in which the interpretation is given. As Walvoord notes, "The phrase 'latter in the time of wrath' may also be rendered 'in the latter part of the time of wrath,' meaning that the events described here will occur at the end of this particular period of judgment."[74] Once again, however, the wording seems obscure. The text with a literal, word-for-word translation is set out below.

Table 20: Daniel 8:19

אֶת־אֲשֶׁר־	מוֹדִיעֲךָ	הִנְנִי	וַיֹּאמֶר
what	I will make known to you	Behold	And he said
כִּי	הַזַּעַם	בְּאַחֲרִית	יִהְיֶה
for	the indignation	in the after	will be
		קֵץ׃	לְמוֹעֵד
		end.	to the appointed time of

Gabriel tells Daniel that the ram is representative of the kingdom of Medo-Persia. In some sense, the kingdom of Medo-Persia relates to the "ap-

74. Walvoord, *Daniel*, 233.

pointed time of the end" since the whole interpretation is set in this context. Since it was during the Medo-Persian Empire that Israel was released from their captivity, a captivity that was precipitated by their rebellion, the "appointed time of the end" may refer to the end of their seventy years of captivity and their release to return to their own land.

The Interpretation of the Vision of the Goat: 8:21–22

21—   "The shaggy goat represents the kingdom of Greece, and the large horn that is between his eyes is the first king.

22—   "The broken horn and the four horns that arose in its place represent four kingdoms which will arise from his nation, although not with his power.

The shaggy goat represents Greece. There may be no particular significance to the additional term "shaggy" or "hairy" other than to identify the kind of goat. Interestingly, the vast majority of uses of the word "hairy" (שָׂעִיר, *śî'ás*) are as a noun by itself indicating a hairy goat, and the majority of these are with reference to a goat for a sin offering. Daniel uses it as an adjective, although spelled the same as the noun, modifying the word "goat" (צָפִיר, *śî'ás*). The adjectival use of "hairy" occurs only twice outside of Daniel, and both are used with reference to Esau as a "hairy man." Isaiah does use the word "hairy" (שָׂעִיר, *śî'ás*) as a noun to refer to a wild goat, which may be the significance here.

Gabriel tells Daniel that the large horn between the goat's eyes is the first king, Alexander. This also fits with previous visions. Like the speedy leopard with four wings, this goat was moving so fast that it never touched the ground. As soon as Alexander conquered the world, he died, and his kingdom was divided among his generals. The four most significant empires that are formed after Alexander's death are represented by the four horns. "The broken horn and the four horns that arose in its place represent four kingdoms which will arise from his nation, although not with his power." Concerning the accuracy of the prophecy, Miller comments, "Also interesting is the correctness of the prophecy in v. 22 that none of the four kingdoms ever attained the power of Alexander's empire."[75]

The Interpretation of the Vision of the Horn: 8:23–25

23—   "In the latter period of their rule, when the transgressors have run their course, a king will arise, insolent and skilled in intrigue.

75. Miller, *Daniel*, 233–34.

24—   "His power will be mighty, but not by his own power, and he will
       destroy to an extraordinary degree and prosper and perform his will;
       He will destroy mighty men and the holy people.

25—   "And through his shrewdness ye will cause deceit to succeed by his
       influence; and he will magnify himself in his heart, and he will de-
       stroy many while they are at ease. He will even oppose the Prince of
       princes, but he will be broken without human agency.

Gabriel explains that another king will arise: "In the latter period of their
rule, when the transgressors have run their course, a king will arise, insolent
and skilled in intrigue." Although the little horn is not specifically identified, the events described were historically fulfilled by the eighth king of the
Syrian dynasty, Antiochus Epiphanes. Some have argued that this cannot refer
to Antiochus because his dates do not fit the "latter period" of the Seleucid
Empire. However, Evans effectively argues,

> In reality, the passage "In the latter part of their reign" can readily
> be interpreted to fit the mainstream conservative view that while
> the small horn of Daniel 8 is Antiochus IV, the little horn of
> Daniel 7 is not. The "their" in "their reign" refers to the kingdoms
> that succeeded Alexander, not just the Seleucid kingdom. When
> Antiochus IV ascended the Seleucid throne in 175, Rome was less
> than thirty years away from incorporating Greece and Macedonia
> into its empire. It had also established a strong presence in Asia
> Minor and turned Egypt into a protectorate. Furthermore, it was
> holding the legitimate heir to the Seleucid throne, Demetrius, the
> son of Seleucus IV, as a hostage in Rome. The Seleucid kingdom
> limped along until Pompey finished it off in 64 BC, but even by
> 175 its territory had been much reduced because of the rise of the
> Parthian Empire I to the east and, to a lesser extent, the advance
> of Rome in the west. Within little more than a decade, Judea ef-
> fectively joined the list of its lost territories.[76]

Lucas adds, "'The last days of their kingship' (23) is, probably, to be
taken as referring to the same period as 'the last days of the time of wrath'
(19), namely the Antiochene persecution."[77] The three directions mentioned
above—south, east, and the beautiful land—indicate that the place from
which the little horn emerged was in fact Syria. The little horn magnifies
himself up to the point of claiming divine honor, which is indicated by his
name Epiphanes that refers to a glorious manifestation of deity. As we have

76. Evans, *The Four Kingdoms*, 173.
77. Lucas, *Daniel*, 220.

seen, the 2300 days probably refers to the time of Antiochus' dominance, from about 171 BC to the time of his death, about 164 BC.

According to the interpretation provided by Gabriel, the little horn will have the following characteristics:

1.   He will appear in the latter time of their kingdom
2.   He will appear when the transgressors have run their course
3.   He will be a king of fierce countenance, and intelligence
4.   He will have great power given to him from another
5.   He will accomplish great exploits including defeating the people of Israel
6.   He will cause wickedness to increase
7.   He will exalt himself
8.   He will exalt many people by deceit
9.   He will oppose the prince of princes
10.   He will be broken without any human agency

As Walvoord points out, "A careful scrutiny of these many points will justify the conclusion that it is possible to explain all of these elements as fulfilled historically in Antiochus Epiphanes."[78] This conclusion has not gone unchallenged, however. We have already dealt with the objection that Antiochus did not arise at the "latter time of their kingdom." Walvoord also points out that some have argued that Antiochus did not "oppose the Prince of princes" (v. 25). But Walvoord responds to this objection by pointing out that, "opposition to God, to Israel, and to the Messianic hope in general, which characterized blasphemers of the Old Testament, can well be interpreted as standing up against 'the Prince of princes.' After all, Christ existed in Old Testament times as God and as the Angel of Jehovah and as the defender of Israel."[79] If we understand Gabriel as not only an actual angel who spoke with Daniel, but also as a symbol of God as the Warrior of Israel, to oppose the army of Israel is to oppose the Warrior of Israel, and, as we have seen from the pre-incarnate appearance of Christ in Joshua, the Captain/Warrior of the Army is Christ Himself, the Prince of princes. Also, it is not necessary that Antiochus be aware that this is what he is doing. However, Antiochus may also function as a type of the Anti-Christ who will appear at the time of the end.

78. Walvoord, *Daniel*, 197.
79. Ibid., 198.

Conclusion of the Vision: 8:26–27

Shut Up the Vision—8:26

26—   "The vision of the evenings and mornings which has been told is true; But keep the vision secret, for it pertains to many days in the future."

It is perhaps significant that when Gabriel commands Daniel to "keep the vision secret," he specifically refers to the "vision of the evenings-mornings." This seems to be a reference back to cessation of the daily sacrifice for 2,300 evening-mornings. Having restated this one point out of the whole vision implies that this is a defining event, or an event of particular importance. Interestingly, in 12:4 and 9, the word translated "keep secret" (סְתֹם, *mātas*) is used in conjunction with the word "seal up" (חֲתֹם, *mātah*) found in 9:24:

Table 21: Daniel 12:4, 9, and 9:24

הַסֵּפֶר	וַחֲתֹם	הַדְּבָרִים	סְתֹם	
the book	and seal	the words	conceal	
	קֵץ	עֵת	עַד־	12:4
	end	time of	until	
הַדְּבָרִים	וַחֲתֻמִים	סְתֻמִים	כִּי־	
the words	and sealed	concealed	for	
	קֵץ	עֵת	עַד־	12:9
	end	time of	until	
	חַטָּאוֹת	לַחְתֹּם		
	the sin	to seal		
	וְנָבִיא	חָזוֹן	וְלַחְתֹּם	9:24
	and prophecy	vision	and to seal	

Miller argues, "'Seal up' is a translation of the verb *mātas*, which means, 'stop up, shut up, keep closed.' Though the NASB renders the term 'keep the vision secret,' ancient documents were sealed for their preservation, and this is the idea here."[80] Miller notes that he takes his lexicographical information from the Brown, Driver, Briggs *Hebrew and English Lexicon of the Old Testament*. However, the word is never used in the OT with reference to "sealing up" a document, and the word is not given this meaning in the more reliable KBH lexicon: "stop up the springs of water, disguise, to shut up words, be aloof, keep secret, be blocked, be shut, to block, to obstruct."[81] Also, the fact that it is used in conjunction with the word (חָתַם, *māṯah*), which is more commonly used of sealing a document, indicates that סָתַם (*māṯas*) does not carry this meaning. Wood argues a sense similar to Miller's: "The word for 'preserve' (*motes*) means literally 'shut up.' The thought is not, however, to shut the vision up in the sense of keeping it secret; but in the sense of preserving it. Daniel was to make sure that a record of the vision would be preserved and not lost."[82] And yet סָתַם (*māṯas*) is never used in the OT in the sense of "keeping safe." Walvoord matter-of-factly says the word indicates that "the vision will not become immediately understandable to Daniel,"[83] but the word itself has no associated sense of being or not being understandable.

Like Miller and Wood, Lucas asserts, "The verb used here (*stm*) is used more of keeping something safe than of keeping it secret."[84] However, Lucas goes on to say, "The reason given here explains why both 'guarding' and 'keeping secret' are necessary. The vision refers to the distant future, not to the reign of Belshazzar. In Ezek. 12:27, it was on the grounds that it referred to the distant future that the prophet's contemporaries dismissed what he said."[85] Even in the case of Hezekiah who, in the prophecy of Isaiah, was told that Jerusalem would be taken into captivity, consoled himself with the realization that the prophecies would not happen in his own day: "Then Hezekiah said to Isaiah, 'The word of the Lord which you have spoken is good.' For he thought, 'For there will be peace and truth in my days'" (Isa 39:8). Concerning this statement, John Oswalt points out, "While it may be that Hezekiah is humbly thankful for God's grace in not bringing the deserved punishment upon him immediately, it is hard to avoid the implication that the real reason for his saying that God's word is good is merely the very human relief that he is not going to be destroyed. Whether his descendants are to be consumed does not seem to affect him. Furthermore, his reaction was quite different when his own demise was imminent (38:3). All this leads me to believe that the

80. Miller, *Daniel*, 236.

81. KBH, s.v. "סתם."

82. Wood, *Daniel*, 229.

83. Walvoord, *Daniel*, 199.

84. Lucas, *Daniel*, 221.

85. Ibid.

picture here is essentially negative."[86] Perhaps Gabriel is commanding Daniel not to divulge the vision at the present because of the possibility of a similar reaction by the people, namely, a response of apathy or disbelief. Also, it may be that this statement is made to Daniel for the purpose of linking it with the subsequent visions of chapters 9 and 12.

Close Up the Understanding—8:27

27—   Then I, Daniel, was exhausted and sick for days. Then I got up again and carried on the king's business; but I was astounded at the vision, and there was none to explain it.

The final statement concerns Daniel's reaction to all that he had seen: "Then I, Daniel, was exhausted and sick for days. Then I got up again and carried on the king's business; but I was astounded at the vision, and there was none to explain it." This is a particularly peculiar statement since in verse 16 the voice commanded Gabriel, "give this man an understanding of the vision." The term translated "explain" (מֵבִין, mēbem) is the same word used in verse 16 and translated "understanding" (הָבֵן, nebah). This implies that there may have been much more to understand than Gabriel actually explained. It is perhaps this still "hidden" understanding that, on top of the experience itself, made Daniel sick for days. Lucas makes an interesting observation: "This vision has a greater physical effect on Daniel than the previous one had (7:28). Once again he is aware of not having fully understood the revelation. This makes further revelation necessary and likely."[87] The final statement of chapter 8 causes the reader to anticipate additional information.

---

86. John N. Oswalt, *The Book of Isaiah: Chapters 1–39*, 697.

87. Lucas, *Daniel*, 221.

10

DANIEL'S VISION OF THE FUTURE OF ISRAEL: 9:1–27

Introduction

In the eschatological debate between Preterists and Futurists, there is no doubt that chapter 9, and especially the prophecy concerning the seventy weeks, is the most frequently discussed passage from the prophecies of Daniel, and perhaps from the entire Old Testament. Right or wrong, the prophecy of the seventy weeks is seen to provide the basic structure into which the events of the end time must fit. Not only is there a divergence of interpretation between these two major camps, but, when it comes to the details of the prophecy, there is often a difference of opinion among the commentators within each camp. These divergences within a given eschatological perspective do not tend to prove that the perspective is faulty as a whole. Especially in prophecy, sometimes the statements are ambiguous, and this engenders various suggestions about fulfillment. Consequently, it is of the utmost importance that each commentator seek to present his case with supporting evidence and not to use language in such a manner as to persuade the reader when the evidence is lacking, or to prejudice the reader before the evidence is presented.

In his introductory remarks on Daniel chapter 9, and before presenting any reasons or evidence for his point of view, Stanley Paher makes several observations that seem to be designed to prejudice the reader toward the view that he wishes to espouse. First of all he states, "Because of chapters 2 and 7–12, his [Daniel's] book is also correctly classed as apocalyptic . . ."[1] He

1. Paher, *Matthew 24*, 41. Concerning the relationship of genre and interpretation, see

307

defines apocalyptic as, "a type of literature which was written in troublous times during periods of trial, sorrow and near despair."[2] First of all, his definition of apocalyptic literature does not conform to the standard definition as one would find this in the literature from those who are scholars in the field of biblical studies. Definitions of apocalyptic literature have to do with the characteristics of the literature itself, not with external conditions in which the piece of literature is written. According to Paher's definition, a genealogical record would qualify as apocalyptic if it was written "in troublous times during periods of trial, sorrow and near despair."

Concerning the nature of apocalyptic literature, J. H. Charlesworth points out, "Unfortunately there is presently no consensus regarding the precise definition of this adjective [apocalyptic]; confusion sometimes arises because it is employed frequently in contradictory ways."[3] Apocalyptic literature is sometimes quite bizarre in its grotesque descriptions, after the manner of many passages in 3rd Enoch.[4] Many commentators classify Daniel as apocalyptic not because of the bizarre descriptions, but because Daniel involves revelation through vision or dreams. Whether Daniel should be classified as apocalyptic is a debated issue in biblical studies. There are portions of Daniel, for example, the visions of beasts in chapter 7, that seem to fit the often bizarre nature of apocalyptic literature. Notwithstanding these issues, and without providing any justification for his claim, Paher has already prepared the reader to accept his upcoming interpretations by suggesting that Daniel ought to be interpreted with a particular perspective, one that does not conform to standard definitions, but one that conforms to the way he has done it.

Paher goes on to declare, "By thus casting aside the principles of 'by whom to whom,' and of assigning primary application to contemporaries or perhaps subsequent generations, the premillennial interpretation offers little comfort and meaning to the faithful Jews of Daniel's day and others throughout the biblical era."[5] However, since the prophecies contained in chapters 7–12 were given at the time of and very shortly after Israel was released by Cyrus from their captivity in Babylon, Paher's criticism is completely deflated. Paher seems to have mistakenly assumed that the "to whom" of his "by whom

---

Thomas A. Howe, "Does Genre Determine Meaning," *Christian Apologetics Journal* Vol. 6, No. 1 (Spring 2007): 1–20.

2. Ibid.

3. J. H. Charlesworth, "Introduction," in *Apocalyptic Literature & Testaments*, vol. 1 *The Old Testament Pseudepigrapha*, 3.

4. *3 (Hebrew Apocalypse of) Enoch*, trans. P. Alexander, in *Apocalyptic Literature & Testaments*, vol. 2, *The Old Testament Pseudepigrapha*, ed. James H. Charlesworth (New York: Doubleday, 1983), 223–315.

5. Paher, *Matthew 24*, 42.

to whom" principle was the nation of Israel in their captivity in Babylon. But, this cannot be the case since they were no longer in captivity when Daniel is given these visions. Perhaps it is not the Premillennialists who have ignored the "immediate historical element" as Paher charges.

Daniel's Prayer: 9:1–19

Daniel Understands the Prophecy of Jeremiah: 9:1–2

1— In the first year of Darius the son of Ahasuerus, of Median descent, who was made king over the kingdom of the Chaldeans—

2— in the first year of his reign, I, Daniel, observed in the books the number of the years which was revealed as the word of the Lord to Jeremiah the prophet for the completion of the desolations of Jerusalem, namely, seventy years.

In the first year of Darius the Mede, while studying the books of the OT, Daniel observes in the prophecy of Jeremiah that the captivity of Israel would last for 70 years. Because Daniel calculated that this period of time had almost elapsed, he began to seek after God to fulfill His promise to restore the people to the land. Walvoord presents a lengthy discussion of the understanding of the phrase "desolations of Jerusalem," considering whether this refers to the restoration of the temple only, to the return of the people to the city of Jerusalem only, or to both. He concludes, "It is most significant that the return took place approximately seventy years after the capture of Jerusalem in 605 B.C., and the restoration of the temple (515 B.C.) took place approximately seventy years after the destruction of the temple (586 B.C.), the later period being about twenty years later than the former."[6] Miller proposes, "Since 605 B.C. was the year when the first captives were taken to Babylon (Daniel and his friends), the year that Judah came under Babylonian domination, and the year the prophecy was first given, it is reasonable to assume that Jeremiah intended this as the beginning date for the seventy-year captivity period. Cyrus issued the decree releasing the captives in 538/537 B.C., and the exiles returned shortly thereafter."[7] Although this is not precisely 70 years, the number is generally held to be a round number. If Daniel came into the land of his captors in 605 BC, and since the first year of Darius the Mede is dated at about 539 or 538 BC, this would mean that Daniel had been in Babylon for approximately 67 years, very close to the end of the 70 years of

6. Walvoord, *Daniel*, 204.

7. Miller, *Daniel*, 241.

captivity. Incidentally, if Daniel was taken into captivity in his mid-teens, he would be some 80 years of age at this time.

Daniel Confesses the Sins of Israel: 9:3–15

ISRAEL'S SIN: 9:3–6

3— So I gave my attention to the Lord God to seek Him by prayer and supplications, with fasting, sackcloth and ashes.

4— I prayed to the Lord my God and confessed and said, "Alas, O Lord, the great and awesome God, who keeps His covenant and loving-kindness for those who love Him and keep His commandments,

5— we have sinned, committed iniquity, acted wickedly and rebelled, even turning aside from Your commandments and ordinances.

6— Moreover, we have not listened to Your servants the prophets, who spoke in Your name to our kings, our princes, our fathers and all the people of the land."

This experience probably took place about 67 years after the captivity. Jeremiah had prophesied in 25:11–12 that Israel would be the servants of Babylon for a period of 70 years. This is probably an approximate number, indicating that the discipline would be complete. However, Daniel took the passage literally and understood Jeremiah's prophecy to mean that there would be about 70 actual years of literal captivity. In other words, Daniel did not understand the prophecy to be allegorical.

Not only had Jeremiah prophesied about the years of captivity, but he also prophesied about the return: "'Then you will call upon Me and come and pray to Me, and I will listen to you. You will seek Me and find when you search for Me with all your heart. I will be found by you,' declares the Lord, 'and I will restore your fortunes and will gather you from all the nations and from all the places where I have driven you,' declares the Lord, 'and I will bring you back to the place from where I sent you into exile'" (Jer 29:11–14). Apparently Daniel took this literally as well and prayed for God's mercy, confessing Israel's sins as if he were a part of them. Daniel confessed the sins of Israel that had led to the captivity. They had acted wickedly by going after other gods and violating the covenant relation, which constituted rebellion against God. Even though God had sent messengers to warn Israel of the path they were following, they did not listen nor heed the warnings.

God's Righteousness: 9:7–15

7—   "Righteousness belongs to You, O Lord, but to us open shame, as it is this day to the men of Judah, the inhabitants of Jerusalem and all Israel, those who are nearby and those who are far away in all the countries to which You have driven them, because of their unfaithful deeds which they have committed against You.

8—   "Open shame belongs to us, O Lord, to our kings, our princes and our fathers, because we have sinned against You.

9—   "To the Lord our God belong compassion and forgiveness, for we have rebelled against Him;

10—   nor have we obeyed the voice of the Lord our God, to walk in His teachings which He set before us through His servants the prophets.

11—   "Indeed all Israel has transgressed Your law and turned aside, not obeying Your voice; so the curse has been poured out on us, along with the oath which is written in the law of Moses the servant of God, for we have sinned against Him.

12—   "Thus He has confirmed His words which He had spoken against us and against our rulers who ruled us, to bring on us great calamity; for under the whole heaven there has not been done anything like what was done to Jerusalem.

13—   "As it is written in the law of Moses, all this calamity has come on us; yet we have not sought the favor of the Lord our God by turning from our iniquity and giving attention to Your truth.

14—   "Therefore the Lord has kept the calamity in store and brought it on us; for the Lord our God is righteous with respect to all His deeds which He has done, but we have not obeyed His voice.

15—   "And now, O Lord our God, who have brought Your people out of the land of Egypt with a mighty hand and have made a name for Yourself, as it is this day-we have sinned, we have been wicked.

Throughout Daniel's prayer there is a confession of the sin of the people and their unworthiness, having rejected God and His covenant. There is a corresponding emphasis on God's righteousness. God had warned the people time and again until finally there was simply no other action to take than that of discipline. Amid all the terrible fortunes which had come upon the people of God, God was still righteous, and the calamities were entirely the fault of the people of Israel.

Daniel points out that the people of Israel are covered with shame. TWOT gives a very insightful explanation of the use of this word:

> The third usage and the one that is most common carries the above thought further expressing the disgrace which is the result of defeat at the hands of an enemy, either in battle or in some other manner. In particular, the awful shame of being paraded as captives is thought of (Mic 1:11; cf. also Jer 2:26). Involved here are all the nuances of confusion, disillusionment, humiliation, and brokenness which the word connotes. The prophets normally use the word with this sense, promising Israel that unless she repents and turns from her idolatrous ways, she will certainly experience the shame of defeat and exile. (Cf. Isa 1:29; 30:5; Jer 2:36; 9:19 [H 18]; Ezr 9:6; Dan 9:7, etc.). Intimately associated with this third use of the word is the question of trust. If Israel seeks to insure her own glory by refusing to trust in God but rather trusts in idols (Isa 1:29) or in foreign nations (Isa 20:5; 30:3,5), she will not get glory, but shame and disgrace. On the other hand, if one will humbly submit to God, he will find his true glory, for God will not let that person come to shame (Isa 29:22; Joel 2:26, 27; Zeph 3:19). It is this promise of which the Psalmist continually reminds God. (Ps 25:3; 31:17 [H18]; 37:19; 119:46)[8]

This is an important point, which is why Daniel uses the word twice, in verses 7 and 8. A point upon which Daniel will capitalize later is that the shame of Israel, which has no doubt been brought upon them by their own sin, nevertheless reflects on the name of God since they are the people of God. A similar point was made by Moses when he interceded for Israel in Ex 32:12: "Why should the Egyptians speak, saying, 'With evil *intent* He brought them out to kill them in the mountains and to destroy them from the face of the earth'?" Here Moses makes the point that because these people are the people whom God brought out of Egypt, if He destroys them, then this will appear to the Egyptians that God had an evil intent all along. The fate of the people of God reflects on the nature of God. That is way Isaiah declared, "'Now therefore, what do I have here,' declares the LORD, 'seeing that My people have been taken away without cause?' *Again* the LORD declares, 'Those who rule over them howl, and My name is continually blasphemed all day long'" (Isa 52:5).

---

8. TWOT, s.v. "בּוֹשׁ."

Daniel Pleads the Glory of God: 9:16–19

16— "O Lord, in accordance with all Your righteous acts, let now Your anger and Your wrath turn away from Your city Jerusalem, Your holy mountain; for because of our sins and the iniquities of our fathers, Jerusalem and Your people have become a reproach to all those around us.

17— "So now, our God, listen to the prayer of Your servant and to his supplications, and for Your sake, O Lord, let Your face shine on Your desolate sanctuary.

18— "O my God, incline Your ear and hear! Open Your eyes and see our desolations and the city which is called by Your name; for we are not presenting our supplications before You on account of any merits of our own, but on account of Your great compassion.

19— "O Lord, hear! O Lord, forgive! O Lord, listen and take action! For Your own sake, O my God, do not delay, because Your city and Your people are called by Your name."

Daniel's petition is that God would restore His holy city and His people to the land, in essence, to fulfill the prophecy which He gave through Jeremiah. It is important that Daniel points out in verse 19 that his petition to God to restore the city and the people was not based on any righteousness of their own, but "because Your city and Your people are called by Your name." As long as the city and the people were defeated, desolate, and in open shame this presented a poor witness for God, and their defeat was a reproach upon God. Quoting the Isaiah passage cited above, Paul points out in Rom 2:24, "The Name of God is blasphemed among the Gentiles because of you."

The action that Daniel took was to seek God in prayer and supplication for the people of Israel. The second part of verse 14 sums up the basis of Daniel's prayer: "the Lord our God is righteous with respect to all His deeds which He has done, but we have not obeyed His voice." Daniel is totally consumed with the plight of his people and the desolation of the holy city and the holy temple. This entire prayer sets the stage for the prophetic pronouncements which would be delivered to Daniel by the angel Gabriel. Not only would God fulfill His prophetic declaration to bring Israel back into the land after the seventy years of captivity, but God would show Daniel His overall plan for Israel. Gabriel now appears with information by which Daniel can understand the plan of God for Israel.

Daniel's Vision: 9:20–27

Daniel is Confronted by Gabriel: 9:20–21

20— Now while I was speaking and praying, and confessing my sin and the sin of my people Israel, and presenting my supplication before the Lord my God in behalf of the holy mountain of my God,

21— while I was still speaking in prayer, then the man Gabriel, whom I had seen in the vision previously, came to me in my extreme weariness about the time of the evening offering.

While Daniel was praying and confessing the sins of his people, the man Gabriel, whom he had seen in the previous vision, came to him. Daniel says the man (הָאִישׁ, *sî'ah*) came to him in his "extreme weariness about the time of the evening offering." Although there had been no evening offering since the destruction of the temple in 586 BC, Daniel notes that is was at this time that Gabriel appeared to him. This may indicate the times that Daniel knelt at his window to pray, that is, at the morning and evening offerings, and prior to sleep.

Daniel is Informed by Gabriel: 9:22–23

22— He gave me instruction and talked with me and said, "O Daniel, I have now come forth to give you insight with understanding.

23— "At the beginning of your supplications the command was issued, and I have come to tell you, for you are highly esteemed; so give heed to the message and gain understanding of the vision.

The man, an angelic figure, appeared to Daniel with the announcement that he had come to give Daniel "insight and understanding" (לְהַשְׂכִּילְךָ בִינָה, *haṇib̄ aklîksah̄el*). The word translated "insight" is the same word used in Gen 3:6: "When the woman saw that the tree was good for food, and that it was a delight to the eyes, and that the tree was desirable to make *one* wise [לְהַשְׂכִּיל, *lîksah̄el*] . . ." or to give insight. The kind of wisdom that the couple sought by their own efforts is the kind of wisdom that must come from God.

In verse 2 Daniel said, "I, Daniel, observed in the books . . ." The word "observed" (בִּין, *n̂ib*) is the same word used here in verse 22 and translated "understanding" (בִינָה, *ḥan̂ib*). Daniel read the prophecy of Jeremiah and understood the meaning of the prophecy and the seventy years of desolations that had come upon his people. Now Gabriel has come to give Daniel insight into the future of Daniel's people. Gabriel informs Daniel, "At the beginning of your supplications the command was issued, and I have come to tell you, for you are highly esteemed; so give heed to the message and gain understanding of the vision."

What about the Hebrew Text, the Septuagint, and Theodotion's Text?

Before the commentary on these crucial verses gets under way, it is important to deal with the claims that have been made regarding the Greek translation of the Old Testament as this relates to understanding the details of Daniel's prophecy. Much has been made of the differences between the Masoretic Text[9] (MT) and the Greek translations. Evans in particular attempts to jettison the MT in favor of Theodotion's (θ) Greek text. For example, Evans presents a standard argument: "Because the MT is in Hebrew, many authorities claim that it should be judged the more authentic version. This argument, however, skips over the fact that the MT was not finalized until the ninth to tenth century AD."[10] This statement is misleading and inaccurate. It is not accurate to say that the MT was "finalized" in the ninth to tenth century. In fact, the Qumran Isaiah scroll is almost identical to the MT version of Isaiah, demonstrating that the text was fixed long before the ninth or tenth century AD. As James VanderKam asserts, "The most famous of all the [Qumran] scrolls, the Great Isaiah Scroll (1QIsaᵃ) was the only one to emerge virtually complete from the caves of Qumran. The orthography (spelling) is very full, and paleographic analysis shows that the manuscript was copied in about 125 BCE. In its fifty-four columns, 1QIsaᵃ preserves all sixty-six chapters of Isaiah, except for small gaps resulting from leather damage (notably in col. 1–9). The text of this scroll is generally in agreement with the Masoretic Text, but it contains many variant readings and corrections, which are of great interest to scholars."[11] VanderKam goes on to state, "With respect to the text of Daniel, all eight scrolls reveal no major disagreements against the Masoretic Text, although 1QDanᵃ is closest to the traditional text. . . . A final question concerns the bilingual nature of Daniel, which in the Hebrew Bible opens in Hebrew, switches to Aramaic at 2:4b, and then reverts to Hebrew at 8:1 . . . the scrolls show us that Daniel existed in this form very early on and was thus most likely compiled in Hebrew and Aramaic."[12] All of this goes to show that Evans'

9. The term "Masoretic Text," or MT, refers to the Hebrew Bible that is the predominate text in Old Testament studies. Theodotion's Greek translation of the Old Testament is identified by the letter *thēta*, θ.

10. Evans, *Four Kingdoms*, 328.

11. James VanderKam and Peter Flint, *The Meaning of the Dead Sea Scrolls*, 131.

12. Ibid., 138.

argument has actually misrepresented the case. What Evans' is alluding to is the fact that the pointing system for representing the vowel sounds was not completed until the sixth to the ninth century. However, the text was stable and fixed many centuries before the vowel pointing system was perfected.

Lucas points out, "Jerome, writing at the end of the fourth century, says that in Christian use the Septuagint (LXX [also referred to as the Old Greek, or OG]) text of Daniel was replaced by Theodotion's version (θ) because the former differed so widely from the Hebrew and Aramaic text."[13] In other words, the Greek translation, which Preterists seem to prefer, replaced the OG in order to bring it in line with the Hebrew text that is substantially the same as the MT. Evans declares, "A fundamental assumption of the preterist approach to the prophecy of the seventy sevens is that translations based on Theodotion are preferable to translations based on the Masoretic Text."[14] But Evans totally ignores the fact that Theodotion's translation was made in order to bring it more into line with the Hebrew text that is substantially the same as the MT. This indicates that even for the Greek translation of θ the MT was the standard of meaning.

Evans is seeking to remove a tool that liberal scholars use to question the meaning of the text. However, liberal interpretations of the MT are not necessitated by the text but by the liberal perspective. It is not inevitable that a translation based on the MT will necessarily arrive at a text that supports a liberal interpretation. Evans argues, "*Many conservatives argue, with good reason, that the MT for Daniel 9:24–27 is not entirely trustworthy because the rabbinical authorities may have altered the punctuation of the text so as to eliminate the implication that Jesus was the Messiah.*"[15] But why does Evans think that Theodotion would be any better at understanding the MT than modern conservative scholars? If the rabbinical authorities altered the punctuation of the text then they did not disturb the consonantal text, and, after all, conservatives believe that the consonantal text is the inspired text. Also, if the rabbinical authorities altered the text of the MT, then the Greek translators would be translating from this altered text. Evans seems to think that somehow Theodotion's text would be immune to errors of its own—that somehow the translator has produced an inerrant text.

The fact of the matter is, there is no good reason wholly to dismiss the MT in favor of the Greek text. Although there may be variant readings in which the evidence goes against the MT, these instances will be subject to judgment on the basis of the evidence. There is no warrant for a wholesale

13. Lucas, *Daniel*, 19.

14. Evans, *Four Kingdoms*, 360.

15. Ibid., 328 (emphasis in original).

rejection of the MT as less authoritative than the Greek, especially since the Greek is a translation of the very text that Evans seeks to jettison. Additionally, as we will see, adopting the reading of θ does not support the Preterist interpretations any more than does the MT.

Daniel is Enlightened by Gabriel: 9:24–27

The importance of this section of prophecy cannot be overstated. In the Old Testament, it is probably the most hotly debated prophetic passage, comparable to the Matthew 24 passage in the New Testament. Because of this we will place the verse or portion of the verse at each new point of the discussion so that we can be reminded of the text. Also, since much of the debate will focus on the language, along with the English translation, we will provide the Hebrew text with word-for-word translation where appropriate.

24— "Seventy sevens have been decreed upon your people and your holy city, to finish the transgression, to make an end of sin, to make atonement for iniquity, to bring in everlasting righteousness, to seal up vision and prophecy, and to anoint the most holy of holies."

25— "So you are to know and discern *that* from the issuing of a decree to restore and rebuild Jerusalem until Messiah the Prince *there will be* seven weeks and sixty-two weeks; it will be built again, with plaza and moat, even in times of distress."

26— "Then after the sixty-two weeks the Messiah will be cut off and have nothing, and the people of the prince who is to come will destroy the city and the sanctuary. And its end *will come* with a flood; even to the end there will be war; desolations are determined."

27— "And he will make a firm covenant with the many for one week, but in the middle of the week he will put a stop to sacrifice and grain offering; and on the wing of abominations *will come* one who makes desolate, even until a complete destruction, one that is decreed, is poured out on the one who makes desolate."

DANIEL 9:24

The "Seventy Sevens"

24—   "*Seventy sevens* have been decreed upon your people and your holy
         city . . ."

Table 22: Daniel 9:24a

נֶחְתַּךְ	שִׁבְעִים	שָׁבֻעִים
are decreed	seventy	Sevens
וְעַל-	עַמְּךָ	עַל-
and upon	your people	upon
	קָדְשֶׁךָ	עִיר
	your holy.	city

The "Seventy Sevens" prophecy is perhaps the most important prophecy in
the book of Daniel, and perhaps in the Old Testament. It is by far the most
frequently discussed Old Testament passage when it comes to the issues of
eschatology. Max King is author of one of the most influential books on eschatology from a Preterist perspective. He stresses the importance of Daniel's
seventy sevens prophecy: "Daniel's prophecy of seventy weeks is important to
us not only because it is the heart of Bible prophecy, but especially because
it is a prophecy with a strong time element."[16] King criticizes much of what
is said about this prophecy: "A weakness of a lot of biblical eschatology is the
tendency to ignore the time element of a prophecy simply because the historical events of that predicted time do not match our concept of what was to
take place. It is more likely, however, that our concept is wrong, rather than
the timing of the prophecy."[17] However, on the very next page King seems to
do what he identifies as a weakness in others—he is determining the time of
the prophecy based on his concept of what could have taken place. He says,

> The first thing we need to consider is the entire time period in-
> volved, which is specified as seventy weeks. The Hebrew here
> means, literally, seventy "sevens"—"seven" being a common desig-
> nation for a week. It also can be a designation for a period of seven
> years (Lev. 25:1–10), and this latter rendering makes the most

16. Max R. King, *The Spirit of Prophecy*, 84.
17. Ibid.

sense in our context. Rendered as seventy seven-day periods the timeframe in question is 490 days, or less than two years. It seems unlikely that Daniel would be told to seal up a prophecy that was only two years from fulfillment. The three major events—the restoration of the city, the advent and rejection of the Messiah, and the eventual overthrow of the city and nation—could not possibly be accomplished in 490 days.[18]

In other words, on the basis of King's concept of how the history should take place, he is formulating what must have been the meaning of the time element. Although his conclusion seems to be correct, it is nevertheless the same methodology for which he criticizes others. Apparently, it is in fact not a weakness to attempt to understand the time elements in terms of our concept of how the history took place. If we cannot appeal to the history to aid in our understanding of the time elements, then the giving of the time elements themselves becomes unintelligible.

Kenneth Gentry provides a helpful argument for understanding the seventy sevens as referring to seventy groups of seven years.

> The seventy weeks represent a period of seventy times seven years, or 490 years: (1) In the preceding context, the original seventy years of Jeremiah's prophecy is in Daniel's mind (Dan. 9:2). Years are suggested, then, by the prior reference which is crucial to the historical context. (2) The sabbath year (the seventh year of the sabbath period) is frequently referred to simply as "the sabbath." Thus, a "sabbath day" (Gen. 2:2; Exo. 20:11) is expanded to cover a year. (3) There is Scriptural warrant for measuring days in terms of years in certain passages (Gen. 29:27–28; Num. 14:34; Deut. 14:28; 1 Sam. 2:19; Eze. 4:6; Amos 4:4). (4) Daniel seems to shift gears and even notify the reader of the change in Daniel 10:2, where he qualifies his situation by saying he mourned "three weeks of days." (Heb)[19]

There seems to be little doubt that the term "sevens" indicates a group of seven years, and, regardless of what eschatological perspective to which they hold, the vast majority of commentators understand these terms as referring to seventy groups of seven years, or 490 years.

John Noē is author of a very popular and influential text promoting the Full Preterist View. He also identifies this as a period of 490 years. He says,

> The Hebrew word (*sha bu'a*), translated above as "sevens," or "weeks" in some versions, literally means a unit, a period or a group

18. Ibid., 85.
19. Gentry, *He Shall Have Dominion*, 322.

of seven of something. It's akin to our English word *dozen*, which
means a unit of twelve of something. The word by itself does not
tell us what the units are. Most interpreters agree that Daniel's sevens of something was sevens of years. They have two good reasons:
1) Jeremiah's original prophecy of "seventy" was an explicit period
of 70 years of Babylonian captivity. This time of deportation was
to serve as both the setting (2 Ch. 36:21) and an uninterrupted
archetype for Daniel's 70 weeks. 2) This concept of time was not
new. God had used the same biblical concept of "weeks of years"
from the beginning of Israel's history under Moses (Lev. 25:8). He
had equated days to years for determining their period of wandering in the wilderness (Nu. 14:34). He had divided the Hebrew
calendar into seven-year periods with every seventh year being a
sabbatical year. Also, the seven years that Jacob worked for Rachel
was called "the fulfilling of her week" (Ge. 29:27, 28 KJV). We
agree with the standard interpretation that "seventy sevens" means
"[*sic*] seventy times seven years, or a total time span equating to
490 years.[20]

The precedent for taking the word "seven" as indicating a group of seven
things, and in this case a group of seven years, is sufficient both within and
outside of the book of Daniel, and is generally held by most conservative
scholars, whether Preterist of Futurist.

There are several factors that are important to note in this section of the
prophecy.

1. The prophecy concerns Daniel's people and Daniel's holy city: "for
    your people and your holy city" (עַל־עַמְּךָ וְעַל־עִיר קָדְשֶׁךָ,
    ⁻akĕsdaq rı̂ˁ laˁᵉwˉakᵉmmaˁ laˁ). This can be a reference only to
    Israel and Jerusalem. This prophecy does not directly relate to the
    Christian church as it is defined and described by Paul in the book of
    Ephesians. The seventy sevens is determined upon Israel. However,
    this does not necessarily mean it will have nothing to do with the
    Christian church at all. That is, although it is directly decreed upon
    Israel, this does not mean it cannot have some implications for the
    church or some impact on the Christian church or other possible
    relations to the Christian church. It means only that the period is not
    decreed upon the Christian church.

2. The "seventy weeks" (שָׁבֻעִים שִׁבְעִים, mı̂ˁbı̂s mı̂ˁ ubăs) is better
    understood as, "seventy sevens." The English term "weeks" tends to
    cause one to think in terms of days rather than years. Also, at this
    point in the chapter the term "seventy" recalls the "seventy" of verse

20. Noë, *Beyond the End Times*, 79.

2. The seventy sevens which are determined upon Israel seem to be related to the seventy years of captivity, which was also determined upon Israel.

3. During this period of seventy sevens, six things will be accomplished. The English translations of these phrases are from the *New American Standard Bible-Updated* and may not reflect the best translation of the Hebrew text. These issues will be taken up in the examination of each phrase in its turn.

   A. "to finish the transgression"
      לְכַלֵּא הַפֶּשַׁע (*lᵉʿǎseppah ʾellaḵ*)

   B. "to make an end of sin"
      לְחָתֵם חַטָּאוֹת (*lᵉtoʾaṭṭah mēṭah*)

   C. "and to make atonement for iniquity"
      וּלְכַפֵּר עָוֺן (*ñowaʿ ñeppaḵlu*)

   D. "and to bring in everlasting righteousness"
      וּלְהָבִיא צֶדֶק עֹלָמִים (*ñumalo ʾqedesʾıbahlu*)

   E. "and to seal up the vision and prophecy"
      וְלַחְתֹּם חָזוֹן וְנָבִיא (*wᵉwʾñozahʾñothalᵉʾıban*)

   F. "and to anoint the most Holy"
      וְלִמְשֹׁחַ קֹדֶשׁ קָדָשִׁים: (*wᵉñısadaqʾsᵉdoqʾhǎŏsmil*)

4. These six phrases are structured similarly: each one consists of an infinitive construct[21] with an inseparable preposition, לְ (lamed, "*l*"), as a prefix, and a noun as its object. Considering the words themselves, there are some features that are not obvious from the English text. These will be discussed at the appropriate point in the commentary.

5. On an infinitive construct, an inseparable preposition prefix can be used to express purpose.[22] In other words, the seventy sevens are decreed for the purpose of accomplishing these six things.

---

21. According to Waltke and O'Connor, an infinitive construct is, "The ordinary Hebrew infinitive . . . a verbal noun used in the ways the English uses its infinitive ('to go) and its gerund ('going')." Waltke and O'Connor, *Biblical Hebrew Syntax*, 36.1.1.

22. See Waltke and O'Connor, *Biblical Hebrew Syntax*, 36.2.3.

The Seventy Sevens are "Decreed"

24—   "Seventy sevens have been *decreed* upon your people and your holy city . . ."

Discussing the word "decreed" or "determined," Kelly Birks, another Preterist author, asserts, "The Hebrew word for 'determined,' is HATAQ."[23] Of this word, Birks says, "An interesting definition of HATAQ is pointed out in Wilson's Old Testament Word Studies. He shows that the word has connotations of 'cutting.' To HATAQ, is to cut or divide something one from another in order to make a decision about it."[24] There are some problems with Birks' claims about this word. First of all, Birks gives an incorrect transliteration of the word. The root is חתך and should be transliterated *kth*. The use of the "Q" is non-standard and does not accurately represent the Hebrew letter. This should alert the reader to be particularly careful in considering Birks' claims about the Hebrew or Aramaic text. Such non-standard transliteration may indicate that Birks is not proficient in the original language.

The word in Daniel's text is נֶחְתַּךְ (*kathen*). This word occurs only in Dan. 9:24 and nowhere else in the Old Testament. According to KBH, there is no sense of "to cut" in the use of this Hebrew word. KBH points out that in Jewish Aramaic and in Middle Hebrew the term had the connotation of "cut," and the Arabic cognate has the sense of "to tear," but the Hebrew word has neither of these senses in the time of Daniel.[25] Emile Nicole and Eugene Carpenter point out that, "This root is common in medieval and modern Heb. with the primary sense 'cut' and the secondary meaning 'decide, pronounce as sentence."[26] Birks, influenced by *Wilson's Old Testament Word Studies*, has read back into the word in Daniel's time a Medieval and Modern Hebrew meaning. The meaning in the time of Daniel is "determine" or "impose," as indicated in KBH.

Birks goes on to declare, "To make a precise determination. (Wilson, Pg. 122) This presents us with the idea that this time was settled in God's plans for the full redemption of His elect, and the complete retribution towards His

---

23. Kelly Nelson Birks, *The Comings of the Christ: A Reformed and Preterist Analogy of the 70th Week of the Prophet Daniel*, 8. Right away the reader should be alerted to the fact that this author has very little if any training in biblical Hebrew. The proper transliteration of this word is *hthk*. Because the word occurs only in the Niphal form, the three letter root, חתך (*kth*) does not actually have vowel points. The letter *kaph* ך (*k*) is transliterated by the English letter "c" or "k," not by the "Q" as Birks has it. In fact, the ק *Joqis* normaly transliterated with the English letter *q*.

24. Ibid.

25. KBH, s.v. "חתך."

26. *New International Dictionary of Old Testament Theology & Exegesis* (1997), s.v. "חתך." Hereafter referred to as NIDOTTE.

unfaithful earthly people, Israel. Like a surveyor would stretch out his line in order to set out the exact boundaries of a piece of property, so God has settled the matter of the exact length of time that the people of Israel would have to exist as God's chosen earthly people, and the exact length of time that was left on the Messianic clock as it ticked toward the first coming of the Son of Man to do the will of the Father."[27] Not only has Birks imposed the incorrect meaning upon the word, but he has extracted quite a bit of meaning out of this one word that occurs only here in the OT. Since the word does not have the "connotations" that Birks thinks, his conclusions do not follow. The word simply indicates that "seventy sevens" have been determined or imposed upon Daniel's people and Daniel's holy city.

Roy Anderson also comments on the term "determined." He says, "Now note Gabriel's message to Daniel: 'Seventy weeks are determined upon thy people.' The word 'determined' *chathak* in Hebrew, has been variously translated as 'decreed,' 'divided,' 'shortened,' 'fixed,' 'cut-off,' 'cut short,' 'apportioned,' and 'allotted.' These variations are significant. Seventy prophetic weeks were allotted to the Jews, during which certain definite things were to happen. The period of time was 'cut off' or 'shortened' from the longer period of 2,300 prophetic days (literal years) of chapter 8, which the prophet said no one understood."[28] In this instance, Anderson is influenced by *Strong's Hebrew and Chaldee Dictionary* which uses an older transliteration scheme. The problem here is that Strong's is not a standard Hebrew Lexicon. Strong's dictionary simply identifies various glosses or words the translation uses and does not actually provide an account of the semantic range as the standard lexicon does. Nevertheless, out of the possible glosses that he finds in Strong's, Anderson simply chooses the one he likes and then attempts to build his interpretation on that. In fact, in his discussion Anderson gives the word two different meanings. He says, "Seventy prophetic weeks were *allotted* to the Jews," then he says, "The period of time was 'cut off' or 'shortened' . . ." If the word in question means "cut off" or "shorten," then where is Anderson getting the idea that the time was "allotted"? Both meanings must have come from the same word. But, the same word cannot have two opposing meanings in the same instance! And, as we have seen, the word cannot mean "cut off" in this context. Based on a faulty understanding of meaning, Anderson constructs an incorrect interpretation of the text.

The word "determined" does not necessarily have the sense of an official decree, as one established by a king. Rather, in this context it has the sense of having been authoritatively fixed as a determined period of time in which

---

27. Birks, *The Comings of the Christ*, 8.

28. Roy Allan Anderson, *Unfolding Daniel's Prophecies*, 113.

the stated goals will be achieved. KBH indicates that it also has the notion of being "imposed."[29] The sense here is that this determinate period of time, seventy sevens, or 490 years, has been set as a determinate period of time, and this determination has been imposed upon Israel and Jerusalem in order to accomplish the six items enumerated.

Upon Your People and Your Holy City

24—   "Seventy sevens have been decreed *upon your people and your holy city . . .*"

Almost all commentators understand this phrase, "upon your people and your holy city" (עַל־עַמְּךָ וְעַל־עִיר קָדְשֶׁךָ, *ʿî laʿw ak̲mmaʿ laʿ ʾak̲ĕsdaq*), to be a reference to the people of Israel and the city of Jerusalem. This fact is not disputed to any significant degree, and among Evangelical authors, it is not disputed at all. The fact that the prophecy of the seventy sevens is decreed upon the people of Israel and the city of Jerusalem is not only indicated by the fact that the angel is talking to Daniel when he says, "your people . . ." but it is also indicated by the prayer and confession of Daniel in the early portion of this chapter. Daniel is interceding for his people and his holy city, confessing the sins of the people of Israel and pleading with God to restore the people and the city of Jerusalem.

The fact that the seventy sevens is decreed upon the people of Israel and the city of Jerusalem is not a matter to be passed over lightly. This fact indicates that the time span is decreed with reference to Israel and Jerusalem, not with reference to the Christian church or the Gentiles. This is not to say that the content of the prophecy does not impact or include Gentiles or Christians in some way, but that the prophecy is not focused on these groups. This implies that other factors relating to the kingdoms of the Gentiles or the Christian church may not be included within the seventy sevens.

To Finish the Transgression

24—   ". . . *to finish the transgression,* to make an end of sin, to make atonement for iniquity, to bring in everlasting righteousness, to seal up vision and prophecy and to anoint the holy of holies."

---

29. KBH, s.v. "חתך."

Table 23: Daniel 9:24b

לַחְתֵּם	הַפֶּשַׁע	לְכַלֵּא
to seal up	the transgression	to finish
עָוֹן	וּלְכַפֵּר	חַטָּאוֹת
iniquity	and to make atonement for	the sin
עֹלָמִים	צֶדֶק	וּלְהָבִיא
eternities	righteousness of	and to bring in
וְנָבִיא	חָזוֹן	וְלַחְתֹּם
and prophet	vision	and to seal up
קָדָשִׁים׃	קֹדֶשׁ	וְלִמְשֹׁחַ
holies.	holy of	and to anoint

In the first phrase, "to finish the transgression," the word translated "finish," כָּלָה, *ḥalak*, (most commentators accept the Qere, כלה, *hlk*, rather than the Ketib, כלא, *ʾlk*, because it fits better with the following statement),[30] can also mean, "complete, bring to an end, use up, consume, or destroy."[31] The verb כלא (*ʾlk*) has the sense of "refrain" or "shut up" or "withhold."[32] Although some commentators take the meaning here as "refrain" or "resist," this does not seem to fit the context. To refrain sin implies that sin is still present and active even though it is being resisted. However, the sense of the other infinitives leads one to expect that sin would be "finished" or "brought to an end," not simply refrained or resisted. The phrase is, לְכַלֵּא הַפֶּשַׁע (*keʾlaʿăseppah ʾell*). The verb כלה (*hlk*) is used in Dan 12:7 in two senses: "I heard the man dressed in linen, who was above the waters of the river, as he

---

30. See *Biblia Hebraica Stuttgartensia*, n24ᵇ: "K a כלא (melius qal) cf K ad ᵈ, Q mlt Mss a כלה cf Q ad ᵈ." The expression "Qere" and "Ketib" are used to make a distinction between "that which is read," Qere, and "that which is written," Ketib (or Ketiv). Emanuel Tov provides a helpful explanation: "In a large number of instances—ranging from 848 to 1566 in different traditions—the *Mp* [*Masorah parva*] notes that one should disregard the written form of the text (in the Aramaic language of the Masorah: כְּתִיב, *kethib*, 'what is written') and read instead a different word or words (in Aramaic: קְרֵי, *qěrê*, 'what is read')." Emanuel Tov, *Textual Criticism of the Hebrew Bible*, 58.

31. KBH, s.v. "כלה."

32. KBH, s.v. "כלא."

raised his right hand and his left toward heaven, and swore by Him who lives forever that it would be for a time, times, and half; and as soon as they cease [(1) וּכְכַלּוֹת] shattering the power of the holy people, all these will be completed [(2) תִּכְלֶ֫ יְנָה]." The first use is the sense of ceasing from the action of shattering, and the second use is the sense of something being brought to completion. The first use is a Piel verb, whereas the second is a Qal. Since the form in Dan 7:24 is also Piel, the sense of "ceasing" or "bringing to an end" fits the context and is probably the sense that should be taken here.

Max King asserts, "'To finish the transgression' is more properly translated 'To restrain transgression.'"[33] However, according to KBH, this is not one of the possible meanings of the word כלה (hlk), although it is one of the meanings of כלא, 'lk. The LXX translates the Hebrew with συντελέω (oeletnus), which does not have the meaning "restrain," and the Syriac uses ܠܡܫܠܡ (mĭsml) from ܫܠܡ (mĭls), which has the same range of meaning as the Hebrew word כלה (hlk), "to cease" or "to bring to an end."[34] Not only does כלה (hlk) fit the context better, but also it is supported by both the LXX and the Syriac.[35] Contrary to the Preterists' claims, the Greek text does not support the Preterist view here. Both θ and the Syriac support the MT.

Birks claims that modern English translations do not "translate the passage correctly" because they do not "follow the Hebrew as direct as [they] should."[36] He therefore offers his understanding of the meaning: "The Hebrew text of the Masorets has, KALA PESHA: 'To hold back the rebellion, or restrict, or restrain the rebellion.' So the correct Hebrew here of what Daniel originally wrote was that the Messiah would arrive in order to 'hold back, or restrain the rebellion.'"[37] First of all, Birks does not inform the reader whether he is commenting on the Ketib or the Qere. Birks transliterates the Hebrew word as "KALA." But Birks has failed to indicate the final letter of the word to which he is referring. Both כָּלָא (kālā) and כָּלָה (kālāh) have the same first four letters, ālak. Without the final letter, Birks' readers can only surmise that he has opted for כָּלָא. But we have already shown that this is the less likely option in this context. Second, Birks does not cite any sources from which he obtained his lexical information. Third, having misunderstood the word,

---

33. King, *The Spirit of Prophecy*, 104.

34. *A Compendious Syriac Dictionary* (1990), s.v. "ܫܠܡ."

35. Even the Vulgate supports this meaning. It uses the word "*consummetur*" meaning "to complete" or "to finish" or "to bring to an end." *A Latin Dictionary Founded on Andrews' Edition of Freund's Latin Dictionary* (1966), s.v. "con-summo." *Oxford Latin Dictionary* (2005), s.v. "consummō."

36. Birks, *The Comings of the Christ*, 15.

37. Ibid.

Birks' interpretation of the text goes in completely the wrong direction, as the following discussion will make clear.

As we pointed out earlier, Dan 12:7 uses the word כָּלָה (*ḥalak*) in two senses. The first instance of the use of the word in Dan. 12:7 indicates that something is finished or ended. A task can cease whether it has fulfilled its goal or not. In the sense of "shattering the power of the holy people," this is analogous to beating someone. When someone is beating another person, we can say, "he stopped beating him up" without implying that he did everything that he could have done to that person. So also, the expression "cease shattering the power" may simply be saying that they stopped doing it without saying whether they shattered the power completely and utterly—they simply stopped doing it. In Ps 31:10(H11), the writer says, "For my life is spent [כָּלוּ, *ulak* from כלה] with sorrow . . ." This is a reference to the fact that the Psalmist's sorrow has virtually brought his life to an end. Of course the Psalmist's life was not brought to an end, since he lived to write the Psalm. If this is the sense in Dan 9:24, the phrase could be translated "to cause the transgression to cease."

The second instance in Dan 12:7 seems to indicate that a task has been completed in the sense of having accomplished what it was supposed to accomplish. If this is the sense in 9:24, the phrase could conceivably be translated, "to bring the transgression to an end" or "to fill it up." In the passages in 12:7 and 9:24 the idea would seem to be to bring something to its end, or cause it to be finished. Either the first or the second sense could be used in Dan 9:24, and in either case, the notion seems at least to be that sin is finished.

The word translated "transgression" is פֶּשַׁע (*'asep*), which occurs in Dan 8:12: "And on account of transgression [בְּפֶשַׁע, *'asaf*b] the host will be given over to the horn along with the regular sacrifice; and it will fling truth to the ground and perform its will and prosper"—and 8:13: "How long will the vision about the regular sacrifice apply, while the transgression [וְהַפֶּשַׁע, *ah*ʷwpʾasep*]causes horror, so as to allow both the holy place and the host to be trampled?" Although the word occurs in these two verses in chapter 8, this does not necessarily mean that the word in 9:24 is referring to the same transgressions that are spoken of there. If such a link exists, it must be demonstrated, not assumed.

Philip Mauro asserts, "Daniel himself had confessed this saying, 'Yea, all Israel *have transgressed Thy law*, even by departing that they might not obey Thy voice. Therefore the curse is poured upon us' (ver. 11)."[38] However, the word that is used in verse 11 for "transgression," עָבַר (*raba'*), is not the same

---

38. Mauro, *The Seventy Weeks*, 44–45.

word used in 9:24, which is פֶּשַׁע (ʿāsep). If these words are used as synonyms, this cannot merely be assumed but must be demonstrated to be the
case. Mauro goes on to assert, "But the angel revealed to him the distressing
news that the full measure of Israel's 'transgression' was yet to be completed;
that the children were yet to fill up the iniquity of their fathers; and that, as a
consequence, God would bring upon them a far greater 'desolation' than that
which had been wrought by Nebuchadnezzar. For 'to finish the transgression'
could mean nothing less or other than the betrayal and crucifixion of their
promised and expected Messiah."[39] The problem here is that Mauro has not
demonstrated that this is the meaning or even an implication of the statement
in 9:24. It seems to make sense in the context, and it may prove to be true,
but this cannot be simply asserted. It must be proven. Mauro's claims are
particularly problematic since the words used are different words.

That the expression "to finish the transgression" may refer to the transgression of Israel concerning which Daniel prayed in the earlier portion of
chapter 9 may be true but must deal with the fact that there are two different
words used in chapter 9 that are translated "transgression." Interestingly, there
is one instance in the Hebrew Bible where these two words seem to be used
in poetic parallelism: Hos 8:1 "*Put* the trumpet to your lips! Like an eagle *the
enemy comes* against the house of the LORD, because they have transgressed
[עָבְרוּ, ʿurba ʿ] My covenant and rebelled [פָּשָׁעוּ, uʿāsap] against My law."
The fact that they can be used as synonyms does not support Mauro's claim
however. Daniel is not praying about a transgression that will happen after his
time—that is, Daniel's prayer is not about the crucifixion of the Messiah. If
the transgression that is to be finished is the transgression of Israel, then it is
the transgression of Israel that happened before Daniel's day. In fact, it may
be a reference to the transgression that led to Israel's captivity. As the passage
in Hosea asserts, and as Daniel confessed, Israel rebelled against Torah, and
they transgressed the covenant by going after false gods. This is the rebellion
that led to Israel's captivity. It is possible, then, that the phrase "to finish the
transgression" is referring to this rebellion that has characterized Israel since
their wandering in Sinai. Notwithstanding these possibilities, the phrase is at
least saying that by the time the seventy sevens is complete, the transgression
will have been brought to an end.

---

39. Ibid., 45.

To Make an End of Sins

24— ". . . to finish the transgression, *to make an end of sins*, to make atonement for iniquity, to bring in everlasting righteousness, to seal up
vision and prophecy and to anoint the holy of holies.

In the second phrase, "to make an end of sins," the word "make an end," in the
Ketib is the Hebrew word חָתַם (*māṭah*). This is the same word that occurs in
the fifth phrase and is translated "to seal up." However, in the Qere the word is
הָתֵם (*mamat*), which means "to be completed, finished," "to come to an end,
expire," or "to come to an end, cease."[40] In support of the Ketib, the Greek of
θ reads, τοῦ σφραγίσαι ἁμαρτία (*aitramah iasigarfs uot*), which means
"to seal up sin." In support of the Qere, the Syriac has ܠܡܓܡܪ (*rmgml*)
from ܪܡܓ (*rmg*) which means "to perfect, finish, accomplish, effect, perform; to cause to become, to put an end to" and others.[41] Also, the OG reads,
τὰς ἀδικίας σπανίσαι (*iasinaps saikida sat*), which means "exhaust, use
up, spend."[42] Although there is slightly more support for the Qere—הָתֵם
(*tamam*)—some commentators argue for the Ketib reading—חָתַם (*mahṭah*).
Miller points out, "'To put an end to sin' may either be translated *mamat*, 'be
complete, come to an end, finish,' or *mahṭah*, 'to seal, affix a seal, or seal up.'
Either translation would make sense and have basically the same meaning,
for 'sealing up' sin could be understood as putting an end to it. Yet Qere,
'to put an end to,' would fit the context better, a reading most scholars and
translations accept."[43] However, the support of θ and the parallelism that is
created within the structure of the six infinitives, as we will show later, seems
to tip the scales in favor of the Ketib reading—חָתַם (*mahṭah*), "to seal up."
Nevertheless, the impact is ultimately the same, as Miller has demonstrated.

There is a similar problem with the word "sin." The Ketib reading is
plural—חַטָּאוֹת (*to'attah*)—and the Qere is singular—חַטָּאת (*t'attah*). In
this instance the difference is probably that the plural adds intensity to the
notion of the sin. Birks asserts, "The Hebrew word translated in our NKJV
that is rendered simply as 'sins,' is the Hebrew word, HAMAT."[44] Once again
Birks has gotten the word wrong. There is no letter equivalent to the "M"
in the Hebrew word. The correct transliteration of the word is *t'attah*☐ or☐
_*to'attah*. Although Birks is correct that the word can be used to refer to a
sin offering, he seems to overlook the fact that it occurs in 9:20 with the

---

40. KBH, s.v. "הָתֵם."

41. *A Compendious Syric Dictionary* (1990), s.v. "ܪܡܓ."

42. *A Greek-English Lexicon* (1996), s.v. "σπανίζω."

43. Miller, *Daniel*, 260.

44. Birks, *The Comings of the Christ*, 23.

simple meaning "sin": "and confessing my sin and the sin of my people Israel,"

וּמִתְוַדֶּה חַטָּאתִי וְחַטַּאת עַמִּי יִשְׂרָאֵל‎ (w □ʾ attah □hedawtimu̱ʿt ʾattah□ leʾ aŕsiy□imma ʿ). It would make no sense to read the text as "confessing my sin offering and the sin offering of my people Israel." Birks' statistics are also incorrect. He says, "HAMAT is so translated as a 'sin-offering,' 116 times in the KJV of the Bible. And it shows up 135 times in the Hebrew Masoretic Text."[45] Actually, the word occurs over 290 times in the Hebrew Bible, and only 75 or so of these are translated "sin-offering" in the KJV. The evidence is against Birks' position.

However, even if we grant Birks' understanding of the meaning of the word, his position still does not work. He asserts, "So, the second reason Messiah the Prince was prophesied by Daniel to arrive at the precise time that He did on the stage of Israeli history, was to make it no longer necessary and thereby obsolete for there to be any kind of a 'sin-offering' at all to be made on behalf of the nation of Israel, or any of the sinning individuals that make up the ones whom God calls 'Israel.'"[46] But contrary to Birks' conclusion, the text does not say that the "sin offering" would be made obsolete or be made unnecessary. The text says, "to make an end of sin," not to make it "unnecessary." The sin offerings were not ended at Christ's coming. They continued to be offered until the destruction of the temple in 70 AD. Birks laments, "Again, the frustration that comes over one who reads this statement in it's [sic] original Hebrew and then compares it against an English translation is a little overwhelming." [47] However, having considered several of Birks' arguments, the frustration is with commentators who attempt to comment on the language and yet seem to have no understanding of it.

This phrase, "*to make an end of sins*," has been interpreted several ways. Kenneth Gentry accepts the Ketib reading as "to seal up sin." He says, "Having finished the transgression against God in the rejection of the Messiah, now the *sins are sealed up* (NASB marg.; *chatham*). The idea here is, as Payne observes, to seal or to 'reserve sins for punishment.' Because of Israel's rejection of Messiah, God reserves punishment for her. . . . The sealing or reserving of the sins indicates that *within* the 'Seventy Weeks' Israel will complete her

45. Ibid.

46. Ibid.

47. Ibid., 22. Birks' claims indicate that he lacks any facility in the Hebrew language. In fact, his frequent appeals to the Hebrew text are fraught with error, misunderstanding, and misrepresentation. As such, we will not spend any more time interacting with Birks' comments on the book of Daniel. This is not meant to be a disparaging remark against Birks' personally. Rather, it is simply an explanation why there will be no more interaction with his claims. His mishandling of the Hebrew language and text would require too much time and space to correct and would led the discussion away from the effort to interpret the text of Daniel.

transgression, *and* with the completing of her sin by crucifying Christ, God will act to reserve (*beyond the seventy weeks*) her sins for judgment."[48] As seems to be the pattern for Gentry, he offers no argument that his interpretation should be considered the correct one. He does not state why he accepts the Ketib over the Qere even though the Qere, "to put an end to," has considerable support. Also, Gentry seems subtly to have altered the text. He begins by taking the phrase to be "to seal up sins," but then he seems to shift the meaning to "to seal up (reserve) punishment." However, the text does not say anything about punishment being "sealed up." Rather it is the sins that are sealed up, and, as we have seen, KBH does not list the meaning "reserve" as one of the possible meanings for this term.[49] Gentry is probably getting the notion of "reserve" from the use of the term "seal up" used 12:4 where the word may be used to indicate preserving the book, although even here the word does not have this meaning.

Even if we accept Gentry's understanding of the meaning, it still does not work in 9:24. The phrase is, "and to seal up sins" (וּלְחִתֹּם הַטָּאוֹת, *to' attah mothalu*). Here the word "sins" is the direct object of the infinitive "to seal up," and therefore is receiving the action indicated by the infinitive. Consequently, the meaning would be "to preserve/reserve sins," not "to reserve punishment," as Gentry proposes. Although Gentry refers to "reserving of the sins" and "to reserve her sins for judgment," this action makes no sense in the Hebrew text. The English expression "reserve her sins for judgment" is an analogical predication or short-cut way of saying that the punishment is reserved in reference to the sins committed, not that the sins are actually reserved. Even in English the expression does not have the meaning Gentry tries to give it, and there is no indication that the Hebrew text is employing an analogical predication.

Other interpretations have also been given. First, if one takes this as strictly referring to the nation of Israel, the end of sins could be the end of Israel's rebellion. As Paul points out in Rom 11:26, "and so all Israel will be saved; just as it is written, 'The Deliverer will come from Zion, He will remove ungodliness from Jacob.'"[50] When "those who pierced Him" see Him,

---

48. Gentry, *He Shall Have Dominion*, 325.

49. Neither TWOT nor the NIDOTTE gives "reserve" as a possible definition of חתם.

50. καὶ οὕτως πᾶς Ἰσραὴλ σωθήσεται, καθὼς γέγραπται, Ἥξει ἐκ Σιὼν ὁ ῥυόμενος, ἀποστρέψει ἀσεβείας ἀπὸ Ἰακώβ. (Rom 11:26). Paul here uses the word *saiebesa*(ungodliness), which does not occur in the Greek text of Daniel. However, in at least two instances in the OT this Greek word is used to translate the Hebrew term חטאת, which does occur here in Daniel.

they will be converted, and Israel's history of wandering away from God in rebellion will be ended.

Another way this phrase has been understood is that Jesus will make an end of all sins at His death, burial, and resurrection. The usual objection to this is that people certainly sin today, so it seems that He has not made an end of sins. However, this phrase can be understood along the lines of the statement in Rom 10:4: "For Christ is the end of the law for righteousness to everyone who believes."[51] Here the notion is that for those who believe, Christ has put an end to the effort to attain righteousness by means of the law. Although He has accomplished this, it does not mean that no one will continue to try to obtain righteousness in this manner. Even Christians often regress in their daily lives to a righteousness/sanctification-by-law approach. This is evidenced by Paul's letter to the Galatians in which he reminds the Galatian Christians, "Having begun by the Spirit, are you now being perfected by the flesh?" (Gal 3:3). In like manner, Christ has brought an end to sins, sin has been overcome, and those who believe are reconciled to God, but the full separation from sin will come when we see Him and are changed to be like Him.

To Make Atonement for Iniquity

24— ". . . to finish the transgression, to make an end of sin, *to make atone-ment for iniquity*, to bring in everlasting righteousness, to seal up vision and prophecy and to anoint the holy of holies.

The word translated "make atonement" is כָּפַר (*kāfar*). It has a wide range of meaning, including, "to make atonement, to appease, to avert."[52] As Miller points out, "Basically, the Hebrew verb *kipper* ('to atone') means 'to make a covering.' This symbolism is drawn from the Old Testament sacrificial system in which the blood was sprinkled over the mercy seat in the temple, depicting that the sin of the people was forgiven because it was covered by the blood (cf. Lev 16:15–16)."[53]

Gentry objects to what he holds to be the Dispensationalists' under-standing of this phrase. He says, "The dispensationalist here prefers to in-terpret this result as *application* rather than *effecting*. He sees it as subjective appropriation instead of objective accomplishment. . . . But on the basis of the Hebrew verb, the passage clearly speaks of the actual *making reconciliation*

---

51. τέλος γὰρ νόμου Χριστὸς εἰς δικαιοσύνην παντὶ τῷ πιστεύοντι. (Rom 10:4).

52. KBH, s.v. "כָּפַר."

53. Miller, *Daniel*, 260.

(or *atonement*)."[54] However, this objection does not stand up to scrutiny. The distinction between the accomplishing of our redemption and the application of all of its benefits is not an uncommon theme in the Bible. In Rom 8:23 Paul states, "And not only this, but also we ourselves, having the first fruits of the Spirit, even we ourselves groan within ourselves, waiting eagerly for *our* adoption as sons, the redemption of our body."[55] It is certainly the case that Christ redeemed our bodies when He redeemed our souls, but the application of redemption to our bodies awaits our resurrection or translation. Here the accomplishing of redemption is distinct from the application of the benefits of that work. So, the Hebrew verb by itself does not require that all the benefits of atonement be applied at once.

In fact, the Hebrew word here translated "atonement" (כָּפַר, *rāfak*) is often translated "forgiveness" or "to forgive" (e.g., Ps 79:9). God forgives our sins, but at that very moment we are not translated to heaven nor are we changed so as never to sin again. Heb 9:26 declares, "but now once at the consummation of the ages He has been manifested to put away sin by the sacrifice of Himself."[56] Although sins have been "put away" (ἀθέτησιν, *nīsetehta*), the benefit of being totally separated from the very presence of sin awaits our resurrection or translation. Rather, we continue to struggle against the world, the flesh, and the devil. Atonement has certainly been accomplished for all of God's people, but the full benefits of that atonement, in the case of Israel, have not yet been applied.

At this point it is important to notice that the first three phrases involve references to the evil, using the synonyms "transgression," "sin," and "iniquity." With the next phrase begins the final three phrases each of which has to do with the good.

To Bring in Everlasting Righteousness

24—   ". . . to finish the transgression, to make an end of sin, to make atonement for iniquity, *to bring in everlasting righteousness*, to seal up vision and prophecy and to anoint the holy of holies.

This phrase is particularly problematic— וּלְהָבִיא צֶדֶק עֹלָמִים (*'ibahlu mumalo' qedes*). The word translated "everlasting" is actually plural (עֹלָמִים,

---

54. Gentry, *He Shall Have Dominion*, 325–26.

55. οὐ μόνον δέ, ἀλλὰ καὶ αὐτοὶ τὴν ἀπαρχὴν τοῦ πνεύματος ἔχοντες, ἡμεῖς καὶ αὐτοὶ ἐν ἑαυτοῖς στενάζομεν υἱοθεσίαν ἀπεκδεχόμενοι, τὴν ἀπολύτρωσιν τοῦ σώματος ἡμῶν. (Rom 8:23).

56. ἐπεὶ ἔδει αὐτὸν πολλάκις παθεῖν ἀπὸ καταβολῆς κόσμου· νυνὶ δὲ ἅπαξ ἐπὶ συντελείᾳ τῶν αἰώνων εἰς ἀθέτησιν τῆς ἁμαρτίας διὰ τῆς θυσίας αὐτοῦ πεφανέρωται. (Heb 9:26).

'*mumalo'*). Perhaps an alternate translation may indicate the meaning: "And to bring in righteousness of the ages."[57] Gentry claims, "Because of this atonement to cover sin the fourth result is that *everlasting righteousness* is effected."[58] Even though Gentry objected to the dispensationalist distinction between objective accomplishment and subjective application, Gentry must resort to this distinction in this instance: "This speaks of the objective accomplishment, not the subjective appropriation of righteousness."[59] Yet all the arguments Gentry used against the dispensationalist can be used against his own interpretation here. If the Hebrew word in the previous phrase speaks of actually making reconciliation, why does not this Hebrew word require the same sense here? Just as Gentry separates the accomplishment from the appropriation here, so the dispensationalist separates the accomplishment from the appropriation in the previous phrase. Indeed, Christ brought in everlasting righteousness and offers it to whomsoever will believe. Eternal life begins when one believes, but all the benefits of this await our final redemption.

To Seal up the Vision and Prophecy

24— ". . . to finish the transgression, to make an end of sin, to make atonement for iniquity, to bring in everlasting righteousness, *to seal up vision and prophecy*, and to anoint the holy of holies.

The word "to seal up" is חתם (*nitah*). It can have the meaning "to seal (up), to keep sealed, to shut, to obstruct."[60] It is used in 1 Kgs 21:8 to refer to sealing a letter with a seal: "So she wrote letters in Ahab's name and sealed them [ותחתם, *mothataw*] with his seal." Interestingly, Isa 29:11 uses the word to indicate a sealed book that cannot be opened and read: "The entire vision will be to you like the words of a sealed [החתום, *mutaheh*] book, which when they give it to the one who is literate, saying, 'Please read this,' he will say, 'I cannot, for it is sealed [חתום, *mutah*].'" The use of this word in the Isaiah passage may indicate a physical sealing shut, or a sealing so that one cannot understand what is written. Concerning this verse Oswalt comments, "They have the technical skills to understand God's word, but they lack the spiritual insight which would enable them to see the plain meaning."[61]

Mauro asserts, "This [Dan. 9:24] we take to mean the sealing up of God's word of prophecy to the Israelites, as part of the punishment they brought

---

57. Wood proposes this translation as well, which see p. 249.

58. Gentry, *He Shall Have Dominion*, 326.

59. Ibid.

60. KBH, s.v. "חתם."

61. Oswalt, *Isaiah 1–39*, 532.

upon themselves."[62] However, if this is taken to indicate punishment, it disrupts the balance between the two sets of three phrases, three indicating what will be done with reference to evil, three indicating what will happen with reference to the good. According to Miller, "'To seal up vision and prophecy' may be interpreted in two ways. Hebrew *mātaḥ* means to 'seal, affix a seal, seal up.' 'To seal' may refer to the closing up of a document, for in ancient times a scroll was rolled up and sealed shut for preservation. A seal was additionally employed as a mark of authentication by a king or another official."[63] We can see both of these uses in the quotes above from Isaiah and from 1 Kings. The idea of authentication is indicated by the writing of letters in Ahab's name and sealing them with his seal, indicating that they are from the king. The idea of shutting up a document is seen in the Isaiah passage.

Interestingly, very few translations use the word "prophet" rather than "prophecy" in the translation of this phrase: וְלַחְתֹּם חָזוֹן וְנָבִיא (*wᵉmothal wᵘ̄ḥōzạhᵉʾ_ıban*). However, the word used here is "prophet," not "prophecy." There is a Hebrew word that means prophecy— נְבוּאָה (*hạʾubᵉn*)—which is used, for example, in 2 Chron 15:8. Miller argues, "In the first case 'to seal up vision and prophecy' would signify that these forms of revelation would be closed, and in the second the idea would be that God will someday set his seal of authentication upon every truly God-given revelation ('vision and prophecy') by bringing about its complete fulfillment."[64] However, since the word here is "prophet" rather than "prophecy," one wonders how a prophet can be "sealed up." Goldingay proposes that the term 'prophet' is a reference to Jeremiah: "Yet it is Jeremiah, not Daniel, whom chap. 9 describes as a prophet (v. 2). The phrase has been taken to suggest that prophecy is to be sealed up and thus silent through this period (Keil), but this is a lot to read out of this phrase. Sealing elsewhere suggests authentication (1Kgs 21:8), and this fits the present context well: the promise is that Jeremiah's prophecy will be fulfilled and thus confirmed."[65] Although it seems rather narrow to confine this reference to Jeremiah's prophecy only, the idea of authentication seems to fit the use of both the word "vision" and the word "prophet." It is easy to understand that the vision and the prophet can both be authenticated by the fulfilling of the prophecy communicated to Daniel. If we take a broader sense here, the phrase can be a reference to all prophecy concerning Israel and the Messiah being fulfilled and authenticated.

---

62. Mauro, *Seventy Weeks*, 50.
63. Miller, *Daniel*, 261.
64. Ibid.
65. Goldingay, *Daniel*, 260.

Gentry holds that this phrase "has to do with the ministry of Christ on earth, which is introduced at His baptism: He comes '*to seal up vision and prophecy.*' By this is meant that Christ fulfills (and thereby confirms) the prophecy (Luke 18:31; cf. Luke 24:44; Acts 3:18)."[66] Of course Daniel's prophecy says nothing about the prophecy being sealed up by Christ, nor does it confine the prophecy to those that have direct reference to Christ. Consequently, Daniel's statement could apply to prophecy that has specific reference to the nation of Israel, or to the world.

To Anoint the Holy of Holies

24—   ". . . to finish the transgression, to make an end of sin, to make atonement for iniquity, to bring in everlasting righteousness, to seal up vision and prophecy, and *to anoint the holy of holies.*

This phrase is difficult in the sense of identifying the referent. The text literally says, "and to anoint holy of holies": וְלִמְשֹׁחַ קֹדֶשׁ קָדָשִׁים: (*seḏoq hāŏsmil^ew mĩsaḏaq*). Young asserts, "The words refer to the anointing of the Messiah. Since the phrase occurs without the definite article, it means *a most holy thing.* In what sense, then, may this be applied to Christ?" After some citations of some OT verses, Young concludes, "Hence, it may be concluded with H, '—the anointing of a Holy of Holies can only denote the communication of the Spirit to Christ, to which prominence is given in other prophecies of the Old Testament, as a distinguishing characteristic of the Messiah.'"[67] Contrary to Young's supposition, the expression "holy of holies" is almost always translated "most holy" in the NASB. In two places in Ezekiel, 45:3 and 48:12, the expression is translated "most holy place." In almost all of the instances of its use, the expression is used with reference to the altar or to the sacrifices or the high priest ministering at the altar. Young's application seems to be too much of a stretch.

Evans argues that this expression must refer to Jesus: "Against this line of argument about 'the most holy' preterists can offer a powerful counterargument that begins with the observation that the Jews were allotted a period of seventy sevens during which to continue their religious practices based on sacrificial worship in the Temple. Toward the end of this period, the ministry of Jesus signaled the replacement of these practices with the New Covenant. *The fact that 'holy of holies' refers to the Temple and the Old Testament worship systems is therefore no barrier to applying it to Jesus in the New Testament.*"[68] But

---

66. Gentry, *He Shall Have Dominion*, 326.

67. Young, *Prophecy of Daniel*, 201.

68. Evans, *Four Kingdoms*, 335–36 (emphasis in original).

this is not an argument for the interpretation. Rather, it is simply an explanation of the Preterist view. Evans does not attempt to demonstrate that his view is correct. Rather, from his perspective he simply explains the words of the text and the use of this phrase in some passages of the Old Testament and then claims that it applies here.

Gentry, on the other hand, actually presents some reasons why he believes this is referring to Jesus' baptism:

> Finally, the seventy years are for the following goal: "*to anoint the Most Holy.*" This anointing [*mashach*] speaks of the Christ's baptismal anointing for the following reasons: (1) The overriding concern of Daniel 9:24–27 is Messianic. The temple that is built after the Babylonian Captivity is to be destroyed after the seventy weeks (v. 27), with no further mention made of it. (2) In the following verses the Messiah (*mashiyach*, "Christ," "Anointed One") is specifically named twice (vv. 25, 26). (3) The "most holy" phraseology speaks of the Messiah, who is "that Holy One who is to be born." It is of Christ that the ultimate redemptive Jubilee is prophesied by Isaiah (Isa. 61:1–2a; cf. Luke 4:17–21). It was at His baptismal anointing that the Spirit came upon Him (Mark 1:9–11). This was introductory to His ministry, of which we read three verses later: "Jesus came to Galilee, preaching the gospel of the kingdom of God, and saying, '*The time* is *fulfilled* [the Sixty-ninth week?], and the kingdom of God is at hand. Repent, and believe in the gospel" (Mark 1:14–15). Christ is pre-eminently *the* Anointed One.[69]

Gentry's arguments are formidable, and we will take up this perspective in more detail below in the section "Have These Six Things Been Fulfilled in the Past?" but Gentry's view is not the only one that has been presented with formidable arguments of support. Walvoord summarizes the views that have been taken on this point.

> The sixth aspect of the prophecy, "to anoint the most Holy," has been referred to the dedication of the temple built by Zerubbabel, to the sanctification of the altar previously desecrated by Antiochus (1 Macc 4:52–56), and even to the new Jerusalem (Rev 21:1–27). Young suggests that it refers to Christ Himself as anointed by the Spirit. Keil and Leupold prefer to refer it to the new holy of holies in the new Jerusalem (Rev 21:1–3). A. C. Gaebelein, expressing a premillennial view, believes the phrase "has nothing whatever to do with Him [Christ], but it is the anointing of the Holy of Holies in another temple, which will stand in the midst of Jerusalem,"

---

69. Gentry, *He Shall Have Dominion*, 326.

that is, the millennial temple. There is really no ground for dog-matism here as there is a possibility that any of these views might be correct.[70]

Walvoord makes a very reasonable point in the conclusion of the above quote. The arguments for various views all have strong support. It may not be possible to be dogmatic about one view over another at this point. A clearer understanding of this phrase awaits an exegesis of the following material in Daniel's vision.

The Structure of the Six Infinitives

Gentry declares, "The six infinitival phrases of verse 24 should be understood as three *couplets* . . . rather than as two triplets."[71] He offers no argument to support this assertion, and the language seems to contradict his claim. As we pointed out earlier, the first three phrases in the list all concern the evil—transgression, sin, iniquity—and the last three phrases concern good—righteousness, vision and prophet, and holy of holies. Also, the balance of concepts is supported by the syntactical structure. The first three phrases are composed of two words each, while the second three are composed of three words each. As D. Dimant points out, this section is "worded in three pairs of parallel terms, each consisting of an infinitive with a nominal object. A triad of terms depicts the contemporary evil situation: transgression (פֶּשַׁע), sin (חַטָּאות) and iniquity (עָוֹן). Three other terms describe the age to come: introducing eternal justice (לְהָבִיא צֶדֶק עֹלָמִים), sealing prophecy (וְנָבִיא לַחְתֹּם חָזוֹן), and anointing the Holy of Holiness (לִמְשֹׁחַ קֹדֶשׁ קָדָשִׁים). However, it has not been sufficiently stressed that the two triads also form three complementary pairs: transgression//righteousness, sin//vision-prophe-cy, and iniquity//Holy of Holiness."[72]

---

70. Walvoord, *Daniel*, 223.

71. Gentry, *He Shall Have Dominion*, 325 (emphasis in original).

72. D. Dimant, "*The Seventy Weeks* Chronology (Dan 9,24–27) in the Light of New Qumranic Texts," in *The Book of Daniel*, 59–60.

Table 24: Three Contrasting Pairs

Evil	Good
to finish the transgression לְכַלֵּא הַפֶּשַׁע	to bring in everlasting righteousness וּלְהָבִיא צֶדֶק עֹלָמִים
to seal up sin וּלַחְתֹּם חַטָּאוֹת	to seal up the vision and prophecy וְלַחְתֹּם חָזוֹן וְנָבִיא
to make atonement for iniquity וּלְכַפֵּר עָוֹן	to anoint the most Holy וְלִמְשֹׁחַ קֹדֶשׁ קָדָשִׁים

There seems to be a dual pattern of relationship here. The chiasm (triplets) is indicated by the repetition of the word "seal up" in the second and fourth phrases. Also, the contrasting pairs are indicated for the reasons argued by Dimant:

Figure 25: Seventy Sevens Chiastic Structure

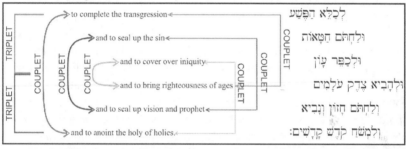

The chiasm seems to direct the reader's focus to the two central phrases, "to make atonement for iniquity," and "to bring in righteousness of the ages." Contrary to Gentry's claim, this section seems to be structured not with one single pattern, but with two groupings of three couplets and two triads. This complex structure stresses the interconnectedness of these six infinitive phrases. One cannot be accomplished unless all are accomplished.

Have these Six Things Been Fulfilled in the Past?

Whether these six phrases indicate tasks that have been fulfilled is a question that relates to Gentry's claim about whether the last infinitive refers to Christ, or to some event future from our perspective. Mauro claims, "Here are six distinct things which were to happen within a definitely marked off period of seventy sevens of years (490 years). These six specified things are closely re-

lated one to the other, for they are all connected by the conjunction 'and.' . . .
It is essential to a right understanding of the prophecy to observe, and to keep
in mind, that the six things of verse 24 were to be fulfilled (and now have been
fulfilled) *by Christ being 'cut off,'* and by what followed immediately thereafter,
namely, *His resurrection from the dead, and His ascension into heaven.*"[73]

There are serious problems with saying they were fulfilled. Mauro's claim
involves the question, how can one claim that an end has been made to sin
since it is still quite apparently with us? Mauro could be claiming that the sin
is ended in the sense of the atonement having been accomplished even though
the full application and separation from sin awaits our full redemption. But
this does not work for all of the six phrases. As we have seen, the anointing
of the holy of holies may refer to the temple, but this cannot be referring to a
partial anointing that awaits some future anointing as well. For Mauro to assert that these have been fulfilled in Christ being "cut off" is an assertion that
derives from Mauro's prior eschatological commitment. This notion must be
demonstrated, not simply asserted. We will deal with this in the following
commentary, particularly the assertion about Messiah being cut off, and we
will consider how Mauro maintains their fulfillment as the occasions arise.

Noë also claims that these six things have been fulfilled. He asserts,
"What's more, it sealed or 'determined' the fulfillment of all six of the redemptive purposes and promises of Daniel's 70 weeks time prophecy stated in
verse 24:"[74] In other words, Noë sidesteps the problem of fulfillment within
the 490 year time frame by claiming that Daniel's prophecy states that the
fulfillment of these are only *determined* within the 70 sevens, not actually
fulfilled in this time frame. But this does not work since these very things were
already determined to be fulfilled by God before the foundations of the earth.
To determine in Daniel's prophecy what has already been determined seems
to be pointless. The syntax of the statement clearly makes the words "seventy
sevens" as that which has been "determined"; "seventy sevens are determined
. . ." The time period of seventy sevens is to accomplish each one of the things
expressed by the infinitives. It is the period of the seventy sevens that is determined, not the tasks. By the end of the time period, they will be fulfilled, not
simply determined. His effort to equate "sealed" and "determined" does not
work either since there is no basis upon which to make this equation. These
are different words, and they mean different things.

Roy Anderson claims that the six items mentioned by the angel were
fulfilled in the past. He says, "Six important predictions mentioned in Dan.
9:24 were all fulfilled during the seventieth week. These six points establish

---

73. Mauro, *Seventy Weeks*, 43–44 (emphasis in original).

74. Noë, *Beyond the End Times*, 86.

without question the timing and the relationship of the great prophecy to our Lord, for not one of these occurred during the preceding sixty-nine weeks of years."[75] Anderson gives the following account of the fulfillment of these six points:

> The first three had to do with the blight of sin, stating that our Lord would (1) "finish the transgression," (2) "make an end of sins [sin offerings]" through His perfect atonement, and (3) "make reconciliation for iniquity" by a substitutionary sacrifice of the Son of God. The last three deal with the glorious realities of the gospel. These are (4) "to bring in everlasting righteousness" as God's free gift of grace to all who will accept it, (5) "to seal up the vision and prophecy," and (6) "to anoint the most Holy" (Berkeley, "to consecrate the Holy of Holies"). This our Lord did following His ascension, when He entered "into heaven itself, now to appear in the presence of God for us." Hebrews 9:24[76]

Anderson does not attempt to explain how to reconcile these six points with the facts of history. For example, Anderson believes that the reference to "sins" in the second point is a reference to sin offerings. Besides the fact that we have already shown that this word does not have this meaning here, Anderson does not explain how Jesus put an end to the "sin offerings" when the historical fact is that the sin offerings were continued until the city and the sanctuary were destroyed in 70 AD. Of course, Anderson alludes to the notion that the sin offerings were "ended" by the fact that they were replaced with "His perfect atonement." In other words, they did not physically cease to be offered. Rather, they no longer were of any value since Christ had offered Himself as the perfect sacrifice to take away sin. However, we have already shown that this understanding simply does not fit the text. Also, Anderson's reference to the anointing of the holy of holies does not fit Heb 9:24 since the text states, "For Christ did not enter a holy place [ἅγια] made with hands, a mere copy of the true one, but into heaven itself, now to appear in the presence of God for us;"[77] It simply does not make sense to say that the heavenly temple in the presence of God needed to be consecrated.

Gentry claims, "The general view of Daniel 9:24 among non-dispensational evangelicals is that 'the six items presented . . . settle the *terminus*

---

75. Anderson, *Unfolding Daniel's Prophecies*, 121.

76. Ibid.

77. οὐ γὰρ εἰς χειροποίητα εἰσῆλθεν ἅγια Χριστός, ἀντίτυπα τῶν ἀληθινῶν, ἀλλ᾿ εἰς αὐτὸν τὸν οὐρανόν, νῦν ἐμφανισθῆναι τῷ προσώπῳ τοῦ θεοῦ ὑπὲρ ἡμῶν· (Heb 9:24).

ad quem of the prophecy,' that is, they have to do with the First Advent."[78]
Gentry goes on to assert, "Dispensationalists, however, hold that these events
are 'not to be found in any event near the earthly lifetime of our Lord.'"[79]
The quote in Gentry's comment is attributed by Gentry to Robert Culver.
However, Gentry seems to be confused about Culver's statement.

Culver is discussing the belief that the prophecy of Daniel 9 is, by what
he identifies as "unbelief," fulfilled "in the time of Antiochus Epiphanies."[80]
Culver opposes this view, and he says, "I caution the reader, however, not
to construe these foregoing remarks to mean that I feel that the *terminus ad
quem* of the full seventy weeks is to be found in any event near the earthly
lifetime of our Lord, for such is not my opinion."[81] In other words, Culver is
not claiming, as Gentry implies, that none of the six items find any fulfillment
in the lifetime of Jesus. Rather, Culver is claiming that the *terminus ad quem* is
itself not to be found at this time. Culver's statement allows for the possibility
that some of these or portions of these six items may have been accomplished
in Jesus' lifetime, but their complete fulfillment awaits the end of the seventy
sevens, which, for Culver, is in the future from his perspective. Culver's statement essentially expresses the view of Futurists that, although some of these
six events have been accomplished in the time of Christ, they await fulfillment
at His return and Kingdom.

Summary of the Six Phrases

From the foregoing discussion, it seems that we may be able to draw the following conclusions:

"To finish the transgression"—This seems to be a reference to Israel's
constant and consistent rebellion against God by going after other
gods. Israel's rebellion/transgression will be brought to an end. This
prophesied by Paul: "and so all Israel will be saved; just as it is written, the Deliverer will come from Zion, He will remove ungodliness
from Jacob. This is My covenant with them, when I take away their
sins." (Rom 11:26–27)

"To make an end of sins"—This seems to refer to the fact that Christ
would pay for the sins of the world. Consequently, Christ would
make an end of sin's reign over us. Israel's sin had separated her from
God, as Isaiah says: "But your iniquities have made a separation be-

78. Gentry, *He Shall Have Dominion*, 324.
79. Ibid.
80. Culver, *Daniel and the Latter Days*, 145.
81. Ibid.

tween you and your God, and your sins have hidden His face from you so that He does not hear" (Isa 59:2). The sins that had separated God's people from Him will be brought to an end.

"To make atonement for iniquity"—There seems little reason to take this as anything other than a reference to the atonement accomplished by Christ.

"To bring in righteousness of the ages"—This seems to refer to the fact that Christ would, by His atonement, make righteousness available to all those who believe. This would be particularly relevent to Israel since, as Paul points out, "For they being ignorant of God's righteousness, and seeking to establish their own righteousness, have not submitted to the righteousness of God. For Christ is the end of the law for righteousness to everyone who believes." (Rom 10:3–4)

"To seal up vision and prophet"—This seems to be a reference to the authentication of the Word of God that Christ is the Messiah of Isarel. This may be what is referred to in Revelation: "Behold, He is coming with the clouds, and every eye will see Him, even those who pierced Him; and all the tribes of the earth will mourn over Him. So it is to be. Amen." (Rev 1:7)

"To anoint the Holy of Holies"—This may be a reference to the anointing of the Millennial temple, although this seems to be the least likely possibility. More probable is the notion that this applies to Christ. However, we are not taking a dogmatic position on this point.

DANIEL 9:25

From the Issuing of a Decree

25— "So you are to know and discern that *from the issuing of a decree* to restore and build Jerusalem until Messiah the Prince there will be seven weeks and sixty-two weeks;"

Table 25: Daniel 9:25a

מֹצָא	מִן־	וְתַשְׂכֵּל	וְתֵדַע
going out of	from	and understand	And know
יְרוּשָׁלַם	וְלִבְנוֹת	לְהָשִׁיב	דָּבָר
Jerusalem	and to build	to return	word

Having given what seems to be the broad parameters in the primary accomplishments of the six phrases, Gabriel begins to present what seems to be a time table of events: "So you are to know and discern that from the issuing of a decree to restore and build Jerusalem until Messiah the Prince there will be seven sevens and sixty-two sevens; it will be built again, with plaza and moat, even in times of distress" (v. 25).[82] Gabriel declares that the seventy sevens will be divided into two sections; 1) seven sevens, and 2) sixty-two sevens, leaving one seven. The chart in Figure 26 provides a graphic depiction of the 69 sevens. The first part composed of the first 7 sevens equals 49 years. Part two is the 62 sevens equals 434 years. These two parts constitute 483 of the 490 years prophesied. Although there are some aspects of the later years of part two, the 62 sevens, that are disputed, the debate between Preterists and Futurists primarily concerns the seventieth seven (which is not included in the following chart), when it will occur and when and how it will end.

Figure 26: 69 Sevens Chart

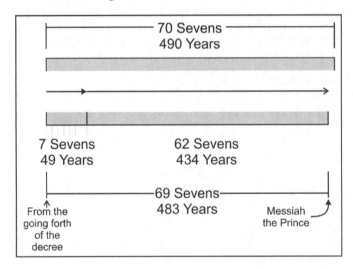

This period of 69 sevens begins with the issuing of a command (דָבָר, *rabad*, lit. "a word") to return and build Jerusalem. First of all, it is important to recognize that the word translated "decree" is actually the word "word" (דָבָר, *rabad*) and does not necessarily indicate a formal decree.

---

82. The Greek of θ reads ἀποκριθῆναι τοῦ οἰκοδομῆσαι which can be translated "to be separated in order to build." Here the idea is to be separated from a throng—see Liddell&Scott—in order to build Jerusalem. To be separated from a throng indicates that the people will be separated from Babylon in order to return to Jerusalem. The word does not mean "to restore."

Pentecost points out that there were four decrees made by Persian rulers in reference to the Jews. The first was Cyrus' decree in 538 BC (2 Chron 36:22–23; Ezra 1:1–4; 5:13). The second was the decree of Darius I (522–486) in 512 BC (Ezra 6:1, 6–12). This decree actually was a confirmation of the first decree. The third was the decree by Artaxerxes Longimanus (465–423) in 457 BC (Ezra 7:11–26). The first two decrees pertain to the rebuilding of the temple in Jerusalem, and the third relates to finances for animal sacrifices at the temple. These three say nothing about the building of the city itself. Since an un-walled city was no threat to a military power, a religious temple could be rebuilt without jeopardizing the military authority of those granting permission to rebuild it. The fourth decree was also by Artaxerxes Longimanus, issued on March 5, 444 BC (Neh 2:1–8). On that occasion Artaxerxes granted the Jews permission to rebuild the city walls.[83]

Although Cyrus issues a command in 583 BC to restore the temple of Jerusalem (cf 2 Chron 36:22–23), it was not until 444 BC that Artaxerxes allowed Nehemiah to return to Jerusalem. This 'word' to Nehemiah specifically gives permission to Nehemiah to return and build the city (cf. Neh 2:1–8). Evans comments, "Ezra 7:12–26 contains the text of a letter from Artaxerxes I to Ezra dated 458/457 that goes into considerable detail regarding the maintenance of the Temple. This document does not specifically mention the rebuilding of the city's fortifications, but it can be inferred from its context and from other passages in Ezra, particularly 4:12, that it must have allowed the rebuilding to get underway."[84] However, the fact that the letter does not contain a "word to rebuild the city" disqualifies it as a possible reference point. Daniel's prophecy does not say, "From the inference that it is permissible to rebuild Jerusalem . . ." Rather, it states, "From the going forth of a decree/ word to return and build Jerusalem . . ." Cyrus' decree simply does not contain a decree/word about building the city.

There is also a serious problem with Evans' reference to Ezra 4:12. In fact, the text argues against Evans' claim that we can infer from the decree of Artaxerxes I that Israel had permission to begin work on the city walls. The text states, "let it be known to the king that the Jews who came up from you have come to us at Jerusalem; they are rebuilding the rebellious and evil city and are finishing the walls and repairing the foundations." This statement was made by Rehum the commander and Shimshai the scribe in a letter to Artaxerxes "against Jerusalem" precisely because they had begun to work on the walls, something to which these enemies of Israel objected. Rehum and Shimshai asked that the king do a search in the archives to discover whether

83. J. Dwight Pentecost, "Daniel," in *The Bible Knowledge Commentary: Old Testament,* ed. John F. Walvoord and Roy B. Zuck (Wheaton, Illinois: Victor Books, 1985), 1362.

84. Evans, *Four Kingdoms,* 372.

or not Israel had been given permission to rebuild the city walls. Artaxerxes' response included these words: "A decree has been issued by me, and a search has been made, and it has been discovered that that city has risen up against the kings in past days, that rebellion and revolt have been perpetrated in it, that mighty kings have ruled over Jerusalem, governing all the provinces beyond the River, and that tribute, custom, and toll were paid to them. So, now issue a decree to make these men stop work, that this city may not be rebuilt until a decree is issued by me" (Ezra 4:19–21). So, not only can we *not* infer from Artaxerxes' decree that Israel had been given implicit permission to rebuild the city, but this is precisely what Artaxerxes denied, and as soon as he heard what the people were doing, he issued a decree to have the work stopped, which is precisely what Rehum and Shimshai did. Table 26 below shows the chronology of the decrees.

Table 26: Chronology of Decrees

King	Date	Passage	Decree
Cyrus	538	2 Chron. 36:22–23; Ezra 1:1–4; 5:13	Rebuild the Temple
Darius I	512	Ezra 6:1, 6–12	Rebuild the Temple
Ahasuerus (Artaxerxes I)	486	Ezra 4:1–21	Stop building the City
Artaxerxes Longimanus	457	Ezra 7:11–26	Rebuild the Temple
Artaxerxes Longimanus	444	Neh. 2:1–8	Build the City

So, the decree of Artaxerxes I cannot be the starting point of the seventy sevens since this king actually decreed that any work that was being done on the city should be stopped. In fact, he decreed that no work be done on the city if and until he should send out a decree specifically allowing this, which he never did.

Roy Anderson argues, "We repeat that the decree or commandment from Artaxerxes was given, not in 445 or 444, but in 457 BC. This is the date for the beginning of the seventy weeks prophecy or the 490 years. It is unfortunate that so many Bible teachers take 445 or 444 BC for the date of the decree, when no decree was given then, nor was it needed, for it had been issued and put into effect thirteen years earlier."[85] Apparently Anderson supposes

---

85. Anderson, *Unfolding Daniel's Prophecies*, 113.

that the English word "decree" indicates that the underlying Hebrew text that requires this translation. However, the text of Dan 9:25 states, דָּבָר מִן־מֹצָא לְהָשִׁיב וְלִבְנוֹת יְרוּשָׁלַם (mialâsur^{e}y tonbil^{e}w bîsah^{e}l r̄abad $^{\sim}$as̄om nim), "that from the issuing of a word [דָּבָר, r̄abad] to return and build Jerusalem." The word translated "decree" in most translations is simply the word דָּבָר (r̄abad), which can mean "word," or "thing," or "message." There are two other Hebrew words that more specifically mean "decree." The first is a Persian loan word, דָּת (r̄ad),[86] the Aramaic form of which is used in Ezra 7:21 to refer to the decree of Artaxerxes. The Hebrew plural form of the word is used in Ezra 8:36 and is translated "edicts," and is used to refer to the same decree of Artaxerxes, now delivered to the satraps of the provinces. Another word that is used in the Aramaic sections is טְעֵם (me^{ce}t).[87] This word is used in Ezra and Daniel to refer to different decrees. The Hebrew equivalent, טַעַם (ma^{c}at) is used once in the Hebrew Bible, Jonah 3:7, to refer to a decree. The word that is used in Dan 9:25 can mean a command or simply a word that is sent out by the king, and does not necessarily mean an official "decree." A word from the king was given to Nehemiah in the form of letters to be sent to the officials in the land to allow Nehemiah to do the work of building Jerusalem. Anderson's apparent lack of facility in the languages has led him to the wrong conclusion and, consequently, to the wrong date.

Stanley Paher holds, "Various expositors widely differ as to when this period [the seventy sevens] begins and ends, and the juggling of historical facts to fit the 490 years shows the fallacy of such assumptions. The seventy sevens more likely represents an indefinite complete fullness of time, perhaps symbolic of the seventy year captivity. When Jesus said to forgive 'seventy times seven' (Matt. 18:22), He obviously had in mind an indefinite number of times."[88] Interestingly, Paher himself cannot seem to abstain from the "juggling of historical facts to fit the 490 years" when he asserts, "The oft-debated verse 25 mentions the event which initiated the seventy weeks 'decreed upon thy people' (v. 24a). This was the 'going forth of the commandment to restore and build Jerusalem.' Likely the decree of Cyrus in 536 B.C. to rebuild Jerusalem is meant, though more than a dozen major interpretations exist, each with its own year as a starting point!"[89] Paher, who chides interpreters, "Any analysis of the book of Daniel surely must consider both its prophetical and historical contexts. Various millennial speculators concentrate

86. KBH, s.v., "דָּת."
87. KBH, s.v., "טְעֵם."
88. Paher, *Matthew 24*, 48.
89. Ibid.

on the former, and generally ignore the latter,"[90] is not reluctant to "ignore the latter himself," since the decree of Cyrus in 536 says absolutely nothing about rebuilding Jerusalem. Notwithstanding his claim that the 490 years is symbolic and representative of an indefinite period of time, without the least consideration that perhaps he is contradicting his own earlier claims, Paher declares, "If the first prophetic time period of 'seven weeks' was fulfilled in 104 literal years, and the second period of '62 weeks' spans about 450 literal years, then the final 'one week' should consistently be a literal time period of less than seven weeks, just as the 62 weeks is more than the seven weeks."[91] Paher's reader is left in confusion by Paher's claims. Which is it? It is symbolic or literal? Is it symbolic of the seventy year captivity, or a prophecy about a literal fulfillment in the future? Is it an "indefinite period of time" or actually fulfilled in a certain number of "literal years"?

Max King holds that the time period begins with the decree of Artaxerxes referenced in Neh 2:1. He argues, "One of our difficulties is determining the exact start of the 70 weeks. There were actually several decrees given in regard to the restoration of Israel (2 Chron 36:22–23; Ezra 6:3–8; Ezra 7:7). In these decrees, however, nothing is said concerning the rebuilding of the city. The first mention of any such decree is recorded in Nehemiah 2:1–8, where, for the first time, permission is granted to rebuild the city. This was in the twentieth year of the reign of Artaxerxes, which becomes our chronological starting point for this prophecy."[92] King then follows the calculations of Robert Anderson: "According to Anderson, the 69 weeks began with the decree to rebuild Jerusalem and terminated at the time of Christ's entry into Jerusalem, just prior to his crucifixion."[93] The chart below is provided by King as an illustration of the timeline as he understands it.[94]

---

90. Ibid., 42.
91. Ibid., 49.
92. King, *The Spirit of Prophecy*, 86.
93. Ibid.
94. Ibid., 83.

Figure 27: Max King's Timeline

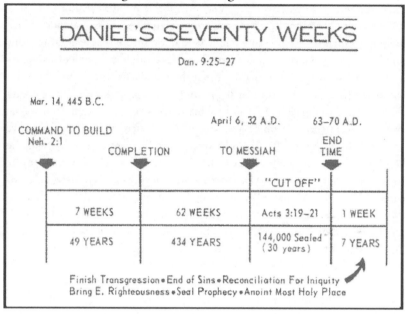

What is particularly interesting about King's time line is that he introduces a gap between the end of the sixty-ninth week and the beginning of the seventieth week that lasts from 32 AD to 63 AD, a gap of about 30 years. In fact, King specifically asserts, "Daniel's vision of the seventy weeks was a prophecy of the time from Israel's release from captivity to the time of the end. A problem we face is that Israel's end did not come in a seven-year period immediately following the crucifixion. Instead, it came nearly forty years later when Rome sacked Jerusalem. This suggests a break in our chronology, a gap between the sixty-ninth and the seventieth weeks."[95] However, King's chart is a bit ambiguous. It is not clear whether the seventieth week begins after 70 AD, or if the seventieth week begins in 63 AD and lasts until 70 AD. In his explanation, King identifies the end as the destruction of Jerusalem, which implies that the seventieth week is indicated in the chart by the designation "63–70 A.D." and the label "END TIME."

What About Cyrus' Decree?

Young argues, "*From the going forth*—This phrase has reference to the issuance of the word, not from a Persian ruler but from God. God is the Author of this word; He has determined the length of the time until the things prophesied

95. Ibid., 91.

in vs. 24 shall be completed. In vs. 23 also this same phrase occurs to describe the issuance of a Divine word."[96] A serious problem with this notion is that it seems to undermine the whole reason for giving the time references. Since there is no such decree presented anywhere in Scripture that occurs after this prophecy was given, the actual decree becomes completely unidentifiable. As Mauro comments, "for it is manifest that the measuring line . . . will be of no use to us whatever unless the starting point be *certainly known*."[97] Recognizing this problem, Young claims, "This issuance of the word is, in itself, an invisible event, yet as H correctly points out, the effects of such an issuance must have appeared upon this earth. 'As the covenant people were then subject to the Persian king, we naturally expect to find an echo of the word of God in the edict of a Persian Monarch' (H)."[98] So, for all of Young's objections against this being a decree from a mere Persian king, he effectively capitulates to this option since otherwise the decree is, as he says, "invisible." Ultimately he argues for the decree of Cyrus in 538–537 BC, which, as we have seen, does not, in fact, issue a single word about rebuilding the city. On the basis of Young's claim that the word is God's, does it make sense that God's word "echoed" through a Persian Monarch would in fact not even give the command that was the substance of God's word, namely, to return and build Jerusalem?

Mauro argues for the Cyrus decree by appealing to the statement in Isa. 44:28: "Turning to Isaiah, Chapters 44 and 45, we find there God's promise that Jerusalem should be *rebuilt* and its captives *restored* to their homes, and not only so but we find that God mentioned *by name* the very man, 'Cyrus,' by whom that promise was to be accomplished. The proof that King Cyrus was the one who should give the 'commandment' (or *word*) for the restoring and rebuilding of Jerusalem, is doubly forceful and impressive, *and designedly so as the Scripture itself declares*, because it was spoken by the mouth of the Lord *two hundred years before Cyrus came to the throne*."[99] There are several problems with Mauro's understanding of the passage in Isaiah, however. But, before we consider that, there is a very serious problem with the fact that, in all the passages in Scripture that refer to all the decrees of Cyrus, not a one says anything about rebuilding the city. Since Mauro believes that certainty can come only from the Scriptures—"It is equally manifest that the starting point cannot be certainly known unless it be revealed *in the Scriptures* and in such wise that the ordinary reader can 'know and understand' it beyond a

---

96. Young, *Prophecy of Daniel*, 201.

97. Mauro, *The Seventy Weeks*, 20.

98. Young, *Prophecy of Daniel*, 201–2.

99. Mauro, *Seventy Weeks*, 25–26 (emphasis in original).

doubt"[100]—it becomes very problematic that, if God said that Cyrus would decree that Jerusalem be built, and since no Scripture records the fact that Cyrus ever made such a decree, either God gave a false prophecy, or Cyrus' decree is not recorded in Scripture and, according to Mauro's principle, we can never have certainty about the starting point.

The real problem, however, is that Mauro has altogether misinterpreted the text of Isaiah. Isa. 44:28 says, "The one saying to Cyrus, 'My shepherd.' All of My desire he will perform. And to say to Jerusalem, 'She will be built, and *the* temple will be established'" (see Table 27 below).

Table 27: Isaiah 44:28

וְכָל־	רֹעִי	לְכוֹרֶשׁ	הָאֹמֵר
and all of	My shepherd	to Cyrus	The one saying
לִירוּשָׁלַ͏ִם	וְלֵאמֹר	יַשְׁלִם	חֶפְצִי
to Jerusalem	And to say	he will perform	My desire
תִּוָּסֵד׃	וְהֵיכָל	תִּבָּנֶה	
will be established.	and temple	She will be built	

The text does not say that Cyrus will decree anything. The word "decree" does not occur in the text. Also, the text does not say God will "commission Cyrus" to build the city. In the text God makes two statements. The first statement is to Cyrus (לְכוֹרֶשׁ, *seŕokᵉl*), "to Cyrus, My shepherd, all of My desire he will perform." The second statement is to Jerusalem (לִירוּשָׁלַ͏ִם, *miǎlǎsuŕil*), "to Jerusalem, she will be built, and *the* temple will be established." These are two separate statements to two different addressees. The text does not say, as Mauro claims, that Cyrus was the one "by whom the promise was to be accomplished." Contrary to Mauro's presumption that "This proof cannot be overthrown,"[101] the fact is there is no proof to be overthrown. It simply does not exist.

Concerning the Isa 45:13 passage, once again the text does not say what Mauro wishes it did. The text states, "'I have aroused him in righteousness, and all of his ways I will make smooth. He will build My city and My exiles he will let go, not for a price and not for a bribe,' says the LORD of Hosts."

---

100. Ibid., 20–21 (emphasis in original).
101. Ibid., 27.

Table 28: Isaiah 45:13

וְכָל־	בְּצֶדֶק	הַעִירֹתִהוּ	אָנֹכִי
and all of	in righteousness	I have aroused him	I
יִבְנֶה	הוּא־	אֲשֶׁר	דְּרָכָיו
he will build	He	I will make smooth	his ways
לֹא	יְשַׁלֵּחַ	וְגָלוּתִי	עִירִי
not	he will let go	and My exiles	My city
אָמַר	בִשְׁחַד	וְלֹא	בִמְחִיר
said	for a bribe	and not	for a price
		צְבָאוֹת׃	יְהֹוָה
		hosts.	LORD of

This may certainly be a reference to Cyrus. However, nowhere in this text does it say that Cyrus will send out a decree to return and build Jerusalem. The text says he will build "My city," but it does not say he would send out a decree or a word of such action. Mauro declares, "No one who believes the Word of God will, with this Scripture before him, dispute for a moment that it was *by Cyrus* that Jerusalem was rebuilt and its captives restored to it."[102] Mauro is certainly correct, but, the question here is not who will and who will not build the city. The question is, who and when was the decree/word sent out. There is no text that says Cyrus would or did do this.

Some may point out that it is legitimate to infer that Cyrus sent out some kind of word to rebuild the city. As true as this may be, the point is that the text of Daniel stated that the starting time for the seventy sevens would be a decree/word to return and build the city. Daniel does not say that the starting time would be on the basis of an inference about a decree/word, and the text of Isaiah does not say that Cyrus made such a decree/word. Regardless of how legitimate the inference may be, the event referred to in Isaiah simply does not meet the criterion established by Daniel's prophecy.

Mauro argues against the decree of Artaxerxes as recorded in Nehemiah as the starting point of the seventy sevens. His first objection is, "the tidings brought to Nehemiah, as recorded in chapter 1, were tidings of *damage freshly done* by the enemies of the Jews to *the walls and gates* of the *rebuilt* city;"[103] He proposed this because he thinks, "The effect of this report upon Nehemiah shows clearly that it was of a fresh and unexpected calamity they

102. Ibid., 28.
103. Ibid., 37.

were speaking. For he relates that, when he heard those words, he sat down, and wept, and mourned certain days, and fasted and prayed before the God of heaven. . . . That could not possibly have been the destruction wrought by Nebuchadnezzar, for that had taken place more than a hundred years previously. Nehemiah had known about *that* all his life."[104] However, just because Nehemiah knew about the condition of Jerusalem all his life and yet was distressed at the report does not necessarily mean that this was recent damage. Nehemiah was no doubt also aware of the fact that many had returned to Jerusalem some years earlier. The report Nehemiah received was distressing because he had expected more progress to have been made. The fact that the walls were broken down and the gates were burned with fire was a condition that, although done in the time of Nebuchadnezzar, Nehemiah had expected to be remedied by now. Since no significant progress had been made on the repair of the walls or gates, Nehemiah was distressed. This explanation is just as reasonable as the one offered by Mauro. Consequently, his argument does not prove that this disqualifies the decree of Artaxerxes as the starting point of Daniel's prophecy. Even granting that this was new damage to the walls and gates, this does not disqualify the decree either. So the walls had been rebuilt, and broken down again, and the gates had been set up, and burned again. They nevertheless needed to be rebuilt. So the decree of Artaxerxes was to repair the walls and the gates, it nevertheless was a decree to return and build Jerusalem. This is no argument against the decree.

Mauro argues, "In chapter 2 [of Nehemiah] we have the account of Nehemiah's request to the king, and the 'letter' given to him. There is no decree, no 'commandment,' nothing whatever about rebuilding the city."[105] This statement is misleading at best. Neh. 2:5 states, "I said to the king, 'If it please the king, and if your servant has found favor before you, send me to Judah, to the city of my fathers' tombs, that I may rebuild it.'" Nehemiah specifically asked for permission to rebuild the city. In the following verses Nehemiah requests letters from the king to permit him to carry out the petition he put before the king, namely, to rebuild the city. So, in fact, Nehemiah does refer to the rebuilding of the city. What is more problematic for Mauro, however, is that no Scripture says anything about Cyrus giving such a decree. If no mention of a decree disqualifies Artaxerxes, then it likewise disqualifies Cyrus. Mauro concludes his argument by declaring, "For the starting point of the prophecy was not the rebuilding of the city, but *the commandment to* restore and to build it. That commandment was, beyond the shadow of a doubt,

104. Ibid., 38.
105. Ibid., 39.

given by Cyrus."[106] In fact, Mauro failed to produce a single text to that effect. He produced texts that referred to Cyrus building the city, but not a decree "commanding to" rebuild it. Even Gentry acknowledges this point: "At first appearance it would seem to refer to Cyrus' decree to rebuild the Temple in 538 BC this command is mentioned in 2 Chronicles 36:22–23 and in Ezra 1:1–4; 5:13, 17, 6:3. Daniel, however, specifically speaks of the command to '*restore* and build *Jerusalem*,' which is an important qualification."[107] Gentry goes on to point out, "It was not until the middle of the fifth century BC [445 or 444 BC] that this [the rebuilding of Jerusalem] is undertaken seriously."[108] Neither Mauro's arguments nor his objections demonstrate his position, and the facts actually disqualify his claims.

What About Ezra's Decree?

MILLER'S ARGUMENTS CONCERNING THE DECREE

Miller argues that the decree is actually a decree given by Artaxerxes to Ezra in 458 BC: "The view accepted here is that the decree of Ezra in 458 B.C. is the correct starting point for the seventy sevens, but a survey of events contained in the first sixty-nine sevens is necessary to demonstrate the appropriateness of this option."[109] But immediately Miller has a problem with his choice as he points out himself. Miller discusses three decrees that have been given as choices for a starting point—1) the decree of Cyrus issued in 538; 2) the first decree of Artaxerxes I given to Ezra in 438; 3) the second decree of Artaxerxes I given to Nehemiah. Miller acknowledges, "Only the third decree [the second decree of Artaxerxes I] specifically refers to the rebuilding of Jerusalem, but it is reasonable to assume that all three orders allowing the Jews to return to their land implied permission to rebuild the city."[110] But the question is not about what was or was not implied, but about who and when was the word given to rebuild the city. Only the decree given to Nehemiah by Artaxerxes in 445 meets this criterion. As Miller admits, "Artaxerxes' words to Nehemiah probably meet the criteria of the *r̩abad*, which may mean 'decree, message, or word.' This decree to Nehemiah specifically mentions the rebuilding of Jerusalem (Neh. 2:5), which is the strongest argument in favor of it."[111] Also, we have already seen that at least in one instance, to infer that a decree

---

106. Ibid., 42.

107. Gentry, *He Shall Have Dominion*, 322 (emphasis in original).

108. Ibid., 323.

109. Miller, *Daniel*, 263.

110. Ibid.

111. Ibid.

to rebuild the temple implied permission to rebuild the city was specifically forbidden. Although Israel was given permission to rebuild their temple, they were forbidden from rebuilding the city because this would lead to their rebellion. So, not only can we not assume that all three orders implied permission to rebuild the city, we must remember that this kind of inference got Israel into trouble.

Another of Miller's arguments is the chronological difficulties that he claims come with the 445 BC date:

> Those who begin the sevens in 445 B.C. are faced with a dilemma; 483 years after 445 B.C. comes to A.D. 39, a date well after the time of Christ. To solve this problem Anderson argued that the 483 years are years of 360 prophetic days rather than years of 365 days. He calculated that from the decree to Nehemiah given on March 14, 445 B.C. (Neh 2:1) until the triumphal entry of Christ on April 6, A.D. 32, there were 173,880 days. At this time Christ presented himself to Israel as their Messiah. Christ was rejected, and the sixty-nine sevens came to an end. Though in some instances in prophecy, notably Daniel and Revelation, a year is rounded off to 360 days, Archer has convincingly demonstrated that the Jews followed a 365-day year. Not only is the 360-day year theory unlikely, but a major problem with Anderson's view is that we must consider that Christ was not crucified in A.D. 32 but in A.D. 30. If so, Anderson's calculations will not work. Hoehner has basically taken Anderson's view and updated it. He begins the seventy weeks on March 5, 444 B.C. and understands the sixty-ninth week to have concluded on March 30, A.D. 33, which he calculates was the day of Christ's triumphal entry into Jerusalem. He continues to accept the 360-day prophetical year, however, with its seemingly insurmountable problems and espouses the date of A.D. 33 as the year of Christ's crucifixion.[112]

Miller's argument is based on speculation and at most claims that if one accepts what some scholars believe, then his calculations might work. Additionally, the calculations presented by Dwight Pentecost consider both the 360 day years and the 365 day years. The chart in Figure 28 below is based on Pentecost's calculations: "Thus the first two segments of the important time period—the 7 sevens (49 years) and the 62 sevens (434 years)—ran consecutively with no time between them. They totaled 483 years and extended from March 5, 444 B.C. to March 30, A.D. 33."[113] The calculation based on

112. Ibid., 265.

113. Pentecost, *Daniel*, 1363. The figure 365.29 figures into the calculation of each year as the extra 140 days that are added into the total for leap years and the difference

365 day years takes into consideration leap years, which adds 116 days to the base total. The 365 days is multiplied by 476 years—it figures out to 476 and not 477 because the calendar goes from 1 BC to 1 AD with no year 0. Since the calculation of 483 years based on 360 day-years extends from March 5, 444 BC to March 30, 33 AD, and since the calculation based on 365 day-years plus 116 days would bring us to March 5, 33 AD, 24 days must be added to the calculation to bring it to March 30, making the total number of days the same in each calculation. Consequently, there is no reason to reject the calculations proposed by Pentecost.

Figure 28: 483 Years Chart

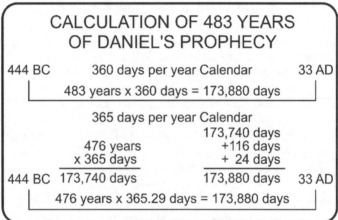

NOË'S ARGUMENTS CONCERNING THE DECREE

John Noë also argues for the decree of Artaxerxes in 457 BC. He begins his speculations with the assertion, "The Bible records three decrees by Gentile kings that affected the restoration and rebuilding of Jerusalem (Ezra 6:14)."[114] At the very beginning of his arguments he makes two fatal assumptions. First, he assumes that there are only three decrees—Cyrus' Decree in 538 BC (recorded in Ezra 1:2–4); Darius' Decree around 520 BC (Ezra 6:3–12); Artaxerxes' Decree, dated by the majority of historians and Bible scholars at 457 BC (Ezra 7:11–26).[115] Second, he assumes that the decree of Artaxerxes given to Nehemiah in 445 BC was merely only "letters of passage issued in

---

between March 5 to March 30.

114. Noë, *Beyond the End Times*, 81.

115. Ibid.

445–444 B.C. (mentioned in Nehemiah 2:5–8) . . ."[116] Also, he confuses that which affects the rebuilding of Jerusalem with specific decrees to do so. Noē even acknowledges this point himself when he says, ". . . both Cyrus' and Darius' decrees, as recorded in Scripture, only called for the rebuilding of the Temple in Jerusalem and made no mention of the city or the restoration of Israel as a people. Big difference."[117] Then he ignores this "big difference" when he elects to begin the calculation with the decree of 457. Without explanation or justification, he does this by collapsing the decree to Nehemiah in 445 BC into the decree to Ezra in 457 BC There is no historical or Scriptural justification for such a move. This seems to be a move to attempt to make the timing fit his prior eschatological scheme. As Hoehner points out, ". . . this decree has not a word about the rebuilding of the city of Jerusalem but rather the temple in Jerusalem."[118]

Noē presents 3 arguments to support his claim that the decree of 457 BC is the best one for beginning the calculation of the seventy sevens:

> It is the best for three reasons: 1) In retrospect, dating from the first two decrees has no literal, future, or chronological significance, or historical prophetic value. But dating from Artaxerxes' Decree does. 2) Some interpreters feel Cyrus' Decree should be the starting point, since the prophet Isaiah, a century and a half before, had foretold that a man by that name would decree the rebuilding of Jerusalem and the Temple (Isa. 44:26–28; 45:1–4). But for some unknown reason, both Cyrus' and Darius' decrees, as recorded in Scripture, only called for the rebuilding of the Temple in Jerusalem and made no mention of the city or the restoration of Israel as a people.' Big difference. A rebuilt Temple would enable the Jews to offer sacrifices and pray for the well-being of the king (Ezra 6:10). But a rebuilt city would provide the Jews with a military fortress. They could then rebel again, and this was a concern of Israel's enemies, as seen in the letter to the king of Persia (Ezra 4:12,15). Using the 538 B.C. date as the starting point would require either a time gap or a symbolic reading of the numbers for the time period to come out with any significant meaning. Note that 538 B.C. plus 490 literal years only works out to 48 B.C., and nothing of significance occurred then. 3) Artaxerxes' Decree, nearly one hundred years later in 457 B.C., and his subsequent letters of passage issued in 445–444 B.C. (mentioned in Nehemiah 2:5–8), covered everything. This is the latest possible date for the

---

116. Ibid., 82.
117. Ibid., 81.
118. Harold W. Hoehner, *Chronological Aspects of the Life of Christ*, 125.

beginning of Daniel's 70 weeks. In addition, these associated letters specifically mentioned both the rebuilding of the city and the
Temple.[119]

Noë has fallen into the same kind of misunderstanding of Isaiah as was
the case with Mauro. As we have seen, Noë attempts to collapse the decree of
457 with the decree in 445. Without any historical or scriptural support, he
matter-of-factly claims that the statements to Nehemiah were merely "letters
of passage." However, this assumption cannot stand the analysis either of history or of the Scriptures. There are several reasons why we should take these as
two distinct decrees, and not merely as one decree with subsequent "letters of
passage." First, the decree of 457 as described in Ezra did not include any statement about rebuilding Jerusalem. However, the decree in 445 did. Second,
although the word "decree" is not used in the Nehemiah passage, letters were
given to Nehemiah specifically requesting that the king "send me to Judah"
(תִּשְׁלָחֵנִי אֶל־יְהוּדָה, ḥaduhᵉy leˇ ı̄ṇeḥaĺsit, Neh. 2:5) and the text asserts,
"So it pleased the king to send me" (וַיִּיטַב לִפְנֵי־הַמֶּלֶךְ וַיִּשְׁלָחֵנִי, baî̇tyyaw□
ˆ ı̄ṇeḥaĺsiyyaw□kelemmah□enfil)). Third, most commentators, including Noë,
identify the statements in Ezra 1:2–4 as constituting the first decree of Cyrus.
However, the word 'decree' is not used with reference to this statement either.
So, the fact that it is not used with reference to Artaxerxes is not an argument
against it being a decree. Fourth, officers were sent with Nehemiah to ensure
that the decree was honored by those governors of the provinces who would
be concerned with Nehemiah's task. This speaks to the official nature of the
letters and treats them as decrees from the king. There is no reason to think
that the events recorded in Nehemiah do not constitute a separate decree.
Finally, even if we take the events in Nehemiah merely to be letters of passage,
the dating must begin here since it was not until these letters were issued to
Nehemiah that permission was given to return and build Jerusalem. So, taken
either way, Noë's attempt to begin the calculation with the decree of 457 does
not fit either history or the biblical text.

ANDERSON'S ARGUMENTS CONCERNING THE DECREE

As we have seen above, Roy Anderson argues that the decree to which the text
refers is the decree of Artaxerxes given to Ezra. After considering the decrees of
Cyrus and Darius and concluding that, "wonderful as these decrees were, they
concerned only the reconstruction of the *temple*, the 'house at Jerusalem,'"
Anderson argues, "Another decree was issued by Artaxerxes Longimanus in
457 B.C., sixty-two years after that of Darius. This third decree authorized

---

119. Noë, *Beyond the End Times*, 81–82.

further rebuilding and restoration, the temple having been finished fifty-eight years earlier, in 515 BC. See Ezra 6:15."[120] Anderson quotes portions of Ezra chapter 7 in which the decree of Artaxerxes is recorded. This is that to which Anderson is referring when he says it was not necessary for a decreed to be issued in 445 BC since a decree "had been issued and put into effect thirteen years earlier."[121] However, Anderson does not quote all of the decree, and his selective reporting leaves the impression that his understanding may be correct. However, once the entire decree is read, it is clear that there is nothing in the decree about restoring and building Jerusalem:

> Artaxerxes, king of kings, to Ezra the priest, the scribe of the law of the God of heaven, perfect *peace*. And now I have issued a decree that any of the people of Israel and their priests and the Levites in my kingdom who are willing to go to Jerusalem, may go with you. Forasmuch as you are sent by the king and his seven counselors to inquire concerning Judah and Jerusalem according to the law of your God which is in your hand, and to bring the silver and gold, which the king and his counselors have freely offered to the God of Israel, whose dwelling is in Jerusalem, with all the silver and gold which you find in the whole province of Babylon, along with the freewill offering of the people and of the priests, who offered willingly for the house of their God which is in Jerusalem; with this money, therefore, you shall diligently buy bulls, rams and lambs, with their grain offerings and their drink offerings and offer them on the altar of the house of your God which is in Jerusalem. Whatever seems good to you and to your brothers to do with the rest of the silver and gold, you may do according to the will of your God. Also the utensils which are given to you for the service of the house of your God, deliver in full before the God of Jerusalem. The rest of the needs for the house of your God, for which you may have occasion to provide, provide *for it* from the royal treasury. I, even I, King Artaxerxes, issue a decree to all the treasurers who are beyond the River, that whatever Ezra the priest, the scribe of the law of the God of heaven, may require of you, it shall be done diligently, up to 100 talents of silver, 100 kors of wheat, 100 baths of wine, 100 baths of oil, and salt as needed. Whatever is commanded by the God of heaven, let it be done with zeal for the house of the God of heaven, so that there will not be wrath against the kingdom of the king and his sons. We also inform you that it is not allowed to impose tax, tribute or toll *on* any of the priests, Levites, singers, doorkeepers, Nethinim or servants of this house

120. Anderson, *Unfolding Daniel's Prophecies*, 112.
121. Ibid., 113.

of God. You, Ezra, according to the wisdom of your God which is in your hand, appoint magistrates and judges that they may judge all the people who are in *the province* beyond the River, all those who know the laws of your God; and you may teach anyone who is ignorant. Whoever will not observe the law of your God and the law of the king, let judgment be executed upon him strictly, whether for death or for banishment or for confiscation of goods or for imprisonment. (Ezra 7:12–26)

Although Anderson's observation is correct that "the temple [was] finished fifty-eight years earlier, in 515 BC," he made the mistake of reading into Ezra's text what is not there. The fact is, there is no statement in Artaxerxes' decree of 515 about restoring and/or building Jerusalem. Anderson must have realized that there is no such statement in the decree, so he attempted to support his argument by declaring, "Artaxerxes in his decree gave in effect a blank check to Ezra."[122] The problem, of course, is that Daniel's prophecy does not say, "from the going forth of a blank check." Rather, the statement in 9:25 declares that the decree/word is for the returning of the people and the building of Jerusalem. The decree to which Anderson is making reference, as Harold Hoehner points out, "encouraged the return of more exiles with Ezra, the further enhancement of the temple and its accompanying worship, and the appointment of civil leaders."[123] There simply is no statement in this decree about building the city.

MATHENY'S ARGUMENT CONCERNING THE DECREE

James Matheny presents several arguments in favor of the first decree of Artaxerxes issued in 458/457 BC. His first argument deals with the language of the decree:

The first reason for adopting this position is the language of the text. This decree, (which appears in Ezra 7:12–26) is written in Aramaic, the trade and diplomatic language of the day and the official language of the Persian Empire. Any decree recorded in God's Word on which God's prophetic countdown for Israel would rest should logically be identified, be set apart, if you will. It is so identified—in the official language of the king issuing the decree. Of the four decrees associated with the return to Jerusalem only this decree is in the Aramaic of the Persian Empire.[124]

---

122. Ibid.

123. Hoehner, *Chronological Aspects*, 124.

124. James F. Matheny and Marjorie B. Matheny, *The Seventy Weeks of Daniel*, 60.

Of course the language of the decree has nothing whatever to do with the characterization by which Daniel, or Daniel's readers, should identify the correct decree. Nowhere in Daniel's prophecy is the qualification established that the decree should be given in a certain language. The statement of Gabriel says, "from the issuing of a decree to restore and rebuild Jerusalem"; it does not say, "from the issuing of a decree in Aramaic to restore and rebuild Jerusalem." That the decree should be in Aramaic is no more or less logical than that it should be issued in Hebrew.

Matheny's second argument is:

> The second point favoring this decree of Artaxerxes grows out of the first. Aramaic occurs again in Ezra 4:6–8 and in 4:18. Verses 6 through 8 refer to a letter written to Artaxerxes when the enemies of Israel wrote "an accusation against the inhabitants of Judah and Jerusalem" in reference to the decree and Ezra 4:7 tells us that the letter was set forth in the "Aramaic language." Ezra 4:18 is Artaxerxes' reference to this letter. Since the enemies of Israel made their protest official, against an official decree of the King, the King returned his answer in the official language of the Persian Empire. The language alone distinguishes this decree and the correspondence relating to it from all the others. A change in language within the divine record is not unique to this circumstance. The tactic is seen again in the book of Daniel, setting apart Daniel 2:4–7:28 in Aramaic to make a prophetic point. Additionally, we will see that the content of verses 25 and 26, as well as the date, makes Artaxerxes' decree the only decree that could fit the details given by Gabriel to Daniel.[125]

This second point is predicated in Matheny's understanding of the word "understand," which he sets forth earlier in the context. Matheny argues, "The word 'biyn' is derived from a verb that means 'to separate mentally' (that is, to perceive or discern or distinguish between), while 'sakal' more properly relates to intelligence or thinking through to a prudent conclusion. 'Biyn' is often used as a preposition between two nouns to make a distinction. Thus 'biyn' in this text could properly be translated 'to distinguish' rather than 'to understand' and would refer to Daniel's perceiving the difference between the seventy years of captivity that Israel had just experienced and the additional seventy sevens (490 years) of suffering and judgment which Daniel was not expecting but was about to learn of."[126] Armed with his speculations about the meaning of the term, Matheny imposes this upon the text as if this is the crite-

125. Ibid., 60–61.
126. Ibid., 52.

rion by which the various decrees are to be differentiated so as to identify the correct one. Because, as Matheny asserts, "The language alone distinguishes this decree and the correspondence relating to it from all the others," this must, according to Matheny, be the correct decree. Once again, however, language was not one of the criteria that was stipulated by Gabriel. Although the word בִּין (nîb) certainly has the idea of "making distinctions between," the word itself does not stipulate the criteria on the basis of which the distinction must be made, and Matheny conveniently ignores the fact that the last decree of Artaxerxes (444/445 BC) is distinguished from all the others by the fact that it is the only one that says anything about rebuilding Jerusalem. All of the other decrees allow only the rebuilding of the Temple and do not allow for the rebuilding of Jerusalem. Matheny has superimposed his prior conclusions on the meaning of the word and then read them into the text.

Matheny also argues against the KJV translation: "from the going forth of the commandment." Matheny argues that the word translated "commandment" is misleading: "The Hebrew word translated 'commandment' in this passage is again 'dabar,' the principal word used in the Old Testament for the Word of God, but used figuratively (of words) to speak; a word or a matter or thing spoken of."[127] From the fact that דָּבָר (rabad) is the most frequently occurring word used to refer to God's Word, Matheny leaps to the conclusion that this must be a reference to the Word of God. He says, "When 'dabar' is translated 'commandment' instead of 'word' the passage loses some of its significance as though the commandment of Artaxerxes was of compelling impetus rather than the Word of God."[128] Matheny offers no argument on which to base his claim except a reference to the fact that he argued earlier, "the first 49 years of the total 490 was to be a period of testing by the Word of God."[129] Whatever substance there may be to this claim, it has nothing to do with whether the use of "word" or "commandment" in this phrase is a reference to the "Word of God." In fact, Gabriel tells Daniel precisely what he means: "know and understand that from the issuing of the word to restore/ return and build Jerusalem." It is the word that is sent out that tells the people of Israel that they can or should or are allowed to return to Jerusalem and rebuild the city. Irrespective of any other speculations floated by Matheny, it simply is not true that the first decree of Artaxerxes in 458/457 said anything at all about rebuilding Jerusalem. Since that is the criterion given by Gabriel, none of the other speculations on the part of Matheny make the decree say what it did not say. Matheny's arguments simply do not establish his thesis.

127. Ibid., 61.
128. Ibid., 62.
129. Ibid.

CONCLUSION CONCERNING THE DECREE

The evidence is overwhelming that the starting point of the prophecy is 445 BC with the word of Artaxerxes as recorded in Nehemiah. None of the other decrees say anything about building the city. The decree of Ahasuerus/ Artaxerxes I in 486 BC, referred to in Ezra 4:1–21, actually includes a decree to stop the work on the city. There is no other decree/word that specifically gives permission to build the city other than the one given to Nehemiah in 445/444 BC. There is no reasonable alternative to this historical point. Consequently, the period of seventy sevens begins at this point in history.

Return and Build

The word translated "restore" is שׁוּב _(bŭs)_ and is frequently used to mean "return" or "repent." Matheny understands this word to have both a physical and a spiritual sense. From the fact that the word can be used to mean "repent," Matheny once again leaps to the conclusion that it must mean that in this context. He says, "From the above, we see clearly that the Word to 'restore' Jerusalem applied not only in the physical sense of rebuilding the city but also to real repentance on the part of the people."[130] The "above" to which Matheny refers are simply a few popular word studies in which the possible meanings are discussed. At the end of one quote from TWOT, Matheny italicizes a statement: "*The association between the ideas of a return from exile and a return to the covenant should be obvious.*"[131] But Matheny conveniently omits an important and qualifying statement in this very quote: "It should be noted that in a number of places _bŭs_ means "to return from exile."[132] In other words, this is a meaning that is used in a number of places, but it is not one that can automatically be assumed in any given text. Simply because the word can mean "repent," and does in many places, does not indicate that it necessarily means this here in Daniel. Matheny neglects to prove his case. He simply assumes it. But, there is no reason to think that Artaxerxes had this in mind when he issued the "word." The word simply is to return to Jerusalem and build the city. Whether there were any spiritual implications along with their return is irrelevant to what the statement itself means. It simply means, "return and build Jerusalem."

The word translated "rebuild" is וְלִבְנוֹת, _(ṭonbilᶜw)_. The notion of *re*-building can be expressed by the phrase, "build again" in which "build" is followed by the adverb "again," עוֹד _(doᶜ)_. This construction occurs twice in

---

130. Ibid., 63.

131. TWOT, 909; quoted in Matheny, *The Seventy Weeks*, 63.

132. TWOT, s.v. "שׁוּב."

the OT (Deut 13:17; Ezek 26:14). The adverb does not appear here in the text Daniel, however, so the word could simply mean "to build." The later part of the verse states, תָּשׁוּב וְנִבְנְתָה (ḥatᵉnbinᵉw̱ būšat), which is translated, "it will be built again . . ." The word translated "again" is actually the verb שׁוּב (būš), and could be translated "it will return." Also, the word translated "restore" (לְהָשִׁיב, bīšaḥᵉl), is the same word, and is often translated simply "return." This may indicate that the phrases could be translated, "to return and build Jerusalem . . . and it will return and be built . . ." Although these may be slight nuances of difference, it is sometimes the small differences that make all the difference. At present it seems best to accept the traditional translation but to keep in mind these alternatives. They may become important later in the prophecy.

Once again Matheny reads into the word unnecessary and unsubstantiated meanings. The word "build" simply means "build." Although it may be used in other contexts in the sense of "set up," even here the word itself does not require that it refer to setting up anything in particular. Matheny has failed to make a distinction between sense and reference. The use of the word in Dan 9:25 does not have the sense of "setting up" the "worship system in the Temple" as Matheny asserts.[133] Matheny seems to be reading into words meanings that he wants to be there in order to make his system work, and yet these meanings are not supported either by the standard Hebrew lexicon or the context. The straightforward use of the word does not include any reference to the worship system, and there is no reason to take this passage as indicating this.

Until Messiah the Prince

25—   "So you are to know and discern that from the issuing of a decree to restore and build Jerusalem *until Messiah the Prince* there will be seven weeks and sixty-two weeks;

Table 29: Daniel 9:25b

עַד־	מָשִׁיחַ	נָגִיד	שָׁבְעִים
until	Messiah	Prince	sevens
שִׁבְעָה	וְשָׁבְעִים	שִׁשִּׁים	וּשְׁנַיִם
seven	and sevens	sixty	and two

133. Matheny, *The Seventy Weeks*, 63. Matheny's consistent eisegesis with the meanings of words would involve too much discussion to address each of his claims, and would take us too far afield. Consequently, we will not refer to Matheny any more unless his arguments offer some substance that needs to be addressed.

Gabriel declares that the seventy sevens will be divided into parts. The first part consists of seven sevens, or 49 years. Part two consists of sixty two sevens and concludes with what the NASB translates as "Messiah the Prince"— מָשִׁיחַ נָגִיד *(dīgan hāīsam)*. Almost every interpreter holds this to be a reference to Jesus Christ. However, William LaSor declares, "It may come as a shock to learn that the word 'Messiah' does not occur in the Old Testament. . . . The Hebrew word *hᵉīšam* is an adjective meaning 'anointed,' often used as a substantive meaning '(the) anointed (one).'"[134] Although the term is technically an adjective, it is treated as a noun, as NIDOTTE indicates: "מָשִׁיחַ *(hāīsam)*, nom. anointed one, Messiah."[135] Of course LaSor is not attempting to deny that the OT contains prophecies of Jesus the Messiah. However, he does deny that Dan. 9:25 and 26 refer to Jesus. He says, "The messianic king is not mentioned here (or possibly elsewhere) in Daniel. However, the deliverance is final and the kingdom to be established is everlasting."[136] However, in the text to which the above quote is a note, LaSor asserts, "The outline [of the prophecy of Jeremiah] is clear: restoration of Judah and Israel to their land, a time of distress, *followed* by salvation and the advent of the messianic king. This is precisely the outline that we can trace in Daniel."[137] If Daniel's text refers to the "advent of the messianic king," then LaSor's understanding amounts to the same outcome—one wonders what the disclaimer is about.

LaSor argues, "It is sometimes claimed that the word 'Messiah' does occur in Daniel 9:25, 26. However, the word in both instances is without the definite article, and the word order in verse 25 requires the reading, 'an anointed one, a Prince.' The adjective must stand *after* the word it modifies."[138] However, this "rule" of Hebrew grammar is not a law of the Medes and Persians. It is often altered for various reasons, such as emphasis of the adjective. In fact, Waltke-O'Connor state, "Sometimes an attributive adjective precedes its noun . . ."[139] Also, if the word מָשִׁיחַ *(hāīsam)* is taken to be a name or a title, it would not be unusual for the word to be anarthrous. There simply is no good reason to reject this as a reference to Jesus the Messiah.

There is also controversy over precisely what event in the life of Christ constitutes the *terminus ad quem* of the sixty-two sevens. Miller points out

---

134. William Sanford LaSor, *The Truth About Armageddon*, 74.

135. NIDOTTE, s.v. "מָשִׁיחַ." KBH also includes "Messiah" as one of the meanings of this term. KBH, s.v., "מָשִׁיחַ."

136. LaSor, *Armageddon*, 133nh.

137. Ibid., 124.

138. Ibid., 86–87.

139 Waltke-O'Connor, *Biblical Hebrew Syntax*, 14.3.1b.

that, "The coming of the Messiah at the end of the sixty-nine sevens could refer to Christ's birth, his baptism, or his presentation to Israel as its promised Messiah on Palm Sunday."[140] Miller holds that the most likely event is Jesus' baptism, "since it was at that time that Jesus officially took upon himself the role of the Messiah and began his public ministry."[141] Gentry likewise asserts, "The second period of sixty-two weeks extends from the conclusion of the rebuilding of Jerusalem to the introduction of Israel's Messiah at His baptism when He begins His public ministry (Dan. 9:25), sometime around A.D. 26."[142] Gentry offers no argument in support of his assertion other than to claim, "This interpretation is quite widely agreed upon by conservative scholars, being virtually 'universal among Christian exegetes'—excluding dispensationalists."[143] Of course, once one excludes dispensationalists, the agreement is not quite so "widely agreed upon," and the fact that non-dispensationalists agree is to be expected. This is tantamount to saying, "It is universally agreed among anti-dispensationalists that dispensationalism is wrong."

Mauro espouses this position as well. He argues,

> We must, of course, look *to the words themselves* to guide us to the information we are seeking; and those words are all we need. We are accustomed to regard the term "the Messiah" as merely a name or a title, but in fact it is a descriptive Hebrew word meaning "the anointed (one)." In Greek the word *Christos* has the same meaning. Therefore, we have only to ask, when was Jesus of Nazareth presented to Israel as the Anointed One? As to this we are not left in any doubt whatever, for it was an event of the greatest importance in the life of Jesus our Lord, as well as in the dealings of God with Israel, and in the history of the world, an event which is made prominent in all the four Gospels. It was at His baptism in Jordan that our Lord was "anointed" for His ministry; for then it was that the Holy Spirit descended upon Him in bodily shape as a dove. The apostle Peter bears witness that "God anointed Jesus of Nazareth with the Holy Ghost and with power." (Acts 10:38)[144]

A serious problem for Mauro's claim is that the text does not say 'until Messiah is anointed.' Daniel's text simply says, "until Messiah the Prince." Neither does the text say, "until Messiah is presented to Israel." Although this may be implied, such a point must be demonstrated, not simply assumed.

140. Miller, *Daniel*, 265.

141. Ibid.

142. Gentry, *He Shall Have Dominion*, 323.

143. Ibid.

144. Mauro, *Seventy Sevens*, 56.

Simply because the word "Messiah" means "anointed one" does not prove that we should look for an anointing event. Additionally, there is no Scripture that states that Jesus' baptism was an "official presentation" of Him as Israel's Messiah. Of course Mauro proposes the day of Christ's baptism because the 3½ years of His ministry seems to fit into the prophecy of the seventieth seven as Mauro understands it.

Noē's position is so contrary to the statements of Daniel's prophecy that they hardly warrant consideration, but because he is a popular Preterist author, we will comment on them. Noē asserts, "An 'anointing' event marks both the conclusion of the second 62-week segment and the beginning of Daniel's 70th and final week of unbroken and uninterrupted years."[145] First of all, Daniel says nothing about an "'anointing' event." Daniel simply says, "until Messiah the Prince." The word "Messiah" מָשִׁיחַ (*hāisam*) is an adjective, not a verb, and here it is being used as a substantive, or as a noun. It simply means, "anointed *one*," or "Messiah." It does not mean "an anointing event." Second, the fact that the statement in 9:27 indicates that the final seven/week will begin with the making firm of a covenant, Noē's claim that the baptism of Jesus—the supposed 'anointing' event—ends the section of 62 sevens and begins the 70th seven makes no sense in light of the text. Noē claims that the crucifixion "did occur during the middle of that 70th week in A.D. 30."[146] However, the text states that the making firm of the covenant would *begin* the last seven/week. This seems to indicate that it would occur at the beginning of the seventieth seven, not in its middle. Noē attempts to circumvent this problem by claiming that, "From the day of his anointing, Jesus moved in the power and authority of the New Covenant."[147] Of course, there is absolutely no scriptural evidence for this claim. In fact, Jesus Himself stated that the New Covenant was not established until His crucifixion: "This cup which is poured out for you is the new covenant in My blood" (Lk 22:20).

Pentecost identifies the Triumphal Entry as the significant event: "The 62 'sevens' (434 years) extend up to the introduction of the Messiah to the nation of Israel. This second period concluded on the day of the Triumphal Entry just before Christ was cut off, that is, crucified. In His Triumphal Entry, Christ, in fulfillment of Zechariah 9:9, officially presented Himself to the nation of Israel as the Messiah."[148] Pentecost does not argue for the notion that Daniel's text must refer to an official presentation of the Messiah to Israel. However, by contrast to Mauro's argument, Zech 9:9 specifically predicts

145. Noē, *Beyond the End Times*, 83.

146. Ibid., 85.

147. Ibid., 84.

148. Pentecost, *Daniel*, 1363.

this day as the day the Messiah would come: "Rejoice greatly, O daughter of Zion! Shout, O daughter of Jerusalem! Behold, your king is coming to you; He is just and endowed with salvation, humble, and mounted on a donkey, even on a colt, the foal of a donkey." Although Daniel's text, as we said, does not specify that the expression "until Messiah the prince" must refer to an official presentation to Israel, the fact that the text uses the word "prince" נָגִיד (dīgan), which, as TWOT points out, "refers to the man at the top, the king, the high priest, etc.,"[149] seems to connect it with the Zechariah passage. Although Jesus' baptism marked the beginning of His earthly ministry, the Triumphal Entry fits better with the reference to the Messiah as "Prince." However, Wood cautions, "Notice should be made that no indication is given as to the particular part of Christ's life, whether birth, baptism, crucifixion, or death, with which the *terminus ad quem* is to be specifically identified."[150] The evidence seems to support the Triumphal Entry, but the reference may be too ambiguous to support any dogmatic stand.

Seven Sevens and Sixty-Two Sevens

25—   "So you are to know and discern that from the issuing of a decree to restore and build Jerusalem until Messiah the Prince *there will be seven weeks and sixty-two weeks;*

The period culminating in "Messiah the prince" is divided into two parts—seven sevens and sixty-two sevens (see Figure 26 on page 344). Concerning this division, Young asserts, "It is best, therefore, to understand (although I am painfully aware of the difficulties) the text as stating that between the terminus a quo and the appearance of an anointed one, a prince, is a period of 69 sevens which is divided into two periods of unequal length, 7 sevens and 62 sevens. To what, then, do these two subdivisions have reference? The 7 sevens apparently has reference to the time which should elapse between the issuance of the word and the completion of the city and temple; roughly, to the end of the period of Ezra and Neh. The 62 sevens follows this period."[151] The notion that the first group refers to the rebuilding of the city and the temple seems to be confirmed by the following statement: "it will be built again, with plaza and moat, even in times of distress" (v. 25).

25—   it will be built again, with plaza and moat, even in times of distress.

---

149. TWOT, s.v. "נָגַד."
150. Wood, *Daniel*, 251–52.
151. Young, *Prophecy of Daniel*, 205.

Table 30: Daniel 9:25c

רְחוֹב	וְנִבְנְתָה	תָּשׁוּב
plaza	and it will be built	it will return
הָעִתִּים:	וּבְצוֹק	וְחָרוּץ
the times.	even in oppression of	and moat

Built Again

The phrase "it will be built" is a translation of the single Hebrew word וְנִבְנְתָה (wᵉnbinᵉḥaṭ). The English pronoun "it" is used to translate the pronominal suffix that serves as the subject of the passive (Niphal) verb. Although the English word 'it' is generally considered to be neuter, the Hebrew pronominal suffix is feminine. Since the antecedent of the pronoun must agree with it in gender, the most likely feminine noun in the context that could serve as the antecedent to "it" is the word "city" (עִיר, ʿîr). This is confirmed by the reference to the "plaza and moat"— רְחוֹב וְחָרוּץ (suraḥᵉw boḥᵉr). As Harold Hoehner points out, "the word וְחָרוּץ [sic] רְחוֹב ('plaza and moat') give weight to the position for a complete restoration of the city."[152] The first word, 'plaza,' indicates "an *open plaza* in the city set against the inner wall of the gate, or gates . . ."[153] The word translated "moat" is, according to KBH, a "town-moat."[154] Hoehner explains: "Commentators are divided on how to apply the two words, וְחָרוּץ [sic] רְחוֹב, to Daniel 9:25, but it is best to take the first word plaza as referring to the interior of the city and the second word trench as referring to a moat going around the outside of the city. Part of Jerusalem's natural defenses consisted of a great cutting in the rock along the northern wall, which is still visible, for the purpose of building a defense wall. Montgomery states that these 'two items present a graphic picture of the complete restoration.'"[155]

There is no indication in the history of the ancient city that there was ever a moat around Jerusalem in the sense that one thinks of a moat, for example, surrounding medieval castles. The arid surroundings would have made a moat in the traditional sense—a large trench filled with water as a deterrent to attackers—very unlikely. Miller reports that the word "has been found in the Dead Sea Copper Scroll with the meaning 'conduit' and would

---

152. Hoehner, *Chronological Aspects*, 119.

153. KBH, s.v. "רְחֹב" (emphasis in original).

154. KBH, s.v. "II חָרוּץ."

155. Hoehner, *Chronological Aspects*, 120–21.

refer to the water system of Jerusalem."[156] Although, as Miller asserts, this
would make sense, it seems unlikely that the city would be rebuilt with a
conduit since Hezekiah's tunnel was designed precisely to eliminate this weakness in the defenses of the city. Lucas argues, "'moat': the vss seem not to have
known the meaning of the word *šūrah*, translating it in various ways: 'length,'
'long' (OG), 'wall' (θ, Vg), 'street' (Syr). It is now attested in Aram. inscriptions, meaning 'trench,' 'moat,' and can be compared with Akk. *uširah*, 'city
moat.'"[157] Of course the problem with this meaning is that there has never
been a "city moat" around Jerusalem if this indicates a traditionally identified
defensive body of water surrounding a city. Ze'ev Herzog describes one sense
of the term "moat": "A deep ditch was cut at the foot of some mounds in order
to increase their height. This method was especially important in places were
[sic] the natural hill was not sufficiently prominent to invest and attack."[158] In
this sense, a moat would be a section of the ground at the base of the wall that
would be cut out in order to make the height to the top of the wall greater
and consequently more difficult to reach. These two terms encompass the two
primary aspects of the city; "plaza" referring to the inner life of the city, and
"moat" to its defenses. The city was not only "rebuilt," but completed even to
the point of being militarily defensible.

Oppression of the Times

The final phrase of verse 25 states, וּבְצוֹק הָעִתִּים (*mittiʿah qoṣbu*), which is
literally translated, "even in oppression of the times." The word "oppression"
(צוֹק, *qoṣ*) occurs only here in the Old Testament. KBH lists the meaning
"distress."[159] The feminine form (צוּקָה, *haqus*) occurs three times in the OT;
Prov 1:27; Isa 8:22 and 30:6. There is, however, no substantial difference in
the meanings of the terms. The history of Israel evidences several periods that
could be characterized as times of distress or oppression, and the phrase in
Daniel is not specific enough to pinpoint a specific period on the basis of the
terms alone. The years of the rebuilding of the Temple and the city could certainly be characterized as times of oppression and distress—oppression from
the opposition and distress created by the failure of the people to continue the
work, which again brought judgment from God.

---

156. Miller, *Daniel*, 267.

157. Lucas, *Daniel*, 230.

158. Ze'ev Herzog, "Fortifications," in *The Oxford Encyclopedia of Archaeology in the
Near East*, 1st ed., 320.

159. KBH, s.v., "צוֹק."

DANIEL 9:26

Cutting Off Messiah

26— "Then after the sixty-two weeks the *Messiah will be cut off* and have nothing, and the people of the prince who is to come will destroy the city and the sanctuary."

Table 31: Daniel 9:26a

וּשְׁנַיִם	שִׁשִּׁים	הַשָּׁבֻעִים	וְאַחֲרֵי
and two	sixty	the sevens	And after
לוֹ	וְאֵין	מָשִׁיחַ	יִכָּרֵת
to Him	and there is not	Messiah	will be cut off

Verse 26 states, "Then after the sixty-two sevens Messiah will be cut off and have nothing . . ." The term "cut off," (יִכָּרֵת, *ŧe̅rakkiy*), is a frequently occurring word being used more than 280 times in the OT. It is commonly used of cutting something down, like a tree. It has several other meanings also: "to cut, cut off, exterminate, cut a covenant, circumcise; ni. be cut down, removed, ostracized, destroyed."[160] Goldingay describes the view that "an anointed one" or "Messiah" refers to Onias III: "Those who connect the seventieth week with the Antiochene crisis generally identify this 'anointed' with the high priest Onias III, who seems to be the one referred to as 'a covenant prince' in 11:22. On the accession of Antiochus in 175 B.C., Onias was displaced as high priest by his brother Jason. In 172 B.C. Jason in turn was displaced by Menelaus, brother of another of Onias's opponents; in 171 Menelaus had Onias killed (see 2 Macc 4). Onias's being 'cut off' could be his displacement/disappearance, or his death . . . his actual death in 171 B.C. marks the beginning of the seven years of trouble."[161] However, as Lucas points out, "If v. 26a refers to Onias' murder, the traditional reading of what follows, 'and the people of the prince who is to come shall destroy the city and the sanctuary,' is problematic because Antiochus IV did not destroy Jerusalem and the temple."[162] Also, Evans points out, "Although 2 Maccabees 4 portrays Onias as a virtuous man, it also points out that he had earlier been replaced as high priest by his brother Jason and that even Antiochus IV denounced his murder and 'was grieved at heart and filled with pity' because of it. Also, 2 Maccabees

160. NIDOTTE, s.v. "כרת."
161. Goldingay, *Daniel*, 262.
162. Lucas, *Daniel*, 244.

4–5 indicate that the murder of Onias was not the proximate cause of the subsequent attacks on Jerusalem by Antiochus, but only an early event (and not the first) in a chain of events that ultimately led to disaster."[163] Evans goes on to point out, "although Onias III was killed in ca. 171, the attempt by Antiochus to suppress Judaism did not begin that early."[164]

. There seems to be no good reason to think that the "Anointed *one*" being cut off in verse 26 is different from the "Anointed *one*" who is the Prince in verse 25. This seems to be a completely natural way to take the reference. Had this been a reference to some other individual, it seems problematic since there was not some identifying characteristic given by Gabriel by which Daniel, and his readers, would have been able to make the distinction. Goldingay argues that the lack of identifiers in the text "is to contribute to the allusiveness appropriate to a vision, which cannot be resolved from within chap. 9 itself."[165] The problem with Goldingay's proposal is that, without any qualifiers that identify this person, the statement cannot be resolved outside of chapter 9 either. That the statement cannot be resolved and therefore cannot be understood, either within or without chapter 9, goes against Gabriel's claim that he came to give Daniel "insight with understanding" (9:22). It seems that without any distinctive qualifiers, the natural insight and understanding from the simple statements of the text are that the two are the same individual. As Walvoord puts it, "The natural interpretation of verse 26 is that it refers to the death of Jesus Christ upon the cross."[166]

EVANS' ARGUMENTS ABOUT THE CUTTING OFF OF MESSIAH

Concerning the "cutting off" of Messiah, Evans proposes, "The 'anointed one' is, of course, Jesus Christ, and the beginning of the last seven coincides with His baptism by John the Baptist, which probably occurred in either AD 26 or 27. Three and one-half years later, in the middle of the last seven, he is crucified."[167] This reading, however, seems particularly problematic. Verse 27 seems to indicate that the seventieth seven begins after the cutting off of Messiah. Of course this notion seems to hinge on the antecedent of the personal pronoun at the beginning of verse 27— "And *he* will make a firm covenant with the many for one seven." However, even if this is a reference to Christ, there still seems to be a problem. Verse 26 states, "Then *after* the sixty-two sevens . . ." indicating that the event about to be identified will take

163. Evans, *Four Kingdoms*, 427–28.
164. Ibid., 428.
165. Goldingay, *Daniel*, 262.
166. Walvoord, *Daniel*, 229.
167. Evans, *Four Kingdoms*, 360.

place "after" the previously related events. The English word "then" translates the Hebrew conjunction ן, pronounced "vav": וְאַחֲרֵי *(er°ha'°w)*. So, the chronology of events so far seems to be:

1. Going out of the word to build Jerusalem
2. Messiah the Prince comes
3. After the sixty-two sevens Messiah is cut off
4. The people of the coming prince will destroy the city and the sanctuary
5. He makes a covenant with the many for one seven
6. Abomination of Desolation

Let's call this chronology F for Futurist. If the covenant referred to was made by Jesus, the chronology would have to be presented in a different way. Let's call this chronology P for Preterist:

1. Going out of the word to build Jerusalem
2. Messiah the Prince comes
3. He makes a covenant with the many for one seven
4. After the sixty-two sevens Messiah is cut off
5. Abomination of Desolation
6. The people of the coming prince will destroy the city and the sanctuary

The problem is, chronology P does not follow the order of the text. If P order is the correct chronological order, then why does not the text follow this order? By not following this order in the text, the passage becomes more obscure. The natural way to take the chronology is one that follows the order of the text. But the chronology is not the only problem. Point 3 in chronology P is the making firm a covenant. Evans, along with most Preterists, claims that this is when the seventieth seven begins. The text states that Messiah is cut off "after the sixty two sevens." Most Preterists also claim that the New Covenant was established at the death, burial, and resurrection of Christ. In other words, the making of the covenant occurs when Messiah is cut off. But, if the making of the covenant begins the seventieth seven, then that would mark the end of the sixty-two sevens. However, that would mean that Messiah's making the covenant and being cut off would refer to the same event. For the Preterist, this is no problem so far. However, the text also says that the coming of Messiah marks the *terminus ad quem* of the sixty-two sevens. So, this means that Messiah's coming, His making firm a covenant, and His being cut off would all have to happen at the same time—that is, they would have to refer to the same event.

1.   until Messiah the Prince = end of the 69 weeks

2.   Messiah is cut off = after the 69 weeks

3.   making firm a covenant = begins the seventieth week

If the beginning of the seventieth week is marked by the making firm of a covenant, and the making of the covenant is the death, burial, and resurrection of Messiah, that is, Messiah being cut off, then the making of the covenant and the cutting off of Messiah are the same event. But, the end of the 69 sevens is marked by the coming of Messiah the Prince. So, either there is a gap between the end of the sixty-ninth week and the beginning of the seventieth week, or these three events refer to the same point in time. But, if they refer to the same event, then the coming of Messiah the Prince cannot refer to His baptism. But all this makes no sense at all.

Evans seems to have a solution to this problem. He argues, "Although verse 26 states that the anointed one is 'cut off' after sixty-two weeks, it does not state that this happens at the *end* of the sixty-two weeks, but only *after* them. In other words, *the 'cutting off' takes place during the seventieth week, but not necessarily—as liberals assume—at its beginning.*"[168] However, what at first seems to be a solution does not actually solve problem. We have already shown that if we accept the Preterist view that the making firm of the covenant is Jesus' establishing of the New Covenant, then that must have occurred at His death, burial, and resurrection—His being "cut off." But, if they are the same event, then the cutting off could not have taken place at the middle of the seventieth week.

Hoehner presents another problem for this view. He contends, "the Messiah was cut off 'after' the sixty-ninth week and not 'during' the seventieth."[169] Hoehner then presents an argument made by Robert Gundry demonstrating this point:

> If the cutting off of the Messiah occurred in the middle of the seventieth week, it is very strange that the cutting off is said to be "after" the sixty-nine weeks (figuring the sum of the seven and the sixty-two weeks). Much more naturally the text would have read "during" or "in the midst of" the seventieth week, as it does in verse twenty-seven concerning the stoppage of the sacrifices. The only adequate explanation for this unusual turn of expression is

168. Ibid., 428.
169. Hoehner, *Chronological Aspects*, 131.

that the seventieth week did not follow on the heels of the sixty-ninth, but that an interval separates the two. The crucifixion then comes shortly "after" the sixty-ninth but not within the seventieth because of an intervening gap. The possibility of a gap between the sixty-ninth and the seventieth weeks is established by the well-accepted OT phenomenon of prophetic perspective, in which gaps such as that between the first and second advents were not perceived.[170]

It certainly seems reasonable to question the notion that the text would, without explanation, suddenly alter its mode of expression. But there is a more serious problem for Evans' apparent solution to the chronology. If the Messiah's being cut off occurred some time after the end of the sixty-two sevens, but not at the beginning of the seventieth seven, then how does this relate to the Messiah making firm a covenant with the many for one seven? There seem to be three possible scenarios in relating these events.

According to the Preterists, the sixty-ninth seven is marked by the baptism of Jesus. Also, the expression in 9:27, "he will make firm a covenant with the many for one seven" refers to Jesus making firm the new covenant. According to this verse, this marks the beginning of the seventieth seven. Also, Preterists claim that the cutting off of Messiah is the crucifixion of Jesus that must have taken place in the middle of the seventieth seven. Preterists also claim there is no gap between the sixty-ninth and the seventieth seven. So, if the sixty-ninth seven is marked by Christ's baptism, and if the seventieth seven begins with Christ confirming the covenant for one seven, then these two events must have occurred at the same time. In fact, unless there is a gap between the sixty-ninth seven and the beginning of the seventieth seven, these two events must have occurred at precisely the same moment. But, if the making firm of the covenant is the same event as the baptism of Jesus, then the making firm of the covenant cannot be the same event as the crucifixion. However, as we have seen, the NT indicates that the establishing of the covenant was the crucifixion of Jesus—"for this is My blood of the covenant, which is poured out for many for forgiveness of sins" (Matt 26:28); "This cup which is poured out for you is the new covenant in My blood" (Lk 22:20)—and it makes no sense to make firm a covenant that has not even been established. Also, since 9:27 indicates that the abomination of desolation must take place in the midst of the seventieth seven, then the abomination of desolation must have taken place at the same time as the crucifixion. But, most Preterists claim that the abomination of desolation occurred in 70 AD, some 30 years after

---

170. Robert H. Gundry, *The Church and the Tribulation* (Grand Rapids: Zondervan Publishing House, 1973), 190; quoted in Hoehner, *Chronological Aspects*, 132.

the crucifixion. This scenario simply doesn't make any sense. The graphic in Figure 29 depicts this scenario:

Figure 29: Preterist Scenario 1

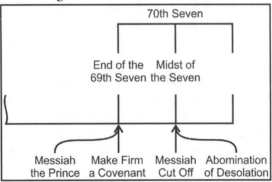

A second scenario might be proposed. As we pointed out, Preterists claim that the end of the sixty-ninth seven was marked by the baptism of Jesus. Since the NT clearly makes the establishing of the covenant as the crucifixion of Jesus, and since it makes no sense to have Christ make firm a covenant that has not yet been established, then the crucifixion and the making firm of the covenant have occurred at the same time. However, since Daniel clearly indicates that the making firm of a covenant marks the beginning of the seventieth seven, then it follows that the crucifixion must have occurred at the beginning of the seventieth seven. But, if there is no gap between the end of the sixty-ninth seven and the beginning of the 70 seven, then the baptism of Jesus, the making firm of the covenant, and the crucifixion must have all happened at the same time (see Figure 30). But this scenario is absurd also.

Figure 30: Preterist Scenario 2

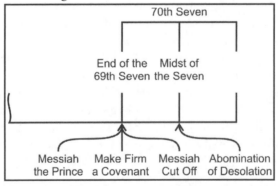

Finally, since the baptism of Jesus and the crucifixion of Jesus clearly were not the same event, nor did they happen at the same time, and since Preterists claim that the crucifixion happened in the middle of the seventieth seven, then this would mean that the making firm of a covenant and the cutting off of Messiah are not the same event. But, we have already seen that it does not make sense to make firm a covenant that has not yet been established. Alternately, if they are the same event, then they must have occurred in the middle of the seventieth seven. But this would mean that the abomination of desolation happened at the same time as the making firm of a covenant and the crucifixion (see Figure 31). But, Daniel clearly states that the making firm of a covenant marks the beginning of the seventieth seven. Also, since Daniel's prophecy states that the abomination of desolation takes place in the midst of the seventieth seven, then this means that it must have taken place some 30 years prior to the events of 70 AD. But, there is absolutely nothing in history that would support this case. So this scenario does not work either.

Figure 31: Preterist Scenario 3

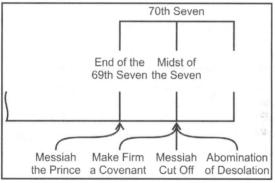

Some Preterists may object that the notion of making firm a covenant is not simply a reference to Jesus making firm the new covenant, but that this is a 7 year covenant with the Jews giving them time to acquiesce to the New Covenant. However, there is no such reference anywhere in Scripture to confirm this interpretation of this statement. Gary DeMar asserts, "As Philip Mauro affirms, using Scripture to interpret Scripture, it is Jesus who 'will make a firm covenant with the many,' not the antichrist. This language is used by Jesus, not the antichrist, in Matthew 26:28 in addressing His *Jewish disciples* in the first century as a fulfillment of the seventieth week."[171] He goes on to assert, "Nothing in the Book of Revelation, a book that supposedly describes a future seven-year great tribulation (Daniel's 'postponed' seventieth

---

171 Gary DeMar, *Last Days Madness: Obsession of the Modern Church*, 328.

week), mentions the antichrist making a covenant with the Jews and then breaking it."[172] Likewise, there is nothing in Revelation, or any other part of Scripture, that indicates that the New Covenant is only seven years long, or that Jesus made some 7 year agreement to give the Jews time to repent.

The juggling of the text and the ad hoc explanations seem to indicate that the Preterists' chronologies simply cannot work. And yet, even if they did make some sense, they still do not explain why the arrangement of the text could be so different from the chronology of events. However, the fixing of the cutting off of the Messiah is predicated on a particular understanding of the remainder of this prophecy. Consequently, we will deal with this issue again as we progress through the material. Nevertheless, it does seem that there is nothing in this particular verse that would necessarily fix the cutting off of Messiah in the middle of the seventieth seven.

PETERSON'S ARGUMENTS ABOUT THE CUTTING OFF OF MESSIAH

Evans presents a different view of the cutting off of Messiah that is proposed by Doug Peterson.

> An interesting insight into the possible meaning of "cut off" appears in a remarkable Internet article by Doug Peterson, which I shall comment about at the end of this chapter and further explore in Appendix B. After informing us that the Hebrew word for "cut off" is *karath* and that this word is *never* translated as "killed" in the OT, Peterson refers us to Isaiah 53:8b: "*For he was cut off from the land of the living; for the transgression of my people he was stricken*" (emphasis added). Contending that this passage is messianic, Peterson suggests that what the words "cut off" and "have nothing" in Daniel 9:26 signify is that because of the transgressions of the Jewish people, Christ "was cut off from the world (i.e., the land of the living)," but not killed, during the period AD 30 to AD 70. For critical commentators, however, *karath* in 9:26 refers to the murder of Onias III.[173]

Evans is a bit charitable with Peterson's statement. What Peterson asserts is, "In Daniel 9:26 the word used to denote 'cut off' in the verse, *karath*, is never translated in the Old Testament to mean 'killed.' Other Hebrew words are translated to mean killed in the Old Testament but *karath* isn't one of them."[174] What Peterson is arguing is that the word "cut off" does not mean

172. Ibid.

173. Evans, *Four Kingdoms*, 360–61.

174. Doug Peterson, "70 Sevenspt. 2," http://www.70sevens.com/id7.html. August 22, 2006.

"to kill" even though it can mean "to be dead." What he wants to argue is that this statement is not about killing Messiah, but simply that, after the sixty-two sevens He would be dead having been killed some time earlier.

First of all, it is simply false that the word כָּרַת *(tārak)* is never translated to mean "to kill." In fact, Gentry points out, "The Hebrew word translated 'cut off' here *(karath)* 'is used of the death penalty, Lev. 7:20; and refers to violent death,' i.e., the death of Christ on the cross."[175] The LXX translated it "to die" in Gen 9:11 (ἀποθανεῖται, *iatienahtopa*),[176] and the *New Living Translation* translated it "kill" in the same verse: "Yes, I am confirming my covenant with you. Never again will floodwaters kill all living creatures."[177] Second, whether a word is given a particular translation does not necessarily indicate its meaning. The same word, כָּרַת *(tārak)* is consistently translated "make" in the expression "to make a covenant," even though technically the word does not mean "make." The literal translation is "to cut a covenant" because establishing a covenant involved cutting an animal to seal the covenant relation.[178] Of course cutting an animal in half would certainly seem to involve killing it! Third, the statement in Isa 53:8b specifically states that he will be cut off from "land of the living," indicating that He will die. In a note on this verse, the NET Bible states, "The 'land of the living' is an idiom for the sphere where people live, in contrast to the underworld realm of the dead."[179] In other words, to be cut off from the land of the living is to be killed. Peterson seems to present this view in order to fit things into his Preterist view that would not fit using a traditional translation.

He goes on to assert, "So what did the author have in mind by the statement 'shall Messiah be cut off, but not for himself'? Likely it simply meant that the Messiah would be 'dead' after those sixty-two sevens. Daniel was indicating that the Messiah would no longer be around after the sixty-two sabbatical years. Of course this was true since Christ was already crucified some thirty years earlier."[180] Peterson's argument suffers from not understanding language in general and the Hebrew language in particular. All standard lexicons assert that the word כָּרַת *(tārak)* can have the meaning "to kill." The NIDOTTE states, "The vb. [כרת] has three basic meanings: (a) to cut

---

175. Gentry, *He Shall Have Dominion*, 327.

176. καὶ στήσω τὴν διαθήκην μου πρὸς ὑμᾶς, καὶ οὐκ ἀποθανεῖται πᾶσα σὰρξ ἔτι ἀπὸ τοῦ ὕδατος τοῦ κατακλυσμοῦ, καὶ οὐκ ἔσται ἔτι κατακλυσμὸς ὕδατος τοῦ καταφθεῖραι πᾶσαν τὴν γῆν. (Gen. 9:11)

177. *New Living Translation* (Wheaton, Illinois: Tyndale House Publishers, 2004).

178. KBH, s.v., "כרת."

179. *NET Bible: New English Translation*, 2d ed. (Dallas, Texas: Biblical Studies Press, 2003), sn15.

180. Peterson, "70 Sevens."

(objects designated); (b) to eradicate, set aside, exclude, cut off (metaphorical), kill, fail, cease; and (c) to enter into, conclude a covenant, agreement, treaty."[181] Peterson's claims are mistaken. In order for the text to say what Peterson claims, the word "cut off" would need to function as a Past Perfect tense—referring to an event that occurred before some other past event. The text would have to say, "after the sixty-two sevens Messiah will have been cut off." The text does not use this form, however. The text uses an Niphal Imperfect form indicating an event that will occur in the future. Also, in order for the word "cut off" to indicate that Messiah is dead, the word would of necessity be a stative verb—a verb indicating a condition or state of being. But, the verb "cut off" is not a stative verb. In fact, it is in this case a passive verb with the subject receiving the action of the verb. According to the text, after the sixty-two sevens, Messiah will be killed. Peterson's arguments simply cannot be supported by the text.

Noē's Arguments about the Cutting Off of the Messiah

Noē addresses the question of what will happen after the sixty-two sevens, and he presents a translation of the relevant verses, which is reproduced below in Table 32. Alongside Noē's translation is the translation from the *New American Standard Updated* version.

Table 32: Noē's and NASBU's Translations of Daniel 9:26–27

Noē's Translation	NASBU Translation
After sixty-two 'sevens' the Anointed One will be cut off and will have nothing. The people of the ruler who will come will destroy the city and the sanctuary. The end will come like a flood: War will continue until the end, and desolations have been decreed [determined] . . . And one who causes desolation will place abominations on a wing of the temple until the end that is decreed [determined] is poured out on him. (Da 9:26 [KJV])	v. 26 Then after the sixty-two weeks the Messiah will be cut off and have nothing, and the people of the prince who is to come will destroy the city and the sanctuary. And its end [will come] with a flood; even to the end there will be war; desolations are determined. *v. 27 And he will make a firm covenant with the many for one week, but in the middle of the week he will put a stop to sacrifice and grain offering;* and on the wing of abominations [will come] one who makes desolate, even until a complete destruction, one that is decreed, is poured out on the one who makes desolate.

181. NIGOTTE, s.v. "כרת."

Noē has omitted a major section, indicated in *italics* in the NASBU Translation. Although by the use of an ellipsis he indicates that a portion of the text has been omitted, he nevertheless gives the reference "(Da. 9:26)" even for that portion which is actually part of verse 27. Noē makes it appear as if the abomination of desolation is part of verse 26. He declares, "The only time restriction here is 'after' sixty-two sevens (the 69th week, 483 years)."[182] Of course, when one considers the actual text of the Scripture one sees that there is in fact another time restriction, namely, the "one week" in the portion that Noē omits.

Noē goes on to argue,

> It is not predicting that all this will happen during the 70th week of years. It is simply saying "after" the 69th week. Nor does it say how long after—just after. However, we know that the final week began with Jesus' anointing 3 years earlier. So, the Messiah being "cut off" so as to "have nothing" meant He was crucified and had nothing befitting the Messiah. This did occur during the middle of that 70th week in A.D. 30. He was without his messianic kingdom. This event is time-restricted in the next verse, and will be addressed in our next section on the middle of the 70th week. Hence, we have separated the "cutting off" (the crucifixion), which is time-restricted to the middle of the final week, from the other events of Daniel 9:26, which are not so restricted, but only named as coming "after" the sixty-two weeks. We know from history that these events occurred 37 years after the crucifixion. The other events that were to come "after" the sixty-two weeks are the destruction of Jerusalem and the Temple, and desolations and abominations. They were "decreed" or "determined" (meaning fixed and unable to be changed) within Daniel's 70th week, when most of Israel did not or would not recognize the time of its visitation by Messiah, just as Jesus had warned (Lk. 19:41–44). These decreed events (the destruction, desolations and abominations) did not take place until the decade of A.D. 60–70 because they were part of the end and were associated with Daniel's other time prophecy, the time of the end. In Daniel's last chapter, Gabriel gave Daniel this second time prophecy for the chronological fulfillment of those predetermined, time-of-the-end events. As we shall discover, it has its own, separate time frame, different time parameters, and different terminology.[183]

182. Noē, *Beyond the End Times*, 84.
183. Ibid., 84–85.

There are a number of problems with Noë's assertions here, besides the fact that he has not accurately presented the biblical text. First, to claim that the text "is not predicting that all this will happen during the seventieth week of years" is a straw man argument and a misunderstanding of the text. Noë does not provide support or argument for this claim. The text does not explicitly state that these events were to happen "during the seventieth week of years," but it does explicitly claim that these events were to happen by the time the 70 weeks of years were completed. The prophecy clearly declares in verse 24, "Seventy sevens have been decreed for your people and your holy city . . ." This is the stated time frame in which these events must occur so that by the completion of the seventieth seven, all that has to do with Daniel's people and Daniel's city would be accomplished. The text does not say, "Seventy sevens are decreed, and any additional time needed to complete the prophecy . . ." Secondly, it is misleading to leave out the reference to making firm the covenant for one seven as stated in verse 27 and then to claim, "It is simply saying 'after' the 69ᵗʰ week." In fact, it does not simply say this. It says "after" the sixty-ninth seven, and then it makes reference to the final seven and the events of the middle of this seven. Third, the fact that verse 27 states that the cutting off of Messiah would happen after the sixty-two sevens but before the seventieth seven argues against Noë's claim that it occurred in the middle of the seventieth seven. As we have seen, the chronology just cannot work. Fourth, Noë has not successfully separated the 'cutting off' of Messiah from the other events precisely because not all of the other events are contained in verse 26, and because those events presented in verse 27 occur with the time restriction of the "one week" occurring in the part of the Scripture Noë omitted.

Again Noë asserts, "The other events that were to come 'after' the sixty-two weeks are the destruction of Jerusalem and the Temple, and desolations and abominations. They were 'decreed' or 'determined' (meaning fixed and unable to be changed) *within* Daniel's 70ᵗʰ week, when most of Israel did not or would not recognize the time of its visitation by Messiah, just as Jesus warned (Lk. 19:41–44)."[184] It is not clear what he means by saying they were "decreed" within the seventieth week. As he explains later, "But these events were only 'decreed' or 'determined' within Daniel's 70ᵗʰ week. Their actual occurrence (fulfillment) lies outside that time period."[185] However, the text does not say this. The text uses the word "decreed" or "determined" (חֶתַךְ, _ḵāṭaḥ). It occurs only once in verses 24–27, and the text states that it is the period of seventy sevens that is decreed, not the events. The period of seventy

184. Ibid., 85.
185. Ibid., 92.

sevens is decreed in which the events are to take place. The text simply does not say, "Certain events are determined during the seventy sevens." To get this interpretation from the text requires the juggling of the text and the addition of words that are not there.

How does Noē justify this reading? He argues,

> How can we be so sure these end-time events were only "decreed" or "determined" *within* Daniel's 70th week and not fulfilled in that time segment? The answer is found in the way the Hebrew word is used elsewhere. In Daniel 11:36, the same Hebrew word (*charats*), translated as "decreed" or "determined," is used in a future fulfillment sense, ". . . for what has been determined must take place." Hence, "decreed" or "determined" (past tense) does not require that all events "happen" during that same time frame, although some did. Others were set, or locked into motion (determined) for future fulfillment. This distinction must be understood. It enables us to maintain the integrity of Daniel's two interrelated and interconnected time frames without resorting to gaps or gimmicks.[186]

Noē claims that because the word used in 11:36 is the same word used in 9:26 (the word in 9:24 is חָתַךְ, *katah*, and the word in 9:26 and 11:36 is חָרַץ, *saṛah*) that it must have the same sense. This is always an assertion that must be made with caution because the same word can have different senses even in the same sentence by the same author. Additionally, the question here is not about the meaning but about the referents. To what is each passage referring? The word is actually used in 9:26 and 9:27 as well as 11:36. In all of these instances it is referring to future events. These verses are set out below with the Hebrew text and the Hebrew word placed in the appropriate spot in the English translation.

Table 33: Daniel 9:26–27; 11:36 Use of "Decreed"

Daniel 9:26	"Then after the sixty-two weeks the Messiah will be cut off and have nothing, and the people of the prince who is to come will destroy the city and the sanctuary. And its end will come with a flood; even to the end there will be war; desolations are determined [נֶחֱרֶצֶת, hen̯'teser]."

וְאַחֲרֵי הַשָּׁבֻעִים שִׁשִּׁים וּשְׁנַיִם יִכָּרֵת מָשִׁיחַ
וְאֵין לוֹ וְהָעִיר וְהַקֹּדֶשׁ יַשְׁחִית עַם נָגִיד
הַבָּא וְקִצּוֹ בַשֶּׁטֶף וְעַד קֵץ מִלְחָמָה
נֶחֱרֶצֶת שֹׁמֵמוֹת:

---

186. Ibid., 85–86 (emphasis in original).

Daniel 9:27

"And he will make a firm covenant with the many for one week, but in the middle of the week he will put a stop to sacrifice and grain offering; and on the wing of abominations will come one who makes desolate, even until a complete destruction, one that is decreed [וְנֶחֱרָצָה, wᵉhnᵉḥaṣar], is poured out on the one who makes desolate."

וְהִגְבִּיר בְּרִית לָרַבִּים שָׁבוּעַ אֶחָד וַחֲצִי
הַשָּׁבוּעַ יַשְׁבִּית זֶבַח וּמִנְחָה וְעַל כְּנַף
שִׁקּוּצִים מְשֹׁמֵם וְעַד־כָּלָה וְנֶחֱרָצָה תִּתַּךְ
עַל־שֹׁמֵם:

Daniel 11:36

"Then the king will do as he pleases, and he will exalt and magnify himself above every god and will speak monstrous things against the God of gods; and he will prosper until the indignation is finished, for that which is decreed [נֶחֱרָצָה, henᵉḥaṣar] will be done."

וְעָשָׂה כִרְצוֹנוֹ הַמֶּלֶךְ וְיִתְרוֹמֵם וְיִתְגַּדֵּל
עַל־כָּל־אֵל וְעַל אֵל אֵלִים יְדַבֵּר נִפְלָאוֹת
וְהִצְלִיחַ עַד־כָּלָה זַעַם כִּי נֶחֱרָצָה נֶעֱשָׂתָה:

What Noë apparently fails to notice is that in 9:26 the same word is used and it indicates an event that in fact *does* take place in the specified period. In the one week that is instigated by the confirming of a covenant, the abomination of desolation, "one that is decreed," takes place in the middle of this week. Also, Noë's argument does not necessarily support his claim. He says, "Hence, 'decreed' or 'determined' (past tense) does not require that all events 'happen' during that same time frame, although some did." But, because it does not "require" that an event happen during the same time frame, neither does it "require" that an event *not* happen during the same time frame. So, since the word does not require either, the appeal to the use of the word does not lend any support to his claim. This case must be made on the basis of other arguments, not simply on the basis of the fact that the same word is used. As a result, Noë's readers are still left without any justification or explanation for why they should understand these events as only "decreed" and not actually fulfilled.

Later Noë attempts to add some support to this argument by declaring,

In his last vision, Daniel sees two others (angels) standing on the bank of a river and talking. One asks the other, "How long will it be before these astonishing things are fulfilled?" (Da. 12:6b). The asking of this time question subsequent to Daniel receiving his 70 week prophecy strongly suggests that the events of this fulfillment

were not included in that previous time period. This is evidently
why Daniel is given another time prophecy for another sovereignly
determined time period. Note that this one uses different time
terminology, which differentiates it from the 490-year time span
covered by Daniel's 70 weeks.[187]

Here Noē is simply reading into the text his prior eschatological commitment. The prophecy of chapter 7 was received after the prophecy of chapter
2, but that does not mean it was "not included in that previous time period."
The prophecy of chapter 8 was received after the prophecy of chapter 7, but
this does not mean it was not included in that previous time period. The
abomination of desolation talked about in chapter 11 was received after the
prophecy of the abomination of desolation prophesied in chapter 9, but not
only does Noē take them as references to the same time period, but holds that
they are discussing the same event.[188] The only reason Noē makes the claim he
does is to attempt to fit the text into his preconceived eschatological scheme.

Don Preston, a Preterist, declares, "Daniel was specifically told that
seventy weeks were determined *on his city and on his people.* The prophecy manifestly encompasses Jerusalem' [*sic*] fate within the predicted events.
. . . What is predicted cannot exclude the determined fate *of the city and the
people.* On the contrary the very fate of the city and people is at stake here."[189] In
other words, against Noē, Preston holds that the prophecy is in fact stating that
these events will actually occur within the specified time period of 490 years.

GENTRY'S ARGUMENT ABOUT PARALLELISM

In order to connect the cutting off of Messiah and the making of the covenant,
Kenneth Gentry attempts to forge a parallelism between verses 26 and 27:

> Given the Hebraic pattern of repetition, we may easily discern a
> parallel between verses 26 and 27; verse 27 gives an expansion of
> verse 26. Negatively, Messiah's *cutting off* in verse 26 is the result of
> Israel's completing her transgression and bringing it to a culmina-
> tion (v. 24) by crucifying the Messiah. Positively, verse 27 states this
> same event: "He shall *confirm a covenant* with many for one week;
> but in the middle of the week He shall bring an end to sacrifice
> and offering." Considered from its positive effect, this confirm-
> ing of the covenant with many makes reconciliation and brings in
> everlasting righteousness (v. 24). *The confirming of a covenant* (v.

187. Ibid.

188. See Ibid., 135.

189. Don K. Preston, *Seal Up Vision and Prophecy: A Study of The Seventy Weeks* of
Daniel 9, 27.

27) refers to the prophesied covenantal actions of verse 24, which come about as the result of the Perfect Covenantal Jubilee (Seventy Weeks) and are mentioned as a result of Daniel's covenantal prayer (cf. v. 4). The covenant mentioned, then, is the divine covenant of God's redemptive grace. Messiah came to confirm the covenantal promises (Luke 1:72; Eph. 2:12). He confirmed the covenant by His death on the cross. (Heb 7:22b)[190]

Although it is true that the Hebrew authors often used the principle of repetition, this device cannot be applied indiscriminately to any passage where an interpreter might need it in order to support his theory. Parallelism in Hebrew literature is a specialized literary device that is used primarily in poetry, and has predictable and identifiable indicators, such as the repetition of key phrases, the balance of line structure, the balance of accents, etc.[191] Gentry offers no literary arguments and cites no indicators that should lead the reader to accept his claim. Rather, Gentry's claim of parallelism is based on his interpretation and prior eschatological commitment, not on the literary structure of the verses in question. In fact, there is no literary parallelism between these verses. Table 34 shows that there is no basis upon which to claim "repetition" between these two verses.

Table 34: Comparison of Daniel 9:26 and 27

	Hebrew Text	NASBU Translation
26	וְאַחֲרֵי הַשָּׁבֻעִים שִׁשִּׁים וּשְׁנַיִם יִכָּרֵת מָשִׁיחַ וְאֵין לוֹ	Then after the sixty-two weeks the Messiah will be cut off and have nothing,
27	וְהִגְבִּיר בְּרִית לָרַבִּים שָׁבוּעַ אֶחָד	And he will make firm a covenant with the many for one week

Having dispatched Gentry's claim to repetition and parallelism, the rest of his argument falls apart. Gentry declares, "Messiah came to *confirm* the covenantal promises (Luke 1:72; Eph. 2:12)."[192] However, the text does not say "he will confirm covenantal promises for one seven." Rather it says, "he will make firm a covenant . . ." Whether the covenant referred to in verse 27

190. Gentry, *He Shall Have Dominion*, 327–28 (emphasis in original).

191. For more information on this point, see Wilfred G. E. Watson, *Classical Hebrew Poetry: A Guide to its Techniques* (London: T&T Clark International, 2001), or Robert Alter, *The Art of Biblical Poetry* (New York: Basic Books, 1985).

192. Ibid., 328 (emphasis in original).

refers to the "*divine* covenant of God's redemptive grace,"[193] as Gentry claims, will be considered in the examination of that verse. Nevertheless, the text simply does not say anything about confirming covenantal promises.

And Have Nothing

26—   "Then after the sixty-two weeks the Messiah will be cut off *and have nothing . . .*"

The phrase, "and have nothing" translates an awkward Hebrew expression: וְאֵין לוֹ (*ol ñe'ᵉw*), which literally reads, "and there is not to him." Young proposes, "These words are exceedingly difficult, but they seem to indicate that all which should properly belong to the Messiah, He does not have when He dies."[194] Miller points out that "the phrase . . . is in Hebrew an idiom for 'not have' (cf. Gen 11:30; Isa 27:4). Therefore the NIV translation ['and will have nothing'] is correct. Thus when Christ died, his earthly ministry seemed to have been in vain."[195] Pentecost argues, "At His crucifixion He would 'have nothing' in the sense that Israel had rejected Him and the kingdom could not be instituted at that time. Therefore He did not then receive the royal glory as the King on David's throne over Israel. John referred to this when he wrote, 'He came to that which was His own [i.e., the throne to which He had been appointed by the Father] but His own [i.e., His own people] did not receive Him' (John 1:11). Daniel's prophecy, then, anticipated Christ's offer of Himself to the nation Israel as her Messiah, the nation's rejection of Him as Messiah, and His crucifixion."[196] Pentecost's explanation works if one has already accepted his eschatological perspective, but it is quite a bit to read out of this small phrase. It seems clear that this is a Hebrew idiom meaning, "he does not have," as Miller points out, but its precise significance at this point is obscure. This is no contradiction to what was stated above about Gabriel giving Daniel understanding. In that situation Goldingay was proposing that the words are obscure in themselves even to Daniel. Here we are simply saying that the idiom is difficult for the modern reader to grasp. They may have been perfectly clear to Daniel, however.

---

193. Ibid. (emphasis in original).

194. Young, *Prophecy of Daniel*, 207.

195. Miller, *Daniel*, 267. For example, אֵין לוֹ דָּמִים "there is not to him blood guilti-ness" (Ex 22:1), he does not have blood guiltiness; אֵין־לוֹ סְנַפִּיר וְקַשְׂקֶשֶׂת "there is not to it fins and scales" (Lev 11:10), the creatures do not have fins and scales; אֵין לוֹ בֵּן "there is not to him a son" (Num 27:4), the man does not have a son.

196. Pentecost, *Daniel*, 1364.

The Coming Prince

26—   ". . . and the people of *the prince who is to come* will destroy the city
        and the sanctuary."

Table 35: Daniel 9:26b

יַשְׁחִית	וְהַקֹּדֶשׁ	וְהָעִיר
will destroy	and the sanctuary	and the city
הַבָּא	נָגִיד	עַם
the coming	prince	people of

PEOPLE OF THE PRINCE, OR DESTRUCTION WITH THE PRINCE?

Gabriel tells Daniel, "and the people of the prince who is to come will destroy
the city and the sanctuary." Matheny raises an important issue in the translation of this verse. The word translated "people of," according to Matheny,
should be translated "with." The difference between the word 'people' and
the word 'with' is a single vowel point: עַם (*maʿ*) with the "a" vowel means
"people," while עִם (*miʿ*) with the "i" vowel is the preposition "with." Using
the preposition, Matheny translates the verse "and the city and the sanctuary
shall be destroyed *with* the prince, the coming one."[197] According to Matheny,
"In addition to being literally accurate, this translation respects the chronology of the Hebrew sentence and echoes both the Syriac and Vaticanus-
Alexandrinus codices of the Septuagint (the Greek translation of the Hebrew
Bible compiled around 200 B.C. and the oldest translation we have of the
Hebrew Old Testament)."[198] There is a serious misrepresentation in the way
Matheny makes his claim. He implies that Vaticanus-Alexandrinus codices
were compiled around 200 BC. This is actually inaccurate. These particular
codices date from the middle fourth century AD, Vaticanus, and some time in
the fifth century AD, Alexandrinus.[199] Matheny also asserts, "The Septuagint,
of course, was the translation of the Old Testament in use during the Lord's
earthly ministry,"[200] but this fact does not prove that this particular reading
was the one that the Greek Bible of that day actually contained.

197. Matheny, *The Seventy Weeks*, 89.

198. Ibid.

199. See Bruce M. Metzger, *The Text of the New Testament: Its Transmission, Corruption,
and Restoration*, 3d ed. (New York: Oxford University Press, 1992), 46–48.

200. Matheny, *The Seventy Weeks*, 89.

Matheny goes on to say, "While the Syriac version uses the Greek term 'meta' ('with the Christ') and 'meta' means 'with' in a broader sense ('in the midst of'), the Vaticanus-Alexandrinus uses 'sun' ('with the coming one') and 'sun' means 'with' in the narrow sense ('together with')."[201] First of all it is simply false that the Syriac uses the Greek term "meta." The Syriac actually reads, ܥܰܡ ܡܰܠܟܳܐ ܕܳܐܬܶܐ (*'t'd 'klm m'*). The problem here is the same as with the Hebrew text. The word ܥܰܡ (*m'*) can be read as the preposition "with" or as the noun "people." So, it is not the case that the Syriac version uses the Greek term 'meta' as Matheny claims. George Lamsa translates the Syriac, "and the holy city shall be destroyed together with the coming king."[202] Lamsa's translation simply reflects Lamsa's choice. It does not necessarily mean that the Syriac term must be translated "with."

The Greek text of θ reads, "καὶ τὴν πόλιν καὶ τὸ ἅγιον διαφθερεῖ σὺν τῷ ἡγουμένῳ τῷ ἐρχομένῳ (*ierehtfaid noigah ot iak nilop ñet iak ‾onemohcre‾ot‾onemuoḡeh‾ot nus*), literally translated is, "and the city and the sanctuary he will destroy together with the one commanding the one coming." In fact, Brenton has almost the same translation as the one given by Methany: "and he will destroy the city and the sanctuary with the prince that is coming."[203]

All of this seems impressive at first glance, but the argument does not hold up to scrutiny. Concerning the Greek text in relation to the Hebrew text, Karen Jobes states, "for most biblical books the MT [Masoretic Text, or Hebrew Bible] has preserved a demonstrably good text, and given its long lineage and uniformity, it can serve us well as the point of departure."[204] In other words, it is a good practice to start with the Hebrew text and then evaluate the differences with the versions in terms of a certain set of criteria. These criteria are technical and involved and would take us too far from our present task even to list. Suffice to say that simply opting for the Greek because one prefers it, as Methany does, is not a sufficient reason to overturn the Hebrew text. Besides the fact that Methany's reading makes little sense in the context, there is no reason to think that these versions present a superior text. As Paul Wegner points out, "One must remember, however, that the LXX is a translation from Hebrew into Greek with the same kinds of difficulties inherent to

201. Ibid.

202. Geroge M. Lamsa, *Holy Bible From the Ancient Eastern Text* (San Francisco: Harper & Row, Publishers, 1968), 896.

203. Sir Lancelot Brenton, *Esdras—Malachias*, vol. 2, *The Septuagint Version of the Old Testament According to the Vatican Text* (London: Samuel Bagster and Sons, 1844), 871.

204. VanderKam and Flint, *Meaning of the Dead Sea Scrolls*, 138.

all translations. Attempting to identify the original Hebrew *Vorlage* of the LXX is much more complicated than earlier scholars thought."[205]

Also, the discoveries at Qumran have yielded a text of Daniel that, according to James Vanderkam and Peter Flint, "reveal no major disagreements against the Masoretic Text, although 1QDan[a] is closest to the traditional text."[206] It is also pointed out that the Qumran Daniel corresponds to the shorter version as contained in the Masoretic Text rather than the longer version contained in the Greek versions.[207] Also, according to Emanuel Tov, the Greek version of Daniel is perceived to be midrashic in character, especially the lengthy additions to the text, and are usually "conceived of as subsequent to the literary compositions included in M [the Masoretic Text]."[208] These characterizations do not necessarily apply down to the level of particular vowel points, but they demonstrate that the burden of proof lies with the one who would abandon the MT for the Greek text. However, Matheny has presented no proof—only his personal preference.

In his further discussion, Matheny also misrepresents the nature of the Hebrew vowel points that were added by the Masorets. Matheny asserts, "With the two possible readings of this single word identified, we should note that the only difference between these two words in our present Hebrew Old Testament (Masoretic text) is basically the vowel of each, ('i' or 'a'). *But the Hebrew vowel system was not added to the language until approximately 900 A.D.* Vowels were *not* a part of the original text but were added much later for clarification. Until 900 A.D., context alone rather than vowel pointing determined the meaning of words and the Greek text of 200 B.C. (the Septuagint versions) followed a literal (normal) reading of the verse, rendering the word as 'with.'"[209]

There are several problems with Matheny's characterization of the reality. First of all, it is not true that the Hebrew vowel points were not added to the language until approximately 900 AD as Matheny claims. In fact, the process that ultimately issued in the acceptance of the Masoretic vowel system was begun centuries earlier. As Waltke-O'Connor describe, "Between 600 and 1000 C.E. schools consisting of families of Jewish scholars arose in Babylon, in Palestine, and notably at Tiberias on the Sea of Galilee to safeguard the consonantal text and to record—through diacritical notations added to the consonantal text—the vowels, liturgical cantillations, and other features of

---

205. Paul D. Wegner, *Textual Criticism of the Bible*, 184.

206. Tov, *Textual Criticism of the Hebrew Bible*, 317.

207. Ibid.

208. Ibid., 317.

209. Matheny, *The Seventy Weeks*, 90.

the text. Until these efforts such features had orally accompanied the text."[210] What this means is that the biblical language certainly had vowels. In fact, without vowels a language could not be spoken since it is primarily the vowels that carry the sound. Rather, it was only that there were no written symbols, like vowel letters in the English language, to represent the vowel sounds. So, the text would have looked something like this, עם נגיד הבא rather than this, עַם נָגִיד הַבָּא. But this fact offered no problem for the native Hebrew reader (in fact, Modern Hebrew is even today written without vowel points). The native English speaker is able to place the accent on a word in its appropriate place even though there are no marks on English words indicating which syllable gets the stress. Native English speakers have no trouble stressing the correct syllable precisely because it is their native language. Similarly, a native Hebrew speaker has no problem knowing which word is being used in a context even though there were no vowel points. The vowel pointing system was not added for the benefit of the native speaker, but for the non-native speaker in order to preserve the language from extinction.

Also, the way Matheny presents the case makes it appear as though the Greek versions somehow preserved a text that pre-dates the text preserved by the Masorets. But this is a complete misrepresentation of the case. As Waltke-O'Connor point out, "The presence of a text type among the Qumran biblical texts (ca. 100 B.C.E. to 130 C.E.) identical with the one preserved by the Masoretes, whose earliest extant manuscript dates to ca. 1000 C.E., gives testimony to the achievement of the later scribes in faithfully preserving the text."[211] And, as they go on to say, "These scrolls [Qumran biblical scrolls] to a large extent lack even the minor variants found in the great recensions of the Greek Old Testament attributed by tradition to Aquila (based on R; ca. 120 C.E.), Symmachus (ca. 180 C.E.), and Theodotion (ca. 180 C.E.); these minor Greek versions were further attempts to bring the Greek translation of the Bible closer to the accepted Hebrew text during the second century C.E."[212] In other words, the Masoretic Text preserves an older and more accurate tradition than the one found in the Greek text that Matheny prefers. What seemed initially as a formidable argument loses all significance once the facts are known, and there is simply no reason to accept Matheny's reading.

Matheny's final argument for his reading is the absence of the definite article before the word translated "people" or "with." He says, "Further grammatical problems with the traditional translation arise when we consider that in normal Hebrew a word is made definite by the addition of the prefix denot-

210. Waltke-O'Connor, *Biblical Hebrew Syntax*, 1.5.4d.

211. Ibid., 1.5.3.

212. Ibid., 1.5.4b.

ing the definite article to the word. But the Hebrew word which we prefer to translate as 'with' ('im') has *no* sign of the definite article prefix. The absence of the definite article rules out the traditional rendering of '*the* people.'"[213] But this statement serves only to accentuate Matheny's lack of familiarity with Hebrew syntax. The word translated "people" is in a construct relation to the word "prince" and as such would never take the definite article anyway. The fact that the participle, "the coming," is definite makes the word "prince" definite, something that Matheny acknowledges: "when the adjective modifying the noun (in this case, the 'ba' [coming] following 'nagid'[prince]), the definite genitive makes the whole expression definite."[214] Since the word "people" is in a construct relation to the word "prince," it is definite also and in fact requires the translation "the coming prince." Ultimately, none of Matheny's arguments supports his claims, and the traditional translation seems to stand well under scrutiny.

WHO IS THE PRINCE?

Perhaps one of the biggest controversies over this passage is who is the coming prince. The text says, "the people of the coming prince." Many commentators have pointed out that the word "prince" (נָגִיד, *dīḡan*) does not have a definite article, that it should be translated "a prince." Although it is certainly true that the word is anarthrous, the following participle, "the one coming" (בָּא הַ, *ʾabah*) does have the definite article, and it is in apposition to the word "prince." The text literally says, "prince, the coming one," or "the coming prince." Therefore, it should be taken as definite.

Who is this prince? At this point in the verse there is no specific identification other than the fact that he the coming prince of the people who will destroy the city and the sanctuary. Although some commentators have attempted to identify this prince with "Messiah the prince" of the first part of verse 25, this cannot be maintained. It is true that the words for "prince" in each case are the same, but there is no historical situation that can be attributed to the people of the Messiah destroying the city and the sanctuary. Since the people of the Messiah did not destroy the city and the sanctuary, and the people of the coming prince did, then the coming prince must be a different prince from Messiah.

Neither can it be claimed that this is referring to the notion that Christ's sacrifice rendered the OT sacrificial system obsolete or no longer effective. First of all, the word does not have this meaning. Second, even if we agree

213. Matheny, *The Seventy Weeks*, 91.

214. A. B. Davidson, *Hebrew Syntax* (Edinburgh: T & T Clark, 1984), 24; quoted in Matheny, *The Seventy Weeks*, 92.

that the word could have this meaning, it makes no sense to say that the city was made obsolete or no longer effective. The text states that the city and the sanctuary will be physically destroyed, and it simply is not true that the people of the Messiah ever destroyed the city and the sanctuary. This prince cannot be the Messiah.

The word translated "destroy" (שָׁחַת, *tạh̄as*) is used three other times before this verse—twice in Dan. 8:24 and once in 8:25.

Table 36: Daniel 8:24–25 "Destroy"

Daniel 8:24	"His power will be mighty, but not by his own power, and he will destroy to an extraordinary degree and prosper and perform his will; He will destroy [וְהִשְׁחִית, *wᵉtịhsih*] mighty men and the holy people." וְעָצַם כֹּחוֹ וְלֹא בְכֹחוֹ וְנִפְלָאוֹת יַשְׁחִית וְהִצְלִיחַ וְעָשָׂה וְהִשְׁחִית עֲצוּמִים וְעַם־קְדֹשִׁים׃
Daniel 8:25	"And through his shrewdness he will cause deceit to succeed by his influence; And he will magnify himself in his heart, and he will destroy [יַשְׁחִית, *tịhsay*] many while they are at ease. He will even oppose the Prince of princes, but he will be broken without human agency." וְעַל־שִׂכְלוֹ וְהִצְלִיחַ מִרְמָה בְּיָדוֹ וּבִלְבָבוֹ יַגְדִּיל וּבְשַׁלְוָה יַשְׁחִית רַבִּים וְעַל־שַׂר־שָׂרִים יַעֲמֹד וּבְאֶפֶס יָד יִשָּׁבֵר׃

In both of these instances the word is used to indicate a physical destruction. So, the text states that the people of the prince who is coming will destroy the city and the sanctuary. It does not say the Prince will do this, but his people will do it. Evans argues, "In the preterist approach, 'the people of a ruler who will come' in 9:26 are the Roman soldiers, and Titus is, of course, their 'prince' or ruler."[215] Evans declares that "although the 490 years covered by the prophecy did not extend past AD 34 or possibly 35, the events that occurred by that time locked into place the catastrophe that followed in 70."[216] However, the history shows that this claim is simply false. As Peter Schäfer points out, "Following the death of Agrippa I, the greater part of Palestine came once more under direct Roman control (44 CE). This last period be-

215. Ibid., 361.

216. Evans, *Four Kingdoms*, 337.

fore the outbreak of war is characterized by a progressive deterioration in the internal political situation, so that war became almost inevitable."[217] In other words, it was not some unidentified events in AD 34 or 35 that precipitated the war. Rather it was the identifiable events in 44 AD, a decade later, that made war inevitable. In fact, Schäfer notes, "Many of the Jewish population may well initially have regarded Roman rule as a liberation from the yoke of the detested Herodians, while others recognized the potential dangers right from the start and fought against the Romans, seeing them as brutal oppressors who were leading the Jewish people irrevocably into slavery."[218] The inevitability of war was not "locked into place" in 34 or 35 as Evans claims. In fact, in 34 or 35 AD, the Romans did not have direct rule of Judea. Judea was under the rule of the Herods. So, there could not have been any events that "locked in" the war with Rome since Rome was not in direct rule at the time.

Also, Evans' claim contradicts the statement of Gabriel in verse 24. Gabriel declared, "Seventy sevens [490 years] have been decreed for your people and your holy city" to accomplish that which is delineated by the following verses. Gabriel did not say, "Seventy sevens, plus an additional period of about 40 years or so, have been decreed upon your people and your holy city." The text indicates that the decree upon the people and the city was to be completed by the end of the seventy sevens, not seventy sevens plus 40.

Additionally, this seems to introduce a gap which has always been the complaint of the Preterists against the Futurists. Evans recognizes this possible criticism and presents a response.

> "Wait a minute!" many will say, "I thought preterists didn't believe in gaps, and here you have a forty-year gap between the first and second halves of the final seven." In reply to this often-expressed opinion, I shall start by conceding that since the passage in 9:26 stating that the "anointed one" will be "cut off" and "have nothing" is immediately followed by the passages in the same verse stating that "the people of a ruler who will come will destroy the city and the sanctuary" and that "War will continue until the end," it seems logical at first sight to assume that the events given in those passages should occur immediately after the anointed one is cut off. That, however, is not how I believe this verse should be understood. As John Noë, Gary DeMar, and others have demonstrated, the fulfillment of the second half of the last seven does not

---

217. Schäfer, *The History of the Jews*, 114.

218. Ibid., 108.

require a forty-year gap between the first half of the last seven and the second half.[219]

The problem with Evans' response is that it ignores the fact that a gap does not need to come between the first and second halves of the last seven in order to be a gap. There would still be a "thirty-year gap" between the end of the seventieth seven and the destruction of Jerusalem no matter how one organizes it. Whether one takes Plan A, Plan B, or Plan C—whether it comes after or between or before, it is still a gap, as Figure 32 illustrates.

Figure 32: Inevitable Gaps

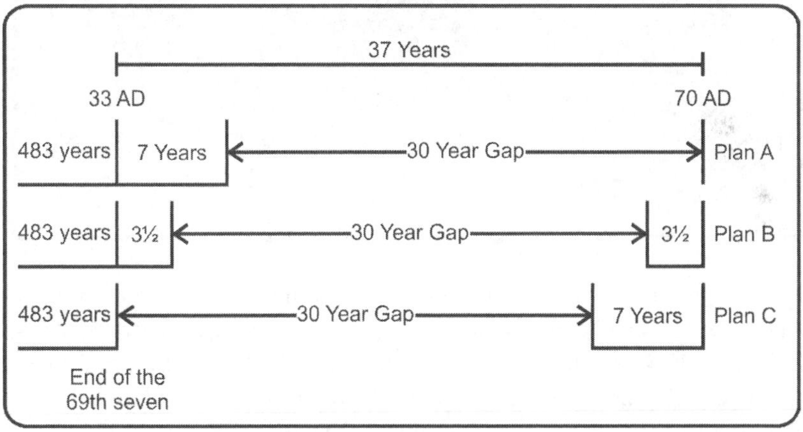

However, historically, Evans seems to be correct that the people of the coming prince are the Romans who actually did destroy the city and the sanctuary in 70 AD. As Miller puts it, "Historically the next destruction of Jerusalem and the temple after the Babylonian period was that perpetrated by the Romans, and Josephus understood Daniel to have prophesied this Roman destruction of Jerusalem."[220] So, it seems clear that the people who destroy the city and the sanctuary are the Romans and that this event took place in 70 AD.

219. Evans, *Four Kingdoms*, 361.
220. Miller, *Daniel*, 268.

Figure 33: Evans' Preterist Gap

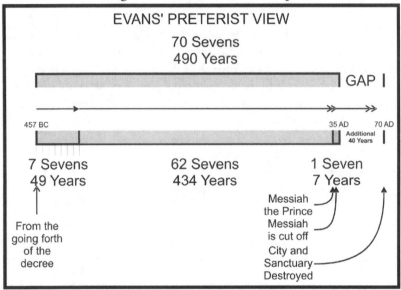

But, regardless of where one puts it in the scheme of the prophecy, there is going to be a gap in the chronology of events. According to Evans' explanation, the 490 years simply does not extend to 70 AD if it is an unbroken chronological progression (see Figure 33 for Evans' Gap). Ultimately, the destruction of the city in 70 AD is outside the scope of the seventy sevens of the prophecy. But this is contrary to the straightforward statement in 9:24: "Seventy sevens are determined upon your people and your holy city . . ." Since the seventy sevens is determined upon the city, it is contrary to the text to claim that the destruction of the city falls outside the seventy sevens. Additionally, it is not at all clear that the "coming prince" is necessarily Titus. Since it was Titus at the head of his army that destroyed the city and the sanctuary, it seems problematic to distance him from the event as the text seems to do: "the people . . . will destroy . . ." In fact, Josephus records how Titus was the one who gave order to set the gates of the Temple on fire.[221] This, and the fact that Titus was the one giving orders to destroy various parts of the defenses of the city, makes it clear that Titus was at least as much a part of the destruction of the city and the sanctuary as were the people. It is possible that the "coming prince" is not Titus but someone who, at the time of the destruction of the city and the sanctuary, was yet to come.

---

221. Josephus, *Wars of the Jews*, 6.4.1.

Its End with a Flood

26—   "And *its end will come with a flood*; even to the end there will be war; desolations are determined."

The Hebrew word "end" has the pronoun, translated "its," as a suffix: וְקִצּוֹ (*ossiqᵉw*). The Hebrew suffix is masculine and might literally be translated "his end." Consequently, its antecedent cannot be the word "city" (וְהָעִיר, *rî‘ahᵉw*), which is feminine. The antecedent could be the word "sanctuary" (וְהַקֹּדֶשׁ, *sᵉdoqahᵉw*), which is masculine. However, the antecedent is probably the whole phrase, "the city and the sanctuary." It is common for a pronoun to take the gender of the last word in a series when referring to that series. The end of the city and the sanctuary will be "in the flood" (בַשֶּׁטֶף, *fetĕssab*). This word does have a definite article. It is possible that the definite article is referring to a specific "flood," yet in Daniel, this word occurs only here and in 11:22 where it also has the definite article (הַשֶּׁטֶף, *fetĕssah*). It is certainly possible that the word in 9:26 can be referring to the word in 11:22, and the reverse. But it is also possible that both 9:26 and 11:22 could be referring to a flood referenced in another part of Scripture. This is not the same word as the one found in Genesis chapter 6. However, it does occur in a passage in Isaiah discussing the fact that God would restore His people and His city even after the destruction: "'In an flood (בְּשֶׁצֶף, *feseseb*) of anger I hid My face from you for a moment, but with everlasting lovingkindness I will have compassion on you,' says the Lord your Redeemer" (Isa 54:8). The flood in the Isaiah passage is a figure of speech for God's anger against His people. He will pour out judgment upon them for a while—"a moment"— but afterwards He will restore them. Similarly, the flood here could be symbolic of the wrath of God.

EVANS ON THE "END WITH A FLOOD"

Evans argues that the end will not take place within the 490 years predicted by Gabriel.

> According to Noē, the first half of the last seven was fulfilled with Christ's ministry following His baptism. That ministry lasted until His crucifixion in the middle of the "week." *The second half consisted of a period of three and one-half years that had to elapse "before Jesus' followers would be free to take the Gospel outside the Jewish realm."* That period "was a time-restricted waiting period in which the New Covenant was to be confirmed with the Jews exclusively." It reached its climax toward the end of AD 33, writes Noē, with the stoning to death of Stephen (Acts 7:54–60). That

event marked the end of the 490 years allotted to Israel. DeMar's analysis follows essentially similar lines, though in less detail. "Wait another minute!" I can hear an imaginary voice of protest exclaiming, "What about 'the ruler who will come' and the other material in verses 26 and 27 that you say refer to the time of the Jewish War?" Noё's answer, with which I completely agree, is that *although the results of the Jewish War are part of the prophecy of the seventy sevens, they are not part of the 490 years because nothing in the prophecy places a time restriction on them stating that they have to occur within that period.* The war and its outcome were decreed by the prophecy, but the prophecy does not state that the war occurs during the final seven.[222]

For Evans, through Noё, to claim that "nothing in the prophecy places a time restriction on them stating that they have to occur within that period" flies in the face of the opening statement of Gabriel's explanation to Daniel—"Seventy weeks have been decreed for your people and your holy city." To deny that this is the time restriction set upon the city renders the entire prophecy completely unintelligible. If it is not a time restriction, setting that which is decreed to happen to the city within the seventy sevens, then all meaning has been set aside. If the event of Stephen's death "marked the end of the 490 years allotted to Israel," then Evans effectively makes the prophecy appear false, because Gabriel declared that the seventy sevens were decreed upon both the people *and the city*.

Evans recognizes this problem and attempts to address it. His defense is quite long, but it is necessary to include it in order to understand his argument in context.

> Daniel 9:24 does state unambiguously that seventy sevens or weeks "are decreed for your people and your holy city" to realize the six delineated items. I believe, therefore, that Preston is on sound exegetical footing in asserting that within the preterist framework of analysis, the realization of these six things requires that the Parousia be included among the events of AD 70. What is at issue is whether or not the language "Seventy 'sevens' are decreed" requires the Parousia to be included within the 490 years as opposed to being decreed during that time and realized somewhat later. In my judgment, the position adopted by Preston requires a gap of thirty-nine to forty-years between the first half of the last seven, which ends with the Crucifixion, and the second half, which ends with the climactic events of AD 70. I am uncomfortable with the gap idea in this context. In the first place, it opens

---

222. Evans, *Four Kingdoms*, 361–62 (emphasis in original).

the door for the argument advanced by the many futurists who believe that a gap of more than two thousand years exists between the end of the sixty-ninth week and the beginning of the seventieth. Although I can find some Scriptural basis for believing in the forty-year gap, I find none whatsoever for the two thousand year gap and prefer to avoid invoking the gap concept to deal with the forty years unless no other way exists for handling it. In the second place, I find the no-gap approach adopted by Noē, DeMar, and others to be Scripturally sound and logically preferable. In the approach followed by Noē and DeMar, the three and one-half years following the Crucifixion represent the time allotted to the followers of Jesus to proselytize among the Jews. That period came to an end with the conversion of Paul and the stoning to death of Stephen. As DeMar puts it, "the Jews, by their stoning of Stephen, in effect cut themselves off from the eternal blessings of inheritance under the newer testament." After Paul's conversion and the death of Stephen, the process of ministering to the Gentiles began, and from that time on, the exclusivity of the relationship between the Jews and Yahweh was finished. Preston points out that distinguished conservative scholars have questioned that the stoning of the Stephen or the beginning of the process of converting the Gentiles qualifies as a suitable ending for the "grand prophetic scheme" presented by the seventy sevens prophecy. "Was God going to consummate such a grand prophecy with a whimper?" he asks, and he immediately adds that the destruction of Jerusalem seems more fitting as a grand climax to the prophecy. I agree that the events of 70 were the grand climax to the prophecy, and I grant that Preston's line of argument has appeal, but I do not agree that the events of that year *must* be construed as having occurred within the period historically covered by the seventy sevens. That means that I accept the idea that 490 years were allotted to the Jewish people for the completion of the Old Covenant and that, with their rejection of Jesus, they locked into place the outcome that Jesus had prophesied for them as destined to occur within "this generation." (Matt 24:34)[223]

What Evans is proposing is that there is no reason necessarily to believe that the Parousia, the "second" coming of Christ, must be fulfilled within the period designated as the seventy sevens by Gabriel. He agrees with Noē and DeMar that the end of the seventieth seven is marked by the conversion of Paul and the stoning of Stephen and that the Parousia takes place some 40 years later at the destruction of Jerusalem in 70 AD. His primary reason is

223. Ibid., 363–64 (emphasis in original).

that he wants to make it fit within his predisposed eschatological framework: "I am uncomfortable with the gap idea in this context. In the first place, it opens the door for the argument advanced by the many futurists who believe that a gap of more than two thousand years exists between the end of the sixty-ninth week and the beginning of the seventieth."[224] In other words, Evans' first reason for rejecting the notion of a gap is not because he believes it is untrue, but because he is afraid it might support Futurists.

In the above quote from Evans, he remarks that the analysis by DeMar follows the same lines of thought. However, DeMar actually offers no analysis. Rather, he simply makes assertions: "A careful reading of 9:27 will show that the destruction of Jerusalem does not take place within the seventieth week. 'Desolations are *determined*' within the seventieth week (9:26)."[225] DeMar's reading is in fact not careful enough, because the text does not say that desolations are determined within the seventieth week. In fact, the text does not say when the desolations are determined. They could have been determined in eternity to take place in the seventieth week. Since the text does not say when the desolations are determined, DeMar has to do more than simply say this. He must support it with exegesis, something he neglects to do.

PRESTON ON THE "END WITH A FLOOD"

Earlier in his discussion of the meaning and significance of the phrase "to seal up vision and prophet," Evans argues that "the idea conveyed is that Daniel is to preserve the record of his visions so that at the appropriate time in the distant future, they can be accurately presented and fully understood. . . . In 9:24, however, the meaning conveyed is that prophecy is finished—there is to be no more of it because the time of the end will have been reached."[226] However, Don Preston specifically contradicts Evans' view that sealing up the prophecy meant preservation for a later time: "We want to clearly elucidate what we believe to be the correct interpretation of this vital prophecy. First, to seal up vision and prophecy means not only to deliver or reveal the inspired message of God, but to confirm it by fulfilling it. We have demonstrated that there is a clear consensus among the scholars, irrespective of their eschatological affiliation, that this is the true meaning of the words."[227]

Also, Preston disagrees with Evans, Noē, DeMar, and others who hold that certain events were not to be fulfilled in the 490 year time frame, but were only determined during this time frame: "The 'vision and prophecy' that

224. Ibid., 363.
225. DeMar, *End Time Madness*, 4th, 334.
226. Ibid., 338.
227. Preston, *Seal Up Vision and Prophecy*, 62–62.

Gabriel said was to be fulfilled was not a specific prophecy, or prophecies, i.e. of the Maccabean period, of the passion of Jesus. We have demonstrated that *God through Gabriel was giving a definite time for which and in which all divine revelation would not only be given but would be fulfilled.*[228] However, Preston agrees with Evans' claim that there will be no further prophecy because all prophecy has been fulfilled. He argues,

> Next, the time for the fulfillment of all prophecy, and yes, we mean *all prophecy*, was the time of the fall of Jerusalem in A.D. 70 that Daniel was told was the "full end."
>
> There are only a limited number of ways to overthrow our interpretation. 1.) Demonstrate that to seal up vision and prophecy does not mean to give and fulfill. The consensus of scholarship is against this. More importantly, Jesus' use of and application of Daniel 9 in Matthew 24 and Luke 21:20–22 is definitive on this point. 2.) Demonstrate that some specific prophecies are in view in Daniel 9. This would allow for the revelation and fulfillment i.e. confirmation of only those specific parts of the inspired corpus which are in view of Daniel. Once again the words of Jesus address this issue. He said in the fall of Jerusalem "all things which are written must be fulfilled." 3.) Demonstrate that the fall of Jerusalem in A.D. 70 was not within the 70 weeks of Daniel. But Daniel is specifically told 70 weeks were determined on his people and *his city*. We have shown that each of the constituent elements of Daniel 9:24 belongs to the Seventy Weeks.[229]

According to Preston, one of the ways to overthrow his interpretation is to "Demonstrate that the fall of Jerusalem in A.D. 70 was not within the 70 weeks of Daniel," which is precisely what Evans has attempted to do. What Evans has effectively done is remove any Scriptural support from Daniel for the claim that the Parousia happened in 70 AD. Since the only Scriptural evidence in Daniel that Preterists had was their interpretation of the prophecy of the seventy sevens, by moving this outside that prophecy, Evans has removed any Scriptural support from Daniel in particular, and from the Old Testament in general. The impact of this for the Preterist view is devastating since this can no longer be used to support their interpretations of various NT passages. Preston goes on to argue,

> The text does not say that those things would be initiated within the Heptads and then consummated at some later time. However, this being true, we have demonstrated that those elements in

228. Ibid., 63.
229. Ibid., 63 (emphasis in original).

Daniel 9:24, while initiated in Jesus' ministry, were still awaiting consummation well after the suggestion [*sic*] time of the end of the Seventy Weeks, i.e. circa A.D. 35. If the constituent elements of Daniel 9 were included in the Seventy Weeks, and they were, and if they were still not fulfilled at any time beyond A.D. 35, then it is patently clear that the Seventy Weeks were not fulfilled in A.D. 35. And this is precisely what we find in the New Testament.[230]

Nevertheless, Evans offers no rebuttal to Preston's position except to say, "In my judgment, the position adopted by Preston requires a gap of thirty-nine to forty-years between the first half of the last seven . . ."[231] (see Figure 34 on page 403). Evans even admits that he sees Scriptural support for Preston's gap: "Although I can find some Scriptural basis for believing in the forty-year gap, I find none whatsoever for the two thousand year gap and prefer to avoid invoking the gap concept to deal with the forty years unless no other way exists for handling it."[232] He claims that there is no gap in the view espoused by Noē and DeMar, "I find the no-gap approach adopted by Noē, DeMar, and others to be scripturally sound and logically preferable."[233] However, it is in fact not a "no-gap" approach since there is a gap between the initiating of the destruction of the city and the consummating of the destruction of the city. Evans as much as acknowledges this when he says, "Preterists believe that the prophecy was completely fulfilled in the first century AD by the combination of Jesus' ministry and the Jewish War. For them, the biggest problems are to decide between a figurative or a literal fulfillment of the 490 years and how to handle the approximately forty-year gap between the Crucifixion and the fall of Jerusalem. The gap problem reflects the fact that the historical difference of about forty years between these two events corresponds in preterist exegesis to the second half of the seventieth seven; i.e. a period of only three and one-half years."[234] And, as Preston points out, "The text does not say that those things would be initiated within the Heptads and then consummated at some later time."[235] It is also instructive that Evans offers no Scriptural support for this position, only citing Scriptures to identify the events themselves. This effort by Evans seems to be nothing other than an attempt to make the text fit the theory.

---

230. Ibid. (emphasis in original).
231. Evans, *Four Kingdoms*, 363.
232. Ibid.
233. Ibid.
234. Ibid., 335.
235. Preston, *Seal Up Vision and Prophecy*, 63.

Figure 34: Preston's Preterist Gap

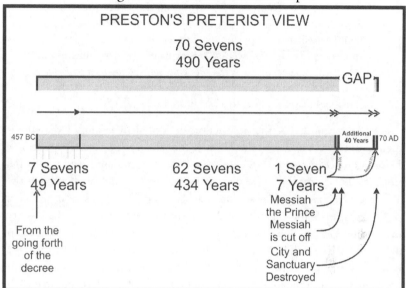

Kenneth Gentry also argues that the destruction of Jerusalem did not occur within the time span of the seventy sevens:

> But how are we to understand the latter portions of both verses 26 and 27? What are we to make of the destruction of the city and sanctuary (v. 26) and the abomination that causes desolation (v. 27), which most non-dispensational evangelical commentators agree occurred in A.D. 70? In verse 26 we learn that *two* events are to occur *after* the sixty-ninth week: (1) The Messiah is to be "cut off," and (2) the city and sanctuary are to be destroyed. Verse 27a informs us that the Messiah's cutting off (v. 26a) is a confirmation of the covenant and is to occur at the half-way mark of the seventieth week. So, the Messiah's death is clearly within the time frame of the Seventy Weeks (as we expect because of His being the major figure of the fulfillment of the prophecy). The events involving the destruction of the city and the sanctuary with war and desolation (vv. 26b, 27b) are the *consequences* of the cutting off of the Messiah and do not necessarily occur *in* the seventy weeks time frame. They are an *addendum* to the fulfillment of the focus of the prophecy, which is stated in verse 24. The destructive acts are *anticipated*, however, in the divine act of sealing up or reserving the

sin of Israel for punishment. Israel's climactic sin – her completing of her transgression (v. 24) with the cutting off of Messiah (v.
26a)—results in God's act of *reserving Israel's sin until later*. Israel's
judgment will not be postponed forever; it will come after the
expiration of the seventy weeks. This explains the "very indefinite"
phrase "till the end of the war": *the "end" will not occur during the
seventy weeks*. That prophesied end occurred in A.D. 70, exactly as
Christ had made abundantly clear in Matthew 24:15.[236]

Gentry claims that the destruction of Jerusalem is one of the consequences of the crucifixion of the Messiah and "do[es] not necessarily occur *in*
the seventy weeks time frame." He claims that this is an "addendum" to the
prophecy. He claims that these destructive acts were anticipated and that the
crucifixion results in God "reserving Israel's sin until later." A serious problem
for Gentry's reasoning is that verse 24 states that the prophecy of the seventy
sevens is determined upon Daniel's holy city, Jerusalem. Since the destruction
of Jerusalem is certainly something that happens to Daniel's holy city, the
natural reading of the text would conclude that this must be included within
the seventy sevens that are determined upon this very city. To claim that such
a momentous event as the destruction of Jerusalem is somehow omitted from
the prophetic statement that claims to be determined upon this city requires
much more evidence and argument that Gentry has presented. Apart from
one's prior eschatological commitment, there is simply no reason to conclude
that the destruction of Jerusalem would not be included in the very prophecy that concerns Jerusalem. Also, nowhere in the prophecy is anything said
about an addendum, nor does the prophecy say anything about an act of God
"reserving Israel's sins until later." We have already seen that the words of the
text do not have this meaning. Gentry declares, "Israel's judgment will not
be postponed forever," and yet the text nowhere says anything about Israel's
judgment being postponed. The fact that Gentry proposes that the destruction of Jerusalem "will come after the expiration of the seventy weeks" flatly
contradicts the straightforward statements of the prophecy. At the beginning
of his comments on Daniel's prophecy, Gentry asserted, "This 'extremely
important prophecy' is the most difficult for dispensationalists to make credible to those outside of their system."[237] But to claim that the destruction of
Jerusalem does not occur in the seventy sevens when the prophetic statement
itself declared that this time frame was decreed upon this very city seems itself
to be incredible in the extreme.

---

236. Gentry, *He Shall Have Dominion*, 330–31 (emphasis in original).
237. Ibid., 320.

Figure 35: Syntax of Daniel 9:26b

KLOSKE ON THE "END WITH A FLOOD"

Tom and Steve Kloske argue a case similar to that of Evans. Holding that Jesus' crucifixion is the event that is indicated by the reference to Messiah the Prince being "cut off," they provide a calculation beginning with what they believe is the date of Christ's crucifixion, AD 30. They argue,

> If we count backwards three and a half years, (486½) since His death occurred in the middle of the last "seven" (see Daniel 9:27), we arrive at November A.D. 26. Now if we count back from November, in the year 26, we arrive at 460½ B.C. Using the Jewish lunar year, which is shorter than our solar year, we subtract two years and that it [*sic*] brings it to 458½ B.C.—the year that Ezra was told by Artaxerxes to rebuild Zion. Of course this mathematical equation still only brings us to A.D. 30 with 3½ years to go. What would be significant by A.D. 33? We suggest that the remaining period of time was used exclusively to evangelize the Jews.[238]

The following chart illustrates the calculations described by Kloske.

---

238. Tom Kloske and Steve Kloske, *The Second Coming: Mission Accomplished*, 499.

Figure 36: Kloskes' Calculations

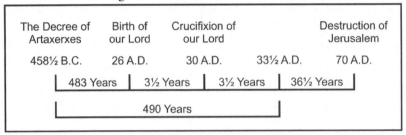

According to the Kloskes' calculation, Daniel's prophecy of the seventy sevens ends without any event that marks its conclusion. As Don Preston says, "Was God going to consummate such a grand prophecy with a whimper?"[239] Also, according to the Kloskes' calculation, the destruction of Jerusalem does not occur within the 490 years as Gabriel predicted. Seeing this problem, the Kloskes devote themselves to further study to "discover how A.D. 70 would fit."[240]

> The final phase of Daniel 9:27 talks about an idea that is difficult to understand. Re-reading the entire seventy "sevens" sections revealed that a "second coming" or return is not specifically mentioned. But what is mentioned is an idea that an apparent promise, prediction, or prophecy is revealed at the time that the Anointed One is about to be "cut off." That prophecy is "on a wing" (or pinnacle) of an abomination that will cause the desolation in the very heart of the people. The temple will be destroyed and this is a promise that will be fulfilled at "the time of the end." So the destruction of Judaism and Jerusalem does not have to fall within the seventy "sevens," but the prophecy of her demise does. Jesus accomplished everything Daniel 9:24 required. The timing of this prophecy began around 458/457 B.C. and culminated with the death of the Anointed One and the beginning of taking the Gospel to the Gentile world. And contained within the time frame of this seventy "sevens" fulfillment was the promise, prediction, and prophecy that Jerusalem would end at the proper time, the time of the end.[241]

What the Kloskes are saying is that their re-reading of 9:27 led them to conclude that the actual destruction would not occur within the seventy sevens, but a promise would occur in the time frame of the seventy sevens that

239. Preston, *Seal Up Vision and Prophecy*, 23.

240. Kloske, *The Second Coming*, 500.

241. Ibid.

the destruction would occur in the future, after the seventy sevens was completed. So, apparently it does not matter that Gabriel said, "seventy sevens are determined on your people and your holy city . . ." And it makes no difference that nowhere in the seventy sevens prophecy is there any statement about a promise, prediction, or prophecy about the end of Judaism. The Kloskes refer to the final phrase in 9:27 as giving rise to this notion of a promise, prediction, or prophecy. The phrase states, "even until a complete destruction, one that is decreed, is poured out on the one who makes desolate" (וְעַד־כָּלָה וְנֶחֱרָצָה תִּתַּךְ עַל־שֹׁמֵם:, *wala‘ kattit ḥaṣar^ehen^ew ḥālak da‘ memŏs*).

First of all, the final phrase in 9:27 says absolutely nothing about a decree happening "at the time the Anointed One is about to be 'cut off.'" Second, the abomination has to do with the desolation of the temple, not the destruction of Jerusalem. Third, not knowing Hebrew, the Kloskes have mistakenly used the English translation to float their hypothesis. The diagrams in Figure 36 on page 406 illustrate the Kloskes' misunderstanding of the syntax. Although Hebrew is difficult to diagram, since it is often composed of forms with prefixes and suffixes that are normally diagrammed as separate words in English, these diagrams should be adequate to demonstrate their error. What the diagramming shows is that the destruction that will be poured out is said to happen at the same time as the "making desolate." This is indicated by the compound conjunction "and even until." The making desolate will occur *even until* the destruction is poured out. The destruction that is poured out is the decreed destruction. So, if the decree occurs within the seventy sevens, so does the abomination that causes desolation. The text does not say the destruction is merely decreed in the period of seventy sevens, but that it occurs within that period.

Figure 37: Diagramming Daniel 9:27

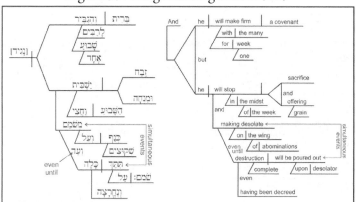

Desolations are Determined

26—   "And its end will come with a flood; even to the end there will be war; *desolations are determined*."

The phrase "desolations are determined" is probably the best translation of the Hebrew: נֶחֱרֶצֶת שֹׁמֵמוֹת *(tomemŏs teser⁽e⁾hen)*. The idea is that it has been determined that there will be desolations, presumably upon the city and the sanctuary. The term "desolations" (שֹׁמֵמוֹת, *tomemŏs*) indicates the results of war that leaves a place uninhabited.[242] Jeremiah describes the scene after the devastation of Judah by the invasion of the Chaldean army as, "formless and void" (תֹהוּ וָבֹהוּ, *uhobaw⁽e⁾uhot*). This is, of course, a picture of the land in Gen 1:2, covered with water, empty and uninhabitable. This is also the picture that is given here in Daniel with the word "desolations" and "war" that constitute the flood upon the land. The term "flood" indicates an overflow of waters. In this case it is a metaphor and a hyperbole emphasizing the extent of the destruction. It will be a total destruction returning the land to a condition reminiscent of the land in Gen 1:2, "empty and uninhabitable." Having rejected their Messiah, Who is none other than the Word of God by Whom all things were created, God will bring the anti-creation beast to devastate the land as a flood and to render the land empty and uninhabitable.

DANIEL 9:27

Who Makes the Week-Long Covenant?

27—   "And he will make *a firm covenant* with the many for one week . . ."

Table 37: Daniel 9:27a

לָרַבִּים	בְּרִית	וְהִגְבִּיר
with the many	a covenant	And he will make firm
	אֶחָד	שָׁבוּעַ
	one	seven

Verse 27 begins with the statement, "And he will make firm a covenant with the many for one seven." To whom or to what does the "he" refer? The English pronoun "he" is part of the form of the verb "will make firm" or "will confirm"—וְהִגְבִּיר *(ribgih⁽e⁾w)*. The verb is גָּבַר *(rabag)*, which, in the

242. KBH, s.v. "שׁמם."

Hiphil form, means "to cause to be strong."[243] It can also indicate the making or establishing of a covenant. The pronoun subject of this verb is indicated by its form—third person, masculine, singular. So there is no independent subject stated. Since it is masculine, its antecedent must be masculine also. Table 38 gives the texts of verses 26 and 27 with a word-for-word translation. The shaded blocks indicate possible antecedents of the pronoun in verse 26.

Table 38: Daniel 9:26–27

verse 26			
וּשְׁנַיִם	שִׁשִּׁים	הַשָּׁבֻעִים	וְאַחֲרֵי
and two	sixty	the sevens	And after
לוֹ	וְאֵין	מָשִׁיחַ	יִכָּרֵת
to Him	and there is not	Messiah	will be cut off
עַם	יַשְׁחִית	וְהַקֹּדֶשׁ	וְהָעִיר
people of	will destroy	and the sanctuary	and the city
בַּשֶּׁטֶף	וְקִצּוֹ	הַבָּא	נָגִיד
by the flood	and its end	the one coming	prince
נֶחֱרֶצֶת	מִלְחָמָה	קֵץ	וְעַד
will be determined	war	end	even until
		שֹׁמֵמוֹת׃	
		desolations	

---

243. KBH, s.v. "גבר."

verse 27			
וְהִגְבִּיר	בְּרִית	לָרַבִּים	שָׁבוּעַ
And he will make firm	a covenant	with the many	seven
אֶחָד	וַחֲצִי	הַשָּׁבוּעַ	יַשְׁבִּית
one	and half	the seven	he will cause to cease
זֶבַח	וּמִנְחָה	וְעַל	כְּנַף
sacrifice	and offering	and upon	wing of
שִׁקּוּצִים	מְשֹׁמֵם	וְעַד־	כָּלָה
abominations	one causing desolation	and until	completion
וְנֶחֱרָצָה	תִּתַּךְ	עַל־	שֹׁמֵם:
and desolations	will pour forth	upon	one desolating.

Three things must be noted in order to understand the text as it is presented. First, in verse 26 the word translated "people" is עַם (maʿ). This is called as collective singular noun. Although its meaning is "people," it is a single group of people, so the noun is masculine singular. This is just like our English word "group." Although a group of people is composed of many individuals, it is a single group, and so the word is singular. As a masculine singular noun in Hebrew, grammatically it can be the antecedent of a masculine singular pronoun. Second, even though the word "people" (עַם, maʿ) follows the verb "will destroy" (יַשְׁחִית, ṭıhsay), עַם functions as the subject of this verb. This is the normal word order for Hebrew sentences—verb + subject + object. In this case, the objects of destruction, the city and the sanctuary, are placed before the verb. This is not an uncommon arrangement, and it is often used to emphasize the objects. Third, the relationship between the word "people" and the word "prince" is called a construct relation where the first word in the relation, in this case "people," is in the construct state and indicates a genitive relation to the second word in the relation, in this case "prince." A construct relation is often used to indicate possession. So, in this instance the relation indicates that the people are the people *of* or *belonging to* the prince, the one who is coming.

What must be stressed from these syntactical factors is that the subject of the verb is "people," not "prince." According to the syntax, it is the people who destroy the city and the sanctuary, not the prince. Young admits this as well: "The city and the sanctuary are to be destroyed, not by a prince, but by the *people* of that prince."[244]

Usually the antecedent of a pronoun is the closest agreeing noun in the text. To make the pronoun refer to an earlier noun, that is, to skip over a perfectly likely noun to refer to an earlier one in the text, there must be some designation or indication of this. For example, if one of the possible antecedents was a person and the other was an inanimate object, even though the noun for the inanimate object is masculine and syntactically likely to be the antecedent because it is closer, it is unlikely that it is the antecedent of a pronoun that is the subject of a verb indicating some action taken by a person. In fact, that is precisely the situation we have here. The word translated "end" (קֵץ, *seq*)—"even to the *end* there will be war"—is a masculine noun, but it is unlikely that it is the antecedent of the "he" since the verb, "he will make firm," implies the act of an intelligent being. Also, even though the word "people" could be the antecedent, syntactically it is not the antecedent since it is not the closest agreeing word. Of course this leaves only the word "prince." It is the coming prince who will make firm a covenant with the many, and since we have already shown that this prince cannot be the Messiah, since the Messiah's people never destroyed the city and the sanctuary, the one who makes the covenant cannot be the Messiah.

Young seeks to dismiss the grammar in order to dismiss the view: "The exposition has already shown that the whole picture of a coming Roman prince who makes a covenant for one week with the Jews is based upon an incorrect interpretation of the Heb."[245] The extent of Young's demonstration about the Hebrew is his claim, "To construe 'prince' as subject, does not appear to be the most natural reading, for the word occupies only a subordinate position even in vs. 26, where it is not even the subject of a sentence."[246] Of course there is no grammatical rule in Hebrew that states that a word that is not the subject of a sentence is somehow "subordinate." But even if we consider it as being subordinate, there is no rule that states that a word in a subordinate position cannot be the antecedent of a pronoun. Young declares, "The *people* are in a more prominent position than is the *prince*. . . . The phrase *of the prince* in vs. 26 is in such a subordinate position that it is extremely unlikely that we are to regard it as antecedent of 'he will confirm.'"[247] But once again there is no such grammatical principle or rule on which to base this claim. The subjective judgment about what is and what is not prominent must be overruled by the

---

244. Young, *Prophecy of Daniel*, 208 (emphasis in original).

245. Ibid., 215.

246. Ibid., 208.

247. Ibid.

objective grammatical and syntactical principles of the language. The reason Young thinks the word 'people' is "in a more prominent position" is because he must find some way to circumvent the actual grammatical and syntactical principles in order to make it fit his eschatological scheme. Far from showing an incorrect interpretation of the Hebrew, Young has actually managed to show that his own explanation is ungrammatical.

Since we have already seen that the "coming prince" is not the Messiah, this must be another prince that is said to be "the coming prince." Mauro claims that this prince is Titus. As he explains, "Taking the words according to their apparent and obvious meaning (which should always be done except where there is a compelling reason to the contrary) it would seem quite clear that 'the prince,' whose people were to destroy the city and the sanctuary, was Titus, the son of the then emperor Vespasian, he (Titus) being the 'prince' or 'leader' who was in actual command of those armies at the time."[248] This seems *prima facie* to be reasonable. However, this creates a problem with the first statement in verse 27. The text states that this prince, "the coming prince," will "make firm a covenant with the many for one seven." There is, of course, no historical evidence that Titus made any kind of covenant with the many of seven years. Why do we conclude that the coming prince is the one who will make the covenant? Because the only syntactically viable antecedent for "he" is "prince" of verse 26: "the coming prince . . . will make firm a covenant . . ." Consequently, the "apparent and obvious meaning," to use Mauro's expression, is that this is not a reference to Titus.

Mauro asserts that the "he" who confirms or makes firm a covenant with the many for one seven is Christ:

> If we take the pronoun "He" as relating to "the Messiah" mentioned in the preceding verse, then we find in the New Testament scriptures a perfect fulfillment of the passage, and a fulfillment, moreover, which is set forth in the most conspicuous way. That pronoun must, in our opinion, be taken as referring to Christ, because (a) the prophecy is all about Christ, and this is the climax of it; (b) Titus did not make any covenant with the Jews; (c) there is not a word in Scripture about any future "prince" making a covenant with them. Other reasons in support of this conclusion will appear later on. But the foregoing are sufficient.[249]

Mauro's first points is, "the prophecy is all about Christ." As true as this may be, this is no proof that the antecedent of "he" is "Messiah." If the prophecy is "all about Christ," does that mean that it is Christ who commits

248. Mauro, *Seventy Weeks*, 74.
249. Ibid., 80.

the abomination of desolation? Mauro's second point, "Titus did not make any covenant with the Jews" likewise is no argument about the antecedent of the pronoun. The fact is, Titus indeed did not make a covenant with the Jews. But, that does not prove that Jesus is the one making the covenant. It can just as easily be an argument for a future Anti-Christ as the one making the covenant with the Jews. Besides, Jesus is nowhere said to have made a seven-year covenant with the Jews. Mauro's final point is, "there is not a word in Scripture about any future 'prince' making a covenant with them," unless of course this is that place, which is precisely what the Futurists claim. Whether it is spoken of anywhere else in Scripture is no argument against it being the case here. Mauro's points turn out to be only the expression of his own view, not proof for his view.

Evans holds a similar position: *"Liberals assume that the 'He' that begins verse 27 refers to the ruler or prince who is to come of verse 26. So do most futurists.* Their grammatical basis for doing this is, as Archer put it, that 'Normally the last eligible antecedent is to be taken as the subject of the following verb.' This does not have to be the case grammatically, however, and *a powerful argument can be made that verses 26 and 27 are structured so as to identify the correct antecedent of 'He' as the 'anointed one.'"*[250] His "powerful argument" is, "In order to see why the context of verse 27 rules out the possibility that Titus or the Roman army is the desolator there, it helps to recognize that verse 27 does not simply follow verse 26 in time. *We have here a parallel structure that intertwines the time order of the different parts of these verses.*"[251] To illustrate this proposal, Evans presents the following re-arrangement of the events delineated in verses 26 and 27:

> Here is how I believe they should be rearranged so as to give the time sequence in which the described events occur:
>
> 9:26. Then after the sixty-two weeks, the Messiah
>
> 9:27. will make a firm covenant with the many for one week.
>
> 9:26. And he will be cut off and have nothing,
>
> 9:27. but in the middle of the week he will put a stop to sacrifice and grain offering;
>
> 9:27. and on the wing of abominations {will come} one who makes desolate,
>
> 9:26. and the people of the ruler who is to come will destroy the city and the sanctuary. And its end (will come) with

250. Evans, *Four Kingdoms*, 429 (emphasis in original).
251. Ibid., 368 (emphasis in original).

a flood, even to the end there will be war; desolations are determined,

9:27. even until a complete destruction, one that is decreed, is poured out on the one who makes desolate.

In this arrangement, the three parts of the prophecy that come after "he will put a stop to sacrifice and grain offering" should be viewed as referring to events that were decreed by the prophecy but were not fulfilled until AD 70. The historical coverage of the last seven of the 490 years is limited to the making of "a firm covenant with the many for one week," the cutting off of the Messiah, and the ending of the covenantal arrangement with God featuring "sacrifice and grain offering" that occurred in the middle of the week with the Crucifixion. Notice that the "one who makes desolate" is not the same person as "the ruler who is to come."[252]

There are a couple of reasons why Evans must rearrange the text in order to make it fit his view. First, he must have Christ as the one making the covenant, else there is no historical figure that can fulfill this prophecy, even up to today, and this flies in the face of his claim that all was fulfilled. Second, since the text presents the events as chronologically progressive, in the sense that the events of verse 26 happen before the events of verse 27, this would mean that Christ is cut off before He makes the covenant. Unfortunately for Evans, however, not even Theodotion's text supports this re-arrangement. There is absolutely no grammatical or textual precedent for such a dislocation of the parts of the text, and contrary to Evans' claim, this is not a grammatical argument, and it leaves the grammar and syntax of the text completely unexamined and unexplained. If Evans' rearrangement is accepted it destroys any reason for following the grammar and syntax of the text and opens the door for any rearrangement that anyone wants to make to fit the text into whatever scheme.

In an effort to bolster his position, Evans presents several translations of Dan. 9:27 in order to accentuate their differences. Having presented them, he asserts, "In this particular instance, my choice among translations is the *New American Standard Bible* (NASB) because it comes closest to being a word-for-word rendering of Theodotion's text."[253] The problem with this proposal is that is it completely inaccurate. Table 39 shows Theodotion's text, a very literal translation of Theodotion's text, and the NASB.

252. Ibid., 368–69.
253. Ibid., 368.

Table 39: Daniel 9:27 Theodotion's Text[254]

Theodotion θ	"καὶ δυναμώσει διαθήκην πολοῖς ἑβδομὰς μία καὶ ἐν τῷ ἡμί σει τῆς ἑβδομάδος ἀρθήσεται θυσία καὶ σπονδή καὶ ἐπὶ τὸ ἱερὸν βδέλυγμα τῶν ἐρημώσεων καὶ ἕως συντελείας καὶ συντέλεια δοθήσεται ἐπὶ τὴν ἐρήμωσιν."
Literal Translation	"And he will strengthen covenant with many, seven one; and in the half of the seven he will take away sacrifice and drink-offering, and upon the sanctuary abominable of the desolations and until completion and completion will be given upon the desolation."
NASB	"And he will make a firm covenant with the many for one week, but in the middle of the week he will put a stop to sacrifice and grain offering; and on the wing of abominations (will come) one who makes desolate, even until a complete destruction, one that is decreed, is poured out on the one who makes desolate."

Further to illustrate the fact that the NASB is not a closer word-for-word translation, Table 40 below sets out the Greek text of Theodotion with the literal translation under each word. The evidence of grammar and syntax, the evidence of the Hebrew text, and even the evidence from Theodotion's Greek text verify that there is no good reason to reject what the grammar and syntax of the Hebrew text dictates, namely, that the "he," the one who makes firm a covenant with the many, is the one whose people destroy the city and the sanctuary. "He" is not the Messiah. Consequently, the covenant is not the "new covenant" as Preterists assert.

Table 40: Daniel 9:27 Literal Translation of Theodotion's Text

καὶ	δυναμώ σει	διαθήκην	πολοῖς	ἑβδομὰς	μία
and	he will strengthen	covenant	with many	seven	one

---

254. The Theodotion text is taken from Jospeh Ziegler, *Susanna, Daniel, Bel et Draco*, vol. 16, *Septuaginta Vetus Testamentum Graecum*, 367, 69. I suspect Evans has mistaken his published LXX text for θ. Even the Greek texts that come with various computer programs are not necessarily the actual θ text.

καὶ	ἐν	τῷ ἡμί σει	τῆς ἑβδομά δος	ἀρθή σεται	θυσία
and	in	the half of	the seven	he will take away	sacrifice

καὶ	σπονδή	καὶ	ἐπὶ	τὸ ἱερὸν	βδέλυγμα
and	drink-offering	and	upon	the sanctuary	abominable

τῶν ἐρημώ σεων	καὶ	ἕως	συντελεί ας	καὶ	συντέλεια
of the desolations	even	until	comple-tion	and	completion

δοθήσεται	ἐπὶ	τὴν ἐρή μωσιν
he will give	upon	the desolation

The grammar and syntax demands that the "he" of the phrase "he will make firm a covenant with the many" must be the "coming prince" of verse 26. And, as Mauro admits, "in order to make the 'he' of Daniel 9:27 refer to antichrist, it is *necessary* to make 'the prince that shall come' of verse 26 to mean a *future* prince."[255] Since the coming prince is the one who makes the covenant for one seven, and since there is no historical evidence of Titus making a seven year covenant with Israel, this argues against the Preterist claim that the coming prince is Titus, and it agrees with Mauro's admission that this prince is a yet future prince.

With Whom is the Covenant Made?

The covenant is with "the many" (לָרַבִּים, *mibaral*). Miller notes, "Walvoord believes the phrase 'the many' refers to unbelieving Jews, whereas Archer and Young contend that these are 'true believers,' the likely meaning of the expression in Isa 53:11–12. In this context, however, 'the many' is best taken as a

255. Mauro, *Seventy Weeks*, 91.

description of the Jewish people as a group, the nation of Israel."[256] There is no indication in the text about whether "the many" are believers or unbelievers, but the expression indicates that this is simply the nation of Israel, whether believers or unbelievers.

What is the Week-Long Covenant?

Contrary to the statement of the text, Noē holds that it is Christ who confirms or makes firm the covenant with the many for one week. He claims that the covenant "was to be confirmed for 'one seven' (one week of years), first and exclusively upon the Jews (Da. 9:24; Ro. 1:16; Jn. 4:22)."[257] Not a single one of these verses supports his claim, however. First, Dan 9:24 says absolutely nothing about a covenant exclusively "upon the Jews": "Seventy weeks have been decreed for your people and your holy city, to finish the transgression, to make an end of sin, to make atonement for iniquity, to bring in everlasting righteousness, to seal up vision and prophecy and to anoint the most holy place" (Dan 9:24).

Rom 1:16 says, "For I am not ashamed of the gospel, for it is the power of God for salvation to everyone who believes, to the Jew first and also to the Greek."[258] Notice that although the text says, "to the Jew first," it then states, "also to the Greek," not "after that to the Greek." There simply is no statement about a covenant to the Jews "first and exclusively." In fact, the word translated "first" (πρῶτος, *soīorp*) does not necessarily mean first in order of time, or "before." According to BDAG, this word can be used to mean "*in the first place, above all, especially*," and this is in fact the meaning given for the use of the word in this verse.[259]

Jn 4:22 states, "You worship what you do not know; we worship what we know, for salvation is from the Jews."[260] Not only is there nothing in this text about a covenant, there is nothing about a covenant being made first and exclusively with the Jews. The text says, "salvation is from the Jews" (ἡ σωτηρία ἐκ τῶν Ἰουδαίων ἐστίν, *nitse ñoiaduoI ñot ke airī̄eīos̄ eh*). Jesus is saying, "salvation comes to the world through the Jews." He is, of course, referring to the Abrahamic covenant and ultimately to Himself Who, as a Jew, a child of Abraham, brings salvation to the world.

---

256. Miller, *Daniel*, 271.

257. Noē, *Beyond the End Times*, 87.

258. Οὐ γὰρ ἐπαισχύνομαι τὸ εὐαγγέλιον, δύναμις γὰρ θεοῦ ἐστιν εἰς σωτηρί αν παντὶ τῷ πιστεύοντι, Ἰουδαίῳ τε πρῶτον καὶ Ἕλληνι. (Rom 1:16).

259. BDAG, s.v., "πρῶτος."

260. ὑμεῖς προσκυνεῖ ὃ οὐκ οἴδατε· ἡμεῖς προσκυνοῦμεν ὃ οἴδαμεν, ὅτι ἡ σωτηρία ἐκ τῶν Ἰουδαίων ἐστίν (Jn 4:22).

Noē argues, "The covenant to be confirmed was the one promised through the prophet Jeremiah (Jer. 31:31–33). The first 3½ years was fulfilled by the earthly ministry of Jesus Christ and his disciples. That meant that 3½ more years were to be fulfilled before Jesus' followers would be free to take the Gospel outside the Jewish realm."[261] There is, of course, no scriptural basis upon which these claims are made. This is simply conjecture in order to make things fit into an eschatological scheme. Noē asserts, "The biblical fact of Jewish preeminence is frequently emphasized throughout the gospels."[262] However, Jewish preeminence does not equal Jewish exclusivity. Noē quotes the statement of Jesus in Matt 10:5–6, "Go not into the way of the Gentiles, and into any city of the Samaritans enter ye not; but go rather to the lost sheep of the house of Israel." He attempts to coordinate this with the Great Commission in which Jesus commanded His disciples to make disciples of all nations. He argues, "Is Jesus' command here in contradiction to his Great Commission command . . . No, it is not. Why? Because there was a time-restriction waiting period in which the New Covenant was to be confirmed with the Jews exclusively."[263] It is extremely peculiar, then, that Jesus made no mention of any "time-restricted waiting period" when He gave the Great Commission. He did not say, "Go into all the nations, after the waiting period, and make disciples." There simply is no basis for such claims. This is eisegesis at its best, or worst. Also, the context of the statement in Matthew 10 has nothing whatever to do with the Great Commission in Matthew 28. The Matthew 10 command was given prior to the rejection of Jesus by the nation and Jesus' denouncing of the cities in Matthew 11. To try to connect these two completely ignores the context of the two events.

In support of his notion of a time restriction on the going out of the Gospel exclusively to the Jews, Noē argues, "Jesus' disciples knew this. How did they know? Quite simply; in Luke we are told that Jesus expounded and explained in all the Scriptures the things concerning Himself. He began at Moses and proceeded through all the prophets (Lk. 24:27)."[264] Besides the fact that this passage occurs in the narrative about Jesus walking with the two on the road to Emmaus, and has nothing to do with teaching His disciples, the biblical fact is that Jesus said nothing about any time-restricted waiting period, either in Lk 24:27 or anywhere else. Noē goes on to assert, "Jesus' teaching would have most certainly included Daniel, the Jews' most copied

261. Noē, *Beyond the End Times*, 87.
262. Ibid.
263. Ibid., 88.
264. Ibid.

book, and Daniel's prophecy of 70 weeks pertaining to the Messiah."[265] As true as this might be, it does not prove that the disciples knew of any time-restricted waiting period. One must assume Noë's position in order to believe this, but then it is circular to use it as proof for the position.

Noë continues, "Toward the end of A.D. 33, Jewish persecution of Christians in Jerusalem reached a climax with the stoning death of Stephen (Ac. 7:54–60)."[266] He offers no historical references to support this claim. Since Hoehner demonstrates that Jesus' crucifixion was in AD 33 and not AD 30, the dates do not match in order to support Noë's claims.[267] This is yet another in the long line of problems that demonstrate that Noë's calculations in his eschatological scheme simply do not fit the facts of history.

As we have seen, Kenneth Gentry also holds that it is Christ who makes firm a covenant with the many for one seven. However, Gentry does not present a very detailed argument for his position. Rather, he bases his interpretation of the dubious claim that there is a parallelism between verses 26 and 27, a claim that we have already shown to be without foundation in the text. Concerning the fact that the covenant will be confirmed for one seven, Gentry asserts, "This confirmation of God's covenant promises to the 'many' of Israel will occur in the middle of the *seventieth week* (v. 27), which parallels 'after the sixty-two [and seven] weeks' (v. 26), while providing more detail. We know Christ's three-and-on-half year ministry was decidedly focused on the Jews in the first half of the seventieth week (Matt. 10:5b; cf. Matt. 15:24). For a period of three and one-half years after the crucifixion, the apostles focused almost exclusively on the Jews, beginning first 'in Judea' (Acts 1:8; 2:14) because 'the gospel of Christ' is 'for the Jew first' (Rom. 1:16; cf. 2:10; John 4:22)."[268] What Gentry seems to be claiming here is that the confirming will last for seven years. This "confirming" begins with Christ's baptism, and in the middle of the seven, at the 3½ year mark, Christ will be crucified and thereby "bring an end to sacrifice and offering."[269] The last 3½ years, according to

265. Ibid.

266. Ibid.

267. Hoehner presents three insuperable problems with the AD 30 date: "(1) it has some (not great) difficulty astronomically; (2) it has difficulty in fitting Luke 3:1–2 into Christ's life unless one reckons according to the Syrian chronology which one is not at all sure Luke was using; (3) it attempts to explain John 2:20 as referring to Herod's rebuilding the temple precincts when actually the passage is talking about the temple edifice; and (4) it limits Christ's ministry to a little over two years which requires a transposition of John 5 and 6 and does not explain the time note of John 4:35 or the unnamed feast of John 5:1." Hoehner, *Chronological Aspects*, 103.

268. Gentry, *He Shall Have Dominion*, 329.

269. Ibid., 328.

Gentry, are concerned with the apostles being "focused almost exclusively on the Jews, beginning first 'in Judea' (Acts 1:8; 2:14) because 'the gospel of Christ' is 'for the Jew first' (Rom. 1:16; cf. 2:10; John 4:22)."[270]

Gentry does not specifically state that the confirming will last for the seven years, but this seems to be initially how he presents his interpretation. The text says that "he" will make firm a covenant for one seven וְהִגְבִּיר בְּרִית לָרַבִּים שָׁבוּעַ אֶחָד (ḏaheʾ ʾubăs mibāral tirᵉb ribgihᵉw). This does not mean that the confirming will last for seven years. Rather, it means that the covenant is a week-long covenant. In order for Gentry's understanding to have any validity at all the "one seven" (שָׁבוּעַ אֶחָד, ʾubăs ḏaheʾ) would have to be the subject of the verb "and he will make firm" (וְהִגְבִּיר, ribgihᵉw): "one week shall confirm the covenant with the many." However, Keil shows that this is not possible here: "But this poetic mode of expression is only admissible where the subject treated of in the statement of the speaker comes after the action, and therefore does not agree with הִגְבִּיר בְּרִית, where the confirming of the covenant is not the work of time, but the deed of a definite person."[271] The structure of the clause indicates that the "one seven" relates to the word "covenant" and indicates the length of the covenant, not the time it takes for the confirming of the covenant.

Later Gentry asserts, "This confirmation of the covenant occurs 'in the middle of the week' (v. 27)."[272] This statement flatly contradicts the text. The text states that "he" will make firm a covenant with the many for one week. In other words, according to Daniel's text, the confirmation must occur at the beginning of the week, not in the middle. If the covenant is a one-week covenant, it makes no sense to make this covenant in the middle of the seven year period. But Gentry's argument can be construed differently.

Confirming the Covenant or Making a Covenant?

Gentry argues that dispensationalists "woefully" misunderstand the confirmation of the covenant in verse 27. He says, "The covenant here is not *made*, it is *confirmed*. This is actually the confirmation of a covenant already extant, i.e., the covenant of God's redemptive grace confirmed by Christ (Rom. 15:8)."[273] In fact, KBH reports precisely the meaning, "to make a strong covenant," as one of the possible meanings of this term.[274] Interestingly, the meaning "to confirm" is not one of the possible meanings of this word in any of its stems.

---

270. Ibid., 329.

271. Keil, *Daniel*, 365.

272. Gentry, *He Shall Have Dominion*, 329.

273. Ibid., 333–34 (emphasis in original).

274. KBH, s.v. "גבר."

And Gentry's appeal to Rom 15:8 does not support his claim. The verse says, "For I say that Christ has become a servant to the circumcision on behalf of the truth of God to confirm the promises to the fathers."[275] The Greek word used in the Romans passage, βεβαιῶσαι (*iasoiabeb*), is not the same word used in the Greek of Daniel, which is δυναμώσει (*iesomanud*).[276] The word in Romans can mean "to confirm,"[277] but the word used in the Greek version of Daniel does not.[278] Consequently, there is no reason to think that these two verses are talking about the same thing or in any way linked because of the use of the same English word. The fact of the matter is, the word translated "make firm" (וְהִגְבִּיר, *ħibgih^e w*) can indeed mean to make a covenant in the sense of institute or establish a covenant. Concerning its use in Dan. 9:27, KBH says, "to make a strong covenant."[279] Also, NIDOTTE asserts, "The meaning of the words *ħibbaral ʾur^e b ħibgih^e w* in Dan 9:27 is debated. If the text be accepted as it stands . . . then the most straightforward translation is, 'And he will make a strong/firm covenant/league/alliance/agreement with many (cf. RSV; NRSV; JB; NEB; REB; TEV; NIV has 'He will confirm a covenant with many')."[280] In other words, he will establish a covenant.

Finally, there simply is no biblical or historical support for the claim that the Messiah "confirmed the covenant for one seven." When did Christ ever confirm a covenant for only seven years? Even if we accept the claim that the disciples focused exclusively on the Jews for three and ½ years, this does not prove the claim. Since there is no statement anywhere in Scripture about such a covenant, to conclude that this is what the disciples are doing assumes that there must have been such a covenant. But, if the covenant is assumed in order to understand the actions of the disciples, then the actions of the disciples cannot be offered as proof of such a covenant. This is circular reasoning. One cannot support the notion that the Gospel went out to the Jews first simply because the text says that the covenant, whether made or only confirmed, was for a period of seven years. The text states that the covenant was a seven year covenant. This implies that after the seven years, the covenant either is no longer in existence or no longer confirmed. This cannot be the case with the

---

275. Theodotion's text (θ) reads, καὶ δυναμώσει διαθήκην πολλοῖς ἑβδομὰς μία . . . The Old Greek text (OG) reads, καὶ δυναστεύσει ἡ διαθήκη εἰς πολλούς . . . (Dan 9:27a). Neither one of these uses the Greek word used in Rom 15:8.

276. καὶ δυναμώσει διαθήκην πολλοῖς ἑβδομὰς μία . . . (Dan 9:27a).

277. BDAG, s.v., "βεβαιόω."

278. See *A Greek-English Lexicon* (1996), s.v., "δυναμ–όω," and *A Greek-English Lexicon of the Septuagint* (1992), s.v., "δυναμόω." In neither lexicon does the word mean "to confirm." It means "to strengthen."

279. KBH, s.v., "גבר."

280. NIDOTTE, s.v., "גבר."

New Covenant. The New Covenant is an eternal covenant (indicated by the statement וּלְחַטָּאתָם לֹא אֶזְכָּר־עוֹד, *doʿ rakzeʾ ʾol maṯ ʾaṭṭaḥlu* "and their sins not I will remember again" Jer 31:34), not a seven year covenant. There is no good reason to take this statement to mean "confirm a covenant" instead of "make a firm covenant," especially without any more argumentation than Gentry has presented.

Additionally, Gentry's argument actually works against his claim. Gentry claims that this is a confirmation of a covenant already extant, "i.e., the covenant of God's redemptive grace . . ." Rom 15:8 does not say anything about a covenant or about confirming a covenant. Of course, to accept Gentry's claim about an extant covenant, one must accept the whole of covenant theology. This is not the place to engage in a debate about covenant theology. Suffice to point out that there is no statement anywhere in Scripture about a covenant of God's redemptive grace. The oft cited statement, "I will be your God and you will be My people," as evidence of a covenant of grace is not in fact a covenant, and does not use covenant language. Gentry's claims about confirming the covenant do not rest on the text of Daniel, but on the prior assumption of the validity of covenant theology. If by "covenant of grace" Gentry is referring to the New Covenant, this does not help his case since we have already shown that the New Covenant is not a seven year covenant, but an eternal covenant indicated by the fact that God will no longer remember our sins.

Concerning the "confirming of the covenant," Mauro asserts, "The sense of the passage then is this: That the one remaining week would witness the confirming of *the covenant* (which could only mean the promised New Covenant) with the many; and that, in the midst of that last week, Christ would cause the entire system of sacrifices appointed by the law to cease, by offering of Himself as the all-sufficient sacrifice for sins."[281] Again, the text simply does not say "he will witness the confirming of the covenant for one seven." Nor does it say, "the covenant will be confirmed for one seven," as we have already demonstrated. Mauro claims that this confirming "gives to the last week of the seventy the importance it should have . . ." and yet the end of the seventieth seven, according to the view of Preterists, comes with virtually no outstanding event.

Along these same lines, Anderson claims that the stoning of Stephen indicates the end of the seventy weeks: "At the end of that prophetic week, Stephen, a deacon and an eloquent preacher, was summoned to appear before the Sanhedrin because his presentation of Jesus as the Messiah was so eloquent that the people 'were not able to resist the wisdom and the spirit

---

281. Mauro, *Seventy Weeks*, 87.

by which he spoke.' Verse 10."[282] He goes on to declare that the stoning of Stephen "brought to an end of [*sic*] the 70 weeks 'determined' or 'allotted' to the Jewish people."[283] Concerning this view, Don Preston notes,

> The view that the 70th week was fulfilled in Stephen's stoning or the conversion of the Gentiles is a rather anti-climactic ending to a grand prophetic scheme. . . . Cited by Walvoord, Leupold writes against the view of the 70 weeks ending in A.D. 34–35, 'For the last week and the consummation of the seventy year-weeks is an unimportant date seven years after Christ's death, when something so unimportant happened that the commentators are at a loss as to what they should point to. The interpretation runs out into the sand.' We concur. It is not that the conversion of the Gentiles [or the stoning of Stephen or the conversion of Paul] is not important *per se*. But, it is the fact that something *climactic* was to consummate the seventy weeks. Was God going to consummate such a grand prophecy with a whimper?[284]

Stopping the Sacrifices

27—   "And he will make a firm covenant with the many for one week, but in the middle of the week he will put a stop to sacrifice and grain offering . . ."

Table 41: Daniel 9:27b

יַשְׁבִּית	הַשָּׁבוּעַ	וַחֲצִי
he will cause to cease	the seven	And the half of
וּמִנְחָה		זֶבַח
and grain offering		sacrifice

The next part of the verse states, "but in the middle of the week he will put a stop to sacrifice and grain offering." A couple of things must be noticed here. First, there are no additional identifying characteristics to the "he" in this verse. This means that the antecedent must be discovered by considering the

---

282. Anderson, *Unfolding Daniel's Prophecies*, 120.

283. Ibid. Again, the text simply does not say that the confirmation is "allotted to the Jewish people."

284. Preston, *Seal Up Vision and Prophecy*, 23.

grammatical and syntactical relationships, and there is no good reason for not taking this "he" to be the same one who makes the covenant. The continuous nature of the syntax through the previous clause into this clause indicates that the "he" referred to here is the same "he" as the "he" referred to in the previous clause, namely, the "coming prince." Second, since in verse 26 the city and the sanctuary were destroyed, the fact that this person causes the sacrifice and grain offering to cease indicates that the sanctuary must be rebuilt, and the rebuilding of the sanctuary implies the rebuilding of the city in which it is contained. Miller argues, "That there will be 'an end to sacrifice and offering' does not necessarily mean that the sacrificial system will be reinstituted in Israel, as Whitcomb thinks, although this is possible. It may only indicate that worship in general is forbidden."[285] However, it seems rather confusing to use this expression if it does not actually mean this. Although the Jews have been worshiping God since the destruction of the temple in 70 AD, the true mode of worship for ancient Israel was the sacrificial system. It is not only possible that the system will be reinstituted, but it seems most improbable that the prophecy would use such an expression without such a reinstitution of the sacrificial system and yet not expect Daniel to understand this implication.

Preterists argue that there is no reason to think that this statement implies a rebuilding of the temple. Rather, they argue that this is a statement that refers to an event that occurs before the city and the sanctuary are destroyed. Hence, this notion is used to support the view that the "he" is the Messiah, not the "coming prince." The problem here is that one's prior eschatological commitment, whether one is a Futurist or Preterist, will predispose the interpreter to take this either as a future event or as a past event. However, since we have seen that thus far the Preterists' view does not fit what the text states, but must force the text, rearranging it to fit into its mold, nor does the Preterists' view fit the actual history, it seems more likely that this statement should be taken from a Futurist perspective.

Additionally, verse 27 begins with a verb that has the waw conjunction: וְהִגְבִּיר בְּרִית (ū^eb rībgih^ew). This is usually translated "And he will make a firm covenant . . ." However, verse 26 also begins with a verb that has the waw conjunction (וְאַחֲרֵי הַשָּׁבֻעִים, w^eha^{ʾa}mî ʿubăssah⊓er), and yet this is translated "Then after the sevens . . ." It is possible to understand the conjunction in verse 27 like the one in verse 26, "Then he will make a firm covenant . . ." indicating a progression of events. This coupled with the impossible re-arrangement of the text and the fact that the history simply does not fit the Preterists' proposals all seem to favor taking this statement as a reference to a future event, not a past event.

---

285. Miller, *Daniel*, 272.

Preterists claim that the "he" who causes the sacrifice to stop is Christ who accomplishes this by His death, burial, and resurrection. Quoting Noē, with whom he has already announced his agreement, Evans states, "With the Crucifixion, Noē writes, 'Even though the Jews continued the practice of animal sacrifices and offerings for another 40 years, Christ's death and resurrection ended the Old Covenant obligation.'"[286] Noē goes on to assert, "It no longer had value and acceptability."[287] Gentry argues, "Thus, the prophecy states that by His conclusive confirmation of the covenant, Messiah will 'bring an end to sacrifice and offering (v. 27) by offering up Himself as a sacrifice for sin (Heb. 9:25–26; cf. Heb. 7:11–12, 18–22). Consequently, at His death the Temple's veil was torn from top to bottom (Matt. 27:51) as evidence that the sacrificial system was legally disestablished in the eyes of God (cf. Matt. 23:38), for Christ is the Lamb of God (John 1:29; Acts 8:32; 1 Pet. 1:19; Rev. 5–7).'" However, the text does not say that "he" will "legally disestablish" the sacrificial system or cause it no longer to have value in the eyes of God. The text states, "he will put an end to/cause to cease sacrifice and offering." The verb here (יַשְׁבִּית, *ayšîtb*) does not have the meaning "legally disestablish" or "to cause not to have value." With reference to this verse, KBH indicates that the meaning is "to cause to disappear." Also, this verb occurs in Dan 11:18: "But a commander will put a stop to [וְהִשְׁבִּית, *tibsihᵉw*] his scorn against him." To think that this word means "to legally disestablish his scorn" or "to devalue it" is absurd. However, simply because the verb has a certain meaning in 11:18 does not mean it must have this meaning in 9:27. The purpose of making reference to the use in 11:18 is to show the sense of the verb. It is the standard lexicon that shows that the word simply does not have the meaning "legally disestablish" or "to cause not to have value." Since it is in the Hiphil form in these two verses, it has the meaning "cause to cease" or "put a stop to." The text says "he will put a stop to the offering of sacrifices and grain offerings." This simply did not happen in the time of Christ. The sacrificial system continued until the temple was destroyed in 70 AD.

Mauro appeals to the LXX in an effort to support the position that the one who stops the sacrifice is Christ: "In further elucidation of the sense of verse 27 we would call attention to the words of the Septuagint Version, 'My sacrifice and drink-offering shall be taken away.' Before the death of Christ the sacrifices of the law were *God's*. But He would never call *His* the sacrifices which apostate Jews might institute under agreement with antichrist. This we deem to be conclusive."[288] Mauro's point is that by the reference to

286. Evans, *Four Kingdoms*, 362.

287. Noē, *Beyond the End Times*, 86.

288. Mauro, *Seventy Weeks*, 87.

"My sacrifice," the text is indicating that even though the sacrifices physically continued after Christ, they were no longer God's sacrifices, therefore fulfilling the prophecy, "he will stop the sacrifice and offering." Unfortunately for Mauro's argument, he wrote his book long before the most recent scholarship on the Greek OT. The reading to which Mauro refers is actually found in only a single Greek manuscript, A Codex Alexandrinus. Interestingly, the most recent scholarship on the text of Theodotion, which Preterists' claim supports their views, omits this as a possible reading of the text.[289] Neither does the Syriac support this reading: ܘܢܘܩܒܪܬ ܕܒܚܐ ܣܘܡܐܝܢ, ('thbd l'thnw 'nbrwqw) "and he will cause to cease sacrifice and oblation."[290] Nor does the Latin text support this reading: *deficiet hostia et sacrificium*, "he will remove animal sacrifice and sacrifice."[291] But, even if we accept Mauro's claims, this does not support his position. The sacrifices were God's, and the text said they would stop, but they did not stop at the time of Christ's crucifixion.

To understand the word "cause to cease" as a spiritual rather than a physical event is unwarranted and is quite a bit to read into the text. The only basis for doing this is a prior eschatological commitment. Since it is simply a fact of history that the offering of sacrifices did not actually stop at Christ's death and resurrection, one can only surmise that when Mauro says, "Christ would cause the entire system of sacrifices appointed by the law to cease," he does not mean that the Jews would actually stop offering sacrifices. Rather, he must have in mind something of their legitimacy or efficaciousness, which he implies when he says, "Christ's death, being a real and proper sacrifice for sin, virtually abolished all those under the law . . ."[292] However, in the beginning of his book, Mauro emphatically declared, "Another guiding principle is that the proof adduced in support of any interpretation should be taken *from the Scripture itself.*"[293] And yet the "Scripture itself" does not say that "he will cause the sacrifices no longer to be of any spiritual value." Rather the text simply says, "he will cause to cease [יַשְׁבִּית, *tibsay*] sacrifice and grain offering." Interestingly, the word used here, שָׁבַת (*tabăs*), is the same word used in Gen. 2:2: "By the seventh day God completed His work which He had done, and He rested [וַיִּשְׁבֹּת, *tobsiyyaw*] on the seventh day from all His work which He had done." God did not keep on creating. When God stopped, He

---

289. See Joseph Ziegler, ed., *Susanna, Daniel, Bel et Draco*, vol. XVI, *Septuaginta*, 367.

290. *Syriac Peshita* (Damascus, Syria: Syrian Patriarchate, 1979).

291. *Biblia Sacra Juxta Vulgatam Clementinam* (Romæ: Typis Societatis S. Joannis Evang., 1927).

292. Mauro, *Seventy Weeks*, 88. These words are not actually Mauro's. Rather, he is here quoting Wm. M. Taylor, albeit he is quoting Taylor approvingly.

293. Ibid., 11 (emphasis in original).

stopped the work of creation. This is the sense of the word here in Daniel, and for Mauro to read into it this additional significance is not to take his interpretation "from the Scripture itself," but rather to base his interpretation on his own prior eschatological perspective. Basing one's conclusion on one's prior eschatological perspective is not necessarily an illegitimate practice in itself. However, an interpreter ought not to claim that he is using "Scripture alone" when what he is actually doing is using his own prior eschatological commitment.

Contrary to Noë's claim that the sacrifices no longer "had value or acceptability," the text does not say that the sacrifices would become invaluable or unacceptable, but that they would cease. Also, we have already shown that the one who stops the sacrifice and offering cannot be Christ, but must be the "coming prince," and without out this major point, Noë's arguments, and the arguments of the others we have discussed, cannot possibly work. However, even if, for the sake of argument, we grant that it was Christ, there simply is no historical event in which Christ confirmed a covenant for seven years. Since this is not Christ, and since there has not been such an event since the destruction of the temple in 70 AD, this must be a future event. As Sherlock Holmes supposedly said, "How often have I said to you that when you have eliminated the impossible, whatever remains, however improbable, must be the truth?"

Abominations and Wings

27—　　". . . and on the wing of abominations will come one who makes desolate, even until a complete destruction, one that is decreed, is poured out on the one who makes desolate."

Table 42: Daniel 9:27c

וְעַל	כְּנַף	שִׁקּוּצִים
and upon	wing of	abominables
מְשֹׁמֵם	וְעַד־	כָּלָה
making desolate	and until	destruction
וְנֶחֱרָצָה	תִּתַּךְ	עַל־
even was determined	it will pour out	upon
שֹׁמֵם:		

The next statement in the text is no less difficult than any of the previous statements: "and on the wing of abominations will come one who makes desolate, even until a complete destruction, one that is decreed, is poured out on the one who makes desolate." This portion of the verse is set out above with a word-for-word translation.

An extremely problematic part of this verse is the reference to the "wing" (כְּנַף, fanᵉk). Lucas surmises, "It is more likely that 'wing' refers to the altar with its four 'horns' at each corner, which could be regarded as winglike."[294] Young claims that the word "apparently refers to the pinnacle of the temple which has become so desecrated that it no longer can be regarded as the temple of the Lord, but as an idol temple."[295] Wood asserts, "The word for 'overspreading' (panᵉk) is normally translated 'wing,' but it comes from the root panak, 'to cover over,' and in Isaiah 8:8 definitely has the idea of 'overspreading,' in a destructive sense."[296] Wood's characterization seems to capture the sense here. The abomination seems to be designed to cover the entire institution of the worship of Israel.

Noē claims, "Earlier, Daniel had referred to 'desolations' (note the plural) that had been 'decreed' or 'determined' (Da. 9:26b), and stated that 'one who causes desolation (note the singular) will place abominations on a wing of the temple until the end that is decreed is poured out on him' (Da. 9:27b). 'Wing' refers to a pinnacle or an extreme point of abominations."[297] Although Noē includes an end note in which he says, "The word 'temple' is not in the original language," to present the text as if this is a translation is misleading. Not only does the word 'temple' not occur in the original text, there is no definitive evidence that the word "wing" has anything to do with the temple. Of the 109 times that word 'wing' (כְּנַף, fañak) is used in the OT, it is never once used with reference to the temple. It is, however, used 16 times with reference to the wings of cherubim, and 2 of those are references to the wings of the cherubim over the Ark of the Covenant. It seems extremely unlikely that the use of the word in the context of Daniel would have anything to do with the temple pinnacles, and there is no reason to think that Daniel would have understood it that way, especially since it is never used that way. The word is used to indicate an edge or extremity, and in this context it more than

294. Lucas, *Daniel*, 245.
295. Young, *Prophecy of Daniel*, 218.
296. Wood, *Daniel*, 261.
297. Noē, *Beyond the End Times*, 94.

likely refers to the extreme nature of the abominations and the fact that, like a wing, it overspreads the whole of the Jewish ritual.[298]

Evans claims, "In Daniel 9:27, the use of the plural *abominations* provides a clear scriptural basis for seeking multiple fulfillments."[299] But this is not necessarily the case. Such comments are commonly made by persons who do not understand the nuances of the language. In Semitic languages, a plural noun is frequently used in order to express emphasis or severity. "Related to the plurals of extension and of abstract reference is a group of *intensive* plurals. In this usage (sometimes called the *pluralis majestatis*) the referent is a single individual, which is, however, so thoroughly characterized by the qualities of the noun that a plural is used."[300] For example, in Gen 4:10 the text states, "The voice of your brother's bloods is crying to Me from the ground." Here the word "blood" is actually plural, "bloods" (דְּמֵי, ʾemʿd). It does not make much sense to a westerner to use a plural: "your brother's bloods . . ." but the plural here is designed to emphasize the intensity and severity of the act. As Waltke points out, "The plural of a singular *collective* noun can indicate *composition*, that is, that the collectivity has been broken apart . . . human blood in its natural state in the body is called דָּם; after it has been spilled, the plural form is used."[301] Such may be the case here. The abomination is so sever and drastic that the author uses the plural form to emphasize this fact. Whether or not this is the case, it nevertheless shows that Evans' claim that it "provides a clear scriptural basis" is simply not true. If there are "multiple fulfillments" as Evans claims, this cannot be based simply on the fact that the word is plural. More argument and evidence will need to be presented than this.

As a result, Evans' effort to separate out various abominations is misdirected at best: "Arguably, therefore, Jesus' singular reference to 'the abomination that causes desolation' refers to 12:11, not 9:27. That does not, however, rule out the possibility that Matthew 24:15 and Mark 13:14 could refer to *one* of the abominations envisioned in Daniel 9:27."[302] There is no reason to suppose that the plural means a multiplicity of events, and Jesus' use of the singular, rather than referring to one of the supposed abominations, is actually using the term in a quantitative sense. Jesus' use confirms that there is only one abomination of desolation and that the plural in Dan 9:27 is for emphasis. This would probably not convince Evans, but it shows that Evans' confidence is misplaced at best and that more evidence must be presented.

---

298. KBH, s.v. "כָּנָף."

299. Evans, *Four Kingdoms*, 290.

300. Waltke and O'Connor, *Biblical Hebrew Syntax*, §7.4.3a.

301. Ibid., §7.4.1

302. Evans, *Four Kingdoms*, 289.

Concerning the abomination of desolation, Roy Anderson declares, "Now, note one or two important details. Jesus said that the 'abomination of desolation' would 'stand in the holy place.' 'Then let them which be in Judaea flee into the mountains.' Matthew 24:15, 16. This is exactly what the faithful Christians did. They fled and saved their lives, whereas the unbelieving Jews remained in the city and most of them perished in the awful siege."[303] Anderson offers no historical testimony supporting his claim. He simply makes it as if this were common knowledge. In fact, Justo González points out, "In A.D. 62 the other James, the brother of Jesus, was killed by order of the high priest, even against the desire and advice of some of the Pharisees. Soon thereafter, the leaders of the Christian community in Jerusalem decided to move to Pella, a city beyond the Jordan whose population was mostly Gentile. This move seems to have been prompted, not only by persecution at the hand of the Jews, but also by Roman suspicion as to the exact nature of the new religious sect. . . . To allay the suspicions that all this created, the church decided to remove to Pella."[304] Anderson's claim about the Christians is simply speculation and is not based on historical facts.

He goes on to assert, "Why do some interpreters overlook the facts of history . . ."[305] But Anderson is not innocent of this charge either. He has completely ignored the very detail that he encouraged his readers to notice, namely, that the abomination of desolation would "stand in the holy place." Yet, in 70 AD at the destruction of Jerusalem, there was no abomination of desolation "standing in the holy place." Anderson asks, "Why do some interpreters . . . look for some future 'abomination of desolation' or antichrist after our Lord's return for His church? Why?"[306] Well, the obvious reason for this is that the abomination of desolation did not occur in 70 AD at the destruction of the city and the sanctuary, nor has it occurred since. Since Jesus said it would occur, it must yet be future. As it turns out, it seems that Anderson is the one who needs to study the facts of history.

Pouring Upon the Desolate

Concerning the final phrase, Wood proposes, "*Even what has been determined shall be poured out upon the desolate:* The thought is that, for the duration of the three-and-one-half-year period in view, all the desolating activity that God has determined before hand would be poured out (the same word as in

303. Anderson, *Unfolding Daniel's Prophecies*, 117.

304. Justo L. González, *The Early Church to the Dawn of the Reformation*, vol. 1, *The Story of Christianity*, 20–21.

305. Ibid.

306. Ibid.

verse eleven [which see]) upon Jerusalem, making it desolate. The nature of
this destructive activity is not described, but a general idea can be taken from
what Antiochus did in his day (cf. chap. 8) and from the horrors wrought by
the Romans in A.D. 70, an occasion intentionally mentioned for its parallel
features in the preceding verse."[307] This proposal, however, makes little sense.
If the desolations are poured out on "the desolate," i.e., Jerusalem, then this
pouring out seems to be redundant and of no real consequence. Why pour
out desolations on that which is already desolate? Also, this seems to conclude
this momentous prophecy with the notion that the desolator has succeeded in
his plans. However, it seems more likely that the culmination of the seventieth
seven is not the victory of the desolator, or the pouring out of desolation on
the already desolated Jerusalem, but the demise of the desolator by means of
the very desolation he determined to bring upon God's people. In fact, the
term translated "the desolate" is in fact a participle: שֹׁמֵם (*m̄emōs*). Since
the definite article is frequently omitted in prepositional phrases, and since
a participle can function as a noun, in this case, the object of the preposition, the phrase could be translated "upon the one desolating" (עַל־שֹׁמֵם, *la*ʿ
m̄emōs). Recall that the prophecy of the seventy sevens is for the purpose of
accomplishing what is expressed in the six phrases in verse 24. By the end of
the seventy sevens, the six things delineated in verse 24 will be accomplished,
and these seem to indicate the end of the evil and the triumph of the good.
The closing phrase here in verse 27 "it will pour out on the one desolating,"
seems to indicate that the destruction will be poured out on the one who has
made the covenant and stopped the daily sacrifices.

Complete Destruction

27—   . . . even until a complete destruction . . .

Verse 27 states that the one who makes desolate will do so until a "complete
destruction" (כָּלָה וְנֶחֱרָצָה, *ḥaṣarʿhenᵉw ḥalak*). This exact phrase is used
two other times in the Old Testament: "For a complete destruction (וְנֶחֱרָצָה
כָלָה, *ḥaṣarʿhenᵉw ḥalak*), one that is decreed, the Lord GOD of hosts will execute in the midst of the whole land" (Isa 10:23): "And now do not carry on as
scoffers, or your fetters will be made stronger; for I have heard from the Lord
GOD of hosts of decisive destruction (כָלָה וְנֶחֱרָצָה, *ḥaṣarʿhenᵉw ḥalak*)
on all the earth" (Isa 28:22). In each instance the predicted destruction is the
judgment of God upon the land in which the land is left completely desolate
so that only a remnant would survive. So also, the destruction referred to
in Daniel would be as complete. However, this hardly fits the events of 70

---

307. Wood, *Daniel*, 263 (emphasis in original).

AD. In fact, S. Safrai points out, "the Jewish people in the Land of Israel was not reduced to total devastation."[308] As we pointed out earlier, the Jews were able to conduct a major war only a few years later. Even Jerusalem itself was not completely devastated. The Roman legion *legio X Fretensis* was actually headquartered in Jerusalem after the end of hostilities, and even many Jews took up residence in the city shortly after the conflict ended. These are hardly indicative of a "complete destruction."

Summary of the Seventy Sevens

The position taken here is a traditional premillennial view. It is possible to become so entangled in the details that one loses sight of the overall flow of the prophecy. In order to give an overall view of the prophecy of the seventy sevens, a summary of the prophecy of the seventy sevens can be found in chapter 14, the final section titled "The Prophecy of the Seventy Sevens" beginning on page 888. Using the same general format of previous charts, the chart in Figure 38 below and Figure 39 on page 434 set out the scheme according to the view adopted here.

Figure 38: Futurist Gap

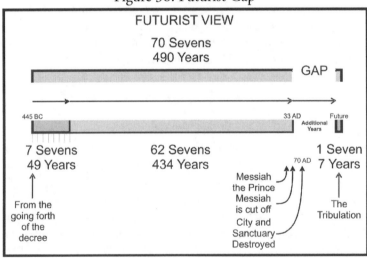

---

308. Safrai, "The Jews in the Land of Israel," 314.

Gap or No Gap

General Criticism

Much criticism has been poured out upon Futurists for proposing a gap that has now lasted for some 2000 years. For example, Evans declares, "Although I can find some Scriptural basis for believing in the forty-year gap, I find none whatsoever for the two thousand year gap."[309] Gentry asserts, "The dispensational arguments for a gap of undetermined length between the sixty-ninth and seventieth weeks are not convincing."[310] Mauro characterizes this position as, "the week which came next after the 69th week from the starting point, and which was in fact *the 70th actual week*, as time is ordinarily reckoned, is not to be taken as the 70th week of the prophecy; but that the prophetic period is to be regarded as having been interrupted at the end of the 69th week, 'the clock of prophecy having stopped.'"[311] Mauro goes on to say, "all the facts and reasons we are now about to set forth in proof that the 70th week was indeed one of the 'seventy,' and not a detached and remote period, avail equally to prove that verse 27 refers to Christ."[312] The purpose of this concluding material is to examine the arguments against the notion of the gap as Futurists have proposed and to offer a critique of Preterists' arguments in order to support the Futurist view. The chart below sets out the seventy sevens and the course of events according to a Futurist, Premillennial perspective.

Gentry's Criticism of the Gap

Gentry has a lengthy argument against the gap theory. Although the section is long, it is necessary to include all of it in order to follow Gentry's reasoning throughout his criticism, but each section will be followed by a response.

309. Evans, *Four Kingdoms*, 363.
310. Gentry, *He Shall Have Dominion*, 331.
311. Mauro, *Seventy Weeks*, 92 (emphasis in original).
312. Ibid., 93.

Figure 39: Seventy Sevens Pre-Mill Chart

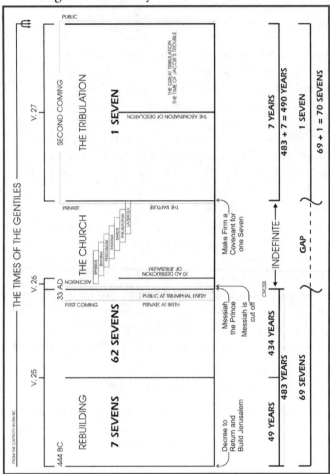

THE PECULIAR PHRASEOLOGY IN DANIEL

Dispensationalism incorporates a gap or parenthesis between the sixty-ninth and seventieth weeks. This gap spans the entirety of the Church Age from the Triumphal Entry to the Rapture. The dispensational arguments for a gap of undetermined length between the sixty-ninth and seventieth weeks are not convincing. Let us consider a few of their leading arguments for a gap. First, *the peculiar phraseology in Daniel*: Daniel places the cutting off of the Messiah "*after* the 62 'sevens,' not in the 70th 'seven.'" This is so stated to allow for a gap between the sixty-ninth and seventieth-weeks. If the cutting-off did not occur during the sixty-ninth week or during the seventieth week, there must be a gap in between wherein it does occur. In response it is obvious that seventy occurs *after* sixty-nine, and thus fits the requirements of the prophecy. Consequently, such an argument does not prove that the "after" *requires* a gap. Besides, Daniel mentions only seventy weeks and, as LaRondelle has pointed out, Daniel most certainly does *not* say "after sixty-nine weeks, but not in the seventieth." Such an explanation is a gratuitous assumption. Since Daniel has yet to deal with the seventieth week, and since he has clearly dealt with the preceding sixty-nine weeks (v. 25), it is quite natural to assume this cutting off of the Messiah must be sometime *within* the seven-year period covered by the seventieth week.[313]

Gentry quotes Pentecost's claim that the cutting off of the Messiah occurs after the sixty-ninth seven, but not within the seventieth seven. Gentry's first response is, "it is obvious that seventy occurs *after* sixty-nine, and thus fits the requirements of the prophecy." This response, however, is not an argument, but simply a restatement of his own eschatological position. Gentry declares that this "does not prove that the 'after' *requires* a gap." Of course neither does the statement that seventy follows sixty-nine prove that there is no gap. Gentry goes on to assert, "Besides, Daniel mentions only seventy weeks and . . . Daniel most certainly does *not* say 'after the sixty-nine weeks, but not in the seventieth.'" Of course neither does Daniel say "after the sixty-nine weeks and in the seventieth." In fact, this latter omission is more telling than the former. We have already quoted from Harold Hoehner's observations concerning this "peculiar phraseology," but it will be helpful again to include a portion of his statement: "If the cutting off of the Messiah occurred in the middle of the seventieth week, it is very strange that the cutting off is said to be 'after' the sixty-nine weeks (figuring the sum of the seven and the sixty-two weeks). Much more naturally the text would have read 'during' or 'in the midst of' the seventieth week, as it does in verse twenty-seven concerning the stoppage of the sacrifices."[314] In other words, if Gabriel meant for Daniel to understand that the cutting off of Messiah took place within the seventieth week, why did he not simply say it that way. The natural reading of the way it is expressed leads one to believe it does not. Also, the fact that the seventieth week is said to begin with the "making firm" a covenant with the many indicates that the final seven does not begin immediately after the end of the sixty-ninth

---

313. Gentry, *He Shall Have Dominion*, 331–32 (emphasis in original).

314. Gundry, *The Church and the Tribulation*, 190; quoted in Hoehner, *Chronological Aspects*, 132.

seven, but that the events described in verse 26 happen between these two time periods. We have already seen that Gentry's appeal to repetition, and his effort to rearrange the text, is untenable (see pages 385 and following). Gentry claims that the gap is a "gratuitous assumption," but it seems much more likely that Gentry's rearranging of the text, forcing parallelism where none is indicated, the reading into the text the notion that the actual destruction of Jerusalem is not within the scope of the prophecy about Jerusalem, and his assumption that the cutting off must occur in the seventieth week are all gratuitous assumptions.

Gentry concludes this criticism by saying, "Since Daniel has yet to deal with the seventieth week, and since he has clearly dealt with the preceding sixty-nine weeks (v. 25), it is quite natural to assume this cutting off of the Messiah must be sometime *within* the seven-year period covered by the seventieth week." But in fact Gentry's argument actually works against his own claim. Granting for the moment that it might be natural to assume that the cutting off would happen within the seventieth week, this could be precisely why the angel states it the way he does. The fact that he does not say that it occurs within the seventieth week and that the seventieth week is not referenced until verse 27 is designed to alert the reader *not* to include the events of verse 26 in the seventieth week as might be the tendency of Daniel and future readers. To assume that these events occur in the seventieth week after the text specifically separates them from the seventieth week is gratuitous in the extreme.

A FATAL ADMISSION

Second, *a fatal admission*: "Historically the destruction of Jerusalem occurred in A.D. 70 almost forty years after the death of Christ." Since this was given in Daniel's prophecy and was to occur within the seventy weeks, "the continuous fulfillment theory [is] left without any explanation adequate for interposing an event as occurring after the sixty-ninth seven by some thirty-eight years."

I have already explained the relation of the seventy weeks to the destruction of the Temple in A.D. 70 (see above). The goal of the Seventy Weeks is not the A.D. 70 destruction of the Temple, which is not mentioned in verse 24. That destruction is *a later consequence* of certain events brought to fulfillment within the seventy weeks. The actual act of God's reserving judgment (v. 24) occurred within the seventy weeks; the later removal of that *reservation* did not. There is no necessity at all for a gap.[315]

315. Gentry, *He Shall Have Dominion*, 332.

Gentry next quotes from Walvoord concerning the fact that the destruction of Jerusalem in 70 AD leaves the continuous fulfillment theory without a way of placing this event within the prescribed time limit. Gentry responds, "The goal of the Seventy Weeks is *not* the A.D. 70 destruction of the Temple, which is not mentioned in verse 24." Of course Walvoord's argument does not rest on whether the destruction of Jerusalem is the "goal" of the seventy sevens. However, since verse 24 does state that the seventy sevens is determined upon Jerusalem, and since the destruction in 70 AD is something that happens to Jerusalem, to place it outside the seventy sevens requires much more argument and proof that Gentry has presented. The only reason for placing the destruction of Jerusalem outside the scope of the seventy sevens is Gentry's prior eschatological commitment. And Walvoord's argument is that since it should belong within the scope of the seventy sevens, the continuous fulfillment theory is indeed left without an adequate explanation of how to incorporate this event, which occurred 38 years later, into the seventy sevens time frame (see pages 403 and following where this is dealt with in more detail).

The General Tendency of the Prophecy

> Third, *the general tendency in prophecy*: Walvoord writes: "Nothing should be plainer to one reading the Old Testament than that the foreview therein provided did not describe the period of time between the two advents. This very fact confused even the prophets (cf. 1 Pet. 1:10–12)." His argument then is: Old Testament prophecy can merge the First and Second Advents into one scene, though separated by thousands of years. Consequently, we have biblical warrant for understanding the sixty-ninth and seventieth weeks as merged into one scene, although separated by a gap of thousands of years. This argument is wholly without merit. The Seventy Weeks are considered as a unit, though sub-divided into three unequal parts: (1) It is *one* period of seventy weeks that must transpire in order to experience the events mentioned. The plural "seventy weeks" is followed by a *singular* verb "is decreed," which indicates the unity of the time period. (2) An overriding concern of the prophecy, in distinction to all other Messianic prophecies, is that it is designed as a *measuring* time frame. If the dispensational gap theory regarding the seventieth week is true, then the gap separating the seventieth from the sixty-ninth week is now almost 2000 years long, or four times the whole time period of the seventy weeks or 490 years. And who know [*sic*] how much longer it will continue. The concept of measuring is thus destroyed.[316]

316. Ibid., 332–33 (emphasis in original).

Gentry next addresses the claim that Old Testament prophecy can merge the first and second comings of Christ into one scene even though they are separated by thousands of years. Gentry responds with two separate points. The first point he makes is that the seventy sevens is "considered as a unit." He argues, "The plural 'seventy weeks' is followed by a *singular* verb 'is decreed,' which indicates the unity of the time period." First, simply because the subject is plural and the verb is singular does not require that the subject be viewed as a unity. In Table 43 below there are two examples of plural subjects followed by singular, Niphal verbs.

Table 43: Plural Subjects with Singular Verbs

Ex. 13:7	"Unleavened breads [מַצּוֹת, *ṭossam*] *it* shall be eaten [יֵאָכֵל, *lֶ̄ka'ey*] throughout the seven days; and nothing leavened shall be seen among you, nor shall any leaven be seen among you in all your borders."

מַצּוֹת יֵאָכֵל אֵת שִׁבְעַת הַיָּמִים־יֵרָאֶה לְךָ
בְּכָל־גְּבֻלֶךָ׃וְלֹא־יֵחָמֵץ וְלֹא־יֵרָאֶה לְךָ שְׂאֹר

Jer. 48:41	"Kerioth has been captured and the strongholds [וְהַמְּצָדוֹת, *wֵ̆mmaḥֵּṭoḏas*] *it* has been seized [נִתְפָּשָׂה, *hāśaphtin*], so the hearts of the mighty men of Moab in that day will be like the heart of a woman in labor.

נִלְכְּדָה הַקְּרִיּוֹת וְהַמְּצָדוֹת נִתְפָּשָׂה וְהָיָה לֵב
גִּבּוֹרֵי מוֹאָב בַּיּוֹם הַהוּא כְּלֵב אִשָּׁה מְצֵרָה׃

In Ex 13:7, the reference to "unleavened breads" followed by a singular verb certainly does not imply that these breads are a unity. It may imply that the breads are to be considered as one in kind, but Gentry's argument is not about "one in kind." In fact, if the plural-subject-singular-verb structure in Dan 9:24 indicates a unity at all, it indicates a unity in kind, not in temporal sequence.

Secondly, even if we grant Gentry's claim that the seventy sevens time period indicates a unity, this does not mean that there cannot be an unperceived gap in the execution of the decree. Evans points out that "both Daniel 2 and 7 treat Babylonia and Nebuchadnezzar as if they were identical, thereby ignoring the interval between the death of Nebuchadnezzar and the fall of Babylon to the Medes and Persians. Also, between verses 2 and 3 in Daniel 11, there is an interval of well over a century if you accept the idea that king of Persia 'who will be far richer than all the others' in verse 2 is Xerxes."[317] So, an unperceived gap exists between Nebuchadnezzar and the fall of Babylon even though the statue is treated as a unity. Once again Gentry's argument does not support his claim.

Gentry's second point in response to the claim that the first and second comings are merged together into one scene is that Daniel's prophecy is "designed as a *measuring* time frame." Gentry argues that a gap of almost 2,000 years destroys the concept of measuring. But this does not follow. The measuring time frame is studded with identifiable events that mark the beginnings and endings of the various segments. The end of the sixty-ninth week is marked by the coming of Messiah, and the beginning of the seventieth week is identified by the making a firm covenant with the many. In fact, in spite of Gentry's efforts to the contrary, the text of Daniel introduces a gap between the end of the sixty ninth week and the beginning of the seventieth week. If a gap destroys the concept of measuring, then it is destroyed by the very text of Daniel. But the fact is, neither the gap in Daniel's prophecy nor the gap proposed by dispensationalists serves to destroy the concept of measuring because the beginnings and endings of the various parts of the time frame are clearly identified by specific events. In fact, Gentry's claim that the destruction of the city actually occurs outside the 70 sevens does more to destroy the concept of measuring than any gap. Since the text stays that the 70 sevens are decreed upon the city, to place the destruction of the city outside the time frame makes all measuring non-sensical. Why even say that the 70 sevens is decreed upon the city if the most catastrophic event since Daniel's day is not included in the very time frame that is decreed upon the city? Additionally, the Preterists themselves introduce gaps at various points to make things fit their own eschatological schemes, as we will now see.

Preterist Gaps

Yet for all the disdain heaped upon Futurists for proposing a gap, the Preterists cannot escape the problem. We have already quoted Evans on this point, but it will serve to present his statement again: "It is true that the Book of Daniel sometimes skips over time from one verse to the next. For example, both Daniel 2 and 7 treat Babylonia and Nebuchadnezzar as if they were identical, thereby ignoring the interval between the death of Nebuchadnezzar and the fall of Babylon to the Medes and Persians. Also, between verses 2 and 3 in Daniel 11, there is an interval of well over a century if you accept the idea

317. Evans, *Four Kingdoms*, 213.

that king of Persia 'who will be far richer than all the others' in verse 2 is Xerxes."[318]

For all his effort to avoid using the word "gap" for his proposal, Preston necessarily introduces a gap in the seventieth week. He declares, "Two things were to happen *after the sixty-ninth week*, Messiah would be cut off, and the city and the sanctuary destroyed. Where is the justification for including one of the events within the seventieth week and another outside? That is illogical and violates the text."[319] Since the seventieth seven can be only seven years in length, and since the cutting off of Messiah is separated from the destruction of the sanctuary by some 40 years, this necessarily introduces a gap in the midst of the seventieth seven (see Figure 32 on page 395).

As we have seen, another Preterist author, Max King, proposes a gap between the sixty-ninth and the seventieth seven. He gave several reasons why one should accept the notion of a gap: "First of all, there is a textual division in Daniel 9:24–27 between the sixty-ninth and the seventieth week. The seventieth week is treated separately. At the end of the sixty-ninth week, Messiah is 'cut off.' Does the expression 'cut off' mean that Christ was through with national Israel? Not at all—the 'day of the Lord' was still to come. Christ, though cut off, would still deal with fleshly Israel:"[320] At this point King ventures off into a study of several NT passages in order validate his understanding. King goes on to assert, "The gap between the sixty-ninth and the seventieth week was from the time of Christ's going into heaven until he came again. His coming, according to Matthew 24, was the time of the end of the world, or the consummation of the age."[321] Of course King's assertion about Jesus going into heaven and coming again is nowhere mentioned in Daniel's prophecy. The point is, King, a Preterist, recognizes the gap between the sixty-ninth and seventieth sevens that is indicated in the prophecy of Daniel.

Since the seventy sevens is decreed upon Israel and Jerusalem, and since the present age is focused upon the Gentiles, it stands to reason that a gap would be introduced between the end of the sixty-ninth and the beginning of the seventieth seven. As Paul points out in Romans, this present age is designed to provoke Israel to jealousy: "I will make you [Israel] jealous by that which is not a nation, by a nation without understanding will I anger you" (Rom 10:19), and, "I say then, they did not stumble so as to fall, did they? May it never be! But by their transgression salvation to the Gentiles, to make

318. Ibid.

319. Preston, *Seal Up Vision and Prophecy*, 36.

320. King, *The Spirit of Prophecy*, 91–92.

321. Ibid., 93.

them jealous" (Rom 11:11).[322] There is nothing other than the acceptance or rejection of a particular eschatological perspective that makes a 2,000 year gap either "surprising" or "startling."[323]

---

322. ἀλλὰ λέγω, μὴ Ἰσραὴλ οὐκ ἔγνω; πρῶτος Μωυσῆς λέγει, Ἐγὼ παρα—ζηλώσω ὑμᾶς ἐπ᾿ οὐκ ἔθνει, ἐπ᾿ ἔθνει ἀσυνέτῳ παροργιῶ ὑμᾶς. Ῥομ.ᵐ. Λέγω οὖν, μὴ ἔπταισαν ἵνα πέσωσιν; μὴ γένοιτο· ἀλλὰ τῷ αὐτῶν παραπτώματι ἡ σωτηρία τοῖς ἔθνεσιν εἰς τὸ παραζηλῶσαι αὐτούς. (Rom 11:11).

323. Young, *Prophecy of Daniel*, 214.

11

PREPARATION OF DANIEL FOR THE FINAL VISION:
10:1–21

Introduction

Literary Structure

THERE APPEARS to be a chiastic structure in chapter ten beginning with verse 7, although it does not seem to fit the usual pattern. The repetition of phrases and topics seems to be haphazard rather than strategically placed as in a usual chiasm.

Figure 40: Structure of Chapter 10

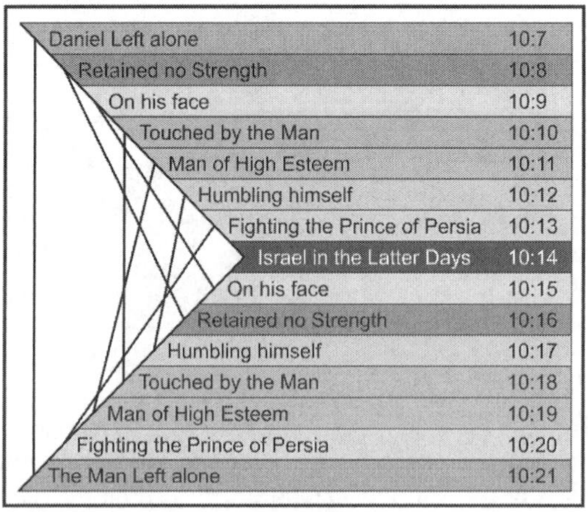

Daniel Left alone	10:7
Retained no Strength	10:8
On his face	10:9
Touched by the Man	10:10
Man of High Esteem	10:11
Humbling himself	10:12
Fighting the Prince of Persia	10:13
Israel in the Latter Days	10:14
On his face	10:15
Retained no Strength	10:16
Humbling himself	10:17
Touched by the Man	10:18
Man of High Esteem	10:19
Fighting the Prince of Persia	10:20
The Man Left alone	10:21

The different colors as well as the lines show the parallelisms between parts of the structure. Although the structure seems unplanned, it does begin and end with the same concept. It begins with Daniel being alone, except for the man, and it ends with the Man left alone, except for Michael. For each item in the first part of the structure, there is a repeating phrase or concept in the second part of the structure. The only item for which there is no repeating item is the focal point in verse 14—what will happen to Israel in the latter days. What appears at first to be a haphazard arrangement of the parts may in fact be designed to communicate the spontaneous nature of the events, though they are purposeful, as the focus indicates—verses 1–6 seem to function as a preparation not only to this chapter, but to the vision as a whole. This vision is introduced by chapter 10 and extends to the end of chapter 12.

Historical Context

An understanding of the historical context in which chapter 10 is placed may be helpful in understanding the purpose for this chapter. Daniel notes that it was in the third year of Cyrus the king of Persia that the revelation came to him. The third year of Cyrus' reign would be about 535 BC. This would place this event shortly after the first wave of captives had returned to Jerusalem to begin the rebuilding of the temple under the direction of Ezra. David Stevens observes that, "Though Cyrus had already allowed some of the Jewish exiles to return to their homeland, many were still dispersed in the Mesopotamian cities of Babylon, Persepolis, Susa, and Ecbatana. The first wave of returnees to Jerusalem encountered opposition in their efforts to rebuild the temple."[1] Ezra 4:4–5 states, "Then the people of the land discouraged the people of Judah, and frightened them from building, and hired counselors against them to frustrate their counsel all the days of Cyrus king of Persia, even until the reign of Darius king of Persia." These counselors were hired to influence Cyrus to discontinue his support of the people's effort to rebuild the temple in Jerusalem. The counselors did their job well, and as Ezra points out, the work was delayed all the days of the reign of Cyrus and did not begin again until the reign of Darius I Hystaspes (521–486 BC).

Stevens argues that it is very likely that Cambyses, the son of Cyrus, was primarily responsible for the halting of the rebuilding of the temple. He suggests that Daniel's prayer and fasting coincides with the enthronement of Cambyses as king of Babylon. Cambyses' reputation as one who despised foreign religions would certainly have been reason enough for Daniel's concerns. As Stevens points out, "Given Cambyses' bellicose character and his hatred of

---

1. David E. Stevens, "Daniel 10 and the Notion of Territorial Spirits," *Bibliotheca Sacra* 157 (October-December 2000): 422.

foreign religions, one can understand why Daniel would have devoted himself to prayer and fasting on behalf of his people and the project of reconstructing the temple already undertaken in Jerusalem."[2]

Terrified by the Angel: 10:1–9

1—   In the third year of Cyrus king of Persia a message was revealed to Daniel, who was named Belteshazzar; and the message was true and one of great conflict, but he understood the message and had an understanding of the vision.

2—   In those days, I, Daniel, had been mourning for three entire weeks.

3—   I did not eat any tasty food, nor did meat or wine enter my mouth, nor did I use any ointment at all until the entire three weeks were completed.

4—   On the twenty-fourth day of the first month, while I was by the bank of the great river, that is, the Tigris,

5—   I lifted my eyes and looked, and behold, there was a certain man dressed in linen, whose waist was girded with a belt of pure gold of Uphaz.

6—   His body also was like beryl, his face had the appearance of lightning, his eyes were like flaming torches, his arms and feet like the gleam of polished bronze, and the sound of his words like the sound of a tumult.

7—   Now I, Daniel, alone saw the vision, while the men who were with me did not see the vision; nevertheless, a great dread fell on them, and they ran away to hide themselves.

8—   So I was left alone and saw this great vision; yet no strength was left in me, for my natural color turned to a deathly pallor, and I retained no strength.

9—   But I heard the sound of his words; and as soon as I heard the sound of his words, I fell into a deep sleep on my face, with my face to the ground.

2. Ibid., 424.

Introduction to the Vision

This entire chapter is an introduction for both Daniel and the reader to the prophetic revelation that will come in the following chapters. Verse 1 of chapter 10 serves as a brief introduction to the extensive vision placing it in its time frame. One result of this is that the reader knows that this is a prophetic declaration, not a historical record. By that is meant, this is not a record of the history by someone who is looking back on these events. Rather, this is prophecy of the history that was yet future from Daniel's point of view. Daniel's Babylonian name is used so that the reader knows that this is not some pseudo-Daniel, but the same Daniel who was given this name under Nebuchadnezzar. All this is designed to authenticate the vision as true prophecy.

When Daniel says, "the message was true" (וֶאֱמֶת הַדָּבָר, *tem^e'ew ṙabadah*), this does not mean only that the vision is true, but that what Daniel relates about what he saw did actually occur just as he saw it. The content is true, but also Daniel's experience of the vision was real. The word translated "conflict" (וְצָבָא, *'abaṣ^{e}w*) indicates also a "military campaign."[3] This is the singular form of the word "Hosts" used in the name "Lord of Hosts." Miller remarks, "Literally the Hebrew text reads simply 'and a great war' or 'conflict,' with the verb to be supplied. The phrase could refer to a great earthly war (or wars) that would occur in the future, or it could even describe spiritual warfare between the forces of God and the forces of Satan. Both interpretations would suit the context well, for a conflict between spiritual forces is described in chaps. 10 and 11, and great wars are prophesied in chap. 11. Probably all the conflicts (or warfare) recorded in these last chapters are involved in the expression, whether conflicts between nations or angels."[4]

When Daniel says, "he understood the message and had an understanding of the vision" (וּבִין אֶת־הַדָּבָר וּבִינָה לוֹ בַּמַּרְאֶה:, *ṙabadah te' ñ̩bu he'rammaḇ'ol ḥañ̩bu*), this seems to indicate not only that Daniel understood the vision that he is about to relate, but that this vision also helped him to understand what was given to him in previous visions that left him in a state of confusion and anxiety. In fact, it may be because of his anxiety at not being able to understand the previous visions that explains not only the giving of this vision, but also why he was mourning for 21 days. Daniel implies that he not only understood the vision as a vision, but he understood the message—the word הַדָּבָר (*ṙabadah*) of the vision—that is, what the vision meant.

---

3. KBH, s.v. "צָבָא."
4. Miller, *Daniel*, 277.

21 Days of Mourning

The relating of the vision begins in verse 2 indicated by the change from third person references in verse 1 to first person reference. Daniel declares that he had been mourning for 3 weeks. This is equivalent to 21 days. Interestingly, the reference to 21 days is repeated in verse 13: "But the prince of the kingdom of Persia was withstanding me for twenty-one days." This implies that the man bringing the information to Daniel was dispatched when Daniel began to mourn, but did not arrive to communicate to Daniel until 21 days later.

Fasting

Daniel "did not eat any tasty food, nor did meat or wine" enter his mouth for the entire period of 21 days. As Miller observes, "He may have existed on bread and water."[5] Nor did Daniel "use any ointment at all until the entire three weeks were completed." This means that Daniel was not partaking of the usual luxuries of his day to make himself comfortable.

On the Banks of the Tigris

While Daniel was at the banks of the Tigris river, there appeared to him a man dressed in linen, "whose waist was girded with a belt of pure gold of Uphaz." Verse 6 says, "His body also was like beryl, his face had the appearance of lightning, his eyes were like flaming torches, his arms and feet like the gleam of polished bronze, and the sound of his words like the sound of a tumult." The sight of this one brought fear to Daniel's heart, and he fell to his face. Many commentators hold that this is an appearance of the Pre-Incarnate Christ. However, that does not seem to fit with the statement that the man was resisted by the prince of Persia and that "Michael, one of the chief princes, came to help me" (v. 13). Miller presents the argument of G. C. Luck: "G. C. Luck offered the proper solution to this problem, which is that the 'man dressed in linen' and the interpreting angel introduced in v. 10 are distinct personalities. At least four holy angels (the interpreting angel [10:10–14 and throughout chaps. 10–12]; Michael [10:13, 21]; and two others [12:5]) appear in this vision, and the 'man dressed in linen' is unquestionably in charge (cf. 12:6–7). Therefore the personage described in 10:5–6 is a theophany, but the contents of the vision are related by the interpreting angel, who is introduced at v. 10."[6] Niehaus points out, "Daniel's description harks back to

5. Ibid., 278.
6. Ibid., 283.

pentateuchal theophanies and also anticipates the revelation of Christ to John on Patmos. It also recalls some of the terminology of Ezekiel's open vision by the River Kebar."[7] Whether this is a Pre-Incarnate Christ is a decision that awaits an understanding of the remainder of this passage.

Daniel was the only one who saw the vision, and the men with him did not see the vision. However, "a great dread fell on them, and they ran away to hide themselves." This statement is parallel to the final statement by the man in this chapter: "Yet there is no one who stands firmly with me against these forces except Michael your prince" (v. 21). Yet Daniel was not completely unaffected: "yet no strength was left in me, for my natural color turned to a deathly pallor, and I retained no strength" (v. 8). The word translated "deathly pallor," according to Lucas, "comes from the same root as *taḥsim* in Is. 52:14, where the word is used to describe the disfigured appearance of the Servant of the Lord."[8] The man dressed in linen spoke to Daniel: "But I heard the sound of his words; and as soon as I heard the sound of his words, I fell into a deep sleep on my face, with my face to the ground" (v. 9). This is the first time a reference has been made in this chapter to Daniel with his face to the ground. A second reference is made in verse 15: "When he had spoken to me according to these words, I turned my face toward the ground and became speechless." Both instances are in response to the words of one talking to Daniel.

Comforted by the Angel: 10:10–17

10— Then behold, a hand touched me and set me trembling on my hands and knees.

11— He said to me, "O Daniel, man of high esteem, understand the words that I am about to tell you and stand upright, for I have now been sent to you." And when he had spoken this word to me, I stood up trembling.

12— Then he said to me, "Do not be afraid, Daniel, for from the first day that you set your heart on understanding this and on humbling yourself before your God, your words were heard, and I have come in response to your words.

13— "But the prince of the kingdom of Persia was withstanding me for twenty-one days; then behold, Michael, one of the chief princes, came to help me, for I had been left there with the kings of Persia.

7. Niehaus, *God at Sinai*, 326.

8. Lucas, *Daniel*, 275.

14— "Now I have come to give you an understanding of what will happen to your people in the latter days, for the vision pertains to the days yet future."

15— When he had spoken to me according to these words, I turned my face toward the ground and became speechless.

16— And behold, one who resembled a human being was touching my lips; then I opened my mouth and spoke and said to him who was standing before me, "O my lord, as a result of the vision anguish has come upon me, and I have retained no strength.

17— "For how can such a servant of my lord talk with such as my lord? As for me, there remains just now no strength in me, nor has any breath been left in me."

Getting the Touch

Someone touched Daniel, and he rose up "trembling on my hands and knees" (v. 10). The text does not say the hand is a hand of the one who had just talked with Daniel. It merely says, "And behold, a hand touched me . . ." (וְהִנֵּה־יָד נָגְעָה בִּי, *ıb haʿgan̠ day hennihʿw*). Miller asserts, "Now the vision of Christ has passed, and the interpreting angel enters the picture."[9] Walvoord asserts, "It is said that the angel 'set me upon my knees' . . ."[10] However, the text does not say "the angel" did this, although this might be assumed. Verse 11 starts out, "He said to me," which translates the two Hebrew words וַיֹּאמֶר אֵלַי (*yāleʾ remʾoyyaw*). The antecedent of the pronoun subject of the verb cannot be "hand," but must be an intelligent being. In the context, the only individual who would be talking to Daniel, since all the other men fled, and no mere human would be able to give Daniel understanding or make him tremble (v. 11), is the "man dressed in linen" of verse 5 (see Figure 41). But, if the one talking to Daniel in verse 11 is the same one as Daniel began describing in verse 5, then this cannot be the Pre-Incarnate Christ since the one talking to Daniel states in verse 13 that "Michael, one of the chief princes, came to help me." The fact that Michael came to help this man does not sound like the man is God the Son.

9. Miller, *Daniel*, 283.
10. Walvoord, *Daniel*, 245.

Figure 41: The Man of Daniel 10:5

5   I lifted my eyes and looked, and behold, there was a certain man dressed in linen, whose waist was girded with a belt of pure gold of Uphaz.

6   His body also was like beryl, his face had the appearance of lightning, his eyes were like flaming torches, his arms and feet like the gleam of polished bronze, and the sound of his words like the sound of a tumult.

11   He said to me, "O Daniel, man of high esteem, understand the words that I am about to tell you and stand upright, for I have now been sent to you." And when he had spoken this word to me, I stood up trembling.

12   Then he said to me, "Do not be afraid, Daniel, for from the first day that you set your heart on understanding this and on humbling yourself before your God, your words were heard, and I have come in response to your words.

13   "But the prince of the kingdom of Persia was withstanding me for twenty-one days; then behold, Michael, one of the chief princes, came to help me, for I had been left there with the kings of Persia.

All of this seems to argue that the man in verse 5ff is not Christ, but an angel with awesome appearance, perhaps giving Daniel a sense of the presence of Deity. That angels have been sent to give the sense of the presence of deity, without themselves being a direct manifestation of God, is seen in the encounter of the three angels with Abraham in Genesis 18. Whether this is a Pre-Incarnate Christ or an angel whose glorious presence gives the sense of the presence of God may not be decidable, however. Nevertheless, the effect and impact upon Daniel is clear.

The Prince of Persia

The man tells Daniel that he has been sent to give Daniel a message. However, before the man gave the word to Daniel, he explained that Daniel's prayer was heard, and from the first day of his prayer, God had sent this messenger. For 21 days the man was engaged with the prince of the kingdom of Persia. There is some controversy over whether the "prince of Persia" is in fact an angelic being or a human being. As David Stevens points out, "Daniel 10 is crucial for the study of cosmic powers over the peoples of the earth."[11] There can be no doubt that the term "prince" (שַׂר, *rás*) can be used to refer to angelic beings. Steven notes, "The angel Michael is called 'one of the chief *princes*' (10:13), 'your prince' (v. 21), and 'the great prince' (12:1)."[12] Since it is clear that the term can be used of angelic beings, the next question is, can it be used of evil angels? Once again Stevens makes the point well: "In this regard the evident parallel between the שַׂר 'prince' of Persia and Michael, the guardian angel of Israel, must not be overlooked. This same parallel is also found in 10:20–21

11.   Stevens, "Daniel 10," 412.

12.   Ibid., 415 (emphasis in original).

between the 'prince of Greece' and 'Michael your prince.' If שַׂר refers in a *context of conflict* to the benevolent angel Michael, who represented God's interests, it is not surprising to find the same term used to designate a malevolent angel (a demon) representing the interests of an earthly kingdom."[13] This must have been an angelic being, since he withstood the man—perhaps one of Satan's demons, a fallen angel. This is of particular interest in light of the events that would be described to Daniel. It was necessary for Daniel to understand that the conflicts that were about to come upon his people would not consist merely of a flesh and blood warfare. Rather, the flesh and blood conflicts would be the physical manifestations of the spiritual warfare that was being waged beyond the senses of men. The movement of nations and the conflicts of peoples would be directed by angelic hosts whose purpose would be either to destroy God's people or protect them.

Daniel may have been told about the 21 days of standing against the prince of Persia because in 9:23 he was told, "At the beginning of your supplications the command was issued, and I have come to tell you." In order to assure Daniel that God had heard and answered his prayer immediately, the man tells him of the delay. But, this may also reveal that the forces of Satan have stepped up their resistance to Daniel. Whereas in chapter 9 the messenger is sent from God and immediately comes to Daniel apparently with no resistance from the evil forces, in chapter 10 the messenger is sent, but it seems that the forces of Satan attempt to prevent the message from getting through. This may indicate the importance of the message, or the fact that the evil forces have begun to realize that they need to try to stop this information from flowing to Daniel—forewarned is forearmed—and the forces of evil do not want the people of God to be forearmed against their efforts.

But there is another possible understanding of this passage as it relates to Daniel's prayer and fasting for 21 days. David Stevens points out that, "the two phrases he 'withstood me' and 'I was left over there' . . . contribute to an understanding of the *reason* for the twenty-one-day period of prayer and fasting by Daniel. Spiritual warfare was being waged in the heavenly places and the angel Gabriel was encountering the malevolent influence of the angelic (demonic) prince of Persia on the contemporary political situation."[14] In other words, the 21 days of confrontation between the man and the prince of Persia was not necessarily a delay in his coming to Daniel, but was rather the man fighting the spiritual warfare while Daniel prayed and fasted. The man was not delayed by the prince of Persia, but was fighting the spiritual war in cooperation with Daniel's prayer and fasting—as an answer to Daniel's

13. Ibid., 415–16 (emphasis in original).

14. Ibid., 420 (emphasis in original).

prayer. While Daniel prayed and fasted for 21 days, the man fought with the prince of Persia to counteract his evil influence for the welfare of Daniel and the people of God.

Kings of Persia

The last phrase of verse 13 states, "for I had been left there with the kings of Persia." Miller argues, "The NIV's 'detained there with the king of Persia' could mean that the angel was prevented from leaving the area ruled by the human king of the Persian Empire. Yet the Hebrew word translated 'king' is plural, and the concept of the angel's being 'detained with' the earthly kings of Persia seems untenable. In the context of angelic warfare, these 'kings' likely were spiritual rulers who attempted to control Persia."[15] The word on which Miller focuses is נוֹתַרְתִּי (*itrâton*), and according to KBH does not have the meaning "detained" as Miller claims. The word is a Niphal verb, which means that it has a passive meaning. According to KBH it means "to be left over,"[16] not "to be detained." What the phrase seems to say is that the man was left behind with the kings of Persia. The word "kings," then, could be a reference to the human kings who ruled Persia over the years, and the man was left there to influence them for the good of God's people. Stevens notes that "מֶלֶךְ [*kelem*, 'king'] is never used in the Old Testament in reference to angels" and that "the term שַׂר [*rás*, 'prince'] is *never* used to designate those who are kings."[17]

Wood argues that this phrase implies a battle between this man and the prince of Persia for preeminence: "The word sometimes carries the thought of being left in a position of preeminence (as on a field of battle), and it is best so taken here. After the struggle with the demon, Daniel's visitor remained preeminent, as victor. That he was thus left 'beside the kings of Persia' means that he remained in a position of influence with the Persian ruler, in place of Satan's representative."[18] This seems to be quite a bit of information to get out of this simple phrase. The word that Wood translates "beside" is translated in the NASB as "with." The word is אֵצֶל (*lēseʾ*) and, according to KBH, is used here "in a hostile sense" with the meaning "facing."[19]

15. Miller, *Daniel*, 284.

16. KBH, s.v. "יתר." Throughout his commentary, Miller references the Brown, Driver, Briggs *Hebrew and English Lexicon of the Old Testament*. This lexicon has been supplanted by KBH and is no longer the standard for Hebrew studies.

17. Stevens, "Daniel 10," 416.

18. Wood, *Daniel*, 273.

19. KBH, s.v. "אֵצֶל."

As we pointed out above, nowhere else are spiritual beings, either good or evil, referred to as "kings." However, this could be the one instance in which they are, and the fact that they are not so called anywhere else does not prove that they could not be called that here. Nevertheless, it does imply that it is less likely that Daniel would have understood the word to have this reference. Although Wood's explanation seems excessive, his notion seems closer to what the text is saying. Similarly Goldingay implies that the word "left" could have the idea, "'I was left over' (i.e., no longer needed; RVmg)."[20] This man was fighting against the prince of Persia and remained there alone beside the human kings perhaps to continue to try to influence them against the influence of the prince of Persia. The kings are probably Cyrus and Cambyses who had been stirred up by the prince of Persia to mount a resistance against the people of God in their efforts to restore the temple. The man must return to fight in behalf of the people of Israel and against the evil prince's influence so that the work on the temple can continue.

Israel and the Latter Days

The whole of this chapter seems to be focused on verse 14: "Now I have come to give you an understanding of what will happen to your people in the latter days, for the vision pertains to the days yet future." This verse with a word-for-word translation is set out below.

Table 44: Daniel 10:14

וּבָ֫אתִי	לַהֲבִ֣ינְךָ֔	אֵ֛ת	אֲשֶׁר־
And I came	to cause you to understand	(sign of the direct object)	what
יִקְרָ֥ה	לְעַמְּךָ֖	בְּאַחֲרִ֣ית	הַיָּמִ֑ים
shall befall	to your people	in the after	the days
כִּי־	ע֥וֹד	חָז֖וֹן	לַיָּמִֽים׃
for	yet	vision	to the days.

---

20. Goldingay, *Daniel*, 276.

This, of course, relates to the material contained in chapters 11 and 12. This does not necessarily mean that everything that will be described in chapters 11 and 12 belong to some period popularly known as "the latter days" (בְּאַחֲרִית הַיָּמִים, *miṁayyaḥ îrªhaʾᵉb*). Although some of the events may belong to that age, this statement does not necessarily relegate all the events to that age. Many events may be preparatory. Walvoord claims, "The expression *in the latter days* is an important chronological term related to the prophetic program which is unfolded in the book of Daniel. As previously considered in the exposition of Daniel 2:28, this phrase is seen to refer to the entire history of Israel beginning as early as the predictions of Jacob who declared to his sons 'that which shall befall you in the last days' (Gen. 49:1) and extending and climaxing in the second coming of Jesus Christ to earth."[21] Lucas says something similar: "In some passages in the Hebrew prophets, the phrase comes to be used of a time in the future when the kingdom of God will be established over Israel and the nations in a definitive way (Is. 2:2; Mic. 4:1; Hos. 3:5; Ezek. 38:16). However, this is not 'the end of history,' but a decisive turning-point in history. That seems to be the sense here in Daniel. What the messenger is about to reveal relates to that decisive turning point."[22]

MAURO'S ARGUMENTS ABOUT THE LAST DAYS

Mauro takes a completely different view of the expression: "We recall again that the one clothed in linen had declared to Daniel that he had come to make him understand what was to befall Daniel's people 'in the latter days' (Dan. 10:14). The prophecy makes it perfectly clear that the period here designated as 'the latter days' is that second term of Jewish history which began at the restoration from Babylon (two years before this vision was given to Daniel in the third year of Cyrus, Dan. 10:1) and ended with the destruction of Jerusalem, and the scattering of the people by Titus, in A.D. 70."[23] To claim that the people were "scattered" by Titus in 70 AD is inaccurate. In fact, the people who survived remained in the land and organized another revolt against the Romans in the Bar Kochba war that took place in 132 to 135 AD. Also, Mauro's view seems necessarily to require that the promises of God to Israel concerning the inheritance of the land be rescinded. In other words, this view implies that Israel will not inherit the land God promised to them, nor will they be the subjects of the kingdom that God promised to establish under David. That, then, seems to call forth the same criticism that Moses

---

21. Walvoord, *Daniel*, 248.
22. Lucas, *Daniel*, 276–77.
23. Mauro, *Seventy Weeks*, 120.

voiced when God said He would destroy the people and raise up a nation from Moses:

> Then Moses entreated the Lord his God, and said, "O Lord, why does Your anger burn against Your people whom You have brought out from the land of Egypt with great power and with a mighty hand? Why should the Egyptians speak, saying, 'With evil He brought them out to kill them in the mountains and to destroy them from the face of the earth'? Turn from Your burning anger and change Your mind about harm to Your people. Remember Abraham, Isaac, and Israel, Your servants to whom You swore by Yourself, and said to them, 'I will multiply your descendants as the stars of the heavens, and all this land of which I have spoken I will give to your descendants, and they shall inherit *it* forever.'" So the Lord changed His mind about the harm which He said He would do to His people. (Gen. 32:11–14)

Whether because of Israel's sins or not, if the people were not brought into the land as God had promised, Moses said this would give the Egyptians grounds for charging God with evil or impotence. Robert L. Saucy expressed this idea well: "'If God has not fulfilled his promises made to Israel, then what basis has the Jewish-Gentile church for believing that the promises will be fulfilled for them?' If God's original election of Israel was as a 'nation,' and that appears to be the teaching of the OT, then a theology affirming the fulfillment of that elective purpose in the nation of Israel seems most supportive of our own election as his people in the church."[24] Are we willing to say that Israel's sins were too much for God? Could not God overcome the sins of Israel to bring them into the inheritance that He promised to give to the descendants of Abraham? And this inheritance, when it was described to Abraham, was not described as a spiritual possession, but a physical one—God even described the physical boundaries of the land that Israel would inherit, a land that they have never yet inherited according to those boundaries. If the promises of God could not be fulfilled for Israel because of Israel's sins, how can we be sure that God can fulfill His promises to us in the face of our sins?

DON PRESTON'S ARGUMENTS ABOUT THE LAST DAYS

Don K. Preston has written a book, *The Last Days Identified*, in which he claims "Our purpose is to demonstrate, through scripture alone, that when the Bible speaks of the last days, that it refers to the last days of the Old

24. Robert L. Saucy, "Israel and the Church: A Case for Discontinuity," 259.

Covenant World of Israel that came to an end with the fall of Jerusalem in A.D. 70."[25] Preston explains his methodology:

> My normal style is to offer extensive bibliographic references. However, for brevity sake, I will keep my references to a minimum. Further, there are some passages that mention the last days that do not directly contribute to our ability to properly define the *framework* of the last days. In the cases where the information is sparse, we will not examine the texts. We will focus our attention on those passages that give us the most defining information. Information that can serve as a "nail" on which to hang our hat, so to speak. In this way, this book can be kept to a smaller format, and be the most beneficial to the reader.[26]

Immediately there are problems. First, Preston says he will not examine those passages that "do not directly contribute to our ability to properly define the *framework* of the last days." However, this maneuver violates the earlier statement about his purpose. Already he has deviated from the notion that he will demonstrate his point "through scripture alone," because, rather than using scripture alone, he has used his own judgment about what "directly contributes." No where does the Scripture alone say what does and does not "contribute to our ability to properly define the framework of the last days." That being the case, it would seem prudent to examine all of them, not simply the ones Preston chooses based on his prior eschatological commitment. On page 25 Preston chides those who, in their study of the notion of the last days in Isaiah, "omit a study of chapters 3–4" because it "is to do a great disservice to proper exegesis."[27] And yet at the outset of his book he "omits to study" many of the verses in which the expression "last days" occurs because, rather than allowing his readers to make this judgment, he makes a prior judgment that they do not "directly contribute." Is this not a "disservice to proper exegesis"? Preston illegitimately assumes that what he thinks "directly contributes" perfectly coincides with what the "scripture alone" might say directly contributes.

Second, he says, "we will focus our attention on those passages that give us the most defining information." But who decides which passages can do this? Again, rather than simply examining "scripture alone," as he purports to do, Preston has used his own prior judgment to decide which Scriptures are relevant to the study. Third, he claims that this methodology will "serve as a 'nail' on which to hang our hat, so to speak." But why does Preston think

---

25. Don K. Preston, *The Last Days Identified*, 1.

26. Ibid., 3 (emphasis in original).

27. Ibid., 25.

that this is a desirable practice? Where does the Scripture alone say that we should examine only enough passages of the Bible in order to find a "nail" on which to "hang our hat"? And how can his reader be assured that a passage or passages that he has deemed "do not directly contribute" are not so judged because they do not support Preston's thesis, or perhaps contradict his thesis? Preston has already deviated from his professed goal of demonstrating his purpose from "scripture alone." Instead, he has employed his prior perspective to decide which Scripture passage and consequently what evidence will be presented. One must wonder if this is a harbinger of things to come.

Last Days in Genesis 49:1

The first passage Preston investigates is Genesis 49:1–10. The expression translated "last days" is contained in verse 1, so we have set it out below with a word-for-word translation.

Table 45: Genesis 49:1

בָּנָיו	אֶל־	יַעֲקֹב	וַיִּקְרָא
his sons	to	Jacob	And called
לָכֶם	וְאַגִּידָה	הֵאָסְפוּ	וַיֹּאמֶר
to you	and I will tell	"Gather yourselves together	and he said
לָכֶם	יִקְרָא	אֲשֶׁר־	אֵת
to you	will happen	what	(sign of the direct object)
		הַיָּמִים:	בְּאַחֲרִית
		the days.	in the future of

The word in this verse that is characteristically translated as "latter" in the expression "the latter days" is translated here as "in the future of" (אַחֲרִית בְּ, *ʾaḥᵃrîtⁿ bᵉ*). This Hebrew form is actually the combination of three elements. The first element is the inseparable preposition בְּ (*ᵉb*), which is translated here as "in." The second element is the definite article "the." The Hebrew definite article is a prefixed *waw* (וְ, *ᵉw*) that is attached to a word. Although the actual Hebrew definite article is not attached to this word, it is to be associated with this word because this word is in a construct relation with the word "the days"

(הַיָּמִים, *mimayyah*). A construct relation is a relationship between two words that usually indicates a Genitive idea. Genitive ideas are usually expressed in English by the word "of," such as in "the children *of* God." In Hebrew, the first word in the construct relation never takes the definite article. It is definite only when the final word in the construct relation has the definite article. So, for purposes of illustration, in the English phrase "the children of God," to mimic the Hebrew construction this phrase would be written with the words "children of" followed by the words "the God." In such a construction in the Hebrew language, the word "children" would also be considered definite, so the meaning would be "the children of the God," or "the children of God." This is what we have here. The word translated "in the future of" is in the construct state and does not have the definite article. The word translated "days" is the final word in the construct relation, and it does have the definite article. Consequently, we can translate this construct phrase as "in the future of the days," or "in the future days."

The word itself, אַחֲרִית _(*tur*ᵃha*ʾ*), according to KBH, can be used to mean "end," "issue," "hind part," "result," "following period," "future," "finally," "descendants," and "least important."[28] KBH cites the Gen 49:1 passage and indicates that the meaning in this instance is "in future days."[29] Interestingly, KBH does not list "latter" as one of the possible meanings of this term in any context. Of course this does not mean that it could not have this translation, but it is up to the commentator to demonstrate that this understanding of the word is applicable in a given context.

Preston lists what he calls "constituent elements" of this prophecy. He says, "1.) The focus, i.e. the sons of Jacob. This means it is not about the end of the Church Age, it is about *the last days of Israel*."[30] He goes on to say, "The topic is not the church, nor the Church Age, yet the topic is what would happen in the last days. Thus, in the first occurrence of the term 'last days,' in an eschatological context, the term has nothing to do with the Christian Age. *It deals with the fate of Israel!*" Of course the text does not say that this has nothing to do with the end of the Church Age or with the Christian age, as Preston claims. Maybe it doesn't, but Preston cannot simply assume this. He must demonstrate it "from scripture alone" as he claimed he was going to do. Just because the text says, "I will tell you what shall happen to you in the last days" does not mean, "I will tell you what shall happen to you, and only you not including the church age or the Christian age, in the future days, which has nothing whatsoever to do with any other group of people who

28. KBH, s.v. "אַחֲרִית."
29. Ibid.
30. Ibid.

might be alive at the time." As we said, Preston cannot simply claim that it has nothing to do with the church age or Christian age. He must show that this is the case, and the straightforward language of the text does not *necessarily* eliminate these possibilities. Since the text does not say "will happen only to you," the last days which "will happen to you" could happen to Israel and anyone else who may be alive at the time. The text simply does not say, "to you and only you," nor does it say, "in this time and not some other." As far as the text is concerned, these things could "happen to you" in the church age, the Christian age, or any other age. The text simply does not specify, and for Preston to specify where the text does not is to violate his promise to demonstrate "from scripture alone."

Also, the fact that Jacob tells his sons that he is going to tell them what will befall them "in the future days" does not necessarily mean that this has *necessarily* anything to do with the last days of Israel. Preston says, "*It deals with the fate of Israel!*" but the text does not use that terminology. It simply does not say, "what will happen to the fate of Israel." It says, "what will happen to you." In the context, this could be referring to these particular individuals in the "last days" of their own lives. In other words, just because it says "you" does not *necessarily* confine these future events to the nation of Israel nor does it *necessarily* have anything to do with Israel's fate. Maybe it does. Maybe it doesn't. The text simply does not specify. But, once again, Preston must demonstrate this, not simply assert it. He has not demonstrated that this has to do with the nation of Israel. He simply claims it. Nor has he, as he proposed, offered any "scripture alone" to show that his assumption is the only way of understanding this passage. Preston is already reading into the text his prior eschatological commitment.

His second constituent element is, "2.) the time frame—the topic of our study, the last days." This is a problematic observation also. What does Preston mean by "the last days"? The text, in fact, does not necessarily say "the last days." As we have seen, the term אַחֲרִית (*tur⁽a⁾ha'*) does not necessarily mean "last." It can be used to mean this, but this is only one of the possible meanings. Why should anyone think that Preston's understanding of the meaning is necessarily the correct one? In fact, this expression can simply mean "in the future." Again, Preston has not demonstrated his point from Scripture alone, as he said he was going to do. Rather, he has simply made unsubstantiated assertions based on his prior eschatological commitment.

Judah and the Scepter

His third constituent element is, "3). The passing of the scepter from Judah." This is a very problematic observation. Preston makes a point of zeroing in on the statement in verse 10: "The scepter shall not depart from Judah, nor a lawgiver from between his feet, until Shiloh comes, and to him shall be the obedience of the people." Preston seems to assume that because the text has been translated "until Shiloh comes," that this means that the scepter will, at this time, be passed from Judah. Because of the importance of the translation, we have set out the verse below with a word-for-word translation.

Table 46: Genesis 49:10

לֹא־	יָסוּר	שֵׁבֶט	מִיהוּדָה
Not	will remove	rod	from Judah
וּמְחֹקֵק	מִבֵּין	רַגְלָיו	עַד
and ruling staff	from between	his feet	until
כִּי־	יָבֹא	שִׁילֹה	וְלוֹ
that	he will come	?	and to him
יִקְּהַת	עַמִּים:		
obedience of	the peoples.		

The reason we have put a question mark in the translation space under the word שִׁילֹה (*holis*) is because its translation is controversial. With reference to the translation "until Shiloh comes," Victor Hamilton points out, "Without emending the Hebrew text in any way, one may read this line as 'until Shiloh comes.' But this reading is strange for several reasons. First, it combines a feminine subject ('Shiloh') with a masculine verb ('comes'). More importantly, what would such an expression mean? As a person, whom would Shiloh represent? Elsewhere in the OT Shiloh is only a place. Why represent an individual by a city, and why represent someone in a message to Judah by a city that falls within the territory of Ephraim?"[31]

John Currid summarizes the difficulties with the translation of this word:

> The meaning of "Shiloh" is a matter of great dispute. Perhaps it is a proper noun (a city in ancient Israel had that name), although the sense of the verse would then be uncertain. Another possibility is to translate it as "he whose it is," although a few changes

31. Victor P. Hamilton, *The Book of Genesis: Chapters 18–50*, 659.

of consonants and vowels are necessary to meet that translation. The manuscript evidence strongly confirms that the reading of the Masoretic Text is the correct one. Another option is to separate the term into two words, which would then mean "tribute to him"—thus the entire clause would read: "until tribute shall come to him." There are difficulties with all three interpretations, and so the meaning remains an enigma.[32]

On top of the problems summarized by Currid, the most serious problem with simply taking the verse the way Preston presents it is that the word "Shiloah" is feminine, and yet the word "comes" is masculine. This cannot be the subject of this verb, so simply accepting Preston's notion goes against the syntax of the text. However, Preston seems to be resting most of his hopes on the word translated "until" (עַד, *daʿ*). Without any argumentation, he treats this as a temporal preposition indicating the *terminus ad quem* of the scepter in Judah. In other words, Preston assumes that the text is saying that the scepter will be in Judah *until* this time, at which time it will no longer be in Judah. It is certainly true that this word can function as a temporal preposition. However, it has other functions as well, and Preston's interpretation is not the only one available. But rather than argue for his understanding, Preston merely assumes that it must be right, and he goes on to build his interpretation on this assumption.

According to KBH, the word עַד (*daʿ*) can be used as a preposition expressing measure or degree, characterized by the translation "up to" or "as far as." An example of this is Gen. 11:31: "Terah took Abram his son, and Lot the son of Haran, his grandson, and Sarai his daughter-in-law, his son Abram's wife; and they went out together from Ur of the Chaldeans in order to enter the land of Canaan; *and they went as far as Haran* [וַיָּבֹאוּ עַד־חָרָן, *nāraḥ daʿuʾobayyaw*], and settled there." Now this did not indicate that their "coming" somehow was no longer theirs, or even that their journey was over. This is simply the point that they reached in their journey. So also, this term does not necessarily mean that the scepter will stop being Judah's or will "pass from Judah," but that the scepter will be in Judah even up to the coming of the one to whom the passage refers. Once again Preston assumes that his understanding is necessarily the only correct one, and he does this without argument or evidence. Even if there was the possibility that Preston's view is correct this cannot be assumed, it must be demonstrated. And, after all, Preston said he was going to demonstrate his view "through Scripture alone," something, again, he has not done.

---

32. John D. Currid, *Genesis 25:19–50:26*, 377.

The fourth of Preston's constituent elements is, "4.) The coming of Shiloh, or Messiah in his kingdom."[33] This element is predicated on the accuracy of the translation and the notion that this is a reference to Messiah. Probably most commentators take the passage as having this Messianic sense. However, we have already shown that this cannot be the meaning since the word "Shiloh" is feminine. It makes no sense to think that a feminine name would be given to the Messiah. Preston completely neglects to deal with these problems and thereby fails to demonstrate his point.

The fifth constituent element, "5.) The gathering of the people to him,"[34] is also a fairly standard way of understanding this phrase. However, since the preposition "him" is masculine (וְל ֹ, *olᵉw*), it cannot be referring to Shiloh, since this word is feminine. In fact, the only masculine noun to which this masculine pronoun could be referring in this sentence is in fact the word "Judah" (יְהוּדָ֔ה, *haduhey*). So, rather than demonstrating his view "from scripture alone," it seems that the "scripture alone" actually contradicts his interpretation. Since the antecedent of the personal pronoun "him" seems to be "Judah," rather than indicating a passing of the scepter from Judah, this passage seems to indicate that the scepter will remain in Judah. At the very least this view is supported by the grammar and syntax of the verse, and Preston has completely omitted any attempt to deal with these issues. Perhaps this is another instance, in Preston's own words, of doing a "great disservice to proper exegesis."

Will God Terminate His Relationship to Jacob?

In his exposition relating to Gen 49:1–10, Preston begins, "Notice again that Jacob made a promise to his sons, and specifically Judah: 'The scepter shall not depart from Judah nor a lawgiver from between his feet, until Shiloh comes and to him shall be the obedience of the people.'"[35] Having brought this again to the attention of his reader, Preston associates another verse with this statement: "There is a fascinatingly similar passage found in Genesis 28:15f concerning the time when God's distinctive relationship with Jacob and his seed would be terminated."[36] Preston then quotes this passage and focuses on the statement, "for I will not leave you until I have done what I have spoken to you." The Hebrew text is set out below with a word-for-word translation.

---

33. Preston, *Last Days*, 3.
34. Ibid.
35. Ibid., 4.
36. Ibid.

Table 47: Genesis 28:15b

כִּי	לֹא	אֶעֱזָבְךָ	עַד
For	not	I will leave you	until
אֲשֶׁר	אִם־	עָשִׂיתִי	אֵת
which	whatever	I have done	(sign of direct object)
אֲשֶׁר־	דִּבַּרְתִּי	לָךְ	
which	I have spoken	to you.	

Once again without argument or support, Preston assumes that the word "until" necessarily indicates a *terminus ad quem* of God's relationship with Israel. He asserts, "Like Genesis 49, it indicates that when Jehovah had fulfilled His promises to the seed of Abraham, to Israel, that the distinctive and exclusive relationship would then be terminated."[37] But, as before, this cannot simply be asserted; it must be demonstrated. And the fact that this word can be taken in other ways requires that Preston make his case, not simply assert it. In fact, in the context, this may not be referring to anything other than the promises that God made to Jacob to be with Jacob during his sojourn outside of the promised land and to bring him back into the land successfully. Preston says, "This passage cannot be speaking of Jacob individually. It is a reiteration of the Abrahamic and Messianic Covenant."[38] It is certainly true that this is a reiteration of the Abrahamic and Messianic Covenant, but that does not prove it cannot be speaking of Jacob individually. As Hamilton explains, "Just as God speaks to Jacob about descendants before Jacob has any, so he speaks to Jacob about 'returning you to this land' even before Jacob has left the land. Thus Jacob will not need to find his own way back. His parents prompted his departure from Canaan; Yahweh will determine and direct his return to Canaan."[39] Hamilton goes on to point out, "The last part of the verse does not mean that once God has wrung from Jacob's life what he wants, he will *abandon (baza ͑)* him. Jacob is of more significance than momentary usefulness to God."[40] In other words, Hamilton proposes that this is in fact not a *terminus ad quem* use of "until."

37. Ibid.
38. Ibid.
39. Hamilton, *Genesis 18–50*, 243.
40. Ibid.

Waltke-O'Connor identify a use of the preposition "until" (עַד, *daʿ*) that indicates "the time *during* which an event takes place."[41] The example they give is 2 Kgs 9:22: "How can there be peace *as long as* [עַד, *daʿ*] the prostitution of Jezebel . . . abound?" This use could be applicable here: "For I will not abandon you *while* I am doing what I have spoken to you." Although Waltke-O'Connor point out that this is not a frequently occurring use, it is a reasonable one to use here. In this case, God is not saying He will abandon Jacob once He has done what He promised. Rather, He is assuring Jacob that while He is doing all the He promised, He will not abandon Jacob. This is quite similar to the kind of things people say to those whom they seek to encourage in difficult times: "I'm going to stay beside you until we get through this together." That does not mean that the friend will not continue to "stay beside" the one he is attempting to encourage. Rather, it is an assurance that the friend will be there to help during this difficult time. Also, Preston has not demonstrated "from scripture alone" that this necessarily has anything to do with Israel rather than, as the context indicates, with Jacob alone in his sojourn outside of the promised land.

There are other possibilities of understanding the verses to which Preston appeals, and yet Preston has not even argued for his view. He simply asserts it as if the asserting is sufficient to establish his position. Preston asserts, "What we have in Genesis 49 specifically is that Judah would remain the focal point of the theocracy *until the appointed Messiah would come*."[42] He then refers to an internet search and the Babylonian Talmud as if the accuracy of an interpretation is simply a matter of counting votes. So what if all these people believe this is what the text is saying? That does not serve as proof that this is what it means. Millions of people do not believe God exists. Does that make it true? Besides, didn't Preston say he was going to demonstrate "through scripture alone"? Polling the community hardly seems like demonstration from Scripture alone. Preston needs to argue from the text, as he promised, that his view is the correct one. He merely asserts it and then continues as if it is a settled issue.

Preston goes on to vilify those who may not accept his view as people who do not believe in the integrity of Scripture: "Now, if the scepter departed from Judah in A.D. 70, for us to maintain a faith in the integrity of scripture, and the faithfulness of God who cannot lie, we must believe, contra the Jews and Moslems, and, we might add, *the millennialists*, that Messiah did indeed come *in the last days*. And, he came when the scepter was removed from Judah, at

41. Waltke and O'Connor, *Biblical Hebrew Syntax*, 11.2.12.

42. Preston, *Last Days*, 4.

the fall of Jerusalem in A.D. 70."[43] But Preston has not proven the point. The only thing Preston has given is unsupported assertion and appeals to other unsupported assertions as if this settles the case. As we have seen, these verses are subject to translation in a way that does not support Preston's claims, and yet Preston continues as if his understanding of the text is the only reasonable one and the only one that those who believe in the integrity of Scripture can hold to. But, this does not amount to demonstration.

This is not the place to deal with all of Preston's arguments in his book. Suffice to say that the rest of his book is more of the same. He builds a structure of belief that is grounded on assumptions the truth of which he has not bothered to demonstrate. Simply appealing to Bible verses does not support his view since his understanding of each one of these verses needs to be demonstrated as well, a task that is simply ignored. Far from "Identifying" the Last Days, Preston has ultimately succeeded only in identifying his own assumptions and how they predispose him to understand the text the way he chooses without argumentation, exegesis, or support. Neither the words themselves nor Preston's arguments demonstrate that the "latter days" are not yet future.

Having dispensed with both Mauro's and Preston's views about the "latter days," it remains that the most natural way to take the statement in Dan 10:14 is that the man is going to explain to Daniel what will happen to his people in future days, and that this expression applies to the material contained in chapters 11 and 12.

Strengthened by the Angel: 10:18–21

18—   Then this one with human appearance touched me again and strengthened me.

19—   He said, "O man of high esteem, do not be afraid. Peace be with you; take courage and be courageous!" Now as soon as he spoke to me, I received strength and said, "May my lord speak, for you have strengthened me."

20—   Then he said, "Do you understand why I came to you? But I shall now return to fight against the prince of Persia; so I am going forth, and behold, the prince of Greece is about to come."

21—   "However, I will tell you what is inscribed in the writing of truth. Yet there is no one who stands firmly with me against these forces except Michael your prince."

43. Ibid., 4–5.

Three times in this chapter Daniel is strengthened by the angel. This is also instructive. If Daniel, or any of the people of God, were to stand firm in the midst of this spiritual conflict, they would need supernatural strength. Neither they, nor we should rely upon human understanding or human strength to resist the evil one and his influence. Now Daniel is prepared for the prophetic revelation. It is very likely that the revelation that the man is about to give to Daniel was in answer to Daniel's prayer and fasting. God would indeed fulfill His promises to Israel, and the revelation of the following chapters gives a detailed account of many historical factors involved in this fulfillment.

12

DANIEL'S VISION OF THE FUTURE OF THE NATIONS: 11:1–45

Introduction

IN CHAPTER 10 the man appeared to Daniel and declared he had come to bring a revelation. Chapters 11 and 12 are the presentation of that revelation. Chapter 11 sets forth in great detail the conflicts between the two great kingdoms of the Seleucids and the Ptolemies, two of the four inheritors of Alexander's Empire. Concerning this chapter, Leon Wood asserts, "The stress of the message is on Antiochus Epiphanes (vv. 21–35) . . . early Persian rulers are set forth and then Alexander the Great who defeated Persia for Greece. After this comes a remarkably detailed presentation of the successive kings, who ruled two of the divisions of Alexander's empire: the Egyptian division, ruled by the Ptolemies, and the Syrian, ruled by the Seleucids."[1]

Philip Mauro makes essentially the same point when he says, "Down to the end of verse 30 there is practical agreement among expositors as to the meaning of the prophecy, and the events by which its several predictions were fulfilled. We are not aware of any sound and competent teacher who does not see, in verses 1–30, the main outlines of Persian history, the rise of Alexander of Macedon, the division of his empire between his four generals, the incessant wars between the Seleucids (kings of Syria, 'the north') and the Ptolemies (kings of Egypt, 'the south'), and the career of Antiochus Epiphanes—that odious persecutor of the Jews, spoken of as the 'vile person' (v. 21)."[2]

1. Wood, *Daniel*, 280.
2. Mauro, *Seventy Weeks*, 119.

The prophetic account of chapter 11 does not end with the conclusion of the chapter, but continues into chapter 12 without a break so that chapters 11 and 12 present one complete prophetic revelation. Since chapter 8 dealt with essentially these same groups, the question might arise, why are these same kingdoms the subject of additional prophetic revelation? Wood proposes, "These two divisions [the Ptolemies and the Seleucids] call for this special consideration because the affairs of Palestine, lying between the two, were so often involved with their activities."[3] In chapter 8, the nature of the revelation was broader in scope and did not extend to the level of detail as is presented here in chapter 11. Also, as was the case with chapter 8, the events leading up to and including Antiochus IV Epiphanes are significant as a type of the Anti-Christ and his career, whether one takes the Anti-Christ to be a yet future person, as do the Futurists, or a person already having passed off the scene, as do the Preterists. Chapter 11 presents the acts of Antiochus in some detail, but also presents the actions of Anti-Christ in even greater detail. Chapters 11 and 12 present a broader historic context in which the actions of these evil forces operate who will oppose the people of God.

Prophecy Concerning the Nations: 11:1–20
The Fall of the Persian Empire: 11:1–2

DARIUS OR MICHAEL

1—   "In the first year of Darius the Mede, I arose to be an encouragement and a protection for him."

In verse 1, the man speaking to Daniel declares that he "arose to be an encouragement and a protection for him [וֹל, *ol*]." Many commentators hold that the "him" is not Darius, but Michael the archangel. Lucas argues, "11:1a has the function of identifying the angel who has been speaking as Gabriel (cf. 9:1). The second half of the verse says that in the first year of Darius the Mede, the speaker (Gabriel) strengthened Michael. This presumably relates to the downfall of Babylon, which resulted in at least some amelioration in the fortunes of the Judeans."[4] Miller asserts, "In 10:13, 21 it is revealed that Michael had helped the interpreting angel; now in 11:1 Gabriel related that he had supported and protected Michael."[5] Young makes the same kind of claim: "The Speaker now relates how He had previously been a help to Michael. During the first year of Darius, when the overthrow of Babylonia by

3. Wood, *Daniel*, 280.

4. Lucas, *Daniel*, 278.

5. Miller, *Daniel*, 289.

Medo-Persia was effected, the Speaker had furnished to Michael the aid and support which he needed. *I stood up*]—lit., my standing up, *Unto him*]—not unto Darius (H) but unto Michael."[6]

Apparently the only justification for the association of this man in chapter 11 with Gabriel in chapter 9 is the similarity of the introductory statements regarding the first year of Darius the Mede. Yet there is no statement in chapter 9 concerning any aid Gabriel might have given to Michael, nor is Michael mentioned in chapter 9. Additionally, *prima facie* the grammar of the sentence seems naturally to make the antecedent of the pronoun "him" to be "Darius the Mede" (see Table 48).

Table 48: Daniel 11:1

אַחַת	בִּשְׁנַת	וַאֲנִי
one	in year	And I
עָמְדִי	עָמְדִי	עָמְדִי
I stood	the Mead	to Darius
	Antecedent of "him" is Darius	
לוֹ׃	וּלְמָעוֹז	לְמַחֲזִיק
to him.	and encouragement	for strengthening

Although the grammar seems to be a strong argument in favor of taking the antecedent of "him" in verse 1 to be Darius, Walvoord's analysis cannot be lightly dismissed on the basis of the grammar alone.

> The statement that the angel "stood" in verse 1 is probably used in *sensu bellico s. militari*, that is, standing as in a military conflict against the enemy, as in 10:13. His stand is usually taken as being in support of Darius the Mede, "to confirm and strengthen him," but it is possible that "him" refers not to Darius the Mede—for the angel must fight against the prince of Persia (10:13)—but to Michael, the prince of Israel, on whose side he contends (10:21). In the first year of Darius the Mede when the world power passed from the Babylonian to the Medo-Persian, the angel stood by Michael, the guardian of Israel, until he succeeded in turning the

---

6. Young, *Prophecy of Daniel*, 231.

new kingdom from hostility to favor toward Israel. The story of chapter 6 demonstrates that efforts were made in the first year of Darius to make him hostile toward Israel. But God sent His angel on that occasion and shut the lions' mouths (Dan 6:22). The miraculous deliverance by the angel caused Darius the Mede to reverse his policies to favor Israel (6:24–27). The beginning of the second great empire with the fall of Babylon in chapter 5 was, then, more than a military conquest or triumph of the armies of the Medes and Persians. It was a new chapter in the divine drama of angelic warfare behind the scenes, and the change was by divine appointment.[7]

Walvoord's analysis seems to be supported by the behind-the-scenes view given to Daniel in chapter 10 concerning the spiritual warfare. The prince of Persia was no doubt attempting to influence the kings of Persia against the people of Israel, and, according to Walvoord, this man tells Daniel how, in the first year of Darius the Mede, he came to strengthen and be an encouragement to Michael in his efforts to sway Darius to a favorable disposition toward the people of Israel. Going back to fight against the prince of Persia implies that he will endeavor to influence the kings of Persia to favor Israel rather than persecute them. Such a notion would seem to be an important aspect of comfort to Daniel since he is most probably aware of the hardships facing his people in the land.

Notwithstanding the argument of Walvoord, almost the same argument can be used to support the notion that the "he" is Darius, not Michael. In chapter 10 the description of the spiritual warfare seems to imply that it was Gabriel who needed the assistance and protection given by Michael, not the other way around. This seems especially to be the case since in 10:13 Gabriel refers to Michael as "one of the chief princes" and that Michael "came to help me" as Gabriel withstood the Prince of Persia. The angel may not have been there to strengthen Michael, but rather to strengthen and protect Darius as he was being influenced by the prince of Persia and to serve to persuade Darius to support Daniel and Daniel's people. In fact, the events of chapter 6 indicate that Darius was already disposed to favor Daniel and his people, but was being manipulated by his administrators. Gabriel perhaps was there to strengthen Darius in the face of this evil influence and manipulation and to provide Darius an opportunity to rid himself of these evil administrators and to save and exalt Daniel.

---

7. Walvoord, *Daniel*, 255.

THREE MORE KINGS

2—   And now I will tell you the truth. Behold, three more kings are going to arise in Persia. Then a fourth will gain far more riches than all of them; as soon as he becomes strong through his riches, he will arouse the whole empire against the realm of Greece.

The angel tells Daniel that there will be three more kings in Persia and a fourth that will be very prosperous. Since the prophecy is given to Daniel in the third year of Cyrus, and since the angel states that these kings are "yet to arise" (עוֹד שְׁלֹשָׁה מְלָכִים עֹמְדִים, *m̲udmoʿ m̲ikaleʿm hằšolʿs doʿ*) this statement probably does not include Cyrus. Since there were in fact more than four kings that followed Cyrus, critical scholars have used this statement to charge the text with error. However, Young responds, "It is perfectly true that there were more than four kings after Cyrus. The fact that the writer mentions but four kings is not that he knew of only four (Hitzig) but apparently because he wishes to lay stress upon four important epochs which will follow that of Cyrus."[8] It is important to note that the man does not say there will be *only* four kings to arise. Rather he simply says there will be four, and if there were more than four, there were certainly four. Most conservative commentators identify these kings as Cambyses, son of Cyrus (529–522), Pseudo-Smerdis (522–521), Darius I Hystaspes (521–486), and Xerxes I (486–465).[9] In fact, the angel's reference to three more kings and a fourth is simply a reference to the immediately following kings, not to those who come after these four.

Table 49: Approximate Dates for Kings of Medo-Persia

539–537	Darius the Mede (or Cyrus)
538–529	Cyrus
529–522	Cambyses
522–521	Pseudo-Smerdis
521–486	Darius I the Great (Hystaspes)
486–465	Xerxes II (Ahasuerus)
465–424	Artaxerxes I (Longimanus)
424	Xerxes II
423–404	Darius II Nothius (The Persian)

8. Young, *Prophecy of Daniel*, 232.

9. The reason Darius Hystaspes is identified as Darius I and not II in light of Darius the Mede is precisely because Darius the Mede is a Mede, not a Persian. Darius I is the 1st Persian Darius.

404–358	Artaxerxes II (Mnemon)
358–338	Artaxerxes III
338–335	Arses
336–331	Darius III (Codomannus)

Some scholars reject the proposal that a ruler named Darius the Mede ever existed. H. H. Rowley argues, "Despite all the efforts to find a place in history for Darius the Mede, therefore, we are compelled to recognize that he is a fictitious creation. No Median king succeeded to the control of the Babylonian kingdom, and no person answering to this Darius is known, or could be fitted into the known history of the period."[10] J. C. Whitcomb has proposed that "Darius the Mede" is another name for Gubaru, who, according to the chronicles of Nabonidus, was the general who actually led the army that captured Babylon.[11] It is possible that Cyrus rewarded Gubaru with the regional governorship of Babylon for capturing this great city. To the contrary, Miller presents convincing evidence, as we have seen, that the name "Darius the Mede" is in fact another name for Cyrus.[12] In this case, the list of Persian rulers would be slightly different. The graphic below depicts the reign of Persian kings beginning with Cyrus who became king of Medo-Persia in 559 BC. The four kings to which Daniel's prophecy refers are indicated by numbers preceding their names. Also, brief references to other events have been added to the chart in order to indicate the chronological relation of these events.

10. Rowley, *Darius the Mede*, 59.

11. John C. Whitcomb, *Darius the Mede: A Study in Historical Identification*, 1959).

12. See Rowley, *Darius the Mede*.

Figure 42: Alternate Dates for the Kings of Persia[13]

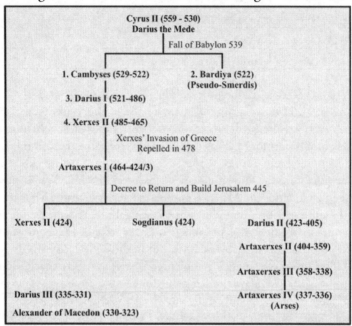

The last of the four kings to whom Daniel's prophecy refers, Xerxes I, mounted a large military campaign against Greece. As Chester Starr describes,

> To the Persians, however, Marathon served only as a warning that a larger force would be needed for what, in the king's eyes, must have seemed merely a matter of punishing a recalcitrant, not very civilized people on one of his far-flung frontiers. Darius accordingly set plans in motion for a full-scale attack but was diverted by an Egyptian revolt. After his death in 486 Xerxes (486–65) first subdued Egypt and a brief revolt in Babylonia, and then renewed preparations. In the fall of 481 he came down to Sardis, where his army assembled. Herodotus gives us the wildly inflated figure of 5,000,000 in all, including camp followers, but the actual fighting force can scarcely have been more than 150,000 or so. The Persian navy, which made itself ready in Ionian harbors, consisted of about 660 Phoenician and Ionian warships.[14]

13. This chart has been adapted from Mieroop, *History of the Ancient Near East*, 314.

14. Starr, *A History*, 285–86.

Ultimately Xerxes' army was defeated and driven out of Greece and back to their homeland. Starr goes on to describe the continued action against Persia by the Greeks: "Down to 449 the Delian league (or, as it soon became, the Athenian empire) waged war almost continuously against Persia. Throughout most of this era its main admiral was the Athenian aristocrat Cimon . . . he drove the Persians out of Europe, eliminated possible Persian Naval bases on the west coast of Asian Minor, and about 469 shattered the restored Persian fleet at the battle of Eurymedon River in Pamphylia."[15]

The angel had said that there would be four kings that would "arise" in Persia. The word translated "arise" is עֹמְדִים (*mudmo'*) from the verb עמד (*dm'*) "to stand." This same verb is used in 10:13 where the man tells Daniel that the prince of Persia was "withstanding" him. The idea here seems to indicate antagonism and has even a military sense, as Walvoord pointed out above. After the defeat of Xerxes by the Greeks, the Persians did not recover the military might to threaten the Aegean again. Soon Alexander the Great would wield the dominate military might in the Near East.

The Rise of the Grecian Empire: 11:3–4

3— "And a mighty king will arise, and he will rule with great authority and do as he pleases."

According to many scholars, the attack of Xerxes upon Greece led to the eventual revenge by Alexander the Great. Once again Starr's description captures the sense of the age: "The victories of 480–79 B.C., which checked the Persians, had been won by only a few of the Greek states under the leadership of Sparta. Yet all Greece had been saved, and many parts of the Aegean world went on in the next few decades to unparalleled heights of prosperity and culture. Above all others towered the state which had suffered most in the Persian invasions, Athens, for this was the *polis* best fitted to draw profit from the Greek triumph."[16] Many historians hold that Alexander's conquest into Persia was at least partly motivated by vengeance. As Walvoord puts it, "Alexander the Great in conquering the Persian Empire was repaying Xerxes I."[17] Also, Philip II (359–336 BC), father of Alexander, had declared war on Persia in 339. However, before he could begin his campaign, Philip was assassinated at the marriage feast of Olympias' daughter Cleopatra to Alexander, King of Epirus. Some scholars propose that Alexander's campaign against Persia was motivated by the desire to fulfill his father's unfulfilled plans.

15. Ibid., 293–94.

16. Ibid., 298.

17. Walvoord, *Daniel*, 257.

Alexander was indeed a mighty king. It is important to note here that from the defeat of Xerxes I, which most date to about 479 B.C., to the rise of Alexander the Great, who "became king at the age of 20 in 336,"[18] is a period of over 140 years. This is only one of the several chronological gaps in the biblical record. Evans observes, "It is true that the Book of Daniel sometimes skips over time from one verse to the next. For example, both Daniel 2 and 7 treat Babylonia and Nebuchadnezzar as if they were identical, thereby ignoring the interval between the death of Nebuchadnezzar and the fall of Babylon to the Medes and Persians. Also, between verses 2 and 3 in Daniel 11, there is an interval of well over a century if you accept the idea that the king of Persia 'who will be far richer than all the others' in verse 2 is Xerxes."[19] Consequently, the charge often leveled by Preterists against Futurists that historical gaps are untenable cannot be sustained from a close reading of the text in comparison to history.

The text points out that this king would "do as he pleases." The word translated "as he pleases" (כִּרְצוֹנוֹ, *oñosrik*), indicates the notion of carrying out one's own will. Starr notes, "Alexander is the first general in history whom we can see thinking out answers to his strategic problems and then doggedly executing his plans."[20] However, the text also points out that as soon as he became strong, his kingdom was broken apart.

4—   "But as soon as he has arisen, his kingdom will be broken up and parceled out toward the four points of the compass, though not to his own descendants, nor according to his authority which he wielded, for his sovereignty will be uprooted and given to others besides them."

As in earlier chapters, the prophecy reveals that Alexander's kingdom was divided. The description of the kingdom as being "broken apart" (תִּשָּׁבֵר, *rebãssit*) is an apt description of the fate of Alexander's empire: "For more than 40 years, the empire Alexander had created and held together by sheer force of personality was ripped apart in his officers' violent power struggles."[21] The expression "four points of the compass" is a figure of speech indicating that the parts were disparate and separated virtually covering the known world of his day (see Figure 43 below). The text also states that this parceling out would not be "to his own descendants." As Starr observes, "Alexander left as his heirs a half-wit half-brother and a posthumous son, born to his new Persian wife,

18. Starr, *History*, 395.

19. Evans, *Four Kingdoms*, 213.

20. Starr, *History*, 397.

21. Alan Fildes and Joann Fletcher, *Alexander the Great: Son of the Gods*, 154.

Roxane. Both were soon swept aside, along with his mother Olympias and all other members of Philip's house; for Alexander's marshals and satraps showed themselves to be extremely ambitious and also extremely able."[22] After the intrigue and power struggles, "Only four great power bases now remained, the separate kingdoms of the ruthless monarchs Ptolemy I of Egypt, Cassander of Greece, Seleucus I of Syria, and Lysimachus, who extended his Thracian territories to include western and central Asia Minor."[23]

Figure 43: Division of Alexander's Empire

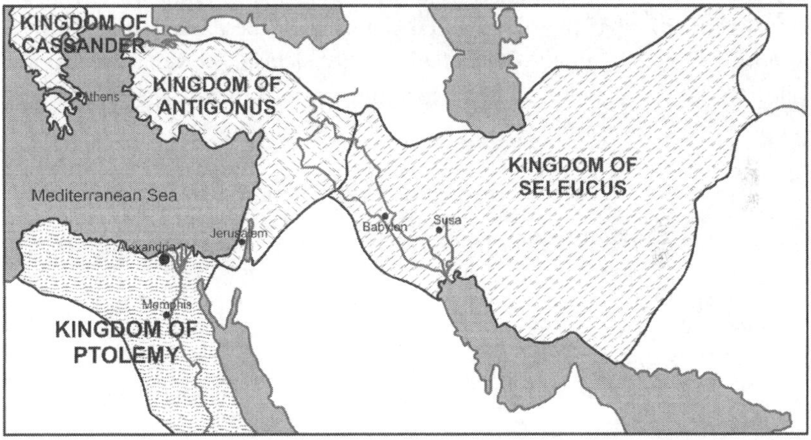

The text points out that the resulting kingdoms of Alexander's empire were not "according to his authority which he wielded" (11:4). Fildes and Fletcher point out, "Yet, as events were to prove, none of them had the ability to control an empire that stretched from Macedonia in the west to India in the east, north to the Danube and south to the borders of Nubia."[24] The two primary players, as far as Daniel's prophecy is concerned, were the Seleucids and the Ptolemys, and they become the primary focus in the succeeding prophecy. As Starr notes, "The Ptolemies and the Seleucids, thus, waged a series of Syrian wars for mastery of the coast of Syria and Palestine."[25] It is because these wars took place in the area of Israel and impacted the people of God that these two kingdoms and their incessant wars are the focus of the following prophetic section.

22. Starr, *History*, 403.

23. Fildes-Fletcher, *Alenander the Great*, 157.

24. Ibid., 154.

25. Starr, *History*, 404.

The Wars of the Divided Empire: 11:5–20

According to Miller, "Verses 5–20 comprise a history of the ongoing conflicts between two divisions of the Greek Empire, the Ptolemaic (Egyptian) and the Seleucid (Syrian), from the death of Alexander (323 B.C.) until the reign of Antiochus IV Epiphanes (175–163 B.C.)."[26] As has been noted by Miller already, "The revelation was limited to these two divisions because Palestine, the home of God's people, lay between them and was continually involved in their later history."[27] The details of this prophecy can be obtained from any reliable and detailed history of this period. The details of the prophecy are so particular that the supernatural character of the revelation is evident. The following chart (Table 50: Ptolemys and Seleucids) sets out the various rulers in the two kingdoms, their dates, and the relevant passages in Daniel's prophecy.

Table 50: Ptolemys and Seleucids

The Ptolemies and the Seleucids in Daniel 11:5–35[28]			
Ptolemies		**Seleucids**	
(Kings "of the South," Egypt)		(Kings "of the North," Syria)	
Daniel 11:5	Ptolemy I Soter (323–285 BC)*	Daniel 11:5	Seleucus I Nicator (312–281 BC)
11:6	Ptolemy II Philadelphus (285–246)		Antiochus I Soter† (281–262)
		11:6	Antiochus II Theos (262–246)
11:7–8	Ptolemy III Euergetes (246–221)	11:7–9	Seleucus II Callinicus (246–227)
		11:10	Seleucus III Soter (227–223)
11:11–12, 14–15	Ptolemy IV Philopator (221–204)	11:10–11, 13, 15–19	Antiochus III the Great (223–187)
11:17	Ptolemy V Epiphanes (204–181)		
		11:20	Seleucus IV Philopator (187–176)
11:25	Ptolemy VI Philometer (181–145)	11:21–32	Antiochus IV Epiphanes (175–163)

*The years designate the rulers' reigns.

†Not referred to in Daniel 11:5–35

---

26. Miller, *Daniel*, 292–93.

27. Ibid., 293.

28. This chart comes from Pentecost, *Daniel*, 1367.

An important observation is that, as we have pointed out, most commentators apply the prophecies down to verse 20 in the same way and to the same historical figures. In other words, the details of the prophecy are related to the historical records of the period in order to discover the most likely individuals to whom the prophecies are referring. This is an important observation because, for many interpreters, this method of relating the prophecies to history suddenly changes after verse 20 and even more so after verse 35. Whereas in these early verses, the methodology is to understand the details of the prophecy and then discover the historical figures to whom the details relate, when it comes to verses 20 and following, many commentators decide to whom the prophecy must be referring and then try to interpret the prophecy in order to make it fit the choices already made. We will see this approach in action as we begin to deal with the details of that later prophecy.

PTOLEMY I SOTER AND SELEUCUS I NICATOR: 11:5

5—   "Then the king of the South will grow strong, along with one of his princes who will gain ascendancy over him and obtain dominion; his domain will be a great dominion indeed."

Rosalie David points out that after the death of Alexander, "Ptolemy, son of Lagos, the Macedonian general in charge of troops in Egypt, became satrap of Egypt, and then, as King Ptolemy I Soter, founded the Ptolemaic Dynasty in 305 BCE. . . . The Ptolemies ruled Egypt until the death of Cleopatra VII and the fall of the country to Rome in 30 BCE."[29] Verse 5 concerns the conflicts between the "king of the South," Ptolemy I Soter, and "one of his princes," who was probably Seleucus I Nicator: "In June 323 Alexander, having created a Macedonian Empire over the whole extent of the old Persian Empire and more, died suddenly in Babylon. About five months later, one of his marshals, Ptolemy, the son of Lagus, appeared in Egypt as the satrap appointed by the new Macedonian king, Philip Arrhidaeus."[30] Seleucus I had obtained power in Babylonia, but fled to Egypt at the threat of the return of Antigonus the satrap of Phrygia who "returned from the eastern provinces in 316, victorious over the remains of the party of Perdiccas."[31] Bevan also points out, "The war with Antigonus, as far as Seleucus was concerned, falls into two phases. In the first, 315–312, Seleucus was merely a subordinate, 'one of the captains' of Ptolemy, as the book of Daniel describes him."[32] Miller adds, "Together, they

---

29. Rosalie David, *Religion and Magic in Ancient Egypt*, 319, 320.

30. Edwyn Robert Bevan, *The House of Ptolemy*, 18.

31. Ibid., 24.

32. Edwyn Robert Bevan, *The House of Seleucus*, 1.52.

[Ptolemy and Seleucus] defeated Antigonus at the Battle of Gaza in 312. After this, Seleucus regained Babylonia. Antigonus was finally defeated and killed in a battle against all the other Diadochi at Ipsus in 301. Seleucus gradually took over Antigonus' territory, extending his realm until it became the largest of the four successor kingdoms of Alexander's empire."[33] As the prophecy had declared, the king of the south, Ptolemy I, Soter, had grown strong by his allegiance with one of his princes, Seleucus. But after the defeat of Antigonus, Seleucus became stronger than Ptolemy.

After the defeat of Demetrius, one of Antigonus' generals, in Palestine near Gaza, Ptolemy gave Seleucus "a body of 800 foot and 200 horse, and with these he set out to recover his old province of Babylonia."[34] Because of his previous work in Babylon under Alexander, Seleucus entered Babylon and was gladly received by the inhabitants who remembered their old governor. Although some supporters of Antigonus resisted Seleucus, they were swiftly subdued. As Bevan states, "*This was the moment which the Seleucid kings regarded as the birthday of their Empire.*"[35]

PTOLEMY II PHILADELPHUS AND ANTIOCHUS II THEOS: 11:6

6—   "After some years they will form an alliance, and the daughter of the king of the South will come to the king of the North to carry out a peaceful arrangement. But she will not retain her position of power, nor will he remain with his power, but she will be given up, along with those who brought her in and the one who sired her as well as he who supported her in those times."

The opening phrase of verse 6 refers to the alliance that was established between Antiochus II and Ptolemy III. The pronoun "they" in this phrase is the pronominal suffix ending on the verb "will form an alliance" (יִתְחַבָּרוּ, *ūrabbaḥtiy*). The verb has the meaning, "to ally oneself" or "to join together." The Hithpael form, which is the form of this verb, indicates "to make an alliance with" or "to have a partnership with."[36] The subject, as we have said, is the pronominal suffix "they." In this instance, there is no antecedent to this pronoun. Although the prefix "ante" in the word "antecedent" means "before," grammatically an antecedent of a pronoun does not always come before the pronoun. In this instance, the pronoun looks forward in the context to the king of the South and the king of the North who are the participants in

33. Lucas, *Daniel*, 280.

34. Bevan, *The House of Seleucus*, 53.

35. Ibid., 54 (emphasis in original).

36. KBH, s.v. "חבר."

the alliance. This is a very common mode of expression. A very good example is the sometimes used phrase, "Let us dance, you and I," where the pronoun "us" looks forward rather than backward for its antecedent.

Miller describes the period intervening between the events prophesied in verse 5 and those prophesied in verse 6: "From the beginning, conflicts arose between the kingdoms of the Ptolemies (Egypt) and the Seleucids (Syria). Ptolemy I died in 285 B.C., and these clashes continued under his son Ptolemy II Philadelphus (285–246 B.C.), who according to tradition instigated the translation of the Hebrew Bible into Greek called the Septuagint. Finally, Ptolemy II made a treaty of peace with the Seleucid ruler, Antiochus II Theos (261–246 B.C.; grandson of Seleucus), about 250 B.C., and it is to this alliance that v. 6 refers."[37]

As Bevan describes,

> According to the arrangement made between Ptolemy II and Antiochus II, the former queen of Antiochus, Laodice, was to be left with her two sons in a secondary position in Asia Minor, whilst Ptolemy's daughter, Berenice, reigned at Antioch and bore children for the Seleucid inheritance. But both Laodice and Berenice were Macedonian princesses true to type. Laodice induced Antiochus to come back to her at Ephesus, and then, after Antiochus suddenly died (in 246) (not without some suspicion falling on Laodice), she sent her emissaries to Antioch to murder Berenice and her infant son. Berenice fought, we are told, like a tigress, but in vain. The double murder was accomplished. Laodice's son, Seleucus II (Kallinikos), was proclaimed king of the Seleucid realm.[38]

According to the historical records, not only were Bernice and her son assassinated, but those Egyptian attendants who had accompanied her were killed. And, as Lucas points out, "In the same year Berenice's father died."[39] As the text prophesied, "she will be given up, along with those who brought her in and the one who sired her . . ."

Ptolemy III Euregetes and Seleucus II Callinicus: 11:7–9

7—   "But one of the descendants of her line will arise in his place, and he will come against their army and enter the fortress of the king of the North, and he will deal with them and display great strength."

---

37. Miller, *Daniel*, 293.

38. Bevan, *The House of Ptolemy*, 189.

39. Lucas, *Daniel*, 280.

8—   "Also their gods with their metal images and their precious vessels of silver and gold he will take into captivity to Egypt, and he on his part will refrain from attacking the king of the North for some years."

9—   "Then he will enter the realm of the king of the South, but will return to his own land."

Verse 7 states that one of the descendants, (הָ‍שָׁרָשֶׁיהָ מִנֵּצֶר‎, rešennim ‾ahyĕšarăs), "of her line," literally, "from the offshoot of her root," will arise in "his" place. The wording of the translation is perhaps confusing and is sometimes taken to refer to one of "her" own children. But the Hebrew makes it clear that this "offshoot" is from her *root*, or from her own ancestors—not her own descendants, but a descendant of her root, in this case, her father. The "her" to whom the verse refers is Berenice, the daughter of Ptolemy II. The "descendant" is Bernice's brother, Ptolemy III Euergetes (246–221), who took over the kingdom in the place of his father, Ptolemy II Philadelphus, as Figure 44 illustrates.

Figure 44: "From the Offshoot of Her Root"

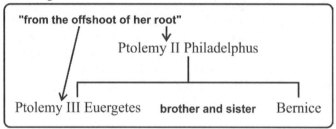

Ptolemy III invaded Syria, the king of the North, in retaliation for the murder of his sister, Berenice. In fact, Bevan states, "According to Justin, Ptolemy III marched from Egypt at the head of his army, whilst Berenice was still alive, besieged at Daphne, near Antioch, but was too late to save her."[40] Bevan goes on to explain, "Then he [Ptolemy III] opened war upon the house of Seleucus—the 'Third Syrian War' modern scholars call it; it seems to have been known at the time as the 'Laodicean War,' the war against the murderess Laodice. Ptolemy himself went forth from Egypt at the head of his army to invade Northern Syria. . . . The expedition which Ptolemy III led into Asia was the greatest military triumph ever achieved by the house of Ptolemy."[41] Lucas gives a synopsis of Ptolemy's campaigns:

40. Bevan, *The House of Ptolemy*, 191.

41. Ibid., 192–93.

He gained control of the major ports of Antioch and Seleucia, seized Syria and campaigned far to the east. Laodice fell into his hands and was killed. He took a great deal of booty, including the images of the gods that Cambyses had carried away from Egypt to Persia in 525. The Egyptians gave him the epithet *Euergetes* ('benefactor') because of this good deed of regaining their gods. However, the need to deal with an uprising in Egypt meant that he was unable to establish total control of the Seleucid Empire. When he returned to Egypt, Seleucus II was able to re-establish himself on the throne. For two years there was no further conflict between the two powers. In 242 Seleucus II was strong enough to mount an invasion of Egypt, but was eventually forced to withdraw.[42]

Interestingly, Miller seems to contradict Lucas' account of the activity of Seleucus II. Miller asserts, "For both grammatical and historical reasons, it is best to take 'the king of the North' as the subject of v. 9 rather than 'the king of the South.' There is no record that Seleucus II ever attempted an invasion of Egypt proper. Evidently this campaign was brief with a swift 'retreat' to Syria."[43] However, Miller's assertion is confusing. On the one hand he says there is no historical record that Seleucus II ever invaded Egypt proper, and on the other hand he asserts that the campaign was "brief with a swift 'retreat' to Syria." Perhaps what Miller is saying is that Seleucus II did mount a campaign against Egypt that never actually penetrated "Egypt proper." Miller's objection is primarily directed against the KJV translation of verse 9: "So the king of the south shall come into *his* kingdom, and shall return into his own land." The text reads,

Table 51: Daniel 11:9

הַנֶּגֶב	מֶלֶךְ	בְּמַלְכוּת	וּבָא
the South	[44]the king of	in the kingdom of	And he will come

אַדְמָתוֹ:	אֶל־	וְשָׁב
his land.	to	and return

42. Lucas, *Daniel*, 280.

43. Miller, *Daniel*, 294.

44. Although there is no definite article on the word 'king' (מֶלֶךְ, *kelem*), Hebrew syntax requires the definite.

Although there is no definite article on the word "king" (מֶ֫לֶךְ, *kelem*), Hebrew syntax requires the definite article. This is because, as we discussed in chapter 9, the word "king" is in a construct relation with the word "the South" (הַנֶּ֫גֶב, *begennah*), and since this second word does have the definite article, this makes the first word, "king," definite. Miller is certainly correct that the subject of this verse is "the king of the North." The reference to the king of the South is grammatically part of the object of the preposition "in" and cannot be the subject of the verb "will come." However, after close examination, it appears that perhaps Miller and Lucas are nevertheless referring to the same event, namely, Seleucus' attempt to invade Egypt which was thwarted and forced him to retreat before actually penetrating Egypt itself. Prior to the campaign of Seleucus II in 242, Ptolemy II had himself captured the land of Palestine and was besieging Damascus. According to Bevan, "In 242–241 the Seleucid counter-attack had apparently reached so far south that the Seleucus was able to deliver Damascus and Orthosia (on the Phoenician coast), which were being besieged by Egyptian forces. But an attempt of Seleucus to penetrate farther south into Palestine itself led to his meeting with a disastrous defeat. Soon after this the two Powers signed a peace (about 240 B.C.)."[45] The text says the king of the North "will enter the realm of the king of the South." This included the outlying areas over which the king of the South had authority, including Palestine as far north as Damascus, but not actually part of Egypt itself.

ANTIOCHUS III, PTOLEMY IV PHILOPATOR, AND PTOLEMY V EPIPHANES: 11:10–19

10—   "His sons will mobilize and assemble a multitude of great forces; and one of them will keep on coming and overflow and pass through, that he may again wage war up to his very fortress."

The text makes reference to "his sons." These are Seleucus III Ceraunus, who succeeded his father Seleucus II in 226, and Antiochus III, The Great, who came to power after Seleucus III in 223. Seleucus III was murdered while on campaign in Asia Minor. "Initially, Antiochus had to deal with revolts in Media and Asia Minor. When Ptolemy IV, renowned as a weak character, came to the throne in 222, Antiochus saw his chance to regain the territory lost to his father in Syria."[46] Miller notes that Antiochus III "was called the 'Great' because of his military successes, and in 219–218 B.C. he campaigned

---

45. Bevan, *The House of Ptolemy*, 204.

46. Lucas, *Daniel*, 280.

in Phoenicia and Palestine, part of the Ptolemaic Empire ('as far as his [the king of the South's] fortresses')."[47]

11—   "The king of the South will be enraged and go forth and fight with the king of the North. Then the latter will raise a great multitude, but that multitude will be given into the hand of the former."

12—   "When the multitude is carried away, his heart will be lifted up, and he will cause tens of thousands to fall; yet he will not prevail."

Although Ptolemy IV was a man of weak character, he attempted to retaliate against Antiochus' re-capture of the lands in Palestine. Antiochus had recaptured much of Palestine and was, according to Bevan, prepared to make an immediate invasion of Egypt. "But accounts received of the Egyptian muster at Pelusium to secure the frontier made him [Antiochus] defer an enterprise which had baffled the companions of Alexander, Perdiccas and Antigonus."[48] Rather than invade, Antiochus proposed to finish the conquest of Palestine, but, as Bevan goes on to point out, "It was, however, in reality a false move. Egypt was in a state of utter unpreparedness, and an immediate attack would probably have succeeded."[49]

It was during the time when Antiochus was finishing his conquest of Palestine that Ptolemy raised a large army and, after the winter, contended with Antiochus at Raphia, a town in the present Gaza Strip on what was at that time the Egyptian border about 50 miles west-southwest of Jerusalem. The Battle of Raphia is also known as the Battle of Gaza. Lucas reports, "According to Polybius (*Hist.* 5.79), Ptolemy had 70,000 infantry, 5,000 cavalry and 73 elephants, and Antiochus had 62,000 infantry, 6,000 cavalry and 103 elephants. Antiochus' 'multitude' was defeated (he lost some 17,000 men) by Ptolemy's (who lost about 2,200 men). Ptolemy was euphoric at this great victory, but, although he regained Palestine and southern Syria (south of the river Eleutherus), he did not press his advantage any further, but made peace with Antiochus. According to Polybius (*Hist.* 14.12.3–4), he preferred to give himself over 'to a life of abandonment.'"[50] Antiochus and Ptolemy agreed to a truce of one year, but Antiochus now faced the prospects of possible rebellion once news of his defeat reached back home. As a result, he made all haste to return to his home country.

---

47. Miller, *Daniel*, 294.
48. Bevan, *The House of Seleucus*, 1.314.
49. Ibid.
50. Lucas, *Daniel*, 281.

13—   "For the king of the North will again raise a greater multitude than the former, and after an interval of some years he will press on with a great army and much equipment."

Ptolemy's victory and the peace that was established between him and Antiochus did not last very long. As Miller describes it, "Approximately fifteen years later (202 B.C.) Antiochus III again invaded Ptolemaic territories with a huge army. The occasion for this invasion was the death of Ptolemy IV in 203 B.C. and the crowning of his young son (between four and six years of age), Ptolemy V Epiphanes (203–181 B.C.), as the new king. Antiochus III took full advantage of the opportunity and attacked Phoenicia and Palestine; by 201 B.C. the fortress in Gaza had fallen to the Syrians."[51] According to Bevan, "Antiochus had not ceased since his repulse at Raphia to burn for a renewal of the contest with the house of Ptolemy,"[52] and, although there is very little information available on Antiochus' invasion, it eventually issued in the transference of Palestine from the power of the Ptolemies to the rule of Antiochus.

14—   "Now in those times many will rise up against the king of the South; the violent ones among your people will also lift themselves up in order to fulfill the vision, but they will fall down."

The king of the North will once again make war against the king of the South. These players are Antiochus III and Ptolemy V. However, there is some controversy about who are the "violent ones among your people." Lucas describes the confusion over this passage:

> It is unclear exactly to what v. 14b refers. According to Josephus (*Ant.* 12.3.3–4), the Jews in Jerusalem at this time were divided into pro-Ptolemaic and pro-Seleucid factions. . . . What is not clear is which group is meant by "the violent among your people." Some have seen it as a reference to pro-Seleucid Jews who joined in resistance to Ptolemy V before and during Antiochus' campaign. But it is then hard to see why they are said to "fail," since, despite one setback, his campaign was a success. If military action is in mind, then the phrase is more likely to refer to a pro-Ptolemaic group. In either case, it is not clear what the "vision" is that they are seeking to establish.[53]

---

51. Miller, *Daniel*, 295.
52. Bevan, *The House of Seleucus*, 2.29.
53. Lucas, *Daniel*, 281–82.

By contrast, Miller seems certain that the "violent ones" refers to "those Jews who aided Antiochus," and he references the same passage in Josephus to which Lucas makes reference—*Antiquities* 12.3.3.[54] Miller argues that the "vision" is this prophecy in Daniel:

> These Israelites "will rebel" against Egypt (or against God) "in ful-fillment of the vision," evidently the prophecy recorded here. Of course, the fulfillment of the prediction was not the intention of these persons, but it was nevertheless the result. "But without suc-cess" reads literally, "But they [those who sided with Antiochus] will fall." Although General Scopas of the Egyptian forces was ultimately defeated, he punished the leaders of Jerusalem and Judah who rebelled against the Ptolemaic government. Scopas's squelching of such a Jewish uprising against Egypt may have been suggested by Polybius.[55]

Miller's treatment seems to answer Lucas' confusion about how to ex-plain the text's reference that the supporters of Antiochus would "fail." In fact, Josephus describes the people of Israel as being at the mercy of the two great forces, "so that they were very like to a ship in a storm, which is tossed by the waves on both sides; and just thus were they in their situation in the middle between Antiochus's prosperity and its change to adversity."[56] Josephus goes on to describe how once Antiochus had driven Scopas from Palestine, "the Jews, of their own accord, went over to him, and received him into the city [Jerusalem], and gave plentiful provision to all his army, and to his elephants, and readily assisted him when he besieged the garrison which was in the citadel of Jerusalem."[57] Bevan also notes that "the bulk of its [Jerusalem's] population . . . received Antiochus with open arms."[58] This certainly seems to indicate that the Jews were all along pro-Seleucid.

Also, the word to which Lucas refers does not necessarily mean "to fail." The word is וְנִכְשָׁל֑וּ (*ûlǎškin^ew*), from the verb כָּשַׁל (*lǎšak*). According to KBH, the word has the meaning "to stumble, stagger."[59] In fact, KBH does

54. Miller, *Daniel*, 295, n54.

55. Ibid.

56. Josephus, *Antiquities*, 12.3.3.130. ὥστ᾽ οὐδὲν ἀπέλειπον χειμαζουμένης νεὼς καὶ πονουμένης ἑκατέρωθεν ὑπὸ τοῦ κλύδωνος, μεταξὺ τῆς εὐπραγίας τῆς Ἀν-τιόχου καὶ τῆς ἐπὶ θάτερον αὐ τοῦ ῥοπῆς τῶν πραγμάτων κείμενοι.

57. Ibid., 12.3.3.133. ἑκουσίως αὐτῷ προσέθεντο οἱ Ἰουδαῖοι καὶ τῇ πόλει δεξάμενοι πάσῃ αὐτοῦ τῇ τε στρατιᾷ καὶ τοῖς ἐλέφασιν ἀφθονίαν παρέσχον, καὶ τοὺς ὑπὸ Σκόπα καταλειφθέντας ἐν τῇ ἄκρᾳ τῶν Ἱεροσολύμων φρουροὺς πολιορκοῦντι προθύμως συνεμάχησαν.

58. Bevan, *The House of Seleucus*, 2.37.

59. KBH, s.v., "כשל."

not list "fail" as one of the possible meanings. The passage, then, does not necessarily say they failed. Rather, it may simply be saying they stumbled and staggered although they did not fall, and Josephus' description of Israel as suffering with the prosperity and adversity of Antiochus fits the description of stumbling and staggering but ultimately surviving. Miller's position seems closer to what the text indicates in this instance and closer to Josephus' account.

15— "Then the king of the North will come, cast up a siege ramp and capture a well-fortified city; and the forces of the South will not stand their ground, not even their choicest troops, for there will be no strength to make a stand."

In 199 BC, the leader of the Egyptian forces was a General Scopas who attempted to retaliate against Antiochus. According to Schäfer, "In the winter of 201/200 BCE, the Ptolemaic general Scopas attempted a counterattack. He succeeded in retaking the southern part of the province and apparently also reached Jerusalem which, following Hyrcanus' retreat, was a pro-Seleucid stronghold and so could hardly have been spared."[60] However, Scopas was pushed back and retreated to the city of Sidon—"a well-fortified city." Antiochus laid siege against the city and forced Scopas to surrender in 198 BC. Scopas returned to Egypt, but retained great power. "He conceived the design of a *coup d'qqtat* which would place him in supreme power."[61] However, Aristomenes had him arrested, and "Scopas, together with a number of his associates, was executed by poison."[62]

16— "But he who comes against him will do as he pleases, and no one will be able to withstand him; he will also stay for a time in the Beautiful Land, with destruction in his hand."

According Lucas, "With Scopas' surrender, Antiochus III became the master of the whole of Palestine, including Jerusalem and Judea, which from then on were in the Seleucid sphere of influence."[63] As Miller points out, "This fact is extremely important because it sets the stage for the reign of terror to follow under the Syrian Greek ruler Antiochus IV Epiphanes."[64] It seems that in a sense, this is one reason for the prophetic descriptions up

60. Schäfer, *The History of the Jews*, 24.
61. Bevan, *The House of Ptolemy*, 259.
62. Ibid.
63. Lucas, *Daniel*, 282.
64. Miller, *Daniel*, 296.

to this point. The history is leading up to this "despicable person" (נִבְזֶה, *hezbin*), Antiochus Epiphanes.

17—   "He will set his face to come with the power of his whole kingdom, bringing with him a proposal of peace which he will put into effect; he will also give him the daughter of women to ruin it. But she will not take a stand for him or be on his side.'"

The concern of Antiochus III about the fact that Rome seemed to be growing as a threat moved him to make peace with Ptolemy V, ruler of Egypt at the time. The text states that he "put into effect" the proposal of peace, and as Miller says, "Backed by Antiochus's army, the Syrians forced terms of peace ('an alliance') upon the Egyptian king."[65] To help establish a permanent alliance, Antiochus "made peace with the seventeen year-old Ptolemy V Epiphanies and in 194/193 BCE gave him his daughter Cleopatra's hand in marriage."[66] One of Antiochus' goals was to gain more influence and power over the Egyptian government by means of his daughter. However, she did not remain loyal to her father. Rather, as Lucas describes, "She became staunchly loyal to her husband, even encouraging an alliance between Egypt and Rome against her father. So his plans did 'not succeed, or come about for him.'"[67]

18—   "Then he will turn his face to the coastlands and capture many. But a commander will put a stop to his scorn against him; moreover, he will repay him for his scorn."

19—   "So he will turn his face toward the fortresses of his own land, but he will stumble and fall and be found no more."

Antiochus' victories propel him to press his advantage, but his advantage is soon taken away. He is killed by an angry mob in 187 BC. Once again Lucas provides a helpful summary of the history corresponding to the prophecy of these verses.

> Despite the peace treaty, Antiochus overran other Egyptian-held areas of the coast of Asia Minor. Philip V of Macedon's power had waned, and Antiochus took advantage of this to occupy Macedonian possessions in Asia Minor and even across the Hellespont in Thrace. Despite warnings from Rome not to attack Greece, he went ahead with an invasion in 192, and was soundly defeated by the Romans at Thermopylae in 191. The Romans then

65. Ibid.
66. Schäfer, *The History of the Jews*, 33.
67. Lucas, *Daniel*, 282.

drove him east of the Taurus Mountains by inflicting on him a
crushing defeat at the Battle of Magnesia in 190. The 'commander'
who did this and so 'put an end to his insolence' was Lucius Scipio.
Antiochus was forced to accept humiliating peace terms at the
Treaty of Apamea in 189. He became a vassal of Rome, and had
to send twenty hostages to Rome (including his son, the future
Antiochus IV) and pay a huge indemnity. Humiliated and short of
funds, he had to return to his 'strongholds' in Syria, Mesopotamia
and lands to the east.[68]

Antiochus III the Great had pressed the Seleucid Empire to its greatest
extent in its history. He had retaken much of Syria and was occupying the
territories of Greece almost to the point of reconstructing the empire as it
had been under Alexander. According to Bevan, "At his accession the Empire
had touched the lowest point of decline; last year it touched its zenith. But
Antiochus seemed born too late, when already a new competitor had entered
the field."[69] Rome had dealt a blow against the Seleucid Empire from which it
would not recover to its previous heights.

SELEUCUS PHILOPATOR AND THE JEWS

20—   "Then in his place one will arise who will send an oppressor through
the Jewel of his kingdom; yet within a few days he will be shattered,
though not in anger nor in battle."

Seleucus Philopator (187–175 BC) is included in this historical material
because of, as Walvoord says, "his oppression by taxation of the people of
Israel."[70] Walvoord goes on to explain, "Because of the rising power of Rome,
he was forced to pay tribute to the Romans of a thousand talents annually. In
order to raise this large amount of money, Seleucus had to tax all the lands
under his domain, including special taxes from the Jews secured by a tax
collector named Heliodorus (2 Mac 3:7) who took treasures from the temple
at Jerusalem."[71] Second Maccabees records how a manifestation from God
prevented Heliodorus from plundering the temple.

> 22 While they were calling upon the Almighty Lord that he would
> keep what had been entrusted safe and secure for those who had
> entrusted it, 23 Heliodorus went on with what had been decided.
> 24 But when he arrived at the treasury with his bodyguard, then

68. Ibid., 282–83.
69. Bevan, *The House of Seleucus*, 87.
70. Walvoord, *Daniel*, 263.
71. Ibid., 263–64.

and there the Sovereign of spirits and of all authority caused so great a manifestation that all who had been so bold as to accompany him were astounded by the power of God, and became faint with terror. 25 For there appeared to them a magnificently caparisoned horse, with a rider of frightening mien; it rushed furiously at Heliodorus and struck at him with its front hoofs. Its rider was seen to have armor and weapons of gold. 26 Two young men also appeared to him, remarkably strong, gloriously beautiful and splendidly dressed, who stood on either side of him and flogged him continuously, inflicting many blows on him. 27 When he suddenly fell to the ground and deep darkness came over him, his men took him up, put him on a stretcher, 28 and carried him away—this man who had just entered the aforesaid treasury with a great retinue and all his bodyguard but was now unable to help himself. They recognized clearly the sovereign power of God. (2 Macc 3:22–28)[72]

Seleucus did not die at the hands of an angry mob or in battle. As Wood describes, "He died quite mysteriously, almost surely by assassination, and probably through poisoning. His only son, Demetrius Soter, had been taken as hostage to Rome, when Heliodorus, his prime minister, evidently sought for the throne himself by committing the act."[73] Schäfer claims, "Seleucus IV was assassinated by that same chancellor Heliodorus whom he had sent to Jerusalem to confiscate the Temple treasury, and his brother Antiochus returned from Rome to become head of state in 175 BCE as Antiochus IV

---

72. 22 οἱ μὲν οὖν ἐπεκαλοῦντο τὸν παγκρατῆ κύριον τὰ πεπιστευμένα τοῖς πεπιστευκόσιν σῶα διαφυλάσσειν μετὰ πάσης ἀσφαλείας 23 ὁ δὲ Ἡλιόδωρος τὸ διεγνωσμένον ἐπετέλει 24 αὐτόθι δὲ αὐτοῦ σὺν τοῖς δορυφόριος κατὰ τὸ γαζοφυλάκιον ἤδη παρόντος ὁ τῶν πνευμάτων καὶ πάσης ἐξουσίας δυνάστης ἐπιφάνειαν μεγάλην ἐποίησεν ὥστε πάντας τοὺς κατατολμήσαντας συνελθεῖν καταπλαγέντας τὴν τοῦ θεοῦ δύναμιν εἰς ἔκλυσιν καὶ δειλίαν τραπῆναι 25 ὤφθη γάρ τις ἵππος αὐτοῖς φοβερὸν ἔχων τὸν ἐπιβάτην καὶ καλλίστῃ σαγῇ διακεκοσμημένος φερόμενος δὲ ῥύδην ἐνέσεισεν τῷ Ἡλιοδώρῳ τὰς ἐμπροσθίους ὁπλὰς ὁ δὲ ἐπικαθήμενος ἐφαίνετο χρυσῆν πανοπλίαν ἔχων 26 ἕτεροι δὲ δύο προσεφάνησαν αὐτῷ νεανίαι τῇ ῥώμῃ μὲν ἐκπρεπεῖς κάλλιστοι δὲ τὴν δόξαν διαπρεπεῖς δὲ τὴν περιβολὴν οἳ καὶ περιστάντες ἐξ ἑκατέρου μέρους ἐμαστίγουν αὐτὸν ἀδιαλείπτως πολλὰς ἐπιρριπτοῦντες αὐτῷ πληγάς 27 ἄφνω δὲ πεσόντα πρὸς τὴν γῆν καὶ πολλῷ σκότε περιχυθέντα συναρπάσαντες καὶ εἰς φορεῖον ἐνθέντες 28 τὸν ἄρτι μετὰ πολλῆς παραδρομῆς καὶ πάσης δορυφορίας εἰς τὸ προειρημένον εἰσελθόντα γαζοφυλάκιον ἔφερον ἀβοήθητον ἑαυτῷ καθεστὼς τὴν τοῦ θεοῦ δυναστείαν ἐπεγνωκότες (2 Mac 3:22–28).

73. Wood, *Daniel*, 294.

Epiphanes."[74] No doubt this intrigue is why Miller adds that this act was "possibly abetted by Antiochus IV."[75]

Prophecy Concerning Antiochus IV Epiphanes: 11:21–35

The Rise of Antiochus: 11:21–24

Most commentators hold that the ruler who is the primary focus of the section beginning in verse 21 is Antiochus IV Epiphanes who ruled in Syria from 175 to 164 BC. He is none other than the little horn of chapter 8. More space is dedicated to this ruler than to any of the previous rulers. The reason for his significance is his persecution of the Jews and his desecration of the temple in Jerusalem.

21—   "In his place a despicable person will arise, on whom the honor of kingship has not been conferred, but he will come in a time of tranquility and seize the kingdom by intrigue."

The text declares that in place of Seleucus IV Philopator, "a despicable person will arise." Accord to TWOT, the word translated "despicable" (נִבְזֶה, hezbin), from the root בָּזָה (hzb), is used to show "that disobedience to the Lord is based on 'contempt, despising' of him. . . . A person who despises the Lord is devious in his ways (Prov. 14:2)."[76] This one will be despised. According to Wood, "He was considered to be a schemer and untrustworthy. He came to call himself 'Epiphanes,' meaning 'the manifest one' or 'illustrious'; but others did not so think of him, giving instead the substitute nickname 'Epimanes,' meaning 'madman.'"[77]

The text not only calls him "despicable," but states, "on whom the honor of kingship has not been conferred." The word "honor" (הוֹד, ôoh) indicates the majesty and splendor that goes with the position of king. Antiochus was not given this position but rather seized it by intrigue, as Lucas explains.

> The exact details of Antiochus IV's route to the throne are not clear (see Mørkholm 1966: 38–50). Just before his death, Seleucus IV sent his eldest son, Demetrius, to Rome as a hostage in place of Antiochus IV. Antiochus IV was in Athens when Seleucus was mur-

---

74. Schäfer, *The History of the Jews*, 35.

75. Miller, *Daniel*, 297.

76. TWOT, s.v. "בָּזָה."

77. Wood, *Daniel*, 294.

dered. Demetrius was the legal heir to the throne, but Heliodorus seized it, ostensibly on behalf of Seleucus' younger son, Antiochus. When Antiochus IV appeared with an army, raised with the help of Eumenes of Pergamum, Heliodorus fled. Antiochus IV assumed the throne, nominally as regent for his nephew Demetrius, with his other nephew, Antiochus, as co-regent. This younger nephew was murdered in 170. This is the background to what is said of him in v. 20. He was not the rightful heir to the throne (20a). By taking swift action, he thwarted Heliodorus' designs on the throne (20b), which he took over initially by the fiction of claiming to act as regent (20c).[78]

Bevan adds, "Antiochus seems to have proceeded with a mixture of calculated mildness and equally calculated bloodshed."[79] Antiochus' scheming can be seen in how he rids himself of one of his rivals, the son of Seleucus. Apparently Antiochus hired an assassin, Andronicus, who killed the child, but then Antiochus turned on him and put him to death for the crime.[80]

22—   "The overflowing forces will be flooded away before him and shattered, and also the prince of the covenant."

Wood explains that the initial phrase of verse 22, "The overflowing forces will be flooded away before him and shattered," has the sense, "armies of those who would invade Syria as an overflowing stream will in turn be overflowed by Antiochus."[81] This is probably a general reference to the kinds of campaigns Antiochus conducted and his successes. Antiochus was able to consolidate his power in Syria and build a large army that swept away opposition, an accomplishment that did not escape the notice of Rome. Antiochus was able to convince Rome that he was "absolutely at the command of Rome. And meanwhile he was quietly contravening the stipulations of the Peace, and new ships of war were being built in the Phoenician docks."[82]

There is a debate about the referent to the description "the prince of the covenant," which in the text reads, נְגִיד בְּרִית *(nreb digen)*. The word translated "prince" is not the same word that is used throughout chapter 10 (רֹאשׁ, *rás*), but it is the same word used for "Messiah the prince" in 9:25 (מָשִׁיחַ נָגִיד, *dıgan haïsam*) and also for "the coming prince" in 9:26 (נָגִיד הַבָּא, *'abah dıgan*). Miller holds that this prince is Ptolemy, "because

78. Lucas, *Daniel*, 283.

79. Bevan, *The House of Seleucus*, 2.127.

80. Ibid., 2.128.

81. Wood, *Daniel*, 295.

82. Bevan, *The House of Seleucus*, 2.134.

he agreed (made a covenant) to become an ally of Antiochus if the Syrians would help him regain his throne in Egypt, which had been taken by his younger brother, Ptolemy VII Euergetes II (Physcon)."[83] Wood holds this view as possible, stating, "The identity of this person, noted in particular as being 'overwhelmed,' is not clear. Reference may be to the king of Egypt at this time, Ptolemy Philometor. . . . In support of this possibility is the propriety of calling him 'prince of the covenant' because of the agreement, noted above, made between his father and the father of Antiochus."[84]

By contrast, Walvoord asserts, "The reference to the 'prince of the covenant' prophesies the murder of the High priest Onias, which was ordered by Antiochus in 172 B.C., and indicates the troublesome times of his reign. The high priest bore the title 'prince of the covenant' because he was *de facto* the head of the theocracy at that time. In 11:28 and 11:32 the 'covenant' is used for the Jewish state."[85] This view is held by Montgomery, Young, and Lucas as well. Goldingay sees this view as a possibility also. Having entertained the possibility of the prince referring to Ptolemy, Wood ultimately opts for Onias III. Almost all commentators who hold this view object to the alternate view on the basis of the fact that one would expect Ptolemy to be referred to as "the king of the South," which has been the consistent mode of reference thus far. It seems problematic to suppose that, without any specific explanation, the angel would have expected Daniel to recognize this title "prince of the covenant" as referring to Ptolemy on the basis of an agreement of which Daniel would have had no knowledge. It is much more likely that Daniel would have recognized the title "prince of the covenant" as a reference to the high priest. Walvoord's position seems more likely for this reason.[86]

23—   "After an alliance is made with him he will practice deception, and he will go up and gain power with a small force of people."

There is some disagreement about whether verse 23 refers to specific events or is a general observation about the character of Antiochus' reign. Walvoord takes the verse as indicating the general character of Antiochus' reign, and, according to Lucas, "The general statements in vv. 22a and 24c favour this, and what is said here is typical of him. He made alliances, but kept

83. Miller, *Daniel*, 299.

84. Wood, *Daniel*, 295.

85. Walvoord, *Daniel*, 265.

86. Schäfer points out that Josephus probably has the chronology regarding Onias incorrect since he places it under the time of Menelaus about two and one-half years later. As a result, Bevan, following Josephus, puts this event at the time of Menelaus. The chronology of the events surrounding Onias' death is, according to Schäfer, a hotly debated issue. See Schäfer, *The History of the Jews*, 37, 59.n28.

them only as long as they suited him. He began with only limited support (from Pergamum). There is ample evidence both of his avarice (as we shall see in his dealings with the Jews) and his prodigality towards his supporters or those whose support he wanted."[87] Concerning the statement, "he will go up," Young claims, "not to Palestine and Syria, nor up the Nile to Memphis but rather a general statement of the king's rise to power," and Young holds that the reference to "the small force of people" or "small nation" (בִּמְעַט־גּוֹי, *ŷog taʿmib*) is a "description of the size of the Syrian nation itself."[88]

Bevan relates the account of a Greek festival of "triumphal games" celebrating the conqueror of Macedonia at which Antiochus received certain ambassadors from Rome. These ambassadors were "on the watch for some sign of ill-will in the Seleucid King, some coolness in their entertainment. But never had Antiochus been more genial and charming. He put his own palace at their disposal, he surrounded them with the state of kings. They returned declaring that it was incredible that this man could be cherishing any serious designs. There were few who could cover so deadly a hate with such disarming manners."[89] Such was the kind of deception Antiochus was skilled at practicing.

24— "In a time of tranquility he will enter the richest parts of the realm, and he will accomplish what his fathers never did, nor his ancestors; he will distribute plunder, booty, and possessions among them, and he will devise his schemes against strongholds, but only for a time."

Most commentators hold that the "time of tranquility" when Antiochus enters "the richest parts of the realm" refers to his tactic of pouncing when least expected. Some commentators, e.g., Pentecost and Wood, propose that this refers to Antiochus attacking the rich provinces of his own kingdom and redistributing the wealth. Wood says, "Apparently he would take good things from the rich districts and give them to the poor, thus building favor with the poorer people, who would have made up the majority of his populace (cf. 1 Macc. 3:29–31)."[90] Although Wood refers to the passage in 1 Maccabees, this passage does not make reference to redistributing to the poor. Rather, it simply states that Antiochus gave gifts "more lavishly than preceding kings" (1 Macc 3:30).[91] On the basis of this reference, Lucas concludes, "1 Macc.

87. Lucas, *Daniel*, 283–84.

88. Young, *Prophecy of Daniel*, 242.

89. Bevan, *The House of Seleucus*, 2.147.

90. Wood, *Daniel*, 297.

91. τὰ δόματα ἃ ἐδίδου ἔμπροσθεν δαψιλῆ χειρὶ καὶ ἐπερίσσευσεν ὑπὲρ τοὺς βασιλεῖς τοὺς ἔμπροσθεν. (1 Macc 3:30).

3:30 tells of Antiochus going on a tribute-gathering campaign in Persia . . ."
implying that the money was to pay tribute rather than to redistribute to the
poor. Miller's view seems to be unique among commentators: "Young notes
that some historical sources indicate that Antiochus gave gifts to the people.
Yet the context of this verse seems to suggest the idea of dividing the spoils of
war ('plunder, loot and wealth') with his followers rather than with the people
generally."[92] The reference is ambiguous and the historical records are not detailed enough at present to decide this question. Bevan describes Antiochus as
one who presented himself to the world as "the radiant champion and patron
of Hellenism. . . . He sustained this character abroad by bestowing magnificent presents upon the old seats of Hellenism in Asia Minor and Greece,
and by throwing open to their artists and craftsmen lucrative employment in
Syria. We may question whether any principal city did not look on some new
embellishment, a temple, an altar, a colonnade, which declared continually
the glory and the munificence of King Antiochus."[93]

The text states that Antiochus will "devise his schemes against strongholds." The word "strongholds" (מִבְצָרִים, miṟaṣbim) indicates military
fortifications. The word occurs only three times in the book of Daniel, all
of them in chapter 11 (15, 24, 39). Wood thinks this refers to Antiochus'
practice of attacking fortified places in his own kingdom "for the purpose
of weakening them. Understandably he did not want to be opposed from
within his own country by possible internal enemies when he would move
out against foreign powers."[94] By contrast, Miller holds that this is a reference
to Antiochus' "Grandiose plans to conquer 'fortresses' (in Egypt, etc.) . . ."[95]
Of course the reason for these interpretive differences is that the prophecy
is not sufficiently detailed to be able to apply it with certainty to the many
aspects of Antiochus' activities. The prophecy is fulfilled either one way or the
other, or perhaps both, but all commentators subscribe to the notion that the
statement "but only for a time" refers to the fact that Antiochus' activities will
be successful only as long as God allows, and that time is fixed. Miller quotes
a comment by Di Lella: "Regardless of his wealth and power, his military
prowess and cunning, Antiochus would not exceed the limits allotted him by
the Lord of history."[96]

92. Miller, *Daniel*, 299.

93. Bevan, *The House of Seleucus*, 2.148.

94. Wood, *Daniel*, 297.

95. Miller, *Daniel*, 299.

96. Ibid.

The Destruction of Egypt: 11:25–27

This section concerns Antiochus' war with Egypt. Miller proposes that this is a reference to Antiochus' first campaign against Egypt that took place in 169 BC: "His victory over Ptolemy VI (described in v. 22) is the subject of v. 25."[97] This view seems to be held by most commentators.

25—   "He will stir up his strength and courage against the king of the South with a large army; so the king of the South will mobilize an extremely large and mighty army for war; but he will not stand, for schemes will be devised against him."

26—   "Those who eat his choice food will destroy him, and his army will overflow, but many will fall down slain.

The description of this time by historians and commentators usually follows the pattern of noting that after making the home base firm, Antiochus prepared to invade other countries, namely Egypt. Ptolemy Philometor was king at this time. However, as Lucas makes clear, in this instance, Ptolemy was the aggressor: "When Cleopatra . . . who had been acting as regent in Egypt, died, her son Ptolemy VI was still a youth. Real power passed to two courtiers, Eulaeus and Lenaeus. They encouraged him to try to recover control of Palestine. Hearing of their plans, Antiochus prepared for battle."[98] Antiochus met Ptolemy's forces at Pelusium, and it was here that Ptolemy was defeated by treachery from his own troops. Bevan indicates that the treachery was accomplished by Antiochus' own guile: "To win Pelusium, Antiochus trusted not less to subtilty than to arms. He had already half-won the hearts of those who served King Ptolemy. In the first battle near Casius, when the horror of flight was upon the Egyptian army, Antiochus had suddenly appeared riding amongst them as an angel of deliverance and ordering his troops to hold their hand. Many of those who 'ate of the meat' of King Ptolemy deserted to the invader."[99]

Many commentators want to change the active voice verb "overflow" for a passive verb. The passive is supported by the Syriac and the Vulgate, but θ uses an active verb (κατακλύσει, *iesulkatak*), "to wash away, to over-whelm, to drown."[100] KBH indicates that the Hebrew term used here and translated "overflow" (יִשְׁטוֹף, *jotsiy* from the root שָׁטַף, *fts*) has the meaning, "to gush,

---

97. Ibid., 300.

98. Lucas, *Daniel*, 285.

99. Bevan, *The House of Seleucus*, 2.137. Bevan footnotes Dan 11:26 at this point.

100. *A Greek-English Lexicon* (1996), s.v. "κατακλύζω."

pour down," "to overflow," or "to flood over."[101] This could be a reference
to the fact that, even though Ptolemy's army was overflowing in size, many
would be killed, and the victory would ultimately belong to Antiochus.

27—   "As for both kings, their hearts will be intent on evil, and they will
           speak lies to each other at the same table; but it will not succeed, for
           the end is still to come at the appointed time."

When Antiochus defeated Ptolemy Philometor at Pelusium, Ptolemy
fled to escape capture, but was nevertheless captured by Antiochus. As Bevan
describes, "The young king [Ptolemy Philometer] was hurriedly packed on
board ship to escape, if he could, to the sacred island of Samothrace. It was
a foolish step. Ptolemy was intercepted by the Syrian vessels, and fell into
the hands of Antiochus."[102] Although Ptolemy was captured by Antiochus,
Antiochus used this as a means of gaining an entry into Egypt. As a result of
Ptolemy Philometor's retreat and capture, his brother Ptolemy Euergetes took
the throne of Egypt. This circumstance offered Antiochus the opportunity for
which he was looking: "He now represented himself as the champion of the
legitimate king against the usurping brother."[103] Antiochus convinced Ptolemy
Philometor to help him in his war against Ptolemy Euergetes by making the
former Ptolemy believe they were friends. The plan was to defeat Ptolemy
Euergetes and restore Ptolemy Philometor to his throne. However, Ptolemy
Philometor was not beguiled by Antiochus ("they will speak lies to each other
at the same table"): "He had been under no illusions as to the real purport
of his uncle's [Antiochus'] friendliness, and the suavity had been equally hol-
low on both sides."[104] No sooner had Antiochus left Ptolemy Philometer in
Memphis than he sent an emissary to his brother Ptolemy Euergetes, and the
two of them reigned together, effectively reuniting the kingdom. Antiochus'
plan did not succeed.

The final statement of verse 27 makes the point again that the time
is measured: "for the end is still to come at the appointed time" (כִּי־עֹוד
קֵץ לַמֹּועֵד: deʿommal ṣeq doʿ ik), literally, "For still the end to the appointed time." Concerning this phrase, Walvoord asserts, "As the last part
of verse 27 makes clear, in spite of all his intrigue, Antiochus was fulfilling
prophecy on schedule."[105] Wood suggests, "'End' appears to carry the thought
of *goal*, rather than *close* of a period of time. The thought is that the goals of

---

101. KBH, s.v. "שׁטף."

102. Bevan, *The House of Seleucus*, 2.136.

103. Ibid., 2.137.

104. Ibid., 2.142.

105. Walvoord, *Daniel*, 267.

the two kings would not be realized because they did not coincide with the 'end' God had in mind—an unidentified end which would come to fruition at the time still future."[106] Young thinks the end has to do with the end of the wars between Syria and Egypt: "Their [Antiochus and Ptolemy] common plan, however, would fail, for God's appointed time for the end of the wars between Syria and Egypt had not come."[107] Apparently the end to which this phrase refers is not a clear cut event or time. The word "for" (כִּי, *ık*) can have the sense of "because."[108] If this is the use here, the statement indicates that the reason their plan will not succeed is "*because* still the end to the appointed time." This sense would seem to support Young's contention that the plan between Antiochus and Ptolemy would fail because there is an appointed time to the end of the conflict between the two powers, and it has not yet come.

The Destruction of the Temple: 11:28–35

According to Miller, "the real purpose of all this historical data [i.e., verses 28 and following]—to set the stage for the persecution of the Jewish people ('the holy covenant')."[109]

28—   "Then he will return to his land with much plunder; but his heart will be set against the holy covenant, and he will take action and then return to his own land."

With much plunder, Antiochus returned to his own land, but "his heart will be set against the holy covenant, and he will take action." First Macc 1:20–28 and 2 Macc 5:11–17 record the terrible atrocities and murder of thousands of Jews at the hands of Antiochus at this time. Antiochus assisted the high priest Menelaus against those Jews who opposed him. Pentecost notes, "After his disappointment in Egypt (he had hoped to take all of Egypt but failed) he took out his frustrations on the Jews by desecrating the temple in Jerusalem. Evidently he opposed (set *his heart . . . against*) the entire Mosaic system (*the holy covenant*)."[110] However, Lucas points out that there is some confusion in the testimony from Maccabees about this event.

> There is some confusion in our sources relating to events in Jerusalem connected with Antiochus' two campaigns against Egypt. According to 1 Macc. 1:20–28, in 169, on his way home

106. Wood, *Daniel*, 299.
107. Young, *Prophecy of Daniel*, 243.
108. KBH, s.v. "כִּי." See §B.1.
109. Miller, *Daniel*, 300.
110. Pentecost, *Daniel*, 1369.

following the first campaign, Antiochus arrived at Jerusalem with a large army and looted the temple. He also 'committed deeds of murder.' No motive is given for this. Josephus (*Contra Ap*. 2.84) attributed it to his need for funds. 1 Macc. 1:29–40 recounts a treacherous attack on Jerusalem 'two years later' by 'a chief collector of tribute' sent by Antiochus. 2 Macc. 5 seems to conflate these two events (naming Antiochus' emissary in the second as Apollonius) and place them both after Antiochus' second Egyptian campaign. In this case, the motive given for Antiochus' attack on the city and looting of the temple is the actions of the former high priest Jason (see below). However, it seems more likely that these actions happened during the second campaign and were the reason for Antiochus' sending a punitive force to Jerusalem after that campaign.[111]

Goldingay makes the same observation about the apparent conflation of the separate events in the sources. He concludes, "It may be that Antiochus indeed took action against Jerusalem in both 169 and 168 (cf. vv 28 and 30) but that on the latter occasion he acted via Apollonius (cf. 1 Macc 1; 2 Macc 5 then conflates the two sets of events into a personal visit in 168). In 169, however, he personally visited Jerusalem and appropriated part of the temple treasury, which functioned as bank and state exchequer, probably viewing it as tribute . . . and acting thus because he simply needed the money."[112]

Bevan recounts the events as two separate actions, both of which took place upon the return of Antiochus from an Egyptian campaign. He describes the first event as having begun "when the intelligence reached him during one of his campaigns in Egypt that Jerusalem had risen for the house of Ptolemy in his rear. Jason had suddenly (on a false report that Antiochus was dead) came back from the Ammonite country with a band he had got together and possessed himself of Jerusalem except the citadel, where Menelaus had taken refuge."[113] It was, according to Bevan, the defection of Jerusalem, a critical city in Antiochus' defensive line against Egypt, that precipitated Antiochus' fury, and it was during this first outburst of anger that Antiochus looted the temple treasury: "Their [the Jews] rebellion had given him the excuse to take into the royal treasury the precious things of the Temple of the Lord, as, on one pretext or another, he had appropriated the riches of the other Syrian temples."[114] However, it was, according to Bevan, the second campaign against the Jews that was precipitated by Antiochus' humiliation at the hands of the

---

111. Lucas, *Daniel*, 285.

112. Goldingay, *Daniel*, 301.

113. Bevan, *The House of Seleucus*, 2.170.

114. Ibid., 2.172.

Roman emissaries led by Gaius Popillius Laenas that Antiochus returned from Egypt and released his anger upon Jerusalem. He defiled the temple and set up the Greek altar of Zeus and sacrificed on it a swine. Bevan also describes the attempt to eradicate the worship of God and the Word of God as part of the goal of Antiochus at this time.

Schäfer notes, "In all probability, Antiochus did not travel himself from Egypt to Jerusalem, but attempted to restore order in the Phoenician coastal cities where the situation had now also become turbulent."[115] Antiochus had no doubt sent officers through the countryside of Israel, and, according to Bevan, "Their instructions were to compel the population to break with the old religion by taking part in the ceremonies of Hellenic worship, especially in eating the flesh of sacrificed swine, and to punish even with death mothers who circumcised their children. The books of which the Jews made so much were destroyed, if found, or disfigured by mocking scribbles, or defiled with unholy broth."[116] Notwithstanding Schäfer's speculation about Antiochus' involvement, the text seems to indicate that Antiochus was the one who perpetrated the atrocities upon Israel

In spite of the confusion in these extra-biblical sources, the prophecy accurately predicts Antiochus' actions against the people of Israel. The term "holy covenant" (בְּרִית קֹדֶשׁ, *sedoq ̄it̨b*) does not necessarily indicate that Antiochus had antagonism toward "the entire Mosaic system," as Pentecost holds. There is no reason to think that Antiochus had any extensive knowledge of the system. Rather, this may be a figure of speech for the people who are part of that holy covenant, as Goldingay takes it: "The 'holy covenant' is a new phrase, here denoting the covenant people . . ."[117]

29—   "At the appointed time he will return and come into the South, but this last time it will not turn out the way it did before."

30—   "For ships of Kittim will come against him; therefore he will be disheartened and will return and become enraged at the holy covenant and take action; so he will come back and show regard for those who forsake the holy covenant."

Verse 29 opens with the phrase, "At the appointed time . . ." (לְמוֹעֵד, *de ̔ommal*). This seems to be a reminder to Daniel and his readers that Antiochus' actions are under God's control, and he comes and goes according to God's plan. This also implies that the evil actions perpetrated upon the Jews by Antiochus are according to God's purpose. This is at once

115. Schäfer, *The History of the Jews*, 40.

116. Bevan, *The House of Seleucus*, 2.174.

117. Goldingay, *Daniel*, 301.

terrifying and comforting. It is terrifying because the horrors executed upon the Jews are according to God's design. It is comforting because Antiochus is not allowed to go beyond what God has ordained to be done, and God has a divine purpose for Israel that can ultimately be only for her good.

In 168 BC, Antiochus again invaded Egypt. This time Antiochus would have no success against Egypt at all. Romans came in ships to aid the Egyptians against Antiochus: "For ships of Kittim will come against him." Lucas explains, "'Kittim' derives from the name of a city, Citium, on the south coast of Cyprus. According to Josephus (*Ant.* 1.6.1), the term came to be used 'for all islands and most maritime countries.'"[118] As mentioned above, Antiochus was met by a Roman emissary, Gaius Popillius Laenas, who presented Antiochus with a letter from the Roman senate forbidding him to make war against Egypt. Antiochus attempted to gain some time in order to develop an alternate plan, but the emissary "drew a circle round him in the sand and insisted on an answer before he stepped out of the circle (Polybius, *Hist.* 29.27)."[119] Having been utterly humiliated by the Romans, on his way home he vented his anger against Israel. In light of the spiritual warfare revealed earlier, there is no doubt that Antiochus' actions were shaped by demonic influence.

Antiochus sought out any Jews who had rejected Jewish law in order to help him in his attempt to stamp out the worship of the God of Israel. Menelaus gave Antiochus his support. Lucas provides a helpful summary of these events.

> Jason's [the high priest and brother of Onias III] actions recorded in 2 Macc. 5 probably took place at this time. He is said to have heard a rumour that Antiochus had been killed in Egypt. This prompted him to attack Jerusalem with a thousand men. Menelaus took refuge in the citadel. Jason killed many in the city, but failed to gain full control of it, and eventually fled to Ammon. When news of the trouble in Jerusalem reached Antiochus, he took it to mean that the city was in revolt, and so sent a force to attack it (30b). 1 Macc. 1:29–40 and 2 Macc. 5:24–26 probably both refer to the same event. Apollonius, commander of the army, pretended to have come in peace. Having lulled the Jews into a false sense of security, he attacked the city on a Sabbath, causing great slaughter.[120]

The text states that Antiochus would "come back and show regard for those who forsake the holy covenant." Apparently, in an effort to increase

---

118. Lucas, *Daniel*, 286.

119. Ibid.

120. Ibid.

the possibility of success in his intended actions against Jerusalem, Antiochus "turned his attention toward" any of the Jews who had already abandoned the Mosaic covenant and would be likely candidates for supporting his plans. Wood points out, "The leader among this group was the apostate high priest himself, Menelaus, who gave full cooperation (cf. 1 Macc. 1:43)."[121]

31— "Forces from him will arise, desecrate the sanctuary fortress, and do away with the regular sacrifice. And they will set up the abomination of desolation."

32— "By smooth words he will turn to godlessness those who act wickedly toward the covenant, but the people who know their God will display strength and take action."

"And forces from him will arise, desecrate the sanctuary fortress, and do away with the regular sacrifice." Miller gives a helpful description of the events to which this prophecy refers:

> Later, in 167 B.C., the suppression of the Jewish religion began on a grand scale (1 Macc 1:41–50; 2 Macc 6:1–6). All Jewish religious practices such as circumcision, possessing the Scriptures, sacrifices, and feast days were forbidden on penalty of death (1 Macc 1:50, 63); and the imperial cult was introduced. Desecration of the Jewish religion reached its climax on 15 Chislev (December) 167 B.C. (1 Macc 1:54) when an altar or idol-statue devoted to Olympian Zeus (Jupiter) was erected in the temple ("the abomination that causes desolation"), and on 25 Chislev sacrifices, probably including swine (cf. 1 Macc 1:47; 2 Macc 6:4–5), were offered on the altar (cf. 1 Macc 1:54, 59). In this manner the temple was desecrated and rendered empty of Yahweh worshipers.[122]

The text states, "And they will set up the abomination of desolation [הַשִּׁקּוּץ מְשׁוֹמֵם, *memŏsᵉm šuqqᵉʾssah*]." The term "desolation" (מְשׁוֹמֵם, *memŏsᵉm*) is actually a Po'el participle. The Po'el stem is another form having significance similar to that of the Piel stem. The Piel stem indicates the cause of an action, but focusing on the resulting state. Here, the abomination causes a state of desolation—that is, the altar is desolated and has become polluted and unusable as a result. Antiochus polluted the sanctuary by offering a sow upon the altar and setting up a statue of Jupiter. Jupiter was the supreme God of the Roman pantheon, equivalent to the Greek Zeus. The name is a combination of the proper name "Jove" and the word "pater" meaning "father." He

---

121. Wood, *Daniel*, 301.
122. Miller, *Daniel*, 301–2.

was known by the name *Jupiter Optimus Maximus*, meaning all-good and all-powerful. This is the difference between Titus in 70 AD and the prince that shall come in 9:27. Whereas Titus completely destroyed the temple but did not set up any kind of defiling altar, the prince of Dan 9:27, like Antiochus, will not destroy the temple, but will desecrate it by presenting a "detestable thing" upon the altar of God.

Verse 32 indicates how Antiochus would actually deceive even those who had pledged loyalty and assistance to his policies: "By smooth words he will turn to godlessness those who act wickedly toward the covenant." As Goldingay describes it, "the sources do not say that the Jews who had sought the establishment of a Hellenistic community actually desired the abolition of the external distinctives of Jewish religion; 1 Macc 1 implies that they found themselves drawn into cooperation with a policy that had gone beyond their original expectations."[123] These events led to the Maccabean revolt, probably referred to in the text by the statement, "but the people who know their God will display strength and take action."

33—   "Those who have insight among the people will give understanding to the many; yet they will fall by sword and by flame, by captivity and by plunder for many days."

Some have proposed that, "Those who have insight" (וּמַשְׂכִּ֣ילֵי, *eliksamu*) were some of the Jews who understood these very prophecies and instructed others how to live in these times. Although the persecution would cause a brief spiritual revival, many Jews were killed. First Macc. 1:62–64 reports how some refused to bow to Antiochus' demands: "But many in Israel stood firm and were resolved in their hearts not to eat unclean food. They chose to die rather than to be defiled by food or to profane the holy covenant; and they did die. Very great wrath came upon Israel."[124] Miller comments, "Tens of thousands were slaughtered in these persecutions, and many others died during the fighting. . . . Though intense, this persecution would last only for a short while."[125] The text simply says, "days," (יָמִֽים, *mumay*), and this short while was in fact several years.

34—   "Now when they fall they will be granted a little help, and many will join with them in hypocrisy."

---

123. Goldingay, *Daniel*, 302.

124. καὶ πολλοὶ ἐν Ισραηλ ἐκραταιώθησαν καὶ ὠχυρώθησαν ἐν αὐτοῖς τοῦ μὴ φαγεῖν κοινὰ καὶ ἐπεδέξαντο ἀποθανεῖν ἵνα μὴ μιανθῶσιν τοῖς βρώμασιν καὶ μὴ βεβηλώσωσιν διαθήκην ἁγίαν καὶ ἀπέθανον καὶ ἐγένετο ὀργὴ μεγάλη ἐπὶ Ισραηλ σφόδρα (1 Macc 1:62–64).

125. Miller, *Daniel*, 303.

35—   "Some of those who have insight will fall, in order to refine, purge, and make them pure until the end time; because it is still to come at the appointed time."

There is some controversy as to how to understand the first statement of verse 34: "Now when they fall they will be granted little help" (וּבְהִכָּשְׁלָם יֵעָזְרוּ עֵזֶר מְעָט, *ta ᶜem reẕe ᶜurẕa ᶜey maīsakkiḫbu*). The focus of the debate is the expression "little help." The phrase literally says, "they will help *with* help little." Both Mauro and Evans assert that the phrase is better translated "by the help of a few."[126] However, syntactically this cannot be correct. The word translated "few" or "little" is an adjective מְעָט (*ta ᶜem*). Their translation is treating this adjective as a noun, i.e., as a substantive. It is certainly true that adjectives can be used as substantives, but this occurs when there is no noun in the phrase for the adjective to modify. In this instance there is a noun that can be modified by the adjective, namely, "help" (עֵזֶר, *reẕe ᶜ*). In fact, the relationship between these two words fits all the criteria for an attributive adjective—the adjective agrees in definiteness with the noun it modifies, and the attributive adjective follows the noun it modifies.[127] Also, the way Mauro and Evans translate the phrase, they are treating the noun "help" (עֵזֶר, *reẕe ᶜ*) as being in a construct relation with the adjective "little." This construct relation is indicated by their translation "*help of* a few." Unlike Greek, in which the "of" would go with the following word, "of a few," which is said to be the genitive, in Hebrew the "of" goes with the preceding word, in this instance "help," and *it* is said to be in the genitive. In this kind of relation, the noun is said to be in the construct state in relation to the adjective. But, in such a relation, the long vowels of the noun, the word in the construct state, are shortened in order to indicate this relation. So, the long "e," called a ͞eres, indicated by the two dots under the letter Ayin, (עֵ, *e ᶜ*), would be shortened to a short "e," called as ͞loges (עֶ, *e ᶜ*), and the short "e," ͞loges, under the *niyaz*(ֶ, *ez*) would be shortened to a *awehs*(ְ, *ᶜz*). The resulting form should be עֶזְר (*rᵉze ᶜ*) as we see in the form יֵעָזְרוּ (*urẕa ᶜey*).[128] In fact, this is the form in which the word is found in the 10 instances in which it occurs in the OT as a construct. But this is not what we find in the text in 11:34. Consequently, the word "help" cannot be translated "help of" as Mauro and Evans suppose, and in fact it is not "better translated" as "by the help of a few." Rather, the phrase should be translated "they will be helped by a little help." Neither Mauro nor

126. Mauro, *Seventy Weeks*, 133; Evans, *Four Kingdoms*, 227.

127. See for example, Russell T. Fuller and Kyoungwon Choi, *Invitation to Biblical Hebrew: A Beginning Grammar* (Grand Rapids: Kregel Publications, 2006), 10.8–10.10.

128. In the textual form, the ͞loges, as in עֶ, is lengthend to a *semaq* עָ.

Evans are students of Hebrew and are not qualified to indicate what is and
what is not a "better translation."

Some take the phrase in a negative sense, that they will not get very
much help, i.e., only a little help. Some take it in a positive sense, that they
will get some help in their efforts. Whichever way one takes this first part of
the verse, the latter part indicates that many Jews would join the revolt against
Antiochus even though they had aided Antiochus earlier. As Bevan describes,
"The effect of his [Judas Maccabaeus'] successes was to rally to the cause all
those who had only unwillingly and from fear accepted Hellenism, and these
together with the refugees, made the mass of the population of Judaea."[129]
Miller points out that "as the strength of the Maccabean revolt grew, many
uncommitted Jews sided with the rebels out of expediency, particularly when
the Maccabean forces, now joined by the Hasidim, began to put to death
those who had collaborated with the Seleucids (cf. 1 Macc 2:42–48)."[130] The
persecutions of Antiochus were for the purpose of making Israel pure "until
the time of the end." This seems to be a reference to the end of the persecution, as Miller notes: "In this context the 'end' that has been 'appointed' by
the Lord denotes the termination of Antiochus's persecutions."[131]

This section ends with a reference to the "appointed time," which serves
to set it off from the following material and thereby introduces a transition to
the following prophecies. That this is the end of this section is evidenced by
the repetition of the reference to the "end" and the "appointed time." Both of
these expressions last appeared in verse 27 marking the end of the first section
beginning in verse 25. The first section, from the transition from the general
flow of history to the focus on Antiochus that began in verse 21, is ended by
a similar expression in verse 24—עַד־עֵת (teʿ daʿ) "but only for a time." This
literary structure is marked by these repeated endings:

---

129. Bevan, *The House of Seleucus*, 2.176.

130. Miller, *Daniel*, 303. The great majority of the Jews, particularly those who lived in
the countryside rather than in Jerusalem, were faithful to the Jewish religion and tradition
and rejected Hellenization. A popular movement of people who wished to preserve Jewish
national and religious values arose who called themselves "Hasidim," meaning "holy ones."
The Hasidim opposed the infiltration of Hellenistic culture because they believed this
would lead to the annihilation of Jewish culture. The opposing group, those who favored
Greek culture and influence, were known as the "Hellenists."

131. Ibid.

Table 52: Literary Structure in Repeated Endings

21–24	"but only for a time"	עַד־עֵת
25–27	"for the end is still to come at the appointed time"	כִּי־עוֹד קֵץ לַמּוֹעֵד
28–35	"until the end time, because it is still to come at the appointed time."	עַד־עֵת קֵץ כִּי־עוֹד לַמּוֹעֵד

Notice, as demonstrated in Table 52, how the final section ending in verse 35 brings together the endings of both the first and the second sections into one concluding expression. This seems to show that verse 35 is not only the conclusion of the section from verse 28, but is the conclusion of the entire section beginning in verse 21.

At this point, Mauro states,

> Verse 35 brings us to within half a century of the nativity of Christ, up to which date the prophetic narrative refers, in regular order, to all the main points of Jewish history, passing over nothing of importance. This creates a strong presumption that the prophecy, in its remaining portion, continues to follow the course of Jewish history without any break. For it is impossible to conceive of any reason why the narrative should follow the course of events for the greater part of the period of 'the latter days,' and then, when the most important events of the period were reached, should abruptly break off and fly away to the remote future, passing over a score of centuries at a single bound.[132]

Of course Mauro's assertion assumes that his interpretation has been correct thus far. However, the fact that it is impossible for Mauro to conceive why the text would "break off" does not mean there cannot be a valid reason or that it could not happen. It seems the height of arrogance to declare that since he cannot conceive a reason, there must not be one. In fact, the text has already "broken off" in a number of instances in the earlier parts of chapter 11. Every time the text, using the same identifying phrase "the king of the South," or "the king of the North," yet jumps, without grammatical notification, from one king and time to another, each of which Mauro himself recognizes, the text "breaks off" and "flies away" to another time. Also, Mauro assumes that the period described in the prophetic narrative is 'the latter days.' But, if the period to which the text "flies away" is in fact 'the latter days,' then to the Futurist it makes perfect sense that the text, having presented the type in Antiochus IV Epiphanes, would "fly off" to the actual 'latter days' in which

132. Mauro, *Seventy Weeks*, 119–20.

the career of the antitype, Anti-Christ, would be described. Mauro's objection is not predicated on the text, but on his own eschatological preference.

Prophecy Concerning the King of the End Time: 11:36–45

With verse 36 we enter the section in which the various eschatological perspectives begin to show themselves much more clearly. Mauro comments, "Here we reach that part of the prophecy in regard to which there is the greatest difference of opinion among expositors;"[133] There are at least three camps with respect to this final major part of chapter 11. 1) There are those who hold that there is no transition in verse 35 by which a new personality is introduced in verse 36, but the section from verse 36 to the end of the chapter concerns Antiochus Epiphanes as does the previous section. 2) There are those popularly known as Preterists who hold that, although these verses were not fulfilled in Antiochus Epiphanes, they were all fulfilled by 70 AD. Preterists differ from Futurists as to the identity of the king introduced in verse 36. 3) There are those who hold that the king introduced in verse 36 is a yet future Anti-Christ. The advocates of this view are usually identified as Futurists.

Eschatological Views and the Identify of "The King"

THE ANTIOCHUS VIEW

Since the principal focus of our commentary is not those who hold the Antiochus view, but is rather those who hold the Preterist view, we will not spend much time on this view. Also, there is sufficient material in print dealing with the problems and countering the claims of the Antiochus view that we need not rehearse this material. We will consider only a few points.

Lack of Correlation

The Antiochus View is the view that verse 36 does not introduce a new and different personality than the one described in verses 21–35. This king who does what he pleases is in fact Antiochus Epiphanes. Miller points out some serious difficulties facing the Antiochus View:

> . . . there are serious problems with this position, not the least of which is the fact that much of the historical data set forth in these verses (even in vv. 36–39) is impossible to harmonize with

133. Ibid., 135.

Antiochus's life. For example, Antiochus did not exalt himself above every god (vv. 36–37), reject 'the gods of his fathers,' or worship 'a god unknown to his father' (v. 38); on the contrary, he worshiped the Greek pantheon, even building an altar and offering sacrifices to Zeus in the Jerusalem temple precincts. Daniel also predicted that this king 'will come to his end' in Palestine (v. 45), but it is a matter of historical record that Antiochus IV died at Tabae in Persia."[134]

In fact, Goldingay, an advocate of the Antiochus view, admits that the material in verses 40–45 do not fit the historical facts: "Porphyry assumed that the quasi-predictive historical account of Antiochus's career continues in these verses. But vv 40–45 cannot be correlated with actual events as vv 21–39 can . . . These predictions, then, are not to be read as if they were mere anticipatory announcements of fixed future events; like the promises and warnings of the prophets, they paint an imaginative scenario of the *kind* of issue that must come from present events."[135] Lucas acknowledges the same disparity between the prophetic descriptions in verses 40–45: "These verses have been a source of perplexity to commentators down the centuries. On the one hand, they seem to continue the story of Antiochus IV, providing the expected account of his downfall and death. On the other, they do not correspond in any way with the events following his second withdrawal from Egypt and the beginning of the persecution of the Jews."[136] The disparity between the text and the actual historical events surrounding Antiochus cannot be dismissed simply as historical inaccuracies on the part of Daniel, especially when there are other candidates that offer more reasonable alternatives.

Antiochus as God

Evans describes how the advocates of the Antiochus View point to the coins "minted during Antiochus's reign with a Greek inscription under the king's image that translates as 'Antiochus God Manifest,'" and conclude that "here we have proof that the passage in verse 36 about the king's exalting and magnifying himself above every god pertains to him [Antiochus IV Epiphanes]."[137] However, Evans goes on to quote a section from Allan MacRae explaining why this claim is overrated: "It is true that he was very proud of his title, 'Epiphanes,' which described him as a god, and he would seem to have been the first of the Seleucids actually to put such a title on his coins. Yet this repre-

134. Miller, *Daniel*, 305.

135. Goldingay, *Daniel*, 305 (emphasis in original).

136. Lucas, *Daniel*, 290.

137. Evans, *Four Kingdoms*, 206.

sented an exaltation of himself above human beings, not an exaltation above the great gods of Greece. The many temples that he built, as well as his attempt to force the Jews to worship Greek gods, make it impossible to think of him as the one described in statements A, C and E [the relevant descriptions in 11:36–37]."[138] In other words, though Antiochus exalted himself above other men, he did not exalt himself above all gods.

The Shift of Subject

As a result of such criticisms, most conservative commentators propose that the king of verses 36–45 is not Antiochus Epiphanes. However, Evans points out that, "because verses 36–45 contain no explicit statement denoting a change of kings after the reference in verse 35 to 'the time of the end,' these last ten verses also constitute a major challenge to conservative exegetes."[139] In fact, Young shows that S. R. Driver objects to the notion that verses 36–45 point to a different subject. "Driver remarks that '—it is contrary to all sound principles of exegesis to suppose that, in a *continuous* description, with no indication whatever of a change of subject, part should refer to one person, and part to another, and that "the king" of *v.* 35, and "the king of the south" of *v.* 45 should be a different king from the one whose doings are described in *vv.* 21–35.'"[140] Those who hold the Antiochus view generally reject the notion that there is a break between verses 35 and 36. In the section below titled "Arguments for a Break," (pages 699ff) we will deal with this issue in more depth.

Inaccurate History or Accurate Prophecy

Walvoord discusses how those who hold to the Antiochus view, identified by Walvoord as liberals, admit that the correlation between the prophecies in this section and the facts of history "are not nearly as accurate as the earlier portion."[141] Those who hold the Antiochus view usually also hold that Daniel was written during the Maccabean revolt by the "wise ones" referred to in verse 33 and therefore is actually history. With reference to the section from verse 35 to 45, these interpreters usually hold that this is an unsuccessful and inaccurate attempt at prophecy, and this accounts for the differences between the text and actual history. However, this assumes what must be proven.

138. Allan A. MacRae, *The Prophecies of Daniel* (Singapore: Christian Life Publishers, 1991), 240; quoted in Evans, *Four Kingdoms,* 207.

139. Evans, *Four Kingdoms*, 205.

140. Young, *Prophecy of Daniel*, 246.

141. Walvoord, *Daniel*, 271.

Whereas these interpreters conclude that the differences are inaccuracies that indicate errors in the prophecy, conservatives point to the same differences and conclude that the prophecy must be about someone else besides Antiochus Epiphanes. The Antiochus view simply does not hold up to scrutiny.

Preterist Views

Preterists believe that the prophecies of Daniel 11 were all completely fulfilled by 70 AD. This includes the second coming of Christ and the establishing of the Kingdom of God. Preterists differ about precisely how these prophecies are fulfilled and to whom they apply. This is not a criticism of the view since all theological systems are likely to have advocates of the overall system who differ in their views about details with others who hold to the same system. Because of these differences, however, a general definition of the position requires a very broad statement. In the following analysis, we will consider in particular the Preterist view as it is expressed by John Evans, although we will mention others along the way, and our focus will be on the relevant verses in Daniel chapter 11 beginning with verse 36.

Gap or No Gap

Evans argues, "A major problem for them [Futurists] is that they insist that there must be a prophetic gap of more than 2,500 years between verses 35 and 36 or between verses 39 and 40, yet the text of Daniel 11 is written as though no such gap exists."[142] But this argument begs the question. To claim that the text is written as though no such gap exists assumes what it must prove. What is there in the text that indicates this? Evans offers no exegetical argumentation to support his claim.[143] Evans has already acknowledged how the text, for example in chapter 2 dealing with the head of gold, skips over periods of history without comment. In fact, Preterist Keith Mathison identifies this practice as

142. Evans, *Four Kingdoms*, 219.

143. This is, unfortunately, characteristic of Preterist writers when it comes to the *Prophecy of Daniel*. We would have appreciated more exegesis, but individuals like Gary DeMar, in his book *Last Days Madness*, mostly offer rhetoric, innuendo, selective reporting, exaggeration, guilt by association, and other tactics rather than actually trying to offer any exegetical argumentation from the text. In fact, in the fourth edition of his book *Last Days Madness*, DeMar devotes an entire chapter to "Daniel's Seventieth Week," and yet not once does he attempt to do any exegesis from the text of Daniel. He makes a good show, quoting verses and talking about what Daniel says, but he does not do any actual exegetical commentary. He makes many claims about what he thinks Daniel means, but he does not offer any sustained exegetical support for his claims. This is unfortunate, for we would have liked very much to see how DeMar actually handles the text, and I am sure we could have learned a lot.

telescoping: "Telescoping occurs when the prophet describes events that are now known to be widely separated in time but does so without giving any indication that they are so separated. . . . Daniel 11:36–12:3 does not provide any indication that the subject has changed, but, unlike the preceding verses, the events described in 11:36–12:3 do not correspond to any known events in the life of Antiochus IV—or anyone else, for that matter. Some suggest that these verses were fulfilled in the first century. Others suggest that they have not yet been fulfilled. In either case, their fulfillment did not occur when the prophecies of Daniel 11:21–35 were fulfilled. The two events were telescoped by Daniel into one continuous prophecy, and no one reading it before any of it was fulfilled would have been able to detect a change of subject at verse 36."[144] Although I disagree that there are no indications in the text of a change of subject at verse 36, the argument of Mathison demonstrates that Evans' arguments are without foundation.

Also, the argument Evans is using against the gap is precisely the argument that liberals used against the change from one subject to another, namely, that there is no indicator in the text to warrant such a shift, an argument to which Evans takes exception. It seems as though Evans rejects or employs this argument as it serves his purpose. The criterion for deciding to whom the "king" refers is not a certain way the text is supposedly written, but whether the events and actions described can be seen as applying to the individual proposed. Just like the actions described in the later verses cannot be applied to Antiochus, so they cannot be applied to the individuals Evans seeks to identify. In fact, Evans' own claim that this must refer to some other individual—in his estimation, Herod the Great—introduces an historical gap of some 100 years or more. If the "gap problem" is merely a question of length or duration, then it is no longer a problem of the gap *qua* gap, and all the rhetorical declarations about an "imaginary 'gap' or 'parenthesis'"[145] are so much smoke.

God of His Fathers

Evans' argument about the expression "gods of his fathers," which he claims could be translated "god of his fathers," is indecisive since it can be translated either way. This argument does not either support or contradict Evans' claims. However, for all of Evans' objections to those whom he claims to be using speculation as a basis for their arguments, Evans employs it quite readily when it supports his position. To argue that "does it not seem probable that the

---

144. Keith A. Mathison, "The Eschatological Time Texts of the New Testament," in *When Shall These Things Be?*, 167.

145. Demar, *Last Days Madness*, 169.

Idumeans and Nabataeans had strong elements of monotheism in their religious practices?" is the height of speculation since historical evidence argues in the opposite direction.

Nevertheless, there are some factors that argue against Evans' understanding of the statement "god of his fathers." The Hebrew text reads אֱלֹהֵי אָבִיו (*wyabᵃʾeholeʾ*). There are only five other places where this expression is used in the OT. Table 53 below presents these verses.

Table 53: God of His Fathers

2 Kings 21:22	"So he forsook the Lord, the God of his fathers [אֱלֹהֵי אֲבֹתָיו *wyaṭobaʾᵭeholeʾ*], and did not walk in the way of the Lord." וַיַּעֲזֹב אֶת־יְהוָה אֱלֹהֵי אֲבֹתָיו וְלֹא הָלַךְ בְּדֶרֶךְ יְהוָה:
2 Chronicles 21:10	"So Edom revolted against Judah to this day. Then Libnah revolted at the same time against his rule, because he had forsaken the Lord God of his fathers [אֱלֹהֵי אֲבֹתָיו, *wyaṭobaʾᵭeholeʾ*]." וַיִּפְשַׁע אֱדוֹם מִתַּחַת יַד־יְהוּדָה עַד הַיּוֹם הַזֶּה אָז תִּפְשַׁע לִבְנָה בָּעֵת הַהִיא מִתַּחַת יָדוֹ כִּי עָזַב אֶת־יְהוָה אֱלֹהֵי אֲבֹתָיו:
2 Chronicles 28:25	In every city of Judah he made high places to burn incense to other gods, and provoked the Lord, the God of his fathers [אֲבֹתָיו אֱלֹהֵי, *wyaṭobaʾᵭeholeʾ*], to anger. וּבְכָל־עִיר וָעִיר לִיהוּדָה עָשָׂה בָמוֹת לְקַטֵּר לֵאלֹהִים אֲחֵרִים וַיַּכְעֵס אֶת־יְהוָה אֱלֹהֵי אֲבֹתָיו:
2 Chronicles 30:19	". . . everyone who prepares his heart to seek God, the Lord God of his fathers [אֱלֹהֵי אֲבוֹתָיו, *wyaṭobaʾᵭeholeʾ*], though not according to the purification [rules] of the sanctuary. כָּל־לְבָבוֹ הֵכִין לִדְרוֹשׁ הָאֱלֹהִים יְהוָה אֱלֹהֵי אֲבוֹתָיו וְלֹא כְּטָהֳרַת הַקֹּדֶשׁ:

2 Chronicles
33:12

"When he was in distress, he entreated the Lord his God and
humbled himself greatly before the God of his fathers
אֱלֹהֵי אֲבֹתָיו, *wyatoba'Ɵehole'*]."

וּבְהָצֵר לוֹ חִלָּה אֶת־פְּנֵי יְהוָה אֱלֹהָיו
וַיִּכָּנַע מְאֹד מִלִּפְנֵי אֱלֹהֵי אֲבֹתָיו׃

In each instance the reference is translated with the singular noun "God,"
and each one refers to the God of Israel. If Dan 11:37 follows this pattern,
the reference here is not to the "gods" of his fathers, or the pagan "god" of his
fathers, but to the God of Israel Who is the God of his fathers. Since Herod's
family was not Jewish, it seems evident that, if this is the correct way to take
this expression, this could not possibly apply to him. Of course it is not conclusive that this is the meaning here, but Evans does not even entertain this
possibility. If this king is a future Antichrist, as many argue, the expression
"God of his fathers" would *not* necessarily require that he be a Jew. The God
of Christianity is in fact the God of Israel, and a Gentile who is reared in a
Christian family could be said to reject the God of his fathers, and this could
still be a reference to the God of Israel. Of course this could not have been
the case with Herod, since Christianity had not yet been established in the
time of Herod.

The Desire of Women

Evans holds that Herod the Great (73 to 4 BC) "is the central figure in Daniel
11:36–45 and the subject of verses 36–39 and 44–45."[146] Evans begins his
effort to demonstrate that Herod fulfills the prophecy by providing a translation of the relevant verses. Below the translation given by Evans is placed
alongside the NASB translation.

146. Ibid., 250.

Table 54: Comparison of Translations of Daniel 11:36–39

	Evans' Translation vv. 36–39	NASB Translation vv. 36–39
1	"The king will do as he pleases.	"Then the king will do as he pleases,
2	He will exalt and magnify himself above every god	and he will exalt and magnify himself above every god
3	and will say unheard-of things against the God of gods.	and will speak monstrous things against the God of gods;
4	He will be successful until the time of wrath is completed, for what has been determined must take place.	and he will prosper until the indignation is finished, for that which is decreed will be done.
5	He will show no regard for the gods of his fathers	He will show no regard for the gods of his fathers
6	or for the one desired by women,	or for the desire of women,
7	nor will he regard any god,	nor will he show regard for any other god;
8	but will exalt himself above them all.	for he will magnify himself above them all.
9	Instead of them, he will honor a god of fortresses;	But instead he will honor a god of fortresses,
10	a god unknown to his fathers he will honor with gold and silver, with precious stones and costly gifts.	a god whom his fathers did not know; he will honor him with gold, silver, costly stones and treasures.
11	He will attack the mightiest fortresses with the help of a foreign god	He will take action against the strongest of fortresses with the help of a foreign god;
12	and will greatly honor those who acknowledge him.	he will give great honor to those who acknowledge him
13	He will make them rulers over many people and will distribute the land at a price."	and will cause them to rule over the many, and will parcel out land for a price.

The translations have been arbitrarily broken up into sections for easier reference. There are some serious problems with Evans' translation, however. For example, in section 6 Evans has, "or for the one desired by women," whereas the NASB has, "or for the desire of women." The Hebrew text is set out in the following arrangement with an English translation below each Hebrew word.

Table 55: Daniel 11:37b

נָשִׁים	חֶמְדַּת	-	וְעַל
woman	the desire of	(Maqqeph)[147]	and unto

The short horizontal line between the two words is identified as a Maqqeph. A maqqeph is for the purpose of bringing two words together in a single pronunciation and indicates some few different relationships. One relationship that this feature indicates is called a construct relation. We have dealt with this before in reference to another of Evans' translations in verse 34. Here Evans has committed exactly the opposite error. In this translation he has unjustifiably translated the noun "desire" (חֶמְדַּת, *tadmeh*) as a participle, "the one desired." Evans' treatment of the noun as a verbal is particularly problematic. The noun חֶמְדַּת (*tadmeh*) is usually spelled חֶמְדָּה (*hadmeh*). The usual spelling is called the absolute state, and the spelling as it appears in verse 36 is called the construct state. The *semaq*, represented by the vowel point that looks like a small 'T' under the letter *telad* (דַ) in the absolute state, has changed to a *hatap*, the vowel point that looks like a short horizontal line under the letter (דְ), which is a short "a," in the construct state. Also, the word in the absolute state ends with a *eh* (ה), while the word in the construct state ends in a *wat* (ת), pronounced "tav." All of these factors demonstrate that the word Evans translates as a participle cannot have the meaning he gives it. The alternate spelling indicates that the word "desire" is in a construct relation to the word "women," and therefore must be translated indicating some kind of genitive sense, such as "desire of women," not "the one desired by women" as Evans has it.

Nevertheless, this expression is ambiguous enough to allow several possible meanings. Walvoord holds that the phrase should be translated "he shall not regard the desire of women," but he takes this to mean "desired by women,"[148] with much the same meaning Evans gives it. By this he means, "The Lord Jesus Christ is here in view. . . . Pious Jewish women in Pre-messianic times had one great desire, they wanted to be mothers, with a view to Him, who is the promised seed of the woman. His birth was desired by those godly mothers of Israel. This king then hates God and hates His blessed Son, the Lord Jesus Christ."[149] This understanding of the meaning fits well into Evans' argument even though Evans has presented a mistranslation the

---

147. "A word may transfer its accent to the following word, marked by a raised dash called Maqqef [Maqqeph is an alternate spelling]." Fuller and Choi, *Invitation to Biblical Hebrew*, 5.5.

148. Walvoord, *Daniel*, 274.

149. Ibid.

passage. Nevertheless, even Walvoord acknowledges, "none of the explanations can be proved beyond question, as Daniel is not specific . . ."[150] In other words, simply asserting that this is the meaning is insufficient to establish one's case.

Additionally, an argument can be made that this expression is in fact not a reference to what women desire, but to the fact that women are desired. First of all, the use of the expression "desire of women" to refer to the Messiah is quite obscure and has no precedent in Scripture or even in extra-biblical use. This expression occurs only here in the entire OT. Second, the word translated "desire" (חֶמְדַּת, *tadmeh*) is used 16 times in the OT, and it is used in the construct state 7 times. Of these instances, only one comes close to the construction found in Dan 11:37, and that is Hag 2:7. Probably the most well known translation of this verse is the KJV translation: "And I will shake all nations, and the desire of all nations shall come: and I will fill this house with glory, saith the LORD of hosts," in which the expression "desire of all the nations" (חֶמְדַּת כָּל־הַגּוֹיִם, *miyogah ʾak tadmeh*) has been traditionally seen to have Messianic expectations. However, this translation is not a correct rendering of the Hebrew text. The NASB translation reads: "'. . . and they will come with the wealth of all nations . . .'" in which the corresponding phrase reads, "the wealth of all nations." This is a much better rendering of the Hebrew, as Joyce Baldwin points out: "The reason is that, whereas the Vulgate (and hence the AV) has a singular subject, the Hebrew verb is plural and requires a plural subject: *the treasures (desirable things, RV) of all nations shall come in.*"[151] The plural verb is וּבָאוּ (*uʾabu*), "they will come," which means that the word "desire," (חֶמְדַּת, *tadmeh*) cannot be the subject. In this instance this phrase identifies what "they" are bringing in, not who is coming in.

However, the point in reference to our verse is the translation "desire of all the nations" indicating the "wealth of the nations." Here the construct relation is not indicating what the nations desire, but to whom the wealth (that which is desired) belongs. Similarly, the expression in Dan 11:37 may not indicate what the women desire. Just like the wealth of nations is referred to by the word "desire" in Hag 2:7 because the wealth of the nations was desired, so the desire of women may refer to the fact that women are desired. This would then be a metonymy, in which the word "desire" is used for the thing desired. Commentators who object to this interpretation do so because Antiochus functions as a type of Anti-Christ, and Antiochus was known to love women. For example, Wood argues, "The thought intended may be the

150. Ibid., 275.

151. Joyce G. Baldwin, *Haggai, Zechariah, Malachi: An Introduction and Commentary,* in *Tyndale Old Testament Commentaries,* ed. D. J. Wiseman (Downers Grove, Illinois: Inter-Varsity Press, 1972), 48.

'desire' which men normally have for women, or the area of 'desire' normally characteristic of women . . . The first is not likely, because the Antichrist is prefigured in Antiochus Epiphanes, and he was known for his profligacy toward women."[152] But this objection does not work since every aspect of the type does not necessarily apply to the antitype. Antiochus was also a Greek, but this does not mean that the Anti-Christ must be Greek. According to Bevan, "Antiochus Epiphanes was seized by a fatal malady—epilepsy, perhaps, or something which affected the brain,"[153] but no one supposes that Anti-Christ will die of epilepsy. Also, Antiochus' relation to women is not part of the description of Antiochus in those verses that deal with him and so does not form part of the type. Once again, however, the expression is ambiguous, so we cannot be dogmatic here.

Since Evans' understanding of the meaning of the phrase seems to be incorrect, this presents a likely argument against these prophecies applying to Herod, assuming we can take the text as stating that this king will "show no regard for the God of his fathers *or for the desire of women*." And as Evans has already pointed out, "Herod never lacked for female companionship, however, for he apparently managed to be married at one time or another to ten women, several of them simultaneously. Clearly, he did not number himself among those Jews who practiced monogamy."[154] Some will perhaps object that we have just eliminated this kind of argumentation with reference to Wood's comments above, yet we are now using it against Evans. But the situation is different. Wood was arguing that since Antiochus was a man who loved women, this meant that the phrase could not indicate that Anti-Christ was a man who would have no regard for the desire for women. On the contrary, we are arguing here that if the expression can be taken to mean a desire for women, then it cannot apply to Herod since he was a man who did in fact desire women.

Others may likewise object that we have just shown that every detail of the type does not necessarily apply to the antitype. But again, the situation is different. Above we were pointing out that every characteristic in the type does not necessarily have a corresponding characteristic in the antitype. Here we are arguing that the characteristics in the prophetic description must certainly be found in the person about whom the prophecy is made. It must be the case that since the prophecy says the Anti-Christ will have no regard for the desire for women, then this must in fact be true of him. The prophecy

---

152. Wood, *Daniel*, 306.

153. Bevan, *The House of Seleucus*, 161.

154. Evans, *Four Kingdoms*, 256.

cannot be false or inaccurate. Evans' arguments simply do not succeed in demonstrating his translation or interpretation.

Time of Wrath

Evans argues that the statement, "He will be successful until the time of wrath is completed," is a more problematic issue. He states, "If the preterist exegesis of Daniel is sound, then the passage referring to this time might well seem to refer to the period immediately preceding and including the destruction of Jerusalem in AD 70. But since Herod died in 4 BC, we have here a gap of seventy-four years for which to account."[155] To resolve this problem, Evans adopts the approach of Philip Mauro who argues that Herod should be equated with his dynasty. If his dynasty lasted until 70 AD, then the prophecy could apply to him. Evans argues, "This may initially seem improbable, but remember that the Book of Daniel interchanges the concepts 'kings' and 'kingdoms.' *If Nebuchadnezzar can stand for Babylonia and Alexander for Greece, why can't Herod symbolize the Herodian dynasty?*"[156] This argument sounds persuasive at first, but it fails once one realizes that this interchanging does not happen in chapter 11. Unlike the other revelations through visions and dreams, chapter 11 uses more straight forward speech and does not employ the symbolism of beasts and statues as do earlier chapters. In this chapter, there is no interchanging of the terms "kings" and "kingdoms." Consequently, Evans' argument falls flat. Additionally, as we will see below, Herod's "dynasty" does not last till 70 AD.

Attacking Fortresses

Evans argues that the statement in verse 38, "He will attack the mightiest fortresses with the help of a foreign god," favors an application to Herod if one adopts certain alternate translations. The alternate translations to which he refers are, "He will act for those who fortify strongholds, the people of a strange god," and "To defend the strongholds he shall station a people of a foreign god."[157] Even though the Hebrew is ambiguous, neither one of these translations is actually possible. The text is set out below with a word-for-word translation.

---

155. Ibid., 262.
156. Ibid., 262–63 (emphasis in original).
157. Ibid., 265.

Table 56: Daniel 11:39

וְעָשָׂה	לְמִבְצְרֵי	מָעֻזִּים
and he will do	to fortresses of	refuge

עִם־	אֱלוֹהַּ	נֵכָר
with	a god	foreign

As can be readily seen, the extra words that are added in order to make Evans' other translations intelligible are not present in the text nor justified by the text. The text simply says, "He will do (act) to (against) fortresses of refuge with a foreign god." There is no instance in which Herod did such a thing. Up to this point it has not been sufficiently demonstrated that Herod fits these prophecies any better than does Antiochus IV, and in fact the evidence seems to be mounting up against Herod. Not a single one of the prophetic descriptions can unambiguously be applied to Herod, and the cumulative effect weighs against Evans' view. Evans has other arguments relating to verses 40–45, and those will be dealt with in the appropriate place.

FUTURIST VIEWS

Futurists believe that most if not all of the prophecies of Daniel 11 beginning with verse 36 are yet future. That is, they do not believe that there has been any historical figure to whom these prophecies can be applied. Consequently, since the prophecies have not been fulfilled in the past, and assuming that the Bible is inerrant, Futurists conclude that these prophecies are yet to be fulfilled. This includes the second coming of Christ and the establishing of the Kingdom of God on earth. Like Preterists, Futurists differ among themselves with reference to the details.

Leon Wood's Arguments

Wood presents eight reasons why he thinks the king in verses 36–45 is the Antichrist of a yet future time. "(1) In the ensuing verses there are statements regarding the character of this king which were not true of Antiochus, but do agree with descriptions given elsewhere of the Antichrist, as the following commentary will show."[158] Unfortunately, Wood does not provide a list of the "descriptions given elsewhere" that he claims refer to Anti-Christ. It is certainly true that the descriptions in verses 36–45 do not correspond to anything known about Antiochus, but other verses about Anti-Christ are subject

158. Wood, *Daniel*, 304.

to interpretation and may not be taken by other interpreters in the same way Wood takes them. In other words, what Wood takes in other texts to be descriptions of Anti-Christ may not be interpreted as such by others. Each one of these would need to be examined and his interpretations defended.

His second reason is, "(2) In verses thirty-six to thirty-nine, policies of this person are reviewed, as if to introduce him for the first time. This would be strange if reference were to Antiochus, whose policies and actual life-history have already been given."[159] This argument is not as formidable as it might sound. The descriptions in these verses go beyond what is presented of Antiochus in the previous verses and can be taken as indicating an escalation in the overt expressions of his defiance and disdain. It is, however, true that nowhere are these kinds of actions reported in history as the actions of Antiochus Epiphanes.

Wood's third reason for taking verses 36–45 as referring to Anti-Christ is, "(3) Numerous historical matters from the life of this king are set forth in verses forty to forty-five; and these do not accord with historical events experienced by Antiochus, but do fit into the life-pattern of all that is stated elsewhere of the Antichrist."[160] This is a fact to which commentators admit regardless of their prior eschatological commitment. As we have seen, even those who espouse the Antiochus view admit that the descriptions in these verses, especially the descriptions in verses 40–45, do not correspond to any historical records or accounts of Antiochus Epiphanes. In fact, as we have pointed out, even some Preterists acknowledge that these descriptions do not apply to any known individual in recorded history.

Fourthly, Wood argues, "(4) Any further treatment regarding Antiochus should not be expected, for his story, as to his oppression of the Jews (the purpose for his mention) has been completed."[161] This is an excellent point to which no commentator, of which I am aware, has attempted to respond. Almost all commentators agree that the reason for including and excluding persons in the prophetic description is the relationship they might have to the nation of Israel. Since Antiochus' relationship to Israel ended after the persecutions recorded in the prophetic description, there would be no more need for any continued prophetic description of his actions.

Wood's fifth reasons is, "(5) The form of reference used in verse thirty-six to introduce this person suggests a change of identity from Antiochus, because Antiochus has not been designated at any time as 'the king' (the form used here, with the article) and Antiochus' predecessors have always been

159. Ibid.
160. Ibid.
161. Ibid.

referred to by the designation 'king of the North.'"[162] This is a particularly interesting argument since already it has been said of Antiochus in verse 21 that he was one "on whom the honor of kingship has not been conferred." However, there is a problem with Wood's thesis. Dan 11:27 states, "As for both kings, their hearts will be *intent* on evil . . ." The verse opens by referring to וּשְׁנֵיהֶם הַמְּלָכִים (mikal^emmah meheñsu), literally, "and both of them the kings." This seems to be a reference to Antiochus and Ptolemy Philometor as they were supposedly working together to restore Ptolemy to the throne of Egypt. If this is an accurate application of this prophetic description, then this is an instance in which Antiochus is referred to as a king. However, strictly speaking, Wood is correct that Antiochus is not referred to precisely as "the king" (הַמֶּלֶךְ, kelemmah) in any of these verses. But this may be a distinction that makes no real difference in light of the statement in verse 27.

Another of Wood's reasons is, "(6) In verse forty this king is actually distinguished from another ruler called 'king of the North,' thus setting him quite apart from a line of kings so called."[163] This is an important observation that we will address when dealing with the relevant verses, so we will save our comments until then. Wood's seventh reason is, "(7) Involved with this person's rule will be a time of trouble for Israel worse than any other period in history, as indicated in 12:1; and this corresponds to Matthew 24:21 (cf. Jer. 30:7) where the Great Tribulation is clearly in view, a time existing when the Antichrist rules."[164] Of course this reason assumes that Wood's interpretation of Matt 24:21 and Jer 30:7 are correct. Since the strength of this reason rests on the interpretation of these other verses, it ends up not being a very formidable argument for Wood's view.

Wood's final reason is, "(8) Since the Antichrist has been presented in the three prior revelational times of Daniel, one should not be surprised to have him set forth in this fourth time as well."[165] Once again this argument rests on the assumption that one accepts the way Wood has interpreted the prior passages to which he refers. If his interpretation of those passages is correct, then perhaps this argument might have some force. But as an argument against a contrary view, it offers no substantive support.

Much of Wood's reasoning is predicated on agreeing with his interpretations of references in earlier parts of Daniel or other parts of the Bible. If one does not accept his interpretations of those passages, this seriously deflates the impact of Wood's reasons. Also, Wood's arguments are against the notion

162. Ibid., 304–5.
163. Ibid., 305.
164. Ibid.
165. Ibid.

that these verses apply to Antiochus IV Epiphanes. They do not address the Preterist view that also rejects Antiochus as "the king" but applies these verses to some other figure in our past.

Stephen Miller's Arguments

Miller presents some arguments for the Futurist position that verses 36 through 45 are describing a different king than the one referred to in earlier verses.

> Exegetical necessity requires that 11:36–45 be applied to someone other than Antiochus IV. The context indicates that the ruler now in view will live in the last days, immediately prior to the coming of the Lord. Verse 40 reveals that this king's activities will take place' at the time of the end' (cf. 10:14), and the 'time of distress' mentioned in 12:1 is best understood as the same 'distress' (the tribulation) predicted by Jesus Christ in Matt 24:21 as occurring immediately before his second advent (Matt 24:29–31; cf. Rev 7:14). But the clearest indication that this 'king' will live in the latter days is that the resurrection of the saints will take place immediately after God delivers his people from this evil individual's power (cf. 12:2). Of course, the resurrection is an eschatological event. Finally, vv. 36–39 seem to introduce this king as if for the first time.[166]

As with the reasons that Wood gave, the arguments that Miller puts forward are directed against the Antiochus view and do not address, for example, Evans' claim that these verses apply to Herod. And like Wood, much of Miller's argument assumes the Futurist view. When he says the "'time of distress' mentioned in 12:1 is best understood as . . . occurring immediately before his second advent," Miller assumes that the second advent is a yet future event. Against the Preterist view, this argument does not conflict with the notion that the second coming took place in 70 AD.

John Walvoord's Arguments

Walvoord also presents some arguments for interpreting these verses from a Futurist perspective:

> Beginning with verse 36, a sharp break in the prophecy may be observed, introduced by the expression *the time of the end* in verse 35. Up to this point, the prophecy dealing with the Persian and Grecian Empires has been fulfilled minutely and with amazing

166. Miller, *Daniel*, 305.

precision. Beginning with verse 36, however, an entirely different situation obtains. No commentator claims to find precise
fulfillment in the remainder of this chapter. Although Zöckler
and others attempt to relate Daniel 11:36–45 to Antiochus, many
students of Scripture have recognized from antiquity that another
king must be in view.[167]

The claim that the prophetic descriptions do not relate to any historical
person or events seems to be Walvoord's strongest argument. The fact that
verse 35 includes the expression "the time of the end" does not seem, by itself,
to be a sufficiently strong argument. However, if one joins this statement to
the literary structures as presented before in Table 52 on page 505, the argument is strengthened considerably. This seems especially the case since these
precise phrases do not occur in verses 36-45. Only one instance is similar to
these, and that occurs in verse 40: "At the end time the king of the South will
collide with him, and the king of the North will storm against him with chariots, with horsemen and with many ships; and he will enter countries, overflow
them and pass through." The phrase in question occurs at the beginning of
the verse: "At the end time." [וּבְעֵת קֵץ, *ṣeqîeʿbu*]. Table 52 is reproduced
below with the added phrase from verse 40.

Table 57: Literary Structures of Daniel 11

v. 24	"but only for a time"	עַד־עֵת
v. 27	"for the end is still to come at the appointed time"	כִּי־עוֹד קֵץ לַמּוֹעֵד
v. 35	"until the end time,	עַד־עֵת קֵץ
	because it is still to come at the appointed time."	כִּי־עוֹד לַמּוֹעֵד
v. 40	"At the end time"	וּבְעֵת קֵץ

The same words are used in verse 40 as in the previous verses, but the
similarity ends there. Only one part of verse 35 has a similar expression to the
one in verse 40, but it is immediately followed by the reference to the "appointed time" (לַמּוֹעֵד, *deʿommal*), which creates the parallelism with verse
27. At most one could claim that there is an inclusio between verses 35 and
40, but this disrupts the structure of the previous group which is based on a
greater parallelism of structures than simply two words. In fact, verse 35 may
function as a hinge connecting the two major parts of the material, but at the
same time signaling a shift or a break in the narrative. On literary grounds
the evidence seems to be in favor of the break between verses 35 and 36.
However, as with Wood and Miller, Walvoord's arguments are directed at the

---

167. Walvoord, *Daniel*, 270.

Amillennialists, not at the Preterists, and even the literary argument would be congruent with claims of some Preterists.

Donald Campbell's Arguments

Campbell presents some arguments that are similar to the one's already mentioned in the previous authors, but they are nevertheless worth recording.

> Though not all have agreed, the evidence seems conclusive that the spotlight now falls on an evil ruler of the last days—Antichrist: (1) according to the angel's words, the scope of this prophecy was to include the "latter days" (see 10:14); (2) in the opening verses of this section (vv. 36–39) introductory statements are made as if this person is being introduced in this context for the first time. This corresponds with the fact that the story of Antiochus in relation to the Jews was brought to completion (v. 35); (3) the prophecies (through v. 35) find fulfillment in history, but there is no historical correspondence with what now follows; (4) this king is actually distinguished from the king of the north (v. 40). Therefore he cannot be Antiochus Epiphanes; (5) the entire section (vv. 36–45) corresponds remarkably with other recognized prophecies of the final Antichrist (see Dan. 7:24–27; 8:23–25; 9:26–27; 2 Thes. 2:4ff; Rev. 13, 17); (6) in connection with this person's rule there will occur the time of Great Tribulation. (12:1)[168]

First, Campbell argues that the scope of the prophecy was to include the "latter days." This is an argument for the Futurist position only if one believes that the latter days are still future. If, as Preterists hold, the latter days refers to the latter days of Judaism and were fulfilled in 70 AD, then this argument has no force. Also, Campbell claims that the prophecies from verse 36 on have "no historical correspondence" with actual history. An important argument, which we have already seen in arguments of other Futurists, is the fact that, as Campbell points out, the king introduced in verse 36 is distinguished from the "king of the North" according to the statement in verse 40: "At the end time the king of the South will collide with him, and the king of the North will storm against him with chariots . . ." However, although this seems to be an important argument against identifying Antiochus as the king, it actually serves to weaken this position. Earlier it was argued that Antiochus is nowhere identified as "the king of the North," which is the designation for all of his predecessors. To argue that the king of verse 36–40 is different from the "king of the North" actually serves to strengthen the argument that this might be Antiochus. Also, it says nothing about the Preterist view since neither do most

---

168. Campbell, *Daniel*, 131.

Preterists hold that this king is Antiochus. We deal with this issue in more detail in the comments on verse 40 below.

Campbell also argues, "the entire section (vv. 36–45) corresponds remarkably with other recognized prophecies of the final Antichrist (see Dan. 7:24–27; 8:23–25; 9:26–27; 2 Thes. 2:4ff; Rev. 13, 17)." However, the strength of this argument rests on interpreting these related passages from a Futurist perspective. If one's opponent does not agree that these verses refer to the Anti-Christ, then this argument is weak. Campbell's final argument has to do with the tribulation: "(6) in connection with this person's rule there will occur the time of Great Tribulation (12:1)." Once again this argument is predicated on accepting the notion of a great tribulation from a Futurist perspective.

Robert Culver's Arguments

Robert Culver presents a lengthy series of arguments why this section of Daniel's prophecy must refer to the Antichrist. We will deal with them one at a time.

> In pursuance of this contention, I present a brief of the evidence that the prophecy concerning the willful king in Daniel 11:36–45 is an eschatological prediction relating to the career of the final Antichrist. 1. The scope of the prophecy, as indicated by the angelic revealer, permits, if it does not demand, an eschatological element in the prophecy. I have reference to Daniel 10:14 (ASV), which reads: "Now I am come to make thee understand what shall befall thy people in the latter days; for the vision is yet for many days." There are two expressions here, designating the scope of the vision: "latter days" and "for many days." The first is a technical term, taken out of the previous prophetical literature of Israel, and always in Scripture includes some eschatological reference. This is recognized by the vast majority of evangelical scholars of all schools of eschatology. Leupold's comment is quite typical: "In all instances that we know of this term reaches out into the Messianic age. Obvious instances are Genesis 49: 1; Numbers 24:14; Isaiah 2:2. We believe that the same is the case in this instance." (See my note on this term in Dan 2:28, p. 115). The other expression, "for many days," is literally "for the days." Whether it be taken as referring to the "latter days" or only as most commentators allow, to long extended futurity, this expression also counts for an eschatological reach to this prophecy.[169]

---

169. Culver, *Daniel*, 176–77.

Culver's first argument is that the prophecies in Dan 11:36–45 are related to the "latter days," which, according to Culver, "is a technical term, taken out of the previous prophetical literature of Israel, and always in Scripture includes some eschatological reference."[170] The testimony that Culver presents from Leupold and the related biblical references seem to substantiate this claim. However, that this term is technical and eschatological does not argue for when it should occur unless one has already decided that eschatological material must relate to our future. For those who hold to the Antiochus view, this may be an important argument, but the Preterist simply acknowledges that it is eschatological and places the eschaton at 70 AD. In order to show that the eschatological element must be understood as future for us, one must present more evidence to support these arguments *vis à vis* the Preterist view.

> 2. For those who believe in the accuracy of predictive prophecy, it is of most importance that the correspondence of the predictions of chapter 11 with now past history breaks down at the end of verse 35. I mean that if verses 36 to 45 were intended to refer to Antiochus, the last great Seleucid king, then the author appears to be guilty of introducing error into the Scriptures. There is nothing known in history which corresponds to the prediction of Daniel 11:36–45. Evidence of this is the utter confusion in the commentaries of those who insist that Antiochus is the chief figure down to the end of the chapter.[171]

This is probably the strongest argument against both the Antiochus view and the Preterist view. If it can be shown that there is no historical material to correspond to the prophecies in a level of accuracy consistent with the previous section in Daniel, this goes a long way to show that these alternate views are incorrect. Although Culver directs his attack toward those who hold that this material relates to Antiochus, the same argument can be directed at the Preterist. The Preterist must show that the text, without distortion or manipulation, can be seen as fulfilled in Herod the great or some other figure in the period leading up to 70 AD. As we go through the individual verses, we will attempt to relate the prophecies to the various views in order to discover if and where there is a correspondence, or lack thereof.

> 3. The statement in 11:36 (ASV) that "he shall prosper till the indignation be accomplished" suggests that the fulfillment of the predictions of the willful king is in eschatological times. "The indignation" is another technical term out of Israel's prophetical literature, referring frequently to the wrath of God on men in the

170. Ibid., 176.
171. Ibid., 177.

last times. We have previously dealt with the Great Tribulation of
Israel in the end time. During the time of that Tribulation of Israel,
God will be dealing in wrath with the Gentiles also, and frequently
that wrath on the nations of men is called *zăʿăm*, "indignation."
The word appears twenty-two times in the Old Testament, and
while it does not always refer to this particular indignation, it
sometimes does. Isaiah 26:20 is a good illustrative passage. It is
not conclusive, of course, but it does bear some weight.[172]

This argument is, once again, primarily directed against those who hold
to the Antiochus view. Since Antiochus died many years before the destruction of Jerusalem in 70 AD, this prophecy could not be referring to Antiochus.
Not only did Antiochus die, but he left no dynasty by which it might be argued that even though he died, his dynasty continued. However, this does not
argue against the Preterist view that Herod is the king to whom these verses
refer. Evans and Mauro argued that Herod's dynasty survived Herod and continued the indignation against the Jews until the destruction of Jerusalem and
the temple in 70 AD. We have already partially considered this interpretation
above. Culver's argument does not apply to this scenario, however.

> 4. Of greater weight is the fact that this predictive section cor-
> responds so precisely with other unquestionable predictions of
> the Antichrist that the identity of the reference can hardly be
> doubted. Leupold, Young, and Keil of the amillennial school
> as well as most of the premillennial writers agree in this. The
> behavior of the "little horn" of chapter 7, the "man of sin" of 2
> Thessalonians, and of "the beast" of Revelation 13 is so strikingly
> similar that on this basis of correspondence alone a strong case
> could be built. This king not only does according to his will, but
> he "shall speak marvellous [*sic*] things against the God of gods"
> (Dan 11:36), just as John reveals of "the beast" (Rev 13:6). He
> also "shall magnify himself above all" (Dan 11:37), just as Paul
> says of the man of sin (2 Thess 2:3–10). He meets his end at the
> end of "the indignation" (Dan 11:36, 45) and that in an unusual
> manner, just as Revelation 19:20 says the "beast" will come to his
> end. Each one of these features also is found, as indicated above,
> in Daniel 7 in relation to the "little horn."[173]

Culver begins this point by saying, "this predictive section corresponds
so precisely with other unquestionable predictions of the Antichrist that the
identity of the reference can hardly be doubted." If one accepts Culver's un-

---

172. Ibid.
173. Ibid., 177–78.

derstanding of those "other unquestionable predictions," then this might be an argument of "greater weight." However, all of these other predictions are subject to the interpretive conclusions of those with contrary views. If someone does not hold to Culver's view that these other predictions are in fact "unquestionable," then this argument loses it "greater weight." Whether the descriptions of this king actually correspond to the descriptions of the "little horn" in Daniel 7 will be considered as we go through the relevant verses. This argument can be important in relation to Evans' arguments about Herod. As Evans declares, "I do not identify Herod with the little horn . . ."[174] If it can be shown that there is a sufficient connection or correlation between these two prophecies, this will go a long way in invalidating Evans' interpretation and application of the chapter 11 material to Herod.

Culver's final arguments are predicated on a Futurist view. However, the reference to the resurrection from the dead is a weightier. One simply has to demonstrate that this is a reference to the physical resurrection of the dead and not simply a reference to the new birth, which is sometimes thought of as a spiritual resurrection from spiritual death and is so argued by some Preterists. Also, the final reward of the righteous can be of importance, but the weight of this argument will need to be postponed until we reach that part of the passage in our analysis.

Conclusions from the Various Views

From the previous arguments and presentations, it seems clear that the king introduced in verse 36 and about whom the prophecy is concerned up to and including verse 45 is a different individual than Antiochus IV Epiphanes. The strongest argument for this conclusion is the fact that virtually all commentators agree that the prophetic descriptions of verses 36–45 do not correspond to any person or events in known history. As Keith Mathison put it, "the events described in 11:36–12:3 do not correspond to any known events in the life of Antiochus IV—or anyone else, for that matter."[175] The literary features of the text described and illustrated in Table 57, and the subsequent discussion with reference to verse 40, support the conclusion that there is a break in the narrative signaling a new subject, a new king. In the following section we will be considering in more detail specific arguments for and against a break, and we will consider various arguments about the identity of the king introduced in verse 36.

---

174. Evans, *Four Kingdoms*, 262.
175. Mathison, "Eschatological Time Texts," 167.

The Rise of the King of the End Time: 11:36–39

Almost all commentators hold that the prophecy beginning in verse 21 applies to Antiochus IV Epiphanies. Many commentators argue that with verse 36 there is a break in the continuous narrative and a new king is introduced. This is a major point of dispute between those who associate these verses with Antiochus IV Epiphanes and those who associate the king depicted in these verses with a later person. As we have seen, Preterists and Futurists generally deny that these verses can be applied to Antiochus, but they differ in respect to the person who they claim is actually the subject of these prophecies. Many Preterists claim that there is a break in the text and that the prophecies in verses 36–45 are fulfilled in Herod the Great. As Evans explains, "The preterist view is that verses 36–45 deal with the life and times of a king who came after Antiochus but before AD 70. *The likely person to be that king is Herod the Great*, who ruled Judea under Roman authority during the years 37–4 BC."[176] Futurists claim that the break indicates the jump in the prophecy from the time of Antiochus IV Epiphanes to the time of Anti-Christ which, according to Futurists, is still future. The sections below will present arguments for and against a break in the text. The Arguments in favor of a break will not make a distinction between Preterists and Futurists, but will simply present the arguments that support a break between verses 35 and 36.

ARGUMENTS FOR NO BREAK

Mauro's Arguments for No Break

Philip Mauro understands what he calls "The 'Break' Theory" to be the Futurist claim that with verse 36, the narrative jumps to the future Anti-Christ. Mauro holds, rather, that the narrative follows the kingdoms of Nebuchadnezzar's dream from Medo-Persia to Greece and to Rome, and that the movement of the narrative to Rome begins with verse 36 with its focus upon Herod the Great. He presents four reasons against what he labels as "The 'Break' Theory," and we will deal with these in turn. Mauro's first argument is: "*First*. The form in which the prophecy is given, that of a straightforward narrative, in continuous historical order, omitting no happening of any importance, precludes the idea of there being any break, such as is supposed."[177]

First, we need to consider a matter-of-fact assertion that Mauro makes before he begins the presentation of his four arguments. He states, "The strongest magnifying glass would fail to reveal the slightest indication of any such

---

176. Evans, *Four Kingdoms*, 205 (emphasis in original).

177. Mauro, *Seventy Weeks*, 138.

'break,' but on the contrary every item of the subject-matter of verses 34, 35 and 36 is connected with the one which precedes it by the conjunction 'and.'"[178] Mauro is referring to the fact that each of the three verses, 34, 35, and 36, begins with the conjunction "and" (וְ, *wᵉ*). There is one decisive reason why this assertion is of no consequence. Hebrew has only one conjunction. Consequently, it must carry the load of indicating the various possible meanings, such as "and," "but," "now," and others. So, even though the Hebrew conjunction is used, that does not necessarily indicate that the meaning must be "and." Often, the meaning is "but," indicating a break with the previous material. Apparently, Mauro is not familiar with the Hebrew language and does not see that his argument is actually built on the English translation, not the original text.

His first argument against the break is that the text is "a straightforward narrative, in continuous historical order, omitting no happening of any importance." Mauro acknowledges that the interpretation of the material beginning in verse 1 is agreed upon almost universally by all commentators, including himself. Yet there are clear breaks in the supposedly continuous narrative throughout the chapter. Verse 5 uses the reference "king of the South" to refer to one king, and in verse 6 the same reference, "king of the South," suddenly refers to another king some years later. This shift through history is followed throughout the chapter. Of course Mauro hedges his bet with the qualification, "omitting no happening of any importance," but this does not help his argument since what he thinks is of "any importance" may be of importance to someone else or in itself. Since this is a subjective qualification, it provides no objective support for his argument. Of course Mauro's rejection is not that there is a break, but that there is a break of such length that it could span 2,000 years. But, the argument, then, becomes not an argument about whether there is a break, but about how long the break can be.

Someone may argue that there is an indicator in verse 6 that there is a break in the narrative but not in verse 36, so verse 6 is not parallel. Verse 6 begins, "After some years . . ." which clearly indicates a break. However, there is a shift in the reference to the "king of the South" between verse 6 and verse 9, but there are no indicators that the text is referring to a different "king of the South" in verse 9 than is referred to in verse 6, yet all commentators, including Mauro, argue that the historical circumstances require a different reference. So, Mauro's claim that this is a continuous narrative does not eliminate the possibility of breaks and changes of reference without any textual indicators. The primary criterion for identifying the referent is the historical

---

178. Ibid., 137.

description, not the nature of the narrative. Of course, his claim that it is a continuous narrative assumes what must be proven.

Mauro's second argument: "*Second.* The prophecy has expressly for its subject the events of 'the latter days' of Jewish history, and the text itself shows this to be the designation of the second term of national life for Israel, which began under Cyrus. This forbids the cutting off of the last (and most important) part of the prophecy and the application of it to a remote age."[179] Of course this argument is predicated on Mauro's assumption that the latter days refers to the period concluding in 70 AD. Since the Futurists take this reference to indicate a time yet in our own future, this argument must be adjudicated on the meaning of that phrase. We have dealt with this to some degree in the section titled "Israel and the Latter Days" beginning on page 596. We will deal with this expression again as the commentary progresses.

Mauro's third argument: "*Third.* After verses 36, 37, 38 and 39, which speak of the character and doings of 'the king,' we find the words, 'And at the time of the end shall *the king of the south* push at (or with) him; and *the king of the north* shall come,' etc. (v. 40). This and succeeding verses (where mention is made of Edom, Moab, and the children of Ammon—peoples which have now long ago ceased to exist) afford clear proof that the prophecy is *still occupied with the era of the wars between Syria and Egypt, which continued till the battle of Actium, B.C. 30.*"[180] This argument assumes that there cannot be any individuals in the future who can be referred to by these designations. In Mauro's day, the latter 1800's and the early 1900's, there were no such individuals. However, since then there are certainly individuals in the Middle East who might qualify for these designations. Whether they do or not is still a question that must be addressed, but it shows that Mauro's assumption is faulty, and therefore his argument is faulty. Also, just because the prophecy refers to Edom, Moab, and the children of Ammon does not require that the events must have taken place while these peoples still inhabited these lands. Rather, it may have been a geographical reference for the benefit of Daniel so that he would be able to understand the geographical areas were these events were to take place, regardless of whether these specific lands were still in existence at the time of the events prophesied.

Mauro's final argument:

> *Fourth.* Finally a conclusive reason for the view we are now presenting is found in the words of the angel recorded in chapter 12:7. It will be observed that the prophecy continues without interruption to verse 4 of chapter 12, where it reaches its end. But then Daniel

179. Ibid., 138 (emphasis in original).
180. Ibid. (emphasis in original).

asked a question concerning "the end of these wonders" which the angel had been foretelling. To this question the angel gives a reply which makes it perfectly certain that the prophecy extends to the dispersion of the Jews at the time of the destruction of Jerusalem by Titus, *and no further*. For he said, "And when He (God) shall have accomplished to *scatter the power of the holy people, all* these things shall be finished." We do not see how it can be contended, in the face of these clear words, that the prophecy has to do with events subsequent to the scattering of the national power of the Jewish people; and it is not open to dispute that that took place in A. D. 70.[181]

Since this argument has to do with the statement in chapter 12 verse 4, we will delay our response until after we have considered that verse in detail at the appropriate place in the commentary. Up to this point, however, we have shown that Mauro's arguments are of no real consequence. This does not prove that there is a break, but it does show that if one is going to argue against a break, one will need to devise other arguments than the one's Mauro uses.

Driver's Arguments for No Break

S. R. Driver presents some few arguments against a break at verse 36. Driver's first argument is that, if there is a break so that verses 36–45 refer to a different person than Antiochus, then the text does not record his demise: "If the contents of vers. 36–45 lie beyond the end of the enemy who has been hitherto spoken of, then bought his destruction to have been mentioned, especially since with the words, 'to the time of the end, because yet for a time appointed,' ver. 35, the words of ver. 27, 'for yet the end of the time appointed,' are resumed."[182] The problem with this objection is that just because Driver thinks the demise of Antiochus ought to have been mentioned does not mean that God thought the same. The question is not what "ought" to have been there, but what is in fact there. There are several reasons that might be proffered for the omission of this material. One reason is that the death of Antiochus has nothing to do with the nation of Israel, and the principle criterion for including material in this chapter is its impact upon the people of God. After the end of Antiochus' persecutions of the Jews, there was no more reason to discuss this person. Another reason may be that, if Antiochus is a type of Anti-Christ, his death is omitted since the death of Antiochus may not have provided any typical significance for the demise of Anti-Christ. Even if

181. Ibid., 39 (emphasis in original).
182. Driver, *Daniel*, 462.

these reasons are not convincing, they are at least reasonable. Simply because Driver may not understand why Antiochus' death was not mentioned is no argument that it must be found somewhere in the text.

Driver also argues, "הַמֶּלֶךְ [*kelemmah*, "king"] with the definite article undeniably points back to the king whose appearance and conduct are described in vers. 21–33."[183] This argument does not work either. Dan 11:4 refers to Alexander the Great, but, without explanation, verse 5 begins, "And the king of the South will grow strong . . ." a reference to Ptolemy I Soter. The fact that the text would abruptly introduce a new person is not unusual. Also, only once throughout all the prophetic descriptions of Antiochus is he referred to as a "king," and this occurs in verse 27 with the opening statement, וּשְׁנֵיהֶם הַמְּלָכִים (*mmah☐meheñšuᶜm̥kal*), literally, "and both of them the kings." This seems to be a reference to Antiochus and Ptolemy Philometor. According to Driver's reasoning, the reference in verse 36 to "the king" could be a reference to Ptolemy Philometer. So, contrary to Driver's claim, this expression does not "undeniably point back to" Antiochus.

Driver's final argument is an objection to the claim that since the prophetic description does not correspond with anything we know about Antiochus it must refer to some other king. Driver argues,

> This is only so far right, that that which is said regarding this king, vers. 36-39, partly goes far beyond what Antiochus did, partly does not harmonize with what is known of Antiochus, and, finally, partly is referred in the N. T. expressly to the Antichrist; cf. ver. 36 with 2 Thess. ii. 4, and ch. xii. 1 with Matt. xxiv. 21. These circumstances also are not satisfactorily explained by the remark that the prophecy regarding Antiochus glances forward to the Antichrist, or that the image of the type (Antiochus) hovers in the image of the antitype (Antichrist); they much rather show that in the prophetic contemplation there is comprehended in the image of *one* king what has been historically fulfilled in its beginnings by Antiochus Epiphanes, but shall only meet its complete fulfillment by the Antichrist in the time of the end.[184]

Driver has actually created a straw man. The argument is not that these verses "partly go far beyond," and "partly do not harmonize," and "partly refer to the N.T." The argument is that there is no correspondence between the history of Antiochus and the prophetic descriptions of these verses. And it does no good to refer to "what has been historically fulfilled in its beginnings by Antiochus Epiphanes." It is not like Antiochus has not completed his life so

---

183. Ibid.

184. Ibid., 462–63 (emphasis in original).

that he might yet finish the fulfillment. The fact is, the prophetic descriptions simply do not find any fulfillment in the life of Antiochus Epiphanes, and, since up to this point the interpretive methodology of commentators, including Driver, has been to identify the historical correlations with the prophetic descriptions, Driver's own admission that the prophetic descriptions do not correspond to anything known about Antiochus eliminates his own view. And it does not help Driver's objection to claim, "in the prophetic contemplation there is comprehended in the image of *one* king what has been historically fulfilled in its beginnings by Antiochus Epiphanes, but shall only meet its complete fulfillment by the Antichrist in the time of the end," because this is precisely what his opponents are claiming. The beginnings of the fulfillment by Antiochus are found in verses 21–35, and the prophetic description of Anti-Christ is found in verses 36–45. Driver's arguments are simply not convincing.

ARGUMENTS FOR A BREAK

Culver Argues for a Break

Culver presents four arguments in favor of a break, and we will deal with each of these in turn. "My reasons for dividing off the directly eschatological prediction at the beginning of verse 36 are four. *First*, a natural break in the thought appears at this point—a break which sets off the last ten verses from the previous narrative. This break is noted by the American Standard Version. The same version also makes a break at the end of verse 39, but the obvious sense of the passage is that the same willful king is discussed on both sides of the break."[185] Culver's first argument seems to be substantiated by the literary features that were discussed earlier and illustrated in Table 57 on page 522 with reference to verse 35. Some have argued that to see a break here is not reasonable. However, there have been similar breaks throughout chapter 11 as we have discussed above. When one verse is making reference to the king of the South and then the next verse uses the same phrase but is suddenly referring to a different king of the South, we see the same kind of break for which Culver argues.

Culver's second argument: "*Second*, as many have noted, the known similarity of the history of the past (during the age of the Antiochus)) [*sic*] breaks off at the end of verse 35. Since nothing in the past is known to correspond with verses 36 to 45, it is quite proper to look for such correspondence in the future."[186] This argument also seems reasonable. Critical scholars argue

185. Culver, *Daniel*, 179 (emphasis in original).
186. Ibid. (emphasis in original).

that this inaccuracy can be attributed to faulty prophesy. However, this assumes what must be proven, and there are equally good if not better reasons to suppose that the historical disparities require the application to a different person rather than to attribute fault to the author.

Culver's third argument: "*Third*, a totally new subject is introduced at the beginning of verse 36. Up to that point, the immediate portion of the chapter is dealing with the king of the south (Egypt), the king (Antiochus) of the north (Syria), and their conflicts one with another, and with Israel. Here, however, the willful king is a third party in conflict with both kings."[187] This argument assumes that Antiochus can be equated with the king of the North. Since this identification has consistently been applied to individuals who have exercised ruling authority of Syria, and since Antiochus is the one exercising this authority since verse 21, it seems reasonable to take the "king" of verse 36 to be a third individual since, according to verse 40, he is in conflict with both the king of the South and the king of the North. The only problem with this is that throughout the verses that clearly deal with Antiochus IV, he is not once referred to as the "king of the North." However, since neither in the prophecy nor in history is there another individual who fits this identification, it is reasonable to assume that Antiochus is functioning in place of the king of the North even though he is not given this identification. Additionally, there is no historical situation in which a king of the South and a king of the North came against Antiochus in the manner described in verse 40. It is again reasonable to conclude that Culver's argument is valid. However, some Preterists argue that in verse 40 there are not three persons discussed, but two, the King of the North and the King of the South, but we will consider this argument at the appropriate point.

Culver's fourth argument: "*Fourth*, since this fourth party may be identified by correspondence with other predictions of the Antichrist as the Antichrist, it seems most likely that the point at which his career is begun in the prophecy (v. 36) is the place at which to begin the eschatological interpretation. Begin somewhere it must, and it is not possible to introduce it later in the chapter."[188] Culver's point here is basically that verse 36 is the most logical and reasonable place to find a beginning to the prophecies that relate to this new king. As he says, "Begin somewhere it must, and it is not possible to introduce it later in the chapter." Verse 36 is not only the most logical and reasonable place to find the beginning of these prophecies, but it is also supported by the literary features to which we have already referred.

187. Ibid., 179–80 (emphasis in original).
188. Ibid., 180 (emphasis in original).

Evans Argues for a Break

Evans presents two arguments for a break between verses 35 and 36: "First, a strong case exists, as I have shown, that the context of 36–45 simply rules out the possibility that the king in these verses is the same as the earlier king."[189] Evans is referring to his analysis and critique of the claims of those who hold that these verses are referring to Antiochus and his arguments that the historical facts relating to the career of Antiochus simply do not fit the prophecies of verses 36–45. We will not deal with those arguments here since we have considered them above, and we will deal with them again as we comment on the various prophecies themselves. Essentially, Evans concludes that the prophecies of verses 36–45, and especially those contained in verses 40–45, are, as he says, "clearly inapplicable to Antiochus IV . . ."[190]

Evans' second argument is, "one can argue that when verse 35 brings in 'the time of the end' and 'the appointed time,' it is signaling the end of the reign of the king who was introduced in verse 21 and, therefore, the end of the vision's concern with that figure."[191] Evans' argument here includes an elaboration of the arguments of Philip Mauro, and we will deal with these arguments and Evans' elaboration in the appropriate section below. A part of this argument is that the references to the "the appointed time" in verse 35 and "the time of the end" in verse 40 are taken by some to refer to the end of the reign of Antiochus IV. Evans argues, "For most conservatives, the 'time of the end' does not always have to be the end of all earthly things before the last judgment, and there is no reason why 11:35 and 11:40 have to refer to the same end time. Most conservatives identify verse 35 with the end of the reign of Antiochus IV and verse 40 with the time of the Antichrist."[192] Basically, Evans' argument is that there is nothing in the text that requires the two references to be talking about the same "end." For the supporters of the Antiochus view, simply to claim that these two verses are referring to the same event is not sufficient argumentation. However, Evans' argument, at least at this point, is much the same. He simply claims that they are not referring to the same event. More of his argument will be examined as we deal with the specific statements in the biblical passages.

189. Evans, *Four Kingdoms*, 213.
190. Ibid., 206.
191. Ibid., 213.
192. Ibid., 214.

Young's Argument Concerning a Break

We have already considered Driver's statement that is quoted by Young (see page 508f). Concerning this statement by Driver, Young comments, "The matter cannot, however, be thus easily dismissed."[193] As we have pointed out on several occasions, Young agrees that the claim that the narrative is continuous is not at all certain: "It is by no means clear that the description is continuous, and because it is by no means clear, many commentators believe that there is a change in the subject."[194] Young goes on to point out, "Again, when Driver asserts that there is no indication of a change of subject, it may be replied that the very fact that the description seems to transcend in large measure what might be applied to Antiochus appears to many earnest expositors to be a very sufficient indication of such a change."[195] Here Young is pointing to the fact that the primary criterion for deciding to whom the various references refer throughout chapter 11, including verse 36ff, is the relationship between the prophetic description and the historical facts as they are known. All commentators use this criterion to argue which king is which, at least up to verse 35. The very fact that the commentators who hold that there is no break take great pains to show that the descriptions can apply to Antiochus IV is evidence that this is the principal criterion, not any supposed "indications" or lack thereof in the text.

Break or No Break

There is in fact precedent for the kind of shift in subject that is the point of contention between commentators, and it can be found even in chapter 11. In verse 5 the reference to the "king of the South" was identified as Ptolemy I Soter. In verse 6 the exact same phrase, "king of the South," is identified by almost all commentators as a reference to Ptolemy II Philadelphus. In fact, in spite of Driver's objection to taking a "continuous description" to refer to two distinct individuals, most commentators, including Driver, do precisely this between verses 5 and 6. With reference to verse 5, for example, Young asserts, "The king of the South is Ptolemy Soter, the son of Lagus . . ."[196] But, with reference to verse 6, the exact same phrase, "the king of the South," according to Young, "is not to Ptolemy Lagi and Seleucus Nicator (as in vs. 5) but probably to Ptolemy Philadelphus and Antiochus II (Theos)."[197]

193. Young, *Prophecy of Daniel*, 246.

194. Ibid.

195. Ibid.

196. Ibid., 234.

197. Ibid., 235–36.

Consequently, Young's exegesis demonstrates that it is not "contrary to all sound principles of exegesis" to suppose that in this *continuous* description the subject can change.

Some may argue that the statement in verse 6, "After some years . . ." was the indicator that the subjects were different. However, this response will not work. The subject of this first verb in verse 6 is the third person plural pronoun, "They" (יִתְחַבְּרוּ, *ūrabaḥtiy*), lit. "they will unite") so that the opening statement of verse 6 is, "And after some years they will unite . . ." The phrase "after some years" is not sufficient to account for a shift in subject, especially since the antecedent of "they" would seem to be the two individuals referred to in verse 5, but is in fact the two individuals whom the prophecy is about to describe. The primary factor by which interpreters, Young included, identify which phrase is referring to which ruler are the prophetic descriptions of the historical events and acts associated with that ruler(s). And so throughout these early verses of the prophecy the phrases "king of the South" and "king of the North," though being the same phrases exactly, refer to different rulers as the prophecy moves through history. So here, even though there is no specific change in the expression from the previous verses, it is the description of events and acts that serve to identify the king that is the referent of the verses. It is primarily the lack of correlation between the prophetic description and any historical person or persons, supported by the literary features already discussed, that indicate that there is in fact a break between verses 35 and 36, and that with verse 36 a new king is introduced. The question now is, who is this king?

THE KING OF VERSES 36–45

Is Herod the King of Verses 36–45?

36— "Then the king will do as he pleases, and he will exalt and magnify himself above every god and will speak monstrous things against the God of gods; and he will prosper until the indignation is finished, for that which is decreed will be done."

Both Mauro and Evans argue that the king referred to in verse 36 is Herod the Great. In fact, Mauro declares, "The proof which enables us to identify 'the king' of Daniel 11:36–39 with Herod the Great and his dynasty, is so convincing that we feel warranted in saying that the prophecy could not possibly mean anyone else."[198] Because Evans refers to Mauro in some of his own arguments, we will first consider Mauro's arguments concerning Herod's dynasty.

198. Mauro, *Seventy Weeks*, 140.

Mauro's first argument is largely based on his subjective evaluations. He says, "It would be strange indeed if, in an outline which gives prominence to Xerxes, Alexander, the Seleucids, the Ptolemies, Antiochus Epiphanes, and the Maccabees, there were no mention of that remarkable personage who exerted upon Jewish affairs and destinies an influence greater than they all, and who sat upon the throne of Israel when Christ was born."[199] This is simply a misrepresentation of the status of Herod. As Bo Reicke points out, "both father [Antipater] and son [Herod] were absolutely dependent on the great individuals who dominate the world: Pompey and Caesar, Antony and Octavian."[200] Herod was not the eminent world figure Mauro supposes. Also, what seems "strange" to Mauro may not be strange at all, and Mauro's argument boils down to his subjective feelings.

Next, Mauro argues from the presence or absence of the definite article "the" to indicate Herod: "The words, 'the king,' should suffice, in the light of the context, without further description, to identify Herod to those who thoughtfully read their Bibles; for Herod alone is called by that title in the Gospels, and he alone had the rank and authority of 'king' in Israel in the days after the captivity, 'the latter days.' The text does not speak of a king, but of the king, the emphatic Hebrew article being used. This is in marked contrast with the terms of v. 40, where the original speaks of 'a king of the north,' and 'a king of the south.'"[201]

Once again Mauro's lack of acquaintance with the Hebrew language leads him to make statements that are contrary to the facts. He argues that since the reference in v. 36 uses the definite article, "the king" (הַמֶּלֶךְ, *kelemmah*), this serves to distinguish "the king" as Herod because this is to be distinguished from verse 40 in which the text supposedly reads, "*a* king of the north," and "*a* king of the south." This is simply a misunderstanding of Hebrew grammar. The actual phrases that occur in verse 40 are "*the* king of the south," (מֶלֶךְ הַנֶּגֶב, *begennah_kelem*), and "*the* king of the north," (מֶלֶךְ הַצָּפוֹן, *ñofassah_kelem*). In both phrases, the word "king" (מֶלֶךְ, *kelem*) is in a construct relation to the words "south" or "north." The words "south" (הַנֶּגֶב, *_begennah*) and "north" (הַצָּפוֹן, *ñofassah*) each have the definite article. In a construct relation, the word in the construct state, in this case the word "king," never takes the article. However, as J. Weingreen states, "When the compound idea is definite, it is (*not* the word in the construct but) the genitive (following it) which takes the article."[202] Since the two words "south" and

199. Ibid.

200. Bo Reicke, *The New Testament Era*, 84.

201. Ibid.

202. J. Weingreen, *A Practical Grammar of Classical Hebrew*, 46.

"north" each have a definite article, this indicates that the idea is definite and should be understood as "the king of the south" and "the king of the north." In fact, this is the pattern throughout chapter 11. Every instance in which the phrase "king of the north" or "king of the south" occurs, it is always "*the* king of the north" and "*the* king of the south." Table 58 below lists all of the uses of the word "king" (מֶלֶךְ, *kelem*) in chapter 11. Of the 18 times that the word "king" (מֶלֶךְ, *kelem*) appears, it appears in the indefinite form only twice, verses 2 and 3. It appears in the definite form either because it has the definite article itself, which occurs in 2 instances, in verses 27 and 36, or it is definite because it is in a construct relation to a word that has the definite article—14 times.

Table 58: The Kings

	I = "indefinite"; D = "definite" — 1 = occurs once in the verse; 2 = occurs twice
1-I	Dan. 11:2 "And now I will tell you the truth. Behold, three more *kings* [מְלָכִים] are going to arise in Persia. Then a fourth will gain far more riches than all of them; as soon as he becomes strong through his riches, he will arouse the whole empire against the realm of Greece."
1-I	Dan. 11:3 "And a mighty *king* [מֶלֶךְ] will arise, and he will rule with great authority and do as he pleases."
1-D	Dan. 11:5 "Then *the king* of the South [מֶלֶךְ־הַנֶּגֶב] will grow strong, along with one of his princes who will gain ascendancy over him and obtain dominion; his domain will be a great dominion indeed."
2-D	Dan. 11:6 "After some years they will form an alliance, and the daughter of *the king* of the South [מֶלֶךְ־הַנֶּגֶב] will come to *the king* of the North [מֶלֶךְ הַצָּפוֹן] to carry out a peaceful arrangement. But she will not retain her position of power, nor will he remain with his power, but she will be given up, along with those who brought her in and the one who sired her as well as he who supported her in those times."
1-D	Dan. 11:7 "But one of the descendants of her line will arise in his place, and he will come against their army and enter the fortress of *the king* of the North [מֶלֶךְ הַצָּפוֹן], and he will deal with them and display great strength."
1-D	Dan. 11:8 "Also their gods with their metal images and their precious vessels of silver and gold he will take into captivity to Egypt, and he on his part will refrain from attacking *the king* of the North [מֶלֶךְ הַצָּפוֹן] for years."

1-D	Dan. 11:9 "Then the latter will enter the realm of *the king* of the South [מֶלֶךְ־הַנֶּגֶב], but will return to his own land."
2-D	Dan. 11:11 "*The king* of the South [מֶלֶךְ־הַנֶּגֶב] will be enraged and go forth and fight with *the king* of the North [מֶלֶךְ הַצָּפוֹן]. Then the latter will raise a great multitude, but that multitude will be given into the hand of the former."
1-D	Dan. 11:13 "For *the king* of the North [מֶלֶךְ הַצָּפוֹן] will again raise a greater multitude than the former, and after an interval of some years he will press on with a great army and much equipment."
1-D	Dan. 11:14 "Now in those times many will rise up against *the king* of the South [מֶלֶךְ־הַנֶּגֶב]; the violent ones among your people will also lift themselves up in order to fulfill the vision, but they will fall down."
1-D	Dan. 11:15 "Then *the king* of the North [מֶלֶךְ הַצָּפוֹן] will come, cast up a siege ramp and capture a well-fortified city; and the forces of the South will not stand [their ground], not even their choicest troops, for there will be no strength to make a stand."
1-D	Dan. 11:25 "He will stir up his strength and courage against the king of the South with a large army; so *the king* of the South [מֶלֶךְ־הַנֶּגֶב] will mobilize an extremely large and mighty army for war; but he will not stand, for schemes will be devised against him."
1-D	Dan. 11:27 "As for both *the kings* [הַמְּלָכִים], their hearts will be intent on evil, and they will speak lies to each other at the same table; but it will not succeed, for the end is still to come at the appointed time."
1-D	Dan. 11:36 "Then *the king* [הַמֶּלֶךְ] will do as he pleases, and he will exalt and magnify himself above every god and will speak monstrous things against the God of gods; and he will prosper until the indignation is finished, for that which is decreed will be done."
2-D	Dan. 11:40 "At the end time *the king* of the South [מֶלֶךְ־הַנֶּגֶב] will collide with him, and *the king* of the North [מֶלֶךְ הַצָּפוֹן] will storm against him with chariots, with horsemen and with many ships; and he will enter countries, overflow [them] and pass through."

Next Mauro argues, "A glance at the context is enough to show that 'the king' of v. 36 cannot mean either of the kings of v. 27. Moreover, these are never spoken of as 'the king,' but always, both before and after v. 36, as 'the king of the north,' or 'the king of the south,' as the case may be."[203] But this

---

203. Mauro, *Seventy Weeks*, 140.

argument does not work either. First, the word "kings" in verse 27 is in fact, "the kings," as has been shown in the chart above. Second, the kings of verse 27, who are the king of the north and the king of the south, are in fact referred to simply as "the kings" in this verse. So, the fact that verse 36 does not use the expression "the king of the north" or "the king of the south" does not prove that "the king" of verse 36 cannot have been either "the king of the north" or "the king of the south." Nevertheless, since verse 40 depicts the king of the south and the king of the north coming against "the king," it is clear that he is not either one of these two individuals. However, this does not show that "the king" of verses 36ff is Herod.

In this same paragraph, Mauro argues, "Nor does the Scripture speak of any 'king' who is to arise at the time of the end of *this present age*, and who answers at all to the description of the prophecy."[204] The problem with this statement is nowhere in the text of these verses, 36–45, does the statement "this present age" occur. Mauro is perhaps referring to the statement in verse 36, "until the indignation is finished." But he has not proven that this refers to the period concluding with the destruction of Jerusalem in 70 AD. His argument here assumes his eschatological framework.

It is not until later, pages 141–42, that Mauro addresses the phrase, "until the indignation is finished." Of this Mauro says, "Moreover, and to this we would specially invite attention, it is said of this king that 'he shall prosper *until the indignation be accomplished*' (or until wrath be completed), in fulfillment of which is the fact that the dynasty of Herod retained, through all the political upheavals of the times, its favor with Rome, and flourished in authority in Palestine, until the destruction of Jerusalem, which is the 'wrath,' or 'indignation,' or 'tribulation,' to which these prophecies of Daniel so frequently refer as 'the end' of Jewish nationality."[205] As we pointed out earlier (see page 517f), Evans claims that when the text states that "he will prosper until the indignation is finished," one might object that Herod died long before 70 AD. However, according to Evans, one can equate Herod's reign with "the dynasty that he founded."[206] So, when the text says "he" will prosper, it indicates that he will prosper through his dynasty. As Evans argues, "*If Nebuchadnezzar can stand for Babylonia and Alexander for Greece, why can't Herod symbolize the Herodian dynasty?*"[207] The text to which Mauro and Evans are referring reads, וְהִצְלִיחַ עַד־כָּלָה זַעַם (*ma'az hālak_ da' hâ1sih^ew*),

---

204. Ibid., 140–41. We will not here deal with his argument about 2 Thess 2:3–10 since that would take us to far afield.

205. Ibid., 141–42.

206. Evans, *Four Kingdoms*, 262.

207. Ibid., 262–63 (emphasis in original).

"and he will prosper until the indignation is finished." The word "prosper" is
וְהִצְלִיחַ (hâṣliḥᵉw). This word occurs in the text in the Hiphil form, and
according to KBH this form of the verb has the meanings, "to be successful,"
or "to make something succeed."[208]

In light of the meaning of the word, and the history of Herod, there are
several problems with the claims of Mauro and Evans. First, Herod did not
in fact found a dynasty *per se*. As Bo Reicke points out, even though Herod
was named King over Judea in 40 BC, he was in fact "a Roman client king
in Palestine."[209] Herod "enjoyed far-reaching domestic and foreign privileges.
He had the right, for example, in some cases to wage war against foreign
nations. But he was responsible to the Romans, and had to furnish troops on
demand and render tribute for certain territories."[210] Peter Schäfer agrees with
Reicke's explanation and further elucidates Herod's actual standing in relation
to Rome.

> The Jewish state under Herod was a *kingdom* under Rome's
> auspices and was identical in every respect to other such client
> kingdoms under Roman sovereignty. Herod received the title of
> king but only as a counter-move to Antigonus' appointment by
> the Parthians. His official status was that of a *rex socius et am-
> icus populi Romani*, that is, a king who was the "ally and friend
> of the Roman people," similar to many other client kings. The
> legal basis for his kingship was his nomination by the Senate on
> Antony's recommendation (in 40 BCE), followed by confirmation
> by Octavian/Augustus after the battle of Actium (31 BCE). Unlike
> the Hasmoneans, there was no official treaty of alliance. His king-
> ship was granted him only *ad personam* [to the person] and for his
> lifetime, whereas Caesar had conferred the office of ethnarch on
> Hyrcanus as a hereditary title. According to Josephus, Augustus
> had indeed granted him the right to nominate his successor, but he
> [Augustus] reserved the right to make the final decision himself, as
> events after Herod's death were to show. Herod's limited minting
> rights (he was allowed to mint only copper coins) were also in no
> way different from those of other client kings of Rome. Apart from
> the tribute, the most important aspect of his political dependency
> on Rome was the fact that he was not allowed to have an indepen-
> dent foreign policy: that is, he could not sign treaties with foreign
> rulers or conduct wars without the consent of Rome.[211]

---

208. KBH, s.v, "צלח."

209. Reicke, *New Testament Era*, 93.

210. Ibid.

211. Schäfer, *The History of the Jews*, 87 (emphasis in original).

In other words, although he had the title of king, Herod was not a king like Nebuchadnezzar and Alexander, or even like David. As Schäfer goes on to point out, "On the other hand, the Romans gave him a totally free hand in internal affairs, and in this respect Herod could rule with unlimited authority."[212] Herod's reign was closer to that of a governor than a king, having authority over the internal affairs of his own realm but subject to the power and authority of Rome in all other aspects. In fact, Schäfer asserts, "The country was essentially the property of the emperor, who had given it to Herod to hold in usufruct."[213] This is distinctly different from the customary practices of actual kings who lay claim to all the property of their realms and lease it out to those who would live on it and work the land. M. Stern adds, "Practically, though, his [Herod's] hands were tied in all matters of political importance and particularly in the sphere in which political independence is characteristically reflected—foreign policy."[214]

It is important to take note of the fact that Schäfer makes a distinction between the hereditary title of ethnarch that Caesar conferred upon Hyrcanus, and the fact that Herod's "kingship was granted him only *ad personam* [to the person] and for his lifetime . . ." This means that Herod could not have founded a dynasty as Mauro and Evans claim. Whether any of Herod's sons would take over his domain after his death was not a function of a dynastic succession, but was rather at the discretion of Augustus.

After Herod's death, his kingdom was divided "in the year 4 B.C., which bound the small princes of Palestine very closely to the *Imperator*."[215] According to the *Latin Dictionary* by Lewis and Short, the term "Imperator" indicates, "The title of the Roman emperors, placed either before or after the name."[216] At this point, Augustus was *Imperator*. In other words, the king of Palestine was not a descendant of Herod, but was in fact the Roman Emperor Augustus himself. Schäfer describes the confusion that followed the death of Herod:

> In his last will and testament, Herod had decreed that Archelaus, the eldest son of his fourth wife Malthace (the Samaritan), was to inherit the title of king, while his brother Antipas, Malthace's younger son, was to become tetrarch of Galilee and Peraea, and

212. Ibid.

213. Ibid., 89.

214. M. Stern, "The Political and Social History of Judea Under Roman Rule," in *A History of the Jewish People*, ed. H. H. Ben-Sasson (Cambridge, Massachusetts: Harvard University Press, 2002), 240.

215. Reicke, *New Testament Era*, 226.

216. *A Latin Dictionary* (1966), s.v. "impĕrātor."

Philip, the son of his fifth wife, Cleopatra the Jerusalemite, would be tetrarch of Gaulanitis, Trachonitis, Batanaea, and Paneas. As was only to be expected, upon his death the brothers quarreled over the inheritance and argued their claims before Augustus in Rome. . . . Augustus hesitated for some time before settling the dispute over the succession. He allowed all the parties concerned to present their cases (including a delegation from the people who requested Augustus to deliver them from the whole Herodian clan and place the country under the direct control of Rome), but ultimately decided to substantially endorse Herod's will.[217]

In other words, the succession to Herod's title did not pass to his sons as a dynastic right, but was allowed by the Roman authority Augustus. This was no dynasty, but was an appointment of Archelaus by Augustus to the position of ethnarch as Peter Richardson notes: "Augustus confirmed Herod's will, with several minor changes. Archelaus was named ethnarch, not king, of Judea, Samaritis, and Idumea, including the important cities of Sebaste and Caesarea Maritima, both lavishly built by Herod. The title 'ethnarch' implied that Archelaus ruled a 'people,' even though the 'peoples' under his control were very disparate. Augustus held back from giving Archelaus the status, dignity, and rule that went with the title 'king.'"[218] After having received this appointment, Archelaus did not function with the authority of a king, as Reicke goes on to point out: "On account of the complaints about Archelaus in A.D. 6, Augustus found it quite natural to change the major portion of the land (Samaria, Judea, and Idumea) into a Roman procuratorship. Indirectly the Jews of the Holy Land were the subjects of the Emperor."[219]

Although Archelaus was the eldest son of Herod whom Herod unsuccessfully appointed in his will to be his successor to the throne as king of Israel, Archelaus' rule as ethnarch lasted only 10 years, from 4 BC to 6 AD when, as Merrill Tenney describes, "The semi-independence of Judea was virtually ended, for Herod had made the assignation of his realm subject to the will of Caesar Augustus, who partitioned the domain as he saw fit. Although Rome had been the real rule of Palestine since Pompey's invasion in 63 B.C., it now asserted its sovereignty more directly and, as the Gospels declare, the Jewish people were compelled to admit that they had no king but Caesar."[220] As Reicke says, "It is noteworthy that Augustus treated the Herodians as a dynasty. Herod I was an upstart; always a vassal, he was not granted a successor of

217. Schäfer, *The History of the Jews*, 101–2.

218. Peter Richardson, *Herod*, 24.

219. Reicke, *New Testament Era*, 226.

220. Merrill C. Tenney, *New Testament Times*, 65.

royal rank. Nevertheless, with Augustus consent, the government of Palestine remained in the hands of Herod's family."[221] In other words, although Herod himself and his descendants considered themselves as having established a dynasty and were actually treated as a dynasty by Augustus, they were in fact simply allowed to rule at the pleasure of Rome, and were not kings after the manner of Nebuchadnezzar and Alexander. History shows that in fact Herod did not establish a dynasty as Mauro and Evans claim, and neither Herod nor his descendants were comparable to Nebuchadnezzar and Alexander, the kind of kings that have been the subject of chapter 11.

A second problem with Mauro's claims about Herod is that neither Herod nor his descendants "prospered." Although Herod "benefited the land and the people by his building activities and by the expansion of trade,"[222] as Tenney points out, "The last years of Herod's life were plagued with frustration and suspicion."[223] Herod grew increasingly suspicious of those around him. He had his wife Mariamne killed, and he imprisoned and eventually had two of his sons, Alexander and Aristobulus, executed. According to Tenney, "The emotional tension and frustration of these dismal years reacted disastrously upon Herod. Mad with suspicion and grief, he rapidly deteriorated physically and mentally. He was almost seventy years of age, broken in spirit, racked by disease, and tortured with doubts and remorse. . . . He attempted suicide but was restrained by his cousin."[224]

A third problem with Mauro's claim that Herod is the king of verses 36–40 is that the career of Herod's descendants was even less prosperous. As Tenney describes, "Archelaus, the son who succeeded Herod, inherited his father's cruelty without his father's ability. His reign was marked by armed rebellion that could be quelled only through the intervention of Varus, the Roman governor of Syria. In A.D. 6, ten years after his succession to the throne, Archelaus was deposed by Augustus and was banished to Gaul. Coponius, a Roman knight, was appointed procurator of Judea . . ."[225] At Herod's request, but with modifications, Augustus divided Herod's kingdom among three of his sons, Archelaus, Herod Antipas, and Philip. Not one of these was designated king in the early stages of his career, and only Philip was elevated to the status of king by Caligula, yet Philip's territory was the Transjordan, not Palestine proper. That Herod did not institute a dynasty is

221. Reicke, *New Testament Era*, 114.

222. Ibid., 105. Reicke remarks, "Herod was certainly, after David, the most powerful ruler of the Holy Land . . ." (105). This, however, is a judgment call on Reicke's part, and many historians dispute such a characterization.

223. Tenney, *New Testament Times*, 62.

224. Ibid., 65.

225. Ibid., 143.

evidenced by the fact that Archelaus, whose claims were upheld by Augustus, "obtained the territory assigned to him: Judea, Samaria, Idumea; only the cities of Gaza, Gadara, and Hippos were severed from these domains and attached to the province of Syria; and instead of the title king, that of ethnarch was given him."[226] So, not only did Herod's eldest son Archelaus not become king after his father, as is the case in a dynasty, but also some of the cities that came under the rule of Herod were taken away from Archelaus, which does not happen to the successor of a dynasty. Archelaus served as ethnarch from 4 BC to 6 AD. Philip was named Tetrarch of the northern Transjordan and served from 4 BC to 34 AD. He died leaving no heirs. Additionally, Augustus ordered that these so-called heirs of Herod were to receive an income from their territories: "Archelaus was to derive from his territories an income of 600 talents, Antipas 200 talents, and Philip 100 talents,"[227] hardly characteristic either of kings or of the inheritors of a "dynasty."

Herod Antipas became Tetrarch of Galilee and Perea, and was in power from 4 BC to 39 AD. Reicke describes the final years of Herod Antipas.

> The last ten years of his reign, however, took a form less happy and serene. Antipas was under the influence of a very ambitious woman, Herodias, infamous for her part in the execution of John the Baptist. . . . In the meantime, the Nabatean king, Aretas IV, was preparing to go to war for the sake of his divorced and humiliated daughter. In 36, he attacked Antipas and defeated him so thoroughly that Vitellius, the Syrian legate, was forced to mount a counterattack, temporarily rescuing Antipas. Herodias was soon to cause his final downfall, for she could not stand Caligula's naming her brother Agrippa I king over the newly independent tetrarchy of Philip in 37, and she drove Antipas to contend for equal rank. The capricious Emperor deposed him in 39 for being too power-hungry, and banished him and his wife to Lugdunum (the modern Lyon), in Gaul, where both of them died.[228]

Emperor Gaius not only exiled Antipas, but, as Hoehner describes, "Antipas' tetrarchy and property were handed over to Agrippa."[229] Although this meant a new beginning, in a sense, for Agrippa I, it marked the end of Herod Antipas. The descriptions of the careers of the sons of Herod certainly

---

226. Emil Schürer, *Political History of Palestin, From B.C. 175 to A.D. 135*, vol. 2, *A History of the Jewish People in the Time of Jesus Christ*, trans. John MacPherson (Peabody, Massachusetts: Hendrickson Publishers, 1998), 6–7.

227. Ibid., 7.

228. Reicke, *New Testament Era*, 125.

229. Harold W. Hoehner, *Herod Antipas*, 262.

do not fit the characterization either of the statement in Dan. 11:36 or that of Mauro. They did not in fact "flourish."

The final and perhaps most devastating problem with the claim of Mauro and Evans that Herod's supposed "dynasty" fulfilled the prophecy is that Herod Agrippa I, the last Herodian to be identified as King of Judea, died in 44 AD, some 26 years before the destruction of Jerusalem in 70 AD, which Mauro identifies with the statement in verse 36, "the indignation is finished." So, contrary to the claims of Mauro and Evans, even if we grant the notion of a dynasty of Herod, this dynasty did not even last until 70 AD. As Reicke points out, "In 44, the Emperor Claudius (A.D. 41–54) brought to an end the kingdom of Judea . . ."[230] Even though Claudius restored Agrippa I to a position of authority in 41 AD, this position was not the position of king, but of procurator, and this lasted only until 44 AD. Even the procuratorship instituted by Claudius did not last until 70 AD, "but was replaced in 67 by the regional military government of Vespasian and in 70 by the imperial province of Judea."[231]

In 44 AD, after the death of Herod Agrippa I, the procuratorship passed to Cuspius Fadus. Although there was a descendant of Agrippa I, Agrippa II, he was never ruler of Judea. Schäfer points out, "He [Agrippa II] was not appointed successor by Claudius, but remained in Rome."[232] Agrippa II was the seventh and last king of the family of Herod the Great and the last of the Herodians. Upon the death of his uncle Herod of Chalcis, Agrippa inherited his uncle's throne and became king of Chalcis. Chalcis was a small town on the road between Damascus and Berytus on the coast of the Mediterranean Sea. However, in 53 even that small kingdom was taken away from him, and he was made governor over the tetrarchy of Philip and Lysanias in Transjordan. Schäfer describes the remainder of his life: "He supported the Romans during the revolution, and after the war Vespasian granted him large new territories in the north, where there were no Jewish inhabitants.

Merrill Tenney points out that Herod Agrippa I "did not succeed to the throne of Judea until after the death of Tiberius in A.D. 37 . . . the entire territory had been placed under a Roman procurator since the deposition of Archelaus in A.D. 6."[233] So, for over 30 years Herod's so-called dynasty did not have any authority over Palestine. As we have pointed out, Agrippa I, the last of Herod's line to rule in Palestine, died in 44 AD. Agrippa II, son of Agrippa I and the last of the Herodians, did not rule in Palestine. The

---

230. Ibid., 202.
231. Ibid.
232. Schäfer, *The History of the Jews*, 113.
233. Tenney, *New Testament Times*, 203.

claim by Mauro and Evans that Herod's "dynasty" "flourished in authority in Palestine, until the destruction of Jerusalem" is simply false.

Above Every God?

Concerning the statement in verse 36, "he will exalt and magnify himself above every god," Mauro claims, "The words 'above every god' may be taken to mean every ruler and authority in Israel, just as 'God of gods' means Supreme Authority above all authorities."[234] However, this is not what the text states. The clause is set out below.

Table 59: Daniel 11:36

כָּל־	עַל־	וְיִתְגַּדֵּל	וְיִתְרוֹמֵם
every	over	and he will make himself great	and he will exalt himself
אֵלִים	אֵל	וְעַל	אֵל
gods.	god of	and over	god

The text does not say that this king would exalt himself above every rule and authority "in Israel." In fact, the text places no such geographical, political, or religious boundaries on the claim. To indicate that this is what the verse "may be taken to mean" is simply reading into the text what is clearly not there. And yet Mauro's diatribe directed at those who do not get their proof from the Scripture alone (see chapter 1 in his book) is conveniently ignored as his own guiding principle: "proof adduced in support of any interpretation should be taken *from the Scripture itself,*" and "His own Word is the *only authority.*"[235] But even if we grant Mauro's understanding of the meaning, this still was not true of Herod as we have seen from his history. Historians repeatedly pointed out that Herod was a vassal of Rome and subject to the demands of the Emperors as this related to Palestine. Herod was required to pay tribute to Rome, and when trouble brewed in Palestine, Herod ran home to Rome for help. It is simply not true that Herod exalted himself above every authority even in Israel. In Israel, Rome was always the ultimate authority.

The historical evidence seems to demonstrate beyond dispute that the description of "the king" in verse 36 simply cannot be applied to Herod with-

---

234. Mauro, *Seventy Weeks*, 144.

235. Ibid., 11 (emphasis in original).

out distortion, manipulation, or simply the ignoring of the facts. Herod did not establish a dynasty in any sense of that term, and his successors did not continually rule in Palestine, nor were they all even designated kings. The last Herodian to exercise authority in Palestine, Agrippa I, died in 44 AD, some 26 years before the destruction of Jerusalem, and the last of the Herodians, Agrippa II never had any authority over Palestine. Herod did not seek to exalt himself above every god, nor did he even seek to exalt himself above every authority in Israel. The description of the king in verse 36 simply cannot be applied to Herod the Great.

37—   "He will show no regard for the gods of his fathers or for the desire of women, nor will he show regard for any other god; for he will magnify himself above them all."

Herod, A Jew?

Verse 37 states that this king will "show no regard for the god(s) of his fathers." We have already dealt briefly with the claims of Evans concerning this phrase (see page 510f). Here we will concentrate on Mauro and others, even though we may review Evans' claims and/or add additional observations about his argument. In an effort to make this statement applicable to Herod, Mauro attempts to make the case that Herod "was virtually a Jew."[236] Mauro has put himself into the awkward position of having somehow to make Herod and his fathers into Jews. He assumes that this statement could not apply to heathens because, "whether or not a heathen king should change his national gods is a matter of no importance whatever."[237] Also, Mauro understands the clause to say "God of his fathers," rather than "gods of his fathers." The Hebrew phrase uses the word "Elohim" (אֱלֹהֵי, 'ĕlōhê'), which is morphologically a plural form but, when used with reference to the true and living God, is always taken as a plural of majesty and understood to refer to the one God. Technically, the word can be translated either as a singular form, "God," or "god," or as a plural form, "gods." Although Mauro does not attempt to justify his translation, he seems to be correct in taking the verse in the sense "God of his fathers," rather than "gods of his fathers." As we have shown in Table 53 on page 511, there are only 5 other instances where this phrase is used, and in each instance the reference is translated with the singular noun "God," and each one refers to the God of Israel. So, if Daniel follows this pattern, we must understand this to be a reference to the God of Israel, as Mauro has taken it.

236. Ibid., 145.
237. Ibid., 144.

Also, it is important to note that the text seems to make a distinction between the God of Israel and the heathen god referred to in the latter part of the verse. In the expression "God of his fathers," the word "Elohim" is used: אֱלֹהֵי אֲבֹתָיו (wᵉyāṭobᵃʾ eholᵉʾ).[238] However, in the latter part of the verse the expression "any other god" uses a different word for "god": אֱלוֹהַּ (hâoleʿ). In Daniel, this form is used only three times (Dan 11:37, 38, 39), and in each instance seems to be referring pagan gods in distinction from the God of Israel. This seems to support the notion that the expression "God of his fathers" is referring to the God of Israel.

Arguing against this view, in a footnote, Miller asserts, "Some commentators have rendered 'the God of his fathers,' and of course אֱלֹהֵי may be singular or plural. Since the phrase 'the God of your fathers' is used elsewhere in the OT to refer to Yahweh, they deduce that the similar expression indicates that Antichrist will be an apostate Jew (so Whitcomb, *Daniel*, 154). Young translates as 'gods of his fathers' but still thinks the phrase indicates Antichrist's Jewish descent (*Daniel*, 249). However, Antichrist will come from the fourth empire, Rome (Gentile), and therefore will not be Jewish."[239] However, as we have pointed out above, this does not work as an argument against the translation since today an individual does not need to be a Jew in order for the God of Israel to be his God or the God of his fathers. Of course this could refer only to the time after Christ's death, burial, and resurrection. Before Christ's first coming, for an individual to claim the God of Israel as his God, it would be necessary for him to become a proselyte to Judaism. However, in the Christian age, the God of a Gentile Christian is the God of Israel. Also, just because this person comes from the fourth Empire, Gentile Rome, does not mean he cannot be a Jew. Jews have obtained positions of great power in gentile kingdoms. One example is Daniel himself. So, Miller's argument is not as forceful as at first it may seem.

Mauro claims, "Now Herod, though supposedly of Idumean (i.e. Edomite) origin, was virtually a Jew; for all the remaining Idumeans, who had come into Judea several centuries previous, had been amalgamated with the Jews."[240] Here again Mauro has made an historical error. Evans points out that, "the Idumeans had been converts to Judaism only since the reign of John Hyrcanus . . ."[241] (134–104 BC), and according to Richardson, "The reassessment of Idumean conversions means that Herod's attachment to Judaism re-

---

238. The word 'Elohey' (אֱלֹהֵי) is in the construct state, which is a shortened form of the word. The absolute state would be אֱלֹהִים (Elohim).

239. Miller, *Daniel*, 307.n90.

240. Ibid., 144–45.

241. Evans, *Four Kingdoms*, 263.

sulted from his grandfather's voluntary adherence and willing 'full' conversion
to the Temple cult in Jerusalem and not from a forced submission to a bare-
bones form of Judaism."[242] In other words, Herod was an Idumean convert to
Judaism, and that tradition did not begin in his family until the time of his
grandfather. His ancestors were probably adherents to the Edomite religion.
The chief god of the Edomites was Cos (Kos or Kaus), whom many scholars
believe to have been the Edomite equivalent to the Moabite god Chemosh.

Ethnically, Herod was not a Jew, nor were his fathers. The text specifically asserts that the king will show no regard to the "God of his fathers." This
expression is used in the OT to refer to the fact that a man's ancestors where
worshipers of the God of Israel. But, this is hardly applicable to Herod or
his ancestors since the conversion to Judaism encompassed only two generations from his grandfather who voluntarily converted to Judaism as an adult,
and, since before his grandfather's conversion, his ancestors could have been
worshipers of many gods. The gods worshiped by the Edomites included El,
Baal, Ashera, and Cos. In other words, there was no "God of his fathers,"
and we have already shown that this phrase is not used in the OT in the
sense of "gods of his fathers." Mauro's claim that "in introducing the worship
of Caesar, Herod conspicuously failed to 'regard the God of his fathers,'"
simply does not fit Herod because his ancestors did not consistently worship
one God, and the Edomite religion of his ancestors, if it was like other poly-
theistic pantheons, would not have forbidden the addition of another deity
into the pantheon. In other words, because Herod's grandfather converted
from Edomite religion to Judaism, the characterization 'God of his fathers' is
simply not applicable to Herod.[243]

The God of Antiochus' Fathers

Montgomery attempts to apply the phrase "gods of his fathers" to Antiochus
Epiphanes. He argues, "For light on the god 'his fathers knew not,' Nestle
(*Marg.*, 42) has called attention to the same work of Babylon, p. xlviii, who
notes that Apollo (the historic deity of the dynasty) seated upon the Cyprian
omphalos disappeared almost entirely from the Seleucid coinage after the
days of Epiphanes, being replaced by Zeus. This replacement of gods, so contrary to antique sentiment, may suffice to explain our writer's bitterness."[244]
Goldingay makes a similar argument: "Antiochus replaced Apollo by Zeus as
the god of the Seleucid dynasty, apparently again for political reasons: it pro-

242. Richardson, *Herod*, 55.

243. Mauro, *Seventy Weeks*, 145.

244. Montgomery, *Daniel*, 461.

vided religious support for the irregularity involved in his accession."[245] Lucas
presents the same argument: "Exactly what lies behind the opening clause of
v. 37 is a matter of debate. . . . Many commentators have argued that, in his
attempt to unify his empire, Antiochus promoted the worship of Zeus, with
whom he began to identify himself, over against local cults. In doing this, he
departed from the Seleucid tradition of worshipping Apollo as their patron.
The main evidence for this has been drawn from his coins, but Mørkholm
(1966: 131) has strongly disputed this interpretation of it."[246] Lucas goes on
to admit however, "Some polemical exaggeration is used here in depicting
this."[247] In fact, concerning this view Young says,

> The embarrassment of those commentators who would apply these
> words to Antiochus is obvious. Bevan admits that we are not told
> the manner in which Antiochus showed disrespect for the gods
> of his fathers but thinks that it may be in his abolition of local
> usages for the sake of centralizing his empire. . . . Driver thinks
> that by paying honor to foreign deities such as Jupiter Capitolinus
> there was implied a depreciation of the gods of his own country.
> Zoeckler is more convincing in suggesting that he will manifest
> his impiety by the robbing of temples and tear [sic] down religious
> systems. All of these are makeshifts, however, which do not do
> justice to the language of the text. The fact is that these words do
> not apply to Antiochus.[248]

Young's argument seems devastating to the Antiochus view. Evans considers the attempt by Collins to make the text apply to Antiochus: "The best
way to interpret the passage in 37, as well as the similar one in 38 referring
to 'a god unknown to his fathers,' Collins suggests, is to make Antiochus appear as impious as possible. One has to wonder, however, if a Maccabean-era
author could have expected to successfully distort the blasphemies committed
by Antiochus to people who knew a good deal about the religious views and
policies of this ruler from personal experience."[249] The evidence against the
Antiochus view is far too great to overcome.

---

245. Goldingay, *Daniel*, 304.
246. Lucas, *Daniel*, 289–90.
247. Ibid., 290.
248. Young, *Prophecy of Daniel*, 248–49.
249. Evans, *Four Kingdoms*, 208.

The Desire of Women

Verse 37 also states that this king will "show no regard . . . for the desire of women." We have dealt with Evans' view when considering his translation of the passage (see page 512f). Here we will consider views of other commentators. Mauro says, "There can scarcely be any doubt that they refer to Christ, and that Daniel would so understand them. For, of course, the 'women' must be understood to be *women of Israel*; and the ardent 'desire' of every one of them was that she might be the mother of Christ."[250] There is no statement in Scripture that Jewish mothers desired to be the mother of the Messiah, and by appealing to this Mauro has once again violated his own principle that "proof adduced in support of any interpretation should be taken from the Scripture itself," and "His own Word is the only authority."[251] Nevertheless, this seems to be the most predominate view. Walvoord takes this perspective as well. He says, "Although Daniel is not specific, a plausible explanation of this passage, in the light of Daniel's Jewish background, is that this expression, *the desire of women*, is the natural desire of Jewish women to become the mother of the promised Messiah, the seed of the woman promised in Genesis 3:15."[252] It is peculiar, however, that Walvoord insisted that it was necessary to use the specific name for the God of Israel in the first part of this verse, but somehow it is not necessary to spell out that the angel is referring to Messiah in this instance.

Nevertheless, Miller makes an important point: "On either side of the phrase are statements concerning Antichrist's contempt for God and religion. It would not be surprising to find a reference to the rejection of the Messiah in this setting."[253] The flow of the verse seems to be, no regard for God, Messiah, or gods—rather exalting himself above all gods. Many have argued that in the context it would be very strange for the flow to be so drastically interrupted in referring to a man's desire of a woman. If we take the phrase to be a veiled reference to Messiah, it would seem to be in accord with the statement in verse 36, "he will exalt and magnify himself above every god." The final phrase in verse 37 is, כִּי עַל־כֹּל יִתְגַּדָּל (*laddagtiy ʾok laʿʾık*), "for over all he will make himself great." The "all" here could refer back to the three things mentioned in the first part of the verse, God, Messiah, gods. It would not seem to make sense to say that he would make himself great over God, desiring women, and gods.

---

250. Mauro, *Seventy Weeks*, 145.

251. Ibid., 11 (emphasis in original).

252. Walvoord, *Daniel*, 274.

253. Miller, *Daniel*, 307.

Concerning the view that this is a reference to the normal desire that men have for women, Wood makes an interesting point against this view: "The thought intended may be the 'desire' which men normally have for women. . . . [this view] is not likely, because the Antichrist is prefigured in Antiochus Epiphanes, and he was known for his profligacy toward women."[254] Yet Wood does not hold that this is a reference to the desire that the Jewish woman would have to be the mother of Messiah. Rather, he holds that this is "the area of 'desire' normally characteristic of women (such as mercy, gentleness, kindness). . . . Moreover, it is very likely that the Antichrist will have little place for such graces as mercy, gentleness, and kindness."[255] This is a particularly odd interpretation and does not seem to fit the text very well. It must overcome the same problem of contextual consistency as the other option. The progression of thought, "God, characteristics of women, gods," does not seem to flow well either. In any case, these graces are not necessarily considered to be "normally characteristic of women" more than of men.

There may be, in fact, too much credence given to the argument by Miller that, "On either side of the phrase are statements concerning Antichrist's contempt for God and religion. It would not be surprising to find a reference to the rejection of the Messiah in this setting."[256] Although it may seem incongruous to take the phrase actually to mean "God and the natural desire of men for women," the use of a reference to both "God" and "Messiah" might be a bit redundant, since the Messiah is God and is depicted as such in many OT prophecies. The text would then read, "God, God, and gods." In fact, the redundancy might be particularly evident if we assume that these events take place in the Christian era and that this king is an individual who has been reared in a Christian environment. Rather, the congruity may be depicting this individual as being both religiously and morally aberrant in his character.

The verse is set out below:

Table 60: Daniel 11:37

וְעַל־	אֱלֹהֵי	אֲבֹתָיו	לֹא
And unto	God of	his fathers	not

יָבִין	וְעַל־	חֶמְדַּת	נָשִׁים
he will pay attention	and unto	desire of	women

254. Wood, *Daniel*, 306.
255. Ibid.
256. Miller, *Daniel*, 307.

וְעַל־	כָּל־	אֱלוֹהַ	לֹא
and unto	all	gods	not
יָבִין	כִּי	עַל־	כֹּל
he will pay attention	for	over	all
יִתְגַּדָּל׃			
he will exalt himself			

Verse 37 is actually composed of two independent clauses. The first states, "And unto God of his fathers not he will pay attention, or unto the desire of women." This is a complete sentence. The second independent clause is, "And unto all gods not he will pay attention for over all he will exalt himself." Because of the construction of this verse, it is not strictly accurate for Miller to depict the situation as, "On either side of the phrase are statements concerning Antichrist's contempt for God and religion . . ." In fact, this statement begs the question. To say that on either side of the statement is contempt for God and religion assumes what must be demonstrated. Also, since the verse is composed of two independent sentences, it is not strictly accurate to talk about "on either side." This is an arbitrary grouping on Miller's part. On this basis we could bring in statements from the previous verse and talk about what is on either side.

Table 61: The Desire of Women

His Character	Spiritual – Rejecting the God of His Fathers
	Natural – Rejecting the Desire for Women
His Ambition	Spiritual – Reject all Gods
	Natural – Exalting Himself as God

The construction of the verse in the form of two independent sentences groups the assertions into two distinct groups: 1) He will not pay attention to the God of his fathers or the desire of women; 2) He will not pay attention to any gods, but will exalt himself above all gods. The first group of assertions then could be a case of merism in which the totality or whole is substituted (expressed) by two contrasting or opposite parts. The whole of this person's character may be expressed by the two encompassing characteristics, the spiritual and the natural. If we could understand the expression "desire of women" to refer to the natural desire of the man for the woman, this first sentence may be expressing this king's rejection of the true God on the one hand, and

godly morality on the other. This also fits Paul's characterization of humanity that has rejected God (Rom 1:24ff). This is not to say that this king will
engage in homosexuality or will himself necessarily be homosexual. Rather,
the extremes represented in the merism indicating a perverting of the spiritual
and the natural characterize the moral and spiritual corruption of this person,
whether it turns out that he is homosexual or not.

38—   "But instead he will honor a god of fortresses, a god whom his fathers
       did not know; he will honor him with gold, silver, costly stones and
       treasures."

The God of Fortresses

The NASB begins verse 38 with the phrase, "But instead . . ." This is used to
translate the simple וְ (ᵉw) conjunction: וְלֶאֱלֹהַּ (hāolᵉʾelᵉw). The conjunction here seems to be saying, "Rather than regarding the God of his fathers,
the desire of women, or any other gods, he will make himself greater than
all gods, and in their place he will honor the god of fortresses." Exactly to
what the phrase "god of fortresses" refers is a matter of some debate. It seems
contradictory for verse 37 to say he will have no regard for any gods, and then
to say in verse 38 that he will honor the god of fortresses. Young makes this
exact point: "If the reference is to some known deity then all that is said in vs.
37 about the king not regarding any god is nullified."[257] It seems more likely
that what is being said here is that by exalting himself above all gods, he will
attempt, by military action, to dominate the world, and thereby make a god
out of war. Again Young makes the same point: "What then is the meaning?
In answer to this question, it must be replied that the reference is not to any
particular god or cult. This seems to be stressed by saying that the god is
one whom the fathers have not known. He is a god who is characterized by
fortresses or strongholds. In other words he is the personification of war."[258]
Miller asserts a similar idea: "Antichrist will not worship the gods (or 'god')
of his ancestors; 'instead of them [i.e., these deities; lit., 'instead of him'],
he will honor a god of fortresses,' that is, military power and might."[259] Keil
asserts, "The 'god of fortresses' is the personification of war, and the thought
is this; he will regard no other god, but only war; the taking of fortresses he
will make his god; and he will worship this god above all as the means of his
gaining world-power."[260]

257. Young, *Prophecy of Daniel*, 249.
258. Ibid.
259. Miller, *Daniel*, 308.
260. Keil, *Daniel*, 466.

Mauro renders it, "god of forces."[261] He argues that this points to Herod the Great.

> Herod's career affords a most striking fulfillment of this verse. The expression, "god of forces, or fortresses," is so unusual that it furnishes a most satisfactory means of identification; for it applies to the Caesars as to none others in history, seeing that the Roman emperors claimed for themselves divine honors, and that it was by "forces," or "fortifications," that they extended and maintained their power, and enforced the worship they demanded. This honor Herod paid to them, and after the most extravagant fashion; and he did it, of course, in order to make himself secure, that is to say, "for his own establishment," as the text of v. 38 may be rendered. This honor paid by Herod, first to Julius Caesar, then to Antony, and then to Antony's conqueror, Augustus, was one of the most conspicuous features of Herod's policy. Josephus records how he sent delegations to Rome, and also to Antony and Cleopatra in Egypt, bearing the most costly presents; also how he converted the ancient Strato's Tower into a magnificent seaport, and named it Caesarea, in honor of Caesar, and how later he rebuilt Samaria, and renamed it Sebaste (Sebastos being the equivalent of Augustus). He built many other fortified cities and named them in honor of Caesar.[262]

Evans takes Mauro's view and expands it somewhat.

> Mauro points out that the Romans placed great emphasis upon fortifications and that Herod made extravagant gifts to Roman leaders and built several forts and/or fortified cities that he named in honor of them. The Roman emperors, he writes, "claimed for themselves divine honors . . . and enforced the worship they demanded" by maintaining a prominent military presence. Jordan views "god of fortresses" as an "odd phrase [that] seems to mean that the king does not honor and fear any personal god at all, but rather honors power itself," and he adds: "A culture that deified raw power, or at least functioned as if raw power were its ultimate deity, is a good description of Rome." To these comments I append that the gifts and honors that Herod bestowed upon his Roman patrons set new records in the history of vassalage and were never even remotely challenged afterwards by any client king.[263]

---

261. Mauro, *Seventy Weeks*, 146.

262. Ibid.

263. Evans, *Four Kingdoms*, 264–65.

But neither Mauro nor Evans does justice to the text. The text does not say that this king will support the wars of others, or will honor what others regard or treat as a god. It says *he* will honor the god of fortresses, which would be the case if Herod worshipped the Caesars. It does not say he will honor those who honor the god of fortresses. As we have seen this seems to indicate a whole-hearted dedication to warfare. Herod was prevented from waging war without the consent of Rome. Also, Herod's own history denies that he held this view of war. As Reicke points out,

> Financially, Herod's regime benefited the land; his buildings provided the clearest evidence of this. Newly established contacts promoted trade with other parts of the Roman commonwealth, especially via the new port of Caesarea, but also quite generally via the wealthy Hellenistic cities and large territories that Herod received from Augustus. A typical example of the relative prosperity was the fishing industry on the Sea of Galilee, mentioned in the New Testament. . . . Thus we may reckon in the New Testament period with an increase in Jewish income that was due in part to the achievements of Herod. . . . Herod assisted his people with generous contributions and relinquished considerable amounts in taxes when the economic system worsened.[264]

Tenney adds, "The Temple which he [Herod] built, the cities which he founded, and the political system which he organized under the aegis of Rome became the cradle of Christianity."[265] Another historian testifies to the building projects of Herod: "Herod . . . erected a magnificent palace, a theatre, a hippodrome, and rebuilt the Temple on a lavish scale."[266] Richardson points out that Herod's building projects "represent an enduring aspect to his career . . ."[267] Even though Herod was hated by much of the populace, he did attempt to do some good in Palestine, and none of the historical descriptions of him and his accomplishments sounds anything like the king who makes a god out of war. As Richardson observes, Herod was "regarded externally as an important patron, a man of kindness, generosity, good will, and piety, a friend of Romans and of the Emperor. These features contrast the usual picture; though none is inconsistent with Josephus's picture, the balance and composition are radically different."[268] Once again the historical facts simply do not support the claim that Herod is the person to whom these prophecies apply. The fact

264. Reicke, *New Testament Era*, 102–3.

265. Tenney, *New Testament Times*, 65,

266. T. Walter Wallbank, et. al., *Civilization*, 154.

267. Richardson, *Herod*, 174.

268. Ibid., 215.

that the text states, "he will honor him with gold, silver, costly stones, and treasures," indicates that he is wholly committed to war, giving every bit of his finances to furthering his efforts to make war. This was not Herod.

Evans argues that such references as "the god of fortresses" cannot apply to some future antichrist because "it so clearly sounds like it pertains to ancient times as opposed to the kind of world in which we live."[269] Of course this argument holds no weight since the text was written by someone in an ancient culture and would be expected to use terminology from that era. Even if the angel is responsible for the precise wording, which seems to be the case, of necessity the angel would communicate with Daniel in words and images that he could understand, i.e., words of ancient times, particularly since this is the reason for speaking to Daniel, namely, "to give you an understanding . . ." (Dan. 10:14). The language of ancient times is indicative of the communication with someone who lives in that time. It does not indicate that the fulfillment must take place in ancient times.

A God Whom His Fathers Did Not Know

That his fathers would not know war as a god fits perfectly with the statement in verse 37, that he will show no regard for the God of his fathers. Those who serve the living God certainly do not aspire to make war their passion. The indication is that this king will not honor any god higher than himself. All of his energies and all of his aspirations are set upon this world and attaining power and wealth in this world. Although there have been rulers in the past who have honored war, this one will be like no other. He will honor war and power in a way that his ancestors did not, and he will worship warfare and power as a god, sacrificing "gold, silver, costly stones, and treasures" to pursue it. Assuming that this evil king is propelled by Satan, his aspirations fit the characterization of the Evil One.

Homer Hailey argues, "The disregard of 'the king' (the fourth empire and the emperors who represented it) of its former gods, the desire of women, and the magnifying of themselves above these, is exemplified to its supreme extent in Nero."[270] Of course this characterization is not indicative either of Rome or of every emperor. In fact, Suetonius declared concerning Nero, "Having tried to turn the boy Sporus into a girl by castration, he went through a wedding ceremony with him—dowry, bridal veil and all—which the whole Court attended; then brought him home and treated him as a wife . . . The world would have been a happier place had Nero's father Domitius married the same

---

269. Evans, *Four Kingdoms*, 211.

270. Hailey, *Daniel*, 235.

sort of wife."[271] In other words, the sentiment and character of Rome is not necessarily exemplified in any one emperor. In fact, one could point to such an emperor as Marcus Aurelius. As Davies points out, "With Marcus Aurelius (r. 161–180) Rome received a true philosopher-king. A disciple of Epictetus, he trained himself to withstand the rigours of constant campaigning, the burdens of office, and the demands of a profligate family."[272] Davies again points out, "Under the emperors Nerva (r. 96–8), Trajan (r. 98–117), Hadrian (r. 117–38), Antonius Pius (r. 138–61), and Marcus Aurelius (r. 161–80), the Empire not only reached its greatest geographical extent but enjoyed an unrivalled era of calm and stability."[273] Holding up Nero as indicative of the character of Rome itself is completely inaccurate and does not fit the context of the prophecy. In our comments on verse 39, we will deal with Hailey's claim about this king being the fourth empire.

39—   "He will take action against the strongest of fortresses with the help of a foreign god; he will give great honor to those who acknowledge him and will cause them to rule over the many, and will parcel out land for a price."

Strongholds of Fortresses

Concerning verse 39, Keil states, "With the help of this god, who was unknown to his fathers, he will so proceed against the strong fortresses that he rewards with honour, might, and wealth those who acknowledge him. This is the meaning of this verse, which has been very differently rendered."[274] Young says, "The mighty conqueror rewards those who have sided with him. This was true of Antiochus, but it is also true of all conquerors."[275] In verse 38 the word "fortresses" is מָעֻזִּים (mîzzuʿam). According to KBH this word can be used to mean a "mountain stronghold," a "place of refuge," or a "fortress."[276] The word in verse 39, however, "fortresses" (מָעֻזִּים, mîzzuʿam) is modified by the word מִבְצָרֵי (erʿshim), which is usually translated "strongest." KBH lists the meanings for this word as "a secure position," or a "fortified city."[277] There certainly seems to be some overlap in meaning, but KBH also indicates

271. Suetonius, *The Twelve Caesars*, 189.

272. Davies, *Europe*, 191.

273. Ibid, 189.

274. Keil, *Daniel*, 466.

275. Young, *Prophecy of Daniel*, 250.

276. KBH, s.v. "מָעוֹז."

277. KBH, s.v. "מִבְצָר."

that the word in verse 38, מָעֻזִּים (*mˆuzzuˁam*), can indicate a temple fortress, whereas the word "strongest" in verse 39 indicates a strongly fortified city. The word "fortress" is used 7 times in Daniel 11 (see Table 62), but nowhere else in the book of Daniel.

Table 62: "Fortresses" in Daniel 11

Daniel 11:1	"In the first year of Darius the Mede, I arose to be an encouragement and a protection [וּלְמָעוֹז, *luˁzoˁam*] for him." וַאֲנִי בִּשְׁנַת אַחַת לְדָרְיָוֶשׁ הַמָּדִי עָמְדִי לְמַחֲזִיק וּלְמָעוֹז לוֹ:
Daniel 11:7	"But one of the descendants of her line will arise in his place, and he will come against their army and enter the fortress [בְּמָעוֹז, *bˁzoˁam*] of the king of the North, and he will deal with them and display great strength." וְעָמַד מִנֵּצֶר שָׁרָשֶׁיהָ כַּנּוֹ וְיָבֹא אֶל־הַחַיִל וְיָבֹא בְּמָעוֹז מֶלֶךְ הַצָּפוֹן וְעָשָׂה בָהֶם וְהֶחֱזִיק:
Daniel 11:10	"His sons will mobilize and assemble a multitude of great forces; and one of them will keep on coming and overflow and pass through, that he may again wage war up to his very fortress [מָעֻזֹּה, *hozzuˁam*]." וּבָנָו יִתְגָּרוּ וְאָסְפוּ הֲמוֹן חֲיָלִים רַבִּים וּבָא בוֹא וְשָׁטַף וְעָבָר וְיָשֹׁב וְיִתְגָּרוּ עַד־מָעֻזֹּה:
Daniel 11:19	"So he will turn his face toward the fortresses [לְמָעוּזֵּי, *lˁezzuˁam*] of his own land, but he will stumble and fall and be found no more." וְיָשֵׁב פָּנָיו לְמָעוּזֵּי אַרְצוֹ וְנִכְשַׁל וְנָפַל וְלֹא יִמָּצֵא:
Daniel 11:31	"Forces from him will arise, desecrate the sanctuary fortress [הַמִּקְדָּשׁ הַמָּעוֹז, *zoˁammah ˆsadqimmah*], and do away with the regular sacrifice. And they will set up the abomination of desolation." וּזְרֹעִים מִמֶּנּוּ יַעֲמֹדוּ וְחִלְּלוּ הַמִּקְדָּשׁ הַמָּעוֹז וְהֵסִירוּ הַתָּמִיד וְנָתְנוּ הַשִּׁקּוּץ מְשֹׁמֵם:

Daniel 11:38

"But instead he will honor a god of fortresses [מָעֻזִּים, *mʿuzzu'am*], a god whom his fathers did not know; he will honor him with gold, silver, costly stones and treasures."

וְלֶאֱלֹהַּ מָעֻזִּים עַל־כַּנּוֹ יְכַבֵּד וְלֶאֱלוֹהַּ אֲשֶׁר
לֹא־יְדָעֻהוּ אֲבֹתָיו יְכַבֵּד בְּזָהָב וּבְכֶסֶף
וּבְאֶבֶן יְקָרָה וּבַחֲמֻדוֹת׃

Daniel 11:39

"He will take action against the strongest of fortresses [לְמִבְצְרֵי מָעֻזִּים, *lʿshimʿmʿuzzu'am ller*] with the help of a foreign god; he will give great honor to those who acknowledge him and will cause them to rule over the many, and will parcel out land for a price."

וְעָשָׂה לְמִבְצְרֵי מָעֻזִּים עִם־אֱלוֹהַּ נֵכָר אֲשֶׁר
הִכִּיר יַרְבֶּה כָבוֹד וְהִמְשִׁילָם בָּרַבִּים
וַאֲדָמָה יְחַלֵּק בִּמְחִיר׃

Throughout the early uses in Daniel 11 the word seems to apply to military installations. Most translations render the phrase in verse 39 so that the word "fortresses" is being modified by the word "strongest," rendering the phrase, "strongest of fortresses." This seems to indicate that the text is referring to a specific place—the place where the strongest fortress is located. However, the word translated "strongest" is not an adjective. It is a noun in the construct state. Consequently, the translation could be "strongholds of fortresses" (לְמִבְצְרֵי מָעֻזִּים, *mʿuzzu'am erʿshimʿl*). In other words, the text may not be talking about a specific fortress, but that this king will not refrain from attacking the strongest fortresses wherever they may be. As Wood puts it, "The Antichrist will not hold back from attacking any stronghold, as he puts his reliance in his war machine."[278] Whichever way the phrase it taken, it is certainly not characteristic of Herod. In fact, Herod did not have authority to conduct war outside of his own immediate realm, and if this verse is merely saying that this king attacked the strongest fortress in Judea, this could hardly characterize someone who makes a god of warfare. This kind of characterization would not be different from any other authority figure who attempted to bring rebellious people under control in his own realm.

Strongholds of Fortresses and Herod

Mauro gives the following translation of verse 39: "'Thus shall he do in the most strongholds [*sic*] with a strange god whom he shall acknowledge and in-

278. Wood, *Daniel*, 307.

crease with glory; and he shall cause them to rule over many, and shall divide the land for gain,' or 'parcel out the land for hire.'"[279] The text of the verse is set out below with a word-for-word translation.

Table 63: Daniel 11:39

מָעֻזִּים	לְמִבְצְרֵי	וְעָשָׂה
fortresses	to strongholds of	And he will do
נֵכָר	אֱלוֹהַּ	עִם־
foreign	a god	with
יַרְבֶּה	הִכִּיר	אֲשֶׁר
he will make great	he will acknowledge	whom
בָּרַבִּים	וְהִמְשִׁילָם	כָּבוֹד
among many	and he will cause them to rule	honor
בִּמְחִיר:	יְחַלֵּק	וַאֲדָמָה
for a price.	he will apportion	and ground

Given the Hebrew syntax, Mauro's translation is simply not possible. First, Mauro uses the preposition "in" in the phrase, "in the most strongholds." The preposition "in" is normally indicated by the use of the preposition בְּ (ᵉb). However, the preposition in this case is actually לְ (ᵉl). Although this preposition can be used to indicate location in, yet, according to Waltke-O'Connor, it is typically a temporal sense of "in"—a point in time—not in the sense of a place: "The temporal uses of *l* include a sense like the simple locational (*in*, *at*, or *during* a period of time . . ." and KBH does not list the meaning "in" in the sense of a place for this preposition.[280] The idea here is not that he will do something "in" the strongholds, which Mauro tries to argue later, but that he will do it *to* the strongholds. Once again Mauro's lack of facility in the Hebrew language leads him to make impossible interpretations.

Second, the translation "most strongholds" is not possible since the word "most" or any equivalent is not even in the text. The phrase is "strongholds of fortresses" as we have indicated above.

Third, Mauro does not make a break between "strange god" and "whom he will acknowledge." However, this creates a problem for his translation in

279. Mauro, *Seventy Weeks*, 146–47.

280. See Waltke-O'Connor, *Biblical Hebrew Syntax*, 11.2.10 and KBH, s.v. "לְ."

the rest of the verse. Mauro has, "and he shall cause them to rule over many." The problem for Mauro's translation is, to whom does the pronoun "them" refer? There is no group of people in the text to whom this pronoun can refer, unless one makes a break between "foreign god" and "whom he will acknowledge." The word translated "whom" (אֲשֶׁר, rĕsᵃ⁾) is an indeclinable relative pronoun.[281] It can function with reference to both singulars and plurals. An example of its use as a plural is given by Waltke-O'Connor from Ezek. 23:28: "בְּיַד אֲשֶׁר שָׂנֵאת into the hand of *those* you hate."[282] Consequently, dividing the phrase before "whom" identifies the antecedent of "them" in the following clause: "Whom he will acknowledge, he will give great honor, and he will cause them to rule among many, and the ground he will apportion for a price." This translation accurately captures the Hebrew syntax. The pronoun "them," then, refers back to the "Whom he will acknowledge."

Mauro goes on to argue that this verse can also be applied to Herod. Although the quote is quite long, it is necessary to present it complete in order to respond to each of his arguments.

> Here we have a reference to one of the most prominent acts of Herod's long reign, namely, his rebuilding of the temple, and his making the temple area a stronghold for Caesar. He made the temple the most famous building in the world for its dimensions, its magnificence, and particularly for the size of the stones whereof it was built, to which the disciples specially directed the Lord's attention (Mk. 13:1), and which Josephus says were 25 cubits long, 12 broad, and 8 thick (Ant. XV II, 3). But, in rebuilding it, Herod took care to convert it into a fortress for his own purposes, this being the "most stronghold" of the land. As a part of this plan he constructed on the north side of the temple, and overlooking it, a strong citadel which he named the Tower of Antonia, after Mark Antony. Josephus says: "But for the Tower itself, when Herod the king of the Jews had fortified it more firmly than before, in order to secure and guard the temple, he gratified Antonius who was his friend and the Roman ruler by calling it the Tower of Antonia" (Ant. XV. 11:4–7). Further this historian says that the fortified places, "were two, the one belonging to the city itself, the other belonging to the temple; and those that could get them into their hands had the whole nation under their power, for without the command of them it was not possible to offer their sacrifices" (Ant. XV. 11:7–8). It was from the stairs leading to this famous Tower, up which the apostle Paul was being taken by the soldiers to save him from the violence of the people, that he stilled them

281. See Waltke-O'Connor, *Biblical Hebrew Syntax*, §19.3ff.

282. Ibid., §19.3c.

by a gesture of his hand, and gained their attention by addressing them in the Hebrew tongue (Acts 21:34–40). Again Josephus says of Herod that, "When Caesar had further bestowed upon him another additional country, he built there also a temple of white marble, hard by the fountains of Jordan"; and also "to say all at once, there was not any place in his kingdom fit for the purpose, that was permitted to be without somewhat that was for Caesar's honour; and when he had filled his own country with temples, be poured out like plentiful marks of his esteem into his province, and built many cities which he called *Caesareas*." (Wars I, 21:2)[283]

We have already shown that Herod is not the king referred to in verse 36 and that the actual history disqualifies his "dynasty" as a possible fulfillment for the statements in verse 37. However, since this is a popular view among Preterists, it is still necessary to deal with Mauro's arguments. First, Mauro's claim that Herod's "rebuilding of the temple" and his "making the temple area a stronghold for Caesar" fulfills the opening statement of verse 39 in fact does not correspond to the historical facts. Goldingay notes, "עשׂה ל: as with other occurrences of עשׂה in chap. 11, the vb's meaning is further defined by the following vb(s), with which it forms a compound idea."[284] In the context, the word "do" also must be understood in light of the previous verbs. In verse 38 the king is described as one who makes a god of war. It fits the context more readily to understand the opening phrase of 39 to indicate that what he "does" to the strongholds of fortresses is to make war with them. There is no indication in the text that he will "build" anything. Hebrew has a word for "to build" (בָּנָה, *hanab*), which does not occur in this text.

Mauro says Herod took care to convert the Temple to a fortress: "But, in rebuilding it [the temple], Herod took care to convert it into a fortress for his own purposes, this being the 'most stronghold' of the land." But in fact, Herod did not make the temple area into a stronghold for Caesar. There is no question that Herod strengthened the walls of the temple area, but had he converted it into a fortress, it would not have been acceptable to the Jews. In fact, as Richardson points out, "Josephus calls it [the rebuilding of the Second Temple] a work of great piety (*War* 1.400–401)."[285] Richardson goes on to describe some aspects of this project:

> The rebuilding's organization and careful preparations, the qual-
> ity and the enormous quantities of materials used, the vast scale

---

283. Mauro, *Seventy Weeks*, 147–48. Mauro's quote from Josephus, *Antiquities*, XV.7.8, actually has nothing to do with Herod building the city or the fortresses.

284. Goldingay, *Daniel*, 280.

285. Richardson, *Herod*, 185.

and drama of the Temple, its innovations, its integration into the existing cityscape, the demand to continue regular worship—all are truly staggering. Determined to leave Judaism richer for his having been king, Herod undertook this project and persuaded the priestly hierarchy of its viability, even gaining their agreement to important innovations such as the courts of women and gentiles. Reactions were varied but generally positive: 'He who has not seen the Temple has not seen a beautiful building' (*b. Baba Bathra* 4a).[286]

None of this sounds even remotely like someone who took care to convert the Temple into a fortress for his own purposes. In fact, Richardson points out that Herod built three temples to Roma and Augustus, and, "Since the Jerusalem Temple offered prayers to God on behalf of the Emperor daily, it could be argued that the temples of Roma were merely an extension of that provision for homage to Augustus."[287] In other words, Herod built the temples to Roma and Augustus because the Temple at Jerusalem was not built for the worship of Caesar. Mauro's characterization that Herod built the Temple as a stronghold to Caesar is simply false.

Mauro mentions the building of Antonia: "As a part of his plan he constructed on the north side of the temple, and overlooking it, a strong citadel which he named the Tower of Antonia, after Mark Antony."[288] But this claim is simply false. Richardson identifies the fortress of Antonia among the primary fortresses that received Herod's attention. However, Richardson goes on to point out, "Without exception these forts went back to Maccabean foundations, when the need for this particular line of defense was pressing. Their genius especially their brilliant locations, was Maccabean."[289] The part of the quote from Josephus that Mauro does not quote indicates the same fact: "Now on the north side [of the temple] was built a citadel, whose walls were square, and strong, and of extraordinary firmness. This citadel was built by the kings of the Asamonean race, who were also high-priests before Herod, and they called it the Tower . . ."[290] According to Josephus, it was a fortress before Herod, and Herod merely "fortified it more firmly than before . . ."[291]

---

286. Ibid.

287. Ibid., 184–85.

288. Mauro, *Seventy Weeks*, 147.

289. Richardson, *Herod*, 180.

290. Josephus, Antiquities, XV.11.4. Κατὰ δὲ τὴν βόρειον πλευρὰν ἀκρόπολις ἐγγώνιος εὐερκὴς ἐτετείχιστο διάφορος ἐχυρος τητι. ταύτην οἱ πρὸ Ἡρώδου τοῦ Ἀσαμωναίων γένους βασιλεῖς καὶ ἀρχιερεῖς ᾠκοδόμησαν καὶ Βᾶριν ἐκά λεσαν . . .

291. Richardson, *Herod*, 180.

Additionally, Richardson points out that Herod's work on these fortresses was not to strengthen them for military purposes:

> The literary and historical evidence confirms that the Hasmoneans were more in need of defense and more anxious about security than Herod. Herod restored, refurbished, modernized, and improved them—especially the water systems and royal apartments— but these were his establishments in neither location nor purpose. (2) In Herod's day the line of defense made little sense. Though some of the forts played a strategic role in the first days of Herod's rule, for the majority of his reign they were irrelevant as fortresses. . . . (3) In refurbishing them, the archaeology makes clear, attention was paid to the living amenities.[292]

The historical facts about Herod hardly depict a man whose god is war or one who honors the "god of fortresses," nor do they coincide with the prophetic descriptions.

Mauro goes on to argue:

> In connection with the prediction of what this king would do in the chief strongholds—"with a strange god," mention should be made of the many images, statues of Caesar, which Herod set up to be worshipped in various fortified places. He even went so far in his sacrilege as to place a huge golden eagle (the adored emblem of imperial Rome) at the very gate of the temple, thus giving rise to a tumult and insurrection among the people. In this way did he, in his estate (office), "honour the god of *forces*" (Caesar) whose statues he everywhere introduced as objects of worship. He fulfilled with literal exactness the words, "Thus shall he do in the most strongholds," (which expression would apply to the citadel of the temple, where he erected the Tower of Antonia) "with a strange god, whom he shall acknowledge, and increase with glory" (Dan. 11:39). The last clause finds a striking fulfillment in Herod's extravagant pains to glorify Caesar, which, as we have shown, went beyond all bounds.[293]

Mauro says, "In connection with the prediction of what this king would do in the chief strongholds 'with a strange god,' mention should be made of the many images, statues of Caesar, which Herod set up to be worshipped in various fortified places."[294] Of course the gods whom Herod honored were not "strange gods" as this seems to be used by Mauro. In fact, the notion here

292. Ibid.
293. Mauro, *Seventy Weeks*, 148.
294. Ibid., 148.

is that the strange or "foreign" god is the god of fortresses mentioned in the previous verse—not "Caesar" or any of the other gods of Rome. There is no historical evidence that Caesar was ever referred to as "the god of fortresses." And Mauro's translation of the word "fortresses" to "forces" is unjustified. Mauro attempts to capitalize on his translation, "in the most strongholds," but as we have shown, this translation cannot be justified from the text.

Mauro then claims, "The words 'dividing the land for gain' (or parceling it out for hire) were fulfilled in the practice adopted by Herod of parceling out among persons favorable to himself, the land adjacent to places which it was important for him to control in case of emergency. Josephus speaks of this (Ant. XV 8, 5)."[295] Mauro makes a note that "Josephus speaks of this (Ant. XV 8, 5),"[296] but once again Mauro has misrepresented the testimony of Josephus. What Josephus actually says is, "Moreover, he parted the adjoining country [adjoining to the city of Sebaste/Samaria], which was excellent in its kind, among the inhabitants of Samaria, that they might be in a happy condition, upon their first coming to inhabit."[297] Josephus says nothing about this being done for gain, hire, or a price. The statement of Josephus is that Herod gave the land to the inhabitants of the city of Samaria.

Although Mauro's translation includes the phrase "he will cause them to rule over many" in verse 39 (וְהִמְשִׁיל, malīsmih‘w), he makes no comment about it in his defense of Herod as the one who supposedly "fulfilled" what was prophesied about the king. In fact, Herod did not cause anyone to rule. Herod was afraid of any other ruler or individual who sought to rule in his territory, even if these were only his own perceptions. Not only did Herod not fulfill this "item," his career was diametrically opposed to the tendency expressed in this phrase.

The NASBU translation sets forth the Hebrew text quite well: "He will take action against the strongest of fortresses with *the help of* a foreign god." The words in italics, "*the help of*," are implied in the preposition "with," עַם (*mi‘*). KBH gives the meanings "in company with, together with" and provides the exposition, "expresses communal action or action in company."[298] The verse seems to be saying that this king will attack the mightiest fortresses with the help of a foreign god. The "god" seems to be a reference to the god of fortresses in verse 38. This could be a reference to the war machine that this king has created. The king has made war his god, a god his fathers did not

---

295. Ibid.

296. Ibid.

297. Josephus, *Antiquities*, XV.8.5.

298. KBH, s.v. "עַם."

know, and he has sacrificed all his resources to building a war machine with which he can storm the mightiest of fortresses.[299]

At the conclusion of this section, Mauro confidently asserts, "We thus find that every item foretold of 'the king' was completely fulfilled in the career of Herod, and that the record of this fulfilment [*sic*] has come down to us in an authentic contemporary history, which is on all hands acknowledged to be trustworthy in an unusually high degree."[300] On the contrary, the historical facts about Herod demonstrate that not a single one of the items foretold about 'the king' was fulfilled in the career of Herod. Since most of the information about Herod was probably discovered long after Mauro's day, one might excuse Mauro for not knowing that his "authentic contemporary history" would turn out to be *untrustworthy* to an unusually high degree. But the fact is, Herod simply is not the one prophesied in these verses in Daniel.

The Foreign God

There has been much controversy over precisely what the phrase "with a foreign god" (אֱלֹוהַ נֵכָר עִם, *raken hâol° mi°*) actually means or to whom or to what it refers. Most commentators argue that the context indicates that the foreign god is the god unknown to his fathers referred to in the previous verse—e.g., Miller states, "This 'foreign god' is the 'god unknown to his fathers' of the previous verse, and Antichrist's god is 'foreign' in the sense that this deity was not worshiped by his ancestors."[301] However, Pentecost makes an interesting suggestion: "The Antichrist will honor a god of fortresses, that is, he will promote military strength. And because of his political and religious power he will be able to accumulate vast wealth. The god unknown to his fathers (ancestors), who will give him strength, may be Satan."[302] If this passage is referring to a future Antichrist, which seems to be the case since no historical figure has been identified who fulfills the prophetic descriptions, then Satan may be the force behind this king's power and advancement. This also fits the notion of a spiritual warfare. The text does not necessarily claim that this king will even be aware of the help of this foreign god. He may in fact be aware, but the text does not require this. So, this proposal cannot be disqualified on the basis that it requires this king to be a worshiper of Satan. A person's dedication to something to the degree that it becomes to him as a god is often not even realized by that person, either actually or by willful ignorance.

---

299. Miller, *Daniel*, 308.

300. Mauro, *Seventy Weeks*, 148.

301. Ibid.

302. Pentecost, *Daniel*, 1371.

The Future Antichrist

Homer Hailey objects to the notion that this king is Anti-Christ. He argues, "It seems that the 'the king' is used here as it was used in chapter seven (review Summary of chapter seven, above). 'The four beasts are four kings' (7:17); 'The fourth beast shall be a fourth kingdom' (v. 23). The conclusion is that the beast equals king equals kingdom; therefore the king is a kingdom, the fourth empire."[303] First of all, Hailey has assumed what he must prove. Why should anyone think that "the king" here is being used as it is in chapter seven? Hailey has not demonstrated this to be the case. He has merely asserted it. Second, his logic is faulty. If 'king' equals 'kingdom,' then the king is a kingdom, and a kingdom is a king. Why conclude that it must be one or the other? If they are equal terms and have the same meaning, then it is just as logical to treat "the king" as a king. Third, Hailey did not use this logic earlier in chapter 11. Concerning the use of the word "king" in 11:3 Hailey said, "Alexander the Great, who should 'stand up'—come to power (539–334 B.C.) and invade Persia."[304] The reason he did not use his logic there is because he knew it would not fit his eschatological scheme. The prophetic description is so specific that all commentators acknowledge this is a reference to Alexander. But, if "king" can be a reference to a person in 11:3, why not in 11:36?

With respect to the identify of the future Antichrist, Walvoord argues that the expression "god of his fathers" cannot be understood as a reference to the God of Israel:

> Gaebelein and others upholding this view, however, overlook a most decisive fact that the word for "God" here is *Elohim*, a name for God in general, applying both to the true God and to false gods. If the expression had been the usual one when referring to the God of Israel, *the Jehovah of his fathers*, the identification would be unmistakable. Very frequently in Scripture, the God of Israel is described as Jehovah, "the Lord God" of their fathers . . . for Daniel to omit the word Jehovah or Lord, (KJV) in a passage where a specific name for the God of Israel would be necessary becomes significant. The expression should be rendered "the gods of his fathers," that is, any god, as most revisions translate it.[305]

However, of the 59 times the expression "God of *x* fathers" occurs, where "*x*" stands for "his," "your," "our," or "their," 38 times it occurs with the word "LORD" (יהוה, *HWHY*) as in 2 Chron. 30:19, "the LORD God of

---

303. Hailey, *Commentary on Daniel*, 234–35.

304. Ibid., 221.

305. Walvoord, *Daniel*, 273–74.

his fathers" (יְהוָה אֱלֹהֵי אֲבוֹתָיו, *wyẚtobᵃᵛ eholᵉᵓ HWHY*), and 21 times it occurs without the covenant name יהוה. Also, as we have shown in Table 53 on page 511, the specific expression "God of his fathers" occurs only five other times in the OT, and in each case it clearly refers to the God of Israel. So, there does not seem to be any reason why there would be greater necessity to find the "specific name for the God of Israel" in this passage in Daniel than in any other passage. The angel who is giving this information is giving it to Daniel, not to the heathen who might require the specific identification.

Also, it seems that Walvoord's argument is motivated by his opposition to the denial that the Antichrist will be a Jew. But, as we have already pointed out, it is not necessary that the Antichrist be a Jew in order for the God of his fathers to be the God of the Jews. Christians worship the God of Israel, and coming from Rome, as Walvoord claims is the heritage of the Antichrist, having Christian ancestors would certainly not be a peculiar situation. Wood alludes to this point in passing: "In verse 37, he is said to turn from 'the God of his fathers' (probably a reference to God as worshiped historically by Rome) . . ."[306] Also, the angel is not saying that the person is a Jew or a Christian or any other thing. He is simply saying that this king will show no regard for the God of his fathers, and Daniel would most likely have understood this as referring to the God of Israel.

Irrespective of the argument about the "God" or "gods of his fathers," Futurists hold that this king will be a future Antichrist. One compelling reason for holding this view is that there is no historical figure to whom these descriptions can be applied. The two most likely candidates to have been proposed are Herod the Great and Antiochus IV Epiphanes, but it has been shown that their lives and experiences simply do not correspond to the prophetic descriptions. Consequently, since there is no historical figure to whom these prophecies apply, one must either conclude that the prophecies are false, as do the critical scholars, a position that we do not take because of a com-

---

306. Leon J. Wood, *The Bible and Future Events*, 103. This is a particularly interesting observation by Wood since, apparently, when writing his *Commentary on Daniel*, he changed his view from this earlier stated position. In his commentary he asserts, "Some expositors see here a reference to Yahweh, as God of Israel (arguing from the characteristic 'God of his fathers'), and take evidence from this that the Antichrist will be a Jew. There is evidence against this view, however, in the plurality of the word 'gods (*ᵛlōhîm*) as here used, which is truly indicative of plurality in this instance, since the singular form *ᵛlōah* is used twice in the next few words." Wood, *Daniel*, 306. Wood's argument about the singular does not work, however, since Elohim can be treated as a singular, and the singular אֵל (*leᵓ*) is much more frequently used for God than אֱלוֹהַּ (*hâolᵉᵓ*). It seems rather that אֱלוֹהַּ (*hâolᵉᵓ*) is used here as a reference to pagan gods, not to the God of Israel. In fact, it is so used in verse 38.

mitment to the inerrancy of Scripture, or that this person is yet to show up in
the course of history.

The Campaigns of the King of the End Time: 11:40–44

With verses 40 through 44 we come to a section that is even more difficult
to apply to any of the historical personages who have been proposed in the
comments of interpreters through the centuries. Since the prophetic descriptions are so drastically different from anything known about Antiochus IV
Epiphanes, those who wish this to apply to Antiochus simply claim that this
section contains inaccurate prophecy. Preterists continue to try to make this
fit into the life Herod the Great, but they run up against the same problem
as do the advocates of the Antiochus view—the history simply does not correspond to the prophetic descriptions.

40— "At the end time the king of the South will collide with him, and
the king of the North will storm against him with chariots, with
horsemen and with many ships; and he will enter countries, overflow
them and pass through.

THE TIME OF THE END

There has, of course, been considerable debate over the phrase "At the end
time." The phrase is וּבְעֵת קֵץ (šeq teʿbu) and literally reads "and in time
of end." Here the definite articles could be used without violating Hebrew
syntax. The definite article is regularly omitted in prepositional phrases even
though the objects of these prepositions may still be definite. This precise
expression occurs only four other times in Daniel.

Table 64: The Time of The End

	"So he came near to where I was standing, and when he came I was frightened and fell on my face; but he said to me, 'Son of man, understand that the vision pertains to the time of the end [לְעֶת־קֵץ, lᵉseq teʿ].'"
Dan 8:17	וַיָּבֹא אֵצֶל עָמְדִי וּבְבֹאוֹ נִבְעַתִּי וָאֶפְּלָה עַל־פָּנָי וַיֹּאמֶר אֵלַי הָבֵן בֶּן־אָדָם כִּי לְעֶת־קֵץ הֶחָזוֹן׃

Dan 11:35

"Some of those who have insight will fall, in order to refine, purge and make them pure until the end time [עֵת קֵץ, *seq ̄e'*]; because still at the appointed time."

וּמִן־הַמַּשְׂכִּילִים יִכָּשְׁלוּ לִצְרוֹף בָּהֶם וּלְבָרֵר
וְלַלְבֵּן עַד־עֵת קֵץ כִּי־עוֹד לַמּוֹעֵד:

Dan 11:40

"At the end time [וּבְעֵת קֵץ, *seq ̄e'bu*] the king of the South will collide with him, and the king of the North will storm against him with chariots, with horsemen and with many ships; and he will enter countries, overflow and pass through."

וּבְעֵת קֵץ יִתְנַגַּח עִמּוֹ מֶלֶךְ הַנֶּגֶב וְיִשְׂתָּעֵר
עָלָיו מֶלֶךְ הַצָּפוֹן בְּרֶכֶב וּבְפָרָשִׁים
וּבָאֳנִיּוֹת רַבּוֹת וּבָא בַאֲרָצוֹת וְשָׁטַף וְעָבָר:

Dan 12:4

"But as for you, Daniel, conceal these words and seal up the book until the end of time [עֵת קֵץ, *seq ̄e'*]; many will go back and forth, and knowledge will increase."

וְאַתָּה דָנִיֵּאל סְתֹם הַדְּבָרִים וַחֲתֹם הַסֵּפֶר
עַד־עֵת קֵץ יְשֹׁטְטוּ רַבִּים וְתִרְבֶּה הַדָּעַת:

Dan 12:9

"He said, 'Go, Daniel, for words are concealed and sealed up until the end time [עֵת קֵץ, *seq ̄e'*].'"

וַיֹּאמֶר לֵךְ דָּנִיֵּאל כִּי־סְתֻמִים וַחֲתֻמִים
הַדְּבָרִים עַד־עֵת קֵץ:

Dan 11:13 is the only instance in the book of Daniel in which the wording is the reverse of the above passages: "For the king of the North will again raise a greater multitude than the former, and after an interval of some years וּלְקֵץ הָעִתִּים שָׁנִים, *mīñas mūti'ah seqlu*, lit. 'and to the end of the times of years'] he will press on with a great army and much equipment." By the time we get to Dan 11:40, most commentators believe that they have sufficiently demonstrated their respective positions that very little argumentation is put forward for one's view on these verses. Most commentators simply assert an understanding of the expression that conforms to the eschatological position taken. Futurists hold that this is a reference to the future end of the age. Walvoord is characteristic of this perspective: "The time of the end introduced in verse 35 is again mentioned in the opening portion of verse 40 to make clear that the military struggle here is that which will characterize the end of the age."[307] Wood specifically identifies this time as "the Tribulation period, when the Antichrist rules."[308] Miller quotes a statement by H. C. Leupold: "There is nothing in the context that would restrict the force of the word 'end,' and so the end of all things must be meant."[309]

Contrary to Leupold's claim that there is nothing to restrict the force of the word "end," Mauro argues, "In order to avoid confusion it is needful to observe that 'the time of the end' may mean one period in one place, and a very different period in another. The meaning is controlled, and is also revealed, by the context. But this is quite frequently overlooked; and we have observed that even careful writers on prophecy have a disposition to take the words 'the time of the end' as meaning the end of the gospel-dispensation, even when the passage in which they occur does not relate to the present dispensation at all."[310] Mauro goes on to declare, "the expression 'time of the end,' where it occurs in these later prophecies, means the last stage of the national existence of Daniel's people, that is to say, the era of the Herods."[311] That the meaning of the expression should be determined by the context is one issue, but that it necessarily refers to the "last stage of the national existence" of the Jews is quite another. Young responds, "Nor is there warrant for Mauro's view, that the words mean 'the last stage of the national existence of Daniel's people, that is to say, the era of the Herods.' There is no intrinsic objection to such an interpretation, but the general context does not warrant it."[312] Not only is Mauro's claim not supported by the general context, the specific details of the prophetic descriptions simply do not correspond to the history of the Herods.

Mauro's claim is predicated on his commitment to the notion that a future re-establishing of the nation of Israel is a heretical belief: "Jewish fables (literally, *myths*) are no new thing. Paul has plainly warned the household of faith not to give heed thereto. He has not given us a list of those grievous heresies; but it is well known that the one that was most fondly cherished, and that constituted the gravest menace to the truth of the gospel, was the notion that the leading purpose of the mission of the coming Messiah would be the reconstitution of the Jewish nation and its elevation to the highest pinnacle of

---

307. Walvoord, *Daniel*, 277.

308. Wood, *Daniel*, 308.

309. H. C. Leupold, *Exposition of Daniel* (Grand Rapids: Baker Book House, 1969), 520; quoted in Miller, *Daniel*, 309.

310. Mauro, *Seventy Weeks*, 149.

311. Ibid.

312. Young, *Prophecy of Daniel*, 251.

earthly dominion and glory."[313] Mauro's position on this question would take us far afield from our primary concern, which is an understanding of the book of Daniel. However, it should be pointed out that Mauro's position, as he describes it, is primarily propelled by his belief that the prophecies of the Old Testament that apply to Israel should be taken to refer, not to earthly realities, but to spiritual realities: "This argument [dispensationalism], however, is utterly fallacious, because based upon a false premise. Those who make use of it take for granted that in order to interpret prophecy 'literally' its fulfillment must be located in the realm of nature, and not in the *spiritual* realm. Thus they assume that the 'literal' interpretation is in contrast with the 'spiritual' interpretation thereof; and they denounce and repudiate what they refer to disparagingly as 'the *spiritualizing*' of the prophecies."[314] Of course this is precisely what Mauro does. He takes the prophecies to Israel that speak of an earthly kingdom and he makes these prophecies fulfilled in only a spiritual way. What is this if not spiritualizing?

On the one hand Mauro acknowledges that Paul did not list the "grievous heresies," but on the other hand he claims that the belief in the re-constitution of the nation of Israel was "well known," and he does this without the least supporting evidence. By whom was this belief "well known"? Where is the biblical, theological, or historical evidence to support this claim? Also, Mauro has in fact created a straw man argument. He characterizes this heresy as believing that "the leading purpose of the mission of the coming Messiah would be the reconstitution of the Jewish nation and its elevation to the highest pinnacle of earthly dominion and glory." But Futurists, or dispensationalists, do not hold this view the way Mauro characterizes it, and Mauro presents no historical evidence that such was a "cherished" view by anyone.

"A" King or "The" King?

Evans presents several arguments that he thinks demonstrate that these verses, 40–45, apply to Herod. The first argument has to do with Mauro's proposal that the references to the two kings ought to be indefinite rather than definite: "In applying verses 40–45 to the time of Herod the Great, the first problem to be overcome is explaining why the king of verses 36–39 is not the king of the North in verse 40. One solution offered by Mauro for this problem was to insist that whereas verse 36 unambiguously refers to '*the* king' (emphasis added), verse 40 should be translated as referring to a king of the South and a king of the North."[315]

313. Mauro, *The Hope of Israel*, 5.
314. Ibid., 15.
315. Evans, *Four Kingdoms*, 267.

This first argument, from the fact that Mauro supposes that the phrases in verse 40 should be translated without the definite article, we have already shown to be contrary to the Hebrew syntax (see page 537ff). Both phrases are definite and must be translated "the king of the South" and "the king of the North." Although Evans does not expound on this argument, he does approvingly assert, "this proposed solution has merit." As a matter of fact, it has no merit at all seeing that it is contrary to the principles of Hebrew grammar. Hebrew grammar dictates that the phrases should be "the king of the south" and "the king of the north."

WHO IS THE KING OF THE NORTH?

Miller argues that the king of the north is not another individual who wars against the king. Rather, Miller takes "the king" to be the king of the north:

> "Some maintain that "the king of the North" and Antichrist should be distinguished. According to this scenario, both the king of the South and the king of the North (presumably allies) will attack Antichrist on two fronts. . . ." Thus a southern force ("the king of the South") will attack Antichrist ("the king of the North"), whereby Antichrist will retaliate and decisively crush his opposition ("against him," then, refers to the king of the South). He "will invade" the "countries" of those who have attacked him and will "sweep through them like a flood."[316]

There seems to be some problems with this view, however. First, what Miller is arguing is that the sense of the passage is, "The king of the South will push against him, and the king of the North will push back." At first, it appears that the clauses *can* be taken this way. The two clauses are set out below.

Table 65: Daniel 11:40

הַנֶּגֶב	מֶלֶךְ	עִמּוֹ	יִתְנַגַּח
the south	the king of	with him	He will push
הַצָּפוֹן	מֶלֶךְ	עָלָיו	וְיִשְׂתָּעֵר
the north	the king of	upon him	and he will sweep

Miller is claiming that in the second clause the phrase "upon him" is referring to the king of the south upon whom the king of the north will "sweep," so that "king" is the subject of the verb "he will sweep." However,

316. Miller, *Daniel*, 309–10.

the two clauses are constructed in precisely the same arrangement, and to take the second clause in the way Miller suggests implies that there is no reason not to take the first clause the same way. So, what one will have, if both clauses are taken the way Miller suggests, is two kings, the south and the north, who are warring against some unidentified "him": "The king of the south will war against him [the king of the north according to Miller], and the king of the north will war against him [the king of the south according to Miller]." Although at first this seems to be a plausible understanding of the arrangement, it seems more natural to take the two phrases as referring to some third "him."

Figure 45: Who is "He" in Verse 40?

v. 36 Then the king will do as he pleases,

and he will exalt and magnify himself above every god
and will speak monstrous things against the God of gods;

and he will prosper until the indignation is finished,
for that which is decreed will be done.

v. 37 He will show no regard for the gods of his fathers
or for the desire of women,

nor will he show regard for any [other] god;

for he will magnify himself above [them] all.

v. 38 But instead he will honor a god of fortresses,

a god whom his fathers did not know;

he will honor [him] with gold, silver, costly stones and treasures.

v. 39 He will take action against the strongest of fortresses
with [the help of] a foreign god;

he will give great honor to those who acknowledge [him]
and will cause them to rule over the many,
and will parcel out land for a price.

v. 40 At the end time the king of the South will collide with him,

and the king of the North will storm against him with chariots,
with horsemen and with many ships;

and he will enter countries, overflow [them] and pass through.

As the graphic in Figure 45 shows, there certainly seems to be syntactical reason why the "him" of verse 40 should be understood to refer back to "the king" of verse 36. All the third person personal pronouns up to and including verse 40 are naturally taken to refer back to "the king" of verse 36. There is no good reason to suppose that suddenly the pronouns in verse 40 should be taken differently. To take the first phrase, "the king of the south will push against him," and then assume that it is understood that the "him" is pointing forward to the king of the north, is awkward at least and contrary to the flow of the narrative.

Miller's additional support comes from his reference to statements by Gleason Archer:

> Grammatically, Wood could be justified in understanding both phrases, "will engage him" and "against him," as referring to Antichrist. Nevertheless, Archer seems correct in stating: "It seems much simpler and more convincing, however, to take the 'king of the North' in this verse to be none other than the latter-day little horn, the Antichrist." Moreover, earlier in this chapter (vv. 6–28) various rulers from the Seleucid line were designated as "the king of the North." Antiochus IV Epiphanes was a Seleucid-Greek monarch (a "king of the North") and probably should be understood as a type of the future Antichrist described in the latter portion of the chapter. It would be appropriate, therefore, to designate both the type and the antitype by the same phrase, "the king of the North."[317]

The problem with the Miller-Archer thesis here is that "the king" of verse 36 is not referred to as the king of the north in verses 36–39, so there is no reason to think that suddenly this phrase is going to be used of him. Also, this creates a problem for the phrase in verse 41, "he will enter the beautiful land." If this king is the king of the north, would he not already be in the beautiful land as a result of passing through the land of Israel to go to war with the king of the south? It seems more problematic to take the verses the way Miller suggests.

Finally, according to Miller, Archer argues, "Antiochus IV Epiphanes was a Seleucid-Greek monarch (a 'king of the North') and probably should be understood as a type of the future Antichrist described in the latter portion of the chapter. It would be appropriate, therefore, to designate both the type and the antitype by the same phrase, 'the king of the North.'"[318] The problem with this assertion is that Antiochus IV Epiphanes is never referred to as

317. Ibid., 310.
318. Ibid.

"the king of the north." Since Antiochus is in fact the type of Anti-Christ, as Miller asserts, it is much more likely that he would not be referred to by this designation either. Consequently, it is not the king of the north that pushes back against the king of the south. Rather, these two kings, the king of the north and the king of the south, push against a third person, "the king." Also, simply because they each push against the same opponent does not necessarily make them allies.

GORING AGAINST OR JOINING WITH?

Evans' second argument to demonstrate that verses 40–45 apply to Herod revolves around the proposed translation of verse 40.

> James Jordan strongly seconds the idea that verse 40 should be translated so as to indicate that the king of the South will battle with the king of 36–39 in the sense of being allied with him instead of fighting against him. Collins's translation of verse 40 is in line with that suggested by Jordan and reads as follows: "At the time of the end, the king of the south will join battle with him, and the king of the north will storm against him with chariots and cavalry and many ships." Curiously, however, Collins interprets this to mean that the king of the South (Egypt) will attack Antiochus instead of being allied with him. In fact, his commentary in verse 40 shows no awareness of its possible contradiction with his translation.[319]

First of all, Evans seems to have misunderstood the expression "join battle with him." This is used by Collins to indicate that the two will go to war against each other. *The American Heritage Dictionary of the English Language* gives the following as one of the definitions of the word "join": "To engage in; enter into: *Opposing armies joined battle on the plain.*"[320] In fact, in the description of a battle between the armies of Vitellius under the leadership of Caecina and the troops of Otho under the command of Titianus and Proclus, Morgan states, ". . . there must have been a time lag between the moment when the two sides became aware of each other's presence and the moment when they actually *joined combat.*"[321] This is an expression that indicates that the two armies have engaged in a battle against one another, an expression, not that they have joined together with one another. Evans has completely misunderstood the expression.

319. Evans, *Four Kingdoms*, 267.

320. *The American Heritage Dictionary of the English Language* (2000), s.v. "join."

321. Morgan, *69 A.D.*, 135 (emphasis added).

Second, Evans' argument ignores the meaning of the key word translated "collide" in the NASB: "At the end time the king of the South will collide with him." The word is נָגַח (ḥagan). It occurs in the OT only 9 other times outside Daniel chapter 11, and there is no instance of its use in the OT in which it indicates "joining together in battle with" anyone or anything (see Table 66 below). It is used of an ox goring someone to death or so that the person is severely injured (Ex 21:28, 31, 32). It is used in Deut 33:17 as a figurative expression, as P. C. Craigie explains: "The blessing of military strength is described dramatically in the imagery of a powerful bull, goring its enemies before it."[322]

First Kgs 22:11 and 2 Chron 18:10 give the same phrase in which the word is used figuratively of goring one's enemies "until they are consumed." Ps 44:6 uses the word for "pushing against" one's adversaries and defeating them, and Ezek 34:21 uses it of thrusting the weak so that they are scattered.

Table 66: Goring and Pushing

Ex 21:28	"If an ox gores [יִגַּח, haggiy] a man or a woman to death, the ox shall surely be stoned and its flesh shall not be eaten; but the owner of the ox shall go unpunished." וְכִי־יִגַּח שׁוֹר אֶת־אִישׁ אוֹ אֶת־אִשָּׁה וָמֵת סָקוֹל יִסָּקֵל הַשּׁוֹר וְלֹא יֵאָכֵל אֶת־בְּשָׂרוֹ וּבַעַל הַשּׁוֹר נָקִי׃
	Ex 21:31 and 21:32 have to do with an ox goring.
Deut 33:17	"As the firstborn of his ox, majesty is his, and his horns are the horns of the wild ox; With them he will push [יְנַגַּח, yᵉhaggan] the peoples, all at once, to the ends of the earth. And those are the ten thousands of Ephraim, And those are the thousands of Manasseh." בְּכוֹר שׁוֹרוֹ הָדָר לוֹ וְקַרְנֵי רְאֵם קַרְנָיו בָּהֶם עַמִּים יְנַגַּח יַחְדָּו אַפְסֵי־אָרֶץ וְהֵם רִבְבוֹת אֶפְרַיִם וְהֵם אַלְפֵי מְנַשֶּׁה׃

322. Peter C. Craigie, *The Book of Deuteronomy*, 399.

1 Kgs 22:11	"Then Zedekiah the son of Chenaanah made horns of iron for himself and said, 'Thus says the Lord, "With these you will gore [תְּנַגַּח, tᵉhaggan] the Arameans until they are consumed."'" וַיַּעַשׂ לוֹ צִדְקִיָּה בֶן־כְּנַעֲנָה קַרְנֵי בַרְזֶל וַיֹּאמֶר כֹּה־אָמַר יְהוָה בְּאֵלֶּה תְּנַגַּח אֶת־אֲרָם עַד־כַּלֹּתָם׃

2 Chron 18:10 This verse is actually a reproduction of the previous verse.

Ps 44:6	"Through You we will push back [נְנַגֵּחַ, nᵉhāeggan] our adversaries; Through Your name we will trample down those who rise up against us." בְּךָ צָרֵינוּ נְנַגֵּחַ בְּשִׁמְךָ נָבוּס קָמֵינוּ׃

Ezek 34:21	"Because you push with side and with shoulder, and thrust [תְּנַגְּחוּ@, tᵉgganᵉuh] at all the weak with your horns until you have scattered them abroad . . ." יַעַן בְּצַד וּבְכָתֵף תֶּהְדֹּפוּ וּבְקַרְנֵיכֶם תְּנַגְּחוּ כָּל־הַנַּחְלוֹת עַד אֲשֶׁר הֲפִיצוֹתֶם אוֹתָנָה אֶל־הַחוּצָה׃

Dan 8:4	"I saw the ram butting [מְנַגֵּחַ, mᵉhāeggan] westward, northward, and southward, and no beasts could stand before him nor was there anyone to rescue from his power, but he did as he pleased and magnified." רָאִיתִי אֶת־הָאַיִל מְנַגֵּחַ יָמָּה וְצָפוֹנָה וָנֶגְבָּה וְכָל־חַיּוֹת לֹא־יַעַמְדוּ לְפָנָיו וְאֵין מַצִּיל מִיָּדוֹ וְעָשָׂה כִרְצֹנוֹ וְהִגְדִּיל׃

Undoubtedly the most significant use of the word for our study is found in Dan 8:4 in which the ram "butts" against the west, north, and south so that "no beasts could stand before him." In the book of Daniel itself we have the use of the word by the angel Gabriel. This is an extremely strong argument against taking the word to mean "join forces with him." The idea here is that "*the* king of the South" pushes against the king in such a manner as to seek to destroy him or injure him severely. There is no lexical support for translating the word as Evans does.

ANTONY THE KING OF THE SOUTH?

In an effort to demonstrate that "the king," whom Evans believes to be Herod, was joined by the king of the south, Evans gives a brief account of the historical situation.

> In historical fact, although Herod was warring against the Nabataeans when the conflict between Antony and Octavian broke into the open, he aided Antony and Cleopatra materially when they moved into Greece to confront Octavian. That move, incidentally, was followed by the Senate's declaration of war against Cleopatra. One can argue, of course, that Cleopatra cannot be the "king" of the South in verse 40 since she was a queen, but the fact that she was allied with Antony allows him to serve as a king substitute. Besides, if "king" is synonymous here with "ruler," Cleopatra would be "eligible" herself to serve as the king of the South. And if Cleopatra alone, Antony alone, or the combination of Cleopatra and Antony qualifies as the king of the South, then Octavian can plausibly be assumed to be the king of the North. Up to this point in Daniel 11, the kingdom of the North has always been Seleucid Syria; but *in the scenario that makes Herod the king of verses 36–39, Rome takes the place formerly held by Greece in the sequence of four kingdoms and becomes the kingdom of the North.*[323]

First of all, all of this is for naught since we have already shown that the text cannot be translated in such a way as to indicate that the king of the South joined with Herod against the king of the North. Additionally, it is not altogether clear from Josephus that Herod actually aided Antony and Cleopatra in the battle of Actium. Josephus describes the circumstances:

> . . . but Herod having enjoyed a country that was very fruitful, and that now for a long time, and having received great taxes, and raised great armies therewith, got together a body of men, and carefully furnished them with all necessaries, and designed them as auxiliaries for Antony; but Antony said he had no want of his assistance; but he commanded him to punish the king of Arabia, for he had heard, both from him and from Cleopatra, how perfidious he was; for this was what Cleopatra desired, who thought it for her own advantage that these two kings should do one another as great mischief as possible.[324]

323. Evans, *Four Kingdoms*, 267–68 (emphasis in original).

324. Josephus, Antiquities, XV.5.1. Ἡρώδης δὲ καὶ τῆς χώρας εὐβοτουμένης αὐτῷ πολὺν ἤδη χρόνον καὶ προσόδων καὶ δυνάμεων εὑρημένων, Ἀντωνίῳ συμμαχίαν κατέλεξεν, ἐπιμελέστατα ταῖς παρασκευαῖς χρησάμενος. Ἀντώνιος δὲ τῆς μὲν ἐκείνου συμμαχίας οὐδὲν ἔφη δεῖσθαι, τὸν δὲ Ἄραβα καὶ γὰρ ἠκηκό

From the testimony of Josephus it appears that Herod did not support Antony and Cleopatra, and in fact Antony actually refused Herod's assistance: "Antony said he had no want of his assistance." As soon as he had planned to provide assistance, Cleopatra convinced Antony to direct Herod to concentrate his efforts and finances to overcoming the Nebateans. This is confirmed by Richardson's understanding of Josephus' account: "Herod intended to join Antony for the final showdown with Octavian (*Ant.* 15.109), but Antony told Herod to deal with Malichus first, about whom he had heard from Herod and Cleoparta (*Ant.* 15.110). Cleopatra, however, was playing each side against the other, expecting to come out ahead whoever won the struggle (*War* 1.365; *Ant.* 15.110)."[325] Once again the historical events in Herod's life just do not correlate with the prophetic descriptions.

Second, Evans takes a particularly interesting approach with reference to the text and how it can be seen to apply in these historical situations. Virtually all commentators, including Evans, understand the first part of Daniel 11, from verse 2 to verse 20, as applying to the historical circumstances leading up to the rise of Antiochus IV. The history is identifiable and the prophetic descriptions depict this history in such a way that identifying the persons described admits of little possibility of difference among commentators. When coming to verse 21, most commentators see the section from verse 21 to verse 35 as applying to Antiochus IV Epiphanes. Although there is a bit more controversy, the association between the prophetic descriptions and the historical accounts indicates that identifying these prophecies as applying to Antiochus is on very good footing. After verse 35 the situation changes radically. Different schools of thought go in different directions concerning to whom these prophecies should apply. Up to this point, however, Evans is content to take the text and find the historical personages based on what the text says and the historical situations that coincide with the prophetic descriptions.

Interestingly, at this point, Evans completely changes his tactic. Now he attempts to manipulate what the text actually says and what history actually records, and he introduces suppositions and speculations in an effort to make things fit. In other words, Evans' tactic is no longer the correlation of what is said with the history. Rather, it is an effort to make what is said fit a preselected personage. Instead of identifying Herod because the text corresponds to his experiences, Evans chooses Herod first, and then tries to make the prophecy fit. Unfortunately for Evans, the history simply does not fit the prophecy.

ει παρ᾽ αὐτοῦ καὶ τῆς Κλεοπάτρας τὴν ἀπιστίαν ἐπεξελθεῖν προσέταττεν. ἠξί ου γὰρ ἡ Κλεοπάτρα ταῦτα, λυσιτελεῖν αὐτῇ τὸν ἕτερον ὑπὸ θατέρου κακῶς πάσχειν ἡγουμένη.

325. Richardson, *Herod*, 167.

Evans argues, "One can argue, of course, that Cleopatra cannot be the 'king' of the South in verse 40 since she was a queen, but the fact that she was allied with Antony allows him to serve as a king substitute. Besides, if 'king' is synonymous here with 'ruler,' Cleopatra would be 'eligible' herself to serve as the king of the South" (see above quote for references). Of course historically Antony is not identified as the king of Egypt, nor as a king at all. Antony was part of the Second Triumvirate whose authority was granted to them by the Roman Senate. Even after the falling out of Antony and Octavian, neither was identified as a king, and, by an act of the Roman Senate, Antony was actually deprived of any power and authority. Not only was Antony not a king—he was no longer even part of the Triumvirate. Evans' attempt to make the prophecy fit in this way is futile.

Also, the word "king" (מֶלֶךְ, kelem), as it has been used in Daniel 11, is the word for "king," not "ruler" in general. In Dan. 2:10 the words "king" and "ruler" are both used in order to cover all possibilities, since "king" refers to kings properly and "ruler" to all others having dominion. In Dan 2:15 Arioch is referred to as the king's "commander," distinguishing "king" from "ruler." God is also referred to as "ruler" of the kingdoms of men, and Daniel states that Nebuchadnezzar would remain in his condition until he recognizes that heaven "rules." In each instance, however, the emphasis is on controlling the affairs of men. Although God is certainly the great King, the term "Ruler" with reference to God is used to emphasize this aspect of God's activity and so is distinguished from God's actions as the King. Ruling is only part of what a king does. Even so, Antony was not a king and could not have bestowed this designation upon Cleopatra by association.

Daniel uses another word that can be used to mean "ruler," namely נָגִיד (dīgan). This word occurs only in chapters 9 and 11. In chapter 9 it is used in verse 25 to refer to "Messiah the prince," and in verse 26 it is used of the "coming prince." In Dan 11:22 it is used with reference to the "prince of the covenant." The notion that Antony would qualify as "the king of the South" does not fit into the flow of Daniel 11 and the way Daniel has been using this expression. Evans is on stronger ground arguing that Cleopatra might qualify as "king of the south" if we take the term "king" to indicate simply "ruler," whether male or female. Of course Hebrew has a word which indicates a female ruler, מַלְכָּה (ḥaklam), the Aramaic cognate of which is used in Dan 5:10. If the text intended to refer to Cleopatra as the ruler, there would be no reason not to use the feminine form of the word. But, as we have seen, this also seems to be against the use and identification of the historical references as this has been done throughout chapter 11. Evans' descriptions sound like a desperate albeit unsuccessful attempt to make things fit into his scheme.

OCTAVIAN AS THE KING OF THE NORTH?

Evans goes much further afield by attempting to argue that Octavian could fulfill the role of "the king of the North" in verse 40. He says "And if Cleopatra alone, Antony alone, or the combination of Cleopatra and Antony qualifies as the king of the South, then Octavian can plausibly be assumed to be the king of the North. Up to this point in Daniel 11, the kingdom of the North has always been Seleucid Syria; but *in the scenario that makes Herod the king of verses 36–39, Rome takes the place formerly held by Greece in the sequence of four kingdoms and becomes the kingdom of the North*" (emphasis in original). Unfortunately for Evans' explanation, the king of Greece is not referred to as "the king of the North." After the struggle among those who would inherit Alexander's kingdom, Cassander actually became king of Greece, and the kings who are referred to as the kings of the north are from the Seleucid kingdom, not the kingdom of Greece. In fact, the first time the expression "the king of the North" is used is in verse 6 with reference to Antiochus II Theos, a Seleucid king. In the scheme of Daniel 11, both the king of the south and the king of the north are "Greece" only in the sense of the four kingdoms that took over Alexander's empire. So, Evans' argument that "Rome takes the place formerly held by Greece in the sequence of four kingdoms and becomes the kingdom of the North" simply does not work. In fact, there is a sense in which Greece included both the king of the north and the king of the south, and so Rome could not "take its place." Even if we grant that the king of the South is a generic reference for Cleopatra, Evans still has the impossible task of identifying the king of the North, which he has already admitted is not a reference to Herod. In fact, there is no historical situation in the career of Herod that corresponds to this prophetic description. Evans is grasping at straws.

THE BATTLE OF ACTIUM

In his further efforts to relate these prophecies to Herod, Evans appeals to the historical account of the battle of Actium, 31 BC.

> It is striking that the passage in verse 40 stating that the king of the North will "storm out against him with chariots and cavalry and a great fleet of ships" bears a close resemblance to the events associated with the battle of Actium and its aftermath. Furthermore, it should be noted that after the disastrous war of Antiochus III with Rome featuring the battle of Magnesia in 190 and disastrous peace terms as a consequence, Seleucid Syria never again achieved prominence as a naval power. Notice that the passage says nothing about infantry. Actium was a naval battle. Although Antony had a decided advantage over Octavian in infantry, at least on the sur-

face, he went along with Cleopatra's desire to avoid a land battle. He may have done so, in part, because of doubts about the loyalty of some of his commanders and their troops. The contacts of the contending armies with each other before Actium were largely restricted to men on horseback. In Egypt after Actium, Mauro claims, it was the failures of their ships and cavalry that sealed the fates of Antony and Cleopatra.[326]

Evans attempts to relate the prophetic description of verse 40 claiming that it "bears a close resemblance to the events associated with the battle of Actium and its aftermath." He comments how after the battle of Magnesia in 190, "Seleucid Syria never again achieved prominence as a naval power," and he specifically points out that "the passage says nothing about infantry. Actium was a naval battle." Earlier Evans criticized Collins for making a claim in his commentary and yet showing "no awareness of its possible contradiction with his translation." One must now ask a similar question of Evans. Is he not aware that the text contradicts his own assertion that the battle of Actium was a naval battle? Evans comments how the text makes no reference to infantry, but the text does make a reference to horsemen and chariots. This does not sound like a typical Naval battle.

Evans is correct that the battle at Actium was a naval battle. Consequently, the prophetic description could not be any more different from the actual battle of Actium than it would be if it had included a reference to infantry. The fact is, the closeness of the prophetic description to the battle of Actium is only in the fact that the text refers to a war. But, the war to which the text refers is a war including ships, horsemen, and chariots. The battle of Actium was a naval battle only. Evans makes reference to confrontations "before Actium" that principally involved horsemen, but that was *before* Actium. Actium was a naval battle, but the text states that the battle, not "before the battle," would involve ships, horsemen, and chariots. Evans must ignore the straightforward statements of the text in order to try to make this fit Herod.

Evans claims that "the Herodian thesis requires that the king of the North of verse 40 has to be someone other than Herod, but there is no clear grammatical pronouncement to that effect."[327] However, the fact that the text refers to three distinct individuals as confronting each other leaves no room for this claim. The statement of the text gives a clear grammatical pronouncement that Herod cannot be identified either as the king of the South or the king of the North. But, rather than support the Herodian thesis, this actually cuts the foundation from under the whole view. There simply is no historical

326. Ibid., 268 (emphasis in original).
327. Ibid., 274.

situation in the career of Herod that corresponds to the prophetic description. The fact that the three are different personages renders the Herodian thesis impossible.

Even if we grant that Octavian might qualify as the king of the north, this still does not correspond to the experiences of Herod. The fact that as soon as it became clear that Antony would lose the war, but before either Antony's death or final defeat, Herod "came to Octavian, now thirty-three, in Rhodes, without his crown and other signs of his royal status. He stressed his integrity and loyalty, saying he would be as loyal to Octavian as he had been to Antony. . . . Octavian travelled triumphantly through Syria and Judea to Egypt in pursuit of Antony and Cleopatra (*War* 1.394; *Ant.* 15.199; Plutarch, *Antony*, 74), confirming publicly that Herod's position had been enhanced by his shift to Octavian."[328] Augustus and Herod were actually friends before the hostilities between Octavian and Antony: "From 40 BCE, when all three [Herod, Antony, and Octavian] had walked arm in arm through the streets of Rome, Antony had been instrumental in Herod's position, and Herod had matched Antony's trust. Octavian had reason for thinking well of Herod . . ."[329]

OVERFLOWING AND PASSING THROUGH

The last part of verse 40 states, "and he will enter countries, overflow them and pass through" (וּבָא בָאֲרָצוֹת וְשָׁטַף וְעָבָר: *fāṭas'w_ṭoŝar'' ab 'abu _ba''war*), lit. "and he will come in the lands and he will overflow and he will pass through." The expression "overflow and pass through" occurs one other time in Daniel, chapter 11 verse 10: "His sons will mobilize and assemble a multitude of great forces; and one of them will keep on coming and overflow and pass through [וְשָׁטַף וְעָבָר, *raba''w fāṭas'w*], that he may again wage war up to his very fortress." The picture here is that the king's army will be so vast and powerful that it will overflow the lands and pass through them, and they will be unable to offer any significant resistance. The lands referred to seem to be the lands over which the king of the South and the king of the North rule.

41—   "He will also enter the Beautiful Land, and many countries will fall; but these will be rescued out of his hand: Edom, Moab and the foremost of the sons of Ammon.

---

328. Richardson, *Herod*, 171.

329. Ibid.

THE BEAUTIFUL LAND

Some translations read "He will invade the beautiful land." The word here is simply "enter" (וּבָא, *ˀabu*). The notion of "invasion" is no doubt inferred from the descriptions of many falling, which seems to be indicative of warfare. This word is often used with the notion of "to invade" in some military sense, but that cannot simply be assumed. The implications in the text seem to support the notion that this person will indeed enter the land as a hostile force. The expression "beautiful land" (בְּאֶרֶץ הַצְּבִי, *ibˀssah sereˀᵉb*) is used in Daniel four additional times (Dan 8:9; 11:16 and 45). In each instance it is taken to refer to the land of Israel. The text indicates that entering into the beautiful land follows upon the over-flowing and passing through the lands. Wood notes that, "having triumphed over the two allied kings, [Antichrist] will move on into 'the glorious land,' meaning Palestine."[330] This seems to be a peculiar statement. Since it has been shown that the king of verse 36 cannot be either Antiochus IV Epiphanes or Herod, but appears to be a reference to a yet future king, there is no specific statement about the location of his headquarters or home country. If one takes this to be a reference to Herod, then this statement makes no sense at all since Herod is already in the beautiful land.

In order to attempt to make sense of this statement and retain the Herodian thesis, Mauro takes the overflowing and passing through to be a reference to Augustus.[331] The text states, "And he will enter the beautiful land." This move serves to make the entire section more confusing. To identify any person one wishes by the third person personal pronouns in this section effectively renders every antecedent of every occurrence uncertain. There is no reason, either grammatically or literarily, that the "he" should refer to anyone else but the king that has been the primary subject since verse 40 and even verse 36. But, Mauro states, "The course pursued by Augustus after his triumph over Antony and Cleopatra follows most literally the predictions of the prophecy. For *he entered into the countries, and overflowed, and passed over them, possessing himself of regions of Africa . . .*"[332] Yet history contradicts Mauro's account. Octavian did not "enter into the countries, and overflow, and pass over them," as Mauro claims. At the battle of Actium, Octavian's army landed north of Antony's and continued to press in on him until he had no escape route but the sea. Once the battle was over, Octavian consoli-

330. Wood, *Daniel*, 311.

331. In 27 BC, the Roman Senate conferred upon Octavian, born as Gaius Julius Caesar Octavianus, the title Augustus, a religious title indicating his authority over mankind and nature.

332. Mauro, *Seventy Weeks*, 153.

dated his position in Egypt and set sail for Rhodes. Herod actually traveled to Rhodes to meet Octavian in order to "clarify his position with Octavian,"[333] and after this meeting Octavian came through Judea, but he came as Herod's ally, not as an invasion force (see Richardson, 172). Once again the history just does not fit the prophetic descriptions. The prophecy is in fact not a reference to Augustus, but to a future king who will overpower these lands. Apparently this king will not have his base of operations in Palestine, but in some other land so that after he overflows and passes through the lands of the king of the South and the king of the North, he will come into the land of Israel as a hostile force. In fact, inadvertently Mauro may have implied what some Futurists argue, that this king will come from Rome.

MANY WILL FALL

The word translated "fall" is יִכָּשֵׁל וּ (*uĕśakkiy*), and in Daniel is used only in chapter 11 (11:14, 19, 33, 34, 35, 41). It can be used to indicate stumbling, but it can also be used to indicate falling in the sense of being put to death. This is particularly the case in verse 33: "Those who have insight among the people will give understanding to the many; yet they will fall by sword [בְּחֶרֶב וְנִכְשְׁל וּ, *berehᵉbⁱ ulᵉskinᵉw*] and by flame, by captivity and by plunder for many days." Here the indication is that they will be put to death by the sword and by the flame. Some commentators assume that the verse is making reference to the fact that many countries/lands will fall. In fact, Mauro gives the following translation of this section: "He shall enter also into the glorious land; and many countries shall be overthrown;"[334] Actually the text simply states, "and many will fall," (וְרַבּוֹת יִכָּשֵׁל וּ, *uĕśakkiy tobarᵉw*) not specifying many what? There is no reason to think that this is a reference to countries exclusively or at all. The sentence states, "He will enter Israel, and many will fall" (see Table 67).

Table 67: Daniel 11:41a

יִכָּשֵׁל וּ	וְרַבּוֹת	הַצְּבִי	בָּאֶרֶץ	וּבָא
will fall	and many	the Beautiful	into land	And he will enter

It seems more natural to take this as a reference to many in Israel. This is the way Wood takes it: "These 'many' must be Jews, since, with the

333. Richardson, *Herod*, 169.
334. Ibid., 150.

three-pronged battle being over by this time, they would not be Russians or Arabs."[335]

EDOM, MOAB, AND AMMON ARE RESCUED

The lands of Edom, Moab, and Ammon are lands to the southeast of Israel. There is no indication in the text how or why these lands will be "rescued from his hand." The word can mean "slip away" or "escape" and may indicate that these people get away before the king can attack. This may also indicate that there is a sense in which they abandon Israel to her fate rather than come to her aid. One reason for mentioning these lands may be to make certain that the reference to the "beautiful land" is understood as Israel, and that it is understood as an actual, not merely figurative or "spiritual" reference. Apparently this king will enter Israel with the intent to kill, and these areas southeast of Israel will escape this fate. Historically there have been antagonisms between the people of Israel and the people of these lands. This may suggest that one reason these people escape or are delivered out of his hand is that his primary aim is Israel, not the surrounding peoples.

As Evans points out, Mauro's explanation of the escape of these lands by associating them with the "expedition . . . under Aelius Gallus" did not actually include these lands. Evans explains, "Unfortunately, Mauro made a careless error in his exegesis of the passage mentioning Edom, Moab, and Ammon. He mistakenly seized upon the failure of an expedition by Aelius Gallus into the Arabian Peninsula ca. 26 BC as proof of the applicability of this passage to the time of Herod. . . . The problem here is that the lands that had once been known as Ammon, Moab, and Edom were far removed from the portions of Arabia where Aelius went."[336] We have already seen that Mauro had a tendency to "seize upon" anything that he might be able to squeeze into his scheme.

Some have argued that this could not be a reference to the future because these areas no longer exist. However, even those who say these prophecies apply to Antiochus IV or Herod have this problem, because in the time of Antiochus and Herod, these lands under these names had already ceased to exist, and Ammon was fading as well. These lands did exist as separate areas in the time of Daniel, and the angel uses these names in order to make sure that Daniel understands the area to which he is referring. He is not claiming, necessarily, that these countries will exist by these names at the time the king invades, although it is possible that they could be reconstituted according to their ancient boundaries and names as Israel has done.

335. Wood, *Daniel*, 311.
336. Evans, *Four Kingdoms*, 270.

42—   "Then he will stretch out his hand against other countries, and the land of Egypt will not escape."

Egypt Will Not Escape

This king will extend his conquest even to the point of attacking Egypt. This verse is problematic in light of the statement in verse 40. Verse 40 indicates that the king of the South, an appellation that has been taken as a reference to Egypt throughout Daniel 11 up to verse 40, has already attacked this king and apparently lost. However, it is possible that the battle was fought in a different location, perhaps the base of operations of the king, indicated by the fact that they attack him, and in retaliation he will now invade the homeland of those he has just defeated.

43—   "But he will gain control over the hidden treasures of gold and silver and over all the precious things of Egypt; and Libyans and Ethiopians will follow at his heels."

He will Control Egypt's Wealth

Apparently the motivation for moving against Egypt is to gain control of Egypt's wealth. The word translated "will follow at his heels" is בְּמִצְעָדָיו (wĕyada ͨ simᵉb). It is better rendered "in his steps." The word "follow" is not present in the text. The NASB translators added it because they understood the word to be indicating participation in the king's activities. However, as Miller points out, this may not indicate that "these nations are allies of (marching with) the king . . ."[337] Rather, it may indicate that they are next on the list of conquests. Miller pinpoints these areas: "Hebrew *bul* ['Libyans,' *mibul*] designates the area in North Africa west of Egypt that includes modern-day Libya, and Hebrew *šuk* ('Nubians,' *mišuk*) was the name of an area roughly equivalent to modern Ethiopia and Sudan."[338]

Mauro's dated comments are revealed in his characterization of Egypt: "Here again are words which make it perfectly clear that the fulfillment of this prophecy must be sought in the days of Egypt's greatness and wealth, and is not to be found in the squalid and poverty-stricken Egypt of later times, which, according to the sure word of prophecy, was to become 'the basest of the kingdoms,' and not to exalt itself any more (Ezek. 29:15)."[339] Since

337. Miller, *Daniel*, 311.
338. Ibid.
339. Mauro, *Seventy Sevens*, 155.

Mauro's day (his text was originally written in the 1920's), Egypt and many of the Middle Eastern countries have become extremely wealthy as a result of oil. So, once again Mauro's argument, which by the way is not based on "Scripture alone" as he claimed he would do, but rather on the historical situation of his own day, fails to support his view.

44—   "But rumors from the East and from the North will disturb him, and he will go forth with great wrath to destroy and annihilate many."

RUMORS

The king will hear rumors from the east and the north that may indicate that he is being attacked from those areas. In fact, the rumors from the east may involve the very countries that earlier escaped from his hand. The text does not indicate who these groups are or the nature of the disturbance. But they are enough to cause the king to respond with great wrath and to go out with the intent to destroy and utterly annihilate those opposing him.

Mauro attempts to apply the reference to rumors from the east to the statement in Matt 2:1: "When Jesus was born in Bethlehem of Judea, *in the days of Herod the king*, behold there came wise men FROM THE EAST to Jerusalem . . . So here we have the exact thing prophesied, namely, '*tidings out of the east*' which '*troubled him.*"[340] Of course Mauro's connection completely breaks down when it is pointed out that Herod did not "go forth in great wrath to destroy and annihilate many." The attempt to connect this phrase with the killing of the children in Bethlehem hardly does justice to the text. Unlike the prophetic description in Dan 11:44, the campaign to kill the children was extremely confined not only in area but in its victims. Also, although these visitors came from the east, the rumor did not come from the east because these visitors were in Jerusalem at the time. Mauro completely ignores the fact that Daniel's text states that the rumors come also from the north. There is no indication in the text of Matthew, or anywhere else, relating to Herod receiving rumors from the north. The response of the king to the rumors from the north and east is the same. He goes forth with great wrath. This implies a similarity in the rumors themselves—they imply the same kind of threat from the two areas. But, there is nothing comparable to what Herod heard from the wise men that could be identified as rumors from the north that "troubled him." The prophetic description simply does not fit Herod.

---

340. Ibid., 158. The Greek text reads, Τοῦ δὲ Ἰησοῦ γεννηθέντος ἐν Βηθλέεμ τῆς Ἰουδαίας ἐν ἡμέραις Ἡρῴδου τοῦ βασιλέως, ἰδοὺ μάγοι ἀπὸ ἀνατολῶν παρεγένον εἰς Ἱεροσόλυμα (Matt 2:1).

Notwithstanding the problems of relating the rumors to Herod, Mauro goes on to attempt to connect the reference to "tidings out of the north" to Herod's son, Antipater, who attempted to deceive his father into killing his brothers. Referring to Rome as having "become the center of what is indefinitely called in this prophecy 'the north'"[341] is not only an enormous stretch of the text, but is not verified by any arguments. Mauro merely asserts this as if it should be obvious to his reader. Of course once again the text and history contradict Mauro's assertions. Having heard of Antipater's plan, Herod did not go forth in great wrath to destroy and annihilate many. He certainly killed his sons, but that can hardly fulfill the notion of "many" in this context.

Mauro's attempt to expand the notion of Herod's "fury" by a reference from Josephus simply does not reach the mark. He says, "Herod's 'great fury' (to use the words of the prophecy) was not confined to the babes of Bethlehem, and to members of his own family. For, says Josephus, 'it was also *during paroxysms of fury*, that, nearly about the same time, he burned alive Matthias and forty young men with him, who had pulled down the golden image of the Roman eagle, which he had placed over the gate of the temple' (Ant. XVII 7)."[342] The account to which Mauro refers is contained in *Antiquities*, 17.6, and, as before, Mauro misrepresents the words of Josephus. What Mauro does not tell his reader is that, although Herod burned these men alive, in the parallel section is Josephus' *Wars of the Jews*, I.33.4, Josephus says, "Whereupon the people were afraid lest a great number should be found guilty, and desired that when he had first punished those that put them upon this work, and then those that were caught in it, he would leave off his anger as to the rest. With this the king complied, though not without difficulty."[343] And Josephus continues, "but delivered the rest that were caught to the proper officers to be put to death by them."[344] In other words, Herod did not go out in great wrath to destroy and to annihilate many. He did not even put to death some that were, according to Josephus, caught in the act. Also, the various events which Mauro characterizes as Herod's "great fury" were separated by many months and perhaps even a few years. Mauro has subtly shifted the rumor from the north, which he claims had to do with Antipater, to the event of taking down the image. Antipater's "rumor" had nothing to do with this event, so it could not have been the "rumor from the north" that caused Herod to kill these young men. In other words, the description of the prophecy simply does not

341. Ibid.
342. Ibid., 159.
343. Josephus, *Wars of the Jews*, I.33.4
344. Ibid.

apply to Herod. Mauro is not only stretching the text and the history, but the credulity of the reader.

Evans' comment about verse 44 is revealing of his methodology. He says, "There is no way that this verse can apply to the career of Augustus, yet there is no explicit language here to suggest that the 'he' in this verse is not the 'he' in the immediately preceding verse. Those who would deny the validity of the Maccabean thesis are thus confronted with the same type of problem that verses 36 and 40 pose for them—how to derive a change in the identity of the person whose actions are described without an explicit grammatical change to suggest it."[345] In other words, Evans' approach is not to let the text indicate what it will, but to make the text fit an already present assumption about what it should mean. Evans rejects the notion that the reference to the king going in great wrath is a reference to military action because he thinks verse 45 nullifies this option.

The Destruction of the King of the End Time: 11:45

45—   "He will pitch the tents of his royal pavilion between the seas and the beautiful Holy Mountain; yet he will come to his end, and no one will help him."

Pitching His Tents

Wood gives the following description as an explanation of the first phrase of verse 45: "The clause is, literally translated, 'he shall plant the tents of his palace.' Ancient conquerors took tents with them for their official dwelling places, when on campaign. At the center of the encampment a large main tent was pitched and around it small ones for personal attendants. The thought here is that the Antichrist would be able to place his official tent where he wanted in Palestine, indicating complete subjugation of the land. The tent would serve both as a symbol of his domination and a base from which to continue his oppression of the Jews."[346] If the "beautiful holy mountain" is Jerusalem, then the seas are the Mediterranean and the Dead Sea. It seems clear that the reference must be to Jerusalem. The expression "beautiful land" has been understood almost universally to refer to Israel, and the expression "holy mountain" is found in Ps 6:2 as a reference to Jerusalem: "Upon Zion, My holy mountain." The expression "beautiful holy mountain" is found only here in Daniel. The statement implies that the king will set up his tent on

345. Evans, *Four Kingdoms*, 271.
346. Wood, *Daniel*, 313.

Jerusalem. Rather than using the name "Jerusalem" the descriptive expression implies that the king sets up his tent there specifically as an affront to the God of Israel.

COMING TO HIS END

Yet he will come to his end, and there will be none to help him. Mauro, quoting Farquharson, claims, "This part of the prediction obviously implies that, in his last hours, the king would apply for deliverance or remedy, from some affliction or disease, but would receive none."[347] The fact is, there is absolutely nothing in the text that would even suggest that this king is applying for deliverance from some affliction or disease. This is imposed on the text in order to make it fit with what is known about the end of Herod's life. Mauro asserts, "He [Herod] died a prey to horrible diseases, and to horrible remorse, just five days after he had ordered the execution of his oldest son."[348] One wonders if Mauro grasped the contradiction between this description and his earlier claim that the "dynasty of Herod retained, through all the political upheavals of the times, its favor with Rome, and flourished in authority in Palestine . . ."[349] Dying in disease and remorse hardly sounds like Herod flourished. As Jonathan Price puts it, "All the charges and complaints against him [Herod]— oppressive taxation, offensive Hellenizing tendencies, violations of Jewish law, constant manipulation of the high priesthood—were symptomatic of a deeper hatred. He died a bitter and generally despised man."[350] This does not fit the glorious picture Mauro attempted to paint earlier in his commentary.

The text simply states that this evil king will come to his end, as all of those before him, yet there would be no escape for him. No one will be able to help him when he faces his end. The word "end" (קֵץ, *ṣeq*) is used 15 times in the book of Daniel (8:17, 19; 9:26 (twice); 11:6, 13, 27, 35, 40, 45; 12:4, 6, 9, 13). However, it is used concerning the end of a king only once, in 11:45. Throughout chapter 11 the expression "time of the end" is used (see Table 63 on page 572). The fact that this one use is unique in its reference to the end of this king may indicate that this is the end toward which all the previous instances were pointing.

---

347. Mauro, *Seventy Sevens*, 160.

348. Ibid.

349. Ibid., 141–42.

350. Jonathan J. Price, *Jerusalem Under Siege*, 5.

Concluding Thoughts on Chapter 11

The material in chapter 11 is detailed and, at least up to verse 35, is discernable in the actual historical events of the period. The nature of the material in these verses sets a precedent for interpreting the remainder of the verses in the chapter. Whereas the procedure for understanding the material in verses 1–35 is to discover the historical events that correspond to the prophetic descriptions, this same procedure ought to be employed throughout the remainder of the chapter. Preterists employ this approach, as do virtually all interpreters, up to verse 35. However, as we have seen, when it comes to verse 36 and following, Preterists suddenly change their methodology. Rather than consistently following the procedure of discovering the historical persons and events that correspond to the prophetic descriptions, Preterists determine who must be the historical person and then attempt to force the prophetic descriptions into the history that they have already concluded must be the time frame of fulfillment.

No better example of this can be found than the attempts to make the prophetic descriptions fit into the life and times of Herod. As we have shown, neither Herod's life nor the history of his supposed "dynasty" corresponds to the prophetic descriptions. Rather than taking the text as it stands and then finding the history that corresponds, the methodology of the Preterist shifts to rearranging the text, reading into the text, arbitrarily opting for meanings that do not fit the context, and other tactics in an attempt to make the prophetic descriptions fit into the history, a history that they have already concluded must be the time frame of the prophecies. In other words, before coming to the text of Daniel 11, Preterists have already decided what period of history must be the time frame in which these prophecies must be fulfilled, and then they go about attempting to make the text fit their prior commitments. This approach is contrary to the approach dictated by the text up to verse 35, and it betrays the fact that they are interpreting the text according to their prior eschatological perspective, not the other way around.

Of course one of the problems with simply locating the history to which the prophetic descriptions correspond is the fact that there is no history to which the prophetic descriptions correspond after verse 35. No historical events or persons fit the actions or persons described in these verses. This seems to suggest that, since the previous verses easily corresponded to discoverable events and persons, that perhaps the persons and events described in verses 36–45 correspond to persons and events that have in fact not yet come on the scene of history. But, since before coming to the text of Daniel, Preterists have already decided that this cannot possibly be the case, they must, because of their prior commitment, make the prophecy fit no matter what violence this does to the text. Contrary to their oft touted claims, Preterists simply are not interpreting the text as they find it. Rather, they alter the text, changing its order and/or its nature, in order to make it fit into their prior eschatological commitment.

Of course Preterists have often claimed that Futurists are in fact imposing their own prior commitments upon the text. It is certainly true that Futurists have their own prior eschatological commitments. However, it is not necessary to impose a Futurist perspective on the text to see that the prophetic descriptions simply do not correspond to any known historical persons or events, at least not without altering the text or history from the way one actually finds it. Also, Futurists do not inexplicably change their methodology of approach once they come to verses 36ff. Rather, the Futurist attempts to discover whether or not there are any historical persons and events that correspond to the prophetic descriptions in these verses, and finding none, see no problem with concluding that these descriptions, which up to this point in the prophecy can be correlated to history without violating the text,[351] are descriptions of persons and events that are yet future. That being the case, as unpleasant as it may seem to the Preterist, the necessities of the text and of history require that one accept the possibility of a prophetic gap in the fulfillment of the prophecy. This conclusion is not the result of imposing a Futurist perspective upon the text. Rather, it is simply a matter of taking the text the way one finds it, discovering that these verses do not correspond to any known history or persons, and, since the material up to and including verse 35 actually does correspond to actual historical persons and events, and since verses 36–45 do not correspond to history, realizing that the historical persons and events prophetically described must be yet future. If Preterists were to do the same, they could no longer be Preterists. However, as we will see, the tactics of the Preterists are not confined to these concluding verses of chapter 11, but extend into the critical prophecies of chapter 12.

351. The expression "violating the text" is not a gratuitous derogatory comment to vilify Preterist approaches, or Preterists themselves. Rather, it is, unfortunately, an accurate characterization of practices, such as arbitrarily rearranging the verses from the order in which they actually occur in the text of Daniel in order to make them fit into one's eschatological scheme, or ignoring the dictates of grammar and syntax in order to connect the words they need to connect in order to make their interpretations work, or imposing the notion of literary parallelism upon the text when there are none of the literary indicators in the text that are used by biblical authors, for example in poetry, to indicate such parallelism. These and other tactics are in fact violations of the text that are necessary in order to make the text fit their eschatological scheme. Simply taking the text as it is found does not support a Preterist approach, and the text must be violated in order to make such a support seem possible.

13

Daniel's Vision of the End of the Age: 12:1–13

Introduction

CHAPTER 12 seems to be structured as a chiasm focusing on the 1,260 days.

Figure 46: Structure of Chapter 12

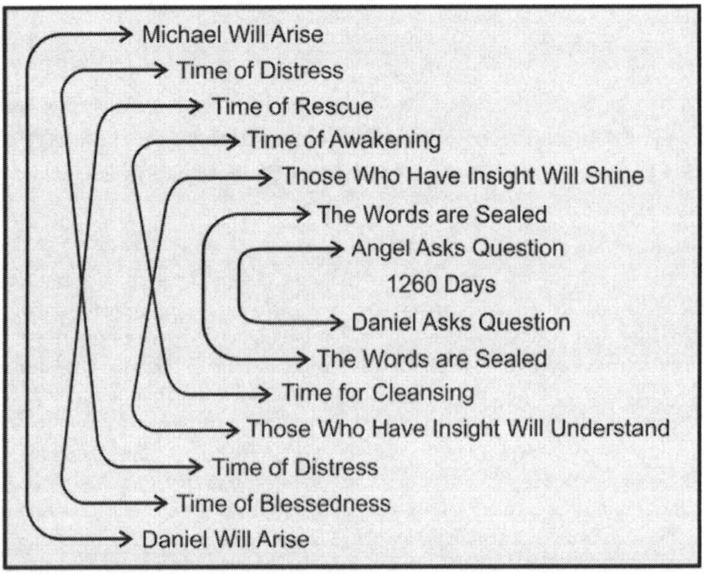

Michael Will Arise
Time of Distress
Time of Rescue
Time of Awakening
Those Who Have Insight Will Shine
The Words are Sealed
Angel Asks Question
1260 Days
Daniel Asks Question
The Words are Sealed
Time for Cleansing
Those Who Have Insight Will Understand
Time of Distress
Time of Blessedness
Daniel Will Arise

According to Miller, "In spite of the chapter division found in both the English and Hebrew Bibles, Daniel's final vision continues from 11:45 through 12:3 without interruption."[1] Similarly, Wood asserts, "There is no change in subject matter in moving from chapter eleven to chapter twelve. In fact, the message of the grand angel to Daniel continues without break through verse four of this chapter, making his uninterrupted message to extend totally from 10:20 through 12:4."[2] This seems to be the consensus. Even Mauro states, "The first four verses of Daniel 12 should not be disconnected from chapter 11, for they are an integral part of the prophecy, there being no break at all at the place where the chapter division has been made."[3]

Prophecy of the Great Tribulation: 12:1

1— "Now at that time will stand Michael, the great prince who stands over the sons of your people. And there will be time of distress which not was done from the days of a nation until that time; and at that time will be rescued your people, everyone who is found written in the book."

That Time

Verse 1 opens with a reference to "that time" (וּבָעֵת הַהִיא, *ıhah te' abu*), lit. "and in the time that one"). The word "time" (עֵת, *te'*) has both the preposition "in" (בְּ, *eb*) and the definite article indicated by the *seṁaq* vowel that appears under the *teb* (בְּ). The presence of the definite article indicates that the man is making reference either to a specifically identifiable time or to a time already discussed in the context. This seems to be a reference to the closing verses of chapter 11 indicating that Michael will stand at the time of the end of the king as described in verse 45. In Table 64: Time of the End Chart, on page 572, we set out the five instances in which the expression "time of end" is used. Mauro claims that verse 1 "connects the passage directly with verse 40 of the preceding chapter, where the words 'at the time of the end' occur."[4] Walvoord takes the same approach: "The opening phrase of chapter 12, *and at that time*, makes clear that this passage is talking about the same period of time as the previous context, that is, 'the time of the end' (11:40)."[5]

1. Miller, *Daniel*, 313.
2. Wood, *Daniel*, 315.
3. Mauro, *Seventy Weeks*, 163.
4. Ibid.
5. Walvoord, *Daniel*, 282.

However, since the opening phrase of chapter 12 does not have the word "end," connecting it back to verse 40 seems unnecessary. If there is any length of time in the events described between verse 40 and verse 45, one would need to propose that Michael is standing the whole time. Although this would not be an impossible situation, it seems better, however, to connect it with verse 45 indicating what will happen at "his end." The fact that Michael "will stand" (יַעֲמֹד, *dom^aʾay*) may indicate that Michael is instrumental in bringing about the end of the king.

Mauro's belief that there is no future for the nation of Israel comes up again in his comment on the expression "time of the end." He says, "The same words are repeated in verse 4 of chapter 12, just quoted. There is, therefore, no room for doubt that the events foretold were to occur during the very last stage of 'the latter days' of Jewish history."[6] We have already shown that 70 AD did not mark the end of Jewish history.

Michael the Archangel

The Hebrew name 'Michael' (מִיכָאֵל, *le^ʾakim*) is the combination of three words. The first is the interrogative pronoun 'who' (מִי, *ʾim*). The second word is the inseparable preposition כְּ (*^ek*), which means "as." The last word is the singular form of the name "God" (אֵל, *le^ʾ*). The resulting meaning is, "Who is as El," or "Who is as God." He is referred to as "the great prince" (הַשַּׂר הַגָּדוֹל, *le^ḏaggah rássah*).[7] As the name of the angel, "Michael" occurs only three times in the entire OT, and all of these are in Daniel: 10:13, 21, and 12:1. One of the reasons for including these references in Daniel's prophecy is to get across the idea that, just like there are spiritual forces that are warring each other, although this is not visible to the human eye, so there are the purposes of God that, though they also may not be visible and sometimes may even seem impossible, they are nevertheless progressing according to His plan. Daniel is to know and understand that although things will become so terrible, such as has never been in the history of mankind, that God is still standing for His people, and He will accomplish His purpose in them.

It is interesting that Michael, the one who "stands over the sons of your people," although he stands, the time is still a time of "distress" (צָרָה, *haras*). Jeremiah compares "distress" to the "agony like a woman in childbirth" (Jer 50:43). The question that arises is, if Michael stands up at this time, is he not attempting to abate the distress? Some propose that Michael is indeed protecting the faithful among God's people. Perhaps Michael's responsibil-

---

6. Mauro, *Seventy Weeks*, 163–64.

7. See C. Fred Dickason, *Angels, Elect and Evil*, for more information on Michael and Gabriel.

ity is previewed in the fiery furnace in chapter 3 in which one having the appearance of a son of the gods protects the three Hebrew youths from the destructive power of the furnace. So, at this time Michael will arise to protect the faithful from the fierce anger of Antichrist. Although the time of distress will be so great, it would be even worse except for Michael being sent by God to stand for God's people.

Mauro on Michael

Mauro proposes four things concerning this time and concerning Michael that he claims are "specified in the passage . . ."[8]

> *First.* The standing up of Michael, the great prince who stands for the children of Daniel's people.
>
> *Second.* A time of trouble such as never was, at which time those found written in the book were to escape.
>
> *Third.* Many to awake from the dust of the earth, some to everlasting life, and some to shame and everlasting contempt, in which connection is given a great promise to those who cause to be wise, and who turn many to righteousness.
>
> *Fourth.* Many to run to and fro, and knowledge to be increased.[9]

Mauro proceeds to structure his comments on the basis of these four specified things, and we will consider each in association with the verse to which it relates. With reference to the first thing, Mauro points to various places in the New Testament in which Michael appears; Jude 9; Rev 12:7. He also proposes that Paul may be referring to Michael in 1 Thess. 4:16 when he talks about the archangel. Mauro points out, "There is no revelation of the precise part taken by Michael, the great prince, in the affairs of God's people in the critical days to which this part of the prophecy relates, that is to say, the beginning of New Testament times; for Michael is not mentioned by name in the Gospels or Acts."[10] Nevertheless, Mauro points to various passages in the Acts to indicate the degree of "angelic activity"[11] that Mauro argues characterized this age. By attempting to characterize the age of the Gospels and Acts as teeming with angelic activity, Mauro hopes to add support to the notion that these events were fulfilled in 70 AD. Of course one fatal problem

8. Mauro, *Seventy Weeks*, 164.

9. Ibid.

10. Ibid., 166.

11. Ibid.

with Mauro's thesis is, if Michael is standing for Daniel's people, and 70 AD marked the end of the nation of Israel, then Michael either completely failed in his responsibility to protect Daniel's people, or it was never his mission to protect them, in which case the angel is simply deceiving Daniel.

The point of the reference to Michael in Daniel's prophecy is to assure Daniel and his readers that the spiritual warfare is always going on behind the visible scene, and the people of Israel should trust that Michael is carrying out the will of God in defending the people of God. This is not relegated to a specific period or specific periods of history. Simply because the angelic activity becomes visible, as it were, at certain times does not mean that there necessarily were times when the activity was greater than at other times. So, this argument does not support Mauro's effort.

A Time of Trouble

Walvoord asserts, "The entire section from Daniel 11:36 to 12:3 constitutes a revelation of the major factors of the time of the end which may be summarized as follows: (1) a world ruler, (2) a world religion, (3) a world war, (4) a time of great tribulation for Israel, (5) deliverance for the people of God at the end of the tribulation, (6) resurrection and judgment, and (7) reward of the righteous. All of these factors are introduced in this section."[12] Walvoord clearly sees the reference to the "time of trouble" as referring to the tribulation period, and particularly the great tribulation, which is, according to the Futurist view, the last three and one-half years of Daniel's seventieth seven. Wood identifies three "matters" that indicate that the reference in 12:1 is to the great tribulation.

> Three matters give evidence that the "time" in view is that commonly called the Great Tribulation: first, the continuance of thought, without break, in this verse from that of the closing verses of chapter eleven, where the subject concerns the rule of the Antichrist, which occurs during the Great Tribulation; second, the logic of identifying it with the reference to the "time of the end" in 11:40, where the period in view, as noted, is the Great Tribulation; and, third, Jesus' reference to the verse in Matthew 24:21, 22, where the context identifies the period in mind as the Great Tribulation. It should be realized, then, that the period in view will not follow the demise of the Antichrist, mentioned in 11:4.5, but will be the same as that in which he is active in bringing his oppressions.[13]

12. Walvoord, *Daniel*, 281.

13. Wood, *Daniel*, 315.

The expression "time of distress" (עֵת צָרָה, *ḥaraṣ ʾēt*) occurs only seven times outside of Daniel's prophecy (see Table 68).

Table 68: Time of Distress

Jdg 10:14	"Go and cry out to the gods which you have chosen; let them deliver you in the time of your distress [בְּעֵת צָרַתְכֶם, *bᵉmektaraṣ◻ēt*]." לְכוּ וְזַעֲקוּ אֶל־הָאֱלֹהִים אֲשֶׁר בְּחַרְתֶּם בָּם הֵמָּה יוֹשִׁיעוּ לָכֶם בְּעֵת צָרַתְכֶם׃
Neh 9:27	"Therefore You delivered them into the hand of their oppressors who oppressed them, but when they cried to You in the time of their distress [וּבְעֵת צָרָתָם, *mataraṣ◻ēt ḇu*], You heard from heaven, and according to Your great compassion, You gave them deliverers who delivered them from the hand of their oppressors." וַתִּתְּנֵם בְּיַד צָרֵיהֶם וַיָּצֵרוּ לָהֶם וּבְעֵת צָרָתָם יִצְעֲקוּ אֵלֶיךָ וְאַתָּה מִשָּׁמַיִם תִּשְׁמָע וּכְרַחֲמֶיךָ הָרַבִּים תִּתֵּן לָהֶם מוֹשִׁיעִים וְיוֹשִׁיעוּם מִיַּד צָרֵיהֶם׃
Ps 37:39	"But the salvation of the righteous is from the Lord; He is their strength in time of trouble [בְּעֵת צָרָה, *bᵉḥaraṣ◻ēt*]." וּתְשׁוּעַת צַדִּיקִים מֵיהוָה מָעוּזָּם בְּעֵת צָרָה׃
Isa 33:2	"O Lord, be gracious to us; we have waited for You. Be their strength every morning, our salvation also in the time of distress [בְּעֵת צָרָה, *bᵉḥaraṣ◻ēt*]." יְהוָה חָנֵּנוּ לְךָ קִוִּינוּ הֱיֵה זְרֹעָם לַבְּקָרִים אַף־יְשׁוּעָתֵנוּ בְּעֵת צָרָה׃
Jer 14:8	"O Hope of Israel, its Savior in time of distress [בְּעֵת צָרָה, *bᵉʾēt◻ ḥaraṣ*], why are you like a stranger in the land or like a traveler who has pitched his tent for the night?" מִקְוֵה יִשְׂרָאֵל מוֹשִׁיעוֹ בְּעֵת צָרָה לָמָּה תִהְיֶה כְּגֵר בָּאָרֶץ וּכְאֹרֵחַ נָטָה לָלוּן׃

"The Lord said, 'Surely I will set you free for good; Surely I will cause the enemy to make supplication to you in a time of disaster and a time of distress [וּבְעֵת צָרָה, $ū b^e h ar a s \bar t e$ ']."

Jer 15:11

אָמַר יְהוָה אִם־לֹא שֵׁרוֹתִךָ לְטוֹב אִם־לוֹא
הִפְגַּעְתִּי בְךָ בְּעֵת־רָעָה וּבְעֵת צָרָה
אֶת־הָאֹיֵב:

"Alas! for that day is great, there is none like it; and it is the time of Jacob's distress [וְעֵת־צָרָה, $w^e e^\varsigma th ar a s$], but he will be saved from it."

Jer 30:7

הוֹי כִּי גָדוֹל הַיּוֹם הַהוּא מֵאַיִן כָּמֹהוּ וְעֵת־
צָרָה הִיא לְיַעֲקֹב וּמִמֶּנָּה יִוָּשֵׁעַ:

Most of the instances seem to be references to difficult times in the history of Israel. However, Jer 30:7 seems to be referring to the same event to which Daniel is referring here in 12:1. Jeremiah calls it "the time of Jacob's distress." In the context of Jeremiah's prophecy, there are many expressions that call up the image of the captivity in Babylon. Jeremiah refers to breaking the "yoke of their servitude to foreign domination" (30:8), tearing off the "chains of captivity" (30:8), and foreigners subjugating them (30:8). Since the "time of distress" to which Daniel refers is certainly not his own time, that is, the Babylonian captivity, this implies that the time of the Babylonian captivity may have some parallel relationship to this time of distress to which 12:1 is referring. The Babylonian captivity may be a type of the future time of distress for the people of Israel.

MAURO ON "A TIME OF TROUBLE"

Concerning this expression Mauro declares, "The prediction of 'a time of trouble such as never was since there was a nation even to that same time,' is the last thing in the chain of national events revealed in this prophecy; and in perfect agreement with it is the well-known fact that the Jewish nation came to its end with a time of tribulation, distress and sufferings, of a severity beyond anything that was ever heard since the world began."[14] Mauro holds that this time of "great tribulation" was fulfilled in 70 AD. He says, ". . . so conclusive to our mind is the proof that the 'great tribulation' of Matthew 24:21 was the then approaching siege of Jerusalem, that we are bound to believe that competent teachers who relegate it to the future have never ex-

14. Mauro, *Seventy Weeks*, 167.

amined and weighted the evidence."[15] The problem with Mauro's argument is that it does not fit the evidence. As disastrous as the events of 70 AD were for the nation of Israel, they affected only the two tribes that remained in the land after the scattering of the ten tribes in the time of the invasion of the Assyrians. So, although one might argue that the Jews in Jerusalem at the time were destroyed, which in fact did not happen, those of Israel who were scattered throughout the world were not the recipients of this devastation. Safrai notes, "As a matter of fact, there is evidence to show that both during and after the war many Jewish farmers stayed on the land, cultivated it and even owned it."[16] Consequently, it simply does not follow that this was "'the end' of Jewish nationality," as Mauro asserts.[17]

Of course, what Mauro and other Preterists mean by the destruction of the nation of Israel is not necessarily the political state or the social structure—although Mauro consistently presents his claims this way—which, although almost destroyed, actually survived even to the point of orchestrating another uprising in the Bar Kochba revolt. What the Preterists seem to be saying is that by the destruction of the Temple, the religion of Judaism was destroyed. Because the Temple was destroyed, the Jews could no longer offer their sacrifices. For the Preterists, this marked the end of the sacrificial system which had been nullified by the death, burial, and resurrection of Christ.

But there is a serious problem with this position as well. The Temple in Jerusalem was utterly destroyed in the past in the invasion of Nebuchadnezzar bringing to an end the sacrificial system at that time. As H. Tadmor describes, "The true end of Judah came with the absolute destruction of Jerusalem and the Temple . . ."[18] Even after this devastation of the Temple—2 Kgs 25:9 declares, "He [Nebuchadnezzar] burned the house of the LORD"—Israel returned to the land, rebuilt the Temple, and re-instituted the sacrificial system. Since the Jews were not annihilated in the destruction of 70 AD, or even in the Bar Kochba revolt of 135 AD, but have in fact returned to their own land, it is possible that again they could rebuild the Temple and re-institute the sacrificial system. In fact, one edition of Mauro's book was published four years before the reconstitution of the nation of Israel in 1948 and following. This negates the claims of Preterists that the nation of Israel was destroyed.

Martin Goodman makes an interesting observation about the rebuilding of the Temple: "In fact, the detailed prescriptions for the sacrifices to be

15. Ibid., 168.

16. Safrai, "Jews in the Land of Israel," 315.

17. Ibid., 142.

18. H. Tadmor, "Judah from the Fall of Samaria to the Fall of Jerusalem," in *A History of the Jewish People*, ed. H. H. Ben-Sasson (Cambridge, Massachusetts: Harvard University Press, 2002), 157.

found in the Mishnah, redacted around 200 CE, presuppose that even at that date rabbis expected, or at least hoped, that the Temple could and would be rebuilt. The hope was entirely reasonable. Jerusalem had lost one Temple in 587 BCE only to see it restored. The more Josephus pointed out the parallels between the two destructions, which had taken place in both cases on the same day of the month of Ab (in late July), the more plausible was a parallel rebuilding."[19] If as late as 200 AD the Jews were still hoping for the rebuilding of the Temple, this hardly supports Mauro's argument regarding the end of Jewish nationality or even the religion of Judaism.

However, the Preterists' claim is primarily that the sacrificial systems was ended because of the work of Christ, and the people of Israel were rejected by God because of their incessant rejection of Him as their king culminating in the killing of the Messiah. Jonathan Price describes this same perspective as the predominate perspective of the early Christians: "After that [defeat of another later uprising], the Jews remained relatively quiet under different empires, struggling desperately to understand God's judgment in 70. The Christians had no difficulty understanding: God, who had been able to forgive all Israel's sins in previous ages, destroyed the Temple and exiled the Jews because of deicide . . . a new epoch had begun."[20] Nevertheless, as in the past, those who thought Israel was finished after the destruction under Nebuchadnezzar did not live to see their return and restoration to the land, and the re-institution of the sacrificial system. But, if what the Preterist is claiming is that the sacrificial system was ended by Christ's work, then it did not happen in 70 AD, but in c. 33 AD with the death, burial, and resurrection of Christ, and 70 AD was in fact not the end of Jewish nationality.

Here is the rub. Preterists claim that the destruction of Jerusalem and the Temple in 70 AD. was the destruction of Jewish nationality as a result of God rejecting Israel. But, since Jewish nationality was in fact not destroyed, then their interpretation of the events is simply wrong. The destruction of the Temple in the time of Nebuchadnezzar was thought to be a sign of God's rejection of Israel, but it was not. God brought them back into the land. So in the early church, and now by the Preterists, the destruction of Jerusalem and the Temple is interpreted as God having rejected Israel. But the fact that Israel survived this destruction and is now back in the land once again is irrefutable evidence that the Preterists, like those in the time of the destruction of the first Temple, are simply wrong. Israel's continued existence as a nation declares that God has in fact not rejected His people. As Paul said: "I say then, has God cast away His people? Certainly not! For I also am an Israelite, of the

19. Martin Goodman, *Rome and Jerusalem*, 427.

20. Price, *Jerusalem Under Siege*, 175–76.

seed of Abraham, *of* the tribe of Benjamin. God has not cast away His people whom He foreknew" (Rom 11:1–2).[21] Since God has not rejected his people, evidenced not only by the testimony of Scripture, but by the historical reality, then the Preterists' claim that 70 AD marked the end of Judaism or of Jewish nationality is simply false.

If Christ's death, burial, and resurrection marked the end of the Jewish sacrificial system, then this should have occurred in AD 30 or 33, not in AD 70, and the Preterists are wrong. If the destruction of Jerusalem is supposed to be a sign of the rejection of the nation of Israel, then the return of the people and the prospect of rebuilding show again that the Preterists are wrong. If the destruction in AD 70 was supposed to signal the end of Jewish nationality, then the fact that the Jewish nation survived to mount another full-scale revolt in 135, and the fact that the Jewish nation exists again today shows again that the Preterists are wrong. If Preterists try to claim that the rejection of the Jewish sacrificial system occurred in AD 30 or 33, but that it was simply the physical destruction of Jerusalem that occurred in 70 AD, we have already shown that this cannot fit into the prophecies of Dan 9:24–27, and once again the Preterists are simply wrong. No matter how one tries to spin the facts, unless the facts are manipulated, they always turn out to demonstrate that the Preterists are simply wrong.

SHEPHERD ON "A TIME OF TROUBLE"

Shepherd sees the reference to a time of trouble as preceding the new age of the establishing of the kingdom of God. According to Shepherd, "The author of Daniel expected the new age to be preceded by 'a time of anguish,' which the persecution of Antiochus certainly fulfilled."[22] However, if this is a reference to Antiochus, then, according to Shepherd's application, the author of Scripture must have been mistaken since Antiochus IV died in 163 BC, over 100 years before the destruction of Jerusalem. Of course Shepherd is trying to say that the time of anguish was the time of Antiochus' activities, not the destruction of Jerusalem. But, this does not work either because the text characterizes the time as a time such as never occurred since there was a nation until that time (Dan 12:1). But the destruction and killing of Jews in the siege of Jerusalem was much more devastating than the persecutions of Antiochus. According to Price, when the upper wall of the city fell, "The Romans showed little mercy. In one incident, a large number of people (Josephus says 6,000),

21. λέγω οὖν, μὴ ἀπώσατο ὁ θεὸς τὸν λαὸν αὐτοῦ; μὴ γένοιτο· καὶ γὰρ ἐγὼ Ἰσραλίτης εἰμί, ἐκ σπέρματος Ἀβραάμ, φυλῆς βενιαμίν. οὐκ ἀπώσατο ὁ θεὸς τὸν λαὸν αὐτοῦ ὃν προέγνω (Rom 11:1–2).

22. Shepherd, *Beasts, Horns, and Antichrist*, 112.

mostly women and children, were burned in a portico of the outer court
. . ."[23] Some have estimated that well over 10,000 Jews were slaughtered just in
the siege of Jerusalem. And when compared to the annihilation of more than
6,000,000 Jews in the Holocaust, the persecutions of Antiochus become less
significant. Besides this, the text states that this time of distress would be more
severe that any kind of distress suffered by any nation in history. It is hardly
the case that the persecutions of Antiochus could be characterized as a time of
distress such as never occurred since there was a nation until that time.

Also, Evans, commenting specifically on this reference, points out, "Did
164 BC—the year generally assigned by critical scholars for the completion
of Daniel 11—constitute such a time [of distress]? Objectively speaking, it
did not since the worst of the persecution by Antiochus was probably about
three years in the past by then and the fortunes of war had turned heavily in
the Maccabees' favor."[24] In other words, applying this to Antiochus is both
much too early and much too late. It is too early because it is over 100 years
prior to 70 AD, and it is too late because by the time Antiochus dies, his worst
persecution had been completed some three years earlier.

EVANS ON "A TIME OF TROUBLE"

Evans argues against the Antiochus view, as we have seen above, but he holds
that this time must have been fulfilled on or before 70 AD. He asserts, ". . .
this verse in Mark [13:19] and the parallel verses in Matthew 24, and Daniel
12:1, I suggest that they are perfectly accurate when applied to the events
that climaxed in AD 70. What happened then was greater than any disaster
that had previously befallen the Jewish nation—and despite the wording of
the passage in the NIV that reads 'from the beginning of nations until then,'
*Daniel 12:1 must be understood as referring to the Jewish nation rather than all
nations*."[25] In support of his contention that this must be a reference to the
nation of Israel and not to "all nations," Evans argues,

> There are several prominent translations of the Bible that have 12:1
> read "nation," not "nations." For example, the RSV translates the
> passage at issue as follows: "And there shall be a time of trouble,
> such as never has been since there was a nation till that time."
> Collins translates it so as to make its meaning even clearer: "There
> will be a time of distress such as has not been from the beginning
> of *the* nation to that time" (emphasis added). I shall use his trans-
> lation to support a conclusion that he does not reach—that this

23. Price, *Jerusalem Under Siege*, 171.

24. Evans, *Four Kingdoms*, 277.

25. Ibid., 277–78 (emphasis in original).

passage points to the culmination of the chain of events associated with the time of the Herodian dynasty, the great destruction of AD 70.[26]

The problem with Evans' argument is that the Hebrew text does not say "the nation." The text is set out below with a word-for-word translation.

Table 69: Daniel 12:1

אֲשֶׁר	צָרָה	עֵת	וְהָיְתָה
which	distress	time of	And there will be
גּוֹי	מֵהְיוֹת	נִהְיְתָה	לֹא־
a nation	from the days of	was done	not
	הַהִיא	הָעֵת	עַד
	that	the time	until

Earlier Evans argued against a view because of the absence of the definite article when in fact the Hebrew syntax required the word to be definite. Here he is trying to argue that a word should be definite when in fact it does not have the definite article, and it is not required by the Hebrew syntax. The text simply says, "from the days of a nation until that time." Some may argue that we have made a point of the fact that the definite article is regularly omitted in prepositional phrases, so why isn't that the case here. The problem is, even though the English uses a prepositional phrase, the Hebrew does not. The Hebrew is actually a construct relation, "from the days of [מֵהְיוֹת, *ŷoyhim*] a nation [גּוֹי, *ŷog*]," and there is no grammatical or syntactical reason for translating this with the definite article. In a construct relation, the definite article is required to appear on the word in the absolute state for the phrase to be definite. As Waltke-O'Connor point out, "The definite of the genitive [the word in the absolute state] specifies the definiteness of the phrase. If the genitive is indefinite, the phrase is indefinite."[27] Not being familiar with Hebrew syntax, Evans has misunderstood the statement and chosen a translation that is simply wrong. It is a completely illegitimate and dangerous practice simply to choose which translation one likes because it supports his prior commitment and then use it to build one's belief. It is illegitimate because the text

---

26. Ibid., 278.

27. Waltke-O'Connor, *Biblical Hebrew Syntax*, 9.7a.

was not originally written in the language of the translation. It is dangerous because one could end up building one's belief on something that the text does not say, which Evans has in fact done here.

The Hebrew text indicates that the reference is not to a specific nation, but to any nation at all. What this implies is that the scope of the distress should not be measured by the greatness of the disaster upon the nation of Israel alone, but upon any nation throughout history. In other words, this prophecy is about a catastrophe so devastating that it will be more wide spread and destructive than anything that has happened to a nation in the history of mankind up to that point. When one compares the destruction of Jerusalem to all the destructions that have ever occurred in history, even up to 70 AD, although there is no minimizing the scale and impact upon the nation of Israel itself, it does not measure up to some of the greater disasters of history, such as Sodom and Gomorrah, or the flood of Genesis 6, for example.

But, even if we grant Evans' claim that this is a measure relative to the nation of Israel alone, the destruction of Jerusalem in 70 AD was not necessarily more disastrous than the destruction of the nation under Nebuchadnezzar. At that time, many died, and many were taken captive so that the land was characterized by Jeremiah as having been returned to the wasteland of the world in the creation account: "I looked on the earth, and behold, *it was* formless and void וָבֹהוּ תֹהוּ,ֵ *whobaw*ˆ *uhot*); and to the heavens, and they had no light" (Jer 4:23). In fact, one could argue that the biblical descriptions of the devastation of Judah and Jerusalem after the Babylonian invasions give a picture of a destruction more devastating than that of AD 70. So, Evans and the Preterists are going to have to do much more research and present much more evidence than they have to make the case that these descriptions in Daniel can be applied to 70 AD.

Evans claims that Mk 13:19 is indicating the same event, and Evans claims that it "displays an even more calamitous tone than Daniel 12:1."[28] The text states, "For those days will be tribulation such as has not occurred since the beginning of the creation which God created until now, and never will."[29] However, the destruction of Jerusalem in 70 AD was not a world-shaking event. These descriptions seem to indicate a calamity that will be so great that it will affect the entire planet. Contrary to Evans' claim that "they are perfectly accurate when applied to the events that climaxed in AD 70,"[30] there have been greater catastrophes in the world before 70 AD, and there have been greater ones since. As we noted before, the siege of Jerusalem did

---

28. Ibid., 277.

29. ἔσονται γὰρ αἱ ἡμέραι ἐκεῖναι θλῖψις οἵα οὐ γέγονεν τοιαύτη ἀπ ς ἀρχῆς κτίσεως ἣν ἔκτισεν ὁ θεὸς ἕως τοῦ νῦν καὶ οὐ μὴ γένηται. (Mk 13:19).

30. Evans, *Four Kingdoms*, 277.

not even affect some of the farmers in the outlying areas: "As a matter of fact, there is evidence to show that both during and after the war many Jewish farmers stayed on the land, cultivated it and even owned it."[31] In other words, the events surrounding the destruction of Jerusalem did not even encompass the whole of Judea. And Safrai goes on to point out, "Ruined towns did not become a feature of the Palestinian landscape until after the Revolt of Bar Kokhba (135)."[32]

However, Daniel's texts speak of something beyond all the expectations and experience of all men and nations throughout history up to that time, and the event in 70 AD simply does not reach that level. In fact, even for the nation of Israel this does not seem to equal the devastation indicated by Zechariah. In Zech 13:8 the text states, "'It will come about in all the land,' declares the Lord, 'That two parts in it will be cut off and perish; but the third will be left in it.'" In 70 AD at most two-twelfths of the people, the two tribes of Judah and Benjamin, were impacted while ten-twelfths, the ten tribes of the north, the Diaspora who were scattered among the nations hundreds of years earlier, were not affected by this event, at least not in the sense of the physical devastation that Daniel's text describes and to which Preterists refer. Shmuel Ahituv points out, "Despite the fierceness of the Romans' war against the Jews from 66 to 73 CE, it was not a war of annihilation. Vespasian as a rule abided by the old Roman maxim: 'fight the proud, spare the meek.' Even towns that were twice destroyed, such as Joppa, rose up again with the cessation of Hostilities. A sparse settlement also remained amid the ruins of Jerusalem, near the camp of the Tenth Roman Legion."[33] Without minimizing the seriousness of the event, the descriptions of the coming time of distress far surpass the devastation and disaster of 70 AD.

Written in the Book

The text states that those who are "written in the book" (כָּל־הַנִּמְצָא :כָּתוּב בַּסֵּפֶר, *refessab būtak ʾasminnah lak*)will be rescued. The term "rescue" (יִמָּלֵט‬, *lelammiy*) is used one other time in Daniel in 11:41: "He will also enter the Beautiful Land, and many countries will fall; but these will be rescued [יִמָּלֵט‬, *uilammiy*] out of his hand:" As we saw in 11:41, the word can mean "slip away" or "escape." Here it may indicate that some will survive those terrible days. In other words, those who are found written in the book

---

31. Safrai, "Jews in the Land of Israel," 315.

32. Ibid., 314.

33. Shmuel Ahituv, *The Jewish People*, 90.

will not necessarily escape before the time of distress begins, but will endure this time and be rescued from destruction.[34]

Miller explains the reference to "the book": "The 'book' is a common figure of speech in the Scriptures and alludes to the 'book of life' in which the names of all saints are written (cf. Exod. 32:33; Ps 69:28; Mal 3:16; Luke 10:20; Rev 3:5; 20:12). Evidently this figure comes from the practice of keeping a record of all the citizens of a town. Those whose names were listed enjoyed the blessings of community membership, whereas the names of those who were excommunicated from fellowship were blotted out."[35] It is important to note that, as Miller describes, a person's name was written in the book because he was born into the community, and was blotted out when excommunicated. A popular view among evangelicals has been that a person's name is written into the book when that person is born again. First of all, this could not have been the meaning when the angel is talking to Daniel. For Daniel, the metaphor would have meant that a person's name would be entered into God's book upon his birth. If this person abandons God and rejects the covenant relation, then his name is blotted out of the book. This is, in fact, how the imagery is employed in Exodus. Second, if the popular view is correct, then the blotting out (e.g., Ex 32:33) would indicate that a person could lose his salvation. The problem is that the popular notion does not reflect the actual practice of the use of the book. The image is that a person's name is written into the book when he is born. If that person becomes born again, then his name remains in the book. However, if that person rejects God and Christ as his Savior, then his name is blotted out of the book. So the corresponding imagery in Daniel's prophecy is that the names of everyone in the nation of Israel are written into the book. But if these individuals reject God as their Savior, their names are blotted out of the book of life and they cannot be rescued. Lucas suggests, "Michael's intervention might be seen as based on this list of those 'recorded for life' (Is. 4:3)."[36] The blotting out of the names of individuals is not equivalent to the blotting out of the nation of Israel. There has always be a faithful remnant in the nation who have trusted in God as their Savior. Because of this, the nation *qua* nation has never been "blotted out" of God's book even though individuals in the nation apparently have been.

---

34. Preterists may want to use this with the fact that we have shown how many people in Judea and outlying areas were not severely impacted by the events of 70 AD to argue that this fits those events. However, unless the Preterist is willing to claim that all the people who survived the events of 70 AD were written in the book of Life, which would be virtually impossible to prove or maintain, this argument will not work.

35. Miller, *Daniel*, 315–16.

36. Lucas, *Daniel*, 294.

The Time of the Final Resurrection: 12:2

2—   "Many of those who sleep in ground of dust will awake, these to life everlasting, but these to disgrace and contempt everlasting."

Awakening from the Dust

LUCAS ON AWAKENING

The statement in 12:2 has been called the clearest declaration of the belief in resurrection in the Old Testament. Lucas observes that the language of this verse "echoes Is. 26:19: 'O dwellers in the dust, awake and sing for joy!'"[37] Lucas goes on to explain,

> In Job 17:16 "dust" stands in parallelism with "Sheol." Although some see the word "land" in Dan. 12:2 as a secondary addition, the result of conflating two synonyms (Talmon 1960: 167–168), it may be an original deliberate allusion to Gen. 3:19: "till you return to the ground, for out of it you were taken; you are dust, and to dust you shall return." There is disagreement over the significance of the word "many" here. Some point out that in Hebrew *rabbîm* can be used in the sense of "all" when the stress is on the numbers involved (J. Jeremias 1968: 536–545). Therefore, they see here a reference to a universal resurrection. However, the following preposition (*min*) is most naturally taken in its partitive sense, implying that only some of those who sleep will awake. The context (11:33–35; 12:3) would suggest that these are the martyred faithful Jews. They will enjoy "everlasting life." This is the only time the expression occurs in the HB. Others, presumably their persecutors, face "everlasting abhorrence." There is no doubt an allusion here to Is. 66:24, the only other place in the HB where the word "abhorrence" (*dir'ôn*) occurs. In Isaiah it is the rotting dead bodies of those who have rebelled against God that are an "abhorrence" to those who see them. Alfrink (1959) has argued that the construction "some . . . some" does not indicate two groups among those who awake, but contrasts those who awake with others who do not. While Hartman & Di Lella (1978: 308) and Lacocque (1979: 243–244) follow him, most commentators see the natural meaning here as two groups who awake to contrasting fates. Dan. 12:2 goes beyond Is. 66:24 to express the belief that the wicked

37. Ibid.

will consciously experience their shame. It does not elaborate on what this may mean.[38]

In the above quote, Lucas asserted that some commentators take this as a reference to a general resurrection, whereas he argues that the preposition *min* (מֵן) meaning "from," which we can see as the first letter on the word מִישֵׁנֵי (*eñeseyîm*), should be taken as a partitive genitive. A partitive genitive indicates a part of the whole. For example, one might refer to a piece of the pie, where the word 'pie' would be a partitive genitive indicating a whole of which one is referring to a piece. In this expression, the statement would be, "Many from the group of those who are asleep will be awakened." So, as Lucas explains, not all of those asleep will be awakened.

Mauro on Awakening

Mauro disagrees that the statement, "Many of those who sleep in ground of dust will awake," refers to the resurrection. Mauro argues, "But there is nothing said here about either death or resurrection."[39] Of course the statement "sleep in the ground of dust" is a euphemism for death. Ps 13:3 (H4) demonstrates this: "Consider, answer me, O Lord my God; Enlighten my eyes, lest I sleep *the sleep of* death."[40] What Mauro argues is that this should be understood in a spiritual sense, not in a physical or natural sense: "On the other hand, it can be abundantly shown that the words 'sleep' and 'awake' are common figurative expressions for the condition of those who are at first oblivious to the truth of God, but who are aroused by a message from Him out of that condition."[41] Referring to Isa 29:10 Mauro states, "Isaiah describes the people of Israel as being under the influence of 'the spirit of *deep sleep.*'"[42] Contrary to Mauro's claim, however, there is no statement in the passage in Isaiah about death, and the word "death" is not used. So, the only reason Mauro appeals to Isaiah is because he assumes already that the verse in Isaiah and the one here in Daniel must be referring to the same thing. But, this cannot be assumed. It must be proven. The word in the Isaiah passage translated "deep sleep" is תַּרְדֵּמָה (*ħamedrat*) from the root רדם (*mdr*). Daniel uses a different word for sleep; מִישֵׁנֵי (*yim̃eñeś*) from יָשֵׁן, so Isaiah and Daniel are

38. Ibid., 294–95.

39. Mauro, *Seventy Weeks*, 169.

40. הַבִּיטָה עֲנֵנִי יְהוָה אֱלֹהָי הָאִירָה עֵינַי פֶּן־אִישַׁן הַמָּוֶת: ‛ħaîbbah³iñen y⁰ hawħ͓ tewammahǔnăŝî'ǔnep⁰yañe‛ǔhaîî'ahǔ̄yahol. (Ps 13:4).

41. Ibid.

42. Ibid.

not even talking about the same thing. Nor is the word "awake" in the Isaiah passage.

Mauro's appeal to the New Testament is anachronistic. Just because the New Testament writers used a phrase a certain way is no proof that the Old Testament writers understood the expression in the same way. The difference of several hundred years can make a huge difference in these cultural metaphors. What Mauro must prove is that the reference to sleep does not ever mean "death." If he cannot show that, then he cannot argue that the Daniel passage cannot possibly mean death. But, that the term "sleep" even in the NT was used to refer to actual physical death is amply demonstrated by Jesus' statement in Jn. 11:11–15: "This He said, and after that He said to them, 'Our friend Lazarus has fallen asleep; but I go, so that I may awaken him out of sleep.' The disciples then said to Him, 'Lord, if he has fallen asleep, he will recover.' Now Jesus had spoken of his death, but they thought that He was speaking of literal sleep. So Jesus then said to them plainly, 'Lazarus is dead, and I am glad for your sakes that I was not there, so that you may believe; but let us go to him.'" Mauro's appeal to the NT is not only anachronistic, it is simply wrong.

But, even if we grant that the sleep and awakening refers to the spiritual rather than the physical or natural, what Mauro says next is simply false: "The whole nation of Israel was 'awakened' out of a sleep of centuries through the ministry of John the Baptist, followed by that of the Lord Himself, and lastly by that of the apostles and evangelists, who 'preached the gospel unto them with the Holy Ghost sent down from heaven.'"[43] If that were true, then Mauro would have a terrible time trying to justify the event of 70 AD. Why did God destroy the nation of Israel if "the whole nation was 'awakened'" as Mauro claims? The fact of the matter is, few in the nation of Israel were awakened from their spiritual sleep.

Also, for Mauro's argument to make sense, it would have to apply only to those who are saved. In other words, Mauro's argument is that the sleep is the sleep of the lost, and the awakening is the reception of the Gospel by faith and the obtaining of salvation. This is what the NT verses are saying to which Mauro appealed. However, the statement in Dan. 12:2 applies to both the saved and the unsaved. The statement says, "Many of those who sleep in the dust of the ground will awake, these to everlasting life, but the others to disgrace and everlasting contempt." Out of the "many" (וְרַבִּים, *mibbarᵉw*) who are awakened, some will be awakened to everlasting life, and others will be awakened to everlasting contempt: "these will be awakened to everlasting life, and these [will be awakened] to everlasting contempt," where the verb is im-

---

43. Ibid.

plied from the first clause to the second. The statement is actually saying that there are many who are asleep. These many who are asleep will be awakened. Some of those awakened from sleep will go into everlasting life. Some of those awakened from sleep will go into everlasting contempt. So, being awakened from sleep cannot be a reference to salvation since no one can be saved to everlasting contempt. Consequently, Mauro's argument is simply false. This is not talking about a spiritual awakening, but a resurrection in which some are raised to everlasting life and others are raised to everlasting contempt.

Evans pinpoints Mauro's reason for rejecting the notion that this verse refers to physical death and resurrection in 12:2 and likewise identifies an insurmountable problem for the Preterist view:

> Why did Mauro adopt such a position, which seems clearly at odds with the plain meaning of Daniel 12:2? He surely did so because he associated the resurrection that it seems to depict with an end-time scenario that places the Second Coming (*Parousia*) in the future rather than with events that transpired in the first century AD. He therefore let his training as an attorney (and he was a very good one) get the better of him and cause him to try to extricate himself from what he saw as a difficult theological position by resorting to the lawyerly technique of arguing that words do not necessarily mean what they appear to mean. If one accepts, as I do, that the Book of Daniel and many passages in the New Testament present an eschatology that finds its fulfillment in events that climaxed in AD 70, then it follows that Daniel 12:2 points to a resurrection that must have been realized around that time. It is beyond the intended scope of this book to explore the theology of this first-century resurrection in these pages, but it is a matter that can readily be investigated by spending a few minutes on the Internet.[44]

What Evans identifies as a "lawyerly technique of arguing that words do not necessarily mean what they appear to mean" is the recognition that Mauro imposed his prior eschatological commitment on the text in order to attempt to make it fit his scheme. Robert Strimple recognizes this motivation in the Hyper-Preterist denial of the bodily resurrection. Although Mauro is not referring to a NT passage, the underlying motivation and methodology is the same:

> Note well the flow of thought. It is not the case that a careful ex-egetical study of a key resurrection passage of the New Testament has caused the hyper-preterist to step back and say, "Oh my! The

---

44. Evans, *Four Kingdoms*, 278–79.

inspired Paul was not teaching a bodily resurrection of believers at the bodily return of their Lord. His words don't say that at all. The entire church has misunderstood Paul throughout her history!" Rather, "the necessary first step" (see Noē above) is to decide that the second coming of Christ and all that was to follow immediately upon it, including the resurrection of "those who belong to him" (1 Cor. 15:23), happened in A.D. 70. Then the second step is to reinterpret all the biblical passages that speak of the coming resurrection in a way that could plausibly have happened at that time.[45]

The point is that Mauro, as well as the Hyper-Preterist interpreters, have committed themselves to an eschatological perspective and then come to the Scriptures to see how they might reinterpret them to make them fit this scheme. Evans recognizes this in Mauro, and Strimple recognizes this in the Hyper-Preterists. But, having observed this methodology in Mauro's argument, Evans then adopts the same process. He says, "If one accepts, as I do, that the Book of Daniel and many passages in the New Testament present an eschatology that finds its fulfillment in events that climaxed in AD 70, then it follows that Daniel 12:2 points to a resurrection that must have been realized around that time." In other words, if you accept the eschatological scheme first, then you must interpret the passage so that it fits. It cannot be the case that the straightforward statement of Dan 12:2 might cause Evans to re-think how he has understood all those other passages.

However, having made reference to Mauro's argument, Evans basically avoids the issue by placing it outside the scope of his book: "It is beyond the intended scope of this book to explore the theology of this first-century resurrection in these pages, but it is a matter that can readily be investigated by spending a few minutes on the Internet."[46] Of course every author is perfectly within his rights to decide the scope of his own book. However, since Evans is attempting to relate the surrounding verses to his view, it seems a bit odd not to offer some explanation of how this verse fits. Since it was impossible to consider a view that Evans does not present, the next best thing is to go to the internet site recommended by Evans. The site to which he pointed contained an article by Daniel T. Silvestri titled, "Futurist Eschatology Unconvincing." The article is not strictly speaking about the resurrection, but this question forms part of what Mr. Silvestri discusses. Essentially he is challenging the Futurists to address various passages that he believes they have avoided; passages he believes support the Preterist view. Close to the end of this article,

---

45. Strimple, "Hyper-Preterism on the Resurrection of the Body," 290.

46. Evans, *Four Kingdoms*, 278–79.

Silvestri brings up the question of the resurrection in the first century. We will present this portion in parts and respond to each part in turn.

How Soon The Resurrection?

Silvestri's first argument concerns how soon the resurrection was to take place. In his effort to argue that the resurrection was expected within the lifetime of Paul and the Apostles, he begins his argument by appealing to some statements made by Paul.

> Speaking of the resurrection, Paul said; "I do fully testify, then, before God, and the Lord Jesus Christ, who is about to judge living and dead at his manifestation and his reign" (II Timothy 4:1 YLT). "And I confess this to thee, that, according to the way that they call a sect, so serve I the God of the fathers, believing all things that in the law and the prophets have been written, having hope toward God, which they themselves also wait for, that there is about to be a rising again of the dead, both of righteous and unrighteous" (Acts 24:15 YLT). Of course, this sounds like Daniel's resurrection; "some to everlasting life and some to everlasting contempt" (Daniel 12:2). Did Paul mean there is about to be a resurrection in a few thousand years? What is the futurist explanation for this passage? Did Paul make a mistake? Was everyone following a "code" (II Peter 3:8) and the saints recognized that Paul was speaking in terms of "God's time" and not man's? Therefore, was the resurrection about to take place in God's time and not ours?[47]

It will of course be necessary to look at the Greek text of the verses to which Silvestri refers. First we will consider the 2 Timothy passage.

---

47. Daniel T. Silvestri, "Futurist Eschatology Unconvincing" http://www.preterist archive.com/Preterism/silvestri-daniel_da_02.html. September 14, 2006.

Table 70: 2 Timothy 4:1

Διαμαρτύρομαι	ἐνώπιον	τοῦ	θεοῦ
I solemnly charge	before	the	God
καὶ	Χριστοῦ	Ἰησοῦ	τοῦ
and	Christ	Jesus	the
μέλλοντος	κρίνειν	ζῶντας	καὶ
being about	to judge	living	and
νεκρούς	καὶ	τὴν	ἐπιφάνειαν
dead	and	the	appearing
αὐτοῦ	καὶ	τὴν	βασιλείαν
of Him	and	the	kingdom
αὐτοῦ·			
of Him.			

The word upon which Silvestri's point rests is the word translated "about to," which in this instance is the participle μέλλοντος (*sotnollem*) from the verb μέλλω (*ollem*). According to BDAG, the word has several possible meanings. The first one given by BDAG is "to take place at a future point of time and so to be subsequent to another event, *be about to*, used w. inf. foll."[48] So, the word can be used to talk about an event that is future with respect to the time of the speaker. The following infinitive indicates that event that is going to take place—in this instance it is "to judge" (κρίνειν, *nienirk*). This phrase does not specify whether the future event is near or far, only that it is future. Consequently, the word can be used in a way that is equivalent to the English, "going to." So, the translation can be, "I do fully testify, then, before God, and the Lord Jesus Christ, who is going to judge living and dead at His manifestation and His reign." Silvestri, not being familiar with the Greek language of the NT, mistakenly took the word to have an English sense, "at the point of happening, very soon," which is not a necessary part of the Greek term.

Another possible meaning that BDAG gives for this word is, "to be inevitable, *be destined, inevitable*."[49] Using this meaning, the verse could be

48. BDAG, s.v. "μέλλω," 1 (emphasis in original).
49. Ibid., 2.a (emphasis in original).

translated, "I do fully testify, then, before God, and the Lord Jesus Christ, who is destined to judge living and dead at his manifestation and his reign." BDAG also points out that the word can be used to refer to something that is at the point of happening; e.g., "*be about to, be on the point of* ἤμελλεν τελευτᾶν *he was at the point of death . . .*"[50] However, BDAG does not include the 2 Tim 4:1 passage under this classification. Rather, 2 Tim 4:1 appears under the next classification concerning which BDAG states, "in a weakened sense it serves simply as a periphrasis for the fut."[51] Concerning this verse in particular, BDAG indicates that this future sense is used "of Christ ὁ μέλλων κρίνειν,"[52] the one who is going to judge sometime in the future. So, the problem here is not for the Futurist, but that this Preterist author has misunderstood the Greek sentence. Paul is not claiming that this was at the point of happening in his time, but that it was something that was going to happen in the future. It seems to be the case that Paul lived as though it could happen at any moment, but planned and worked as if he were going to live out his life on earth before it occurred. In other words, Paul's attitude apparently was, "It could happen today, tomorrow, or many years from now. But it will definitely happen."

Concerning the phrase in Acts 24:15, "that there is about to be a rising again of the dead, both of righteous and unrighteous," Mr. Silvestri makes the same error. The verse is set out below with a word-for-word translation.

Table 71: Acts 24:25

ἐλπίδα	ἔχων	εἰς	τὸν
hope	having	unto	the
θεὸν	ἣν	καὶ	αὐτοὶ
God	which	also	themselves
οὗτοι	προσδέχονται	ἀνάστασιν	μέλλειν
these	wait for	resurrection	to be going to
ἔσεσθαι	δικαίων	τε	καὶ
to be	of righteous	and	also
ἀδίκων			
unrighteous			

50. Ibid., 1.c.α (emphasis in original).
51. Ibid., 1.c.β.
52. Ibid.

Once again, BDAG cites this passage as indicating that μέλλω is used here to assert that this event *"will certainly take place* or *be* Ac 11:28; 24:15; 27:10 . . ."[53] not that it was at the point of taking place. In this passage, Paul is not claiming that the rising of the dead was *soon* to occur, but that it was *certain* to occur. Mr. Silvestri's argument is based on his lack of understanding of the Greek text.

Silvestri's next argument is,

> The futurists charge preterists with the same heresy of Hymenaeus and Philetus of the first century; "And their word will eat as doth a canker: of whom is Hymenaeus and Philetus; Who concerning the truth have erred, saying that the resurrection is past already; and overthrow the faith of some." (II Timothy 2:17–18). This passage, by implication, appears to speak very loudly in support of preterist eschatology. One strong implication of this passage is the fact that no one expected the resurrection to be visible in the normal worldly sense. If they did, no one could have possibly been convinced the resurrection already occurred, for Abraham, Isaac, Jacob, and the rest of the dead, were not observed as being present citizens dwelling upon the earth. Another logical implication is that no one expected the resurrection to occur thousands of years later. On the contrary, they must have expected the resurrection to occur rather soon. That would explain why some could be convinced that it had already passed. In addition, they must have understood that usual earthly life would continue after the resurrection of the dead, which they all understood from Jesus, would occur at the "last day." Therefore, the resurrection of the dead did not signify the last day of life on earth as we know it when every single person who ever lived would be judged for eternity.[54]

First, it is extremely difficult to see how one can get from the statement that Hymenaeus and Philetus erred by saying the resurrection is already past to the notion that "no one expected the resurrection to be visible in the normal worldly sense." In fact, the implication is that because they did expect the resurrection to be visible they could identify the error of these two heretics who said it was already past. Their response was basically, "We didn't see it!" Second, the claim that "no one could have possibly been convinced" ignores the history of religion and the fact that people will believe what they want whether there is evidence or not—Silvestri being a case in point. But to claim that they would not have believed it because they did not see Abraham, Isaac,

---

53. Ibid., 1.a.

54. Silvestri, "Futurist Eschatology Unconvincing."

Jacob, and the rest of the dead "as being present citizens dwelling upon the earth" assumes that the physical resurrection and the timing of the raising of different groups of people is necessarily the same. Not seeing Abraham, etc., could have been easily explained by the fact that their resurrection is yet to come. There are probably many other ways that these conditions could have been explained away by the heretics so as to convince someone that the resurrection was already past.

Silvestri isn't the only hyper-preterist to pose this approach to these verses. Strimple notes that Daniel Harden proposes a similar notion. Harden makes the following argument: "How could this errant belief of an already-come parousia and resurrection have arisen within the church if the apostolic teaching of the resurrection were a *physical* one? . . . If the apostle taught such a resurrection, how could anybody possibly have come up with the notion that it had already happened?"[55] Strimple's response is quite direct: "Why, in the same way that the hyper-preterists have come up with that 'errant belief,' despite the apostle's having taught such a resurrection and the church having confessed her faith in such a resurrection for two thousand years!"[56] It is patently absurd to suppose that simply because the truth is taught, there is no explanation for the propagation of error.

Third, Silvestri argues, "Another logical implication is that no one expected the resurrection to occur thousands of years later. On the contrary, they must have expected the resurrection to occur rather soon. That would explain why some could be convinced that it had already passed." Once again this is simply false. Not only is Silvestri's "implication" illogical, since it is a *non sequitur*, the logical implication is that they in fact did expect the resurrection to occur in the future, and that is yet another way the writer recognized that the teaching was false. In other words, the orthodox teaching about the resurrection was that it was in the future was the basis upon which they could recognize the error of claiming that it had already happened. It is simply *non sequitur* that because some were convinced of the error that everyone must have expected the resurrection to occur soon. But, even if we grant that they expected the resurrection soon, this says nothing about whether it was actually going to occur soon. In fact, all Christians should live as if the resurrection could occur at any moment, just like we should live as if today we might die, so that we take advantage of the opportunities that come our way. But, just because we expect something to happen soon does not mean that it necessarily will. Silvestri's inference simply does not follow, but even if it did,

55. Daniel E. Harden, *Overcoming Sproul's Resurrection Obstacles* (Bradford, Pennsylvania: International Preterist Association, 1999), 34–35; quoted in Strimple, "Hyper-Preterism on the Resurrection of the Body," 314.

56. Ibid.

it does not support his view. What people expect and what actually occurs are sometimes quite different.

Finally, he asserts, "In addition, they must have understood that usual earthly life would continue after the resurrection of the dead, which they all understood from Jesus, would occur at the 'last day.' Therefore, the resurrection of the dead did not signify the last day of life on earth as we know it when every single person who ever lived would be judged for eternity." This is a misunderstanding of the problem. It was those who believed the error that may have expected earthly life for Christians to continue after the resurrection. In fact, it was precisely because earthly life for Christians was continuing in its corruptible state that the orthodox identified the teaching as an error. Also, Silvestri's conclusion, that "Therefore, the resurrection of the dead did not signify the last day of life on earth as we know it when every single person who ever lived would be judged for eternity," is a straw-man argument since Futurists do not necessarily believe this.

HAILEY ON AWAKENING

Homer Hailey advocates a view similar to Mauro's. He says, "The better explanation is that through the preaching of the word by Jesus, many were brought to spiritual life. But because iniquity abounded, the love of many waxed cold, they gave up the faith and went back into Judaism, or back into the world. They were raised by the Gospel, some to everlasting life, some to everlasting contempt, so not all of them remained faithful to Jesus Christ."[57] First, the text says nothing about some being raised and then turning back. Second, the text says nothing about being "raised by the Gospel." The text states that some will awaken from sleep. If to be "raised by the Gospel" simply means that some heard the Gospel and followed after Jesus, but in fact did not receive salvation, then this hardly does justice to the text or to the notion of salvation. According to the text, the "awakening" happens to both groups, and there is no distinction made in the text as if one group had one kind of awakening and another group had another kind of awakening. The same "awakening" happened to both groups. If by being "raised by the Gospel" Hailey understands that the same thing happened to each group, then Hailey is indicating that some lost their salvation. Third, the text does not indicate that these were raised to life and then turned back to the world and to everlasting contempt. The text indicates that some were awakened unto everlasting contempt. This was that to which they were awakened. But, Hailey's scenario requires that these were actually raised for one reason, but then did not fulfill the reason for which they were raised. This is contrary to the clear statements of the text.

57. Hailey, *Commentary on Daniel*, 244.

CULVER ON AWAKENING

Quoting Biederwolf, Culver summarizes the various views taken with reference to this statement:

1.   To the general resurrection at the end of all things.

2.   To a limited resurrection immediately after the Tribulation, and prior to the last and general resurrection, and one confined to Israel.

3.   To a resurrection of the righteous just before Christ's second coming, and of the wicked at the end of time, no notice being taken by the angel of the hiatus between them.

4.   To a resurrection of all that sleep in the dust after the time of Great Tribulation; the good, at that very time (immediately after), and the wicked later, at the end of all time, with no notice taken by the angel of the hiatus or intervening time.[58]

After some brief discussion, Culver goes on to express his view and to provide a justification for his preference: "1. The language favors a selective, or limited, resurrection rather than a general resurrection. . . . 2. The Hebrew of the passage permits and, according to many of the best authorities, demands a translation favoring this view."[59]

Culver argues that the ones who awake are only the righteous, and he accepts the translation given by Tregelles: "And many from among the sleepers of the dust of the earth shall awake; these shall be unto everlasting life; but those the rest of the sleepers, those who do not awake at this time, shall be unto shame and everlasting contempt."[60] The problem with this translation is that the clause, "those who do not awake at this time" is not present in the text, but is, rather, an inference based on the prior theological commitment of the translator. The verse is set out below with a word-for-word translation.

Table 72: Daniel 12:2

עָפָר	אַדְמַת־	מִיְשֵׁנֵי	וְרַבִּים
dust	ground of	from the sleepers of	And many
עוֹלָם	לְחַיֵּי	אֵלֶּה	יָקִיצוּ
everlasting	to contempt	to the disgrace	but these

---

58. Culver, *Daniel*, 185.

59. Ibid., 185–86.

60. Ibid., 186.

וְאֵלֶּה	לַחֲרָפוֹת	לְדִרְאוֹן	עוֹלָם׃
but these	to the disgrace	to contempt	everlasting

Culver refers to the Brown, Driver, Briggs Hebrew lexicon (BDB), which he says is the "most authoritative in the English language."[61] This was before KBH was translated and made widely available. He refers to BDB in an effort to support his understanding of the two terms "these . . . and these" (וְאֵלֶּה . . . אֵלֶּה, *helle'ᵉw . . . helle'*). He says BDB "gives this as one of the possible uses and lists Deuteronomy 27:13."[62] However, KBH gives the translation of this very same verse as "these . . . and these," but does not give "the other" as a possible meaning.[63] The point of this question was to attempt to separate "these," namely, the ones awakening, from "those," the ones not awakening. However, the text simply states, "Many from the sleepers of the ground of dust will awake, these . . . and these," which seems to indicate that both groups will awake, some to eternal life and some to eternal contempt. In other words, the text is not ascribing any time relationship between these two groups. Rather, it is differentiating on the basis of the result of the resurrection of those in the respective groups. "These" will be raised to life, and these to death, not making any reference to when these events will occur in the scheme of history. It is beyond the scope of this commentary to enter into an exposition and defense of the temporal relations of the various resurrections, but, since our argument is not based on the temporal question, this is sufficient to demonstrate that this event did not take place in 70 AD, and this statement cannot be talking about a spiritual awakening since it indicates that both groups will awake.

Walvoord points out that some have taken this to be a reference, not to a resurrection from the dead, but rather is a metaphor for the revival of Israel. Walvoord quotes A. C. Gaebelein who asserts this view: "Physical resurrection is not taught in the second verse of this chapter. . . . We repeat, the passage has nothing to do with physical resurrection. Physical resurrection is however used as a figure of the national revival of Israel in that day."[64] Of course, to point to a national revival of Israel the reference does not have to be only a figure, but can be a reference to the actual physical resurrection which also serves to point to the revival of Israel. In response to Gaebelein's assertion,

---

61. Ibid.

62. Ibid. BDB, s.v. "אֵלֶּה": "b. repeated, וְאֵלֶּה . . . אֵלֶּה, *these . . . those* Dt 27¹²,¹³."

63. KBH, s.v. "אֵלֶּה."

64. A. C. Gaebelein, *The Prophet Daniel* (New York: Our Hope Publishers, 1911), 200; quoted in Walvoord, *Daniel*, 286.

Culver emphatically declares, "Gaebelein's categorical assertion is so utterly without foundation that it does not merit further attention. As Robinson says, 'If a resurrection of the body is not here declared, it will be difficult to find where it is, or to imagine words in which it can be.' Tregelles asks, 'If the language of this verse be not declaratory of a resurrection of the dead, actual and literal, is there any passage of Scripture at all which speaks of such a thing as a resurrection?'"[65] Whether this statement is being used as a figure for the revival of Israel or not, it seems unreasonable to refuse to see a reference to the physical resurrection.

Resurrection—Spiritual or Physical?

Concerning the bodily nature of the resurrection, Geerhardus Vos declares, "Bodily the resurrection certainly is, and every attempt to dephysicize it . . . amounts to an exegetical *tour de force* so desperate as to be not worth losing many words over."[66] Nevertheless, in order to make the text fit his Preterist assumptions, Silvestri must propose that the resurrection is only a spiritual event, not a physical event: "There is a bodily resurrection described in the scriptures, but it is 'a spiritual body.' Nowhere in scripture do we find the expression, 'resurrection of the body' although the phrase is commonly used. Expressly addressing the question, 'How are the dead raised up, and with what body do they come,' Paul identifies a spiritual body (I Corinthians 15:44), and states that, 'Howbeit that was not first which is spiritual, but that which is natural; and afterward that which is spiritual' (vs. 46)."[67] This is a common misrepresentation of Paul's statements. Silvestri assumes that his interpretation of these few verses is able to overturn the history of orthodoxy and the abundance of biblical evidence for the physical nature of the resurrection. To the contrary, these verses do not say what Silvestri supposes. 1 Cor 15:44 states, "it is sown a natural body [σῶμα ψυχικόν], it is raised a spiritual body [σῶμα πνευματικόν]. If there is a natural body, there is also a spiritual." Paul does not say that the body is *not* raised a physical body. A spiritual body can still be physical as was Jesus' body after His resurrection. Norman Geisler points out, "A 'spiritual' body denotes an immortal one, not an immaterial one. A 'spiritual' body is one dominated by the spirit, not one devoid of matter. The Greek word *pneumatikos* (translated 'spiritual' here) means a body directed by the spirit, as opposed to one under the dominion

65. Culver, *Daniel*, 184.

66. Geehardus Vos, *The Pauline Eschatology* (Grand Rapids: William B. Eerdmans Publishing Company, 1953), 154; quoted in Strimple, "Hyper-Preterism on the Resurrection of the Body," 288.

67. Ibid.

of the flesh. It is not ruled by flesh that perishes but by the spirit that endures (vss. 50–58). So 'spiritual body' here does not mean immaterial and invisible but immortal and imperishable."[68] Also, the contrast here is not between a material body and an immaterial body, but between the spiritual and the natural. Again Geisler puts the point succinctly: "'Spiritual' also denotes a supernatural body, not a nonphysical body."[69]

Verse 46, which Silvestri quotes, does not say that the natural/physical ceases to be with the coming of the spiritual. In fact, Jesus' resurrection body was physical. The Gospels testify to the fact that Jesus could be seen with the physical eyes of the disciples and touched with their physical hands. In Jn. 20:27 Jesus told Thomas, "Reach here with your finger, and see My hands; and reach here your hand and put it into My side; and do not be unbelieving, but believing." In 1 Cor 15:20 Paul declares, "But now Christ has been raised from the dead, the first fruits of those who are asleep," indicating that our resurrection will be like His, material, physical, and supernatural.

Flesh and Blood and the Kingdom

Silvestri continues his argument by appealing to Paul's statement about flesh and blood: "Paul goes on to say, 'flesh and blood do not inherit the kingdom of God' (vs. 50)."[70] Geisler points out, "As early as the second century Irenaeus noted that this passage was used by heretics in support of their 'very great error' (Irenaeus, 30.13), that the resurrection body will not be a body of physical flesh."[71] What Silvestri fails to do is continue on from verse 50 to include all of what Paul says. Paul is not talking about flesh as such, but of corruptible flesh. Paul is not saying that the resurrection body will not be a body of flesh. Rather, he is saying that the resurrection body will not be a body of *corruptible, and mortal, and perishable* flesh. It will be a body of incorruptible, immortal, and imperishable flesh.

Silvestri goes on to argue,

> Apparently Paul understood the nature of the resurrection as taught by Jesus; "For in the resurrection they neither marry, nor are given in marriage, but are as the angels of God in heaven" (Matthew 22:30). According to the scriptures, angels have qualities much different than physical beings. For one thing, they suddenly appear and disappear (sounds like Christ after the resurrection). Angels

68. *Baker Encyclopedia of Christian Apologetics*, (1999), s.v. "Resurrection, Objections to."
69. Ibid.
70. Silvestri, "Futurist Eschatology Unconvincing."
71. *Baker Encyclopedia of Christian Apologetics* (1999), s.v. "Resurrection, Objections to."

have "supernatural" qualities. Christ says those in the resurrection,
"are as the angels of God in heaven."[72]

Once again Silvestri has committed a *non sequitur* fallacy. The fact that
angels do not marry nor are given in marriage says nothing about whether the
resurrection body will be material or immaterial. The point of comparison
was not the materiality or immateriality of an angel's body, but the capacity to
join in marriage. In the resurrection we will be like the angels in that we will
not be joined in marriage. By contrast, if we employ Silvestri's method, we
must also conclude that we will have wings like the Seraphim and Cherubim.
In other words, if the comparison extends to the whole nature of angels, then
this implies that we will become angels. But, that was not the point of the
comparison. The point of Jesus' comparison had nothing to do with comparing the nature of angels and the nature of men, or with materiality and
immateriality, but with joining in marriage. Of course Selvestri will respond
that the reason angels could not marry is because they did not have physical
bodies. Be that as it may, it makes no difference to the argument. Jesus is
not comparing the *cause* of the incapacity to marry. He is comparing the *fact*
of the incapacity to marry. Perhaps it is true that the angels cannot marry
because they do not have physical bodies. But this is irrelevant to the fact that,
when we get to heaven, we will be like them in that we won't marry either,
regardless of what the cause is.

Selvestri makes a comment about the angels appearing and disappear-
ing. However, in His physical, resurrection body Jesus was able to appear and
disappear, but that did not mean His body was not a material body. Do we
conclude that because Jesus walked on water that His body was made of balsa
wood? In Jn 20:19 the disciples were in the room with the doors shut, and
suddenly Jesus stood in their midst: "So when it was evening on that day, the
first of the week, and when the doors were shut where the disciples were, for
fear of the Jews, Jesus came and stood in their midst and said to them, 'Peace
with you.'" The reason He could do this is because after His resurrection His
physical body was now a supernatural body, but it was still a material, physical
body evidenced by the fact that He showed them His crucifixion scars, and
Thomas was able to touch Him. Silvestri's last quote is a misrepresentation of
what Jesus said. Jesus did not say, "those in the resurrection, 'are as the angels
of God in heaven.'" Rather, He said, "those in the resurrection, 'are as the angels of God in heaven in that they will not marry nor be given in marriage.'"
By leaving off the description that provides the point of comparison, Silvestri
misrepresents the text.

---

72. Silvestri, "Futurist Eschatology Unconvincing."

Heavenly and Bodily

But Silvestri is not finished yet. Again he appeals to a statement by Paul to attempt to support his view.

> This is why Paul says; "The first man is of the earth, earthy: the second man is the Lord from heaven. As is the earthy, such are they also that are earthy: and as is the heavenly, such are they also that are heavenly. And as we have borne the image of the earthy, we shall also bear the image of the heavenly. Now this I say, brethren, that flesh and blood cannot inherit the kingdom of God; neither doth corruption inherit incorruption" (I Corinthians 15:47–50). The futurist must convincingly explain how it can possibly be interpreted that Paul explained a physical body resurrection of the dead.[73]

What Silvestri ignores in the above quote is that "the second man" who is "the Lord from heaven" came to earth *in a physical body*. When Paul says, "And as we have borne the image of the earthy, we shall also bear the image of the heavenly," he does not say we will stop bearing a physical body. The fact that Jesus' resurrection body still had the scars of His crucifixion indicates that our bodies, though transformed into supernatural bodies, will still be physical bodies. Silvestri's challenge has been met throughout the history of the church. A strong point in support of the claim that Paul is teaching a physical body resurrection of the dead is the fact that this has been the orthodox position of the church throughout its history, and the notion that the resurrection body will not be a material/physical body has been considered heretical and has been condemned by the church even in our modern age.

In order to make the text fit the Preterist view, Dan 12:2 must be interpreted either as referring to a spiritual awakening (Mauro's approach), or as a non-material, non-physical resurrection (Silvestri, and apparently Evans' approach), which is in fact a heretical belief. But, as we have shown, Mauro's approach does not work because the awakening is an awakening not only of those who gain eternal life but also of those who are condemned to everlasting contempt. Those who are condemned to eternal disgrace and contempt will also "awake from sleep." So, this cannot be a reference to spiritual awakening. Also, since we have shown that the resurrection will be a physical and bodily resurrection, Silvestri's position is proven to be an error. Since the resurrection will be physical and bodily, and since this simply did not happen in 70 AD, nor to our present day has it yet happened, it must be future, and once again

---

73. Ibid.

the Preterist position cannot be maintained in the face of the evidence of history or the text.

When the Resurrection?

Walvoord supports the notion that the text indicates that this resurrection includes both the righteous and the unrighteous. He also points out that this creates a problem for those who hold to a premillennial-pretribulational view. He says, "The problem arises, however, in that the passage states that the resurrection will extend to 'some to shame and everlasting contempt.'"[74] The specific problem is that the premillennial view holds that there will be a resurrection of the righteous before the beginning of the millennial kingdom, but there will not be a resurrection of the unrighteous until after the millennial kingdom has been completed. Walvoord resolves this problem by appealing to Revelation: "Here, premillenarians appeal to the clear distinction provided in Revelation 20 which states, after revealing the resurrection of the righteous, 'But the rest of the dead live not again until the thousand years where finished. This is the first resurrection' (v. 5)."[75] So, Walvoord basically sees a prophetic gap here. He asserts, "Accordingly, premillenarians consider the revelation to Daniel as a statement of fact that after the great tribulation and the second coming of Christ many, of both the righteous and of the wicked, will be raised. It is not at all unusual for the Old Testament in prophecy to include events separated by a considerable span of time as if they concurred in immediate relation to each other."[76]

Some have seen this as a convenient manipulation of the text to make it fit the premillennial position, and therefore the arguments against Mauro's view fail as a result. However, the timing of the resurrection is not the issue with Mauro's position. Mauro confined the notion of "awakening" only to the righteous, yet the verse assigns it to both the righteous and the unrighteous. Regardless of when the resurrection occurs, this verse assigns the awakening to both, and Mauro's association of the awakening with salvation is thereby demonstrated to be false.

A much more pertinent question relating to the Preterist-Futurist debate is that if Futurists are going to introduce a gap between the awakening of the two groups, why not simply relegate the whole to some future time. In this case, the Futurist cannot use this verse as an argument against the Preterists because there was no resurrection in 70 AD. If the Futurists can introduce a gap between the two groups, then the Preterists can argue that the fact that

74. Walvoord, *Daniel*, 288.
75. Ibid.
76. Ibid., 288–89.

there was no resurrection in 70 AD is simply a matter of the gap placing the resurrection of both groups in the future (see Figure 47 below).

Figure 47: Resurrection Views

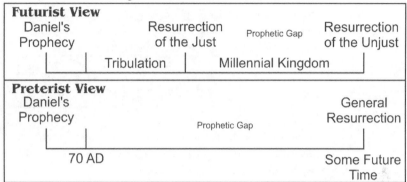

Although this seems to be a reasonable objection to the Futurist interpretation, the Preterist must deal with the fact that the abundance of evidence from the earlier chapters in Daniel seem to disprove the Preterist view altogether, and assuming that the Preterist could make his case in Daniel, he would need to deal with other Scriptures that seem to indicate that the resurrection of the just and the unjust does not occur at the same time (e.g., Rev 20:5ff). In other words, the question of the chronology of the resurrections is a subsequent question in the Preterist-Futurist debate and cannot be called upon to settle the question. If the Preterist view as a whole can be shown to be false, which we have done by showing that the Preterists' claim cannot be sustained when compared to the actual historical facts, then the claims of resurrection chronology associated with that view are likewise shown to be false.

Reproach and Contempt

According to TWOT, the term "reproach" (לַחֲרָפוֹת, *hal⁺tofar*) indicates scorn "with the specific connotation of casting blame or scorn on someone."[77] The word occurs two other times in Daniel (see Table 73).

---

77. TWOT, s.v. "חָרְפָּה."

Table 73: "Reproach" in Daniel

Dan 9:16	"O Lord, in accordance with all Your righteous acts, let now Your anger and Your wrath turn away from Your city Jerusalem, Your holy mountain; for because of our sins and the iniquities of our fathers, Jerusalem and Your people have become a reproach [לְחֶרְפָּה, *haprehel*] to all those around us."

אֲדֹנָי כְּכָל־צִדְקֹתֶךָ יָשָׁב־נָא אַפְּךָ וַחֲמָתְךָ
מֵעִירְךָ יְרוּשָׁלִַם הַר־קָדְשֶׁךָ כִּי בַחֲטָאֵינוּ
וּבַעֲוֹנוֹת אֲבֹתֵינוּ יְרוּשָׁלִַם וְעַמְּךָ לְחֶרְפָּה
לְכָל־סְבִיבֹתֵינוּ׃

Dan 11:18	"Then he will turn his face to the coastlands and capture many. But a commander will put a stop to his scorn against him; moreover, he will repay him for his scorn [חֶרְפָּתוֹ, *ōtapreh*]."

וְיָשֵׁב פָּנָיו לְאִיִּים וְלָכַד רַבִּים וְהִשְׁבִּית
קָצִין חֶרְפָּתוֹ לוֹ בִּלְתִּי חֶרְפָּתוֹ יָשִׁיב לוֹ׃

The idea here seems to be that those who awake to reproach will suffer the blame for their evil deeds. The fact that the word is plural indicates the intensity of the reproach. Keil refers to it as "a plural of intensive fullness."[78] The contrast is between the everlasting life of the just (לְחַיֵּי עוֹלָם, *ahe^lyey mālo‘*), and "the reproaches of contempt everlasting" which awaits the unjust (לַחֲרָפוֹת לְדִרְאוֹן עוֹלָם, *mālo‘ ño'rid^el tōfar^ahal*). The word "contempt" (לְדִרְאוֹן, *ño'rid^el*) occurs nowhere else in Daniel's prophecy, and it occurs only one other time in the Hebrew Bible, Isa 66:24. Concerning the Isaiah passage Oswalt asserts, "The world in which we live all too often sees the triumph of the wicked and the defeat of the righteous. Does that not call the veracity of God into question? Isaiah assures his readers that the true servants of God, whether they be Jew or Gentile, will indeed triumph, and the rebels, likewise Jew or Gentile, will be manifestly defeated. God's promises will not fail. If God's own people will come before him with joy perpetually, those who rebel against him will die perpetually."[79]

78. Keil, *Daniel*, 483.
79. John N. Oswalt, *The Book of Isaiah*, 693.

Shining Brightly: 12:3

3— "Those who have insight will shine brightly like the brightness of the expanse of heaven, and those who lead the many to righteousness, like the stars forever and ever."

Verse 3 involves a parallelism in its structure (see Table 74).

Table 74: Daniel 12:3 Parallelism

Those who have insight	will shine brightly	like the brightness of the expanse
and those who lead to righteousness the many	(verb implied)	like the stars forever and ever

כְּזֹהַר הָרָקִיעַ	יַזְהִרוּ	וְהַמַּשְׂכִּלִים
כַּכּוֹכָבִים לְעוֹלָם וָעֶד:	verb implied	וּמַצְדִּיקֵי הָרַבִּים

In this kind of parallelism, the verb in the fist line may be omitted in the second line but implied or carried over from the first line. Here the verb "will shine brightly" (יַזְהִרוּ, *urihzay*) is used in the first part and implied in the second. Both those who are wise and those who lead the many to righteousness will shine brightly.

The English phrase "those who have insight" comes from a single Hebrew word (וְהַמַּשְׂכִּלִים, *miliksammahᵉw*). Besides its occurrence in 12:3, it occurs 8 additional times in the book of Daniel and always in the Hiphil form. It is used to refer to the insight that was given to Daniel and his friends.

Table 75: "Insight" in Daniel

"youths in whom was no defect, who were good-looking, showing intelligence [וּמַשְׂכִּילִים, mîliksaṁu] in all wisdom, endowed with understanding and discerning knowledge, and who had ability for serving in the king's court; and to teach them the literature and language of the Chaldeans."

Dan 1:4

יְלָדִים אֲשֶׁר אֵין־בָּהֶם כָּל־מְאוּם וְטוֹבֵי
מַרְאֶה וּמַשְׂכִּילִים בְּכָל־חָכְמָה וְיֹדְעֵי
דַעַת וּמְבִינֵי מַדָּע וַאֲשֶׁר כֹּחַ בָּהֶם
לַעֲמֹד בְּהֵיכַל הַמֶּלֶךְ וּלֲלַמְּדָם
סֵפֶר וּלְשׁוֹן כַּשְׂדִּים:

"As for these four youths, God gave them knowledge and intelligence [וְהַשְׂכֵּל, wᵉleksah] in all literature and wisdom; Daniel even understood all visions and dreams."

Dan 1:17

וְהַיְלָדִים הָאֵלֶּה אַרְבַּעְתָּם נָתַן לָהֶם הָאֱלֹהִים
מַדָּע וְהַשְׂכֵּל בְּכָל־סֵפֶר וְחָכְמָה וְדָנִיֵּאל
הֵבִין בְּכָל־חָזוֹן וַחֲלֹמוֹת:

"As it is written in the law of Moses, all this calamity has come on us; yet we have not sought the favor of the Lord our God by turning from our iniquity and giving attention [וּלְהַשְׂכִּיל, lıksaḥlu] to Your truth."

Dan 9:13

כַּאֲשֶׁר כָּתוּב בְּתוֹרַת מֹשֶׁה אֵת כָּל־הָרָעָה
הַזֹּאת בָּאָה עָלֵינוּ וְלֹא־חִלִּינוּ אֶת־פְּנֵי
יְהוָה אֱלֹהֵינוּ לָשׁוּב מֵעֲוֺנֵנוּ
וּלְהַשְׂכִּיל בַּאֲמִתֶּךָ:

"He gave instruction and talked with me and said, 'O Daniel, I have now come forth to give you insight [לְהַשְׂכִּילְךָ, aklıksahel] with understanding.'"

Dan 9:22

וַיָּבֶן וַיְדַבֵּר עִמִּי וַיֹּאמַר דָּנִיֵּאל עַתָּה
יָצָאתִי לְהַשְׂכִּילְךָ בִינָה:

"So you are to know and discern [וְתַשְׂכֵּל, w^eleksaṭ] from the issuing of a decree to restore and rebuild Jerusalem until Messiah the Prince seven sevens and sixty-two sevens; it will be built again, with plaza and moat, even in times of distress."

Dan 9:25

וְתֵדַע וְתַשְׂכֵּל מִן־מֹצָא דָבָר לְהָשִׁיב וְלִבְנוֹת
יְרוּשָׁלַם עַד־מָשִׁיחַ נָגִיד שָׁבֻעִים שִׁבְעָה
וְשָׁבֻעִים שִׁשִּׁים וּשְׁנַיִם תָּשׁוּב וְנִבְנְתָה
רְחוֹב וְחָרוּץ וּבְצוֹק הָעִתִּים:

"Those who have insight [וּמַשְׂכִּילֵי, eliksaṁu] among the people will give understanding to the many; yet they will fall by sword and by flame, by captivity and by plunder for days."

Dan 11:33

וּמַשְׂכִּילֵי עָם יָבִינוּ לָרַבִּים וְנִכְשְׁלוּ בְּחֶרֶב
וּבְלֶהָבָה בִּשְׁבִי וּבְבִזָּה יָמִים:

"Some of those who have insight [הַמַּשְׂכִּילִים, miliksammah] will fall, in order to refine, purge and make them pure until the end time; because still at the appointed time."

Dan 11:35

וּמִן־הַמַּשְׂכִּילִים יִכָּשְׁלוּ לִצְרוֹף בָּהֶם וּלְבָרֵר
וְלַלְבֵּן עַד־עֵת קֵץ כִּי־עוֹד לַמּוֹעֵד:

"Many will be purged, purified, and refined, but the wicked will act wickedly; and none of the wicked will understand, but those who have insight [וְהַמַּשְׂכִּלִים, w^emiliksammah] will understand."

Dan 12:10

יִתְבָּרֲרוּ וְיִתְלַבְּנוּ וְיִצָּרְפוּ רַבִּים וְהִרְשִׁיעוּ
רְשָׁעִים וְלֹא יָבִינוּ כָּל־רְשָׁעִים וְהַמַּשְׂכִּלִים
יָבִינוּ:

Its use in verse 3 and again in 12:10 is in contrast with the statements in 11:33 and 35. In the two verses in chapter 11 the prophecy states that some who have insight will fall, whereas 12:3 declares that those who have insight "will shine brightly like the brightness of the expanse of heavens." The statement in 12:1 seems to refer to those who are raised to eternal life. Of those who are raised, some will be those who have shown insight in their earthly lives, these will "shine brightly" in the resurrection.

The term "they will shine" is the verb יַזְהִרוּ (urihzay) from זָהַר (raḥaz). In this verse, the verb is followed by the same root in its noun form זֹהַר

(*rahoz*): "they will shine as the shining of" (כְּזֹהַר יַזְהִרוּ, *rahoz^ek urihzay*). In the entire OT, the verb occurs only in Dan 12:1. The noun form occurs here and in Ezek 8:2.

Table 76: Ezekiel 8:2

Ezek 8:2	"Then I looked, and behold, a likeness as the appearance of a man; from His loins and downward the appearance of fire, and from His loins and upward the appearance of brightness [זֹהַר, *rahoz*], like the appearance of glowing metal."

וָאֶרְאֶה וְהִנֵּה דְמוּת כְּמַרְאֵה־אֵשׁ מִמַּרְאֵה
מָתְנָיו וּלְמַטָּה אֵשׁ וּמִמָּתְנָיו וּלְמַעְלָה
כְּמַרְאֵה־זֹהַר כְּעֵין הַחַשְׁמַלָה׃

In the Ezekiel passage, the shining was an indication of the glory of the person Ezekiel was seeing. So also, the shining of those who have insight and those who lead many to righteousness is a sign of their glorification. They will be glorified and will shine as bright as the sky to show forth the glory that has been given to them.

Concerning the End Period: 12:4–13

4—   "But you, Daniel, conceal the words and seal up the book until time of end; many will go back and forth, and knowledge will increase."

Seal and Conceal

The word "conceal" is the same word used in 8:24, "The vision of the evenings and mornings which has been told is true; But keep the vision sealed up [סְתֹם, *mot^es*, lit. "seal up"], for *it* pertains to many days." It is different from the word used in chapter 9—חָתַם (*matah*). However, this word is used also in 12:4: "conceal [סְתֹם, *mot^es*] the words and seal [חֲתֹם, *matah*] up the book." The first word indicates the notion of cutting off the supply. It is usually used to refer to stopping the supply of water. The second word indicates applying an official seal so that only those who are authorized may open the scroll. Miller states, "As in 8:26 this admonition concerned the preservation of the document, not its being kept 'secret; (NRSV)."[80] Lucas makes a similar

---

80. Miller, *Daniel*, 320. The initials NRSV refer to the New Revised Standard Version Bible.

assertion: "The verb used here (*stm*) is used more in keeping something safe than of keeping it secret."[81] Evans takes a similar position: "Gleason Archer points out that it was customary in the ancient Near East to seal the original of an important document and store it in a safe place. Copies might be made, but the original was the ultimate authority should any future challenge be made about the document's content. The fact that Daniel is told to 'close up and seal the words of the scroll until the time of the end' thus does not necessarily mean that the scroll's contents were to be kept secret. More probably, the idea was to keep the original version of his work under seal while allowing copies to circulate until the time to which it refers was at hand."[82] Perhaps this has to do with the fact that this book is composed while Israel in general and Daniel in particular are in captivity in a foreign land. The command to seal the book would have been special instruction to make sure that the book is preserved through the time of captivity so that it can be brought back to the land of Israel.

Concerning the sealing of the book, Pentecost says, "Understandably Daniel and his immediate readers could not have comprehended all the details of the prophecy given in this book (cf. v. 8). Not until history continued to unfold would many be able to understand these prophetic revelations."[83] Pentecost relates the notion of sealing the words and the book to the increase of knowledge. He says, "But God indicated that an increased understanding of what Daniel had written would come. People today, looking back over history, can see the significance of much of what Daniel predicted."[84] In fact, the word used for "sealing" the words can have the meaning "to shut up words, be aloof, keep secret."[85] However, assuming the term does not mean "to preserve" as other commentators take it, the problem with Pentecost's evaluation is that the text seems to indicate that the cause of not being able to understand is the sealing the words, not simply the lack of historical background. Additionally, the angel commanded Daniel to seal the words "until the time of the end." Pentecost's interpretation would imply that the time of the end encompasses an extensive time period. Also, for Pentecost to take the increase of knowledge to apply to the understanding of Daniel's book seems to make the statement "many will go back and forth" (יְשֹׁטְטוּ רַבִּים, *mibar uṭṭŏsᵉy*) almost nonsensical. Wood refers to Leupold who takes this to mean "a reader's eye running

---

81. Lucas, *Daniel*, 221.

82. Evans, *Four Kingdoms*, 279.

83. Pentecost, *Daniel*, 1373.

84. Ibid.

85. KBH, s.v. "סתם."

to and fro in Daniel's book, reading it."[86] But, Wood points out that every other time the verb is used in the Old Testament in this particular form, it "refers to movement of one's body to and fro, in search of something, especially information (cf. 2 Chron. 16:9; Jer. 5:1; 49:3; Amos 8:12; Zech. 4:10) . . ."[87]

Also, if this statement refers to keeping the content secret until a future time, then how can anyone know when this time has been reached? Just because we think we know what the text means, if the text is still secret, we can never know that our interpretation of it is either correct or incorrect, and no future generation could ever know this until after everything has already happened. If the content is secret, then why does the angel say that he is going to give Daniel understanding?

Walvoord seems to hold the view that these words were sealed in the sense of kept from Daniel's understanding. He says, "In this statement, it is made plain that the revelation, although enlightening and reassuring even to Daniel, was not intended primarily to interpret these events to him alone. The prophecies thus revealed were to have primary application to those living in "the time of the end."[88] Walvoord's explanation is not very clear, however. It is not clear whether he is referring to understanding the words or merely applying them.

Interestingly, Goldingay proposes an understanding similar to Pentecost's: "Daniel is to 'close up' and 'seal' them: the expressions suggest not merely conserving them but withholding them (cf. 8:26). This is confirmed by the next words: because they are withheld, 'many will hurry to and fro,' unable to find a word from God: see Amos 8:11–12. When Daniel's book is unsealed, during the Antiochus crisis, the famine ends . . ."[89] The famine to which Goldingay refers is the famine predicted in Amos 8:11: "'Behold, days are coming,' declares the Lord God, 'When I will send a famine on the land, not a famine for bread or a thirst for water, but rather for hearing the words of the Lord.'" Contrary to Goldingay's proposal, the New Testament, particularly the opening of John's Gospel, indicates that this famine was ended with the coming of the Logos (Λόγος, logos), the Word of God, in the flesh. And, since the text does not say that the book will be unsealed at any particular time, how can Goldingay verify that it was unsealed in the time of Antiochus? He cannot rely on his own interpretation or understanding of the book since he would have to assume that it has been unsealed for his understanding in

86. Wood, *Daniel*, 321.

87. Ibid.

88. Walvoord, *Daniel*, 291.

89. Goldingay, *Daniel*, 309.

order to support the notion that it was unsealed in Antiochus' time. But that is circular reasoning.

The Time of the End

We have dealt with this expression somewhat already (see page 572ff). Of course the identification of the time of the end is usually predicated on the eschatological perspective of the one making the identification. Evans, for example, asserts, "That time arguably arrived with the advent of the Jewish War of AD 66–70, which erupted thirty plus years after the disciples of Jesus began going 'here and there to increase knowledge.'"[90] However, through the analysis of the prophecy, we have shown that the Preterist view does not stand up to the facts of the text or the facts of history.

Don Preston claims, "Daniel's prophecy is about *the end of Israel's history*, not the end of human history."[91] Of course the error Preston makes is assuming that Israel's history ended in 70 AD, which we have already seen simply is not the case. Preston asserts, "When was the power of the holy people completely shattered? That is easy for anyone with a knowledge of history. In A.D. 70, when the Romans conquered Israel. Jerusalem and the Temple, the center of Jewish life, was destroyed. The Temple was the heart and the core of Israel. To destroy the Temple was to destroy the nation."[92] If this were true, then Israel was destroyed with the destruction of Solomon's Temple, and the people who were defeated in 70 AD was not even the nation of Israel. Of course, Preston's claim is simply false. At the beginning of his book Preston said he was going to demonstrate his position "through scripture alone," but nowhere in the Scripture is it ever said that the Temple was the heart and core of Israel. In fact, the heart and core of Israel was the LORD God as Solomon himself acknowledged in the dedication of the Temple: "But who is able to build a house for Him, for the heavens and the highest heavens cannot contain Him? So who am I, that I should build a house for Him, except to burn *incense* before Him?" (2 Chron 2:6). Neither does Scripture anywhere say that 70 AD was the end of the Jewish people, and since the Temple was rebuilt after its destruction by Nebuchadnezzar, so it can be rebuilt today, and its rebuilding demonstrates that this was not the end of Jewish history.

This exact expression, "until *the* time of *the* end" (עֵד־עֵת קֵץ, *ʿeʿ daʿ ṣeq*), occurs only three times in the entire OT, and all three are in the book of Daniel: 11:35, 12:4, and 12:9. In fact, the same expression minus the word "until" occurs in only two additional passages: Dan 8:17; 11:40. This seems

90. Evans, *Four Kingdoms*, 279.

91. Preston, *Last Days Identified*, 56.

92. Ibid.

to indicate that these expressions must be connected in some way. This is especially the case with the fuller expression. Dan. 11:35, 12:4, and 12:9 seem to be referring to the same period.

Table 77: "Until the Time of the End" in Daniel

Dan 11:35	"Some of those who have insight will fall, in order to refine, purge and make them pure until the end time [עַד־עֵת קֵץ, *seqīte ʿĪdaʿ*]; because still at the appointed time." וּמִן־הַמַּשְׂכִּילִים יִכָּשְׁלוּ לִצְרוֹף בָּהֶם וּלְבָרֵר וְלַלְבֵּן עַד־עֵת קֵץ כִּי־עוֹד לַמּוֹעֵד:
Dan 12:4	"But as for you, Daniel, conceal these words and seal up the book until the end of time [עַד־עֵת קֵץ, *seq Īteʿ Īdaʿ*]; many will go back and forth, and knowledge will increase." וְאַתָּה דָנִיֵּאל סְתֹם הַדְּבָרִים וַחֲתֹם הַסֵּפֶר עַד־עֵת קֵץ יְשֹׁטְטוּ רַבִּים וְתִרְבֶּה הַדָּעַת:
Dan 12:9	"He said, 'Go, Daniel, for words are concealed and sealed up until the end time [עַד־עֵת קֵץ, *seqĪte ʿĪdaʿ*].'" וַיֹּאמֶר לֵךְ דָּנִיֵּאל כִּי־סְתֻמִים וַחֲתֻמִים הַדְּבָרִים עַד־עֵת קֵץ:

Verse 35 of chapter 11 refers to those who have insight as falling, and verse 3 of chapter 12 refers to them as being raised to life eternal and shining as the brightness of the expanse. In addition to the precise duplication of wording, these factors indicate that these two verses may be referring to the same period. Of course the question is; when is the time of the end? Walvoord holds that the time of the end is the end of the age. He says,

> After experiencing the broad expanse of the revelation—beginning as it did with the kings of Persia, extending through the Maccabean period, then leaping to the end of the age and the great tribulation, and including the resurrections and reward of the righteous— Daniel is now instructed to "shut up the words, and seal the book." In this statement, it is made plain that the revelation, although enlightening and reassuring even to Daniel, was not intended primarily to interpret these events to him alone. The prophecies thus

revealed were to have primary application to those living in "the time of the end." In fact, the entire revelation, even the portions already fulfilled through Daniel 11:35, are designed to help those seeking to trust in the Lord in their affliction at the climax of the age. It is significant that in the twentieth century, even though twenty-five hundred years have elapsed, the prophecies of Daniel have never been more relevant to an attempt to understand the course of history and impending future events.[93]

As we have seen, the times of the Gentiles is a period of history that begins with Nebuchadnezzar and extends into the future of human history. The same may be true of the expression "time of end." The time of the end may be an extended period of time rather than a single day or a range of days. Peter announced at his preaching to the multitude that the last days were upon them. Consequently, the last days seems to be a period that began at Pentecost and extends to the end of the age. Miller asserts, "Gabriel therefore was instructing Daniel to preserve 'the words of the scroll,' not merely this final vision but the whole book for those who will live at 'the time of the end' when the message will be needed. This future generation will undergo the horrors of the tribulation ('time of distress') and will need the precious promises contained in the Book of Daniel—that God will be victorious over the kingdoms of this world and that the suffering will last for only a brief time—to sustain them."[94] If Miller's view is correct, then the notion that the book is to be kept secret makes little sense. If the book was to be sealed until the time of the end, and if it was to be kept secret until then, there would be no way to explain the fact that commentators are able to expound upon and exegete much of the text. Since we have shown that the prophecies of Daniel cannot be applied either to the time of Antiochus Epiphanes or Herod, we must conclude that the prophecies of Daniel are ultimately fulfilled in a future time of trouble. Consequently, the sealing of the book cannot mean to keep it secret, but rather to preserve it so that it will be available to those who will need it in those days.

Running To and Fro

Mauro attempts to relate the statement "many will go back and forth, and knowledge will increase" to the great commission. He says, "These words bring the prophecy to an end; and it is not difficult to see the resemblance they bear to the final words of the first Gospel, '*Go ye, teach* (or make *disciples*

93. Walvoord, *Daniel*, 291.
94. Miller, *Daniel*, 321.

of) all nations.'"[95] By appealing to several verses, Mauro attempts to establish the point that the "running to and fro" necessarily means to encompass the whole earth. He says, "By these scriptures, therefore, it appears that the words we are considering are most appropriate to describe that world-wide activity in spreading the truth of the gospel which the Lord specially pressed upon His disciples, and to which the apostle Paul refers in the words, 'How shall they believe in Him of whom they have not heard, and how shall they hear without a preacher? . . . The Gospel messenger is frequently figured as one who *runs*, because of the urgency of the tidings he bears (Hab. 2:3, 3)."[96] Once one examines the use of the words, however, one can see the error of Mauro's attempt to force this into his eschatological framework.

All the passages from the OT containing the word שׁוּט (*tŭs*) translated "going to and fro" are in the same form as it appears in Dan 12:4. These are included in the following table.

Table 78: "Running To and Fro" in Daniel

	"For the eyes of the Lord move to and fro [מְשֹׁטְטוֹת, *ʾoṭṭŏsem*] throughout the earth that He may strongly support those whose heart is completely His. You have acted foolishly in this. Indeed, from now on you will surely have wars."
2 Chron 16:9	כִּי יְהוָה עֵינָיו מְשֹׁטְטוֹת בְּכָל־הָאָרֶץ לְהִתְחַזֵּק עִם־לְבָבָם שָׁלֵם אֵלָיו נִסְכַּלְתָּ עַל־זֹאת כִּי מֵעַתָּה יֵשׁ עִמְּךָ מִלְחָמוֹת:
	"Roam to and fro [שׁוֹטְטוּ, *uṭŏs*] through the streets of Jerusalem, and look now and take note. And seek in her open squares, if you can find a man, if there is one who does justice, who seeks truth, then I will pardon her."
Jer 5:1	שׁוֹטְטוּ בְּחוּצוֹת יְרוּשָׁלַ͏ִם וּרְאוּ־נָא וּדְעוּ וּבַקְשׁוּ בִרְחוֹבוֹתֶיהָ אִם־תִּמְצְאוּ אִישׁ אִם־יֵשׁ עֹשֶׂה מִשְׁפָּט מְבַקֵּשׁ אֱמוּנָה וְאֶסְלַח לָהּ:

---

95. Mauro, *Seventy Weeks*, 171.
96. Ibid., 172.

"People will stagger from sea to sea and from the north even to the east; They will go to and fro [יְשׁוֹטְטוּ, *uṭ̄ōsey*] to seek the word of the Lord, but they will not find."

Amos 8:12

וְנָעוּ מִיָּם עַד־יָם וּמִצָּפוֹן וְעַד־מִזְרָח
יְשׁוֹטְטוּ לְבַקֵּשׁ אֶת־דְּבַר־יְהוָה וְלֹא
יִמְצָאוּ׃

"For who has despised the day of small things? But these seven will be glad when they see the plumb line in the hand of Zerubbabel— the eyes of the Lord which range to and fro [מְשׁוֹטְטִים, *miṭ̄ōsem*] throughout the earth."

Zech 4:10

כִּי מִי בַז לְיוֹם קְטַנּוֹת וְשָׂמְחוּ וְרָאוּ אֶת־
הָאֶבֶן הַבְּדִיל בְּיַד זְרֻבָּבֶל שִׁבְעָה־אֵלֶּה
עֵינֵי יְהוָה הֵמָּה מְשׁוֹטְטִים בְּכָל־הָאָרֶץ׃

Of the four uses outside the book of Daniel, two of them refer to God's eyes roaming to and fro throughout the earth. This, no doubt, is an anthropomorphism depicting God's omniscience. In the other two instances the word is used of the actions of men. In Jeremiah it has to do with attempting to find at least one man in Jerusalem who does righteousness, and in Amos it has to do with seeking the Word of the Lord but not finding it. In other words, in the instances in which the word is used of the actions of men, the situation is always unpleasant.

Mauro claims, "The word 'run' in Daniel 12:4 is not the usual word for the *action* of running."[97] There is indeed another Hebrew word that occurs more than 100 times in the OT with the predominate use being to indicate the act of running: רוּץ (*ṣur*). However, simply because the word used in 12:4 is not the usual word for the meaning "run" does not mean it does not have a similar meaning. In fact, the use in both Jeremiah and Amos seems to give the idea of frantically going back and forth, i.e., running. In the case of Jeremiah's prophecy, the people are frantically going about to find a righteous man so as to avert the coming judgment. In Amos they are frantically going about to find a word from God. In fact, as Miller points out, "In a number of Old Testament passages . . . Hebrew *uteʾōsey* denotes 'to go here and there' in search of a person or thing, and that is the meaning here. An 'intense' searching seems indicated by the verb form. The purpose of this search will

97. Ibid., 171.

be 'to increase knowledge.'"[98] This hardly sounds like the spreading of the Gospel. This text is simply not referring to the spreading of the Gospel as Mauro claims.

Increase of Knowledge

There is no statement in the text that tells the reader what is the content of the knowledge. The Hebrew word translated "knowledge" (הַדַּעַת, taʿad) is not an unusual word. Having attempted to relate the going to and fro with the spreading of the Gospel, Mauro asserts that the knowledge "is *the knowledge of the true God* that is spoken of . . ."[99] However, the implication of the text is that this effort will be futile. In fact, the sense seems to be quite similar to that spoken by Paul in 2 Tim 3:7: "ever learning, and never able to come to the knowledge of the truth."

When Will These Wonders End?

5— "And I, Daniel, looked and behold, two others standing, one on this bank of the river and the other on that bank of the river."

6— "And one said to the man dressed in linen, who was above the waters of the river, "How long will it be until the end of these wonders?"

7— "I heard the man dressed in linen, who was above the waters of the river, as he raised his right hand and his left toward heaven, and swore by Him who lives forever that it would be for a time, times, and half a time; and as soon as they finish shattering the power of the holy people, all these events will be completed."

How Long Will it Be?

As Daniel was looking, he saw two other beings standing on each bank of the river, and the man dressed in linen was standing above the waters of the river. One of those on the bank asked the one standing above the river, "How long will it be until the end of these wonders?" The Hebrew text reads, עַד־מָתַי קֵץ הַפְּלָאוֹת (toʾalʿppah šeq yaʾtam daʿ), lit. "until when end of the wonders?" The word "wonders" (הַפְּלָאוֹת, toʾalʿppah) occurs nowhere else in Daniel, but it does occur 12 times outside the book of Daniel. According to TWOT, "Preponderantly both the verb and the substantive refer to the acts of God, designating either cosmic wonders or historical achievements on behalf

98. Miller, *Daniel*, 321.
99. Mauro, *Seventy Weeks*, 172.

of Israel. That is, in the Bible the root *ᵓlp* refers to things that are unusual, beyond human capabilities. As such, it awakens astonishment (*ᵓlp*) in man."[100] Mauro argues that the expression "How long the end of these wonders?" is in fact "concerning *the duration of those days of unparalleled distress for Israel* that the question was asked,"[101] not when the end of these wonders will arrive. However, Mauro's argument hardly seems to make any difference. The answer to the question would seem to be the same: "These wonders will last for a duration of time, times, and half a time"; or, "These wonders will end in time, times, and half a time." Mauro argues, "This makes it certain that the *entire prophecy* spoken to Daniel by the one clothed in linen, including the time of trouble such as never was, and the awakening of many from the dust of the earth, was fulfilled *at and prior to the destruction of Jerusalem, and the scattering of the power of the holy people by the Romans in A.D. 70.*"[102]

We have already seen that Mauro's understanding of the awakening is false. Also now he argues specifically that the scattering of the "holy people" took place in 70 AD as a result of the Romans' destruction of Jerusalem. However, the historical facts do not support Mauro's speculations. First, there was no scattering of the holy people in 70 AD. The majority of the Jews had been scattered among the nations back in the time of the fall of the nation of Israel (c. 721 BC) and the deportation of people. Second, the terrible event of 70 AD was principally a destruction of Jerusalem and the people rather than a scattering of them. Also, as we have seen, those who survived the destruction of Jerusalem actually remained in Israel so as to mount another rebellion in 135 AD, the Bar Kochba revolt. We have quoted from Safrai already on this point, but it will serve to do so again: "In the Hellenistic cities where the Jews were slaughtered or expelled by their neighbors (only in four of them, Antioch, Epimea, Sidon and Gerasa, did the Jews remain unharmed), we find a large Jewish population by the end of the first century. Both Jewish and non-Jewish literature show that a normal farming economy had been restored by the end of the first and the beginning of the second centuries, with the highly developed cultivation of field crops, and gardens. Many orchards had been rehabilitated and new ones planted."[103] So, not only has Mauro gotten the prophecy wrong, but he has gotten the history wrong as well.

---

100. TWOT, s.v. "פֶּלֶא."
101. Mauro, *Seventy Weeks*, 174 (emphasis in original).
102. Ibid., 175 (emphasis in original).
103. Safrai, "The Jews in the Land of Israel," 315.

TIMES, TIME, AND HALF A TIME

Evans, following Mauro, argues, "Preterists . . . see that 'the shattering of the power' to which 12:7 refers is, as Mauro wrote, 'the destruction of Jerusalem, and the scattering of the power of the holy people by the Romans in A.D. 70.' The 'time, times and half a time' of 12:7 are thus to be associated with the first century AD, not the Maccabean era. In Mauro's view, however, what has generally been translated as 'half a time' should be rendered as 'a part,' and the meaning of the passage in 12:7 is actually 'three full years and a part (not necessarily the half) of a fourth.'"[104] Evans refers to the fact that Mauro asserts, "This is given by the angel as 'a time, times, and a part,' which is understood by nearly all expositors to be three full years and a part (not necessarily the half) of a fourth."[105] Mauro's argument is summarized by Evans:

> Mauro's "three full years and *a part* ran from November 66, the month he assigned for the invasion of Judea by Cestius Gallus, the governor of Syria, to July 70, when the daily sacrifice was taken away because the besieged Jews in Jerusalem ran out of men who were qualified to conduct it. He then noted that the 1,290 and 1,335 days of 12:11–12 both satisfy the requirement of three years and a part. The 1,290 days, he claimed, correspond to 43 months of 30 days each and represent the time elapsing between the invasion by the Roman army, which he took to be the "abomination that causes desolation," and the ending of the daily sacrifice. The difference of 45 days between 1,335 and 1,290 days represents the additional month and a half between the ending of the daily sacrifice and the fall of the city to the Roman force commanded by Titus.[106]

A fact devastating for Mauro's argument is that the Hebrew word "half" (חֵצִי, *ḥēṣ^ah*) is never used to mean "a part," but is always used to mean either a half or the middle.[107] In order to make the time frame fit into their Preterist assumptions, they must alter the wording from the Hebrew text from what it actually reads. Also, Mauro's argument has been critiqued by Young, and he has demonstrated that Mauro's reasoning and calculations cannot fit the historical facts as they are presently known.

> Mauro says that it was exactly 43 months between the taking away of the daily sacrifice during the siege of Jerusalem and the appear-

---

104. Evans, *Four Kingdoms*, 281–82.

105. Mauro, *Seventy Weeks*, 175.

106. Evans, *Four Kingdoms*, 282 (emphasis in original).

107. KBH, s.v. "חֵצִי"

ance of the Roman army (the abomination), if the days of the month in which the two events occurred be not reckoned. Thus: A.D. 66. Coming of the Romans under Cestius. A.D. 70. Taking away of the Daily Sacrifice. It must be noted, however, that upon this scheme the two events are reversed. If this were correct, we should expect the text to read, *from the abomination to the taking away of the continual sacrifice is 1290 days*. Hence, this construction does not do adequate justice to the text. Furthermore, the period between these two events is not 1290 days, but possibly 60 days more. The coming of the Romans took place about the 15–22 of Tishri (i.e., October, 66), and on the 30th of Hyperberetmus (i.e., c. 17th November, 66) Cestius led his troops into Jerusalem. On the 17th of Panemus 70 A.D., (i.e., Tammuz in the Jewish calendar—our August) Titus learned that the continual sacrifice had ceased to be offered (See Josephus, *The Jewish Wars* II:19:1ff. and VI:2:1). Now the interval between these two events was not 1290 days or 43 months but about 1350 days. Note that 1290 days would carry us from November 17, 66 to June 17, 70. There still remains the interval (at least more than a month) up to August 17, 70. This view, therefore, must be rejected.[108]

Evans acknowledges that Young's criticisms "are fatal to Mauro's exegesis of 12:11. Mauro's belief that the 1,290 days are the gap between the appearance of an abomination that causes desolation (the Roman army) in 66 and the ending of the daily sacrifice at the Temple in 70 cannot be reconciled with either the language of 12:11 or the facts of history. Furthermore, in insisting on the wording 'three full years and a part' for 12:7, Mauro brought himself into conflict with the Book of Revelation."[109] However, Evans believes that it is possible to reconcile the language of the text with a Preterist view. Since his argument principally revolves around 12:11–12, we will consider Evans' presentation under those verses.

Miller holds that the time, times, and half a time "reveals the duration of the period. . . . Thus the sovereign Lord of the universe is promising directly and emphatically that the Antichrist's horrors (the 'time of distress' of 12:1) perpetrated upon God's people and the whole world will last but a brief time—three and a half years."[110] Walvoord concurs: "What is the meaning of the phrase *a time, times, and an half.* This expression, also occurring in Daniel 7:25, apparently refers to the last period preceding the second coming

---

108. Young, *Prophecy of Daniel*, 262.

109. Evans, *Four Kingdoms*, 282–83.

110. Miller, *Daniel*, 323.

of Christ which brings conclusion to the time of the end."[111] According to the premillennial view, the three and a half years are the second half of the seventieth seven of Daniel' prophecy in chapter 9. The angel declared, "but in the middle of the week he will put a stop to sacrifice and grain offering." The middle of the seven—the three and one-half year point—marks the beginning of the period referred to with the expression "time, times, and half a time."

SHATTERING THEIR POWER

The angel declares that by the end of the three and one-half year period, the "shattering the power of the holy people" will have been accomplished. The text does not indicate that this "shattering" will occur *at* the end of this period, but implies that it will be by this time—the process of shattering will occur during this time to be completed by its end. The text states, "as soon as they finish shattering the power of the holy people" (וּכְכַלּוֹת נַפֵּץ יַד־עַם־קֹדֶשׁ, *(seḏoq ma ͨ day šepan ͨollakku)*. The word translated "shattering" is the root נפץ (*nfs*). According to KBH, this is the root of two distinct lexical entries. The one, identified as I, means "to smash to pieces," and the other, identified as II, means, "to be scattered, dispersed."[112] There are at least two good reasons why the word should be taken as "to smash to pieces," hence "to shatter" as in the NASBU. First, the word in the text appears in the Piel form. I appears in the Piel form in other passages in which it clearly means "to shatter." For example, in Ps 2:9 it is used in the phrase, "to shatter like earthenware." II never occurs in the Piel form, unless of course the Daniel passage is the only one. Second, in the text the word is used in conjunction with the word "hand" (יָד, *day*). Literally the phrase is, "shatter the hand of the holy people." It is nonsensical to speak of *scattering* someone's hand, and this is not an OT metaphor. However, the word "hand" is often a metaphor to indicate power, and speaking of shattering someone's hand as a metaphor for power makes good sense. Even speaking of scattering someone's power makes little sense. Miller asserts, "During these three and one-half years, 'the power of the holy people' will be 'finally [probably better, "completely"] broken [or "shattered"].' The 'holy people' in this context is a specific reference to Israel; therefore their 'power' being 'broken' signifies that the nation will be utterly defeated by their enemies."[113]

John Noë claims that the "power" referred to was "the biggest power anyone could have—the power of biblical Judaism (i.e., their exclusive relationship with God) as manifested by the Temple complex (Isa. 2:2–5; 56:7)."[114]

111. Walvoord, *Daniel*, 293.

112. KBH, s.v. "נפץ," I and II.

113. Miller, *Daniel*, 323.

114. Noë, *Beyond the End Times*, 93.

He goes on to argue, "The final breaking of this power was to be both the historical setting and defining characteristic for Daniel's 'time of the end.'"[115] Unfortunately for his reader, in this book Noë does not attempt to explain what it means "to shatter the power" of the holy people. Nevertheless, the claim that this power is biblical Judaism is without foundation and makes no sense in the context. The text indicates that this power will be shattered. To suppose that some external force could shatter the power of biblical Judaism assumes that the purposes of God can be resisted. It makes no sense to suppose that had Israel at this time been committed to biblical Judaism, that it would have been in the plan of God for this commitment to be shattered. This is not spoken of in the text as something that Israel does to or for themselves, but is done to them. To the fact that individuals can refuse the grace of God is sufficiently testified. To the fact that some evil force can shatter the power of the commitment of God to His people is not only rejected in the text, but makes no sense.

In Richard Pratt's arguments against the Hyper-Preterists, he offers some interesting insights.[116] His proposals begin with a recounting of the

---

115. Ibid.

116. Richard L. Pratt, Jr., "Hyper-Preterism and Unfolding Biblical Eschatology," in *When Shall These Things Be?* ed. Keith A. Mathison (Phillipsburg, New Jersey: P&R Publishing, 2004), 124. Notwithstanding Pratt's views on eschatology, we must strongly object to his view on and comments about immutability. Pratt asserts, "When we speak of historical contingencies affecting the fulfillment of prophecies, we have in mind a concept of contingency that complies with the emphasis of traditional Reformed theology on the sovereignty of God. In the first place, this study affirms the doctrine of God's sovereign immutability. Unfortunately, this doctrine is often misunderstood to teach that God is unchangeable in every way imaginable. But such an outlook denies the biblical portrait of God's ability to have meaningful interaction with the creation (to judge, redeem, answer prayer, become flesh, etc.). It is for this reason that Reformed theologians have distinguished ways in which God is immutable from ways in which he is not. For example, Louis Berkhof puts the matter succinctly: 'The Bible teaches us that God enters into manifold relations with man and, as it were, lives their life with them. There is no change in His Being, His attributes, His purposes, His motives or actions, or His promises.' We can summarize Berkhof by saying that Reformed theology has identified at least three ways in which God is unchanging: (1) God's character does not change; he cannot become something other than what he is. (2) God's covenant promises are immutable. He will not break his covenant oaths. (3) God is immutable in his eternal counsel or plan for all of history. God has an unchangeable plan, and this plan governs every detail of history." Contrary to Pratt's claim, his view does not conform either to the traditional Reformed view of immutability nor to the current Reformed view. Francis Turretin, a 17th century Reformed theologian, for example states, "Immutability is an incommunicable attribute of God by which is denied of Him not only all change, but also all possibility of change, as much with respect to existence as to will" (*"Immutabilitas est attributum Dei incommunicabile, quo negatur de Deo non tantum omnis mutatio, fed etiam possibilitas mutationis, tam quoad existentiam, quam quoad voluntatem."*). Francisco Turrettino, *Institutio Theologiæ Elencticæ*

eschatological expectations of Moses and the early prophets. He points out, "According to Deuteronomy 4:25–31; 28:1–30 and Leviticus 26:3–45, the judgments and blessings of the covenant would not simply come and go in endless cycles. Moses expected that Judgments would increase as Israel went further and further away from God. This increase in judgment would culminate in the exile of Israel from the Promise Land (Deut. 4:25–28; Lev. 26:14–39)."[117] Pratt mistakenly understands these passages as referring to the Babylonian exile. However, the text states that God would "scatter you among the peoples . . ." This, perhaps, includes the Babylonian captivity, but it must

---

(Amstelodami: Ant. Schouten, & Th. Appels., 1696), Third Topic, Q. XI.225. Thomas Ridgley, an 18th century Reformed theologian, asserts that God is immutable not only in His essence but also in His will: "That God is unchangeable in his will: thus it is said of him, *He is of one mind, and who can turn him?* Job. xxiii. 13. this is agreeable to his infinite perfection, and therefore he does not propose to do a thing at one time, and determine not to do it at another." Thomas Ridgley, *A Body of Divinity: Wherein the Doctrines of the Christian Religion, are Explained and Defended* (Glasgow: John Bryce, 1770), 38. John Dick, a 19th century Reformed Pastor and Theologian affirms the same view: "I proceed to speak of his immutability, by which we understand not only that his duration is permanent, but that his nature is fixed, immoveable, unaffected by external causes; in every respect the same from eternity to eternity." John Dick, *Lectures on Theology* (Oxford: David Christy, 1836), 102–3. Herman Hoeksema, a twentieth century Reformed Theologian avers the same position: "He does not grow older, does not increase or decrease in Being or power, is from eternity to eternity the same in essence and in all His virtues, in His mind and will. His love and life, the absolute fulness and Self-sufficient God. When in the Scriptures we read that God repents, or when He speaks a word which at a later moment is changed into the very opposite, as in the case of Hezekiah's sickness, or of Jonah's commission concerning the destruction of Nineveh, these instances may never be explained as presupposing a change in God. Rather must we remember that the eternal and immutable God reveals Himself in time, and that what is thus revealed to us in a succession of moments is eternally and unchangeably in the mind of God." Herman Hoeksema, *Reformed Dogmatics* (Grand Rapids: Reformed Free Publishing Association, 1966), 76. Even Pratt's quote from Berkhof does not tell an accurate story. Although Pratt quotes from Berkhof, he fails to quote enough, so the reader gets a distorted view of Berkhof's position. Berkhof goes on to assert, "And if Scripture speaks of His repenting, changing His intention, and altering His relation to sinners when they repent, we should remember that this is only an anthropopathic way of speaking. In reality the change is not in God, but in man and in man's relation to God. It is important to maintain the immutability of God over against the Pelagian and Arminian doctrine that God is subject to change, not indeed in His Being, but in His knowledge and will, so that His decisions are to a great extent dependent on the actions of man;" L. Berkhof, *Systematic Theology*, 4th ed. (Grand Rapids: Wm. B. Eerdmans Publishing Company, 1976), 59. Pratt's view is not consistent either with the traditional Reformed view or with the current Reformed view. The contingencies he describes are perfectly consistent with the traditional view of immutability and do not require any sense in which God changes.

117. Ibid., 140.

also include the earlier scattering of the 10 tribes who did not return to the land after the Babylonian captivity.

Pratt goes on to quote Deut 4:30–31: "When you are in distress and all these things have come upon you, in the latter days you will return to the Lord your God and listen to His voice. For the Lord your God is a compassionate God; He will not fail you nor destroy you nor forget the covenant with your fathers which He swore to them." Pratt provides a good summary of the eschatological expectation of Moses, provided one makes allowance for Pratt's tendency to locate these promises to the Babylonian captivity. He says, "Moses anticipated that Israel would go into exile from the land. But once the people repented of their sins, they would be forgiven. And then, in the latter days, or the eschaton, they would be brought back to the land of promise and receive tremendous blessings. This basic outlook of Moses was never forgotten in biblical history; it set the stage upon which eschatology unfolded in the Scriptures."[118]

Pratt goes on to argue from the prophets that there was a similar expectation. Pratt relates this to the destruction of Jerusalem and to the return from Babylonian exile. He says, "They [the prophets] believed that forgiveness would take place during the Exile (Isa. 43:25–26; 44:21–22; Jer. 31:34). They also affirmed that a repentant people would be gathered back to the land of Israel for a great restoration (Jer. 31:1–25; 32:26–44; Ezek. 36:16–38)."[119] None of these verses indicates that there was an expectation of forgiveness "during the Exile." There was, however, the promise of forgiveness should Israel repent, and the promises of the great restoration refer, not to the restoration from Babylonian captivity, which in fact did not involve the entire nation, but only the two tribes of Judah and Benjamin, but to the final restoration to the land in the eschaton.

Pratt takes these promises, which he relates to the Babylonian captivity, and proposes that the unrepentance of Israel caused God to alter His plans for restoration. He argues, "Moses and the prophets had announced that exile would be reversed only when the people of God repented from their sins. But an unexpected intervening historical contingency had taken place. The Israelites had gone into exile, but they still had not repented of their sins. Israel's recalcitrance led to a major adjustment in the way that eschatological expectations unfolded."[120] But it is not necessary to see this as an "unexpected historical contingency." Rather, this was all part of God's plan from the very beginning, and the passages that Pratt confined to expectations regarding the

118. Ibid., 141–42.
119. Ibid., 142.
120. Ibid., 145.

Babylonian exile were actually addressing the ultimate repentance and return of the people in the last days precisely because God had planned things to happen this way. According to Pratt's view, there is no way to explain why after the Babylonian exile God brought Israel back into the land in spite of their lack of repentance. However, since this is all planned by God from the beginning, and there are no "unexpected historical contingencies" that cause God to make any "major adjustment," God brought Israel back into the land in order to prepare them for the next step in His plan.

The threats of Judgment throughout the history of the nation were designed to bring Israel to repentance, but they would not (cf. Isa 1:5ff). The Babylonian exile was the next step in leading Israel to repentance, an episode in their history that they likewise failed to understand so that they might bring about the appropriate response—repentance. Pratt rightly identifies Daniel's prayer as a recognition that Israel had refused to repent. So, Daniel's prayer, prompted by his realization that the seventy years of captivity prophesied by Jeremiah was almost fulfilled, was not, as Pratt observes, "a prayer of rejoicing in the certainty that the eschaton was about to be realized,"[121] rather his prayer was a prayer of repentance and contrition. Consequently, Pratt sees the prophecy of the seventy sevens as an extension of the exile: "Simply put, Gabriel said that the Exile had been extended from seventy years to seventy weeks of years, or about 490 years. Because the people had refused to repent, God decided to multiply the length of the exile by seven. The idea that God would cause a sevenfold increase of judgment against his rebellious people was already known from the covenant of Moses. As God said in Leviticus 26:18, 'If after all this you will not listen to me, I will punish you for your sins seven times over.' Here, God applied this sevenfold increase to the Exile itself. He delayed the restoration of Israel for seven times seventy years."[122]

At this point, Pratt introduces a concept that has been the argument of many Futurists with reference to the establishing of the kingdom. Pratt argues, "At a time when other prophets were speaking of the imminent fulfillment of eschatological expectations, Daniel learned that the eschaton had been postponed because of a lack of repentance. As a result, the early postexilic community faced an anomalous situation. The imminent eschatological expectation of Jeremiah had been realized in part, but it had also been delayed."[123] The eschatological expectation of the complete restoration of the people to their land, and the complete fulfillment of the inheritance of all the land specified in the Abrahamic covenant, were "delayed" because of Israel's

121. Ibid., 144.
122. Ibid., 145.
123. Ibid., 145–46.

lack of repentance. God brought them back into the land to prepare them for the next step in His plan to bring Israel back to the relationship they had rejected.

Pratt argues that the Hyper-Preterists have "collected an impressive number of passages which at least appear to indicate that New Testament writers predicted that Jesus was returning within one generation."[124] Pratt rejects the Hyper-Preterists' understanding of these passages and presents a summary of eschatological expectation that fits very well into a Futurist perspective.

> Our proposal is that the New Testament eschatological expectations unfolded in ways that roughly parallel the three levels of eschatological expectation that developed among Israel's prophets after the destruction of Jerusalem. These three levels may be summarized in this way: (1) Jeremiah offered an imminent eschaton upon the assumption of repentance, and a measure of this expectation was realized; (2) Daniel came to realize that the fullness of the eschaton was delayed because of a lack of repentance; (3) Haggai and Zechariah called for repentance after the delay had begun, to hasten the fullness of eschatological promises. The New Testament makes a similar presentation. (1) The initial eschatological perspective was that the blessings of the eschaton had been realized to some measure, and the imminent return of Christ was offered as a benefit of repentance. (2) The lack of repentance within the covenant community caused an indefinite delay of Christ's return. (3) Nevertheless, the hope and prayer of every true believer is that through their repentance and faithful living the return of Christ may be hastened.[125]

124. Ibid., 148.
125. Ibid., 149.

Figure 48: Flow of Israel's History

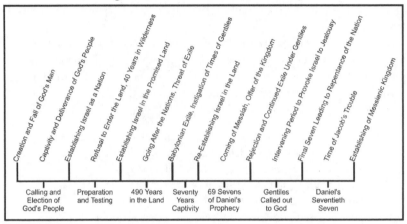

When Jesus comes to offer to Israel the promised kingdom, He is rejected by His people due to the unrepentant heart of the nation. Consequently, that kingdom was delayed. The intervening period is designed to provoke Israel to jealousy to cause them to repent and return to God. One way of looking at the major events in Israel's history is depicted in the graphic in Figure 48 above. The shattering of the power of the holy people may not be a reference only to some military opposition that overcomes the people of God. Rather, this may also be a reference to the fact that, by the fierce persecution of Israel during the time of Jacob's Trouble, God has finally broken the power of their stiff neck and iron forehead that has prevented Israel from repenting. This may go back to the mission given to Isaiah: "Then I heard the voice of the Lord, saying, 'Whom shall I send, and who will go for Us?' Then I said, 'Here am I. Send me!' He said, 'Go, and tell this people: "Keep on listening, but do not perceive; Keep on looking, but do not understand." Render the hearts of this people insensitive, their ears dull, and their eyes dim, otherwise they might see with their eyes, hear with their ears, understand with their hearts, and return and be healed.' Then I said, 'Lord, how long?' And He answered, 'Until cities are devastated without inhabitant, houses are without people and the land is utterly desolate'" (Isa 6:8–11). Even in the time of Jesus this judgment was upon Israel with no hint that it was about to be revoked: "And the disciples came and said to Him, 'Why do You speak to them in parables?' Jesus answered them, 'To you it has been granted to know the mysteries of the kingdom of heaven, but to them it has not been granted'" (Matt 13:10–11). Through this time of trouble, the Tribulation, God brings Israel to the point that they can no longer resist God, but must turn to him in repentance and faith. As Paul put it, "For I do not want you, brethren, to be uninformed of this mystery–so that you will not be wise in your own estimation–that a partial hardening has happened to Israel until the fullness of the Gentiles has come in; and so all Israel will be saved; just as it is written, 'The Deliverer will come from Zion, He will remove ungodliness from Jacob'" (Rom 11:25–26).

All Will Be Completed

Interestingly the NASBU reads, "and as soon as *they* finish," making the verb a third person plural. However, the text uses וּכְכַלּ֣וֹת (*tollakku*), which is an infinitive construct. Infinitives do not have person. The translation should be, "And when brought to completion the shattering of the power of the holy people . . ." There is no indication in the word that this shattering is attributed to many or to one. This could be speaking of the forces that complete their persecution of the people, or it could be speaking of God Who uses these forces to bring Israel to the point of crying out to God in repentance and faith. The fact that Israel will be defeated and shattered by their enemies is presented in the Isaiah passages cited above: ". . . until cities are devastated without inhabitant, houses are without people and the land is utterly desolate" (Isa 6:11). Miller points out, "That the Jewish state will be attacked by many nations and crushed by them is taught elsewhere in Scripture (e.g., Zech 12–14)."[126] The crushing of Israel under the power of a foreign nation leading to Israel's repentance and calling upon the Lord is the pattern in Judges. Isaiah refers to this also:

> How the faithful city has become a harlot, she was full of justice! Righteousness once lodged in her, but now murderers. Your silver has become dross, your drink diluted with water. Your rulers are rebels and companions of thieves; everyone loves a bribe and chases after rewards. They do not defend the orphan, nor does the widow's plea come before them. Therefore the Lord God of hosts, the Mighty One of Israel, declares, "Ah, I will be relieved of My adversaries and avenge Myself on My foes. I will also turn My hand against you, and will smelt away your dross as with lye and will remove all your alloy. Then I will restore your judges as at the first, and your counselors as at the beginning; after that you will be called the city of righteousness, a faithful city." Zion will be redeemed with justice and her repentant ones with righteousness. But transgressors and sinners will be shattered together, and those who forsake the Lord will come to an end. Surely you will be ashamed of the oaks which you have desired, and you will be embarrassed at the gardens which you have chosen. For you will be

---

126. Miller, *Daniel*, 323.

like an oak whose leaf fades away or as a garden that has no water. The strong man will become tinder, his work also a spark. Thus they shall both burn together and there will be none to quench them. (Isa. 1:21–31)

The idea is that God will bring judgment on Israel. Although this may initially have been a reference to the invasion of the Assyrians who scattered the northern nation of Israel and to the Babylonians who took the two tribes of the south into exile, these events were foreshadows of the ultimate judgment upon the people "in order to refine, purge and make them pure until the end time" (Dan. 11:35). God will bring Israel to a point that they will "Stop trusting in men, whose life's breath is in their nostrils" (Isa. 2:21).

Concealed and Sealed

8—   "And I heard but I understood not; and I said, 'My lord, what the after these *things?*'"

9—   "He said, 'Go, Daniel, for these words are concealed and sealed up until time of end.'"

Although most commentators held the view that the concealing of the words and the sealing of the book stated in verse 4 meant to preserve rather than keep secret, the statement in verses 8 and 9 seems to belie that understanding. Daniel states that he did not understand what he heard, so he asked, "My lord, what the after these *things?*" (אֲדֹנִי מָה אַחֲרִית אֵלֶּה, *ᵃham̂ m̂od helle᾿ ᵕ̄rᵉha᾿*). The response to Daniel seems to indicate that Daniel did not understand because the words were concealed from him and sealed up so that he could not access the words. The angel said, "Go, Daniel, for these words are concealed [סְתֻמִים, *m̂umutᵉs*] and sealed up [וַחֲתֻמִים, *m̂umutᵉhaw*] until time of end." These are the same two words used in verse 4. There is a difference in this verse, however. Whereas in verse 4 the command was to "conceal the words and seal up the book," verse 9 is not a command, it is, rather, a statement, and the statement is that the words are both concealed and sealed up. It is as if the command that was given to Daniel in verse 4 has been fulfilled by the time we get to verse 9.

Table 79: Comparison of Daniel 12:4 and 12:9

v. 4	"conceal the words and seal up the book until time of end."	סְתֹם הַדְּבָרִים וַחֲתֹם הַסֵּפֶר עַד־עֵת קֵץ
v. 9	"these words are concealed and sealed up until time of end."	סְתֻמִים וַחֲתֻמִים הַדְּבָרִים עַד־עֵת קֵץ׃

Miller holds that verse 9 is also referring to the preservation of the prophecy: "This is not a rebuke . . . but simply indicates that the prophet should go on about his life and not be concerned about his lack of knowledge because the vision related to the far distant future. Yet Daniel was assured that these prophecies would be preserved ('closed up and sealed'; cf. v. 4) for those who will need them, that is, the persons who live at 'the time of the end.'"[127] Wood holds to a view quite similar to that of Miller. He says,

> *Words are preserved and sealed*: The words of this element were used in verse four, showing an intentional reference back to it. The thought is that because the information Daniel had received is securely preserved and sealed, Daniel did not need to be concerned regarding his inquiry. These are words of both comfort and rebuke. The comfort consists in the fact that Daniel did not need to worry, since the events involved were far in the future; and, further, he could know that, since the information he had would be faithfully preserved, those who would then live, whose welfare might otherwise have been a matter of anxiety for him, would have it and be able to profit accordingly. Implied is the fact also, that further information, such as that for which Daniel had just asked, would be available for them by that time, and in the book of Revelation this has been revealed, as we now know. The rebuke consists in the fact that Daniel should not have asked for this information, which really was only for the satisfaction of his curiosity. He did not need to know all these matters at the time he lived, and he should have rested content in what God Himself had seen appropriate to relate. So often today, too, Christians want to know more details regarding some doctrine, especially concerning the last things, than God has revealed in His Word; but they also should rest content with what God has chosen to make clear.[128]

However, the statement by the angel that the words are concealed and sealed up does not seem to be simply a word of assurance, as Wood claims.

127. Ibid., 324.
128. Wood, *Daniel*, 325.

Daniel does not seem to be worried about whether the words will be preserved. Rather, he seems to be concerned because he does not understand.
Also, whereas Wood asserts that the statement of the angel is a rebuke—"The
rebuke consists in the fact that Daniel should not have asked for this information, which really was only for the satisfaction of his curiosity"—most other
commentaries assert emphatically that this was not a rebuke, and Daniel was
not seeking to satisfy his curiosity. Additionally, there seems to be a causal
relation between Daniel not understanding and the fact that the words are
concealed and sealed. The word "for" (בִּי, *ik*) can indicate a causal relation, as
KBH indicates. In fact, it is so used in Gen 3:14:[129]

Table 80: בִּי as Causal in Genesis 3:14

> "The Lord God said to the serpent, 'Because [בִּי, *ik*] you have done
> this, cursed are you more than all cattle, and more than every beast of
> the field; On your belly you will go, and dust you will eat all the days
> of your life;"

Gen 3:14

וַיֹּאמֶר יְהוָה אֱלֹהִים אֶל־הַנָּחָשׁ כִּי עָשִׂיתָ
זֹּאת אָרוּר אַתָּה מִכָּל־הַבְּהֵמָה וּמִכֹּל
חַיַּת הַשָּׂדֶה עַל־גְּחֹנְךָ תֵלֵךְ וְעָפָר תֹּאכַל
כָּל־יְמֵי חַיֶּיךָ:

In Gen 3:14 בִּי (*ik*) is translated "because." There seems to be good
reason to translate it this way in 12:9: "Go, Daniel, because these words are
concealed and sealed up until time of end.'" If the concealing and sealing of
the words merely meant that they were preserved, this does not seem to be a
cause for Daniel going his way, as Miller puts it. Lucas states, "The messenger
begins by making clear that no further revelation is going to be given. He
then more or less recapitulates what has been said in 11:32–35. Because the
revelation is 'sealed,' true understanding is available only to 'the wise.' It is
not available to 'the wicked.'"[130] But Lucas' position on this statement sounds
contrary to the way he took almost the same statement in verse 4: "The verb
used here (*stm*) is used more in keeping something safe than of keeping it
secret."[131] If the words are merely in safe keeping, and there is nothing here
indicating keeping them secret, then why the statement about the wise understanding and the wicked not? Whereas Walvoord's position regarding the

129. KBH, s.v. "כִּי."
130. Lucas, *Daniel*, 297.
131. Ibid., 221.

statement in verse 4 was somewhat unclear, he seems to be more precise in his comment on verse 9: "In verse 9, Daniel is once again informed that the revelation given to him will not be completely understood until the time of the end. . . . The primary purpose of the revelation, however, was to inform those who would live in the time of the end. The confirming interpretation of history and prophecy fulfilled would be necessary before the final prophecies could be understood."[132] By putting it this way, Walvoord is implying, either intentionally or unintentionally, that the time he is writing his commentary is the very "time of the end" to which the angel referred, evidenced by his assumption that he has understood the prophecies.

Young argues that only some of the prophecies were concealed: "God wished some of His predictions to be partially understood, and the rest to remain concealed until the full period of the complete revelation should arrive" (Calvin).[133] By citing Calvin as holding this view, does this not also imply that Calvin understood these prophecies, and if so, does this not imply that the "time of the end" was in the time of Calvin as well? Young goes on to assert, "*Go!*]—i.e., inquire no further, leave this matter alone. The reason for this command is stated in the fact that the words are preserved in security against destruction so that they may be read and understood at the time of their fulfillment. It is not necessary that Dan. himself should understand the answer to this question, for it does not have immediate application to him. There will come a time, however, when the words are needed and then they will be understood. Therefore, they are shut up and sealed until the time of the end."[134] Here again this seems to imply, whether Young intended this or not, that the time Young is writing his commentary is the time of the end when these prophecies are needed. Yet this does not seem to be that time, since that time is characterized by unprecedented persecution and disaster. Either Young and Walvoord must admit that they do not understand either, since the words are sealed until the time of the end, or the time of the end was/is the time of their writing.

When Daniel asks his question, he seems to be asking something specific, not simply for a clarification concerning the prophecy. The NASBU translates Daniel's question as, "what *will be* the outcome of these *events*?" The KJV gives the following translation: "what *shall be* the end of these *things*?" The NET Bible translates the question as, "what will happen after these things?" The Hebrew text reads, מָה אַחֲרִית אֵלֶּה, *helle' 'tur*ᵃ*ha' ham*), lit. "what after these?" The NET Bible seems to have captured the sense of this phrase. Daniel

---

132. Walvoord, *Daniel*, 294.

133. Young, *Prophecy of Daniel*, 260.

134. Ibid.

does not seem to be asking for clarification about the prophecy already given, but about what will happen after the events just described. If this is correct, then what is sealed and shut up may not be the words of the prophecy, but the information that Daniel was seeking, namely, what will happen after these events. Daniel does not seem to be asking simply to satisfy his curiosity, but the foreboding nature of the prophecy provokes Daniel to inquire what the outcome of these disasters will be. But the angel informs Daniel that this information is not for him, but is for the time of the end. This may be a hint about the further revelation given in the NT, particularly the book of Revelation. If the time of the end is referring to a period of time roughly coincident with the "latter days," as Culver seems to argue, then, as Peter announced, the latter days began at Pentecost, and the book of Revelation provides the very information that Daniel sought to know, namely, what will happen after the time of Jacob's trouble.

Purging, Purifying, and Refining

10—   "Many will be purged, purified, and refined, but the wicked will act wickedly; and none of the wicked will understand, but those who have insight will understand."

Wood points out that the verbs here parallel the verbs used in 11:35.

Table 81: "Purge," "Refine," and "Make Pure"

Dan 11:35	"Some of those who have insight will fall, in order to refine [לִצְרוֹף, *liṣrôf*], purge [וּלְבָרֵר, *ûləḇārēr*] and make them pure [וְלַלְבֵּן, *wᵉnēḇlal*] until the end time; because it is still to come at the appointed time.
	וּמִן־הַמַּשְׂכִּילִים יִכָּשְׁלוּ לִצְרוֹף בָּהֶם וּלְבָרֵר וְלַלְבֵּן עַד־עֵת קֵץ כִּי־עוֹד לַמּוֹעֵד׃
Dan 12:10	"Many will be purged [יִתְבָּרֲרוּ, *raḇtiyᵃur*], purified [וְיִתְלַבְּנוּ, *wᵉbbaltiyᵉun*], and refined [וְיִצָּרְפוּ, *wᵉufraṣṣiy*], but the wicked will act wickedly; and none of the wicked will understand, but those who have insight will understand."
	יִתְבָּרֲרוּ וְיִתְלַבְּנוּ וְיִצָּרְפוּ רַבִּים וְהִרְשִׁיעוּ רְשָׁעִים וְלֹא יָבִינוּ כָּל־רְשָׁעִים וְהַמַּשְׂכִּלִים יָבִינוּ׃

Although the word order is different—refine, purge, and make pure—purge, make pure, refine—and the forms of the verbs are different—in 11:35 the words are all infinitives, while in 12:10 they are all finite verbs in the Hithpael form—the two passages seem to be referring to comparable events. In fact, Wood goes on to state, ". . . many Jews will experience being 'cleansed,' 'made white,' and 'refined'; and, since he employed the same verbs as are used in 11:35, it is clear that he intentionally paralleled this development with that of Antiochus' day. As many Jews then were 'cleansed,' 'made white,' and 'refined,' for a new and more devoted walk before God, so will this be true of Jews in the last days to come (Zech. 13:8, 9)."[135]

If, as Wood asserts, the two events are comparable, it seems to indicate that these Jews are refined for a "more devoted walk before God" by severe persecution. In 11:35 these Jews "fall" (יִכָּשְׁל֖וּ, *uⁱsakkiy*) in order to be refined. The word translated "fall" can indicate physical stumbling as a result of some force. Also, if this association is deliberate on the part of the angel, then this implies that the interpreter should see the career of Antiochus as illustrative of the career of this evil king who will persecute the Jews at the time of the end.

Walvoord declares that, ". . . the prophet [Daniel] is informed in verse 10 that the time of the end will have a two fold result: first, it will result in the purification of the saints; second, it will manifest the true character of the wickedness of the human heart. Likewise, understanding the events of the time of the end will be possible for 'the wise' who 'shall understand,' but 'none of the wicked shall understand.'"[136] Miller adds an interesting observation: "Wicked persons will continue in their sin till the end, never discerning the signs of the times or the spiritual truths God has revealed. There seems to be little room here for the prospect held out by some that the world will turn to the Christian gospel and thereby bring in the kingdom of God upon the earth (postmillennialism)."[137] Of course Miller's observation is predicated on his identification of the time when these actions are occurring. If in fact they are prophesied as taking place at the end of the age—a yet future time according to the Futurist scheme—then his analysis is pertinent. Postmillennialists would, however, dispute the conclusion that these events are yet to occur. Notwithstanding the assertions of the Postmillennialists, the text thus far seems to support Miller's contention and conclusions.

135. Wood, *Daniel*, 326.

136. Walvoord, *Daniel*, 294.

137. Miller, *Daniel*, 325.

Table 82: Words for Offering in Daniel and Josephus

Word	הַתָּמִיד	ἐνδελεχισμοῦ	δῶρον θυσίαν
Refers to	continual burnt offering	continual burnt offering	daily sacrifice for Caesar
Dan 12:11 HB	•		
Dan 12:11 LXX		•	
Josephus, *Antiquities*		•	
Josephus, *Wars*			•

One Thousand, Two Hundred, Ninety Days

11— "From the time that the regular sacrifice is abolished and the abomination of desolation is set up, there will be 1,290 days."

12— "How blessed is he who keeps waiting and attains to the 1,335 days!

Following John Noë, Evans holds that the abolishing of the regular sacrifice refers to the "ending of the sacrifices for Caesar within the Temple complex, which occurred in the summer of 66, rather than the ending of the traditional Jewish sacrifices in the Temple in the summer of 70."[138] Noë, while discussing these events, says, "Next, they massacred a garrison of Roman soldiers. And to top it off, they stopped performing the twice-daily Temple sacrifices for Caesar and the Roman people. Josephus states that this cessation of the daily sacrifice was the true beginning of the Roman-Jewish War."[139] Noë refers to Josephus, but he does not give any specific references to any passages in Josephus' writings. Josephus actually describes these events in *The Wars of the Jews*, II.17.2. He does refer to the gifts and sacrifices offered in behalf of the Emperor, but he does not state that there was a twice-daily sacrifice for Caesar. Josephus says,

> And at this time it was that some of those that principally excited the people to go to war, made an assault upon a certain fortress called Masada. They took it by treachery and slew the Romans

138. Evans, *Four Kingdoms*, 293.

139. Noë, *Beyond the End Times*, 94.

that were there, and put others of their own party to keep it. At the same time Eleazar, the sons of Ananias the high priest, a very bold youth, who was at that time governor of the temple, persuaded those that officiated in the divine service to receive no gift or sacrifice [δῶρον ἢ θυσις̔αν] for any foreigner. And this was the true beginning of our war with the Romans; for they rejected the sacrifice of Caesar on this account; and when many of the high priests and principal men besought them not to omit the sacrifice which it was customary for them to offer for their princes, they would not be prevailed upon. These relied much upon their multitude, for the most flourishing part of the innovators assisted them, but they had the chief regard to Eleazar, the governor of the temple.[140]

That Josephus is referring to the sacrifices offered by the Jews in behalf of the Emperor seems to be clear. Schäfer holds this to be Josephus' meaning also: "The Zealots captured Masada (under the leadership of Menaham, son of Judas the Galilean), while in Jerusalem the Temple Captain (*segan*) Eleazar, son of Ananias the High Priest, ordered the suspension of the daily sacrifices for the emperor. This was the decisive act of the rebellion and constituted an official breach in relations between the Jerusalem religious community and their Roman overlords."[141] Noē seems to be saying that the sacrifice, in 12:11, that is said to be "abolished" is not a reference to the Jewish sacrifices, but is in fact referring to the sacrifices offered in behalf of Caesar. Evans takes this to be Noē's meaning also when he says, ". . . the sacrifices for Caesar within the Temple complex . . . rather than the ending of the traditional Jewish sacrifices in the temple . . ."[142]

However, Noē and Evans have incorrectly associated the actions reported by Josephus with the reference in Dan 12:11. The expression in 12:11, "regular sacrifice" הַתָּמִיד *(dīmatah)*, occurs also in Dan 8:11, 12, 13; 11:31,

---

140. Flavius Josephus, *The Wars of the Jews*, in *The Works of Josephus*, trans. William Whiston (Peabody, Massachusetts: Hendrickson, 1996), 2.17.2.408–10. Κἂν τούτῳ τινὲς τῶν μάλιστα κινούντων τὸν πόλεμον συνελθόντες ὥρμησαν ἐπὶ φρούριόν τι καλούμενον Μασάδαν, καὶ καταλαβόντες αὐτὸ λάθρα τοὺς μὲν Ῥωμαίων φρουροὺς ἀπέσφαξαν, ἑτέρους δ᾽ ἐγκατέστησαν ἰδίους. ἅμα δὲ καὶ κατὰ τὸ ἱερὸν Ἐλεάζαρος υἱὸς Ἀνανία τοῦ ἀρχιερέως, νεανίας θρασύτατος, στρατηγῶν τότε τοὺς κατὰ τὴν λατείαν λειτουργοῦντας ἀναπείθει μηδενὸς ἀλλοτρίου δῶρον ἢ θυσίαν προσδέχεσθαι. τοῦτο δ᾽ ἦν τοῦ πρὸς Ῥωμαίους πολέμου καταβολή· τὴν γὰρ ὑπὲρ τούτων θυσίαν καὶ Καίσαρος ἀπέρριψαν. καὶ πολλὰ τῶν τε ἀρχιερέ ων καὶ τῶν γνωρίμων παρακαλούντων μὴ παραλιπεῖν τὸ ὑπὲρ τῶν ἡγεμόνων ἔθος οὐκ ἐνέδοσαν.

141. Schäfer, *The History of the Jews*, 121.

142. Evans, *Four Kingdoms*, 293.

and here in 12:11. It is important to note that this form has the definite article, "the continual *offering*." In this form it occurs only 19 times outside of Daniel. Of the 19 times it occurs, 16 are rendered "continual burnt offering," 2 are rendered "continual grain offering," and 1 is rendered "continual bread" (see Table 83 below). In the 4 times the form is used in Daniel outside of chapter 12, each time it is rendered "regular sacrifice" and is a reference to the Jewish sacrifices according to the Mosaic law. The text of θ uses the word ἐνδελεχισμοῦ (*uomsiceledne*), to translate the Hebrew, while Josephus uses the terms δῶρον (*norod*, "gift") and θυσίαν (*naisuht*, "sacrifice") in his description. According to Liddell and Scott, ἐνδελέχισμός means "*persistence*" and is used "esp. of daily sacrifices."[143] In fact, this word is used by Josephus in *Antiquities of the Jews*: "They also celebrated the festival of Tabernacles at that time, in the manner which the lawgiver had ordained, and after that they brought the offerings and the so-called continual burnt-offerings [ἐνδελέ χισμούς, *suomsiceledne*] and the sacrifices of the sabbaths and all the sacred festivals."[144] Here Josephus clearly uses the term to refer to the Jewish sacrifices, and the fact that he uses the term θυσίας (*saisuht*) to refer to the "sacrifices of the sabbaths," and earlier in this context to refer to the "customary sacrifices to God" (νομίμους θυσίας τῷ θεῷ, *oehī̄ ot saisuht suomimon*), indicates that he understands θυσίας (*saisuht*) to be a more general term, and ἐνδελέ χισμούς (*suomsiceledne*) to be specifically referring to the "continual burnt-offerings" ordained by "the lawgiver," namely, Moses. Even Evans takes this meaning in the other places in Daniel. In other words, Josephus makes it clear that the action in AD 66 was the cessation of the offerings in behalf of Caesar, whereas the action referred to in Dan 12:11 is the regular sacrifice offered by the Jews according to the Mosaic law. There is no justification for taking the 12:11 statement to refer to sacrifices offered to Caesar. The only motivation for such a claim is the effort to make the text fit their eschatological scheme.

143. *A Greek-English Lexicon* (1968), s.v. "ἐνδελέχ-εια."

144. Josephus, *Jewish Antiquities*, 11.4.1. ἤγαγον δὲ καὶ τὴν σκηνοπηγίαν κατ' ἐκεῖνον τὸν καιρὸν ὡς ὁ νομοθέτης περὶ αὐτῆς διετάξατο, καὶ προσφορὰς μετὰ ταῦτα καὶ τοὺς καλουμένους ἐδελεχισμοὺς καὶ τὰς θυσίας τῶν σαββάτων καὶ πασῶν τῶν ἁγίων ἑορτῶν...

Table 83: הַתָּמִיד _(dimatah)_ "The Continual"

	"Continual Burnt Offering"	"Continual Grain Offering"	Other
1	Num 28:10	Num 4:16	"continual bread" Num 4:7
2	Num 28:16	Neh 10:34	"regular sacrifice" Dan 8:11
3	Num 28:23		"regular sacrifice" Dan 8:12
4	Num 28:24		"regular sacrifice" Dan 8:13
5	Num 28:31		"regular sacrifice" Dan 11:31
6	Num 29:6		
7	Num 29:11		
8	Num 29:16		
9	Num 29:19		
10	Num 29:22		
11	Num 29:25		
12	Num 29:28		
13	Num 29:31		
14	Num 29:34		
15	Num 29:38		
16	Neh 10:34		

In his argument to separate the events referred to in 11:31 and 12:11, Evans criticizes the Futurists for proposing that 11:31 is a type of which 12:11 refers to the fulfillment. He says, "Although it is arguable that 11:31 is a prophetic type that duplicates features of 12:11, this does not necessarily mean that the former has a *dual fulfillment*."[145] He goes on to argue, "Perhaps a prophecy can have a dual fulfillment, but invoking that concept without a clear scriptural warrant for doing so is a dangerous procedure that can too readily be used to explain one's way out of an exegetical corner into which he has painted himself."[146] But Evans has done precisely that by proposing that the reference to the regular sacrifice refers to the sacrifice to Caesar. Not only is there no "clear scriptural warrant," there is no warrant of any kind to suggest this. Evans' maneuver is precisely to extricate himself from the exegetical corner into which the Preterist view has painted him. In fact, Evans as much

145. Evans, *Four Kingdoms*, 290.
146. Ibid.

as declares that this is his methodology: "Fitting 12:11–12 into a preterist framework requires that verse 11 be understood as allowing the abolition of the daily sacrifice to precede the abomination that causes desolation by 1,290 days instead of having the two events occur simultaneously, or almost simultaneously."[147]

Evans argues for the separation of the abolishing of the daily sacrifice and the setting up of the abomination of desolation by a period of 1,290 days, or 3 years of 360 days each, and 7 months of 30 days each. He argues,

> From the preterist perspective, it would be wonderful if the language of 12:11 explicitly stated that one event follows the other, but it does not. On the other hand, neither does it say unambiguously that both events occur at the start of the 1,290 days. Look again at that verse: "From the time that the daily sacrifice is abolished and the abomination that causes desolation is set up, there will 1,290 days." Although this seems to imply that both events precede the 1,290 days, again one must ask, "1,290 days until what?" Critical-historical scholars say the answer is 1,290 days until the time of the end that was supposed to take place early in 163 BC. If that interpretation must he rejected, the path is clear for concluding that the 1,290 days are the time between the abolition of the daily sacrifice and the setting up of the abomination that causes desolation.[148]

In this instance, Evans' argument seems to be supported by the language of the text. The text is set out below with a literal, word-for-word translation.

Table 84: Daniel 12:11

הַתָּמִיד	הוּסַר	וּמֵעֵת
the regular sacrifice	is abolished	And from the time
שֹׁמֵם	שִׁקּוּץ	וְלָתֵת
making desolate	abomination	and to set

---

147. Ibid.
148. Ibid., 290–91.

מָאתַיִם	אֶלֶף	יָמִים
two hunderd	one thousand	days

וְתִשְׁעִים:

and ninety.

The important word is the word translated "and to set" (וְלָתֵת, *tetal'w*). This is an infinitive construct with the inseparable preposition לְ (*'l*), which can certainly have the sense of a movement toward. As Waltke-O'Connor state, "The *temporal* uses of *l* include a sense like the simple location (*in*, *at*, or *during* a period of time; ##5–7) and a sense like the terminative (*to*, *by*, or *after* a period of time, ##8–11)."[149] An example of this use given by Waltke-O'Connor is Deut 16:4, which they translate, "None of the flesh . . . shall remain *until* morning."[150] Here the sentence could be translated, "And from the time that the regular sacrifice is abolished *until* the abomination of desolation is set up . . ."

But, as Evans acknowledges, the text is not absolutely clear in this statement, and there are other functions of the *lamed* preposition. Another function of the terminative use is to indicate the *terminus ad quem* of an event. One example Waltke-O'Connor give is Gen 8:11.[151] The Hebrew structure of this passage is וַתָּבֹא . . . הַיּוֹנָה לְעֵת עֶרֶב, *(te'l hañoyyah . . . 'obataw _bere')*, "The dove came . . . *at the time of* evening." So, the text could be saying, "And from the time that the regular sacrifice is abolished *at the time that* the abomination of desolation is set up . . ." indicating that these two events happen almost simultaneously. Because the text is ambiguous on this point, it is necessary to consider other factors, particularly the historical events, to see whether the history fits into what the text asserts, rather than attempting to fit the text to the history we have already chosen.

Evans declares, "My position is that the Crucifixion rendered Jewish religious rituals obsolete in the eyes of God. This very point is implied by Matthew 27:51, where we read that when Jesus 'gave up his spirit' on the cross (v. 50), 'At that moment the curtain of the temple was torn in two from top to bottom.' The temple itself had become an idol, and the sacrificial system had degenerated into a form of idol worship. That being the case, although the daily sacrifice to which Daniel 12:11 refers was at the Temple, it could

149. Waltke, *Biblical Hebrew Syntax*, §11.2.10.c.
150. Ibid., #11.
151. Ibid., #6.

have been pagan as well as Jewish."[152] The absurdity of this kind of assertion requires no response. There is absolutely no biblical or historical support for such claims. They are conjured up in order to make the Preterist view sound reasonable, but they actually depict the view as unhistorical and unbiblical. Evans may not be typical of Preterist views on this point, but these kinds of assertions serve to diminish the view as a whole. The text says absolutely nothing about the Temple sacrifices becoming equivalent to pagan worship or whether it was rendered obsolete in the eyes of God. These are all impositions upon the text that are necessary for Evans who is "Fitting 12:11–12 into a preterist framework . . ." by any means possible.[153]

Since historically the abolishing of the daily sacrifice occurred almost simultaneously with the abominable acts of Antiochus IV that caused the holy place to become desolate, Evans must attempt to re-define the term "regular sacrifice" to indicate some other event in order to make it fit into his predetermined scheme. But, as we have seen, there is no "clear scriptural warrant" (Evans' own criterion) for attempting this re-definition.

What is an Abomination that Causes Desolation?

Preterist View

Again following John Noē, Evans holds that the abomination of desolation is the "factional fighting among Jews at the site of the Temple, which made a mockery of its religious function . . ."[154] Unfortunately for Noē and Evans, there is no "clear scriptural warrant," to employ Evans' criterion, nor is there any historical evidence to support the claim that an abomination consisted of factional fighting among the Jews. Of the 28 times this word 'abomination' (שִׁקּוּץ, šuqqîs) is used in the OT, 25 of them occur outside of the book of Daniel, and as TWOT points out, "This noun is always used in connection with idolatrous practices, either referring to the idols themselves as being abhorrent and detestable in God's sight, or to something associated with idolatrous ritual."[155] In fact, Evans quotes Noē's definition of the term 'abomination' which is very much like the definition from TWOT: "'In Jewish terminology,' Noē writes, 'an "abomination" was anything that involved the worship of false gods or the false worship of their God in sacred places.'"[156]

---

152. Evans, *Four Kingdoms*, 293.

153. Ibid., 290.

154. Ibid., 292.

155. TWOT, s.v. "שֶׁקֶץ."

156. Ibid.

The problem is that factional fighting hardly constitutes idolatrous worship or something associated with idolatrous rituals.

If Antiochus Epiphanes is a type of the Antichrist, then his actions indicate the kinds of acts of Antichrist. As TWOT point out, "Antiochus Epiphanes, as prophesied in Dan 11:31 . . . set up an altar to, and image of, Zeus in the temple. This is called the 'abomination that causes desolation,' a desecration of the altar which destroys its true purpose."[157] Noë's own definition quoted by Evans and the one given by TWOT argue against the notion that the abomination had anything to do with factional fighting.

Shepherd deals with the abomination of desolation in his discussion of chapter 9 and the seventy sevens of Daniel. He says, "The event marking the midpoint of the last week confirms that the Seventy Weeks Prophecy finds literal fulfillment in the second century B.C. Daniel's author says that for half of the week the 'sacrifice and offering' will stop. . . . Unmistakably this is a reference to the period of Jewish persecution (167–164 B.C.) when Antiochus outlawed Judaism and defiled the sanctuary. . . . In place of the Jewish sacrifices, Antiochus placed the infamous 'abomination that desolates.' This phrase, also known as the 'abomination of desolation,' is a direct reference to pagan sacrifices that defiled the Temple in December 167 B.C. According to I Maccabees, the abominable act occurred as 'they offered sacrifice on the altar which was upon the altar of burnt offering' (I Maccabees 1:59)."[158] It is not difficult to show the error of this conclusion. In Matthew's Gospel, Jesus spoke of the abomination of desolation as an event that was yet future from His perspective: "Therefore when you see the abomination of desolation which was spoken of through Daniel the prophet, standing in the holy place (let the reader understand) . . . For then there will be a great tribulation, such as has not occurred since the beginning of the world until now, nor ever will" (Matt 24:15, 21).[159] Consequently, since Jesus spoke of this as yet future, it is not possible that Daniel's prophecy, either in 9:27 or 12:11 could be a reference to the actions of Antiochus Epiphanes.

Futurist View

Pentecost argues that the abomination of desolation is the erecting of an image on the altar in the temple. This conclusion comes, according to Pentecost,

---

157. Ibid.

158. Shepherd, *Beasts, Horns, and the Antichrist*, 102–3.

159. ῞Οταν οὖν ἴδητε τὸ βδέλυγμα τῆς ἐρημώσεως τὸ ῥηθὲν διὰ Δανιὴλ τοῦ προφήτου ἑστὸς ἐν τόπῳ, ὁ ἀναγινώσκων νοείτω . . . ἔσται γὰρ τότε θλῖψις μεγάλη οἵα οὐ γέγονεν ἀπ᾽ ἀρχῆς κόσμου ἕως τοῦ νῦν οὐδ᾽ οὐ μὴ γένηται. (Matt 24:15, 21).

from the typological act of Antiochus Epiphanes who, "erected on December 16, 167 B.C. an altar to Zeus on the altar of burnt offering outside the temple, and had a pig offered on the altar."[160] Pentecost goes on to argue,

> The angel said that 1,290 days will be measured off from the time that the daily sacrifice is abolished (cf. 9:27, "he will put an end to sacrifice") and the abomination that causes desolation is set up (cf. 9:27, "one who causes desolation will place abominations on a wing of the temple"). The last half of the 70th "seven" of years is "a time, times, and half a time" (7:25; Rev. 12:14), which is three and one-half years. It is also designated as 42 months (Rev. 11:2) or 1,260 days (Rev. 11:3). How then can the variance of 30 days (1,290 compared with 1,260) be explained? Some suggest that the 30 days will extend beyond the end of the Tribulation, allowing for the judgment of Israel and the judgment of the nations. Another possibility is that the 1,290 days will begin 30 days before the middle of the 70th "seven" of years when the world ruler will set up "the abomination that causes desolation" (Matt. 24:15). The 1,290 days could begin with an announcement (about the abomination) made 30 days before the abomination is introduced. This abomination, as stated earlier, will be an image of himself (Rev. 13:14–15) and will be symbol of this religious system.[161]

Miller states, "Jesus spoke of this 'abomination' (Matt 24:25) and indicated that it would be placed in the 'holy place' (temple) immediately before his return. Antiochus IV also erected an 'abomination that causes desolation' (cf. 11:31), which was an altar or statue of Zeus. The exact nature of the Antichrist's 'abomination' is unclear, but its presence in the temple will cause believers to cease worshiping there and thus render the temple desolate, that is, empty of worshipers."[162] Whereas Pentecost holds that the abomination of desolation will be the construction of an image of Antichrist in the temple, Miller believes that the description is not specific enough to make a statement about precisely what the act will entail.

Walvoord seems to hold yet a different view. He says,

> The time that the daily sacrifice is taken away is equated with "the abomination that maketh desolate." This expression originating in the revelation of Daniel 9:27 has reference to the stopping of sacrifices in the middle of the seven-year period. The predicted event had its corresponding anticipation in the desolation of the

160. Pentecost, *Daniel*, 1370.

161. Ibid., 1374.

162. Miller, *Daniel*, 325.

temple by Antiochus Epiphanes in the second century B.C. (Dan 8:11–14). That this event is future and not a reference to the historic desecration by Antiochus is apparent from the prophecy of Christ in Matthew 24:15 where "the abomination of desolation, spoken of by Daniel the prophet," is given as a sign of the great tribulation.[163]

Walvoord is not definitive in his statement about precisely of what the abomination consists, but earlier in his commentary he expressly stated that the abomination was the cessation of the daily sacrifice: "The word *abomination* used by Christ in Matthew 24:15 may be an allusion to Antiochus in Daniel 11:31, but in Daniel 12:11, it clearly refers to the future stopping of the daily sacrifices, forty-two months before the second advent of Christ."[164] Futurists disagree on precisely what this act entails, but they are agreed that it will occur at the mid-point of the tribulation, initiating, in a sense, the time of the Great Tribulation, or the Time of Jacob's Trouble.

What are the 1,290 Days?

Precisely to what the angel is referring when making the statement about 1,290 days has been another point of controversy. As before, we will consider the Preterist views and the Futurist views in turn.

Preterist Views

Evans basically adopts the view proposed by John Noë. He asserts, "Noë's explanation of how the time prophecies of Daniel 12 should be interpreted is the most plausible one I have seen. No other explanation with which I am familiar has succeeded to such an extent in tying the 1,290 and 1,335 days to historically verifiable events."[165] Noë starts his explanation of these time periods with the following observation: "In his last vision, Daniel sees two others (angels) standing on the bank of a river and talking. One asks the other, 'How long will it be before these astonishing things are fulfilled?' (Da. 12:6b). The asking of this time question subsequent to Daniel receiving his 70 week prophecy strongly suggests that the events of this fulfillment were not included in that previous time period."[166] We have already dealt with this part of Noë's assertion in our exegesis of chapter 9, but our comments there

---

163. Walvoord, *Daniel*, 294–95.
164. Ibid., 236.
165. Evans, *Four Kingdoms*, 295.
166. Noë, *Beyond the End Times*, 92.

bear repeating. The prophecy of chapter 7 was received after the prophecy of chapter 2, but that does not mean it was "not included in that previous time period." The prophecy of chapter 8 was received after the prophecy of chapter 7, but this does not mean it was not included in that previous time period. The abomination of desolation talked about in chapter 11 was received after the prophecy of the abomination of desolation prophesied in chapter 9, but Noë takes them as not only references to the same time period, but discussing the same event.[167] The only reason for making the assertion that the asking of this time question subsequent to Daniel receiving his 70 week prophecy strongly suggests that the events of this fulfillment were not included in that previous time period is to fit the text into the preconceived eschatological scheme.

Noë begins his calculations with the events which he claims took place in 66 AD, the most significant of which is the reference in Dan 12:11 to the "time that the daily sacrifice is abolished." We have already seen that Noë's understanding of the reference to daily sacrifice as the sacrifice of Caesar is not only an misunderstanding of Josephus, but also a misunderstanding of the text of Daniel (see page 662ff). Consequently, there is no event in 66 A.D. that corresponds to the abolishing of the daily sacrifice as Noë and Evans claim, and therefore Noë's calculations are completely erroneous.

Noë attempts to show that the 1,290 days refers to the time between 66 AD and AD 70 and the desolation of the Temple by the Jews themselves. Noë argues, "Early in the year of A.D. 70 (approximately—if not exactly—three years and six months, or 1,290 days, after the cessation of the twice-daily sacrifice for Caesar and Rome), Josephus reports that a major abomination that all in Jerusalem could see took place in the Temple. . . . There can be no doubt that the warring of the three Jewish factions inside the city walls (and particularly in the Temple area) was one of the many abominations and desolations spoken of by Daniel."[168] First of all, the 1,290 days is not equal to three years and six months as Noë implies, but is actually three years and seven months. This may seem a trivial difference, but the fact that Noë does not bother to make this distinction prejudices the reader to believe that these two quantities are equal and that his calculation supports Noë's assertions. The difference in the quantities is not explained by Noë. Second, the cessation of the daily sacrifice did not occur, as we have seen, at the time Noë assumes. Third, Noë offers no argumentation why the reader should accept his claim that the warring in the Temple is that to which Daniel referred in his prophecy. Fourth, the use of the plural, as we saw in chapter 9 (see page

167. See Ibid., 135.
168. Ibid., 95.

427ff), does not necessarily indicate a multiplicity of events. Also, even if we take the word as a quantitative plural, it does not necessarily indicate several separate events. Rather, the text seems to indicate that by extreme abominations, this one will make a desolation. In other words, there is one event, the abomination of desolation, which is composed of several abominations which constitute the desolation.

Table 85: The Wing of Abominations Making Desolate

מְשֹׁמֵם	שִׁקּוּצִים	כְּנַף	וְעַל
one causing desolation	abominations	wing of	and upon

The word translated "one causing desolation" (מְשֹׁמֵם, *memŏs^em*) is a masculine, singular participle. This participle is probably functioning as a substantival participle, and because it is singular, this implies that there is one individual who is causing the desolation, not separate groups of people.

Noē declares, "A strong argument can be made that the Jews brought the final desolation upon themselves."[169] He asserts, "The question of who destroyed Jerusalem has been equated with the age-old question of who crucified Christ?"[170] But, of course, this is the age-old practice of misdirection. The question of who crucified Christ is a different question from who actually carried out the physical act. The biblical text makes clear that certain Roman soldiers actually carried out the act of the physical crucifixion of Christ. This is a separate question than who was morally and spiritually responsible for the event. So also, there is no question that the Roman soldiers actually carried out the act of destroying the city and the sanctuary. That is a different question from who was morally and spiritually responsible for the whole problem in the first place. It is quite possible that the Jews were morally and spiritually responsible for the ultimate demise of the Temple, but it was the Romans who carried out the acts of destruction. The text does not state the case in terms of who is ultimately responsible. Rather, the text states that "one" will carry out the actual abomination causing desolation. This was not the Jews. But, in order to make the calculation fit, Noē must make the text fit his scheme. In support of his speculations, Noē comments, "When all the facts are known, the Jews were 'the people of the ruler [i.e., the people of Jesus, and not the Roman army under Titus' command or some future Antichrist ruler] who

169. Ibid.
170. Ibid., 95–96.

will come and destroy the city and the sanctuary' (Da. 9:26)."[171] But we have already shown in our exegesis of chapter 9 that this statement cannot refer to Jesus, but must be the Roman ruler. One error cannot be used to imply the truth of another.

Having shown that Noë's beginning point, AD 66, and his assertions concerning the 1,290 days are fallacious, his claims about the 1,335 days, which he deems to be the ending point, must also be rejected. Of Noë's time scheme Evans asserts, "Noë's explanation of how the time prophecies of Daniel 12 should be interpreted is the most plausible one I have seen. No other explanation with which I am familiar has succeeded to such an extent in tying the 1,290 and 1,335 days to historically verifiable events."[172] Assuming Evans to be familiar with the several Preterist views, we may conclude that no other Preterist has offered another scenario that rivals the one proposed by Noë. That being the case, we can dismiss all Preterist claims to have any reasonable account of the prophecies of Daniel chapter 12.

Futurist Views

Wood presents the following argumentation from a Futurist view.

> *From the time:* A period of 1,290 days is designated here, and the occasion which begins it is indicated; namely, the time when the regular ceremonies (same word, *āimat*, as is used in 11:31 and 8:11 [which see]) of the restored Jewish Temple will be taken away by the Antichrist and the abomination of desolation (altar and/or image of Jupiter [Zeus] Olympius, cf. 9:27) will be set up. This means the middle of the Tribulation week, as noted under 9:27 (which see). *A thousand two hundred and ninety days:* This is the length of the period in view, but the termination occasion is not indicated. One might assume that the termination point would be the cessation of the last half of the week, but this number of days is thirty too many to fit; and, moreover, verse seven has already given the length of that period as three and one-half years, or 1,260 days (figuring thirty-day months, as sustained by a comparison of verses six and fourteen of Revelation 12 and verses two and three of Revelation 11). The question must be asked as to the significance of the thirty additional days. . . . The right answer can only be in terms of literal days, which somehow concern the Tribulation week. A clue as to how they fit this week is found in Matthew 25:31–46, which describes a time of judgment by

---

171. Ibid., 95.

172. Evans, *Four Kingdoms*, 295.

Christ immediately after He comes in power at the close of this period. The purpose of the judgment is to determine those who will be permitted to enter into and enjoy the blessedness of the millennial period. The passage shows that those so honored will be only the people who have treated the Jews properly, and have thus demonstrated a true relation to Christ through personal salvation. But such an act of judgment will take a period of time for its accomplishment. The added thirty days in question would seem appropriate. The cessation point in view, then, for the full 1,290 days may be the completion of this time of judgment. Judging will begin, apparently, soon after the defeat of the Antichrist and could, indeed, continue for those thirty days.[173]

Walvoord takes a view quite similar to that of Wood. He holds that the 1,290 days, "actually forty-three months, seem to extend beyond the second advent to the beginning of the millennial kingdom."[174] Later he argues,

Although Daniel does not explain these varying durations, it is obvious that the second coming of Christ and the establishment of His millennial kingdom requires time. The 1,260 day period or precisely forty-two months of thirty days each, can be regarded as culminating with the second advent itself. This is followed by several divine judgments such as the judgment of the nations (Mt 25:31–46), and the regathering and judgment of Israel (Eze 20:34–38). These great judgments beginning with the living on earth and purging out of unbelievers who have worshiped the beast, although handled quickly, will require time. By the 1,335 days, or seventy-five days after the second advent, these great judgments will have been accomplished and the millennial kingdom formally launched. Those who attain to this period are obviously those who have been judged worthy to enter the kingdom. Hence, they are called "blessed."[175]

Wood and Walvoord are representative of Futurists in their understanding of the significance of the reference to the 1,290 days. Briefly, the Tribulation is the final seven years of Daniel's prophecy. The beginning is marked by the making of a covenant. The mid-point of this period marks the beginning of the calculation of days. The 1,260 days equals 3½ years. The 1,290 days, calculated from the mid-point of the Tribulation, extends beyond the 3½ year point by 30 days. This period is for the judgment of the nations described in Matt 25:31–46. One reason this is not explained in Daniel's prophecy may be

173. Wood, *Daniel*, 327–28.
174. Walvoord, *Daniel*, 236.
175. Ibid., 295–96.

because the angel has already told Daniel that the things that will occur "after these things" are sealed and will not be made known to Daniel. This information is then revealed by Christ in the Gospels, effectively unsealing that which was sealed—since He is the one worthy to break the seal.

What About the 1,335 Days?

We have seen that the Preterists make an unsuccessful attempt to relate these days to the destruction of Jerusalem. It is particularly telling that Noē relates the 1,335 days to the destruction of Jerusalem in 70 AD. He says, "Shortly before Passover in the spring of A.D. 70 (approximately— if not exactly—45 days following the previously-cited Temple desecration), Titus' Roman legions advanced toward Jerusalem from the Northwest through Samaria (the invader from the 'north' of Ezekiel 38 and 39)."[176] It is beyond peculiar that the text calls those who attains to the 1,335 days blessed (אַשְׁרֵי, 'ešra'), and yet Noē takes this to be the destruction of Jerusalem. He does not even attempt to explain how someone who attains to this date could be considered blessed—unless, of course, he wishes to apply this to the Roman soldiers.

In the previous quote from Walvoord we found that he made mention of the 1,335 days marking the end of the great judgments referred to in other passages. Wood has a slightly different take on that to which these days are referring.

> *A thousand three hundred and thirty-five days:* This figure is forty-five days longer than the one just considered and seventy-five more than the duration of the last half of the Tribulation week. What is the significance of the additional days this time? The idea of the preceding phrase, speaking of being "blessed," shows that whatever occasion falls at the conclusion of these days is something good and desirable. There will be blessing for those who attain to it. The thought is thus suggested that it will be the actual starting point of the Millennium. Those who will have passed the judgment of Christ, during the preceding thirty days, would be those who will attain to it, after these forty-five additional days. What will be the need of these forty-five days? It may be the time necessary for setting up the governmental machinery for carrying on the rule of Christ. The true and full border of Israel (from the River of Egypt to the Euphrates, Genesis 15:18) will have to be established, and appointments made of those aiding in the government. A period

176. Noē, *Beyond the End Times*, 96.

of forty-five days would again seem to be reasonable in which to accomplish these matters.[177]

Whereas Walvoord holds that the 1,335 days constitutes the time needed to complete the judgments, Wood holds that the 1,335 days constitutes the time needed to set up the Millennial Kingdom. Both hold that by the end of this time, the Millennial Kingdom will begin. The following chart depicts the basic progression of events from a Futurist perspective.

Figure 49: End Time Chart

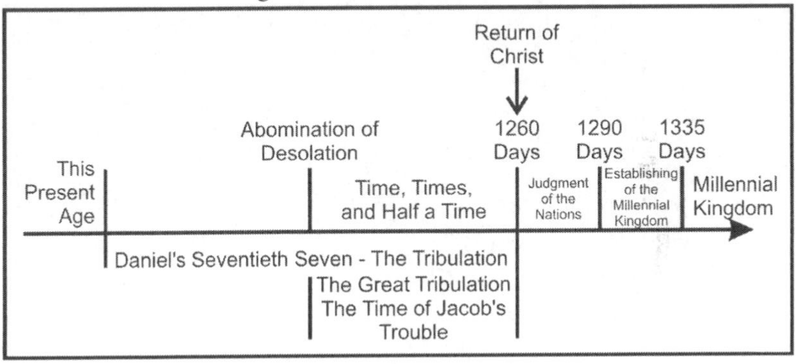

13—   "But as for you, go to the end; then you will enter into rest and rise again for your allotted portion at the end of the right hand."

The expression "go to the end" (לֵךְ לַקֵּץ, *šeqal ḳel*) probably indicates something like, "go on until the end," or "go your way to the end." Wood proposes that the meaning is "parallel with that of verse nine, giving the paraphrase, 'cease being anxious concerning these matters, Daniel, but be satisfied with what you do understand, for as long as you live.'"[178] Concerning this statement Walvoord asserts, "Anticipating that Daniel would not completely understand these additional revelations, the angel informs him, 'But go thou thy way till the end be.' The angel predicts that Daniel will 'rest,' that is, die, and 'stand in thy lot at the end of the days,' that is, be resurrected in the resurrection of Daniel 12:2 and participate in the glorious triumph of Christ as the Millennial kingdom is inaugurated."[179] Daniel will rest and rise again. As Pentecost points out, "Because of Daniel's faith in God he led a life of faithful service for Him, and for that faith and that obedience he will receive a

177. Wood, *Daniel*, 328–29.

178. Ibid., 329.

179. Walvoord, *Daniel*, 296.

glorious reward. All who like Daniel trust the Lord will share in the blessings of His millennial kingdom."[180]

---

180. Pentecost, *Daniel*, 1374.

14

Conclusion

Daniel in the Preterists' Den

Preterists hold a high view of Scripture, and they take the prophecies of Daniel quite seriously. Because they believe in the inerrancy of the text, they do not believe that it is legitimate to alter the wording of the text in order to make things fit a preconceived eschatological framework. They also believe that an interpreter ought to be consistent in the application of his hermeneutical principles. Preterists are committed to the truth of the Gospel of salvation by grace through faith, and many of them are diligent students and scholars. Some Preterists believe that most or all of Bible prophecy, especially the second coming of Christ, the resurrection, and the judgment, have been fulfilled in Christ and the expansion of His Kingdom throughout this age. What this means with reference to Daniel is that the events that are prophesied have all been fulfilled in the years leading up to and including the destruction of Jerusalem in 70 AD. This study of Daniel has demonstrated the inability of Preterism to explain the prophecies of Daniel in terms of the claims of Preterism. The primary failure of Preterism has been its unsuccessful attempts to relate Daniel's prophecies to the historical events of the period leading up to and including AD 70.

For example, Preterists attempt to explain the relationship between the statue in Nebuchadnezzar's dream and the events of history. Although Preterists and Futurists agree that the four metals represent the four world kingdoms, Babylon, Medo-Persia, Greece, and Rome, the Preterists fail to explain how the interpretation fits with their scheme. For example, Nebuchadnezzar's dream and Daniel's interpretation indicate that the final form of the Roman

Empire, represented by the feet and toes of the mixture of iron and clay, is struck by the stone that is cut out of the mountain without hands. When the stone strikes the statue, the entire statue is pulverized as one unit, and the residue is blown away without a trace left. This indicates that the establishing of the Kingdom of God will involve a sudden and catastrophic end to the world powers at the time. However, such an end did not occur in 70 AD. Rather, the Roman Empire continued to exist for at least another 400 years. Preterists try to explain this by claiming that the kingdom of God is spiritual and not earthly, and that the destruction of the Roman Empire is a gradual demise as the kingdom of God grows. These attempts simply do not fit with the description and interpretation of the dream by Daniel. Preterists' interpretations fail to account for the text as it stands.

Preterists have a particularly difficult time with the prophecy of the seventy sevens. Verse 24 states that the seventy sevens, or 490 years, is decreed upon the people of Israel and the city of Jerusalem. If follows that whatever the prophecy predicts about Jerusalem will occur within the 490 years that are decreed upon Jerusalem. Verse 26 of the prophecy clearly states that the end of the first two divisions of the 490 years decreed upon Israel and Jerusalem, the seven sevens and the sixty-two sevens, will be followed by the cutting off of Messiah and the destruction of the city and the sanctuary. Since the cutting off of Messiah occurred in either 30 or 33 AD, and the destruction of the city and the sanctuary did not occur until 70 AD, there is a span of almost 40 years that divide these two events, and there is only one seven-year week left in the 490 years that is decreed on Jerusalem in which to fit these events. Every attempt by Preterists somehow to include these events within the 490 years fails. For example, one Preterist commentator argues that it was not the actual destruction that was to occur within the 490 years. Rather, it was only the decree concerning Jerusalem's destruction that was to occur within the 490 years. Such attempts to reword the text violate their own claims of faithfulness to the text.

Also, verse 27 states, "he will make firm a covenant with the many for one seven." Preterists attempt to make this apply to Christ and the new covenant. However, these attempts fail also. Their attempts to make the chronology of the prophecy fit their eschatological framework range from rearranging the text to imposing upon the text characteristics that are properly applied to poetry. They sometimes ignore the principles of grammar and syntax and sometimes try to redefine these principles in order to make things work out in a way that will coincide with their system. Once again such tactics contradict their high view of Scripture.

Preterists attempt to make the ten horns of the fourth beast in Daniel seven coincide with the Roman Republic and the Roman Empire calculating from Pompey to Vespasian—Vespasian supposedly being the little horn. However, as we have shown, beginning the calculation with Pompey is arbitrary, and the attempts to related the actions of Vespasian to the descriptions of the actions of the little horn do not stand up to scrutiny. Preterists also try to relate the descriptions of the king in Dan. 11:36–45 to Herod the Great. As it is with every other attempt Preterists make, the correlation of the life of Herod with the prophetic descriptions fail miserably. Since, apart from Vespasian and Herod whose histories have been shown not to correspond to the prophetic descriptions, there are no other historical persons to whom these prophecies relate, the prophetic descriptions must relate to the future. Both Preterists and Futurists acknowledge the foundational nature of the prophecies of Daniel, and since the Preterists' schemes with reference to Daniel have been shown to be erroneous, it does not matter what they try to argue from the New Testament, their system simply cannot be true. Having failed to explain the foundational prophecies of Daniel in terms of their system, Preterism must be rejected as a viable eschatological approach.

At every point, Preterists' attempts to interpret Daniel's prophecies so that everything prophesied is fulfilled by 70 AD fail as this commentary has shown. The prophecy simply does not fit their scheme. These criticisms are not designed as an attack on any person who holds to this eschatological perspective. Although some Preterists who hold to a Full Preterist view advocate positions that have been condemned as heresy in the church—for example, some Full Preterists believe that the resurrection is already past, that there is no future resurrection, and that the resurrection was only a spiritual resurrection and not a bodily resurrection—those who hold to Partial Preterism do not advocate these beliefs, and should not be treated as if they were enemies of the Gospel. Notwithstanding the fact that Preterists are no less committed Evangelical Christians than Futurists, their system simply fails adequately to explain the prophecies of Daniel.

Synopsis of the Daniel's Prophecies

This commentary is quite detailed, and much time is spent analyzing and critiquing various views. Consequently, it is easy for the reader to get immersed in the details and lose sight of the whole. This section will provide a summary of the key prophetic passages of Daniel according to a Futurist perspective in order to give the reader an understanding of the flow of the prophecies and how it all fits together.

Nebuchadnezzar's Dream of the Statue

Chapter two presents the prophecy of the gentile world powers from the time of Nebuchadnezzar to the establishing of the Kingdom of God. Beginning with the head of gold, the nations follow in chronological progression throughout world history. The head of gold represents the Babylonian empire particularly under the headship of Nebuchadnezzar. With Nebuchadnezzar's kingdom, the times of the Gentiles begins. The breast and arms of silver represent the kingdom of Medo-Persia that succeeded Babylon. The change from gold to silver indicates the movement from a superior to an inferior kingdom. The loins and hips represent the empire of Greece, and the legs of iron and the feet of iron and clay represent the Roman Empire. The stone cut out of the mountain represents the establishing of the kingdom of God. The fact that it is cut out without hands indicates that this kingdom will not be the product of man, but of God.

The vision of the statue depicts the kingdoms of man as one unit, indicating that there is something about all these kingdoms that holds them together as one. The legs of iron and the feet of iron and clay, represent the Roman Empire from the time of its establishment to its demise. The legs of iron represent the earlier instantiation of the empire while the feet and ten toes of iron mixed with clay represent a form of the Roman Empire that has yet to be seen. Consequently, the Roman Empire represented in this way is yet future from the perspective of the twentieth century. The prophecy of Daniel passes over the intervening historical period that has traditionally been identified as the church age. Although the notion of a gap of some 2,000 years has been severely criticized, it is the only explanation that actually fits the details of the prophecy without distortion, rearranging, or rewording the text. This period, which has been identified as the church age, is the time when God is calling out a people to Himself from among the Gentiles. This time is also a time to stir up Israel to jealousy in order to motivate them to return to their God.

When the stone strikes the statute, it strikes it on the feet. At that point, the entire statue is pulverized as one thing, and its residue is blow away with the wind so that nothing is left of the kingdoms of men. This indicates that the kingdom of God will not in any way be the admixture of man's kingdoms, but will be completely the work of God. The description of this event indicates that the destruction of the kingdoms of men, and particularly the Roman Empire that is the specific kingdom existing at this time, will be a sudden and complete end of the world's kingdoms. The kingdom of God that is depicted by the stone will be none other than the Messianic kingdom. Once the kingdoms of men are destroyed, the Messianic kingdom will grow to encompass the entire earth. There is no room in the prophetic picture for a gradual demise of the Roman Empire and a simultaneous gradual growth of the Kingdom of God. The prophetic picture clearly shows that the Kingdom of God begins to grow only after the kingdoms of men have been destroyed and swept away.

Daniel's Vision of the Beasts

Daniel's vision of the beasts in chapter seven covers the same period of human history as is predicted in chapter two. Whereas chapter two presented the kingdoms of man from the point of view of man, chapter seven presents these kingdoms from God's point of view. The prophecy of chapter seven also adds details that were not present in chapter two. Consequently, they are presented as four destructive beasts that kill and destroy one another. These beasts come out of the sea indicating that they will arise out of the world of mankind. The first beast presented as a lion having two wings represents the Babylonian Empire. The second beast presented as a bear represents the Medo-Persian Empire. The third beast represents Greece and is presented as a leopard having four wings. More is said about the fourth beast than any of the others. The fourth beast represents Rome and is depicted by a beast that defies any earthly categories.

When the fourth beast comes out of the sea, it has ten horns. The ten horns correspond to the ten toes of the statue and represent ten kings who will reign at the same time in this future form of the Roman Empire. Out of one of the horns another horn arises. This horn represents Anti-Christ who will rise to power out of the Roman Empire. He will subdue three of the kings and will exalt himself against God. He will war against the people of God, the Jews, to the point of overcoming them for a time. This time of warring against the Jews is known as the Time of Jacob's Trouble and will last for three and one-half years. However, God will judge this blasphemous king, and he will be annihilated. This event corresponds to the stone striking the statue on the feet and toes as depicted in the dream in chapter two. The people of God will inherit the kingdom of God that is established after the destruction of the fourth beast.

Daniel's Vision of the Ram and the Goat

Daniel's vision as presented in chapter eight is a vision that focuses on the kingdoms of Medo-Persia and Greece. Daniel first sees a ram, representing the kingdom of Medo-Persia. Next he sees a goat coming across the land at great speed. The goat represents the kingdom of Greece, and the speed represents the rapidity with which the army of Alexander the Great carried out their campaigns. This goat has one conspicuous horn, representing Alexander the Great. When the kingdom of Greece had become mighty, Alexander died, and his empire was divided into four major parts, represented by the four horns that come up after the large horn was broken. Out of one of these horns came a little horn that grew to become powerful. This little horn represents Antiochus IV Epiphanes.

One purpose for this vision is the focus that is given to the little horn that arises out of one of the horns on the head of the Goat. Antiochus will become mighty and will persecute the people of God. By these activities, Antiochus foreshadows the Anti-Christ who will not only oppose the people of God, but will oppose the Messiah, Christ Jesus. However, Antiochus would come to his end, as will also Anti-Christ.

The Prophecy of the Seventy Sevens

The prophecy of the Seventy Sevens is without doubt the most frequently discussed prophetic passage in the Old Testament. It presents a panoramic view of the future history of Israel consisting of the 490 years. The following is a summary of the points from the seventy sevens prophecy in chapter 9.

1.   Seventy groups of seven years is determined upon the people of Israel and upon the city of Jerusalem. This constitutes a 490 year time frame.

2.   The seventy sevens is decreed in order to accomplish six things.

    a.   "to finish the transgression"—Recall the thrust of Daniel's prayer. One of Daniel's tasks was to confess the sins of Israel. The seventy sevens is for the purpose of bringing an end to the transgressions/rebellions of Israel. This answers Daniel's petition for God to restore Israel.

    b.   "to make an end of sin"—In relation to Daniel's prayer, this indicates that God will completely remove sin so that Israel will no longer sin against their God. God will completely end sin altogether. This is also indicated in Jer 31:34 "and their sins not I will remember again."

    c.   "to make atonement for iniquity"—This is a prophetic announcement that God would atone for the sins of His people. The seventy sevens is for the purpose of accomplishing the momentous work of justification.

d. "to bring in everlasting righteousness"—This is most probably a reference to the millennial kingdom. In the prophetic literature of the OT, the establishing of righteousness is frequently associated with the establishing of the Messianic kingdom (Isa 11: 2–5; Jer 2:3:5–6). Remember also that the seventy sevens are determined "upon thy people and upon thy holy city." More broadly, the work of Christ has made righteousness available to everyone who believes, to the Jew first and also to the Greek.

e. "to seal up the vision and prophet"—This probably indicates that all the prophetic promises relating to His covenant with Israel will be finally and completely fulfilled.

f. "to anoint the most Holy"—The term "place" is not in the original. It may be a reference to the anointing of the most holy place in the millennial temple prophesied in Ezekiel 41–46. However, in view of the primary concern of most of the prophecies of the book of Daniel, it seems just as reasonable to understand this as the anointing of the Messiah as king of the everlasting kingdom which has been presented in almost every prophecy in the book.

3. The command to return and build Jerusalem was given by Artaxerxes in 445 BC. This is the starting point of the seventy sevens.

4. The seventy sevens will be divided into three distinct periods.

a. The seven sevens, or 49 years, covers the period of the building of the city.

b. The sixty-two sevens stretches from the completion of the city to the coming of the Messiah into the city at the Triumphal Entry to declare Himself the Messiah, King of Israel.

c. The seventieth seven is marked by the establishing of a covenant between the coming prince and the nation of Israel. This event is yet future, so the seventieth seven has not yet begun.

5. By the end of the first period of seven sevens, the city of Jerusalem will be completely rebuilt, even to the point of constructing military defenses.

6. After the end of the sixty-two sevens, Messiah will be crucified, "cut off," having been rejected by His own people as the Messiah.

7. After the end of the sixty-two sevens, and before the inauguration of the seventieth seven, the people of a prince that is going to come in

the future will destroy both the city of Jerusalem and the sanctuary. This event occurred in 70 AD.

8.   The coming prince is not Titus, but some future prince who will be connected to the Roman Empire seeing as he is identified as a prince of the Romans who destroyed the city in 70 AD.

9.   This coming prince will make a covenant with Israel for one seven. This event has not yet occurred. This is not the New Covenant, but is some kind of arrangement with the nation of Israel.

10.   In the middle of this seven, at the 3½ year point, this prince will stop the sacrifice and offering. Since verse 26 has declared that the city and the sanctuary will be destroyed, an event that took place in 70 AD, the statement here necessitates the rebuilding of both the city and the temple.

11.   At this time, the Desolator will desolate the temple by some means, but his plans to completely desolate the worship of the God of Israel will be turned upon him, and the very desolations he intended will be poured out upon him.

The Message Given to Daniel

Chapter 10 begins the final section of Daniel's prophecy. The final message (דָבָר, *rabad*) given to Daniel stretches from the beginning of chapter 10 to the end of chapter 12. The actual prophecy does not begin until chapter 11 and extends to the end of the book. Throughout verses 1–35 of chapter 11, the message focuses upon the events surrounding the wars between the kings of the South and the kings of the North, referring to the Ptolemys and the Seleucids respectively. Beginning with verse 36, the Anti-Christ is introduced and becomes the focus of the remainder of chapter 11. This material covering verses 36 through 45 describes the character and the exploits of Anti-Christ in the final days before the return of Christ. Anti-Christ will be an evil king who will be dedicated to war and the accumulation of ultimate power. His exploits will ultimately revolve around Jerusalem, and it is there that he will meet his demise, and there will be none to rescue him.

The Conclusion of Daniel's Prophecy

Chapter 12 is the conclusion of Daniel's prophecy. Its focus is the final days before the conclusion of this age and the establishing of the Millennial Kingdom at Christ's return. The prophecy begins by making reference to the Tribulation period and the great distress that will characterize the last 3½ years known as the Great Tribulation and the Time of Jacob's Trouble. After this time, many of those who are dead will be raised to eternal life. The rest of the dead will not be raised at this time, but will be raised at a future point to face eternal condemnation.

The last 3½ years of the Tribulation period is a span of 1,260 days. Verse 11 makes reference to a period of 1,290 days. This period, beginning at the middle of the Tribulation, is 30 days longer. It will include an additional 30 in which will take place the judgment of the nations described in Matthew 25. Verse 12 refers to the 1,335 days and to those who will be blessed who attain to this point. This period also begins at the middle of the Tribulation and extends 75 additional days past the end of the Tribulation period. It is also 45 days longer than the previous period referred to in verse 11. The end of the 1,335 days marks the official establishing of the Millennial kingdom. The additional 45 days will probably include preparations for this momentous occasion. The chart in Figure 52 on page 699 is the same one found at the end of the commentary on chapter 9, but here it includes the periods referred to in chapter 12 of 1,290 days and 1,335 days demonstrating their relations to the overall period of the seventy sevens.

Structure of Daniel's Prophecies

Functions and Arrangement of the Prophecies

One issue that could not be addressed until the commentary was completed is the issue of the function of the various chapters and their arrangement in the book of Daniel. For example, since chapter 2 deals with the four world empires and the establishing of the kingdom of God, what is the purpose of chapter 7 that covers the same historical period? One reason for including chapter 7 is the depiction of these kingdoms in their true character as mutually destructive beasts. Man's effort to establish a lasting kingdom of peace on earth is ultimately futile because of man's own sinful nature. Another reason is to include greater details about these kingdoms and their ultimate destruction.

That being the case, one wonders what is the function of chapter 8. Chapter 7 has given greater details about the four kingdoms, and since chapter 8 covers the Medo-Persian and Greek empires, it seems to be redundantly reporting the same history. One function of chapter 8, however, is to focus the reader's attention on these two kingdoms and how a more detailed view of their history leads up to the rise of Antiochus IV Epiphanes, the type of the Anti-Christ. The greater detail and focus upon these empires seems to be designed to make it difficult for future generations to mistake the evil Antiochus as ushering in the final days of the world empires. Although Antiochus is a type of Anti-Christ, as a result of this chapter, the history leading up to and the exploits of Antiochus can be distinguished from the career of the final opposer of Christ.

Chapter 9 addresses the question of the Babylonian captivity and its goal. God had sent the tribes of Judah and Benjamin into captivity because, having followed the example of the northern kingdom of Israel, these remaining tribes had broken the covenant relation with God by going after foreign gods. The question is, did the Babylonian captivity rehabilitate the people of God to return to the worship of the God of Israel exclusively. When Daniel received the angelic messenger in Daniel 9, the people had already begun to return to the land. Yet God's people had not completely returned to God. Already in the post-exilic prophets we see the people abandoning God and repeating the same mistakes as their fathers. The prophecy of the seventy sevens sets out God's ultimate plan for turning His people back to Him. This prophetic timetable is a response to Daniel's intercession for his people and his request that God would restore them to the land and to Himself. God will do this, and this prophetic overview sets out the course that this restoration will take.

Chapter 11contains the major amount of prophetic material of the remaining vision. Although this prophecy begins with a brief statement about the four kings of Medo-Persia, the text immediately focuses in even greater detail than before on the kingdom of Greece and the two branches of Alexander's empire, the Ptolemaic and the Seleucid, which developed after Alexander's death. This material leads up to Antiochus IV Epiphanes and then focuses on the career of Anti-Christ. One function of this chapter is to set forth in great detail the method by which the wise can understand the times. From the beginning of the prophecy down to verse 35, the almost universal method for understanding the prophecy is to relate the prophetic descriptions to the historical events in order to identify the persons and times that constitute the subject of the prophecy. This same methodology should continue through to the end of the prophetic declarations so that those who have understanding can understand the times. Also, this chapter provides much greater detail about the exploits of Anti-Christ. Chapter 12 concludes the prophecy of Daniel and provides details about the end of the age.

Although other interpreters may certainly find additional functions of these chapters and other reasons why they are arranged as we find them, this seems to be at least a plausible account of the role that these chapters play in the overall organization of the book of Daniel.

Logical and Thematic Structure of Daniel

As we pointed out in our introduction to the book of Daniel, we have made a distinction between the literary structure of Daniel's book and its logical structure. There are some charts in the introductory material that are designed to illustrate the literary structure (see Figure 2 on page 41). The Logical-Thematic Structure of Daniel (see Figure 50 below) illustrates the relationships of the earlier chapters of Daniel—chapters 1–6—to the Prophetic chapters of Daniel—chapters 7–12. Chapters 1 through 5 focus on the judgment of Babylon, the false garden in the false city, the city of man. Although Jerusalem is destroyed and the people of God are taken into captivity—the content of chapter 1—the faithful remnant will understand the plan of God and remain faithful. The kingdoms of men will ultimately yield to the kingdom of God, chapter 2. Although the people of God have been defeated by the kingdom of men, this is all part of God's plan to return His people to Himself. Even though the kingdoms of men will persecute the people of God, chapter 3, He will protect the faithful remnant, and He will bring them through the fiery trials. God is the one who rules in the kingdoms of men, and all the nations will ultimately acknowledge and bow before the God of Israel, chapter 4. Even though the kingdoms of men appear to encompass the whole earth, they have power only at the discretion of the God of Israel, so the people of God must remain confident and faithful. Ultimately, the city of man will be judged, chapter 5.

Figure 50: Logical-Thematic Structure of Daniel

Ch	X	Content	Theme
1	A	Captivity of Jerusalem Looting of the Temple Vessels Testing of Daniel Exaltation of Daniel	Judgment of Jerusalem

2	B	Dream of Nebuchadnezzar
		  Grand Statue
		    Statue Destroyed
		Interpretation of Daniel
		  World Kingdoms
		  Kingdom of God
			Kingdoms of Men

3	C	Statue of Nebuchadnezzar Testing of Three Hebrews Victory over Furnace and Nebuchadnezzar Praise of God	Deliverance From Destruction

4	B'	Dream of Nebuchadnezzar
		  Grand Tree
		    Tree Cut Down
		Interpretation of Dream
		  Nebuchadnezzar's Kingdom
		  Kingdom of God Acknowledged
			God Rules In the Kingdoms of Men

5	A'	Captivity of Babylon Defilement of Temple Vessels Testing of Daniel Exaltation of Daniel	Judgment of Babylon
6	A	Organization of Babylon Exaltation of Daniel Plot Against Daniel Rescue of Daniel Judgment on Plotters	Distress and Rescue
7	B	World Kingdoms as Beasts Rise of Little Horn Judgment of Fourth Beast	Kingdoms of Men and The Rise of Anti-Christ
8	C	Medo-Persian Empire Grecian Empire Rise of Insolent King	Physical Warfare
9	D	Prayer of Restoration Appearance of Gabriel Prophecy of Seventy Sevens	Purification of God's People
10	C'	Prayer and Fasting of Daniel Appearance of the Man Spiritual Warfare	Spiritual Warfare
11	B'	Kingdoms of Men at War Rise of Antiochus Rise of Anti-Christ Judgment of Anti-Christ	Kingdoms of Men and The Rise of Anit-Christ
12	A'	Distress and Rescue of the People Resurrection and Judgment Shattering of the People Resurrection and Exaltation of Daniel	Distress and Resurrection

The people of God will be persecuted, and the forces of evil will attempt to put them to death, but God will protect them from destruction, chapter 6. The kingdoms of men will become worse, more evil, and more defiant leading up to the one who will oppose God, Anti-Christ, chapter 7. The warfare will encompass the world, but the physical warfare, chapter 8, is only the outward appearance. God has a plan to purify the people of God and bring them back to him, chapter 9. Behind the scenes the spiritual warfare is raging, and the people of God must be in constant prayer, chapter 10. Anti-Christ is an integral part of God's plan to bring His people back to Him. Anti-Christ will be revealed by his actions, prefigured in Antiochus, chapter 11. There will be a time of distress and persecution such as has never been seen, but those who remain faithful will be delivered, and those who die will be raised to a new life, chapter 12.

There are many other relationships between these chapters forming a complex web of inter-relations. For example, there is a pattern of A B A B between chapters 3 through 6. Chapter 3 depicts the pride and arrogance of the king, but the king is humbled by God in chapter 4. Chapter 5 also depicts the pride and arrogance of the king who, in chapter 6 is humbled by God.

A	Pride and Arrogance of the King	Nebuchadnezzar	Chapter 3
	B Appropriate Response to God	Humility	Chapter 4
A	Pride and Arrogance of the King	Belshazzar	Chapter 5
	B Appropriate Response to God	Faith	Chapter 6

If we divide chapter 9 into 9a and 9b, there seems to be another chiasm that emerges. Chapter 7 depicts the reign of the world powers. Chapter 8 depicts the two kings, Medo-Persia and Greece. Chapter 9a is Daniel's prayer for the restoration of Israel. Chapter 9b is God's answer. Chapter 10 is Daniel's prayer for intervention. Chapter 11 presents two kings, Antiochus and Anti-Christ, and chapter 12 depicts the end of the world kingdoms. This chiasm is illustrated below.

A	Reign of World Kingdoms		7
	B	Two Kings	8
		C Prayer of Restoration	9a
		D Seventy Sevens	9b
		C′ Prayer of Intervention	10
	B′	Two Kings	11
A′	End of World Kingdoms		12

These relations and inter-relations demonstrate that the function of chapters 1–6 is not merely to provide a historical setting for the prophetic chapters. Rather, these chapters provide an integral part of the thematic structure of the book. The relationship between the literary structure and the logical structure of the book of Daniel is illustrated in Figure 51 below. The point here is that the whole notion of the end of Jewish history as this is proposed by Preterists is contrary to the Logical-Thematic Structure of Daniel's book. Everything points to the faithfulness of God ultimately to restore His people to the place and the land that He promised and to which He covenanted Himself when He brought Abraham into the land.

We have demonstrated that the Preterists' interpretations of the prophecies of Daniel cannot stand up to examination. Attempts to make the prophecies of Daniel apply to the events of 70 AD simply fail. The structure of Daniel's prophecies demonstrates that, as Paul said, "God has not rejected His people" (Rom 11:1f). Daniel's prophecy, including all 12 chapters, points to the ultimate restoration of God's people, Israel in the land that He covenanted to give to them.

Figure 51: Comparative Structures of Daniel

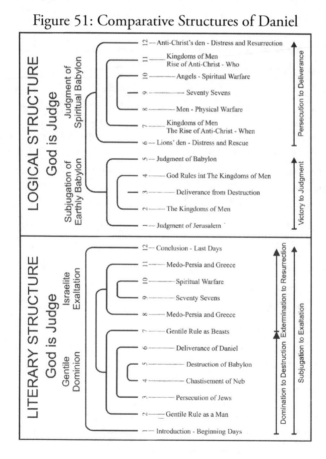

One Final Problem for the Preterists

Rejection of Israel

There is one final problem that faces the Preterist interpretation. A frequent claim made by many Preterists, and a point that is a critical part of the Preterist view, is that God has finished His work with Israel, evidenced by the destruction of Jerusalem in 70 A.D. that supposedly marked the "destruction of Judaism . . ."[1] Commenting on the vision of the stone destroying the earthly kingdoms as described by Daniel in chapter 2, Jessie Mills argues that the kingdom of God is spiritual, not earthly, and that, "The spiritual kingdom would destroy Judaism and the Hebrew kingdom."[2] Preterists argue that Dan 8:17 is referring to the time when Christ came, died, was buried, and rose again bringing an end to Judaism and establishing the kingdom of God. Again, Jessie Mills asserts, "In the future time when the divine indignation shall be manifested toward the Hebrew people, the beginning of these calamities would therefore bring forth the end, seen in chapter 8 as beginning with Antiochus. It therefore pertains to a series of events which are to introduce the latter days, when the kingdom of God (Christ) will be established, and Judaism abolished."[3]

In a note on the definition of Dispensationalism, Gentry asserts, "It is remarkable that this statement allows the *religion of Judaism* (not just Israel the people) to have an equal role in history with the Christian religion—even in the future, post-Christian millennium!"[4] Gentry's statement betrays a misunderstanding of the term "Judaism" as it is used in dispensationalist literature. There are two concepts surrounding this term. In the way Gentry is using it, "Judaism" indicates the worship of God by the people of Israel according to the system of laws and ritualistic requirements set forth in Torah. Gentry's misunderstanding is the assumption that by the term "Judaism," dispensationalists are referring to the system followed by those who refuse to acknowledge Jesus as the Messiah, and seek to continue to worship God according to the Old Testament prescriptions. This kind of Judaism is contrary to God's plan and God's will. In fact, salvation has always been by grace through faith. The sacrificial system was never designed to take away sin or to bring salvation to Israel or its people. What the sacrificial and ritualistic system foreshadowed has been fulfilled in Christ. The kind of Judaism that believes that the sacrifices of animals can take away sin was never the purpose

1. Kloske, *The Second Coming*, 500.

2. Mills, *Daniel*, 19.

3. Ibid., 116.

4. Gentry, *He Shall Have Dominion*, n39, 117.

of the Law, and this is not the kind of Judaism to which dispensationalists are referring. This is, in fact, not Judaism at all.

The true function of the sacrificial system was not abolished, however, but was rather fulfilled, as Christ states: "Do not think that I came to abolish the Law or the Prophets; I did not come to abolish but to fulfill" (Matt 5:17).[5] Jesus came as the Messiah to fulfill the law and the prophets and to make the final and everlasting atonement for the sins of mankind, including the sins of Israel. Israel's great sin was their self-righteousness that led to their rejection of their own Savior. The true worship of God as expressed in the Old Testament was not abolished, but was fulfilled in Christ and now continues in Him. The true Judaism that truly worships God and recognizes in Christ their Messiah and the fulfillment of the law and the prophets continues in those Jews who are born again. God has not ended His work among Israel. Ultimately Israel will recognize their Messiah and return to the pure worship of God in Christ as His distinct people, as Paul asserts, "and so all Israel will be saved; just as it is written, 'The Deliverer will come from Zion, He will remove ungodliness from Jacob'" (Rom 11:26).[6] It is this Judaism, the Judaism that is converted, born again, that will continue.

Also, Gentry is simply mistaken when he claims that dispensationalists believe that Judaism will have an equal role in history with the Christian religion. This introduces a bifurcation where there is none. Judaism as the true worship of God through the Messiah, Christ Jesus, is not a *different* "religion," as Gentry implies. Rather, it is the same worship of God in the same way on the same basis—salvation by grace through faith. It is rather a different people who are God's chosen people. Christians and Jews who have recognized the Messiah will worship God in the same way, but they are nevertheless two distinct people groups according to the plan of God for His chosen people. During this time that God is calling out a people to Himself from among the Gentiles, individual Jews who are born again become part of the Bride of Christ. However, there will be a time when God will return to His people Israel and restore them to faithfulness, and Israel, as the chosen people of God, will recognize their Messiah, "even those who pierced Him" (Rev 1:7).[7] God will fulfill the promises He made to Abraham, and Israel will inherit the kingdom according to the covenant God made with the descendants of Abraham.

---

5. Μὴ νομίσητε ὅτι ἦλθον καταλῦσαι τὸν νόμον ἢ τοὺς προφήτας· οὐκ ἦλθον καταλῦσαι ἀλλὰ πληρῶσαι. (Matt 5:17).

6. καὶ οὕτως πᾶς Ἰσραὴλ σωθήσεται, καθὼς γέγραπται· ἥξει ἐκ Σιὼν ὁ ῥυό μενος, ἀποστρέψει ἀσεβείας ἀπὸ Ἰακώβ. (Rom 11:26).

7. καὶ οἵτινες αὐτὸν ἐξεκέντησαν (Rev 1:7).

Rejected Because of Their Sin

But, what the Preterists claim is that God has finished with Israel altogether as His distinct people, and will never reconstitute them as His people so as to fulfill the promises He made to them in the Old Testament. Although actually enumerating the key elements of a postmillennial eschatology, Gentry's statement about Israel is a necessary part of a Preterist view. He says, "The kingdom which Christ preached and presented was not something other than that expected by the Old Testament saints. In postmillennialism, the Church becomes the fulfilled/transformed Israel, being called 'the Israel of God' (Gal. 6:16)."[8] According to this view, Israel as the distinct people of God have not simply been transformed. Rather, they have been rejected by God because of they have rejected their Messiah. Gentry asserts, "While on earth Christ clearly and forthrightly teaches that God would soon set aside national Israel as a distinctive, favored people in the kingdom."[9] Gentry points to Matt 21:43 to support his claim: "Therefore I say to you, the kingdom of God will be taken away from you and given to a people, producing the fruit of it."[10] On the basis of this and many other verse, Gentry asserts, "He [Jesus] parabolically teaches the rejection of national Israel . . ."[11] Gentry goes on to explain, "Israel's demise from dominance is directly related to her ethical conduct. *Israel crucified the Messiah.* Jesus makes this the point of His Parable of the Householder mentioned above (Matt. 21:33ff). The constant apostolic indictment against the Jews pertained to *this gross, conclusive act of covenantal rebellion.*"[12] In other words, the Preterists in general, and Gentry in particular, are claiming that God has rejected Israel because of her sin.

A serious problem with these assertions is they seem to be saying that in order for Israel to continue as the distinct people of God, they would have had to, as it were, do the right thing. But this smacks of works salvation. Because of Israel's sins, they will not be saved. Gentry as much as declares this when, discussing the destruction of Jerusalem, he says, "The destructive acts are *anticipated,* however, in the divine act of sealing up or reserving the sin of Israel for punishment. Israel's climactic sin—her completing of her transgression (v. 24) with the cutting off of Messiah (v. 26a)—results in God's act of *reserving*

8. Gentry, *He Shall Have Dominion*, 72.

9. Ibid., 237.

10. διὰ τοῦτο λέγω ὑμῖν ὅτι ἀρθήσεται ἀφ᾿ ὑμῶν ἡ βασιλεία τοῦ θεοῦ καὶ δοθήσεται ἔθνει ποιοῦντι τοὺς καρποὺς αὐτῆς. (Matt 21:43).

11. Gentry, *He Shall Have Dominion*, 237.

12. Ibid., 238.

Israel's sin until later. Israel's judgment will not be postponed forever; it will come after the expiration of the seventy weeks."[13]

If this is an accurate understanding of Gentry's position, that Israel is rejected for her sins, particularly crucifying the Messiah, this bodes ill for the rest of humanity. How was Israel more guilty for the crucifixion of Jesus than any other human being? Is their sin greater simply because they were responsible for the physical act? Does not the Scripture declare that Jesus died because of the sins of the whole world? Then we are all guilty of crucifying the Messiah. Why does God not reject all humans? Is God unable or unwilling to forgive the sin of crucifying His Son? Neither Gentry nor most Preterists believe in a works salvation. They would certainly reject the notion that God could not or would not forgive the sin of crucifying the Messiah. The very fact that we are all morally and spiritually guilty of crucifying the Messiah and yet many are saved demonstrates that God could and would forgive those who repent. But, if God could and would forgive those individuals who repent, could He not also forgive Israel should they repent? But according to Paul, that is precisely what they will do.

Did God Have an Evil Intent for Israel?

This also raises another very problematic issue for the Preterist. Was God unable to overcome the sin of Israel? The idea that God has rejected Israel for rejecting the Messiah is analogical to the rejection of Israel in Exodus on the basis of their rejection of God by the creation of and worship of the golden calf. In Exodus 32, while Moses is on the mountain receiving from God the law written on stone tablets, Israel is at the foot of the mountain committing spiritual adultery. Because of this great sin, God tells Moses, "I have seen this people, and behold they are a stiff-necked people. So, now, leave Me, that My anger might burn against them and I might destroy them. But I will make you a great nation" (Ex 32:9–10). After Moses' intercession for the people, the text states, "So Yahweh had compassion regarding the harm that He had said He would do to His people" (Ex 32:14).

John Currid gives a helpful explanation of Moses' intercession for the nation:

> Moses presents three arguments to God as to why his wrath ought to turn away from the Hebrews. First, he says, the Israelites are "your people"—that is, they were the ones whom God had chosen and had delivered from the land of Egypt. Secondly, he points out that the Egyptians would surely mock both God and

---

13. Ibid., 330–31.

Israel, saying that Yahweh had merely been toying with Israel and that his plan all along had not been to deliver them, but to destroy them. One of the principal purposes of the exodus and, in particular, the series of plagues, was so that the Egyptians might know who Yahweh was, his power, and his redeeming hand (see 7:5; 8:10; 9:14). If God were now to destroy Israel, Egypt would be convinced of nothing! And, thirdly, Moses makes the point that these Israelites embodied the fulfillment of the promises God had made to Abraham, Isaac and Jacob. God should not go back on his word. It is interesting to note that nowhere does Moses attempt to justify the sins of the Hebrews. That is because they are unjustifiable. Moses rather pleads for the mercy of God on the basis of God's character and promises.[14]

The important argument of Moses for our consideration is the second one in which Moses argues, "Why should the Egyptians speak, saying, 'With evil *intent* He brought them out to kill them in the mountains and to destroy them from the face of the earth'?" (Ex 32:12). Moses is arguing that if God destroys Israel, the nations will claim that either God had planned evil for Israel all along or that God was impotent and unable to fulfill His promises. But this same argument can be lodged against the Preterists' claim that God has abandoned Israel as a result of their sin of rejecting their Messiah. Had God planned all along to destroy Israel? Does this imply, at least as far as the nations would think, that God had an evil intent with reference to Israel? This kind of response to God's rejection of Israel is implied in God's statement in Isa 52:5: ""*Again* the Lord declares, 'Those who rule over them howl, and My name is continually blasphemed all day long.'" With reference to this verse, Oswalt points out, "God's name is held in contempt because it appears to the watching world that Israel's belief in God was false. He had been forced by the superior power of the gods to surrender his people."[15] In Romans, Paul applies this text to the sins of Israel: "You who boast in the Law, through your breaking the Law, do you dishonor God? For 'the name of God is blasphemed among the Gentiles because of you,' just as it is written" (Rom 2:23–24). As John Murray observes, "The thought in the apostle's application of the text is that the vices of the Jews give occasion to the Gentiles to blaspheme the name of God. The reasoning of the Gentiles is to the effect that a people are like their God and if the people can perpetrate such crimes their God must be of the same character and is to be execrated accordingly. The Jews who claimed to be the leaders of the nations for the worship of the true God had

14. John D. Currid, *Exodus 19–40*, 275–76.
15. Oswalt, *The Book of Isaiah: Chapters 40–66*, 363.

become the instruments of provoking the nations to blasphemy."[16] In the same manner, would not God be subject to blasphemy by the watching nations if He rejected Israel as the Preterists claim? Is God not able or not willing to overcome the sin of His chosen people so as to establish them in the land and give to them the inheritance as He promised? And if God is either unable or unwilling to overcome Israel's sin, will he do the same to us who believe? If God alters the parameters of His promises to Israel because of their sin, will He not alter the parameters of His promises to us because of our sins? The Preterist claim that God is finished with Israel provokes the watching world to have a distorted view of who our God is.

The fact is, and this commentary has shown, that God has not rejected His people. As Paul emphatically declares, "I say then, God has not rejected His people, has He? May it never be! For I too am an Israelite, a descendant of Abraham, of the tribe of Benjamin. God has not rejected His people whom He foreknew" (Rom 11:1, 2). God will restore Israel to a right relationship with Him. Neither their sins nor ours are too great that God cannot overcome and save. God is faithful concerning His promises, and He will complete the work that He began in the nation of Israel. As God declares, "Is My hand so short that it cannot ransom? Or have I no power to deliver?" (Isa 50:2). John Matheny makes an interesting and informative correlation between the experience of Israel and the experience of Peter as recorded in Matt 18:21–22.

> But while Israel has been living in rebellion since shortly after the return from the Exile, God will still be faithful to His word and will restore them to His favor on the day they turn to Him in faith. Witness the Lord's answer to the Apostle Peter's query as to how often forgiveness should be extended: Matthew 18:21 "Then came Peter to him and said, Lord, how often shall my brother sin against me, and I forgive him? Till seven times? 22 Jesus saith unto him, I say not unto thee, until seven times; but, until seventy times seven."
>
> Israel will experience this gracious forgiveness at the end of the seventy sevens.[17]

All Israel will be saved, and because God will fulfill His promises to the nation of Israel, as He has said, we also can trust God to fulfill the promises He has made to us. The prophecies of Daniel declare not only the faithfulness of God to fulfill His promises to Israel, but they provide us with a peek at God's plan by which He will yet accomplish His will for Israel and for all humanity.

16. John Murray, *The Epistle to the Romans*, 85.

17. Matheny, *The Seventy Weeks* of Daniel, 21–22.

Figure 52: Seventy Sevens Chart

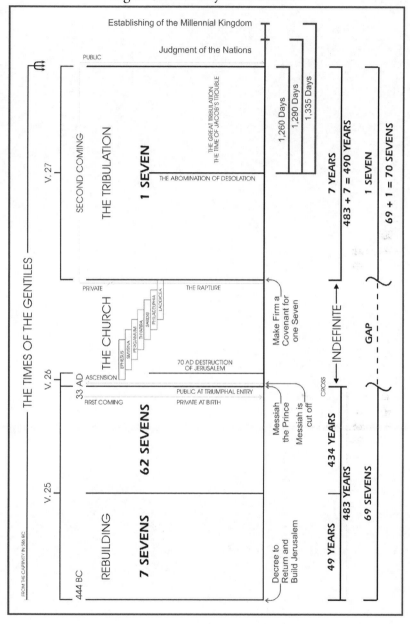

Bibliography

Adams, Jay E., and Milton C. Fisher. *The Time of the End: Daniel's Prophecy Reclaimed.* Woodruff, South Carolina: Timeless Texts, 2000.

Ahituv, Shmuel, ed. *The Jewish People: An Illustrated History.* New York: Continuum International Publishing Group, 2006.

Anderson, Roy Allan. *Unfolding Daniel's Prophecies.* Mountain View, California: Pacific Press Publishing Association, 1975.

Anderson, Sir Robert. *The Coming Prince: The Marvelous Prophecy of Daniel's Seventy Weeks Concerning the Anti-Christ.* Grand Rapids: Kregel Publications, 1977.

Archer, Gleason L., Jr. *A Survey of Old Testament Introduction.* Chicago: Moody Press, 1974.

Avi-Yonah, Michael, and Zvi Baras, ed. *Society and Religion in the Second Temple Period.* Jerusalem: Massada Publishing, 1977.

Ben-Sasson, H. H., ed. *A History of the Jewish People.* Cambridge, Massachusetts: Harvard University Press, 2002

Bevan, Edwyn Robert. *The House of Ptolemy.* London: Methuen Publishing, 1927.

_____. *The House of Seleucus.* Chicago: Ares Publishers, 1985.

Birks, Kelly Nelson. *The Comings of Christ: A Reformed and Preterist Analogy of the 70th Week of the Prophet Daniel.* Bloomington, Indiana: 1st Books Library, 2002.

Black, Jeremy, and Anthony Green. *Gods, Demons and Symbols of Ancient Mesopotamia: An Illustrated Dictionary.* Austin, Texas: University of Texas Press, 1992.

Bottéro, Jean. *Religion in Ancient Mesopotamia.* Translated by Lavender Fagan. Chicago: The University of Chicago Press, 2001.

Brown, Francis, S. R. Drive, and Charles A. Briggs. *A Hebrew and English Lexicon of the Old Testament.* Oxford: Clarendon Press,1980.

Bringmann, Klaus. *A History of the Roman Republic.* Translated by W. J. Smyth. Cambridge, England: Polity Press, 2007.

Campbell, Donald K. *Daniel: Decoder of Dreams.* Wheaton, Illinois: Victor Books, 1977.

Carter, John M. *The Battle of Actium: The Rise & Triumph of Augustus Caesar.* New York: Weybright and Talley, 1970.

Charlesworth, J. H., ed. *Apocalyptic Literature & Testaments.* Vol. 1, *The Old Testament Pseudepigrapha.* New York: Doubleday, 1983.

Clouse, Robert G., ed. *The Meaning of the Millennium: Four Views*. Downers Grove, Illinois: InterVarsity Press, 1980.

Collins, John J., and Craig A. Evans, ed. *Christian Beginnings and the Dead Sea Scrolls*. Grand Rapids: Baker Academic, 2006.

Craigie, Peter C. *The Book of Deuteronomy*. Grand Rapids: William B. Eerdmans Publishing Company, 1976.

Culver, Robert Duncan. *Daniel and the Latter Days*. 2d ed. Chicago: Moody Press, 1977.

_____. *The Earthly Reign of our Lord with His People: Biblical Millennialism without Covenantal or Dispensational Presuppositions*. Rushford, Minnesota: Vinegar Hill Press, 1998.

Currid, John D. *Exodus 19–40*. Vol. 2, *A Study Commentary on Exodus*. Darlington, England: Evangelical Press, 2001.

_____. *Genesis 25:19–50:26*. Vol. 2, *Genesis: An EP Study Commentary*. Darlington, England: Evangelical Press, 2003.

David, Rosalie. *Religion and Magic in Ancient Egypt*. London: Penguin Books, 2003.

Davies, Norman. *Europe: A History*. New York: HarperPerennial, 1998.

DeMar, Gary. *Last Days Madness: The Folly of Trying to Predict When Christ Will Return*. Brentwood, Tennessee: Wolgemuth & Hyatt, Publishers, 1991.

_____. *Last Days Madness: Obsession of the Modern Church*, 4th ed. Powder Springs, Georgia: American Vision, 1999.

Dickason, C. Fred. *Angels, Elect and Evil*. Chicago: Moody Press, 1975.

Dungan, David Laird. *A History of the Synoptic Problem: The Canon, the Text, the Composition, and the Interpretation of the Gospels*. New York: Doubleday, 1999.

Elliger, K., and W. Rudolph, ed. *Biblia Hebraica Stuttgartensia*. Stuttgart: Deutsche Bibelstiftung, 1977.

Elwell Walter A., and Barry J. Beitzel. *Baker Encyclopedia of the Bible*. Grand Rapids: Baker Book House, 1988.

Evan, Craig A., and Peter W. Flint, ed. *Eschatology, Messianism, and the Dead Sea Scrolls*. Grand Rapids: William B. Eerdmans Publishing Company, 1997.

Evans, John S. *The Four Kingdoms of Daniel: A Defense of the "Roman" Sequence with AD 70 Fulfillment*. Longwood, Florida: Xulon Press, 2004.

Feinberg, Charles L. *Jeremiah: A Commentary*. Grand Rapids: Zondervan Publishing House, 1982.

_____. *Millennialism: The Two Major Views*. Chicago: Moody Press, 1980.

Feinberg, John S., ed. *Continuity and Discontinuity: Perspectives on the Relationship Between the Old and New Testaments*. Westchester, Illinois: Crossway Books, 1988.

Fildes, Alan, and Joann Fletcher. *Alexander the Great: Son of the Gods*. Los Angeles: The J. Paul Getty Museum, 2002.

Frankfort, H., et. al. *The Intellectual Adventure of Ancient Man*. Chicago: The University of Chicago Press, 1977.

Gadamer, Hans-Georg. *Truth and Method*. Translated by Joel Weinsheimer and Donald G. Marshall, 2d ed. New York: Crossroad, 1992.

Gage, Warren Austin. *The Gospel of Genesis: Studies in Protology and Eschatology*. Winona Lake, Indiana: Carpenter Books, 1984.

Geisler, Norman L. *Baker Encyclopedia of Christian Apologetics*. Grand Rapids: Baker Book House, 1999.

_____. *Church, Last Things*. Vol. 4, *Systematic Theology*. Minneapolis: Bethany House, 2005.

Gentry, Kenneth L., Jr. *He Shall Have Dominion: A Postmillennial Eschatology*, 2d ed. Tyler, Texas: Institute for Christian Economics, 1997.

Goldingay, John E. *Daniel*. Vol. 30, *Word Biblical Commentary*. Dallas, Texas: Word Books, Publisher, 1989.

González, Justo L. *The Early Church to the Dawn of the Reformation*. Vol. 1, *The Story of Christianity*. San Francisco: Harper & Row, Publishers, 1984.

_____. *From the Beginnings to the Council of Chalcedon*. Vol. 1, *A History of Christian Thought*. Nashville: Abingdon Press, 1970.

Goodman, Martin. *Rome and Jerusalem: The Clash of Ancient Civilizations*. New York: Alfred A. Knopf, 2007.

Greidanus, Sidney. *The Modern Preacher and the Ancient Text*. Grand Rapids, Michigan: William B. Eerdmans Publishing Company, 1988.

Hailey, Homer. *A Commentary on Daniel: A Prophetic Message*. Las Vegas, Nevada: Nevada Publications, 2001.

Hale, Bob, and Crispin Wright, ed. *A Companion to the Philosophy of Language*. London: Blackwell Publishers, 1997.

Hamilton, Victor P. *The Book of Genesis: Chapters 18-50*. Grand Rapids: William B. Eerdmans Publishing Company, 1995.

Hanegraaff, Hank. *The Apocalypse Code*. Nashville: Thomas Nelson, 2007.

Harris, R. Laird, Gleason L. Archer, Jr., and Bruce K. Waltke, eds. *Theological Wordbook of the Old Testament*. Chicago: Moody Press, 1980.

Hendricksen, William. *Exposition of the Gospel According to John*. Grand Rapids: Baker Book House, 1976.

Hirsch, E. D., Jr. *Validity in Interpretation*. New Haven: Yale University Press, 1967.

Hitchcock, Mark L. "A Critique of the Preterist View of Revelation and the Jewish War." *Bibliotheca Sacra* 164.653 (January-March 2007): 89–100.

Hoehner, Harold W. *Chronological Aspects of the Life of Christ*. Grand Rapids: Zondervan Publishing House, 1977.

_____. *Herod Antipas: A Contemporary of Jesus Christ*. Grand Rapids: Zondervan Publishing House, 1980.

Holland, Tom. *Rubicon: The Last Years of the Roman Republic*. New York: Anchor Books, 2003.

Hoyt, Herman A. *The End Times*. Chicago: Moody Press, 1969.

Ice, Thomas, and Randall Price. *Ready to Rebuild: The Imminent Plan to Rebuild the Last Days Temple*. Eugene, Oregon: Harvest House Publishers, 1992.

Ironside, H. A. *Lectures on Daniel the Prophet*. Neptune, New Jersey: Loizeaux Brothers, 1974.

Jobes, Karen H., and Moisés Silva. *Invitation to the Septuagint*. Grand Rapids: Baker Academic, 2000.

Jones, Lindsay, ed. *Encyclopedia of Religion*. 2d ed. Detroit: Thomson Gale, 2005.

Josephus, Flavius. *Jewish Antiquities*. Translated by Ralph Marcus. Cambridge, Massachusetts: Harvard University Press, 1998.

_____. *The Jewish War*. Translated by J. Thackeray. Cambridge, Massachusetts: Harvard University Press, 1927.

Kaiser, Walter C., Jr. *The Uses of the Old Testament in the New*. Chicago: Moody Press, 1985.

Keil, C. F., and F. Delitzsch. *Ezekiel, Daniel*. Vol. 9, *Commentary on the Old Testament in Ten Volumes*. Grand Rapids: William B. Eerdmans Publishing Company, 1978.

Kik, J. Marcellus. *An Eschatology of Victory*. Carlisle, Pennsylvania: The Presbyterian and Reformed Publishing Company, 1975.

Kline, Meredith G. "The Covenant of the Seventieth Week." In *The Law and the Prophets: Old Testament Studies in Honor of Oswald T. Allis*, ed. by J.H. Skilton. Nutley, NJ: Presbyterian and Reformed, 1974, 452–69.

King, Max R. *The Spirit of Prophecy*. Colorado Springs, Colorado: Max R. King, 2002.

Kloner, Amos. "Underground Hiding Complexes from the Bar Kokhba War in Judean Shephelah." *Biblical Archaeologist* (December 1983): 210–21.

Kloske, Tom, and Steve Kloske. *The Second Coming: Mission Accomplished*. St. Louis, Missouri: K. and K. Publishing, 2003.

Koehler, Ludwig, and Walter Baumgartner. *The Hebrew & Aramaic Lexicon of the Old Testament*. Leiden: Brill, 2001.

LaSor, William Sanford. *The Truth About Armageddon: What the Bible Says About the End Times*. New York: Harper and Row, Publishers, 1982.

Lenski, R. C. H. *The Interpretation of St. John's Gospel*. Minneapolis, Minnesota: Augsburg Publishing House, 1943.

Liddell, Henry George, and Robert Scott. *A Greek-English Lexicon*. Oxford: At The Clarendon Press, 1968.

Lucas, Ernest C. *Apollos Old Testament Commentary: Daniel*. Leicester, England: Apollos, 2002.

Lust, J., E. Eynikel, and K. Hauspie. *A Greek-English Lexicon of the Septuagint*. Stuttgart: Deutsche Bibelgesellschaft, 1992.

Martin, Brian L. *Behind the Veil of Moses*. Napa, California: The Veil of Moses Project, 2004.

Matheny, James F., and Marjorie B. Matheny. *The Seventy Weeks of Daniel: An Exposition of Daniel 9:24-27*. Brevard, North Carolina: Jay and Associates, Publishers, 1990.

Mathison, Keith A. *Postmillennialism: An Eschatology of Hope*. Phillipsburg, New Jersey: P&R Publishing, 1999.

Mathison, Keith A., ed. *When Shall These Things Be? A Reformed Response to Hyper-Preterism*. Phillipsburg, New Jersey: Presbyterian and Reformed Publishing Company, 2004.

Matyszak, Philip. *Chronicle of the Roman Republic: The Rulers of Ancient Rome from Romulus to Augustus*. London: Thames & Hudson, 2003.

Mauro, Philip. *The Hope of Israel: What Is It?* Swengel, Pennsylvania: Reiner Publications, n.d.

_____. *The Seventy Weeks and the Great Tribulation*. 2d ed. Dahlonega, Georgia: Crown Rights Book Company, 1998.

McGee, J. Vernon. *The Prophecies of Daniel*. Nashville, Tennessee: Thomas Nelson Publishers, 1991.

Metzger, Bruce M., and Roland E. Murphy, ed. *The New Oxford Annotated Apocrypha*. New York: Oxford University Press, 1991.

Meyers, Eric M., ed. *The Oxford Encyclopedia of Archaeology in the Near East*. New York: Oxford University Press, 1997.

Mieroop, Marc Van De. *A History of the Ancient Near East: ca. 3000–323 BC*. 2d ed. Malden, Massachusetts, 2007.

Miller, Stephen R. *Daniel: An Exegetical and Theological Exposition of Holy Scripture*. Vol. 18, *The New American Commentary*, ed. E. Ray Clendenen. Nashville: Broadman & Holman Publishers, 1994.

Mills, Jessie E., Jr. *Daniel Fulfilled Prophecy*. Bradford, Pennsylvania: International Preterist Association, 2003.

Montgomery, James A. *A Critical and Exegetical Commentary on the Book of Daniel.* New York: Charles Scribner's Sons, 1927.

Morgan, Gwyn. *69 A.D.: The Year of the Four Emperors.* Oxford: Oxford University Press, 2006.

Moulton, James Hope. *Prolegomena.* Vol. 1, *A Grammar of New Testament Greek,* 3d ed. Edinburgh: T. & T. Clark, 1978.

Murray, John. *The Epistle to the Romans.* Grand Rapids: Wm. B. Eerdmans Publishing Co., 1977.

Nash, Ronald. *Christianity and the Hellenistic World.* Grand Rapids: Zondervan Publishing House, 1984.

Neusner, Jacob, Alan J. Avery-Peck, and William Scott Green, ed. *The Encyclopedia of Judaism.* New York: Continuum, 1999.

Newman, Robert C. "Daniel's Seventy Weeks And The Old Testament Sabbath-Year Cycle." *Journal of the Evangelical Theological Society* 16.4 (1973): 229-34.

Niehaus, Jeffrey J. *God At Sinai: Covenant and Theophany in the Bible and Ancient Near East.* Grand Rapids: Zondervan Publishing House, 1995.

Noē, John. *Beyond the End Times: The Rest of the Greatest Story Ever Told.* Bradford, Pennsylvania: International Preterist Association, 1995.

Nöldeke, Theodor. *Compendious Syriac Grammar.* Translated by James A. Crichton. Eugene, Oregon: Wipf and Stock Publishers, 2003.

Oppenheim, A. Leo. *Ancient Mesopotamia: Portrait of a Dead Civilization.* Chicago: The University of Chicago Press, 1964.

Oswalt, John N. *The Book of Isaiah: Chapters 1 – 39.* Grand Rapids: William B. Eerdmans Publishing Company, 1986.

_____. *The Book of Isaiah: Chapters 40–66.* Grand Rapids: William B. Eerdmans Publishing Company, 1998.

Paher, Stanley W. *Matthew 24: First Century Fulfillment or End-Time Expectation?* Las Vegas: Nevada Publications, 1996.

Pannekoek, A. *A History of Astronomy.* New York: Dover Publications, 1961.

Patterson, Richard D. "Holding On To Daniel's Court Tales." *Journal of the Evangelical Theological Society* 36/4 (December 1993): 445-54.

Payne, J. Barton. "The Goal of Daniels Seventy Weeks." *Journal of the Evangelical Theological Society* 21.2 (1978): 97-115.

Pentecost, J. Dwight. *Things to Come: A Study in Biblical Eschatology.* Grand Rapids: Zondervan Publishing House, 1977.

Peters, George N. H. *The Theocratic Kingdom.* Grand Rapids: Kregel Publications, 1978.

Peterson, Doug. "70 Sevens pt. 2." [Online]. Available: <http://www.70sevens.com/id7.html.> [August 22, 2006].

Pierce, Ronald W. "Spiritual Failure, Postponement, And Daniel 9." *Trinity Journal* 10.2 (1989): 211-22.

Poythress, Vern S. "Hermeneutical Factors in Determining the Beginning of the Seventy Weeks (Dan. 9:25)." *Trinity Journal* 6.2 (1985): 131-49.

Preston, Don K. *The Last Days Identified.* Ardmore, Oklahoma: JaDon Productions, 2004.

_____. *Seal Up Vision and Prophecy.* Ardmore, Oklahoma: JaDon Productions, 2003.

Price, Jonathan J. *Jerusalem Under Siege: The Collapse of the Jewish State 66–70 C.E.* Leiden: E. J. Brill, 1992.

Poythress, Vern S. *Understanding Dispensationalists,* 2d ed. Phillipsburg, New Jersey: P&R Publishing, 1994.

Pusey, E. B. *Daniel the Prophet: Nine Lectures.* New York: Funk and Wagnalls, Publishers, 1885.

Rahlfs, Alfred. *Septuaginta.* Stuttgart: Deutsche Bibelgesellschaft, 1979.

Reicke, Bo. *The New Testament Era: The World of the Bible from 500 B.C. to A.D. 100.* Translated by David E. Green. Philadelphia: Fortress Press, 1964.

Richardson, Peter. *Herod: King of the Jews and Friend of Rome.* Minneapolis: Fortress Press, 1999.

Rosenthal, Franz. *A Grammar of Biblical Aramaic.* Wiesbaden, Germany: Otto Harrassowitz, 1983.

Roth, Cecil, ed. *Encyclopedia Judaica.* New York: The Macmillan Company, 1971.

Rowley, H. H. *Darius the Mede and the Four World Empires in the Book of Daniel: A Historical Study of Contemporary Theories.* Cardiff, UK: University of Wales Press, 1964. Reprint, Eugene, Oregon: Wipf and Stock Publishers, 2006.

Russell, James Stuart. *The Parousia: The New Testament Doctrine of Christ's Second Coming.* Bradford, Pennsylvania: International Preterist Association, 2003.

Ryken, Leland, James C. Wilhoit, and Tremper Longman, III, ed. *Dictionary of Biblical Imagery.* Downers Grove, Illinois: InterVarsity Press, 1998.

Ryrie, Charles C. *The Basis of the Premillennial Faith.* Neptune, New Jersey: Loizeaux Brothers, 1953.

_____. *Dispensationalism Today.* Chicago: Moody Press, 1965.

Saggs, H. W. F. *Civilization Before Greece and Rome.* New Haven, Connecticut: Yale University Press, 1989.

Sailhamer, John H. *Biblical Prophecy.* Grand Rapids: Zondervan Publishing House, 1998.

_____. *The Pentateuch as Narrative: A Biblical-Theological Commentary.* Grand Rapids: Zondervan Publishing House, 1992.

Saucy, Robert L. "Israel and the Church: A Case for Discontinuity." In *Continuity and Discontinuity: Perspectives on the Relationship Between the Old and New Testaments,* ed. John S. Feinberg, 239-59. Westchester, Illinois: Crossway Books, 1988.

Schäfer, Peter. *The History of the Jews in the Greco-Roman World.* London: Routledge, 2003.

Schürer, Emil. *The History of the Jewish People in the Time of Jesus Christ.* Translated by John Macpherson. Peabody, Massachusetts: Hendrickson Publishers, 1994.

Shepherd, Brodrick D. *Beasts, Horns, and the Antichrist.* Grassy Creek, North Carolina: Cliffside Publishing House, 1994.

Silvestri, Daniel T. "Futurist Eschatology Unconvincing." n.p.: PreteristArchive.Com. [Online]. Available: http://www.preteristarchive.com/Preterism/silvestri-daniel_da_02.html.> [September 14, 2006].

Smith, J. Payne, ed. *A Compendious Syriac Dictionary.* Oxford: At The Clarendon Press, 1990.

Smyth, Herbert Weir. *Greek Grammar.* Cambridge: Harvard University Press, 1984.

Stanton, Gerald B. *Why I Am a Premillennialist.* West Palm Beach, Florida: Gerald B. Stanton, 1976.

Starr, Chester G. *A History of the Ancient World,* 3d ed. New York: Oxford University Press, 1983.

Stevens, David E. "Daniel 10 and the Notion of Territorial Spirits." *Bibliotheca Sacra* 157 (October-December 2000): 410–31.

Stevens, Ed. "What is the Preterist View of Bible Prophecy?" Bradford, Pennsylvania: International Preterist Association. [Online]. Available: < http://www.preterist.org/whatispreterism.asp [14 July 2006].

Stiebert, Johanna. "Shame and Prophecy: Approaches Past and Present." *Biblical Interpretation* 8:3 (July 2000): 255–75.

Strauss, Lehman. *The Prophecies of Daniel.* Neptune, New Jersey: Loizeaux Brothers, 1969.

Strayer, Joseph R., and Hans W. Gatzke. *The Mainstream of Civilization*, 4ᵗʰ ed. San Diego, California: Harcourt Brace Jovanovich, Publishers, 1984.

Suetonius Tranquillus, C. *The Lives of the Twelve Caesars.* In *Loeb Classical Series.* Translated by J. C. Rolfe. Cambridge, Massachusetts: Harvard University Press, 1914.

Syriac Bible. Damascus, Syria: Syrian Patriarchate, 1979.

Tenney, Merrill C. *New Testament Times.* Grand Rapids: William B. Eerdmans Publishing Company, 1975.

Terry, Milton. *Biblical Hermeneutics.* Vol. 2, *Library of Biblical and Theological Literature*, ed. George R. Crooks and John F. Hurst. New York: Phillips & Hunt, 1883.

Thomsen, Marie-Louise. "Witchcraft and Magic in Ancient Mesopotamia." In *Witchcraft and Magic in Europe: Biblical and Pagan Societies.* Philadelphia: University of Pennsylvania Press, 2001.

Toit, A. B. du, ed. *The New Testament Milieu.* Halfway House: Orion, 1998.

Tov, Emanuel. *Textual Criticism of the Hebrew Bible*, 2d ed. Minneapolis: Fortress Press, 2001.

Towner, W. Sibley. *Daniel.* Atlanta: John Knox Press, 1984.

_____. "The Poetic Passages of Daniel 1–6." *Catholic Biblical Quarterly* 31 (1969): 317–26.

Unger, Merrill F. *Beyond the Crystal Ball.* Chicago: Moody Press, 1973.

VanGemeren, Willem A., ed. *New International Dictionary of Old Testament Theology & Exegesis.* Grand Rapids: Zondervan Publishing House, 1997.

Van Kampen, Robert. *The Rapture Question Answered: Plain and Simple.* Grand Rapids: Fleming H. Revell, 1997.

_____. *The Sign: Bible Prophecy Concerning the End Times.* Wheaton, Illinois: Crossway Books, 1992.

VanderKam, James, and Peter Flint. *The Meaning of the Dead Sea Scrolls.* San Francisco: HarperSanFrancisco, 2002.

Wallace, Daniel. *Greek Grammar Beyond the Basics.* Grand Rapids: Zondervan Publishing House, 1996.

Wallbank, T. Walter, Alastair M. Taylon, Nels M. Bailkey, George F. Jewsbury, Clyde J. Lewis, and Neil J. Hackett. *Civilization: Past & Present*, 8th ed. Glenview, Illinois: Scott, Foresman and Company, 1981.

Waller, J. C. *The Second Coming of Christ.* Louisville, Kentucky: John P. Morton and Company, Printers, 1863.

Waltke, Bruce K., and M. O'Connor. *An Introduction to Biblical Hebrew Syntax.* Winona Lake, Indiana: Eisenbrauns, 1990.

Walvoord, John F. *Daniel: The Key to Prophetic Revelation.* Chicago: Moody Press, 1971.

_____. *Israel in Prophecy.* Grand Rapids: Zondervan Publishing House, 1962.

_____. *The Millennial Kingdom: A Basic Text in Premillennial Theology.* Grand Rapids: Zondervan Publishing House, 1977.

_____, and Roy B. Zuck, ed. *The Bible Knowledge Commentary: Old Testament.* Wheaton, Illinois: Victor Books, 1985.

Wegner, Paul D. *Textual Criticism of the Bible: Its History, Methods, & Results.* Downers Grove, Illinois: IVP Academic, 2006.

Weingreen, J. *A Practical Grammar of Classical Hebrew*, 2d ed. Oxford: At The Clarendon Press, 1979.

Whitcomb, John C. "Daniel's Great Seventy-Week's Prophecy: An Exegetical Insight." *Grace Theological Journal* 2.2 (Fall 1981): 259–63.

_____. *Darius the Mede: A Study in Historical Identification*. Grand Rapids: William. B. Eerdmans 1959.

_____. *Everyman's Bible Commentary: Daniel*. Chicago: Moody Press, 1985.

Wood, Leon J. *The Bible and Future Events: An Introductory Survey of Last-Day Events*. Grand Rapids: Zondervan Publishing House, 1976.

_____. *A Commentary on Daniel*. Grand Rapids: Zondervan Publishing House, 1990.

Woude, A. S. Van Der, ed. *The Book of Daniel in the Light of New Findings*. Leuven: Leuven University Press, 1993.

Yamauchi, Edwin M. "Hermeneutical Issues in the Book of Daniel." *Journal of the Evangelical Theological Society* 23.1 (1980): 13-21.

Young, Edward J. *The Prophecy of Daniel*. Grand Rapids: Wm. B. Eerdmans Publishing Company, 1949.

Ziegler, Joseph, ed. *Septuaginta Vetus Testamentum Graecum*, vol. 16, *Susanna, Daniel, Bel et Draco*, 2d ed. Göttingen: Vandenhoeck & Ruprecht, 1999.

Zuck, Roy B. "Highlights in the History of Hermeneutics," *Classnotes*. Dallas: Dallas Theological Seminary, n.d.

Author Index

SCRIPTURE INDEX

The Apocrypha Index